WORLD CHRISTIANITIES

C.1914–C.2000

The twentieth century saw changes as dramatic as any in Christian history. The churches suffered serious losses, both through persecution and through secularisation, in what had been for several centuries their European heartlands, but grew fast in Africa and parts of Asia. This volume provides a comprehensive history of Catholicism, Protestantism and the Independent churches in all parts of the world in the century when Christianity truly became a global religion. Written by a powerful team of specialists from many different countries, the volume is broad in scope. The first part focuses on institutions and movements which have had a worldwide impact, including the papacy, the Ecumenical movement and Pentecostalism. The second provides a narrative of Christian history in each region of the world. The third focuses on selected themes from an international perspective, including changes in worship, relations with Jews and Muslims, science and the arts, gender and sexuality.

HUGH MCLEOD is Professor of Church History at the University of Birmingham. His publications include *Piety and poverty: working class religion in Berlin, London and New York 1870–1914* (1996) and *Secularisation in western Europe 1848–1914* (2000). He is president of CIHEC, the international organisation of historians of Christianity.

CHRISTIANITY

The *Cambridge History of Christianity* offers a comprehensive chronological account of the development of Christianity in all its aspects – theological, intellectual, social, political, regional, global – from its beginnings to the present day. Each volume makes a substantial contribution in its own right to the scholarship of its period and the complete *History* constitutes a major work of academic reference. Far from being merely a history of western European Christianity and its offshoots, the *History* aims to provide a global perspective. Eastern and Coptic Christianity is given full consideration from the early period onwards, and later, African, Far Eastern, New World, South Asian and other non-European developments in Christianity receive proper coverage. The volumes cover popular piety and non-formal expressions of Christian faith and treat the sociology of Christian formation, worship and devotion in a broad cultural context. The question of relations between Christianity and other major faiths is also kept in sight throughout. The *History* will provide an invaluable resource for scholars and students alike.

List of volumes

Origins to Constantine
EDITED BY MARGARET M. MITCHELL AND FRANCES M. YOUNG

Constantine to c.600
EDITED BY WINRICH LÖHR, FRED NORRIS AND AUGUSTINE CASIDAY

Early medieval Christianity c.600–c.1100
EDITED BY THOMAS NOBLE AND JULIA SMITH

Christianity in western Europe c.1100–c.1500
EDITED BY MIRI RUBIN AND WALTER SIMON

Eastern Christianity
EDITED BY MICHAEL ANGOLD

Reform and Expansion 1500–1660
EDITED BY RONNIE PO-CHIA HSIA

Enlightenment, Reawakening and Revolution 1660–1815
EDITED BY STEWART J. BROWN AND TIMOTHY TACKETT

World Christianities c.1815–1914
EDITED BY BRIAN STANLEY AND SHERIDAN GILLEY

World Christianities c.1914 to c.2000
EDITED BY HUGH McLEOD

THE CAMBRIDGE HISTORY OF
CHRISTIANITY

*

VOLUME 9
World Christianities c.1914–c.2000

*

Edited by
HUGH McLEOD

CAMBRIDGE
UNIVERSITY PRESS

CAMBRIDGE UNIVERSITY PRESS
Cambridge, New York, Melbourne, Madrid, Cape Town, Singapore, São Paulo

CAMBRIDGE UNIVERSITY PRESS
The Edinburgh Building, Cambridge CB2 2RU, UK

Published in the United States of America by Cambridge University Press, New York

http://www.cambridge.org
Information on this title: http://www.cambridge.org/9780521815000

First published 2006

Printed in the United Kingdom at the University Press, Cambridge

A catalogue record for this book is available from the British Library

ISBN-13 978-0-521-81500-0 hardback
ISBN-10 0-521-81500-2 hardback

Contents

Contents

PART II
NARRATIVES OF CHANGE

Contents

Contents

Maps

Illustrations

Notes on contributors

CHRISTOPHER ABEL teaches Latin American history at University college, London, and has written extensively on Latin America and the Caribbean of the nineteenth and twentieth centuries. He has research interests in the history of religion, politics, social policy and health-care; he has published *Politica, iglesia y partidos en Colombia* (Bogotá, 1987), various co-edited books on the history of social policy, and contributions to such multi-volume works as the Cambridge History of Latin America and the UNESCO General History of Latin America.

ALLAN ANDERSON is Professor of Pentecostal Studies at the university of Birmingham, specialising in Pentecostalism and Independency in Africa and Asia. He is the author of *An introduction to Pentecostalism* (Cambridge, 2004), *African reformation* (Trenton, NJ, 2001) and *Zion and Pentecost* (Pretoria, 2000), and co-edited *Pentecostals after a century* (Sheffield, 1999) and *Asian and Pentecostal* (Oxford, 2005).

PETER J. BOWLER is Professor of the History of Science at Queen's university, Belfast. He is a Fellow of the British Academy and a Member of the Royal Irish Academy. His publications include *Reconciling science and religion: the debate in early twentieth century Britain* (Chicago, 2001).

ANDREW CHANDLER is Director of the George Bell Institute, Senior Research Fellow at the Queen's foundation, Birmingham, and Honorary Lecturer in the school of historical studies, university of Birmingham. He has edited *The moral imperative: new essays on the ethics of resistance in National Socialist Germany 1933–45* (Boulder, 1998), *Brethren in adversity: Bishop George Bell, the Church of England and the crisis in German Protestantism, 1933–39* (Woodbridge, 1997), and *The terrible alternative: Christian martyrdom in the twentieth century* (London, 1998). He has published in many journals, including *English historical review* and *Leo Baeck institute yearbook*.

DAVID CHEETHAM is Lecturer in Theology and Inter-Religious Relations in the department of theology and religion, university of Birmingham. He is the author of *John Hick* (Aldershot, 2003) and numerous academic articles.

EDWARD L. CLEARY, OP is Professor of Political Science and Director of the Latin American Studies Program at Providence college, Providence, Rhode Island. He has published several books on religion in Latin America, including *Power, politics and Pentecostals in Latin America* (Boulder, 1997), *Crisis and change* (Maryknoll, 1985), and *Resurgent Voices in Latin America* (New Brunswick, NJ, 2004). He was President of the Bolivian Institute of Social Study and Action, and editor of *Estudios Andinos*.

MARTIN CONWAY is Fellow and Tutor in Modern History at Balliol College, Oxford. He has published widely on twentieth-century Catholicism, including *Catholic politics in Europe 1918–45* (London and New York, 1997).

DUNCAN B. FORRESTER taught in India, at Madras Christian college, in England at Sussex university, and from 1978 until retirement in 2001 was Professor of Christian Ethics and Practical Theology in the university of Edinburgh. His recent publications include *On human worth: a Christian vindication of equality* (London, 2001) and *Truthful action: explorations in practical theology* (Edinburgh, 2000).

ROSWITH GERLOFF holds a PhD from Birmingham university on the African and Caribbean church movement in Britain 1952–90, based on intensive field studies in Europe, America and the Caribbean, and was the founder and first director of the Centre for Black and White Christian Partnership, a model of inter-cultural theological training between different traditions, and a Yale Research Fellow 2001. At Leeds university she continued with a major study of the social, cultural and missiological significance of the African Christian diaspora in Europe. Her various publications in the field of Black Christianity, Pentecostal studies and inter-cultural learning include her doctoral dissertation, *A plea for British Black Theologies: the black church movement in its cultural and theological interaction* (Frankfurt am Main, 1992), the 89/354 (July 2000) issue of the *International review of mission* ('Open space – the African Christian diaspora in Europe and the quest for community') as guest editor, *Mission is crossing frontiers* (Pietermaritzburg, 2003), as editor, and *Das schwarze Lächeln Gottes: Afrikanische Diaspora als Herausforderung an Theologie und Kirche* (Frankfurt am Main, 2005).

STEVE DE GRUCHY is the Director of the Theology and Development Programme at the university of Kwa-Zulu-Natal, where he teaches, researches and writes in the area of Christian social ethics in southern Africa. He has an interest in the history of the church struggle against racism and apartheid in South Africa, and has recently collaborated with his father to publish a twenty-fifth anniversary revised edition of *The church struggle in South Africa* (London and Minneapolis 2004). He is also editor of the *Journal of theology for southern Africa*.

DAVID HILLIARD is Reader in History at Flinders university, Adelaide, Australia. He has published in many different areas of the religious history of Australia and the Pacific Islands and on modern Anglican attitudes to homosexuality.

DAVID JASPER is Professor of Literature and Theology at the university of Glasgow. He was awarded a Doctorate of Divinity by the university of Oxford in 2002. His most recent book is *The sacred desert* (Oxford, 2004).

OGBU U. KALU was for many years Professor of Church History at the University of Nigeria, Nsukka. He is currently the Henry Winters Luce Professor of World Christianity and Missions, McCormick theological seminary, Chicago. His publications include *Power, poverty and prayer: the challenges of poverty and pluralism in African Christianity* (Frankfurt am Main, 2000); *Embattled gods: Christianization of Igboland, 1841–1991* (Trenton, NJ, 2003); and (as editor) *African Christianity: an African story* (Pretoria, 2004). Forthcoming is *Clio in sacred garb: essays on Christian presence and African responses, 1900–2000* (Pretoria).

DIANNE KIRBY lectures in the school of history and international affairs at the university of Ulster. Author of *Church, state and propaganda* (Hull, 1999), she also edited *Religion and the Cold War* (Basingstoke, 2003), a ground-breaking collection of essays about the significant global role assigned to religion in the critical Cold War period. She is currently working on a monograph exploring President Harry Truman's efforts to create a religious front against Soviet communism.

DANIEL R. LANGTON is Lecturer in Modern Jewish–Christian Relations at the university of Manchester. His doctoral studies were at the centre for Jewish/non-Jewish relations at the university of Southampton. His significant publications include *Claude Montefiore: his life and thought* (2002), a biography of the co-founder of Anglo-Liberal Judaism, religious scholar and pioneer of inter-faith relations; and a series of articles on the apostle Paul in the Jewish imagination.

CHANDRA MALLAMPALLI is Assistant Professor of History at Westmont college. He is the author of *Christians and public life in colonial South India, 1863–1937* (London, 2004). His areas of research include religious nationalism, secularism, conversion, post-colonialism and the history of Christianity in south Asia.

PIRJO MARKKOLA is Academy Research Fellow (Academy of Finland), department of history, university of Tampere. Her publications include *Synti ja siveys. Naiset, uskonto ja sosiaalinen työ Suomessa 1860–1920* (Helsinki, 2002) (Sin and morality: women, religion and social work in Finland, 1860–1920); and (as editor) *Gender and vocation: women, religion and social change in the Nordic countries, 1830–1940* (Helsinki, 2000).

KATHARINE MASSAM is Head of the department of church history in the united faculty of theology at the university of Melbourne. Her publications include *Sacred threads: Catholic spirituality in Australia, 1922–1962* (Sydney, 1996).

DAVID MAXWELL, Senior Lecturer in International History, Keele university, is editor of the *Journal of religion in Africa*. He is author of *Christians and chiefs in Zimbabwe. A social history of the Hwesa people ca. 1870s–1970s* (Edinburgh, 1999), and *African gifts of the Spirit: Pentecostalism and the rise of a Zimbabwean transnational religious movement* (Oxford, forthcoming). With Ingrid Lawrie he edited *Christianity and the African imagination: essays in honour of Adrian Hastings* (Leiden, 2002).

COLLEEN MCDANNELL is the Sterling M. McMurrin Professor of Religious Studies and Professor of History at the university of Utah in Salt Lake City. She is the author of *Picturing faith: photography and the Great Depression* (New Haven, 2004), *Material Christianity: religion and popular culture in America* (New Haven, 1998), *The Christian home in Victorian America: 1840–1900* (Bloomington, 1986), and co-author with Bernhard Lang of *Heaven: a history* (New Haven, 1988). In 2000 she received a Guggenheim Foundation Fellowship.

HUGH MCLEOD is Professor of Church History at the university of Birmingham. His publications include *Piety and poverty: working class religion in Berlin, London and New York 1870–1914* (New York, 1996) and *Secularisation in western Europe 1848–1914* (London, 2000). He is president of CIHEC, the international organisation of historians of Christianity.

JOHN POLLARD is Fellow in History at Trinity Hall, Cambridge. He has published extensively on the history of the modern papacy, most notably *The unknown pope: Benedict XV (1914–1922) and the pursuit of peace* (London, 1999), and *Money and the rise of the modern papacy: financing the Vatican, 1850–1950* (Cambridge, 2004).

JOHN ROXBOROGH is Coordinator of Parish Leadership Training at the Presbyterian school of ministry, Dunedin, New Zealand. He has previously taught in Malaysia and at the Bible College of New Zealand. He is convenor of the documentation, archives and bibliography study group of the International Association for Mission Studies.

MICHAEL SNAPE is Lecturer in History at the university of Birmingham and a member of the university's centre for First World War studies. His research is currently focused on religion and conflict in the English-speaking world c.1700–1950. Publications include *The Church of England in industrialising society: the Lancashire parish of Whalley in the 18th Century* (Woodbridge, 2003) and *God and the British Soldier 1914–1945* (London, 2005).

BRYAN D. SPINKS is Professor of Liturgical Studies at the Yale institute of sacred music and Yale divinity school. His most recent books are *Sacraments, ceremonies and the Stuart divines: sacramental theology and liturgy in England and Scotland 1603–1662* (Aldershot, 2002) and *Rituals and theologies of baptism: beyond the Jordan* (Aldershot, 2005). He served on the Church of England liturgical commission from 1986 to 2000, and is a former President of the Church Service Society, Scotland.

EDMOND TANG is Head of the research unit for the study of east Asian Christianity at the university of Birmingham. He is editor of *China study journal* and author of articles on contemporary Chinese Christianity. He is now working on emerging christologies in China, Japan and Korea.

ADRIAN THATCHER was Professor of Applied Theology at the college of St Mark and St John, Plymouth, until his retirement in August 2004. He is now part-time Professorial Research Fellow in Christian Ethics at the university of Exeter.

DAVID THOMAS is Reader in Christianity and Islam in the department of theology and religion, university of Birmingham, where he specialises in the history of Christian–Muslim relations. Among his recent publications are *Early Muslim polemic against Christianity* (Cambridge, 2002) and *Muslim–Christian polemic during the crusades*

(Leiden, 2005). He is general editor of the Brill book series 'The History of Christian–Muslim Relations'.

DAVID M. THOMPSON, Reader in Modern Church History, university of Cambridge, and President of Fitzwilliam college, is author of *Nonconformity in the nineteenth century* (London, 1972), *Let sects and parties fall* (London, 1980), and 'The unity of the church in twentieth century England: pleasing dream or common calling?', in *Studies in church history* 32 (London, 1996). He was President of the Ecclesiastical History Society, 1994–6, and Moderator of the General Assembly of the United Reformed Church, 1996–7.

JUTTA VINZENT is Lecturer in Modern and Contemporary Art and Visual Culture in the department of art history, university of Birmingham. Her publications include *Identity and image. Refugee artists from Nazi Germany in Britain* (Weimar, 2005), and 'Ars Memoriae und das Exil', in Wolf-Friedrich Schäufele and Markus Vinzent (eds.), *Theologen im Exil – Theologie des Exils* (Mandelbachtal and Cambridge, 2001).

MICHAEL WALSH was formerly Librarian at Heythrop college, University of London. He has published on a variety of topics in the history of the church in late antiquity and on the contemporary church. He is currently revising the late J. N. D. Kelly's *Oxford dictionary of the popes*.

PHILIP WALTERS obtained his doctorate in Russian religious thought at the London school of economics. Since 1979 he has worked at Keston institute (formerly Keston college), the research and information centre on communist and post-communist countries; since 1984 he has been Head of Research. He is author of numerous articles and chapters on aspects of church–state relations and religious life in the Soviet Union, Russia and eastern Europe and editor of the journal *Religion, state & society: the Keston journal* (formerly *Religion in communist lands*).

KEVIN WARD is Senior Lecturer in African Religious Studies in the department of theology and religious studies at the university of Leeds. He lectured for many years in Uganda, and his research interests focus on the history of Christianity in east Africa. He is presently engaged in writing a history of the worldwide Anglican communion.

ANDREW WILSON-DICKSON is now a freelance musician, having been teaching in higher education for many years. He is a composer, conductor, keyboard player and author. His book *The story of Christian music* (Oxford, 1992) has been translated into more than ten languages.

NIGEL YATES is Professor of Ecclesiastical History and Director of the university research centre at the university of Wales, Lampeter. His publications include *Buildings, faith and worship: the liturgical arrangement of Anglican churches 1600–1900* (1991, revd edn 2000), *Anglican ritualism in Victorian Britain 1830–1910* (Oxford, 1999), and a forthcoming study for Oxford University Press of *The religious condition of Ireland 1770–1850*. Between 1981 and 1991 he served on the executive committee of the Council for the Care of Churches and he is currently Provincial Archives Advisor to the Church in Wales.

RICHARD FOX YOUNG is the Timby Associate Professor of the History of Religions at Princeton theological seminary (Princeton, NJ, USA). A former member of the faculty of Meiji Gakuin university (Tokyo/Yokohama, Japan), his studies of interactions, historical and contemporary, between Christianity and the new religions of Asia (Chinese, Japanese and Korean) have appeared in journals such as the *Japanese journal of religious studies*, *Japanese religions*, and *Monumenta nipponica*.

Introduction

HUGH McLEOD

At the beginning of the twentieth century it is estimated that about a third of the people in the world were Christians – which meant that Christianity was by far the largest of the world's religions. During the century the numbers of Christians increased rapidly, but so of course did the world's population, with the result that the proportion who were Christians may have fallen slightly. By the end of the century Christians still outnumbered the followers of any other religion, but Muslims were a strong second.[1] Meanwhile, there had been a dramatic shift in the distribution of Christians between the different regions of the world. It has been estimated that at the beginning of the twentieth century about 80 per cent of the world's Christians lived in Europe, the Russian empire and North America, and a mere 5 per cent in Asia and Africa. By 2000, according to the same authors, the proportion living in Europe, the former Soviet Union and North America had dropped to around 40 per cent, while the proportion living in Asia and Africa had jumped to 32 per cent.

These figures neatly summarise two of the central themes of this volume: in the twentieth century Christianity became a worldwide religion; yet at the same time it suffered a series of major crises in what had been for many centuries its heartlands. Nonetheless, these familiar points may conceal two others, which are equally important. First, power within international Christianity was still at the end of the twentieth century mainly concentrated in Europe and North America. Second, in spite of the crises brought about in the West both by attacks from totalitarian governments and by broader and more gradual processes of secularisation, Christianity and the Christian churches continued to play a major political, social and cultural role in their former heartlands, at least up to the 1960s. This role remained important

---

1 All the figures in this paragraph are based on the estimates (admittedly in many cases speculative) in David B. Barrett, George T. Kurian and Todd M. Johnson (eds.), *World Christian encyclopaedia*, 2 vols. (Oxford: Oxford University Press, 2001), vol. I, pp. 4, 12.

in the last three decades of the century, though varying between countries, and being more significant in some areas of life than others.

Catholics, Protestants, Independents

Christianity has historically been divided between East and West, and the modern history of Eastern Christianity is the subject of another volume in this series. The present volume is devoted entirely to Western Christianity, and to newer movements that grew out of Western Christianity in the nineteenth and twentieth centuries. Since the sixteenth century, Western Christianity has been divided between Catholics, who recognise the primacy of the bishop of Rome, and Protestants who do not. In the nineteenth and twentieth centuries, new forms of Christianity emerged in the United States and, more especially, in Africa and Asia, sometimes led by prophets claiming to have received new revelations, sometimes driven simply by the motive to be free of any kind of Western control. In Africa and Asia they are generally referred to collectively as 'Independent churches'. Part I of this volume provides an overview of five institutions or movements that have been of international significance in the twentieth century, namely: the papacy; the Ecumenical movement, in which the driving forces have been the older Protestant churches; the missionary movement; Pentecostalism, the most expansive branch of twentieth-century Protestantism; and Independency.

Roman Catholicism has remained throughout the twentieth century by far the largest branch of Christianity, about half the Christians in the world being members of that church. At the beginning of the century, it dominated southern, and much of central and eastern, Europe. Baptised Catholics formed the overwhelming majority of the population in France, Belgium, Spain, Portugal and Italy. They were a substantial majority in Ireland and in the Austro-Hungarian empire. There were large Catholic minorities in Germany, Switzerland and the Netherlands, and a significant minority in Great Britain. Catholics were also an overwhelming majority in nearly all parts of South and Central America, in several Caribbean islands and in the Philippines. They were nearly half the population in Canada and there were substantial Catholic minorities in the United States and Australia. There were also long-established Catholic enclaves in various parts of Asia and Africa, and recent missionary efforts had led to significant numbers of conversions, notably in Uganda and in Indo-China.

The Vatican Council (1869–70), culminating in the definition of the dogma of papal infallibility, had set the dominant tone for Catholic life in the later nineteenth and early twentieth centuries. The church was increasingly centralised, strongly conservative in theology and often in politics, and bound together by Ultramontane piety and intense loyalty to the pope. There had, however, been a significant dissenting minority of liberal Catholics, Gallicans, and others at the time of the Vatican Council. Some had left the church; most had suppressed their doubts. But dissenting currents continued beneath the surface. At the beginning of our period the church had just passed through the so-called 'modernist crisis', in which Pope Pius X had clamped down on Catholic biblical scholars who used 'modernist' methods of biblical criticism pioneered by Protestants, and had required the clergy to take an 'anti-modernist' oath. Apart from these internal divisions, the church had also faced serious external challenges from anti-clerical governments and broader trends towards 'dechristianisation' – the alienation of significant sectors of the population – in some European countries, notably France.

In the sixteenth century, Protestantism had become the religion of the state in large parts of northern Europe. There were already three main branches of Protestantism: Lutheranism became the official religion of many of the German states and throughout Scandinavia; the Reformed faith (also known as Calvinism or, in the English-speaking world, Presbyterianism) was victorious in many of the Swiss cantons, in some German states, in Scotland, and, after many years of warfare, in the Dutch Republic; Anglicanism became the established religion of England and Wales, as well as of Ireland (where most of the people nonetheless remained Catholics). In the early twentieth century the religious establishments set up in the sixteenth century were still intact (except in the Netherlands and in Ireland) and generally commanded at least the nominal allegiance of the majority of the population.

But the religious situation in the Protestant world had been greatly complicated by the emergence of many new forms of Protestantism from the seventeenth century onwards. Already in the sixteenth century the Anabaptists had tried to initiate a Reformation from below without any support from the state, but they had been largely wiped out by persecution. However, seventeenth-century England gave birth to the Baptists, Congregationalists and Quakers; eighteenth- and nineteenth-century England to the Methodists, the Unitarians and the Salvation Army; nineteenth- and twentieth-century America saw the emergence of the Adventists, Mormons, Jehovah's Witnesses and Pentecostalists. The most important new development in the twentieth century was Pentecostalism, a collective term for a plethora of denominations, some large, some very small, which have sprung up since the Azusa Street revival in Los Angeles in 1906.

As Protestantism moved beyond Europe it took a great variety of forms. In the United States the largest branches of Protestantism in the twentieth century were the Baptists and Methodists; in Australia, the Anglicans and the Uniting church (a union of Methodists, Congregationalists and Presbyterians); Nigeria and Uganda were Anglican strongholds; while Presbyterianism was strong in Malawi, and Methodism in Ghana and South Africa – reflecting the continuing relevance of earlier missionary geographies – though, as almost everywhere in Africa, these long-established churches were competing with many newer forms of Protestantism. Pentecostalism is now by far the largest branch of Protestantism in Latin America and, as is shown in chapter 6, it has grown impressively in various parts of Africa and Asia and to a lesser extent in most other parts of the Christian world.

The nineteenth century brought new theological differences to Protestantism. Very often these divided denominations and brought together those of similar theological tendencies in different churches. The biggest driving forces in the later eighteenth and early nineteenth centuries had been Evangelicalism (the term used in the English-speaking world) and Pietism (the name given to related movements in Germany and Scandinavia). Evangelicals believed in the inherent sinfulness of all human beings, and their absolute need to repent, to seek God's forgiveness, and to undergo an experience of conversion. They emphasised the authority of the Bible, usually interpreted literally.[2] But the nineteenth century also saw the development of a powerful liberal movement within Protestantism. While still regarding the scriptures as their supreme authority, liberal Protestants believed that the sacred text should be subject to critical scrutiny; and, rather than seeing the Bible as a cohesive whole, they recognised tensions within it, and treated some parts, notably the gospels and the Old Testament prophets, as more authoritative than others. They emphasised the ethical more than the doctrinal teachings of Christianity, and they had a very positive view of science and education. A third major division arose from the high-church movements in Anglicanism and Lutheranism. 'High-church' indicated an emphasis on the sacraments, especially the eucharist, on the priestly office, on ritual and ceremony, on church tradition. It often led to more sympathetic attitudes to Roman Catholicism and Orthodoxy: indeed, high-church Anglicans often

---

2 David W. Bebbington, *Evangelicalism in modern Britain: a history from the 1730s to the 1980s* (London: Unwin Hyman, 1989), pp. 2–3, offers an influential definition of Evangelicalism.

called themselves 'Catholics' or 'Anglo-Catholics', and denied that the Church of England was a Protestant church.

The early twentieth century brought further theological divisions within Protestantism. Two developments need special mention. Fundamentalism, which by the later twentieth century had become largely a term of abuse, originated with the publication in the United States between 1910 and 1915 of a series of volumes called *The Fundamentals*, and the subsequent formation of a World's Christian Fundamentals Association. The authors were conservative Evangelical Protestants, hostile to the growth of liberalism. Many of their tenets were common to conservative Christians generally, but they had certain distinctive beliefs and concerns. Their central principle was commitment to what they called the 'inerrancy' of scripture. This led to two other points: rejection of Darwin's theory of evolution became a favoured shibboleth; and their interest in biblical prophecies led to a distinctive interpretation of history known as 'premillennial dispensationalism' and an expectation of Christ's imminent Second Coming.[3] Fundamentalism had a big influence on popular religion in the United States and, via American missionaries, in other parts of the world. A second important new development around the same time was Neo-Orthodoxy, which had minimal influence on Christians at large, but a huge influence on academics and church leaders. Its leading exponent was the Swiss theologian Karl Barth, and its first major statement was his commentary on Paul's epistle to the Romans (1919). It was 'orthodox' in that it reaffirmed many of the classical Reformation doctrines and emphasised the radical gulf between God and sinful humanity, bridgeable only through God's self-revelation in Jesus Christ. It was 'neo' in the fact that it took for granted some of the major theological innovations of the previous century, such as the critical approach to the Bible.[4]

Five major themes

Five themes run right through parts I and II of this volume: the development of Christianity from a mainly European and American religion to a worldwide

---

3 See George M. Marsden, *Fundamentalism and American culture: the shaping of twentieth century Evangelicalism 1870–1925* (New York: Oxford University Press, 1980).

4 For a comprehensive guide to Christian theology in the twentieth century, including sections on the various regions of the world, on individual theologians, on feminist and postmodern theologies, on relations between theology and science, and much else, see David F. Ford (ed.), *The modern theologians: an introduction to Christian theology in the twentieth century*, 2nd edn (Oxford: Blackwell, 1997).

religion; the major challenges faced by Christianity in its European and North American heartlands; the diminishing importance of denominational boundaries within Christianity, together with the growth in contacts between Christians and adherents of other faiths; the huge role of war in twentieth-century history; and the relationship between Christianity and movements for the emancipation of oppressed groups. A sixth theme is seldom mentioned explicitly, but is part of the essential background to most of the chapters, namely the revolution in communications. I will comment briefly on each of these points.

Christianity becomes a worldwide religion

The great growth of Christianity in Africa and Asia has to be seen in ambivalent relationship to European and American power. In the 1920s nearly all of Africa, nearly all of south and south-east Asia, and much of the middle east was under European rule. This offered Christian missions two major advantages: physical protection both for missionaries and for native converts, and funding for mission schools. On the other hand, none of these things guaranteed a response to Christian missionary efforts. In most of south Asia and in some parts of Africa the response was small, and, in many parts of Africa, Islam was also growing during the colonial era. On the other hand, Korea, the Asian country where Christianity progressed fastest, was under Japanese rule. And, of course, as David Maxwell points out in chapter 22, Christianity has grown faster since the end of colonial rule than it did during that era. It seems likely that continuing processes of social change set in motion by colonialism have done more to create the conditions in which Christianity might flourish than anything inherent in colonial rule as such.

In the late twentieth century, with the end of the European empires, American power continued to have an important influence on the growth or non-growth of Christianity. Perceptions of the United States, as well as the efforts of American missionaries and such resources as books, tapes, videos and so on, provided by American denominational headquarters, have influenced the spread of Pentecostalism and other forms of conservative Protestantism across the world. The prestige of American culture makes many people more open to other American products, such as American religion. On the other hand, American economic and cultural power, like European colonialism, is two-edged: anti-Americanism can take the form of hostility to Christianity, or at least to Protestantism, as happened, for instance, in China in the 1950s and 1960s, and was happening in various parts of the Muslim world at the end of the century. From 1945 until *perestroika* in the later 1980s there was also an anti-Christian super-power, with considerable influence in other parts of the world, especially Africa. In the 1960s and 1970s numerous Marxist governments were set up, sustained ideologically, and to some extent financially, by the Soviet Union, and in some cases, as in Ethiopia, pursuing violent anti-Christian policies.

Crisis in the West

In Europe and the United States in the nineteenth century the truth of Christian doctrines had been fiercely debated. Equally fierce was the political debate about the position of the church in relation to the state. These political debates became particularly intense during the first four decades of the twentieth century. At the beginning of the century, most European countries had an established church and Christianity was deeply implicated in the exercise of political and economic power. Paternalist businessmen and land-owners often practised Christian charity, but also used Christian preachers to legitimate their authority. Schoolteachers often mixed religion with patriotism, and soldiers were required to attend church parades.

Most of this was under attack from liberals and socialists. France separated church and state in 1905, Portugal followed in 1911, Russia did so in 1918, Germany in 1919, Spain in 1931. The establishment of totalitarian, or at least highly authoritarian, governments in large parts of Europe in the 1920s and 1930s, and the prestige that some of these regimes enjoyed even in democratic countries, posed serious problems for the churches. These governments differed widely in their attitude to religion and the churches. Only the Soviet Union was completely and openly opposed to any kind of religion. At the other extreme, some dictators such as Salazar in Portugal or Dolfuss and Schuschnigg in Austria were very friendly to the Catholic church – though, of course, the high-handed methods of even the friendliest dictators could be a source of tension. The Nazis were in principle anti-Christian, and at the local level often openly so, but their official policies were mainly determined by tactical considerations.[5] Pope Pius XI, as John Pollard points

---

5 The classic text is John S. Conway, *The Nazi persecution of the churches* (London: Weidenfeld & Nicolson, 1968). This has now been challenged by Richard Steigmann-Gall, *The Holy Reich: Nazi conceptions of Christianity 1919–45* (Cambridge: Cambridge University Press, 2003), who argues that militantly anti-Christian Nazis, such as Heydrich, were untypical, and that the mainstream position, though anti-Catholic and anti-clerical, was not anti-Christian. Their attitude to Protestantism was relatively favourable. His study is well documented and provides a more nuanced picture than was previously available, but his central argument is, in my view, considerably overstated.

out in chapter 3, was no democrat, and had indeed helped Mussolini into power; but his relations with the Italian dictator were often tense, he never had any sympathy for the Soviet Union, and he soon lost all sympathy for Nazi Germany. International Protestant leaders were mostly convinced democrats, but they asked themselves whether Christianity was losing the battle against new 'political religions', which seemed to offer a more exciting faith and practical solutions to economic and social problems.

After 1945, communist governments were established through most of the eastern half of Europe, and all pursued anti-religious policies. In western Europe, on the other hand, church–state relations entered an exceptionally harmonious phase – one reason being that so many of the key political figures in the period c.1945–65 were practising Catholics. In the United States, which in 1791 had become the first Christian nation to separate church and state, questions of church–state relations gained a new prominence in the last quarter of the century. The so-called 'religious right', emerging in the later 1970s, consisted mainly of conservative Protestants, who believed that Christianity was under threat from recent Supreme Court decisions and from more general changes in the moral climate. They in turn had a galvanising effect on liberals and secularists, who claimed that this 'religious right' endangered the constitutional separation of church and state.

The changing moral climate, deplored by American conservatives, had in fact affected the whole Western world in the 1960s. Religious controversy now focused not so much on politics as on Christian teachings concerning sexual ethics and gender, and on criticism of Christian exclusiveness. There was a growing demand for greater individual freedom in questions of religion and ethics, with each person claiming the right to choose their own 'path', to draw inspiration from a variety of sources, and to decide which parts of their church's teaching they would accept and which they would reject or ignore. The religious and moral ferment of these years is fully described in chapters 17, 18 and 29. There is no doubt that the 1960s and 1970s mark a turning point in the religious history of Europe and North America – though historians, sociologists and theologians are divided as to how the changes in this period should be interpreted. Some see this as a time of definitive secularisation; some see it as the beginning of a era that is 'post-Christian', but not 'post-religious'; and others see it as a period of 'spiritual awakening' from which Christianity has emerged transformed and also in some ways strengthened.[6]

---

6 For a variety of perspectives, see Grace Davie, Paul Heelas and Linda Woodhead (eds.), *Predicting religion: Christian, secular and alternative futures* (Aldershot: Ashgate, 2003);

Relations with other Christians and other faiths

In the nineteenth century, conflict between Catholics and Protestants intensified and Protestant churches were bedevilled by schism, leading to the formation of many new denominations. Religious divisions were partly caused by social and political factors, but they were justified by exclusivist theologies that insisted that salvation depended on orthodoxy. Overseas missions gained their urgency from the belief that the 'heathen' were destined to hell. This latter expectation was modifed as liberal theologians in the later nineteenth century questioned traditional teachings concerning eternal punishment. Yet, while doing so, they often placed even greater emphasis on the humanitarian motives for mission: Christianity would bring an end to a multitude of cruel practices that wrecked lives in the present world.

In the twentieth century, in spite of important counter-currents, the overall trend, as is shown in chapters 4 and 27, has been towards closer contacts between Christians of different denominations, and between Christians and those of other faiths. Collaboration between Protestant denominations, sometimes extending to proposals for union between them, was developing rapidly from the late nineteenth century. But collaboration between Protestants and Catholics made little progress until the papacy of John XXIII (1958–63) and the Second Vatican Council (1962–5). The 1960s, when 'dialogue' became one of the the most popular slogans of a slogan-loving decade, also mark a key stage in the development of contacts between Christians and members of other faiths.

It is a frequent criticism of such 'dialogues' that they take place at the top and have little impact on 'ordinary people'. In the case of Catholic–Protestant relations the opposite was true. Dialogue between leaders often stalled, but the council opened the way for major changes at the local level. For instance, discussion and prayer meetings, pulpit exchanges, participation in ecumenical social action and, especially important, a more positive approach to inter-marriage all brought about a revolution in relationships. A further rapproche-ment was that between the older Protestant churches and the Pentecostal and African Independent churches, some of which joined the World Council of Churches in the 1970s. An important factor here was the discrediting of European imperialism, and a recognition by Western Christians that they had to take non-Western forms of Christianity more seriously.

Grace Davie, *Religion in modern Europe: a memory mutates* (Oxford: Oxford University Press, 2000); Amanda Porterfield, *The transformation of American religion: the story of a late-twentieth-century awakening* (New York: Oxford University Press, 2001).

The perception that secularisation poses a common threat has encouraged co-operation between churches, and more recently between faiths. Equally significant at the beginning of the twenty-first century is a recognition of the destructive potential of religious hatred, and the dangers it poses to all. As one example, Buddhist, Christian, Jewish, Muslim and Sikh leaders in the religiously very mixed English city of Birmingham marked the European elections in 2004 by issuing a joint statement affirming support for 'our multi-ethnic, culturally and religiously diverse community in Birmingham' and concluding: 'We expect all members of our faith communities to practise and promote racial justice and inclusion and reject any political party that attempts to stir up racial and religious hatred, discrimination and fear of asylum-seekers.'[7] The recognition of 'faith communities' as being among the essential components of contemporary British society is a means both of diminishing the danger of conflict between these communities and of combating demands for a more thorough secularisation.

The biggest reason for the erosion of denominational boundaries within Christianity has been the fact that many of the issues that led to the emergence of new Christian denominations in the sixteenth, seventeenth and eighteenth centuries had lost much of their urgency by the twentieth. Meanwhile, new issues had arisen that caused division within rather than between denominations – for instance, attitudes to the Charismatic movement, to Liberation Theology, to the role of women in church and society, and to sexuality (especially homosexuality). The Roman Catholic church in particular has suffered bitter internal conflicts since the Second Vatican Council. And in the latter years of the century, the Anglican communion was being torn apart by the questions first of women's ordination and then of homosexuality, as is shown in chapter 29. Christians still disagree fundamentally on certain issues, but the grounds for disagreement have changed. Thus a liberal Catholic is likely to have a lot in common with a liberal Methodist, though conservatism is often more denominationally specific.

---

7 *Birmingham ecumenical news*, June–August 2004. It is notable how many items in this issue of the journal have an inter-faith character or theme: for instance, there are notices of an annual Jewish–Christian study day, meetings organised by the Birmingham Council of Faiths, meetings of the Council of Christians and Jews, a course on 'Understanding Islam', and an inter-faith peace walk. Similarly, a report on the placing of a work of Christian art in a public place in the city, with support from the city council, noted that opposition came 'not from Jews, Hindus, Sikhs or Muslims', who encouraged Christians 'to celebrate the hope Jesus offers', 'in return inviting us all to support their public celebrations when their turn came', but from 'old-fashioned liberal secularists, who pretend that faith is a private affair at best, and irrelevant to our public life'.

The impact of war

The twentieth century has often been termed the most terrible in human history,[8] and war casts its shadow over all areas of the century's history. The two world wars bought death and destruction on a vast and unprecedented scale, and both had enormous political consequences. The Spanish civil war in the 1930s, the Vietnam war in the 1960s and 1970s, the wars in former Yugoslavia in the 1990s, and the persisting Arab–Israeli conflict all had a huge international impact, and shaped thinking about religion as well as politics. Now, at the start of the twenty-first century, the war in Iraq in 2003 promises or threatens (according to one's assessment) to have equally far-reaching implications. War has been a central fact of life for a large part of humanity in the twentieth century, and inevitably plays a major part in this volume. In particular, chapters 8 and 15 focus on the role of the Christian churches in the two world wars, and on the ways in which Christians have related their faith to their experiences of war and to the moral dilemmas that these presented. Twentieth-century history has brought questions of theodicy to the fore, leading some to 'protest atheism', but equally often causing a loss of faith in purely human solutions to human suffering. It is no accident that Neo-Orthodoxy became the fashionable theology of the era of the two world wars.

Wars have also had contradictory effects on people's understanding of the relationship between religion and patriotism. As in the nineteenth century, religion often underpinned national identity in the twentieth century. Wars have often brought an upsurge of patriotic religiosity and of claims that the national cause is God's cause. In Britain it is often a reason for naive surprise that this patriotic religiosity is to be found not only among those fighting in 'just' wars, but also in evidently 'unjust' wars, as with the Germans in World War II. Certainly at the time of World War I (as Michael Snape shows in chapter 8), and to a large extent at the time of World War II, the belief that fighting in defence of the Fatherland is both a moral and religious duty was so deeply engrained that only people of exceptional independent-mindedness (and often of exceptional courage) were able to resist it. On the other hand the horrors of war have also led to mass disillusion. In the 1990s, the violence in Ireland, in former Yugoslavia and in the middle east led to a perception that

---

8 Eric J. Hobsbawm, *Age of extremes: the short twentieth century 1914–1991* (London: Michael Joseph, 1994), pp. 1–2.

religion 'causes wars'.[9] This view was reinforced by the increasing association of terrorism with religious extremism. According to one expert on terrorism, none of the terrorist groups operating in 1968 could have been termed 'religious', whereas in 1995 nearly half of the known terrorist groups in the world had a religiously based ideology.[10] Alienation from Christianity has been caused both by church support for unpopular wars, as happened in the United States in the 1960s and 1970s,[11] or by vaguer and more general perceptions of the dangers of religious fanaticism. These concerns have also given rise to Christian pacifism, which became, perhaps for the first time since the pre-Constantian era, a major Christian option in the twentieth century.

Emancipation

The French revolutionary slogans of liberty and equality continued to have immense resonance in the twentieth century, and have inspired emancipatory movements by oppressed groups of all kinds, ranging from the working class, to colonised peoples, to women. These movements have often been anti-Christian, or at least anti-church. The most powerful and effective criticism of Christianity in the twentieth century has been the charge that it has been too closely identified with the rich and powerful, and too ready to legitimate the status quo. These political criticisms have had a far wider impact than those deriving from scientific or philosophical objections to religion. In the first half of the century, the most frequent accusation against Christianity in Europe and the Americas was that it was allied with the capitalists and was involved in the oppression of the workers. Since the 1970s the most common charges have been that it has been involved in the oppression of women or of sexual minorities. In Asia and Africa, opponents of Christianity have focused mainly on claims that Christianity is an alien import or an arm of Western imperialism (claims which, as Chandra Mallampalli shows in chapter 23, are bitterly resented by Indian Christians, with their nearly two-thousand-years-long history).

---

9 This claim was made in a radio broadcast in 1995 by Richard Dawkins, Professor of the Public Understanding of Science at Oxford, and Britain's best-known atheist, prompting the sociologist David Martin to attempt a more sophisticated analysis of the issue in *Does Christianity cause war?* (Oxford: Oxford University Press, 1997).

10 Charles Townshend, *Terrorism: a very short introduction* (Oxford: Oxford University Press, 2002), p. 97.

11 American churches were in fact deeply divided by the Vietnam war. For instance, Christian ministers were prominent both among supporters of the war, such as Cardinal Spellman and Billy Graham, and among opponents, such as Martin Luther King Jr and the Berrigan brothers.

However, as many chapters in this volume demonstrate, the relations between Christianity and emancipatory movements have been highly varied. For instance, anti-colonial movements were often anti-Christian in Asia, but seldom in Africa. Marxism, the most influential radical ideology of the twentieth century, has generally been resolutely anti-Christian; but by the 1970s and 1980s Marxists in Latin America were realising that the prospects of overthrowing their rulers were much better if they worked together with Christians, as happened in the Sandinista revolution of 1979 in Nicaragua. Out of the feminist movement of the late 1960s and early 1970s, with its mainly anti-Christian ethos, there soon developed a Christian feminism, dedicated to transforming the churches, as well as society. As Steve de Gruchy shows in chapter 21, the confrontation between antagonistic understandings of Christianity was particularly vivid in the struggles in South Africa, since Christianity was central both to the defence and to the critique of apartheid. Duncan Forrester in chapter 28 highlights the tensions between Christian socialism and Christian neo-liberalism. And Pirjo Markkola concludes her analysis of patriarchy and women's emancipation by noting that Christianity has been a factor both in women's emancipation and in opposition to women's emancipation. Twentieth-century Christians have come to radically different conclusions about the political and social implications of their faith.

The revolution in communications

Many centuries have brought revolutions in communications, but probably none has brought so many within a relatively short period of time as the twentieth century. Motor cars and aeroplanes, the cinema, the radio, television, computers and, most recently, the internet have all had implications for Christianity. They have provided governments with powerful tools for the repression and indoctrination of the population. They have forced remote communities with their own distinctive way of life out of isolation. On the other hand they have provided means of gaining access to forbidden ideas of all kinds. This is most obviously true of the situation in totalitarian states, where dissidents can be sustained by listening to radio broadcasts from outside. But now the internet means that the dissidents can themselves find a public voice. This is happening in China. It is also happening in churches, where the leadership has *its* official website, and those who have been marginalised or thrown out can also have *their* website. A case in point is the bishop of Partenia, Mgr Jacques Gaillot. His persistent questioning of official teaching on such issues as compulsory clerical celibacy led the pope to transfer him from Evreux to this uninhabited diocese located in the Sahara.

However, the outspoken prelate then continued to lambast the Vatican through his internet site.[12]

At the end of the twentieth century the religious impact of the internet was only beginning to be felt, but it seems likely that it will be very considerable. A minor example is the vogue for 'online worship', including communion services where participants provide their own bread and wine and consume them simultaneously, each in front of their own screen. More significantly, the internet is likely to reinforce the trends towards religious diversity, both by helping to sustain scattered religious communities[13] and by giving religious seekers information about a vast range of often esoteric alternatives.

12 Brenda Brasher, *Give me that online religion* (San Francisco: Jossey Bass, 2001), pp. 30–1.
13 David Nash, 'Religious sensibilities in the age of the internet: freethought culture and the historical context of communication media', in Stewart M. Hoover and Lynn Schofield Clark (eds.), *Practicing religion in the age of the media: explorations in media, religion and culture* (New York: Oxford University Press, 2002), pp. 276–90.

Being a Christian in the early twentieth century

HUGH McLEOD

Christendom

Limerzel is a large village in the Morbihan department of western France. In the first half of the twentieth century most of the population were employed in agriculture and the overwhelming majority were churchgoing Catholics. Its reputation for devotion was such that Catholic journalists referred to it as 'the pearl of the diocese of Vannes'. The rector was the most powerful figure in the village and he was accustomed to wielding the big stick. Children were brought up from an early age to realise that the clergy were special. When a priest visited, the adults showed respect and the children were afraid. In 1962, concerned at a relatively small decline in churchgoing, the rector was still warning in the parish bulletin: 'The presence of man here below has no other reason than preparation for eternal salvation of which the Church has received charge.' Religious symbols were prominent in the home, as well as in the village and the surrounding countryside. The weekly mass, from which in the 1930s only 'one or two' villagers were said to be regularly absent, was a central event in the weekly cycle. News was exchanged on the church steps, and bereaved families then headed in a group to the cemetery, while men gathered in the bar. Processions, pilgrimages and the various church festivals were major events in the annual cycle.

Nearly everyone was educated in a Catholic school. In fact the state school, popularly known as 'the devil's school' or 'the school for dogs', was only saved in the 1920s by the secret intervention of the rector, who persuaded a family to transfer their children to the secular establishment. His reasons were partly personal – his nephew was married to the teacher's daughter – but partly ideological: he feared that if the school closed, it might reopen later under the direction of a militant anti-clerical. The Catholic school tried to socialise its pupils into a total view of the world, which included a distinctive under-standing of French history (France as 'eldest daughter of the church'), a strong awareness of the boundaries between sacred and profane, and complete loyalty to the church. Catholic allegiance also had political consequences. This region of France had a long history of royalism and of voting for the right. Bastille Day, inaugurated as the supreme national festival in 1881, evoked little enthusiasm: the real national festival here was the feast of Joan of Arc.[1]

Limerzel was one of the rural 'Christendoms', still numerous in Catholic Europe, and indeed in Quebec and parts of Latin America in the first half of the twentieth century. They were concentrated in countries such as Ireland and Poland, in regions such as Brittany or Flanders, where the Catholic church had become identified with national struggles against foreign rule or with the struggles of disadvantaged regions against Protestantising or secularising governments. In such situations, an influential and respected clergy, powerful Catholic institutions and a public opinion that condemned any kind of open dissent combined to give the Catholic religion the force of something taken for granted.

A typical example would be Quebec, a huge Catholic and French-speaking island in the middle of a Protestant, English-speaking, sea. After the failure of the uprising against British rule in 1837–8, the Catholic church made common cause with the often anti-clerical 'Patriots' who had supported the rising, and for the next 125 years the church was the central institution of Quebec society, enjoying at least the nominal loyalty of the great majority of the French-speaking population. The church controlled education and welfare, and the archbishop of Montreal was rector of the two leading French-language universities, Laval and Montreal. Churches and Catholic institutions dominated the townscape of Montreal, the provincial metropolis; high levels of recruitment to the clergy and to female religious orders permitted a very strong clerical presence in rural and urban areas alike; and the large number of French Canadian missionaries was a telling reflection of the province's Catholic commitment. Overwhelmingly high levels of Catholic observance were maintained until the 1960s – a poll in 1965 found that 83 per cent of Catholics in Quebec claimed to have attended church during the previous week. By that time, reforms introduced by the Liberal government had weakened the power of the church. But up until 1960 it was well integrated into the political establishment through its close links with the dominant *Union Nationale*.[2]

---

1 Yves Lambert, *Dieu change en Bretagne* (Paris: Editions du Cerf, 1985), pp. 23–98, 246–7.
2 Kenneth McRoberts, *Quebec: social change and political crisis*, 3rd edn (Toronto: McClelland & Stewart, 1988), pp. 47–127; Reginald W. Bibby, *Fragmented gods: the poverty and potential of religion in Canada* (Toronto: Stoddart, 1990), p. 17.

The Protestant churches found it harder to achieve this kind of dominance. They had a persistent tendency to split into rival denominations, and these splits deepened where they were linked with other cleavages such as those of class or politics. For instance, the old division between 'church' and 'chapel' in England and Wales, or between the national church and the free churches in Scotland or Sweden, still counted for quite a lot at the local level, even if at the top the emerging ecumenical movement was aiming to sweep away such differences. However, there were regions such as north Wales or the highlands and islands of Scotland, or the north-east of Ireland, or many rural regions of the United States, Canada or the Netherlands, where Protestantism, in spite of its many divisions, was a dominant cultural influence. This seldom meant the unanimous churchgoing seen in Limerzel, but it meant certain standards of behaviour that were seen as Christian and open defiance of which could bring ostracism. Perhaps the most conspicuous symbol of this Protestant way of life was the observance of Sunday, 'the sabbath', as a day apart. This included a ban not only on work and travel, but on most forms of amusement. Attendance at churches could not be enforced, and any such attempt might be seen as an infringement of religious liberty. But any kind of conspicuous sabbath-breaking was social suicide. Abstention from alcohol was also widely seen as a necessity of Christianity, and indeed of respectability. While not all Protestants were convinced teetotallers, and many did drink in spite of the disapproval they were likely to encounter, they were generally agreed in condemning gambling. An ethos of hard work, saving, and unostentatious dress also gave these Protestant cultures a somewhat dour reputation. Religious life focused on Bible-reading, and the scope this allowed for conflicting individual interpretations of the sacred text meant that Protestant unity was always at risk and frequently collapsed. Here being a Christian meant especially adherence to a set of moral rules, generally accepted by the community and enforced through various forms of socially imposed discipline.[3]

In northern Scotland where the overwhelming majority of the people were Protestants, they were also very conscious of the divisions between those belonging to the Church of Scotland, the United Free church, the so-called 'Wee Frees' (who claimed to be the 'true' Free church), the Free Presbyterians, the Congregationalists, the Baptists, the Methodists, the Brethren, the

---

3 See, for example, the comments on life in Scottish fishing communities in Paul Thompson with Tony Wailey and Trevor Lummis, *Living the fishing* (London: Routledge, 1983), pp. 264–307 and *passim*.

Salvation Army, the Episcopal church, and others besides. In the north-east of Ireland, on the other hand, the deep split between Catholic and Protestant had come by the early twentieth century to supersede all other religious distinctions. Here too, Protestants were divided into many denominations, but the differences, once bitterly contested, were by now of secondary importance. The sectarian divide in Ireland revolved primarily round differing responses to Irish nationalism. In the course of the nineteenth century, nationalism had come to be closely identified with Catholicism, and most Protestants had rallied to the defence of the Union with Great Britain. But theological and cultural differences also played a part. The rise to dominance of the Evangelicals meant that there was a powerful faction within the Protestant churches that wanted no compromise with the Roman 'antichrist'. Catholics and Protestants tended to live amidst their own kind: for instance, in the industrial metropolis of Belfast the east was mainly Protestant, the west Catholic. The children went to different schools, and to a large extent their parents went to different places of work: in the larger enterprises, skilled jobs were mainly given to Protestants and unskilled jobs to Catholics. Small businessmen preferred to employ their co-religionists. Every area of life had a sectarian dimension. Football and cricket were seen as Protestant sports, while hurling and Gaelic football, promoted by the Gaelic Athletic Association, were more or less exclusively Catholic. 'Mixed' marriages were opposed not only by the churches, but even more by parents and neighbours, for whom they were a form of betrayal. Mutual stereotyping was rife. Catholics accused Protestants of sexual laxity. Protestants claimed that Catholics were drunkards – 'Smell a man's breath and tell his religion.'

Sectarian conflict in Ireland reached a terrible climax in the years 1912–23, which began with the Liberal government's Home Rule bill, offering Ireland partial autonomy under a parliament in Dublin. Home Rule was bitterly opposed by Irish unionists, for whom it meant 'Rome Rule'. Their opposition culminated in a 'Solemn League and Covenant', calling in aid 'the God whom our fathers in days of stress and trial confidently trusted'. Over 200,000 men (supported, in a separate document, by an even larger number of women) announced their determination to use 'all means which may be found necessary to defeat the present conspiracy' and their refusal to accept the authority of a Home Rule parliament. The unionists' implied threat of violence set in train a sequence of events: the formation of rival nationalist and unionist paramilitary groups, the Easter Rising by republicans in Dublin, the 'Black and Tan war' between the Irish republicans and British forces, the partition of Ireland between the overwhelmingly Catholic south and the predominantly Protestant north, and finally the Irish civil war. In the latter part of this period, ethnic cleansing, mixed with murder, was commonplace. The high degree of correlation between religious and political affiliation meant that it was hard to disentangle the political and the religious motives for this violence. The two political entities that emerged from this turmoil each had a distinctive religious character. Northern Ireland was described by its first prime minister as having a 'a Protestant Parliament for a Protestant people',[4] and its legitimacy was consistently rejected by a large part of the Catholic minority. The Irish Free State, though professedly non-confessional, was dominated by Catholicism, and a large part of the Protestant minority responded by emigration. Being a Protestant or a Catholic in Ireland was about Christian faith – and there were many people who took that faith very seriously. But it was also about intense loyalty to a particular community, a lively awareness both of its history and of its present situation, and a willingness to defend its rights by any method deemed necessary.

Belfast was only an extreme example of a situation that was found in many parts of the world in the first quarter of the twentieth century. The Irish conflicts were uniquely violent because religious differences were so deeply bound up with the principal political question of the day, namely Ireland's relationship with Great Britain. However, in Germany, Switzerland and the Netherlands, the divide between Protestant and Catholic remained a major fact of life, as it had been for centuries. And in the nineteenth century Irish emigration to the great cities of England and Scotland, North America and Australasia, challenged Protestant religious, political and cultural domination, and established a major fault-line, cutting through most areas of life.

In the immigrant cities of North America, relatively high levels of religious involvement were partly sustained by the links between religion and ethnicity. 'The point about the melting pot', wrote Glazer and Moynihan in their famous study of ethnic groups in New York city, 'is that it did not happen.'[5] At least in the first and second generation a large proportion of immigrants and their descendants lived in ethnic neighbourhoods, chose a marriage partner of the same ethnicity, belonged to churches or benefit societies that brought them into regular contact with those of similar origins, found work through ethnic networks, and voted for politicians from a similar

---

4 Paul Bew, Peter Gibbon and Henry Patterson, *Northern Ireland 1921–1996* (London: Serif, 1996), p. 242.
5 Nathan Glazer and Daniel P. Moynihan, *Beyond the melting pot*, 2nd edn (Cambridge, MA: Harvard University Press, 1970), p. xcvii.

ethnic or religious background. Not that this always promoted involvement in the church: in New York in the early twentieth century, the Irish were overwhelmingly Catholic and had high levels of churchgoing; Italians were equally strongly Catholic, but their Catholicism was tinged with anti-clericalism, and they were much less regular in attendance at mass and confession; and Germans were not only divided between Protestants, Catholics and Jews, but the Protestants, in particular, were noted as infrequent churchgoers.[6]

While few crossed the frontier that separated Catholic, Protestant and Jew, Protestants and Jews more readily crossed denominational boundaries, and the cities of North America, like those of Britain, the Netherlands, Sweden and Australasia, offered a wide range of choices. So, for instance, if most German Protestant immigrants to New York remained Lutherans, there were also considerable numbers (especially of those who were successful in business) who became Episcopalians, while others became Baptists or Methodists, or joined groups like Ethical Culture.[7] Competition was thus an essential part of the urban religious scene. The doctrine, the liturgy and the reputation of the preacher were the three basic factors that influenced the choice of one church rather than another. 'Pulpit princes' could still attract huge congregations, and the pronouncements by prominent preachers on political and social issues, as well as on theological questions, received extensive coverage in the press. But there were many people inclined to spend their Sundays in bed, in a pub, or visiting relatives, and who thus needed to be persuaded to come to church at all. Some denominations pinned their hopes on aggressive evangelism, whether in the form of mass rallies, preaching in parks or at street corners, or knocking on doors. Most churches offered a range of associated attractions and services, ranging from creches and parish nurses to evening classes and a gymnasium. Some offered more subtle rewards, such as enhanced social status or business contacts. In the 1890s it had been said that: 'A steady young man commencing life in Liverpool without capital or good friends could not do better for his own future than by becoming active, useful and respected in a large dissenting congregation.'[8]

6 Hugh McLeod, *Piety and poverty: working class religion in Berlin, London and New York, 1870–1914* (New York: Holmes & Meier, 1996), pp. 49–80.
7 Ibid., p. 97.
8 Hugh McLeod, 'White collar values and the role of religion', in Geoffrey Crossick (ed.), *The lower middle class in Britain 1870–1914* (London: Croom Helm, 1977), p. 74.

Secularisation

Even in the English-speaking countries, where urban religion had flourished most vigorously in the nineteenth century, the churches were encountering serious secular competition by the early twentieth century. These challenges were even more evident in the cities and industrial regions of Germany and France. Berlin was said in the 1880s to be 'the most irreligious city in the world',[9] and indeed it had a history of widespread alienation from the Protestant church, going back at least to the time of the 1848 revolution – and perhaps even further, since the notorious scarcity of churches in the city dates back to the second half of the eighteenth century. To be a churchgoing Christian in Berlin was to be part of a small and sometimes beleaguered minority. This sense of isolation was nowhere greater than in working-class districts, such as Wedding, a centre of heavy industry in the city's proletarian north. In 1913 the parish helper, a working-class man, employed as a visitor, complained of 'being treated as a criminal . . . just because he belonged to the church'. 'One has the feeling', he wrote, 'of working among a people who know nothing of Christianity, and it has been suggested that a "Society for Missions to the Heathen" is needed in the national capital.'[10] The biggest reason for hostility to the church was political. The working-class districts of Berlin were dominated by the social democrats in the years before 1914, and became communist strongholds in the 1920s. The social democrats included some 'religious socialists', as well as others who wanted the party to avoid religious controversy. But on the whole they shared the communists' militant hostility to the church which they saw as a stronghold of political conservatism. Until the fall of the monarchy in 1918, this antipathy was exacerbated by the Protestant church's close links with the state and with the Hohenzollern dynasty. Moreover, intellectual criticisms of religion, which had a large audience in the German bourgeoisie, also influenced politically conscious workers. From about the 1830s, philosophical questioning of religion, radical biblical criticism and scientific materialism had all established a wide following. Alienation from the church in Berlin was also in some ways a response to the apparent religious unanimity of many rural areas. Migrants who had resented the links between religious and civil authority in their native villages and the strong social pressures to attend church sometimes revelled in the freedom that the big city offered.

9 McLeod, *Piety*, p. 6.   10 Ibid., p. 26.

Those who remained loyal to the Protestant church included some who were positively attracted by its traditions, its conservatism and its links with the state. Two groups among them seem to have been particularly numerous: artisans, shopkeepers and small employers, from old Berlin families, often with longstanding links to a particular parish church; and state employees, ranging from army officers and bureaucrats to postmen and railway workers, for whom going to church was partly a matter of loyalty. In Berlin, as indeed in many other parts of early twentieth-century Europe, going to church contained a message – whether intended or not – about one's attitude to the state. This would become even more apparent in the 1930s. When Hitler came to power he was courting the churches, especially the Protestant churches, and going to church, or at least becoming a member of the church, looked like a way of expressing solidarity with the new regime. The year 1933 saw a big return to church membership by those who had earlier resigned, as well as a significant number of conversions of Catholics to Protestantism. By 1937 the churches were out of favour and the years 1937–9 saw record numbers of resignations from the churches.[11]

Berlin was an extreme case of wider tendencies in the cities and industrial regions of early twentieth-century Europe. In many countries there was a contrast between a devout countryside and a more secular city, and alienation from the church was usually most frequent in the working class.[12] Political factors were a major reason for this. But other factors contributed, especially the tardiness with which the church had responded to rapid urban growth by building churches, schools and parish centres and by transferring clergy to the new centres of population. Of course, lower levels of churchgoing in the cities partly reflected the availability of a huge range of alternative activities, as well as the fact that anti-religious or sceptical ideas were more easily available.

Even in Berlin, however, those who seldom or never went to church were not necessarily agnostics or atheists. More common probably was what an Anglican bishop called 'diffusive Christianity'.[13] A working-class Londoner, born in 1899, told an oral historian that his parents were 'one hundred

---

11 Lucian Hölscher (ed.), *Datenatlas zur religiösen Geographie im protestantischen Deutschland*, 4 vols. (Berlin, Walter De Gruyter, 2001), vol. IV, p. 705.
12 Hugh McLeod, *Religion and the people of western Europe, 1789–1989* (Oxford: Oxford University Press, 1997), pp. 75–97, 118–31.
13 Jeffrey Cox, *English churches in a secular society: Lambeth 1870–1930* (Oxford: Oxford University Press, 1982), p. 93.

per cent Christians but not churchgoers'.[14] All over Europe – and indeed all over the Americas and Australasia – in the early twentieth century there were probably large numbers of people who would have accepted this description. It was particularly characteristic of the urban working class. Acceptance of some form of Christian ethics, strong attachment to the rites of passage and observance of certain festivals often went hand in hand with indifference to doctrine, and disapproval of more regular churchgoing as being an objectionable form of super-piety.[15] But the situation in many rural areas was not so different. There were large parts of rural Catholic Europe, and even more of Latin America, where the culture was strongly Catholic, but attendance at mass and confession was infrequent, and anti-clericalism was widespread. In such places, the major focus of Catholic practice was on devotion to the saints and especially Mary. Pictures of the saints adorned the walls at home, and their devotees carried cards and medallions with them as they worked, travelled, or went to war. Annual processions in honour of the patron saint of the community were the biggest event in the calendar. Times of crisis brought pilgrimages to local shrines, or sometimes to a major national or international shrine, such as Lourdes or La Salette.

Conversion

Even in Europe, with its long history of close ties between church and state and between higher clergy and other social elites, there were also situations in which being a Christian was an act of conscious rebellion. This was notably so in France during the years around World War I. The anti-clerical republicans had come to power in 1879. In the years up to the formal separation of church and state in 1905 they had pursued a wide-ranging programme of secularisation, supported by many of the literary and scientific intelligentsia, as well as by the tens of thousands of doctors, lawyers and teachers who formed the bedrock of republican electoral strength. But, beginning slowly in the 1880s and then becoming much more rapid after 1905, there was a movement of conversion to Catholicism among the younger generation of intellectuals, especially writers and artists.[16] Some had been brought up in freethought,

14 Hugh McLeod, 'New perspectives on Victorian working class religion: the oral evidence', *Oral history* 14 (1986), p. 32.
15 See especially S. C. Williams, *Religious belief and popular culture: Southwark c.1880–1939* (Oxford: Oxford University Press, 1999).
16 Frédéric Gugelot, *La conversion des intellectuels au catholicisme en France (1885–1935)* (Paris: CNRS, 1998).

while others were returning to a childhood faith that they had rejected in adolescence. The most prominent figures in this movement were the poets Paul Claudel and Charles Péguy and the philosopher Jacques Maritain, though many more obscure figures were also involved. Several themes recur in these conversions. Science was criticised for having excluded important areas of human experience. Catholicism was seen as providing a better basis for morality than positivism, and as offering a more realistic understanding of human nature: while the latter seduced people by its promises of boundless progress, the former recognised that human beings are sinful and that suffering is an inescapable part of life. Catholicism was also valued because of its role in art, architecture and literature, and even more because of its central place in French history and its association with national identity. Péguy was typical here: his conversion was followed by the adoption of a romantic nationalism, expressed in the cult of Joan of Arc.

In 1914 the only place where Christians faced a major risk of martyrdom was the Turkish empire, in which recurrent attacks on Christian minorities culminated in the massacre of several hundred thousand Armenians in 1915. Yet in other places martyrdom was a part of the recent past, or would become familiar in the near future. Buganda in the 1880s had seen the killing both of the English-born Anglican Bishop Hannington and of hundreds of Bugandan Christians. In China, the Boxer rebellion of 1900 had targeted both missionaries and Chinese Christians. The 1920s would see not only the communist attack on religion in the Soviet Union, but persecutions of the Catholic church in Mexico and uprisings by Catholic peasants in the west of the country.

In China and in some parts of Africa there was in this period a first generation of Christians, very conscious of having broken with the traditions of their ancestors, sometimes radically critical of these traditions, and confident that Christianity offered not only personal salvation, but the foundation for a modern and progressive society. So, for instance, in Northern Rhodesia and Nyasaland in the early twentieth century both hereditary chiefs and the British authorities, who were trying to operate a system of indirect rule, found themselves in conflict with a generation of militant youth, many of them associated with Presbyterian missions, who poured scorn on all aspects of traditional belief and ritual. One of their leaders was David Kaunda, father of the later Zambian president. In 1904 or 1905 he started preaching in the area of the sacred burial groves of the Bemba kings, in defiance of an official ban. In 1908 another young evangelist was flogged for speaking disrespectfully to a headman who tried to stop his preaching.

As Karen Fields comments, 'African evangelists employed by missions were notorious radicals who did not hesitate to scandalize village opinion by destroying ancestor shrines, breaking ceremonial beer pots, disrupting communal rituals, insulting and disobeying "heathen" elders, and aggressively advertising and displaying the material advantages of mission membership.' Furthermore, 'Christianity gave people principled grounds for denying customary obligations of all kinds – arranged marriages, prescribed remarriages, customary labor', and it could justify wives in disobeying their husbands.[17]

Whereas in Europe the socially marginal were often leaving churches which they regarded as part of the social and political establishment, in many parts of Asia the opposite was happening. Generally speaking, it was the marginalised – ethnic minorities, 'hill-peoples', 'untouchables' – who were most responsive to Christian missions. Indeed it was often they who took the initiative in seeking out missionaries whose attention was focused elsewhere. A typical story is that of Samuel Pollard, a Cornish Methodist who was making little progress in his missionary labours among Han Chinese in north-eastern Yunnan but who, one day in 1904, was approached by four men belonging to the Miao minority. They had travelled some distance to find him, and they wanted to be taught to read. After several hundred more visitors had followed, Pollard transferred his base to a Miao hamlet, where he took a leading part in devising the first Miao script and translating the New Testament into their language. Christianisation and education went hand in hand, and the Miao became known for very high levels of adherence to Christianity and of both female and male literacy. As Norma Diamond comments, the Chinese regarded the Miao as 'an inferior and rootless people', and as 'newly pacified barbarians': education and conversion to Christianity gave them a new degree of self-confidence and an ability to defend their own identity and culture.[18]

A somewhat similar story can be seen in the Punjab, where between about 1880 and 1930 there was a mass movement of conversion to Christianity among members of the sweeper caste, one of the most deprived and despised sections of the rural poor. Here again the movement started with an American missionary being approached by a man called Ditt, previously unknown to him, who asked for baptism and then secured the conversion

---

17 Karen E. Fields, 'Christian missionaries as anticolonial militants', *Theory and society* 11 (1982), pp. 96–9.
18 Norma Diamond, 'Christianity and the Hua Miao: writing and power', in Daniel H. Bays (ed.), *Christianity in China from the eighteenth century to the present* (Stanford, CA: Stanford University Press, 1996), pp. 138–57.

of several family members and neighbours. Converts often came in groups. Thus in 1925 an Anglican missionary reported: 'I baptized the greater part of the Mazhabi Sikh community in three hours. They are a bright lot of people and decidedly above the the level of the ordinary Chuhra. It was through relatives of the headman having become Christian in another part of the Punjab that these people decided to enrol themselves as catechumens.' Again, conversion was seen as going hand in hand with greater educational opportunities and a new sense of self-worth. In the 1930s a Salvation Army journalist asked a spokesman for Punjabi village Christians what difference Christianity had made to their lives. He received the reply that 'Christianity had brought them many benefits: cleanliness, self-respect, cessation of eating animals which died, schooling for the children, the privilege of free approach to their officials to whom they could freely tell their troubles and get helped. But what about the moral character of the People? We have learned to pray. There is now no gambling amongst us, no drink, no murder. The women sing praises to Jesus.'[19]

So, in spite of much that Christians in different parts of the world and in different parts of the same country shared, the meanings of being a Christian also varied radically. In the course of the twentieth century these meanings would often change again. In some parts of the world periods of severe persecution would alternate with periods of optimism, or even triumphalism. Some areas would see the gradual decline of a once powerful Christian culture, and in others Christianity would advance from marginality to dominance.

19 Jeffrey Cox, *Imperial faultlines: Christianity and colonial power in India, 1818–1940* (Stanford, CA: Standford University Press, 2002), pp. 129–30.

PART I

★

INSTITUTIONS AND MOVEMENTS

3

The papacy

JOHN POLLARD

Introduction

By the end of the reign of Pius X in August 1914, the construction of the modern papacy was virtually complete. Nearly all of its most typical characteristics were in place – papal infallibility, the 'Romanisation' of national hierarchies through the appointment of increasing numbers of bishops at least partially educated in Rome, bureaucratic centralisation of decision-making in all ecclesiastical affairs in Rome via the agency of papal nuncios and apostolic delegates, and the use of papal encyclicals and apostolic letters to enforce the magisterium in matters not only of dogmatic theology and moral theology, but of social doctrine, liturgy, popular piety and those touching upon church–state relations in individual countries. Perhaps most important of all, the cult around the personality of the reigning pontiff had been fully developed, underpinned by the mobilisation of lay support through the Catholic press, Peter's Pence, pilgrimages and early forms of 'Catholic Action' organisation. The only major elements of modern papal absolutism over the Roman Catholic church that were still lacking were the codification of canon law, which would be promulgated by Benedict XV in 1917 but which in point of fact had been inaugurated by his predecessor ten years earlier, and the Catechism of the Catholic Church, to replace national/regional variants of basic Christian doctrine taught to the laity, which would first be prospected by Benedict XV in 1921 but not brought to fruition until the reign of John Paul II in 1992.

The pontificates that followed that of Pius X, between 1914 and 1958, would do little more than confirm and consolidate the unchallenged authority of the papacy over the church, but in the reigns of John XXIII and Paul VI, in the twenty or so years after 1958, that authority would be seriously challenged by the decisions of the Second Vatican Council (1962–5) and the responses of clergy and laity to them, and by the more broadly cultural and social changes that took place in North America and western Europe in the 1960s and 1970s. It thus makes sense to talk about the pontificate of John Paul II, after 1978, as constituting a conservative reaction to the developments that flowed out of the council, or perhaps even as a 'preventive counter-revolution'.

This chapter has been built around an analysis of the key events in successive pontificates, with obviously only a brief mention of the thirty-three-day reign of John Paul I in 1978, and will concentrate on the impact of successive pontiffs in the following areas of the life of the church:

1 Christian doctrine, liturgy and ecclesiastical organisation;
2 moral theology;
3 social doctrine.

It will also examine the papacy in its relations with the Eastern churches in communion with Rome, its missionary outreach and its relations with non-Catholic churches, and the papacy's response to important developments in national politics and in international relations and, in regard to the latter, through the workings of Vatican diplomacy.

Each section on a pontificate will be prefaced by a brief account of the conclave that elected the pope, and each will close normally with a summative judgement of his achievements and the longer-term significance of his reign. Finally, the chapter will conclude with an analysis of the state of the papacy at the beginning of the third Christian millennium.

Benedict XV (1914–1922)

Despite being largely unknown before his election, Cardinal Giacomo Della Chiesa, archbishop of Bologna, was the frontrunner from the start, indeed much of the 1914 conclave was taken up by attempts on the part of his opponents to prevent his elevation.[1] This indicates that the election of the Genoese pope, who had been exiled from his post as substitute secretary of state in the Vatican in 1907 and who had spent the next seven years as pastor of the major diocese of Italy's 'red belt', was a break with the previous pontificate. Though Della Chiesa was not a 'modernist', despite suspicions to the contrary, he deplored the persecution of alleged 'modernists' during his predecessor's reign and sought actively to heal the wounds in the church

---

1 J. F. Pollard, *The unknown pope: Benedict XV (1914–1922) and the pursuit of peace*, (London: Cassell, 1999); P. Levillain (ed.), *The papacy: an encyclopedia*, (London: Routledge, 2002), vol. I, pp. 172–7.

that it had caused, starting with his first encyclical *Ad Beatissimi*, 1914.[2] As pupils of Cardinal Rampolla, Leo XIII's secretary of state, Benedict and his secretary of state, Cardinal Pietro Gasparri, broke with the policy of Pius X and Cardinal Rafael Merry Del Val, and pursued a more active and concilia-tory line in Vatican diplomacy, commencing with a cordial letter announcing the new pope's election to the president of France.

The previous diplomatic experience of both pope and secretary of state were absolutely vital for the Holy See because Benedict's pontificate was, of course, dominated by the First World War which had broken out a month before the 1914 conclave. Benedict and Gasparri established a neutral and impartial stand from the start: with millions of Catholics fighting on both sides, they could hardly have done otherwise, though it has to be said that events sometimes placed a terrible strain upon that policy.[3] They not only organised considerable humanitarian relief work to alleviate the suffering of soldiers and civilians alike, spending 82 million gold lire in the process,[4] they also engaged in active diplomacy to bring about peace, seeking to prevent the entry into war of Italy in 1915 and the USA in 1917. Their greatest effort took the form of dispatching Mgr Eugenio Pacelli (substitute secretary of state and later Pope Pius XII) to Bavaria in May 1917 to win German support as a prelude to the 'Peace Note' of August that year in which Benedict laid down a series of proposals as a starting point for peace negotiation.[5] The negative response of all the belligerents was a bitter disappointment to Benedict. Despite the lack of success, Benedict had established a tradition in which the papacy was henceforth committed to being an active international peace-maker.

Benedict and Gasparri were not happy with the subsequent Versailles Peace Settlement of 1919, which they regarded as dangerously harsh and punitive in the terms it imposed upon Germany in particular.[6] They also regretted the disappearance of the Habsburg empire, the last Catholic great power in Europe and a former bulwark against Russia and Orthodoxy, yet the prestige of Vatican diplomacy benefited greatly from the establishment of relations with the successor states to the vanquished empires. Perhaps their only major consolation was the enormous improvement in relations between the Holy See and Italy, which nearly resulted in resolution of the

---

2 For the texts of all the encyclicals cited in this chapter, see C. Carlen, IHM (ed.), *The papal encyclicals, 1846–1978*, 5 vols. (Ann Arbor: Pierian Press, 1990–7).
3 Pollard, *The unknown pope*, ch. 4.   4 Ibid., pp. 112–16.   5 Ibid., pp. 117–28.
6 S. Stehlin, *Weimar and the Vatican, 1919–1933: German–Vatican diplomatic relations in the interwar years* (Princeton: Princeton University Press, 1983), chs. II and III.

'Roman Question' in 1919. But the political situation in Italy during the 'red two years' of 1918 to 1920, when the militancy and violence of the working-class movement seemed to presage a revolution on the lines of that which had succeeded in Russia in 1917 and which had been less successfully attempted in parts of central and eastern Europe, led Benedict to condemn socialism and communism in two major public letters. He also showed no sympathy for an even more violent and radical movement which emerged during his pontificate, Italian fascism.[7]

While Benedict did not have the same impact upon the organisational structure and worship life of the worldwide church as his predecessor, he did continue Pius X's reform of the Roman curia, he promulgated the Code of Canon Law in 1917 and he established both a commission to interpret it and an ecclesiastical institute to study it. He also launched the first steps towards the creation of a uniform catechism for the church.[8] His most important ecclesiastical innovations were in the area of relations between the Holy See and Eastern churches in communion with it and in the church's missionary outreach. He created a separate congregation for the Eastern churches with himself as prefect, and in his apostolic letter *Maximum illud* of 1921 he sought to distance missionary activities from the interests of colonial administration.[9] Though highly suspicious of the 'Protestant' churches, like most Rome-trained clergy, he allowed the Malines ecumenical conversations between the British Anglo-Catholic Lord Halifax and the Belgian Cardinal Mercier.[10]

Benedict died at a very early age for a pope – sixty-eight years – and this partially accounts for his not being well known and remembered. Despite the failure of his peace efforts, his was clearly one of the key pontificates of the twentieth century, given his achievements in healing the wounds left by the 'modernist' crisis, his humanitarian response to the First World War, his revitalisation of papal diplomacy – the number of countries having relations with the Vatican had doubled by the end of his reign – and his anticipation of the role of the missions in the event of decolonisation. The greatest evidence of the importance of Benedict's reign is to be found in the fact that his successor continued and developed the majority of his policies and initiatives and even kept on his secretary of state, Gasparri, a decision unprecedented in the modern history of the papacy.

---

7 Pollard, *The Unknown Pope*, pp. 166–70.   8 Ibid., pp. 178–9.   9 Ibid., pp. 201–4.
10 B. Pawley and M. Pawley, *Rome and Canterbury through four centuries* (London and Oxford: Mowbray, 1981), chs. 15 and 16.

Pius XI (1922–1939)

The election of Achille Ratti, cardinal archbishop of Milan, in the conclave of 1922 can only be explained as being that of a compromise, between Merry Del Val who was trying to make a comeback and reverse the policies of the previous reign, and Gasparri, who clearly represented continuity but who was damaged by allegations of nepotism.[11] Like his predecessor, Pius XI had both diplomatic and pastoral experience, though his stint in Milan was short to say the least, seven months. His faithfulness to Benedict's policies may have been a reflection of the fact that he had in a real sense been his 'creation', owing to the Genoese pope his sudden transfer from the Vatican library to a diplomatic posting in Poland and his elevation to the cardinalate and to the archbishopric of Milan. In temperament, his dictatorial personality was more akin to that of Pius X than to Benedict's.

If Pius continued many of Benedict's policies, he also developed them, as in the way in which he changed the attitude of the Vatican to Mussolini and fascism, accepted the consequences of the March on Rome of October 1922, and implicitly supported the Fascist government during the Matteotti Crisis of 1924 which nearly brought it down.[12] Fascism claimed to have saved Italy from communism, restored political stability of a sort after the chronic instability of parliamentary government in the post-war period, and ultimately delivered a solution to the 'Roman Question'. In his policies towards the Catholic Italian People's Party on the one hand and fascism on the other, Papa Ratti revealed a deep-seated mistrust of liberal democracy, and of Catholic participation in politics. His willingness to forgive the adolescent excesses of fascism was typical of the Italian episcopate and clergy. More broadly, his attitudes reflect the initial, very sympathetic, response of many Catholics to the rise of fascist movements, and authoritarian regimes, in Europe in the 1920s.[13]

The long 'courtship' of fascism resulted in the Lateran Pacts of February 1929: the Lateran Treaty finally resolved the 'Roman Question' and restored the temporal power in the form of the tiny state of the Vatican City; the Financial

---

11 There is no good, full biography of Pius XI in English: see Levillain, *The Papacy*, vol. II, pp. 1199–210 and C. Falconi, *The popes of the twentieth century* (London: Weidenfeld & Nicolson, 1967), pp. 151–234.

12 J. N. Molony, *The emergence of political Catholicism in Italy: Partito Popolare: 1919–1926* (London: Croom Helm, 1977), chs. 6 and 7.

13 See the entry for 'Facism' (*sic*) in J. A. Dwyer (ed.), *The new dictionary of Catholic social thought* (Collegeville, MN: Liturgical Press, 1994), pp. 381–8.

Convention gave monetary compensation to the Holy See for the loss of revenues from the former Papal States, and the Concordat restored much of the property and many of the rights and privileges of the Italian church which it had lost during the unification process, including religious instruction in schools and a form of marriage that effectively precluded divorce.[14] While some contemporary Catholic observers, including Mgr Giambattista Montini, the future Paul VI, criticised the Lateran settlement as a dangerous endorsement of fascism, it brought many long-term benefits, including a stronger influence in Italian civil society and new diplomatic prestige. Moreover, under the management of Bernardino Nogara, the financial compensation paid by the Italian government was used to lay the foundations of Vatican financial independence.[15]

Pius XI used his authority to drive forward Benedict's new policy of establishing a native clergy and even episcopate in the colonial territories of the European powers, and in 1926 issued another encyclical on the missions, *Rerum ecclesiae*, ordained six Chinese bishops in St Peter's Basilica, and declared unequivocally: 'The missions must have nothing to do with nationalism. They must be solely concerned with Catholicism, with the apostolate ... nationalism has always been a calamity for the Missions, indeed it would be no exaggeration to say that it is a curse.'[16]

Pius XI's most important pronouncement in the field of theology and morals was undoubtedly the encyclical *Casti connubi*, of 1930. The encyclical, while largely a reiteration of existing church teaching on marriage, divorce and related sexual questions, with its firm condemnation of artificial contraception and its emphasis on the role of women as wives and mothers, was in a real sense a response to the relaxation of sexual mores and the changing of the role of women that had followed the end of the First World War. In the field of social doctrine, a year later he published *Quadragesimo anno* to commemorate the fortieth anniversary of Leo XIII's great social encyclical, *Rerum novarum*. *Quadragesimo anno* was not simply a reiteration of Leo's teaching, but displayed both innovative thinking on the part of its real author – the Jesuit Nell-Brunning – and a felt need on the part of the pontiff to give guidance to Catholics in a period of economic crisis, the Great Depression,

---

14 J. F. Pollard, *The Vatican and the fascist regime in Italy, 1929–1932: a study in conflict* (Cambridge: Cambridge University Press, 1985), chs. 2 and 3, and pp. 197–215 for the text of the pacts.

15 J. F. Pollard, *Money and the rise of the modern papacy: financing the Vatican, 1850–1950* (Cambridge: Cambridge University Press, 2004), chs. 6–9.

16 As quoted in Pollard, *The Vatican*, p. 89.

which Pius XI described as the 'greatest human catastrophe since the flood'. It was condemnatory of communism, but was also highly critical of capitalism's failures and of those of finance capital in particular. And though critical of some aspects of the Italian fascist corporate state, in broader terms it welcomed 'corporatist' experiments, like that in Austria, and could thus be said to be giving support to fascist movements in general in the 1930s.[17]

While Pius XI was tolerant of undemocratic, even fascist, regimes, the rise and consolidation of totalitarianism in Europe – Mussolini's Italy, the Nazi regime in Germany and Stalin's Soviet Union – increasingly preoccupied him from the end of the 1920s.[18] The first signs of tension and disagreement between the Vatican and the fascist regime appeared shortly after the signing of the Lateran Pacts, and in that year Pius took his first swipe at the totalitarian pretensions of fascism, this time in the area of education and youth. Two years later, during a full-blooded crisis over fascist attacks on both Catholic youth and trade union organisations, Pius XI came close to rejecting fascist ideology *tout court* in his encyclical *Non abbiamo*.[19] The outcome was a draw and the church and fascism settled down to an uneasy 'marriage of convenience' that lasted until 1938. Having signed a *Reichskonkordat* with the new Nazi government in 1933, the Vatican had to grapple with successive, increasingly serious, violations of it by Hitler's government. These led to the publication of a condemnatory encyclical, *Mit brennender Sorge*, in 1937.[20] The rejection of National Socialist racialism in that encyclical was repeated in another encyclical, *Humani generis unitas*, which Pius commissioned from the American Jesuit John Lafarge to address the question of racial anti-semitism. This was prompted by Mussolini's introduction of the Racial Laws into Italy in the autumn of 1938.[21] The text was suppressed by Eugenio Pacelli when he succeeded Papa Ratti: thus was lost a crucial opportunity to publicly oppose Nazi racialism before it descended into the Holocaust. As far as communism was concerned, in 1929 Pius had abandoned attempts to negotiate some sort of *modus vivendi* with the Soviets, another continuation of the policy of his predecessor, and in 1930 he condemned communism anew in the encyclical *Divini redemptoris*.

17 See the entry on *Quadragesimo anno* in Dwyer, *New Dictionary*, pp. 802–13.
18 See A. Rhodes, *The Vatican in the age of the dictators* (London: Hodder & Stoughton, 1973), chs. 8, 9, 11 and 14.
19 Pollard, *The Vatican*, ch. 5.
20 G. Lewy, *The Catholic church and Nazi Germany* (London: Weidenfeld & Nicolson, 1964), chs. 2–6.
21 G. Passalecq and B. Suchecky, *The hidden encyclical of Pius XI* (New York & London: Harcourt Brace, 1997).

The rise of the dictators, and the emergence in particular of the Rome–Berlin Axis from 1936 onwards, prompted Pius XI to change course. He had hitherto encouraged both the development of better relations between Italy and France and the emergence of a Catholic bloc of countries led by Fascist Italy, as a third force between Britain and France on the one hand and Nazi Germany on the other.[22] In the late 1930s, the cardinal secretary of state, Pacelli, now travelled widely in his attempts to develop closer relations with the democracies, Britain, France and the United States.[23]

Pius XI's achievements were considerable, most notably the settlement of the 'Roman Question' and the securing of the Vatican's finances. But they were overshadowed by his mistakes, such as his trust in concordats, most especially the *Reichskonkordat*, and in the apolitical lay organisations of Catholic Action rather than in political parties to protect the church's rights. By the end of his reign the unwisdom of that policy was plain for all, including the pope, to see.

Pius XII (1939–1958)

Eugenio Pacelli was the clearly designated *dauphin* by the end of his predecessor's reign. Pius XI believed that in a turbulent world, almost certainly heading for war, a diplomat like Pacelli was needed to lead the papacy.[24] Certainly, Pacelli was the only twentieth-century pope to lack almost completely the pastoral experience necessary to complement his bureaucratic/diplomatic expertise. He used that expertise in his peace efforts before the outbreak of war in 1939, and in his attempts to keep Italy out of the war once it had started.[25] In his pursuit of peace, Pius XII enjoyed a number of advantages over Benedict XV. Papal diplomatic influence was much stronger and more widespread in 1939 than it had been at the beginning of the First World War and by the end of the Second World War the Vatican had relations with all the major belligerents except the Soviet Union.

Pius XII was in a much stronger position than Benedict from even before his election in 1939. He was quite well known before his election: as cardinal

22 P. C. Kent, *The pope and the duce* (London & Basingstoke: Macmillan, 1983), chs. 6, 9, 10 and 11.
23 P. C. Kent and J. F. Pollard (eds.) *Papal diplomacy in the modern age* (Westport, CN: Praeger, 1994), p. 18.
24 There is no satisfactory biography of Pius XII in English. For biographical essays see Falconi, *The popes*, pp. 234–303 and Levillain, *The Papacy*, vol. II, pp. 1210–20.
25 O. Chadwick, *Britain and the Vatican during the Second World War* (Cambridge: Cambridge University Press, 1986), especially chs. 3–5.

secretary of state, he had been at the centre of affairs in the Vatican for nine years and, moreover, had visited North and South America and was personally known to President Roosevelt. Thanks to the growth in the numbers of American Catholics, and their consequent pre-eminent position among the financial supporters of the Vatican's activities, Pius XI and Pacelli had been able to strengthen both their financial and their political links with the USA from about 1936 onwards. This paid off in 1939 when Francis Spellman, archbishop of New York, brokered a deal whereby a 'personal representative' of the US president was accredited to the papal court in late 1939. Pius thus had what one could almost describe as a 'special relationship' with the USA, and though this did not prevent serious difficulties arising between the Vatican and the Allies from time to time, the relationship was to stand Vatican diplomacy in good stead.[26] Yet, despite all these advantages, Pius XII's peace diplomacy was no more successful than that of Benedict. His 'five peace points' plan of 1940, which, it has to be said, was a much more vague formula for peace-making than Benedict's 'Peace Note', has hardly been remembered, even though it evoked much greater support in the belligerent countries, especially those of the Allies, than Benedict's 'Peace Note' of 1917.[27]

In any case, Pius XII's peace-making efforts have been overshadowed by the bitter controversies surrounding his response to the Holocaust and the genocide practised by the Ustasha regime in Croatia from 1941 to 45. The controversy began over Hochhuth's play *The Deputy* which was first staged in German in February 1963. Since then, dozens of monographs and articles in scholarly journals and probably hundreds of articles in newspapers have been published on it and related subjects.[28] The controversy is, therefore, by any standard, one of the longest running and most bitterly contested of historiographical debates and at least half of the monographs have been produced in recent years, prompted by the publication of John Cornwell's *Hitler's pope* in 1999.[29] The issues are complex, and involve not only the personal role of Pius XII but, more importantly, the extent of anti-semitism in the Catholic church in general before the outbreak of war in 1939, the difficulties faced by

26 J. F. Pollard, 'The papacy in two world wars: Benedict XV and Pius XII compared', in G. Sorensen and R. Mallett (eds.), *International fascism, 1919–1945* (London: Frank Cass, 2002), pp. 83–97.
27 Ibid., pp. 89–91.
28 For an excellent summary of the debate, from a liberal Catholic point of view, see J. Sanchez, *Pius XII and the Holocaust: understanding the debate*, (Washington: Catholic University of America Press, 2002).
29 J. Cornwell, *Hitler's pope: the secret history of Pius XII* (London: Viking, 1999).

the Holy See in its wartime diplomacy, and the vexed question of whether it would really have been counter-productive to have denounced genocide at the time.

At the end of the war, there was no immediate questioning of Pius XII's role and therefore the papacy emerged in 1945 in a strong moral and diplomatic position to face the onset of the Cold War, with isolation of the persecuted 'Church of Silence' behind the Iron Curtain in eastern and central Europe and the challenge of large, well-organised communist parties in western Europe, especially in France and Italy.

In the early period of the Cold War, Pius could rely upon the 'special relationship' with the USA, and co-operation between Washington and the Vatican was quite close in such places as Belgrade and Bucharest.[30] However, he had opposed the divisions of Europe sanctioned by Yalta, and the subsequent policy of 'containment' towards the USSR and its satellites practised by the West, and avoided being trapped into the role of 'the chaplain of NATO'.[31] In the battle against communism in western Europe, Pius endorsed the rise to governmental power of Christian Democratic parties in the Benelux counties, France, Germany and Italy, and encouraged European integration.

In the years after the war, Pius XII initiated some important theological and liturgical innovations, the infallible definition of the doctrine of the Assumption of the Blessed Virgin Mary into Heaven in 1950 and changes to the liturgy of Holy Week. He also warned against the 'Nouvelle Théologie' in Humani generis, 1950.

This year was the highpoint of Pius XII's reign. The celebration of Holy Year and the proclamation of the dogma of the Assumption took place against a background of a massive mobilisation of Catholics against communism and the exaltation of the cult of the pope. Having refused to replace Maglione as cardinal secretary of state when the latter died in 1944, thereafter he insisted on conducting virtually all major business personally, and pronouncing upon all sorts of matters, theological, scientific, economic and political. He was, therefore, truly as Spinosa has described him, 'the last real pope'.[32] But after his serious illness in 1954, Pius began to withdraw from

---

30 C. Gallagher, 'The United States and the Vatican in Yugoslavia', in D. Kirby (ed.), *Religion and the Cold War* (Basingstoke: Palgrave, 2003), pp. 118–44.
31 P. C. Kent, *The lonely Cold War of Pius XII* (Toronto: McGill-Queen's University Press, 2002).
32 A. Spinosa, *Pio XII: l'ultimo papa* (Milan: Mursia, 1992).

the world and the activity of the Roman curia stagnated, and the general air of decay was reflected in the rather bizarre circumstances of his funeral.

John XXIII (1958–1963)

The election of Cardinal Angelo Giuseppe Roncalli as pope in August 1958 was the outcome of a divided conclave, a split between supporters of the conservative Cardinal Siri of Genoa and the progressive Archbishop Montini of Milan.[33] Since Montini was not a cardinal, the conclave was loath to break precedent and elect him. On the other hand, Roncalli was known as a friend of Montini; moreover he was old and was thus seen by Montini's supporters as a safe pair of hands who would keep the seat warm for Montini. But it did not work out entirely that way. Roncalli's had hardly been a spectacular career. After thirty years in Vatican diplomacy as apostolic delegate in Bulgaria, Greece and Turkey and then nuncio in Paris – a difficult posting in which he had to sort out the problem of the worker priests, as well as De Gaulle's demands for the sacking of thirty-two bishops who had collaborated with Vichy – he was appointed patriarch of Venice in 1954. But the career encompassed experiences which influenced the direction of his pontificate, most especially his contacts with the Orthodox and Muslim worlds, not to mention his role in saving Balkan Jews. As important as these influences was his charismatic personality, humble, open, affable, affectionate and down-to-earth, which well suited the 'democratic' world of the 1950s and 1960s. These, and his inspired decisions to call an ecumenical council and seek better relations with the communist world, transformed what should have been a transitional (albeit short) papacy into a 'revolutionary' one, marking a clear break with what had gone before.

Hebblethwaite has dubbed John XXIII 'the pope of the Council', and in view of his success in launching the great venture of Vatican II, that seems to be apt and appropriate. He seems to have been motivated into calling it by two concerns, a feeling that the apparent drift and stagnation of the latter years of Papa Pacelli's reign needed to be offset by a show of vitality and activity and that the church needed to face the challenges of the modern world and go through a process of *aggiornamento* (updating). As important as his decision to call the council was the way in which he did so, in particular his decision to allow the potential council fathers, the bishops, superiors of

---

33 The definitive biography of John XXIII is P. Hebblethwaite, *John XXIII: pope of the council* (London: Geoffrey Chapman, 1984).

religious orders and experts, to create the agenda. In this, he was moving firmly away from the projects of both Pius XI and Pius XII, who had both considered calling a council and had had second thoughts, but who seem to have been clear what the agenda would have been.[34]

He must well have foreseen that some elements in the Roman curia, most notably conservatives like Pizzardo, prefect of the congregation for seminaries, and Ottaviani, secretary of the Congregation of the Holy Office (the pope was traditionally the prefect) would not have been enthusiastic; nor would Tardini, who had not thought much of Roncalli as a Vatican diplomat but who, nevertheless, allowed John XXIII to make him a cardinal and secretary of state.[35] What eventually, and inevitably, ensued was a battle between the curia, which initially had the upper hand since it had responsibility for the preparation of the council, and the more progressive and independent bishops who, if they did not come to Rome as organised groups, very quickly became so after they arrived, in particular the Americans and the French and Germans.

By the time of John XXIII's death in June 1963, the council had not even agreed on a major constitution (*Sacrosanctum concilium* on liturgical reform), and the battle lines between the 'conservatives' and the 'progressives' had been drawn. It was not clear which side was going to win, or on exactly which side Papa Roncalli stood. But he had achieved his aim of opening up the church, of letting in some light and air. His other notable achievements were to adapt Catholic social teaching to the changed circumstances of the post-war and post-colonial world in his encyclical *Mater et magistra*, 1961, and to proffer the hand of peace to 'all men of good will'. In the encyclical *Pacem in terris* of 1963, written in the wake of his intervention in the Cuban missile crisis of the previous October, he declared that there was no such thing as a just war in a nuclear age and set out a clear distinction between Marxist *philosophy*, which was unChristian, and the practical policies which might flow from it. He thus began the 'opening to the East' which would eventually become the *Ostpolitik* of Mgr Casaroli in the next pontificate and which gave Italian Catholic politicians permission to embark upon an 'opening to the left'.

Clearly, by the end of his reign, John XXIII had changed the agenda of the papacy, and the fact that his death agonies in the spring of 1963 were followed by huge numbers of people through newspapers, radio and television demonstrated that he had changed its image as well.

---

34 Levillain, *The papacy*, vol. III, pp. 1570–83.
35 Hebblethwaite, *John XXIII*, pp. 288–90.

Paul VI (1963–1978)

There are a significant number of parallels between Benedict XV and Paul VI. One was that both had had long careers (thirty years apiece) in the curia and Vatican diplomacy. The second was that they had both been effectively 'exiled' from the Vatican by their opponents. The third was that the 'exile' involved a useful period of pastoral ministry as ordinaries of major Italian sees, and the fourth was that their election to the papacy had been bitterly contested by their opponents. Where the parallels end is that like Pacelli in 1939, Montini in 1963 was clearly the designated *dauphin*, hence he was committed to a continuation of Papa Roncalli's policies, most importantly the council which he had done so much to promote and in whose opening session he had played such a prominent and important part, and this almost certainly helped his election.[36]

The new pope summoned the second session of the council to meet in September 1963, and a further two sessions in 1964 and 1965: throughout all of the sessions he attempted to guide the council from behind the scenes and, in particular, to reconcile the conservative minority with the progressive majority. Serious tensions developed as the work of the council progressed, over the constitution on the liturgy,[37] the constitution on the church (*Lumen gentium*) and the collegiality of bishops (*Christus Dominus*). Further controversy was aroused by the declaration on religious freedom – between Cardinal Ottaviani's fiercely held belief that 'error has no rights' and the liberalism of the Americans in particular, led by Cardinal Alfred Meyer of Chicago – and by disagreement over the role of Jews.[38] In the end, the point of view of the progressives largely prevailed and the council ended in December 1965 with the proclamation of *Gaudium et spes* on the church in the world and Paul VI's announcement that the first episcopal synod of the worldwide church would be held in 1967. As part of the longer-term legacy of the council, curial secretariats for Christian unity, non-believers, the laity and social communications were set up. Paul VI had fulfilled the major mission of his pontificate.[39] The last session of the council coincided with the pope's visit to the United Nations, which symbolised one of the great innovations of his pontificate – the pope as traveller or pilgrim visiting all five continents,

---

36 The best biography of Paul VI is P. Hebblethwaite, *Paul VI: the first modern pope* (London: HarperCollins, 1993).

37 Levillain, *The papacy*, vol. III, pp. 1583–5.   38 Hebblethwaite, *Paul VI*, pp. 400–2.

39 See A. Hastings (ed.), *Modern Catholicism: Vatican II and after* (London: SPCK, 1992) ch. 9, 'Institutional renewal'.

including a visit to the Philippines in 1970 when an attempt was made on his life. These travels were part of Paul's strategy to bring the pope to the peoples, thus reinforcing the efficacy of rather more impersonal papal diplomacy. The trips to Africa, Asia and Latin America were meant to underline his commitment to the further development of Catholic social teaching: in *Popolorum progressio* of 1967 he laid emphasis on the need for social justice *between nations* with an eye to the economic plight of the third world in the wake of decolonisation. The visit to the UN was part his peace offensive, in particular his urgings for a negotiated peace in Vietnam which were to lead to conflict with the Johnson administration in the USA.

The energies of papal diplomacy, in keeping with John XXIII's 'opening to the East', were also engaged in the Vatican's version of *Ostpolitik*, to establish dialogue with regimes in eastern Europe and in particular a sustained campaign by the indefatigable Mgr Casaroli to alleviate the conditions of the church in Czechoslovakia, Hungary and Yugoslavia by negotiating the agreement of the communist rulers for the filling of episcopal sees left vacant by the death or imprisonment of their incumbents.[40] Casaroli had most success in Yugoslavia, but in recent years the whole *raison d'être* of *Ostpolitik* has been challenged.[41]

The latter years of Paul VI's pontificate were increasingly clouded by disappointment and dissent. The fundamental problem was the mixed responses to the work of the council. On the one hand, there were those like Archbishop Lefebvre who denounced the council and all its works as a 'satanic plot'. He set up a schismatic organisation continuing to use the Latin Tridentine Mass, abolished in 1963, and to train priests in defiance of Rome, which eventually excommunicated him. On the other hand, many more liberal Catholics' expectations of the council were not fulfilled, and probably never could have been fulfilled. Moreover, the secularising influences of economic 'miracles' in several European countries, with consequent processes of migration and urbanisation, the impact of the great 'cultural revolution' in Western society in the 1960s and 1970s, and in particular such ideologies and movements as Marcusian libertarianism, Women's Liberation and Gay Liberation, all challenged Catholic discipline and sexuality. The numbers of priestly vocations fell, and large numbers of men left the priesthood to marry, unconvinced by Paul's encyclical reaffirming clerical celibacy,

---

40 See S. Stehle, *The eastern politics of the Vatican, 1917–1979* (Athens, OH: Ohio University Press, 1981), chs. IX and X.
41 See J. Luxmoore, 'The cardinal and the communists', *The Tablet*, 2 September 2000 and a reply by D. O'Grady, 'Casaroli's long march', *The Tablet*, 9 September 2000.

Sacerdotalis caelibatus, 1967. Even more important, *Humanae vitae* of 1968, restating the ban on 'artificial' birth control, opened up a gulf between the magisterium of the church and millions of Catholic laypeople which saddened the pope. The declaration *Personae humanae* of 1975 also reaffirmed Catholic teaching on the immorality of homosexual acts.

The worst blow for Paul came from the 'apostasy' of his homeland, Italy, which legalised divorce for the first time in 1970, and then endorsed it by a large popular majority in a referendum effectively called by the church to repeal the law, in 1974. The progress of the broader process of secularisation in Italy was such that even before Paul's death the Italian bishops' conference had declared their country 'mission territory'. Paul's last months were further tormented as terrorism in Italy reached its high point: in March 1978 the Red Brigades kidnapped Aldo Moro, a friend of his youth, many times premier of Italy and president of the ruling Christian Democratic Party. The refusal of the Italian political class (including the Christian Democrats) to negotiate, and Moro's brutal murder in May, despite Paul's own impassioned pleas to the terrorists, left him bitter and saddened. His funeral, at which his bare coffin had only an open Gospel book to adorn it, fittingly symbolised Papa Montini's other efforts to dismantle the 'imperial' papacy: his giving away of his tiara and his abolition of the papal court with all its trappings and flummery. For this alone, Hebblethwaite's description of Paul VI as the 'first modern pope' is probably correct.

John Paul I

The reign of Paul's successor, John Paul I, lasted only thirty-three days, during which he had no time to make great decisions or issue momentous encyclicals, yet for several reasons it deserves analysis.[42] His was the classic background of twentieth-century Italian popes, coming as he did from the Catholic heartlands of rural, small-town, north-eastern Italy, in his case the Veneto region. He was the third pope to have been patriarch of Venice: two others were archbishops of Italy's second largest city, Milan. His election was a compromise between the Siri and Benelli factions, and the expression of a heartfelt desire for a 'pastoral' pope. John Paul, in the very unusual name that he chose, demonstrated that the church was now firmly on the route his two predecessors had set. His eschewing of a papal coronation, and choice of a public ceremony to 'inaugurate his supreme pastorate', also confirmed his

---

42 The best biographical sketch is in Levillain, *The Papacy*, vol. II, pp. 857–9.

commitment to Paul's vision of the papacy. But it was his sudden and tragic death that refocused world attention on the papacy. In addition, the book by David Yallop which alleged that he had been murdered,[43] and the Vatican's mishandling of the aftermath of the death, revived memories of previous scandals associated with the Vatican like the Sindona and the Roberto Calvi, Banco Ambrosiano and Vatican 'Bank' affairs of Paul VI's reign.[44]

John Paul II (1978–2005)

John Paul II was the first Slav pope and the first non-Italian since 1522.[45] His election testifies to the efficacy of John XXIII's and Paul VI's efforts to internationalise both the Roman curia and the college of cardinals. It was also a product of the fact that, with John Paul I dead, Cardinal Benelli of Florence dead, and Siri moving into his seventies, there was a feeling that the Italian choices were limited. Karel Josef Wojtyła, cardinal archbishop of Cracow, also had many factors in his favour: youth (he was only fifty-eight), vigour, a certain reputation as an intellectual and the fact that he had become known to many other cardinals and bishops through the council and the 1967 synod. In electing a Polish pope, the conclave was also giving especial recognition to the 'Church of Silence'.

His initial impact on the Catholic faithful and the world was very favourable. This former actor exuded charm and had a forthrightness, matter-of-factness and humour that were very appealing: he roused much enthusiasm in St Peter's Square in January 1979 when he announced to the waiting crowds, 'God bless you: and your umbrellas.' But the charisma was accompanied by a steely conservatism. He would indeed carry forward the work of John and Paul, particularly in relation to the council, but in a conservative key. The synods held during his reign – national, regional and worldwide – were all carefully stage-managed: episcopal collegiality marched hand in hand with Roman primacy, and the American and Dutch national synods were used very cleverly to restore 'order' in those churches.[46] Subsequently, John

43 D. Yallop, *In God's name: an investigation into the murder of Pope John Paul I* (London: Corgi, 1984): Yallop's theories were convincingly debunked by J. Cornwell, *Like a thief in the night: the death of Pope John Paul I* (London: Viking, 1989).

44 See C. Raw, *The money-changers: how the Vatican bank enabled Roberto Calvi to steal $4250 million for the heads of the P2 masonic lodge* (London: HarperCollins, 1992).

45 For an interesting, if controversial, biography see C. Bernstein and M. Politi, *Holiness: John Paul II and the hidden history of our time* (London: Doubleday, 1996); also Levillain, *The papacy*, vol. II, pp. 859–67.

46 M. J. Walsh, *John Paul II* (London: Geoffrey Chapman, 1994), ch. 4.

Paul directed a careful policy of episcopal nominations to all national hierarchies that ensured theological and disciplinary soundness, and conformity with the wishes of Rome.

The appointment of Cardinal Ratzinger, formerly archbishop of Munich, as head of the Congregation for the Doctrine of the Faith (ex-Holy Office) was the key to bringing doctrinal and disciplinary dissent under control. Ratzinger carried out a crackdown on radical Catholic theologians, and in their public pronouncements both Ratzinger and Wojtyła repeatedly denounced 'Liberation Theology': during his visit to Nicaragua in 1983, the pope publicly rebuked priests who served as ministers in the Sandinista regime. Papa Wojtyła rejected the notion of married priests, and also of women priests. In May 1994, in the statement *Ordinatio sacerdotalis*, which the Vatican claimed had been written by the pope himself, the future possibility of the ordination of women was ruled out on theological grounds, as was further discussion of the subject.

The Vatican under John Paul also followed an uncompromising line in its pronouncements on matters of sexual morality, especially artificial contraception, abortion, bioethics and homosexuality: indeed, in regard to the latter, it published *two* statements, one in 1986 denouncing homosexual acts as 'intrinsically disordered' and a second nearly twenty years later expressly warning Catholic legislators against voting for legal recognition of homosexual unions. In 1994 the Vatican representative made himself extremely unpopular at the Cairo Conference on Population and Development by his stand on family planning and abortion, and a year later the Vatican took an equally unpopular stand, in alliance with various Islamic countries, on 'female reproductive rights' at the Beijing Conference. The encyclical *Veritatis splendor*, 'The splendour of truth', 1993, and the *Catechism of the Catholic church*, published the same year, were also used to reiterate traditional teaching on all these matters.

Inevitably under the Polish pope, the Vatican's *Ostpolitik* changed somewhat, as Cardinal Wyszinski of Warsaw and Wojtyła had preferred to deal with the Polish communist regime in their own way, without Vatican interference. But its architect, Agostino Casaroli, became a cardinal and was secretary of state from 1979 until 1991. Wojtyła arguably became his own secretary of state in relation to eastern Europe and especially Poland. The election of a Polish pope inevitably had a profound impact there and in the Soviet Union. The Soviet rulers could not have been much less shocked than Metternich was at the election of a 'Liberal pope' in 1846. The ongoing unrest in Poland, the Soviet invasion of Afghanistan, and the successive elections of Margaret Thatcher and Ronald Reagan gave rise to a 'second Cold War' in which Papa Wojtyła was to play a key role. That role has probably been exaggerated by some,[47] but the influence he exercised in crucial events in Poland, especially his support of Lech Wałęsa and *Solidarnosc*, was crucial in assisting the latter to achieve a share of power peacefully in early 1989.[48] In their turn, those events helped precipitate the key event in the collapse of communism, the coming down of the Berlin Wall later that year.

In the wake of the collapse of communism, the Vatican has achieved a major goal of the 'foreign policy' of popes from Pius XII onwards, the cancellation of Yalta and the reuniting of the European continent. Though its efforts to rebuild and even expand the church in the former Soviet Union have met with hostility and obstruction from local nationalists and the Orthodox, in the wider world Vatican diplomacy, buttressed by John Paul's one hundred foreign journeys, has extended its network to include virtually all Muslim states, and only the 'bamboo curtain' impedes its progress in the cluster of Asian communist countries – China, Laos, Vietnam and North Korea.[49] Yet prestigious though this network is, it did not enable Vatican diplomacy to prevent the Gulf or Iraq wars or adequately defend Catholic interests in the former Yugoslavia.

The death of John Paul II and the election of Benedict XVI

The pontificate of John Paul II reached a dramatic climax in his long-drawn-out final illness of February and March, and his death in April, 2005. He was determined to continue working to the end and his death agonies became a worldwide media spectacle, reinforcing one of the key messages of his reign, that death and suffering are, and should be, natural parts of the life experience, as well as attracting much sympathy from Catholics and non-Catholics alike, evidenced by the two million people who flocked to Rome for his funeral.

---

47 See Bernstein and Politi, *Holiness*, esp. chs. 5 and 7: for an alternative view, see J. Luxmoore and J. Babiuch, *The Vatican and the red flag: the struggle for the soul of eastern Europe* (London: Geoffrey Chapman, 1999), esp. chs. 10–13.
48 Luxmoore and Babiuch, *Vatican*, ch. 11.
49 For an analysis of the determining factors in the papacy's relations with communist China, see B. Leung, *Sino–Vatican relations: problems in conflicting authority, 1976–1986* (Cambridge: Cambridge University Press, 1992).

The election as his successor of Cardinal Joseph Ratzinger came quickly – on the second day of the conclave – and not altogether unexpectedly, though the size of Cardinal Martini's vote proved that the liberal element in the Sacred College is far from negligible. Events during the first month of Benedict XVI's pontificate were entirely predictable – the confirmation in office of all the heads of the Roman curia, the decision to 'fast-track' the beatification of his predecessor, and the appointment of Archbishop William Levada to succeed the pope as a 'safe pair of hands' at the head of the crucially important Congregation for the Doctrine of the Faith.

The papacy, 1914–2005

The development of the papacy in this period has been striking for the changes it has instituted or presided over. Most striking has been the change in the ecclesiology of the church after the Second Vatican Council. The church is now seen less as a hierarchically organised community and more as 'the people of God', and the introduction of the vernacular into the celebration of the mass and the reordering of Catholic churches back towards arrangements reminiscent of ancient Roman basilicas has given visible expression to this change. Similarly, the removal of many of the monarchical trappings of the papacy and the change of title of the pope from 'Supreme Pontiff' to 'Supreme Pastor' express a new sense of humble ministry of the papacy towards the whole church and to the world. Perhaps most important of all has been the attempt to re-establish the authority of the episcopacy alongside papal primacy.

But despite appearances to the contrary, the development of the papacy in this period has been most strongly characterised by *continuity*. In the matter of doctrine, the deposit of the faith, there has been little innovation – the proclamation of the doctrine of the Assumption in 1950 was arguably simply a definition of a belief that had existed in the Catholic church for centuries. And the statements in recent decades excluding the possibility of married or women priests (the latter on ostensibly theological grounds) are simply reiterations of long-held belief, admittedly against a rising tide of dissent. In moral theology too the papacy has stuck to traditional teaching. Only in the area of social doctrine can it be argued that John XXIII and Paul VI have *developed* the ideas of their predecessors to meet the needs of the times. Moreover, neither Vatican II, nor the changes in ecclesiology, nor even the theory and practice of episcopal collegiality and the ecumenical activity to which it gave rise, have undermined the structural authority of the papacy inside the Catholic church in the longer run. Paul VI, who so frequently humbled himself in the acts of his ministry, and who did so much to foster ecumenism, did not fail to assert the special authority of the Holy See in a document on ecumenism entitled, significantly, *Tu es Petrus*. In practical terms he reserved to himself, rather than the council, the decision to pronounce on the morality of artificial birth control and priestly celibacy. And John Paul II demonstrated this not only by his insistence upon making decisions regarding matters of this kind, but also by his oft-repeated statement that the 'church is not a democracy'. His whole reign was an exercise in the reassertion of centralised control over the church from Rome.

The papacy at the beginning of the third millennium

Indeed, in so many ways, John Paul II resembled no one so much as Pius IX. That pope reasserted the authority of the papacy against the spirit of the modern age, refusing, in his Syllabus of Errors, to conform to the many 'modern' liberal propositions which the syllabus condemned. Using infallibility as the conceptual key and the mobilisation of the Catholic episcopacy, clergy and laity, Pius IX managed to challenge the 'modern world' and survive. Above all, the papacy, whose demise had long been predicted by its enemies, also managed to survive and to emerge as a powerful centralised institution with almost absolute reliance on the loyalty of Catholics worldwide.

John Paul II similarly defied the present modern world, confidently reasserting traditional Catholic teaching not only on Catholic doctrinal belief, but also, more strikingly, on matters of ecclesiastical discipline – clerical celibacy and the ordination of women – as well as Catholic morals – artificial contraception, abortion, divorce, bio-ethics and homosexuality. The problem for John Paul II's successor is that there is nowadays nowhere near the kind of support for the teaching of the papacy on these matters as there was for Pius IX in his battles 120–150 years ago. On the contrary, substantial majorities of Catholics in their daily practice reject the ban on artificial contraception, and smaller groups tacitly accept the unfortunate necessity of divorce and abortion.[50] Large numbers of heterosexual Catholics, though definitely a minority, are tolerant towards homosexuality and others have little or no clear understanding of the moral issues involved in modern genetic science.

50 D. Willey, *God's politician: John Paul at the Vatican* (London: Faber&Faber, 1992), p. 86.

The gulf, therefore, between the teaching authority of the church and a large proportion of its members is growing. This problem has been exacerbated in recent years, in the United States and Europe, by the almost continuous succession of priestly paedophile scandals and the revelations about the way in which diocesan authorities have covered them up. Admittedly, dissident movements in conflict with the magisterium have flourished within the church since the end of Vatican II, especially in Italy, and 'We are church', in conflict with the episcopal hierarchy on similar matters, has developed robustly in Austria and Germany. But the paedophile scandals have shaken the loyalty and confidence of large numbers of American Catholics in their bishops and clergy, a confidence that will be difficult to rebuild. The Vatican has been deeply and directly involved in the problems of the American church, so at heart the crisis thus engendered is also about *papal* authority, as many question the way in which Rome has treated the problem. A further spin-off of the paedophile scandals is *financial*: American Catholics provide one-third of the offerings from Peter's Pence, the only other major source of income for the Vatican beyond the profits on its investments. As the reserves of American dioceses are employed to satisfy litigants, and American Catholics hold back on giving, even the short-term effects on the functioning of the central headquarters of the Catholic church could be serious.

The 'Hitler's pope' controversy has put the church in general on the defensive, especially in America, reopened old wounds between Catholics and Jews, and damaged the prestige of the papacy. John Cornwell's declared agenda in publishing his book on Pius XII was preventing the beatification of that pope. He has largely succeeded. (Ironically, Pius IX, the pope of the Edgardo Mortara affair, in which a Jewish boy was brought up as a Christian against the wishes of his parents, has been beatified instead!) But his ultimate target was John Paul II and his brand of papal absolutism and Roman centralisation. The question now is whether, with the election of a new pope who was so close to John Paul II, that kind of papacy can long survive in the twenty-first century.

4

Ecumenism

DAVID M. THOMPSON

In what Horton Davies described as 'the ecumenical century' the most decisive steps were taken in the twenty-five years after 1945. The inauguration of the World Council of Churches in 1948 brought together the major Protestant churches, the Ecumenical patriarchate, the Church of Greece and Orthodox churches in North America; in 1961 the Russian Orthodox church and other Orthodox churches from 'Iron Curtain' countries joined. The Roman Catholic church had remained outside that movement between the wars, with the papacy holding that schismatic churches should return to the mother church. However, the election of John XXIII in 1958, the establishment of the Secretariat for Promoting Christian Unity in 1960 and the Second Vatican Council (1962–5) substantially changed relationships between the Roman Catholic church and other churches.[1] Like his predecessor, Pope Paul VI met with other church leaders; the mutual anathemas of 1054 between East and West were revoked, and a similar agreement was reached with the Coptic church. It proved easier to bring churches together in organisations where their individual identity was not lost than to inaugurate structural reunion. Thus the pace of ecumenical advance seemed to slacken in the last quarter of the century.

Edinburgh 1910

The World Missionary Conference held at Edinburgh in June 1910 is regarded as the starting point of the modern ecumenical movement. From this are traced the people and institutions that became characteristic of twentieth-century ecumenism.[2] Although the word 'ecumenical' was dropped from the title of the conference at the last minute (it had been in the title of the

---

1 See S. Schmidt, *Augustin Bea, the cardinal of unity* (New York: New City Press, 1992).
2 I. Bria and D. Heller, *Ecumenical pilgrims* (Geneva: WCC Publications, 1995).

New York Missionary Conference in 1900), the essential meaning is expressed in the title *World* Missionary Conference. This refers to the primary meaning of the Greek *oikou mene*, 'the whole inhabited earth'. When William Temple, in his enthronement sermon as archbishop of Canterbury in 1942, spoke of the worldwide Christian fellowship as 'the great new fact of our era' he was not only referring to the new inter-church meetings.[3] In noting that this worldwide fellowship was the result of the missionary enterprise of the previous 150 years he made the crucial link between the missionary and ecumenical movements. This was a significant insight for someone as steeped in a national and established view of the church as Temple. The only archbishop of Canterbury to be the son of a previous archbishop, Temple had actively co-operated with other Christians since his time as an Oxford don before the First World War. As bishop of Manchester (1920–9) and archbishop of York (1929–42) he was active in the Faith and Order and Life and Work movements that led to the formation of the World Council of Churches. No longer for him was either the Church of England or even the Anglican communion at the centre of his understanding of the church. Overseas missions were the key to a broader understanding of the church for many nineteenth- and early twentieth-century Christians.

The coming together of missionary societies rather than churches indicates the early movement's essentially voluntarist character, and this is reflected in two other features: the evangelical inheritance and the role of student and youth work. The great English missionary societies of the 1790s were the result of evangelical activity; and even the high Anglican Society for the Propagation of the Gospel (1701) was a society. The Young Men's Christian Association (1844) and the Young Women's Christian Association (1854), which began in Britain, spread to the USA and had spectacular success in the numerous colleges and universities there. Dwight L. Moody, the American evangelical preacher, was a former YMCA member, and after his Cambridge mission of 1882 Christian Unions were formed in several British universities, leading to the formation of the Student Volunteer Movement for Foreign Missions in 1886 and the World Student Christian Federation in 1895.[4] These agencies provided opportunities for lay leadership in what was otherwise the clerical preserve of the churches. Moody was a layman, as were many missionaries; and so was John R. Mott, an American Methodist,

---

3 F. A. Iremonger, *William Temple* (London: Oxford University Press, 1948), p. 387.
4 R. Rouse and S. C. Neill, *A history of the Ecumenical movement, 1517–1948*, (London: SPCK, 1954), pp. 327–30.

converted by Moody, president of the World Alliance of YMCAs, general secretary and later chairman of the WSCF, chairman of the International Missionary Council, and first honorary president of the World Council of Churches.[5]

The Edinburgh conference was planned as a deliberative occasion, to take account of the significant changes in the context of mission (especially because of the shattering impact on missionaries of the Boxer uprising in China in 1900 and the Japanese defeat of Russia in 1905). Eight commissions were appointed on different topics, and their reports were the agenda of the conference.[6] Although more representative than previously, the membership of the conference was overwhelmingly north Atlantic: more than 500 each from Britain and North America, about 170 from Europe, and 26 from South Africa and Australia. Only 17 or 18 delegates were from younger churches. Mott's confident slogan, 'The evangelization of the World in this generation', reflected a new sense that such a goal could be achieved. This evangelistic context was reflected in the two most significant emphases of the conference reports, on the church and on unity.

Missionaries had avoided competition through comity agreements, which gave missions different geographical areas. The ease with which mission stations were transferred from one society to another is surprising in view of the competition between the same churches in Britain or North America. The success of missionary work raised the question of its ecclesiological status. Were these new churches? How were they related to the societies that established them? Were they to be independent? Who were to be the ministers? How soon could 'natives' (a word much discussed in 1910) be ordained? Although the ultimate independence of the newly established churches had been a clear goal in the early nineteenth century, there was a move away from that view later. Such questions enabled churches like the Church of Scotland, which did not have a separate missionary society, to emphasise that mission was the task of the whole church, and the churches established were churches in their own right.

Unity was also emphasised. The report on *Co-operation and unity* quoted the unanimous declaration of members of the Centenary Missionary Conference in Shanghai in 1907 that in planting the church of Christ on Chinese soil, it was their desire 'only to plant one Church under the sole

---

5 C. H. Hopkins, *John R. Mott 1865–1955, a biography* (Grand Rapids: Eerdmans, 1979), pp. 696–8.
6 W. H. T. Gairdner, *Edinburgh 1910* (Edinburgh: Oliphant, Anderson and Ferrier, 1910), pp. 68–258.

control of the Lord Jesus Christ, governed by the Word of the living God and led by his guiding Spirit'.[7] Organic union and federation were carefully discussed as paths followed in different places, the former by churches with a common polity, the latter by a variety of different churches in the same geographical area. This was the first systematic discussion of the concepts: they were not originally conceived as alternatives, but rather as appropriate to different situations. The report affirmed the Shanghai ideal 'to plant in every non-Christian nation one united Church of Christ'.[8] It suggested that the church in Western lands would reap a glorious reward from its missionary labour if the church in the mission field pointed the way to a healing of its divisions. Five of the ten speakers in the discussion spoke about the Chinese experience of united action.

That commission also proposed that the conference establish a continuation committee. The new committee was asked to continue the discussions initiated by the conference, to consider when another world missionary conference should be held, and to confer with the societies and boards on the best method of working towards the formation of the permanent international missionary committee suggested by the commission. All the speeches were favourable, and when it was passed unanimously the doxology was sung.[9]

The formation of the continuation committee was therefore the first result of the Edinburgh conference. Mott and J. H. Oldham became chairman and secretary. The First World War disrupted progress but in June 1920 a preliminary meeting was held at Crans, Switzerland, to discuss the formation of an International Missionary Council. The various missionary boards accepted the proposals, and the council was officially formed at a meeting at Lake Mohonk, New York in October 1921. The IMC eventually merged with the World Council of Churches in 1961 after a decade of discussions.

A second consequence of Edinburgh was the gradual recognition of the importance of the younger churches. Of the seventeen member councils of the IMC only four were representative of the mission field itself. V. S. Azariah's intervention at Edinburgh was profoundly significant. He pleaded for truly *mutual* respect and co-operation from foreign missionaries: 'Through all the ages to come the Indian Church will rise up in gratitude to attest the heroism and self-denying labours of the missionary body. You have

---

7 *World Missionary Conference 1910: Report of Commission VIII, co-operation and the promotion of unity* (Edinburgh: Oliphant, Anderson and Ferrier, 1910), p. 83.
8 Ibid., p. 131.   9 Ibid., pp. 202–18.

given your goods to feed the poor. You have given your bodies to be burned. We also ask for love. Give us FRIENDS.'[10]

A third consequence of Edinburgh was the emergence of a core of international church leaders who became friends, and were involved in what became the Faith and Order and Life and Work movements. The significant new feature here was the involvement of Anglo-Catholics: Charles Gore, bishop of Birmingham, for example, was chairman of Commission III on 'Education and the Christianisation of National Life'; and Edward Talbot, bishop of Southwark, was also actively involved.[11] Oldham had worked hard to achieve this.[12] However, Roman Catholics and Orthodox were not present at Edinburgh.

The movements towards church union most directly inspired by Edinburgh came in India and China. In India Anglican participation in talks for union led to the formation of the Negotiating Committee for union in South India, whose work occupied the whole inter-war period.[13] C. Y. Cheng had told the Edinburgh conference, 'Speaking plainly, we hope to see, in the near future, a united Christian Church without any denominational distinction.'[14] The Continuation Committee Conference in China in 1913 adopted the title of 'Chinese Christian Church' as a title for all Christian churches in China.[15] Moreover, China, which was the largest mission field at this time, was not a Western colony.

Nevertheless there were different perceptions of ecumenism in 'North' and 'South'. The Indian theologian, P. V. Devanandam, said at the WCC First Assembly in 1948, 'To us of the younger Churches it is the international nature of our faith that strikes the imagination: to you of the older Churches it is the inter-denominational character of ecumenical Christianity that compels admiration.'[16] This tension explains the significance of Roman Catholic involvement from the 1960s, which both changed and restored a particular emphasis on unity.

---

10 Gairdner, *Edinburgh 1910*, p. 111.
11 Tissington Tatlow emphasised this in his chapter in Rouse and Neill, *History*, p. 406.
12 K. Clements, *Faith on the frontier: a life of J. H. Oldham* (Edinburgh: T&T Clark, 1999), pp. 79–90.
13 B. Sundkler, *Church of South India: the movement towards union, 1900–1947* (London: Lutterworth, 1954).
14 *Co-operation and the promotion of unity*, p. 196.
15 Rouse and Neill, *History*, pp. 379–80.
16 H. Ruedi-Weber, *Asia and the Ecumenical movement*, (London: SCM, 1966), p. 38.

Faith and Order; Life and Work

In October 1910 at the General Convention of the Protestant Episcopal Church in the USA, Charles Brent, bishop of the Philippines, persuaded the House of Bishops to appoint a commission to bring about a conference to consider questions touching faith and order. All Christian communions throughout the world 'which confess Our Lord Jesus Christ as God and Saviour' were to be invited to join in arranging such a conference. Simultaneously Dr Peter Ainslie, president of the General Convention of the Disciples of Christ in the USA, proposed the establishment of a Council on Christian Union,[17] which immediately contacted the Episcopal church. Robert Gardiner was the secretary of the Episcopal Church Commission, an American lawyer who bore much of the cost of this exercise personally. Members of the commission visited the Anglican churches in Great Britain and Ireland in 1912; and a conference of interested churches was held in 1913. A second deputation visited the English free churches and the Scottish Presbyterian churches in 1914. A representative of the head of the Russian Orthodox church in the USA attended the 1913 conference; and Pope Benedict XV, whilst declining Roman Catholic participation, encouraged the efforts. The North American Preparatory Faith and Order Conference took place in January 1916.[18]

Archbishop Söderblom of Uppsala appealed to both sides to consider a negotiated peace on various occasions during the First World War without success. The conference of the World Alliance for Promoting Friendship among the Churches at Oud Wassenaar, 30 September–3 October 1919, was therefore the first occasion on which Christians from both sides met again; and it was dominated by war guilt problems. Nevertheless Söderblom persuaded the conference to pursue the idea of an ecumenical council, and gathered a conference at Geneva in 1920, immediately before the meeting of the Faith and Order Preparatory Conference. He had corresponded with various Orthodox leaders in 1918 and his idea of a council was favourably received by the Ecumenical patriarchate. This contact probably influenced the content of the letter of the Ecumenical patriarchate 'to all the Churches of Christ wheresoever they be' in January 1920, largely composed by Metropolitan Germanos of Seleukia. By inviting members of the Orthodox

---

17 In 1913 its name was changed to the Association for the Promotion of Christian Unity, and later to the Council on Christian Unity.

18 Rouse and Neill, *History*, pp. 407–17.

delegation to Faith and Order to come to his conference, Söderblom secured their support for the proposed Life and Work Conference.[19]

The Faith and Order Continuation Committee, appointed in Geneva in 1920, proposed a World Faith and Order Conference in Washington, DC in 1925, with a Conference on Life and Work following immediately afterwards. However, the Life and Work Committee preferred the two conferences to be separate. The Faith and Order Committee prepared a series of questions for the churches on the degree of unity in faith regarded as necessary for a reunited church, and the relation to that of creeds and confessions of faith. As a result the Life and Work Conference happened first in Stockholm, Sweden in August 1925. The main topics discussed were: the obligations of the church in the light of God's plan for the world; economic and industrial problems; social and moral problems; international relations; education; and ways to promote co-operation between churches and their association on federal lines. It proved difficult to keep theological differences out of the discussion – for example, whether the kingdom of God was to be regarded as a present or a future reality. The patriarchs of Alexandria and Jerusalem attended, representing a significant Orthodox presence, which facilitated Anglican commitment to the process. But there were only six representatives from India, China and Japan.

There was a significant discussion over the follow-up to Stockholm. Söderblom wanted an International Christian Council on Life and Work, and strongly believed that the churches should act as if they were one.[20] But the delegates settled for a continuation committee, on the Edinburgh lines. An office was established in Geneva from 1928. After the Lausanne Faith and Order Conference in 1927 and the Jerusalem Conference of the International Missionary Council in 1928, Söderblom revived his idea of a council, and persuaded the continuation committee to reconstitute itself as the Universal Christian Council for Life and Work in September 1930, not long before he died.[21]

The Faith and Order Conference met at Lausanne, Switzerland for three weeks in August 1927, with 108 churches represented. The first six reports were adopted, but there were reservations over the last one, which proposed the formation of a council of the churches 'for practical purposes'

19 B. Sundkler, *Nathan Söderblom: his life and work* (London: Lutterworth, 1968), pp. 217–52, 323–9.
20 R. C. D. Jasper, *George Bell, bishop of Chichester* (London: Oxford University Press, 1967), p. 63; Sundkler, *Söderblom*, pp. 220–2, 229–33.
21 Sundkler, *Söderblom*, pp. 413–18.

(Söderblom's proposal), and the matter was referred to the continuation committee.[22] The preamble to the Lausanne reports emphasised that they were for the consideration of member churches, with no intention to define the conditions for future reunion. The first report on 'The call to unity' made several affirmations that have been regularly repeated: 'God wills unity . . . We can never be the same again . . . More than half the world is waiting for the Gospel'.[23] The agreements on faith recorded in the reports on 'The gospel' and 'The common confession of faith' pushed the ecclesiological issues into the forefront. Thus the reports on 'The church', 'The ministry' and 'The sacraments' became central.

Although the Lausanne conference identified the crucial problems it did not offer any obvious solutions. The churches' responses to the Lausanne reports were reviewed by a Theological Committee chaired by Bishop Headlam of Gloucester, and a selection of them was published under the title *Convictions* in 1934. Three Theological Commissions were appointed, and the most important result of this was a report, *The ministry and the sacraments*, published for the second World Faith and Order Conference in 1937.

The Life and Work movement also worked through various commissions. The International Christian Social Institute was set up in 1927: there was a Commission on the Church and Labour, under Élie Gounelle of France; a Theological Commission under Adolf Deissmann and Martin Dibelius to work on the kingdom of God and the church; a Youth Commission; and the International Christian Press Commission, which was the predecessor of the Ecumenical Press Service. American and Swiss co-operation produced the European Central Bureau for Inter-Church Aid, with Adolf Keller as director – the predecessor of Inter-Church Aid. The International Christian Council for Refugees was established in 1933 under George Bell, bishop of Chichester (1929–58), as a response to the problems caused by the Nazi government's policy towards non-Aryans. Peace questions remained the responsibility of the World Alliance for Promoting International Friendship through the Churches, which was independent until 1948.

A shift of theological emphasis took place among Life and Work supporters from the kingdom of God (characteristic of the Stockholm and Lausanne meetings) to the church (as studied at the Oxford and Edinburgh meetings in 1937). Contemporary biblical and theological scholarship supported this,

---

22 H. N. Bate (ed.), *Faith and Order: proceedings of the world conference, Lausanne, August 3–21, 1927* (New York: SCM, 1928), pp. 321–66, 397–403, 435–9.
23 Ibid., pp. 460–1.

and the German Church Struggle crystallised what might otherwise have remained an abstract theological discussion. The Universal Council on Christian Life and Work decided at Fanø, Denmark in 1934 to back the Confessing Church in Germany and to make the subject of the world conference in 1937 'Church, community and state'. The explanation of this noted that the emergence of the totalitarian state was focusing the debate between Christian faith and the secular tendencies of the time: 'In this struggle the very existence of the Christian Church is at stake.'[24] The idea that the church stretched beyond individual nations gained importance, and was reflected in the slogan of the conference, 'Let the Church be the Church'.

The Oxford Conference on Church, Community and State met in July 1937. Three hundred out of 425 delegates were from the USA or the British commonwealth; there were about 40 Orthodox and Oriental Orthodox, and about 30 from younger churches in Asia and Africa. The Edinburgh Faith and Order Conference followed in August, with 443 delegates and 53 youth. There were four sections: the grace of our Lord Jesus Christ; the church of Christ and the word of God; ministry and the sacraments; and unity in life and worship. The report of the conference was fuller than that from Lausanne, representing a higher level of agreement on the various issues discussed. The proposal to form a World Council of Churches was put to both the Oxford and Edinburgh conferences. At Oxford only two voted against; at Edinburgh the proposal came up towards the end of the day's business, and was approved with one dissentient. Headlam wrongly suspected vote-rigging, though Temple would have preferred a longer discussion.[25]

A draft constitution for the World Council of Churches was prepared in Utrecht in May 1938. As churches accepted it, the World Council of Churches in Process of Formation came into being. William Temple was appointed chairman, Willem Visser 't Hooft general secretary and William Paton associate general secretary.[26] Visser 't Hooft from Holland had been general secretary of the World Student Christian Federation; Paton, a former Presbyterian missionary in India, was secretary of the International Missionary Council.

In December 1938 the International Missionary Council met in Tambaram. (It had been intended to meet in Hangchow, but the Sino-Japanese war made this impossible.) More countries were represented at this conference than at

24 Rouse and Neill, *History*, pp. 583–4.
25 R. C. D. Jasper, *Arthur Cayley Headlam: life and letters of a bishop* (London: Faith Press, 1960), pp. 275–9.
26 Rouse and Neill, *History*, pp. 704–5.

Jerusalem in 1928 (or indeed the first assembly of the WCC in 1948). There was outstanding representation from China, and and also from Japan despite the war. There was a similar emphasis upon the church to that at Oxford and Edinburgh; and the conference is remembered for the challenge posed by the book, *The Christian message in a non-Christian world*, written for it by Hendrik Kraemer. This marked a sharp swing from the more open-ended attitudes of the Jerusalem meeting.[27]

The World Council of Churches

The first assembly of the World Council of Churches met at Amsterdam, Holland in August 1948. A total of 147 churches in 44 countries were represented by 351 delegates. Mott provided a link with the Edinburgh conference of 1910. An early issue was the nature and authority of the council. Some feared that the council might try to speak for the churches. Leonard Hodgson's letter to William Temple in August 1935, when the proposals to bring Faith and Order and Life and Work together were first mooted, stated the view of a significant number of people, even though it misrepresented Life and Work. Hodgson contrasted the 'prominent people much engaged in international affairs' associated with the Stockholm movement with 'the numberless simple church people all over the world' who constituted the strength of the Faith and Order movement. Whereas Faith and Order only wanted to go on quietly doing its own work, the Stockholm movement had repeatedly tried to draw them 'into the general current of "an ecumenical movement"', which it was difficult to resist without seeming to be non-co-operative. The key point followed:

> . . . our movement is essentially a conference in which churches talk to one another. If there is to be an ecumenical movement which shall claim to speak for Christendom as a kind of super-church we shall have to be extremely careful not to get tied up in it or we shall compromise the guarantee given to all the churches we invited to be represented in Faith and Order that they shall not be committed by any of our activities.[28]

Temple drafted the constitution of the WCC so that its statements did not bind member churches and had only the authority that their contents deserved; but the phrase 'super-church', coined by Hodgson, returned regularly to haunt the council.

27 Ibid., pp. 369–70.
28 E. Jackson, *Red tape and the gospel* (Birmingham: Phlogiston, 1980), pp. 232–3.

It is not surprising that the issue was a problem, since there was no Protestant model for an international church council. The Lambeth Conferences (which were of bishops not churches) had only moral authority for Anglicans. The Lutheran World Federation did not exist until 1947. The International Methodist Council, the World Alliance of Reformed Churches, the International Congregational Council and the Baptist World Alliance were all consultative bodies only.

Section IV of the WCC constitution adopted at Amsterdam, subtitled 'Authority', stated that

> the World Council shall offer counsel and provide opportunity of united action in matters of common interest. It may take action on behalf of constituent churches in such matters as one or more of them may commit to it ... The World Council shall not legislate for the churches; nor shall it act for them in any manner except as indicated above or as may hereafter be specified by the constituent churches.[29]

The assembly also adopted a Report on Policy, which made two key points on authority. Whilst the council wished to be an instrument for the common witness of its member churches, it did not intend to usurp the functions of the churches nor to become a single unified church structure, independent of its member churches. On public pronouncements, the report said that it was necessary for the council to address its members on matters that might require united action or on issues affecting church and society. It was undesirable that such pronouncements be made often: 'But such statements will have no authority save that which they carry by their own truth and wisdom' – echoing Temple's phraseology earlier. Nor would they be binding on any church unless that church confirmed them.[30] These points were incorporated in the council's rules.

Nevertheless the central committee had to return to the question at its meeting in Toronto, Canada in 1950. The committee had been concerned with issues of religious freedom, racial discrimination in South Africa and the Korean war, where its support for the United Nations led to the resignation of Dr T. Chao of China as one of its presidents. Its statement began by saying what the council was not: it was not a super-church; its purpose was not to negotiate unions between churches; it was not based on any one conception of the church (and therefore did not pre-judge the ecclesiological problem);

---

29 W. A. Visser 't Hooft, *The first assembly of the World Council of Churches* (London: SCM, 1949), p. 198.
30 Ibid., pp. 127–8.

membership in the council did not imply that a church viewed its own conception of the church as relative; and no particular doctrine of the unity of the church was implied in membership. There followed a series of positive affirmations: conversation, co-operation and common witness were based on the recognition of Christ as the divine head of the church; the member churches believed that on the basis of the New Testament the church is one; member churches recognised that membership of the church of Christ was more inclusive than the membership of any particular church; membership of the council did not imply that member churches accepted one another as churches in the full sense; member churches did recognise elements of the church in other churches; member churches wished to consult together to learn from Christ what witness he would have them bear to his name; member churches should recognise their solidarity with one another, assist each other in times of need and refrain from unbrotherly actions; member churches sought to learn from and help one another in order to build up the Body of Christ and renew the life of the churches.[31] That remains the council's position.

The original Basis of the World Council was that of the Faith and Order movement, which in turn had copied the Edinburgh conference of 1910: 'The World Council of Churches is a fellowship of churches which accept our Lord Jesus Christ as God and Saviour.' Various suggestions for an amplification of this were made in the early 1950s; and a trinitarian draft was first discussed at the central committee at New Haven in 1957. The central committee at St Andrew's in 1960 agreed to put a new text to the assembly at New Delhi, which approved it: 'The World Council of Churches is a fellowship of churches which confess the Lord Jesus Christ as God and Saviour according to the Scriptures, and therefore seek to fulfil together their common calling to the glory of the One God, Father, Son and Holy Spirit.' The reference to the 'common calling' brought out the missionary dimension of the church; and the new references to the scriptures and the Trinity filled gaps felt by several.

In 1961 too the Russian Orthodox church and the other Orthodox churches in the Soviet bloc of eastern Europe became members of the council. This significantly strengthened the Orthodox voice within the council. It was almost certainly permitted by the Soviet government with the hope of strengthening the 'peace voice' internationally, and possibly of bringing

---

31 G. A. K. Bell, *Documents on Christian unity: fourth series* (London: Oxford University Press, 1958), pp. 219–23.

pressure on Western governments from their internal church constituencies. On the other hand, Western church leaders were clearly aware of the Soviet agenda.

Finally the assembly approved a statement 'On the Nature of the Unity We Seek'.

> We believe that the unity which is both God's will and his gift to his Church is being made visible as all in each place who are baptized into Jesus Christ and confess him as Lord and Saviour are brought by the Holy Spirit into one fully committed fellowship, holding the one apostolic faith, preaching the one Gospel, breaking the one bread, joining in common prayer, and having a corporate life reaching out in witness and service to all and who at the same time are united with the whole Christian fellowship in all places and all ages in such wise that ministry and members are accepted by all, and that all can act and speak together as occasion requires for the tasks to which God calls his people.[32]

Lesslie Newbigin, one of the first non-Anglican bishops of the Church of South India, had been involved in the process of bringing the WCC and the IMC together, and this sentence reflected his concern for a restatement of the council's goal. The emphasis on 'all in each place' was balanced by an emphasis on 'all in all places' at the Uppsala assembly in 1968.

Ecumenical organisations also developed at the national level. The Protestant Federation of France was founded in 1905, and was probably the first example of a national council of churches. (The English National Council of the Free Churches, formed in 1896, had as its members local free church councils, not churches.) The Federal Council of the Churches of Christ in America was formed in 1908, and by 1910 thirty-one churches had joined. It was renamed the National Council in 1941 after it had joined with a number of other specialised councils. Councils were formed in Switzerland in 1920, Germany in 1922, Holland in 1935, and Great Britain in 1942. Similar councils were formed in Australia and New Zealand after 1945.[33]

There were also councils at the continental level. The first was the East Asian Christian Conference in Bangkok in December 1949. The All Africa Church Conference met first at Ibadan in January 1958. The Near East Christian Council, which had been exclusively Protestant since 1927, changed its name to the Near East Council of Churches in 1964 and welcomed the Orthodox. The Conference of European Churches, developing out of

---

32 W. Visser 't Hooft (ed.), *The New Delhi report* (London: SCM, 1962), p. 116.
33 Rouse and Neill, *History*, pp. 620–30.

informal meetings from 1957, was formally constituted in 1964. Finally the Pacific Conference of Churches was inaugurated in 1966.[34]

Church unions

Alongside international ecumenical developments there were church union schemes in particular countries.[35] Several United churches involving Reformed and Lutherans came into existence in Germany in the nineteenth century. The two major Unions of Reformed Churches in France, together with several of the free churches and Methodist churches, joined to form the Eglise Reformée de France in 1938.[36] A union between the two Reformed churches and the Lutheran church in Holland was agreed in 2002. But no unions in Europe bridged the episcopal/non-episcopal divide.

From the late nineteenth century there were several reunions among Presbyterians and Methodists. In 1907 the Methodist New Connexion, the Bible Christians and the United Methodist Free Churches in Britain came together in the United Methodist church; and this subsequently joined with the Wesleyan Methodist and Primitive Methodist churches to form the Methodist Church of Great Britain in 1932. Similar unions took place in the various British dominions and colonies, often before those in Britain itself. In 1900 the Free Church of Scotland and the United Presbyterian church united in the United Free Church of Scotland, and this in turn united with the Church of Scotland in 1929, though in each case a small minority remained outside.

The first union across confessional lines was the United Church of Canada, formed from Methodists, Congregationalists and Presbyterians in 1925, though a Presbyterian minority remained outside. The same church traditions were involved in the formation of the United Church of Zambia (1965) and the Uniting Church in Australia (1979). Presbyterians and Baptists formed the United Church of Siam (later Thailand) in 1934, and were subsequently joined by Disciples of Christ. Congregationalists and Presbyterians formed the United Church of Jamaica in 1965, also later joined by Disciples. After

34 H. Fey (ed.), *The ecumenical advance: a history of the Ecumenical movement, volume 2, 1948–1968* (London: SPCK, 1970), pp. 67–91.
35 The WCC Faith and Order Commission publishes regular reports on church union negotiations in different countries, and from the 1970s has organised regular conferences of united and uniting churches.
36 Rouse and Neill, *History*, p. 465; M. Boegner, *The long road to unity* (London: Collins, 1970), pp. 92–107.

unsuccessful conversations in the 1930s and 1940s, the Presbyterian Church of England united with the majority of the Congregational Union of England and Wales in the United Reformed church in 1972; the majority of Churches of Christ in Great Britain and Ireland joined in 1981 and the majority of the Congregational Union of Scotland joined in 2000.

In the USA the Congregational churches united with the Evangelical and Reformed churches to form the United Church of Christ in 1957.[37] This also brought together church traditions among immigrants from different European countries – in this case, British and German or Dutch. The other main church divisions in the USA derived from the civil war, and were usually internal. The United Methodist church was formed in 1968 by a union between the Methodist church and the Evangelical United Brethren, and the northern and southern Presbyterians united in 1983. Involvement of the main black churches in union discussions came with the Consultation on Christian Union, initiated in 1962, but with a pre-history going back to the Greenwich Plan of 1949. The member churches established a covenanted fellowship with the title Churches of Christ Uniting in January 2002.

The Church of South India, involving the South India United church (itself a union of Congregational, Presbyterian and Reformed churches), the four southern dioceses of the Church of India, Burma and Ceylon, and the British Methodist church was the first union scheme to tackle episcopacy. It was agreed that all ministerial ordinations after union would be episcopal, but existing ministers did not have to be episcopally reordained. High-church Anglicans in the Church of England were not pleased, but their opposition failed to stop the inauguration of the church in 1947. The non-episcopal churches sending missionaries to India agreed that new ordinands should be ordained in the Church of South India, rather than their sending church. Nevertheless the 1948 Lambeth Conference declined to remain in full communion with the Church of South India, and this did not change until 1988.

The discussions which had begun in north India (and Pakistan and Ceylon) therefore aimed to secure a united ministry from the beginning. This was achieved in 1970, with services of inauguration which brought the ministries of the constituent churches together. Unfortunately, although great care was taken in India not to define these services as constituting episcopal ordination, the Judicial Committee of the Privy Council ruled that, for the purposes of English law, this was how they should be regarded. The Church of North

---

37 L. H. Gunneman, *The shaping of the United Church of Christ* (New York: United Church Press, 1977).

India was also different from its southern neighbour in including Baptists and Churches of Christ, which required a resolution of the relationship between infant and believers' baptism. It was agreed that anyone who had been baptised as an infant should not subsequently be rebaptised as an adult.

Archbishop Geoffrey Fisher suggested in a Cambridge university sermon in 1946 that non-episcopal churches might consider 'taking episcopacy into their system', as a way of avoiding the problems of south India. Conversations along these lines took place between the Church of England and the Church of Scotland, but broke down in 1957. Simultaneous conversations between the Church of England and the Methodist church produced a scheme to bring the two churches together in 1967. Although approved by the Methodist Conference, it failed to gain a sufficient majority in the Convocations of the Church of England. A slightly modified proposal failed again in the new General Synod of the Church of England in 1972. The proposals for a covenant between the main English churches in 1981 also failed to gain a sufficient majority in the Church of England. An Anglican–Methodist covenant was eventually inaugurated in 2003.

The growing number of church union schemes inevitably resulted in a concentration on institutional issues rather than mission, however much the latter might be affirmed as a goal.[38] It also meant that church leaders became much more involved. Although this was valuable, it also meant that the role of enthusiasts, many of them lay, was diminished. It was easier to say that ecumenism was simply a way of increasing church bureaucracy rather than renewal. The failure of church union schemes sometimes resulted in even more local experiments in co-operation, such as Co-operating Parishes in New Zealand and Local Ecumenical Partnerships in England and Wales from the 1960s.

Theological dialogue

The Second Vatican Council's Decree on Ecumenism of 1964 marked a new commitment to ecumenism by the Roman Catholic church. It also led to some changes of emphasis. The Roman Catholic church did not join the WCC, but established a joint working group with the council. This avoided some delicate questions – for example, the number of delegates the church might have had, since it would have dominated the council numerically, and

38 See N. Ehrenstrom and W. G. Muelder (eds.), *Institutionalism and church unity* (London: SCM, 1963).

also whether they should be nominated by local hierarchies or the Vatican. (The church did, however, join many national or regional councils of churches.) The main emphasis was placed on theological dialogue, particularly at the international level. This gave a new significance to the various Christian world communions, which became the dialogue partners rather than national churches. Dialogues were established first with the Orthodox churches and with the Anglican communion in the late 1960s; and since then they have extended to all the major World Communions.[39]

Similar dialogues took place between other World Communions at international and regional levels. These produced some important agreements, notably the Leuenberg agreement of 1973, which established pulpit and table fellowship between the majority of Reformed and Lutherans in Europe, and was later extended to include the Methodists. The Meissen agreement between the Church of England and the Evangelical churches in Germany (1992), the Porvoo agreement between the Anglican churches in the British Isles and the Scandinavian Lutheran churches (1996), and the Reuilly agreement between the Church of England and the Reformed and Lutheran churches in France (2000) each in their different ways represented important ecumenical milestones. There was less success in the discussions between the Anglican communion and the Roman Catholic church. Despite the important Agreed Statement of 1980, the Vatican insisted on further agreements before any action could be taken. The Roman Catholic church and the Lutheran World Federation signed an agreement on justification on 31 October 1999.

Yet although official progress seems slow, local inter-church relations have often changed beyond recognition from the situation before 1939. In France the informal Groupe des Dombes brought together Roman Catholic and Protestant theologians, and published several important statements, some of which are cited in official texts. In Holland the effect of the vernacular mass after Vatican II almost made people wonder what the difference between the Roman Catholic and Protestant churches was, and Cardinal Jan Willebrands was moved from the Secretariat for Promoting Christian Unity to the archdiocese of Utrecht to sort things out. Protestant–Catholic relations remain difficult in Ireland, though they are often better officially than at the popular level. Generally the picture is one of transformation.

---

39 The results are to be found in H. Meyer and L. Vischer (eds.), *Growth in agreement* (Geneva: World Council of Churches, 1984), and H. Meyer and W. G. Rusch (eds.), *Growth in agreement II* (Geneva: WCC Publications, 2000).

Probably the main exception lies in Roman Catholic–Orthodox relations. Since the end of communism and the revival of conservative Orthodoxy, the issue of the so-called Uniate churches in eastern Europe (Orthodox churches in communion with Rome) has revived in significance. This is partly because the agenda of the Papal Secretariat of State has prevailed over that of the Pontifical Council for Promoting Christian Unity. But the opportunity to reverse state-imposed absorption of Uniate churches into Orthodox churches and questions over the rightful ownership of church property caused significant problems, which are not easily resolved. Moreover, state encouragement of Orthodox involvement in the ecumenical movement in the former communist Europe made it easier for conservative voices to represent ecumenism as a legacy of communism.

Ecumenism, church and state, and secularisation

The ecumenical movement also highlights the shift in the balance of power in the churches away from Europe towards North America on the one hand, and Africa, Latin America, and to a lesser extent Asia, on the other. The encyclical letter from the Ecumenical patriarchate of January 1920 referred to the establishment of the League of Nations as a reason for thinking that greater co-operation between the churches was opportune.[40] The international ecclesiastical co-operation which developed was similar to that embodied in the League of Nations with the important difference that the churches of the United States were involved. (It is interesting that the Greek *koinonia* was translated as 'League', rather than 'Fellowship' or 'Communion', particularly in view of the development of an ecclesiology of *koinonia* in recent decades.) Whereas the United Nations moved to New York after 1945, the World Council of Churches remained in Geneva, the headquarters of the old league and of many international non-governmental organisations. Although the possibility of constituting the council from the World Christian Families was rejected, the formation of the WCC did encourage them. The Lutheran World Federation was formed in 1947 from the previous looser international association, and the temporary eclipse of Germany allowed North American influence to come to the fore. The United States already dominated both the World Methodist Council and the Baptist World Alliance.

---

40 G. K. A. Bell, *Documents on Christian unity 1920–24* (London: Oxford University Press, 1924), pp. 44ff.

There are different reasons for the enhanced significance of Africa, Latin America and Asia. Whereas in Asia the end of empire involved a resurgence of south Asian religious traditions such as Hinduism, Buddhism and Islam, in Africa (with the significant exception of Islam) Christianity remained dominant. The development of African Instituted churches in some ways corresponded to the position of Hinduism and Buddhism in India. Moreover, in both Africa and Latin America, the development of Pentecostal churches affected the traditional balance of Christian power.

Generally the churches were better prepared for the end of empire than colonial governments; but they faced similar problems over the indigenisation of leadership, and church life more generally. Mission churches became independent, and even where white missionaries remained they did not always continue to occupy positions of leadership. The multiplication of newly independent churches also meant that the number of churches in the WCC doubled between 1948 and 1998. This created problems for the Orthodox, since the number of their churches did not increase significantly; and they felt increasingly overwhelmed in the World Council, particularly since they were hostile to evangelistic efforts by some Western evangelists in eastern Europe. Thus even before the collapse of communism led to changes in Orthodox leadership, a gap was opening up.

Ecumenism represented a further step in the differentiation of church from state, because of its emphasis on what churches have in common across national boundaries. The slogan of the 1937 Oxford conference, 'Let the Church be the Church', lies at the heart of the issue. Earlier differentiations between church and state usually identified 'church' with the hierarchy or clergy, rather than the total *laos* or membership. Indeed, the identity of membership between church and state in western Europe had made differentiation difficult, as is seen in the uneasy way in which Jewish and Muslim minorities were described. Religious pluralism in continental Europe after the Peace of Westphalia (1648) and in Britain after the 1689 revolution made the total identification of church and state increasingly difficult. After the French revolution, the exercise of the papal office in the Roman Catholic church developed in a new way, emphasising the church's international character and its separation from the state. The Evangelical Revival among Protestants produced a new emphasis on what they held in common, which was reflected in co-operation in overseas missions, but not in any centralised authority.

One consequence of the Life and Work movement was that the private dreams of a few enthusiasts about international affairs and peace-making became a primary concern of the churches. The German Church Struggle marked this shift. Although the official German churches generally stayed out of the ecumenical movement, members of the Confessing Church were involved. Moreover, during the war their links with church leaders involved in the World Council in Process of Formation were vital. This made possible the Stuttgart Declaration of 1945, when a representative group of German church leaders, in a meeting with leaders of the World Council, declared that the German churches had shared in the responsibility for the Hitler years. This facilitated the integration of the German churches into international bodies after 1945, by contrast with the longer isolation of the German churches after 1919.

Another consequence was the increased readiness to comment on internal affairs of various countries. Bishop Headlam, the first chairman of the Church of England Council for Foreign Relations from 1933, believed that it was inappropriate to interfere in the affairs of other countries, which explains his suspicion of the Life and Work movement. There had been protests before, as over the Bulgarian and Armenian massacres in the nineteenth century, but they were essentially political rather than ecclesiastical. After 1945 such protest came to be regarded almost as an ecclesiastical obligation. The first example was South Africa. Later concerns were imperialism, disarmament and international economic development. Although the Amsterdam assembly of the WCC had envisaged that the council's statements on church and society would be infrequent, this has proved to be difficult in practice.[41]

The international character of ecumenism challenges one view of its relationship to secularisation. Bryan Wilson argued quite strongly in the early 1960s that ecumenism was a response to decline among the mainline churches, which he attributed to secularisation.[42] For him the liveliness embodied in Pentecostalism had no need for or interest in ecumenism. Wilson was one of the earliest writers to draw attention to the phenomenon of Pentecostal growth; and developments since the 1960s in many ways seem to reinforce his arguments. However, France, which is the earliest example of secularisation, offers no support for Wilson's argument. Is that because ecumenism is primarily a Protestant phenomenon? Possibly: but church attendance is also low in Scandinavia, yet there has been no significant ecumenical response there. The thesis almost seems plausible only in multi-denominational Britain. If so, is ecumenism better understood as a response to multi-denominationalism rather than secularisation?

---

41 D. Hudson, *The Ecumenical movement in world affairs* (London: Weidenfeld & Nicolson, 1969).
42 B. R. Wilson, *Religion in secular society* (London: Watts, 1966), pp. 125–41.

Again, how is decline measured? There have been significant variations in the level and type of religious practice in Europe from one generation to another since the Roman empire. Arguments about rise and decline generally assume a 'revivalist' model of practice, such as in the Reformation, or the Evangelical Revival, when there is a general rise in attendance or membership – rather than a life-cycle model, when religious practice is more common among certain age-groups than others. This raises once more the question of whether the church is a separate community within or beyond national society, and also the issue of establishment. Both France and Scandinavia have dominating national churches, albeit Roman Catholic in one case and Lutheran in the other. In Britain the non-established churches have declined more rapidly than the established, so that Britain is becoming more like France and Scandinavia.

However, a different kind of non-established Christianity has developed in Britain, as in the United States, which is generally unsympathetic to ecumenism. This is the Charismatic or Pentecostal movement, which is almost the twentieth-century form of the Evangelical Revival. Its significance in Africa and Latin America has already been noted; it is equally significant in the United States. Since 1960 it has grown in mainland Europe, because of the reinforcement of Baptists, Adventists, and other evangelicals and Pentecostals by North American missionaries in post-war Europe. Nowhere is this clearer than in eastern Europe, where groups that had emigrated to North America felt an urge, if not to return, at least to support missionary activity in their homelands. Even without a conservative reaction against ecumenism, it is easy to understand the Orthodox churches' concern; and fundamental issues about freedom of religion have been raised.

This is a paradoxically unecumenical note upon which to end. However, it exposes quite sharply an issue that has been with the church since Constantine. His reign brought a uniformity and coherence into the life of the Christian church that it had lacked, so long as there was periodic persecution and only limited interchange between different territories. The nineteenth century forced the Roman Catholic church to rethink its relation to the state, and the twentieth century forced the same reflection upon Protestants. Ecumenism was and is a strategy that enables the church to hold together as an institution with an existence distinct from that of political society. Inevitably, after so many centuries when the norm has been different, ecumenism has been a tender plant. Nevertheless, the history of the churches since 1945 indicates that ecumenism offers an alternative to continuing conflict in the church.

Christianity, colonialism and missions

KEVIN WARD

Introduction

In 1910 Rennie McInnes, an Anglican missionary in Cairo, enthusiastically pointed out that King Edward VII ruled over more Muslims than Persia and the Ottoman empire combined. 'Who would doubt the issue of this glorious conflict?' he concluded, confident that Islam would wither away under the combined onslaught of Christian mission and colonial rule.[1]

As a result of the 1914–18 war the Ottoman empire collapsed and many of its territories came under control of Western powers. The independence of Persia was further eroded. But the war also brought a loss of confidence in the ability of Christianity, even with the support of colonialism, to undermine Islam. In 1909 McInnes' colleague in Cairo, William Temple Gairdner, had produced a little book, *The reproach of Islam*, designed to convince Christian students in British and American universities of the need for evangelism to the Muslim world. Yet Gairdner was already developing a more sober realism, a less assertive style, a humbler approach, qualities which he was to develop further in the decade between the end of the war and his death in 1928 and which were to make him one of the great Christian Islamists of the twentieth century.[2] McInnes himself became Anglican bishop in Jerusalem in 1914. He became an outspoken critic of the Balfour Declaration and of the abrasive politics (as he saw it) of Dr Weizmann and the Zionist settlers in Palestine. Bishop McInnes supported a moderate Arab delegation of Muslim and Christian Palestinians who were sent to Britain to voice their concerns about Jewish settlement, incurring the wrath of Winston

---

1 Quoted in Samy Shehata, 'An evaluation of the mission of the Episcopal church in Egypt 1918–1925', MA dissertation, Birmingham university, 2001, p. 12.
2 Michael T. Shelley, 'The life and thought of W. H. T. Gairdner 1873–1928: a critical evaluation of a scholar-missionary', PhD dissertation, Birmingham university, 1988, p. 44.

Churchill.[3] In 1925 the choir of St George's school (which Edward Said,[4] author of *Orientalism*, the pioneer work on post-colonialism, would briefly attend a decade later) threatened to boycott the cathedral service if Lord Balfour, who was visiting Jerusalem, read a lesson. The identity of interest of empire and mission could no longer be taken for granted.

After 1918 a greater area of the globe came under colonial rule than ever before or since. In many ways the inter-war years saw the apogee of colonial–missionary co-operation. But increasingly Christianity's reliance on Western political power appeared to be deeply questionable. Britain and France were the chief colonial beneficiaries. Britain obtained the League of Nations mandate for Palestine – the presence of the Anglican bishopric in Jerusalem was not totally irrelevant to this award. France received a mandate for Syria and Lebanon: France had long claims to be the defenders of Levant Catholics and Uniate (Orthodox in communion with Rome) communities like the Maronites. In the inter-war period Britain continued its longstanding policy of a disinterested, general, tolerance of Christian mission, regardless of denomination. Britain had two Protestant established churches in England and Scotland: Anglican and Presbyterian. In Ireland, before the creation of the Free State in 1922, Britain still ruled an overwhelmingly Catholic population. The complexities of British church–state relations meant that, even in places of British settlement overseas, the Church of England was rarely a legal establishment, though it was often criticised for being too closely allied to the state. Barbados was one of the few places overseas where the Anglican church was established – it remained so until 1968. India was an anomaly. The church there was established in so far as the British Indian civil service and army were concerned. But the authorities were quite clear that this did not apply to India as a whole. Even this attenuated establishment was formally ended in 1930. In its non-settler dominions, Britain consistently refused to grant any special privileges to Anglicanism. She welcomed Roman Catholic missions, and non-British missions, whether Protestant or Catholic, thus giving mission in the British empire a rare diversity. Britain was keenly aware of the sensitivities of Christian mission in Islamic areas. In places like the northern Sudan and northern Nigeria Christian mission work of any kind was strictly circumscribed.

---

3 Rariq Farah, *In troubled waters: a history of the Anglican church in Jerusalem 1841–1998* (Dorset: Christians Aware, 2002), pp. 86–92.
4 Edward Said, *Out of place: a memoir* (New York: Alfred Knopf, 1999).

France's attitude to missionaries was characterised both by a greater hostility and a greater intimacy. An overwhelmingly Catholic country, France still deployed in 1914 by far the greatest number of Catholic missionaries throughout the world. But France was a secular state, marked by antagonistic relations with the church. However, the militant secularism of the early years of the twentieth century was not revived in the inter-war period, not least because the strong patriotic support of the church during the war had given it credibility even to parties of the left.[5] Even anti-clerical regimes in France were acutely conscious of the utility of French overseas missions for the furtherance of French colonial ambitions. 'Anti-clericalism is not for export.' For their part, French missions often identified themselves strongly with a French cultural chauvinism.[6]

Germany had a long tradition of mission going back long before Bismarck's creation of the German empire. Missions had been a useful tool in Germany's search for a colonial empire, and they paid the penalty of defeat in 1918. German missionaries in Ruanda-Urundi and in Kenya were not allowed to return. Other missions, in Tanganyika, Togo, Cameroon and South West Africa (Namibia), now found themselves under the colonial control of Germany's former enemies. The other Protestant colonial power in 1918 was the Netherlands. The East Indies (Indonesia) were important as the last remnant of the Dutch seaborne empire. The late nineteenth century had seen the rise of the Anti-Revolutionary Party of Abraham Kuyper, a conservative confessional Protestant movement in the Reformed tradition. Kuyper stressed the responsibility of the state to promote Christianity in the colonies, even in the face of an overwhelming Islam. As Kuyper's famous manifesto *Our programme* put it: 'the tendency of our policies to selfishly exploit the colonies for the benefit of the state or private persons should give way to policies of moral obligation.' The Christian governor of the Dutch East Indies from 1909 to 1916, A. W. F. Idenburg, had attempted to combine this moral vision with a policy of support for Christianity. But he found opposition from planters and the press in the colony and the secular forces of the left at home. After 1918 there was a succession of religious coalition governments in the Hague, in which Catholics were a greater (and much more cohesive) force than the Protestant parties. For the first time the Netherlands had a Catholic premier in Ruys de Beerenbrouck. In the East

5 Patrick J. N. Tuck, *French Catholic missionaries and the politics of imperialism in Vietnam, 1857–1914* (Liverpool: Liverpool University Press, 1987), p. 301.
6 Frederick Quinn, *The French overseas empire* (Westport, CN: Praeger, 2000).

Indies this meant that both Catholic and Protestant missions were given parity of treatment and anti-clerical forces declined within the Dutch expatriate community. But, in a situation where the colonial government had increasingly to take into account the rise of Islamic nationalism, there could now be no question of the government expressing a purely Protestant vision.[7]

Portugal continued to hold on tenaciously to its waning colonial possessions, notably in Africa (Mozambique, Angola and Guinea Bissau) and East Timor. For much of the twentieth century Portugal was controlled by the fascist regime of Salazar, who emphasised the alliance between church and state in the colonies. The Catholic church was a privileged and somewhat reactionary establishment. Protestant missions were recognised only reluctantly and in a niggardly fashion. The Belgian government, both in the Congo and in the new League Mandate of Ruanda-Urundi, strongly favoured Belgian missionaries. Even non-Belgian Catholics were discriminated against. Fascist Italy belatedly began a new imperial venture by invading Abyssinia (Ethiopia) in 1936. The war led to the execution of the *abuna* (patriarch) of the Ethiopian Orthodox church and the expulsion of non-Italian Catholic missionaries, as well as Protestants. This proved a short and harrowing interlude – in 1941 Italy was expelled from Ethiopia by the Allies.

Ireland occupied a special place in Catholic missionary work. Independent from Britain in 1922, the Irish Free State was a European Catholic state with no colonial responsibilities or ambitions. It played with renewed vigour the vital role that it had assumed in the nineteenth century – providing Catholic missionary personnel for English-speaking colonies. The Irish were well represented in French and British Catholic mission societies, and in a growing number of indigenous Irish missionary societies. The importance of the Irish nationalist struggle against Britain did not necessarily translate into sympathy for anti-colonialism in Africa or Asia. But in the post-colonial era it did give the Irish missionary movement a special importance. Significantly, support for mission societies in Ireland remained stronger than in other European countries.[8] The Scandinavian countries, with their strong Lutheran missionary traditions, played a similarly important role in the Protestant world. They had inherited a number of German missions after the First World War – for example the Bukoba district of north-eastern Tanganyika. Interestingly, both

7 Pieter Holtrop, in Pieter N. Holtrop and Hugh McLeod, *Missions and missionaries* (Woodbridge, Suffolk: Boydell Press, 2000), pp. 142–56.
8 Edmund H. Hogan, *The Irish missionary movement: a historical survey 1830–1980* (Dublin: Gill & Macmillan, 1990).

Ireland and the Scandinavian countries have been active in development issues in the post-colonial world.

The most important non-colonial great power in 1914 was the United States of America. Since the 1898 war against Spain, America too had the trappings of imperial power, formally in the Philippines and informally in parts of Latin America. But in its own self-understanding the USA remained resolutely 'anti-colonial', at least rhetorically. The USA saw itself as modelling an alternative way of relating to the world from that of old Europe. The American attachment to China, mediated extensively by Protestant missions, was particularly deep. The Chinese authorities resented America as much as the Europeans for the unequal treaties that had been imposed upon China in the nineteenth century. But the reform movements that provoked the 1911 revolution drew inspiration from American political institutions and the American Protestant Christian colleges in China provided models for a modern Chinese patriotism. Both Sun Yat Sen and Chiang Kai-shek were trained in Protestant schools and colleges. Despite American shock at the communist victory in China in 1949, America's anti-colonial instincts remained strong in the middle east and Africa, only to be destroyed by the Vietnam war.

The missionary movement in the early twentieth century

In the twentieth century, the Catholic church regained, to a large extent, the missionary momentum it had lost to the Protestants in the previous century. Catholic missionaries in 1914 were just as liable as Protestants to support their own European national interests. But the Catholic church could never simply be identified with a particular nation. Rome acted as a counterpoise to Catholic states too eager to utilise Catholic missions for their own purposes. Benedict XV was elected pope just as war was breaking out in 1914 and was greatly exercised by the perils of unrestrained nationalism. In 1919 Benedict produced one of the great mission encyclicals, *Maximum illud*. Speaking to the text of Psalm 45:10, 'Forget your nation and your ancestral home', Benedict warned against the missionary appearing 'to further the interests of his own country'. This led to the false impression that 'the Christian religion is the exclusive property of some foreign nation', and that acceptance of Christianity entails 'submission to a foreign country' and 'the loss of one's own national dignity'. The encyclical went on to encourage the development of a local clergy and hierarchy and appropriate theological training.[9] Benedict's appointment of the Dutch Cardinal Van Rossum as head of Propaganda Fidei was critical for the implementation of a policy that fostered the growth of local church hierarchies and put limits to missionary nationalism. Although the papacy itself did not always live up to this ideal of independence and critical distance, especially during the fascist era, it did, cumulatively, increase the church's scope for independence from colonial regimes. Nevertheless, Rome itself could demonstrate equal forms of colonial arrogance and repression in its relation to mission churches.

Protestant missions tended, even more than Catholics, to be composed of members of a single nation. Even as an international movement, the Protestant missionary enterprise was dominated by the English-speaking world. One legacy of the Edinburgh Missionary Conference of 1910 was the creation, in 1921, of the International Missionary Council. J. H. Oldham (1874–1969), a Scot and member of the United Free Church of Scotland, became secretary. He dominated international Protestant missionary life for thirty years.[10] Oldham's first area of concern, in the aftermath of the war, was to assist German missions, where possible, in re-establishing their shattered work. But his most important work was to facilitate a dialogue between Protestant missions and colonial governments. Oldham was the efficient, paternalist, mission statesman *par excellence*, mildly progressive within the colonial context, but, by the 1940s, eager to look beyond colonialism. The other great figure in Protestant mission was the American John Mott (1865–1955). Older than Oldham, he had been a pioneer of the Student Volunteer Movement and of international missionary co-operation in the two decades before the war. In the inter-war years his particular concern was for a Protestant Christianity sensitive to the awakening of nationalism in Asia. Mott represented an important strand of liberal Protestant thinking in this period, encapsulated in William Hocking's *Rethinking mission* of 1933, the report of the (American) Laymen's Foreign Missions Inquiry. The report was widely criticised for its emphasis on mission as a process of social and political enablement rather than direct evangelism, especially at the third mission conference in Tambaram, near Madras, in 1938, when the terrors of an 'ungodly' nationalism in Germany and Japan were seen as a major threat both to world peace and Christian mission.

---

9 Quoted in Adrian Hastings, 'The clash of nationalism and universalism within twentieth-century missionary Christianity', unpublished paper, 2001.
10 Keith Clements, *Faith on the frontier: a life of J. H. Oldham* (Edinburgh: T & T Clark, 1999).

One area of particular insensitivity in inter-war Protestant missionary ecumenism was the way in which it collaborated with colonial authorities in discouraging black American missionary endeavour. Max Yergan was excluded from work for the YMCA in east Africa. He settled in the Union of South Africa, where he was an important role model for an aspiring black Christian educated class.[11]

The Protestant ecumenism with which Oldham and Mott were associated was challenged by a different sort of Protestantism: that of the faith missions, such as the China Inland mission, the Africa Inland mission, the Sudan Interior mission. Much more likely to be international than the traditional Protestant mission movement, they were also less concerned with the institutional development of the church, and on theological grounds feared the ecumenical movement. Pentecostals also rapidly became involved in missionary work, in seemingly spontaneous ways that contrasted with the formalised mission structures of the older Protestantism.

By the early twentieth century, the majority of missionaries were women: wives, single women, or, in the case of the Catholics, members of a wide variety of religious orders. In the period after the First World War women demanded, and in many case obtained, full recognition as missionaries and representation on their local and central boards. Their role in education, medicine and evangelism, as well as in fostering Christian family life, was crucial to the whole mission enterprise.

Africa and education

The inter-war period was one of high colonialism in Africa. Colonial officials generally saw themselves as a permanent fixture. But the League of Nations concept of 'trusteeship' brought a typically missionary concern for the welfare of subject peoples to the fore in international affairs. Oldham's *Christianity and the race problem* of 1924 was a 'realist' tract, excessively cautious in its concern that Christianity work within the inequalities essential to colonialism, while mitigating their worst features. Education was for Oldham crucial in training native peoples, in the distant future, to rule themselves. He arranged for the Phelps-Stokes commissions to enquire into mission education in Africa, and facilitated the Le Zoute Conference on educational and social issues and on co-operation with colonial governments.

11 Rodney Orr, 'African American missionaries to east Africa, 1900–1926: a study in the ethnic reconnection of the gospel', PhD dissertation, university of Edinburgh, 1999.

'The whole work of the Conference was done under a sense that a human drama of absorbing interest and deep significance was being enacted with the African continent as its stage.'[12]

Governments often despised the mission 'school in the bush' for its narrow religious aims and crude pedagogy. But they had nothing like the network of schools provided by Christian missions. Oldham's achievement was to convince government, and particularly the British government, that it should utilise the Christian schools in the establishment of colonial educational systems. The advantage for the missions was that this protected the Christian ethos of the school, while providing the funds (grants in aid) without which the missions could not develop educationally. By the end of the colonial period Christian missions were utterly reliant on state aid to maintain their schools. In British Africa, funding was open to all denominations. Catholics were presented with the dilemma of whether to build up their own system independently of the colonial state, or to accept state inspection and government-imposed curricula in order to qualify for grants. In the late 1920s the apostolic delegate to British Africa, Mgr Arthur Hurley (later to become head of the Catholic church in England and Wales), came down decisively on the side of co-operation: 'Collaborate with all your power and where it is impossible for you to carry on both the immediate task of evangelisation and your educational work, neglect your churches in order to perfect your schools'.[13] Already, in Nigeria, the Irish Bishop Shanahan had pursued a vigorous policy of co-operation, a highly successful enterprise which had gone a long way to making the Catholics the dominant voice in Igboland.[14]

The Protestant high schools such as Trinity college, Achemota (Gold Coast), King's college Budo (Uganda), the Alliance high school (Kenya), trained the political leaders who were to lead British African colonies into independence. Despite the wholehearted collaboration of Catholics at the primary level, Catholic secondary education tended to be much more directed towards establishing seminaries for the training of Catholic priests. In British Africa, this often meant that Catholics, despite their numerical superiority, were under-represented in political leadership. The exceptions were the Catholics Kwame Nkrumah of Ghana and Julius Nyerere of Tanzania.

---

12 Clements, *Faith on the frontier*, p. 36.
13 Roland Oliver, *The missionary factor in east Africa* (London: Longmans, 1952).
14 Adrian Hastings, *The church in Africa 1450–1950* (Oxford: Clarendon Press, 1994), pp. 450–1.

The French were less willing to devolve education entirely to missions. Their *écoles primaires supérieures* and *écoles normales* were often the breeding ground for national leaders such as Félix Houphouet-Boigny of Côte d'Ivoire. Léopold Senghor, by contrast, trained for the priesthood in Dakar, but was expelled for his protests against the racism endemic in the seminary and in society at large. He fought for the French during the war and was a POW in Germany, before eventually becoming the first president of Senegal – a Catholic leader in a predominantly Muslim country. In Burkino Fasso the importance of Catholic education also created a Christian Catholic elite in a predominantly Muslim country. By contrast, in the Portuguese African colonies the powerful alliance between Catholic church and state led its nationalist leaders to emerge from Protestant schools; while one of the chief failures of the Belgians in the Congo was their lack of support for any credible secondary school system.

Colonial labour policies in Africa

Colonial regimes in Africa were desperate to make their colonies pay. Whether their economies were based on plantation cash cropping, white settler farming, or local peasantry, governments looked to the churches to encourage Africans to join the labour market and to instil the disciplines of time-keeping and a work ethic. In Kenya colony after 1918, war and influenza had severely reduced the African population at a time when white settlers were taking over land and were desperately looking for labour. Settlers persuaded the British authorities in Nairobi to introduce regulations to force young African men to abandon subsistence farming in their own fields to become workers on European farms. The Kikuyu, whose land had been alienated to provide farms for settlers in the early years of the century, were now expected to provide labour for those farms. Methods of compulsion included the requirement to pay poll tax only in cash rather than in kind, and leaning on government-appointed chiefs to recruit a regular supply of labour. Missionaries, with their history of anti-slavery, were naturally critical of government policies that seemed to amount to coercion and forced labour. But Kenya missions had also acquired land and their missionaries were potential settlers. They had cultivated social links with the settlers, shared their hopes and fears to a large extent and were sympathetic to their economic necessities. When the Colonial Office became alarmed at reports of forced labour practices in east Africa, the missionaries turned to Oldham to defend the honour of the white community. Oldham negotiated with the

Colonial Office what it was hoped would be a well-regulated and 'humane' system, but nevertheless one that still had strong elements of compulsion. This in turn created a protest from the Anglican bishop of Zanzibar, Frank Weston, against 'the serfs of Great Britain'. As the immediate post-war labour shortage abated, less obviously coercive methods of recruiting labour began to operate. But land and labour remained crucial areas of controversy throughout the colonial period in Africa, especially where widespread European settlement created a conflict of economic interest. A number of missionaries conducted long painstaking campaigns: in Southern Rhodesia the Anglican Shearly Cripps and the Methodist John White; in Kenya, Archdeacon Walter Owen of Kavirondo, whose letters to the *Manchester Guardian* about African conditions and rights so infuriated the Kenya settlers.

In French colonial Africa, labour policies tended to be ruthlessly policed by the colonial government, even secularist governors adopting religious terminology to justify compulsion: the *apostolat du travail*.[15] British colonies experienced an influx of Africans into their territories as a result.

Missionary views on Africa's development, indeed colonial views generally, were not consistent. Colonial economic policies and missionary schooling disrupted traditional life and values. But colonial and missionary rhetoric simultaneously exalted traditional life and actively tried to preserve it. In south-west Tanganyika the high-church Anglicans of the Universities' Mission to Central Africa provided Christian alternatives to traditional initiation rites (*jando*), stressing the positive appropriation of what was good in the tradition rather than an entirely negative condemnation. The most consistent and impressive example was in the Lutheran church among the Chagga of north-east Tanganyika. Under the inspiration of the German missionary Bruno Gutmann, church structures were developed in a thoroughgoing way, to reinforce and parallel traditional tribal models. The aim was to create an African *Volkskirche*. Such experiments drew from German philosophical roots about the uniqueness of racial identity, but they were far from the crude racism of National Socialism, and were deeply respectful of Chagga culture and sensibilities. But, by and large, missionary attempts at 'adaptation' were regarded with as much suspicion by African Christians as wholesale condemnation. An example of this was seen in Kenya, where the decision of the Protestant missions to launch a radical attack on female circumcision in 1929 was taken by the Kikuyu as a general attack on Kikuyu culture and tribal

---

15 Frederick Cooper, *Decolonization and African society* (Cambridge: Cambridge University Press, 1996), pp. 77ff.

integrity, part of a process that had deprived the Kikuyu of land and auto-nomy. But those who left the mission churches in protest also resented missionary attempts to limit the use of English in primary schools: they rightly discerned that a differentiated education was an inferior education and designed to inhibit political advance. The most insidious example of this occurred in the working of the apartheid doctrine in South Africa after 1948. The Bantu Education Act of 1953 combined a cynical façade of respect for African culture with a ruthless suppression of African rights and opportun-ities, as well as dismantling a mission school system that had been developed over the generations.

Training of indigenous clergy

The Protestant emphasis on training pastors drawn from a peasant back-ground to serve the rural base of mission Christianity had many positive aspects. But it did produce a dichotomy between a clergy of small educational achievements and a tiny elite of highly educated laymen and -women. This was to cause the Protestant churches some headache in the era of independ-ence. It provided a plausible reason for delaying the Africanisation of church leadership. In 1950 there were still no African Anglican diocesan bishops anywhere in Africa, and the situation was little different for the leadership of other Protestant churches. The move towards the creation of autonomous church structures was then hurriedly accomplished in little more than a decade, creating an indigenous church leadership which, initially at least, lacked the training or the confidence to handle the social and political crises of the early years of independence. On the other hand, the concentration of Catholic resources on major seminaries was, by the 1930s, producing a high calibre of local priests. It facilitated the development of an African hierarchy: Joseph Kiwanuka of Uganda became the first African diocesan bishop when in 1939 he was made bishop of Masaka. This was some twenty years before a Ugandan Anglican had such responsibility. The weakness of the Catholic system was that it failed during the colonial period to produce educated leaders in secular callings. Moreover, the highly specialised seminarian train-ing aimed at producing only a small number of priests. Consequently the Catholic church continued to rely heavily on missionary parish priests long after they had disappeared from Protestant church life.

In areas of strong settler influence (in Congo, the Portuguese territories, Kenya, South Africa and the Rhodesias) the mainline missionary churches were often too readily identified with white interests, inhibiting the development of the African church. Some Africans responded to white dominance by forming independent churches. But the remarkable thing is that, despite the colonial dominance of the church, African Christians did manage to create and sustain an African space within the missionary-formed churches. Great spiritual movements like the *Balokole* movement, which swept through east African Protestantism from the 1940s, utilised a strongly Westernised form of Holiness Evangelicalism (inspired by the Keswick movement) to create a thoroughly African style of Christianity, emphasising African ideals of community and solidarity, and engaging with distinctively African concerns, for example in relation to the spirit world. In Congo, a parallel movement called *Jamaa* (a Swahili word for 'family'), pioneered by the Flemish Franciscan missionary Placide Tempels, spread rapidly within the Catholic church of Katanga and Kasai in the 1940s and 1950s. Tempels developed what he called a 'Bantu philosophy of Being'. He may have over-interpreted his data, constricting it into Thomist categories. But he was genuinely appreciative of African thought and life and tried to articulate these in ways that he hoped were expressive of authentic African culture. Tempels was an important forerunner for post-independence Zairean Catholic theologians, stressing *authenticité*. He also influenced the great Tutsi Rwandan cultural philosopher, Abbé Alex Kagame.

Asia and nationalism

India

Decolonisation only became an active policy issue in Africa after the Second World War. In Asia it was of vital concern a generation earlier. African nationalism generally, and Pan-Africanism as a movement, were invented and sustained largely by African Christians. In Asia much of the dynamic of anti-colonialism came from a revival of Islam or Hinduism or Chinese religion. Nevertheless, Christians did play an important role in the Asian renaissance at many points. Crucial for Asian Christian leaders in the mid-twentieth century was to show that Christianity and nationalism could co-exist. Many missionaries were sceptical or hostile to this project, at least when it became too 'political' and radical. There were always exceptions, missionaries who did break out of the 'caste' mentality in which the missionary community was so often confined, physically and psychologically. C. F. Andrews (1871–1940), an Anglican priest, taught at St Stephen's college in Delhi in the years before the First World War. Increasingly frustrated by racial prejudice, in 1912 he met Gandhi in South Africa and became a devoted disciple. For the rest of his life he was associated with the struggle for *swaraj* (independence) in India, and also campaigned for the rights of Indians in Fiji and South Africa. Later he formed a strong friendship with the Bengali poet Rabindranath Tagore, staying at his ashram at Shantiniketan, and further absorbing a Hindu religious sensibility to nationalist questions. The immersion of Andrews in the nationalist struggle took him far from institutional forms of Christianity. An American Methodist, E. Stanley Jones, by contrast, remained more closely attached to the missionary movement in India, while calling for a revisioning of the Christian missionary movement so that it fulfilled Indian aspirations. His *Christ of the Indian road* (1925), and his espousal of Christian ashrams (spiritual centres, common in the Hindu tradition), remain important milestones for this process. The need to transcend the Western heritage of Christianity animated the long negotiations for a unified Protestant church in south India. At times the debates seemed dominated by issues of Western ecclesiology. But Indian leaders such as Bishop Azariah (1874–1945), the first and the only Anglican Indian bishop until just a few years before independence, were also wholeheartedly committed to the creation of an ecumenical Indian church. The Church of South India, uniting churches of the Anglican, Methodist and Reformed traditions, came into being on 27 September 1947, a month after independence. It has played an important role in asserting an Indian, post-colonial, character to Protestantism in India.

China

The transition to independence in India in 1947 was traumatic, accompanied as it was with communal displacement and killings. Not least, the creation of separate Muslim states in Pakistan and, eventually, in Bangladesh had grave consequences for the status of Christians, as followers of a minority religion, throughout the sub-continent. Nevertheless, Indian independence did not entail the chronic disorder and upheaval that occurred further east. China was in an almost constant state of turmoil. The anti-Christian campaigns of the 1920s were followed by the Japanese invasion of the 1930s and the communist triumph of 1949. All put severe stresses on Christianity in China and called into question the missionary role. By the late 1950s the communist regime was insisting that Christians cut off all ties with foreign mission societies. The resulting union of Protestant churches was very different from that accomplished under missionary management a decade earlier in India. Yet the Three Self Patriotic movement did in many ways build on the ecumenical impulses of the early years of the century. Its architect Y. T. Wu (1893–1979) and Bishop K. H. Ting, his successor as chief apologist for the movement, saw the 'post-denominational' situation as the only realistic way for Chinese Protestants to demonstrate their full commitment as patriotic Chinese to the creation of a new China. Significantly, the very term 'Three Self movement' looked back to Henry Venn and Rufus Anderson, missionary strategists of the nineteenth century, as well as incorporating John Nevius and Roland Allen's critique of the slowness in creating a Chinese Christianity. In the Cold War politics of the 1950s and 1960s American missionaries in particular found it difficult to reconcile themselves to a Christian acceptance of communism. But there were other missionary voices calling for a more sober and humble reappraisal of the Western missionary enterprise in China. David Paton's book *Christian missions and the judgement of God* (1953) was of great significance, as was the unpopular stand of the Anglican bishop of Hong Kong, R. O. Hall (1895–1975), in keeping open channels of communication with the Three Self movement, and in speaking positively about the communist regime in China. Bishop Hall had earlier shown his flexibility when in 1942 he had ordained a Chinese woman, Florence Li Tim Oi, as the first woman priest in the Anglican communion, a response to the pastoral emergency during the war and the Japanese occupation, but one of immense importance for the church worldwide.

The Catholic church in China had even more difficulty than Protestants in adjusting to communism. One important earlier missionary figure was, however, crucial for developing Chinese forms of Catholicism. Frederick Vincent Lebbe (1877–1940), a Belgian Vincentian priest, identified himself totally with his adopted country. He took a Chinese name (Lei Ming Yuan) and became a Chinese citizen. He worked hard to overcome the suspicions between missionaries and Chinese Christians that still persisted as a result of the ancient Rites controversy (the dispute about how far Chinese customs, and particularly Chinese names for God, could be utilised in Christian practice and worship). Lebbe was delighted when in 1926 the pope consecrated six Chinese bishops. Imprisoned by the communists, he died soon after his release in 1940, as a result of the hardships he had endured. His Belgian compatriot, Cardinal Suenens, saw him as a crucial inspiration for the Second Vatican Council.[16]

The Dutch East Indies

The Japanese occupation of east Asia and the Pacific during the Second World War resulted in the large-scale deportation, imprisonment and execution of

---

16 Entry in Scott W. Sundquist, *A dictionary of Asian Christianity* (Grand Rapids: Eerdmans, 2001).

missionaries. It greatly speeded up the process of decolonisation, and the development of independent indigenous churches in the area. After the war, the Dutch were never seriously able to reoccupy Indonesia. Under Dutch colonialism, missions in the Reformed tradition had been favoured. The greatest missionary of the inter-war period was Hendrik Kraemer (1888–1965), a missiologist of worldwide importance who at Tambaram introduced a Barthian perspective on mission.[17] But he was also the proponent of indigenisation for Dutch Protestantism. Catholics were comparatively weak in the Dutch colony. The first Indonesian bishop, Albertus Soegijapranata (1896–1963), was only consecrated in 1941, on the eve of the Japanese occupation. Soegijapranata was to play an important part during the early years of independence in securing a firm niche for the Christian churches in the largest Muslim country in the world.

French Indo-China

Nowhere was the transition from colonialism to independence more fraught and dangerous for Christians than in French Indo-China. The relationship between the French colonial government and the French Catholic missionaries was particularly intimate. Both were agreed on the importance of the French cultural civilising mission. Even during periods of anti-clericalism at home, there tended to be a truce in Vietnam. The alliance was, however, problematic for the development of a Vietnamese Catholicism. Catholics in Vietnam went back long before formal French colonialism. After the First World War Catholic intellectuals, including priests, participated in the development of a Vietnamese nationalism.[18] They resented the strongly pro-French attitude of the hierarchy. Ironically, French governments had been converted to a much more sympathetic attitude to the church, just at a time when Vietnamese Catholics were concerned to distance themselves from French values. Pope Benedict's encyclical of 1919 was welcomed in Vietnam as giving tacit support for a Catholic Vietnamese patriotism. The consecration of the first Vietnamese bishop, Nguyen Ba Tong (1868–1949), by Benedict's successor, Pius XI, in Rome in 1933 was an important landmark. During the war French Indo-China was controlled by Vichy France and collaborated with the Japanese. The Japanese finally threw out the French

---

17 Hendrik Kraemer, *The Christian message in the non-Christian world.*
18 Huy Lai Nguyen, 'Vietnam', in Adrian Hastings (ed.), *The church and the nations* (London: Sheed & Ward, 1959), pp. 171–92.

in 1945, but by this time their position was precarious. A national rising, led by Ho Chi Minh and the communists, occurred before the French were able to reassert control, the prelude to a bitter war and the partition of Vietnam into a communist north and a French-backed but nominally independent south. The decolonisation process was particularly traumatic for the Catholic church. There was a large exodus of Catholics to the south after the ceasefire of 1954 and the division of the country. But even in the south, nationalism became identified with a strong Buddhist identity that marginalised Catholics. In both parts of Vietnam, the Catholic place in society was insecure. Harassment and persecution was nothing new for the Vietnamese church.

The transformation of mission in a post-colonial world

With the rapid demise of colonialism in Asia in the years immediately following the Second World War, and with independence increasingly dominating the agenda in Africa, missionary attitudes were of necessity profoundly transformed – within missionary societies themselves, if not in the churches of the West that sponsored them, or in general Western attitudes. The image of missionary as destroyer of local culture, as part and parcel of the imperial project and as unsustainable in a post-colonial world, has tended to persist in the popular European secular mind.

In the 1950s, the final decade of colonialism, a 'colour bar' still persisted in social relations between Europeans (including missionaries) and 'natives' in Africa. By the early 1960s this had been eroded beyond all recognition. South Africa was the exception. It was not formally a colony, having attained self-rule from Britain in 1910. But the systematic implementation of a rigorous form of segregation after 1948 meant that it was here that Western missionaries most clearly continued their role as critics of colonialism. The protests of such missionaries as Trevor Huddleston, Michael Scott and Bishop Ambrose Reeves relied on widespread support in Britain, particularly co-ordinated by Canon John Collins and the Anti-Apartheid movement. Their witness, valuable as it was, should not obscure the importance of local black African and Afrikaner initiatives in this period of the 1960s.

In the rest of Africa and in Asia, as former mission churches became autonomous, the mission societies underwent a transformation. They still endeavoured to provide professional expertise for the young churches, but it was in the context of serving churches whose leadership was in the hands of local Christians. The emphasis was on partnership and mutual responsibility and inter-dependence. Max Warren, the general secretary of the Church Missionary Society from 1941 to 65, and his successor, John V. Taylor, were important figures in working out a new theology of mission that emphasised support for Christians in the national struggle and engagement in dialogue. Warren used the language of 'Christian presence' and a 'theology of attention' (i.e., respectful listening). One thing that Warren particularly regretted, however, was the merging in 1961 of the International Missionary Council with the World Council of Churches. He passionately held that Christianity should never forget its distinctive missionary calling, and that the dynamic nature of mission could never be adequately expressed in ecclesiological structures.[19]

In the Catholic world, Vatican II played an enormous part in enabling newly independent churches to discover their own identity, to develop indigenous forms of worship and 'being church'. 'Probably in no other continent did the Vatican Council coincide quite so neatly and sympathetically with a major process of secular change as in Africa.'[20] Missionaries such as Aylward Shorter and Adrian Hastings in Africa were important as midwives of this movement towards an authentic African Catholicism.

Meanwhile, the ability of mission societies to recruit missionaries (or 'mission partners') has declined, along with their financial basis (always precarious even at the height of the missionary movement). Western Christians, at least in Europe, have turned towards international aid organisations as a new and more acceptable way of relating to the world. But these newer institutions often replayed the mistakes of the earlier missionary movement: colonial arrogance, sidelining the local churches and indigenous forms of knowledge. Meanwhile new forms of missionary work, particularly associated with American Evangelicalism and Pentecostalism, became common. Ironically, both America and Pentecostals were commonly associated at the beginning of the twentieth century with a new world, an anti-colonial mentality. By the end of the twentieth century America seemed to be the chief bearer of a form of Western, Christian, neo-imperialism. Pentecostalism often does seem unashamedly to promote capitalism in its American expression. The gospel of wealth and prosperity may seem to appeal to crass forms of materialism. But just as the people of Asia, Latin America and Africa did

---

19 Timothy Yates, *Christian mission in the twentieth century* (Cambridge: Cambridge University Press, 1994), pp. 155ff.
20 Alberic Stacpoole (ed.), *Vatican II by those who were there* (London: Chapman, 1986), p. 315.

not passively accept the older forms of mission from Europe, so they are not now in the process naively of accepting American values. There are acute problems of globalisation that go beyond Christian mission and the question of whether American forms of conservative Evangelicalism and Pentecostalism are liberative or stultifying. But in emphasising the importance of local appropriation, there are important traits in Pentecostalism which resonate with local cultural understandings and which seem to be solutions to local poverty and powerlessness. The Charismatic movement characteristically generates a local leadership that is responsive to local congregations in ways that foreigners cannot control.[21] It is characteristic of all the churches of the South (Catholic, Protestant, Evangelical, Charismatic) that they are concerned with mission, with evangelism and with conversion. But this should not be seen as primarily a conservative movement, a reversion to older forms of Western Christianity. The expansive, missionary Christianity of the non-Western world has its own dynamic.[22]

---

21 David Martin, *Pentecostalism: the world their parish* (Oxford: Blackwell, 2002).
22 Philip Jenkins, *The next Christendom: the coming of global Christianity* (Oxford: Oxford University Press, 2002).

6

The Pentecostal and Charismatic movements

ALLAN ANDERSON

Revivals preceding Pentecostalism

Although sporadic outbursts of 'spiritual gifts' and ecstasy have occurred throughout Christian history, the idea developed particularly in the Protestant missionary, healing and 'Holiness' movements in the late nineteenth century that there was an experience after conversion called 'baptism in the Holy Spirit', the key doctrine of classical Pentecostals. Wesley's doctrine of a 'second blessing', a crisis experience subsequent to conversion, had a significant influence on the emergence of Pentecostalism. Increasingly the phrase 'baptism with the Spirit' was used to indicate the 'second blessing', but towards the end of the nineteenth century in the English Keswick Conventions and elsewhere it was no longer understood in terms of holiness, but as empowering for service. A new expectancy was created through various revivals and the 'second blessing' was linked with a worldwide revival, the 'latter rain' that would precede the return of Christ. At the same time, the experience of the Spirit was linked with a search for the 'power' of Pentecost, a new development that was to overtake the earlier emphasis on 'perfection'.[1] The divine healing movement, whose theology was taken over almost completely by early Pentecostalism, gave further impetus to these ideas.

The Welsh Revival (1904–5) emphasised the Pentecostal presence and power of the Spirit, as meetings were long, spontaneous, seemingly chaotic and emotional, focusing on the immediacy of God in the services and in personal experience. This revival was declared to be the end-time Pentecost of Acts 2, the 'latter rain' promised by biblical prophets that would result in a worldwide revival. These ideas were continued in other revival movements.

---

1 Donald W. Dayton, *Theological roots of Pentecostalism* (Metuchen, NJ and London: Scarecrow Press, 1987), pp. 88–9, 95–100; D. William Faupel, *The everlasting gospel: the significance of eschatology in the development of Pentecostal thought* (Sheffield: Sheffield Academic Press, 1996), pp. 73–5, 84–7.

Pentecostal-like movements had been known in south India since 1860, when glossolalia and other manifestations of the Spirit's presence were reported. In 1905 revivals broke out in north-east India where Welsh Presbyterian missionaries were working and at Pandita Ramabai's Mukti mission in Pune near Mumbai, which lasted two years, where speaking in tongues and other ecstatic phenomena occurred. Azusa Street revival participant Frank Bartleman documents the influence reports of the Welsh and Indian revivals had on their expectations for Los Angeles.[2] The 'Korean Pentecost' of 1907–8 commenced at a Presbyterian convention in Pyongyang and soon spread throughout Korea, and was likened by eyewitness William Blair to the Day of Pentecost. All these revivals were characterised by emotional repentance with loud weeping and simultaneous praying,[3] and had the effect of creating an air of expectancy and longing for revival in many parts of the evangelical world. The signs that this revival had come would be based on the earlier reports: an intense desire to pray, emotional confession of sins, manifestations of the coming of the Spirit, successful and accelerated evangelism, and spiritual gifts to confirm that the Spirit had come. This coming of the Spirit was linked to a belief that the last days had come and that the gospel would be preached to all nations on earth before the imminent coming of Christ. The stage was set for the coming of a new Pentecost to spread across the world in the new (twentieth) century.

The beginnings in the USA

Charles Parham (1873–1929), a former Methodist preacher in Topeka, Kansas, began Bethel Gospel school in 1900, enrolling thirty-four students to train for world evangelisation, where the only textbook was the Bible. Parham convinced his students that they had still to receive the full outpouring of Pentecost and to seek this with fasting and prayer. They reached the conclusion that the biblical evidence of Spirit baptism was speaking in tongues, and they set aside 31 December 1900 to pray for this experience. The next night, Agnes Ozman was first to speak in tongues, followed by others including Parham three days later. By 1905 several thousand people had received Spirit baptism in Parham's new movement known as the 'Apostolic Faith'. He

2 Frank Bartleman, *Azusa Street* (S. Plainfield, NJ: Bridge Publishing, 1980), p. 35; Gary B. McGee, '"Latter rain" falling in the east: early-twentieth-century Pentecostalism in India and the debate over speaking in tongues', *Church history* 68:3 (1999), pp. 649, 653–9.
3 Allan Anderson, *An introduction to Pentecostalism: global charismatic Christianity* (Cambridge: Cambridge University Press, 2004), pp. 35–8.

began a school in Houston, Texas, where through a half-opened door an African American Holiness preacher, William Seymour (1870–1922), was to hear his teaching of evidential tongues, the doctrine that became the hallmark of classical Pentecostalism. Although Parham believed that tongues were authentic languages given for the proclamation of the gospel in the end times, he was responsible for the theological shift in emphasis to glossolalia as 'evidence' of Spirit baptism in early North American Pentecostalism. This remains its central emphasis today.

Seymour was invited to Los Angeles in 1906 to a small Holiness church, which was locked against him when he preached that tongues was the sign of Spirit baptism. People continued meeting with Seymour in prayer in a house, where several people including Seymour received Spirit baptism. Within a week this rapidly growing group moved into a former African Methodist Episcopal church building on Azusa Street, where daily meetings commenced in the morning and usually lasted until late night, spontaneous and emotional, without planned programmes or speakers. Singing in tongues and people falling to the ground 'under the power' or 'slain in the Spirit' were common phenomena. The racial integration in these meetings was unique at that time and Seymour led a fully integrated leadership team.[4] Seymour became spiritual leader of thousands of early Pentecostals as he directed the most prominent centre of Pentecostalism for the next three years, further promoted by his periodical *The apostolic faith*. Visitors came to be baptised in the Spirit, and many of these began Pentecostal centres in other cities. Parham came to 'control' the revival in October 1906 and was disgusted particularly by the inter-racial fellowship and what he termed 'hypnotism' and the 'freak imitation of Pentecost'.[5] He was never reconciled with Seymour and went into relative obscurity.

The first schisms and Pentecostal denominations

Under Seymour the Apostolic Faith movement took on international dimensions. But from 1908, several competing Pentecostal missions drew away members from Azusa Street. The North Avenue mission of William Durham in Chicago, who received Spirit baptism at Azusa Street, became

4 Faupel, *Everlasting gospel*, pp. 194–7; S. M. Burgess and E. M. van der Maas (eds.), *New international dictionary of Pentecostal and Charismatic movements* (Grand Rapids: Zondervan, 2002), pp. 344–50, 1053–8; Anderson, *Introduction*, pp. 39–42.
5 Robert M. Anderson, *Vision of the disinherited: the making of American Pentecostalism* (Oxford: Oxford University Press, 1979), p. 190.

a revival centre that helped create several European immigrant congregations. In 1911 Durham went to Los Angeles during Seymour's absence to preach at Azusa Street on his 'Finished Work' doctrine. Seymour on his return to Los Angeles asked Durham to stop teaching his doctrine and, when Durham refused, locked the mission against him. Durham continued in a nearby hall with about two-thirds of Seymour's workers.[6] Durham had declared the Holiness teaching of 'entire sanctification' embraced by Seymour and most early Pentecostals to be 'unscriptural' in 1910, and taught that sanctification was not a 'second blessing' or a 'crisis experience', but was received at conversion by identification with Christ by faith. His influence was enormous, as many leaders of Pentecostal churches came to Durham to embrace his doctrine, which became the basis upon which the Assemblies of God (AG), the later 'Oneness' churches and several other smaller Pentecostal denominations were founded. By 1914, some 60 per cent of North American Pentecostals had accepted Durham's position and, at the launch of the AG that year, the first address was entitled 'The finished work of Calvary'.[7] Seymour's mission after this split became a small black congregation, but at least twenty-six different Pentecostal denominations trace their origins to Azusa Street.

There were many subsequent divisions. A more fundamental schism erupted in 1916 over the doctrine of the Trinity, when several Pentecostals grouped around what was called 'New Issue', 'Jesus' Name' or 'Oneness', and 'Jesus Only' by its opponents. Some 'Finished Work' Pentecostals began teaching that the correct formula for baptism was 'in the name of Jesus', but this developed into a dispute about the Trinity. Oneness Pentecostalism, which has a Modalism that rejects the Trinity and believes that Jesus is the revelation of God the Father and that the Spirit proceeds from the Father (Jesus), was destined to remain isolated from the rest of Pentecostalism. The United Pentecostal church (UPC) became the largest Oneness group in North America, a white denomination formed in 1945 from a union of two groups. Oneness Pentecostals are found all over the world today and account for up to a quarter of all classical Pentecostals.[8]

By 1916, North American Pentecostalism was divided theologically into three mutually antagonistic groups: 'Second Work' (Holiness) Trinitarian, 'Finished Work' Trinitarian and 'Finished Work' Oneness Pentecostals. The

---

6 Bartleman, *Azusa Street*, p. 151.
7 Faupel, *Everlasting gospel*, pp. 230–63; Robert Anderson, *Vision*, pp. 169–73.
8 Robert Anderson, *Vision*, pp. 166, 176; Faupel, *Everlasting gospel*, pp. 273–88, 301–6; Allan Anderson, *Introduction*, pp. 47–50.

process of schism and proliferation of new sects was established as segregated denominations formed in North America during the next fifty years, beginning as associations for fellowship and accreditation that became increasingly institutionalised. Charles H. Mason (1866–1961) visited Azusa Street in 1907 and received Spirit baptism, becoming presiding bishop of the Church of God in Christ (COGIC) from 1908 until his death in 1961, the largest African American and Holiness Pentecostal church by 2000 with an estimated five million members. The AG was organised in Hot Springs, Arkansas in 1914 with an emphasis on regional government to counter the extreme individualism developing in Pentecostalism. The new organisation did not adopt either a constitution or a statement of faith, but as a result of the doctrinal disputes formulated a 'Statement of Fundamental Truths' in 1916 enshrining the doctrine of the Trinity and (later) 'initial evidence' as essential teachings. In 1942 the AG joined the newly formed National Association of Evangelicals, a move that was to hasten their transition to a middle-class evangelical denomination, with over two million members in the USA in 2000. By this time the main areas of its growth were among Hispanic and Korean congregations, whereas many white congregations were in a state of stagnation or decline. Hispanic Pentecostalism was the fastest growing form of Pentecostalism in the USA in 2000, with some 20 per cent of Hispanics found in Pentecostal churches, some six million people. Their increasing numbers, improving economic status and political power in society make them a force to be reckoned with in the changing face of North American Pentecostalism.[9]

The Church of God (Cleveland) (CGC) is a Holiness Pentecostal church with roots in revival movements from 1886 in Tennessee and North Carolina and organised in 1907 in Cleveland, Tennessee with A. J. Tomlinson (1865–1943) as bishop. In 1908 the CGC became Pentecostal and Tomlinson became the CGC's first general overseer. Leadership tensions led to Tomlinson's expulsion and his founding in 1923 what was called the Church of God of Prophecy (CGP) from 1952. Aimee Semple McPherson (1890–1944) was founder of the International Church of the Foursquare Gospel (ICFG) in 1927, another 'Finished Work' denomination. 'Sister Aimee' was a talented public speaker, writer, musician, administrator and media star who fought against crime and poverty, encouraged women to enter the ministry and began a crusade against drug trafficking. She created the prototype of a new kind of Pentecostalism able

---

9 Burgess and van der Maas, *NID*, pp. 333–40, 535–7, 715–23; Walter J. Hollenweger, *The Pentecostals* (London: SCM, 1972), pp. 33–40.

to use and adapt the prevailing popular culture of its day for its purposes. Over 40 per cent of the ICFG's ministers in 2000 were women, probably a higher proportion than in any other Pentecostal denomination.[10] McPherson was one example of a host of Pentecostal women who were leaders, pioneers and missionaries in these early years. Women, far more than men, have been promoters of Pentecostalism, and were accorded more authority as ministers than that offered by other churches at the time. Although with the 'evangelicalism' of Pentecostal denominations has come a more limited role for women and a hierarchical male clergy, it is still true to say that Pentecostals have led the way in the ordination and use of women with charismatic gifts.

William Branham's (1909–65) sensational healing services, which began in 1946, formed the pattern for those that followed. The evangelistic healing campaigns had their peak in the 1950s with support from most Pentecostal denominations. By 1960, Oral Roberts (b.1918) had become the leading healing evangelist, increasingly accepted by 'mainline' denominations, while denominational Pentecostals were becoming increasingly critical of the evangelists' methods (particularly their fundraising) and lavish lifestyles and had begun to distance themselves from them.[11]

Latin American Pentecostalism

Pentecostal missionaries were sent out from Azusa Street from 1907, reaching over twenty-five nations in two years.[12] Parham, Seymour and many of the first North American Pentecostals believed that they had been given foreign languages through Spirit baptism so that they could preach the gospel throughout the world. The first North American missionaries who went out when the Azusa Street revival began were self-supporting and the majority were women. The first Pentecostals in Latin America were Chileans, associated with Willis C. Hoover (1858–1936), a US American revivalist minister in Valparaiso who had been in Chile since 1889, pastor of the largest Methodist congregation in Chile and a district superintendent. In 1907, the Hoovers learned of the Pentecostal revival at Ramabai's mission in India and were stirred to pray for such a revival. It broke out in April 1909 when many unusual and ecstatic manifestations occurred. After the Methodist Conference charged Hoover with conduct that was 'scandalous' and 'imprudent' and with propagating teachings that were

---

10 Burgess and van der Maas, *NID*, pp. 530–5, 539–42, 793–4, 856–9.
11 Ibid., pp. 440–1, 713, 950–1, 1024–5.
12 Faupel, *Everlasting gospel*, pp. 182–6.

'false and anti-Methodist', the revivalists formed the Methodist Pentecostal church (MPC) with Hoover as superintendent. Hoover resigned from the MPC in 1933, and his supporters formed the Evangelical Pentecostal church, the first of over thirty subsequent schisms.[13]

There are more Pentecostals in Brazil than in any other country, with roots in the ministry of Durham. His associate since 1907, Luigi Francescon (1866–1964), established Italian congregations in the USA and Argentina in 1909 and formed the Christian Congregation (CC) in São Paulo in 1910, the first Pentecostal church in Brazil. The formation of the AG in Brazil began with two Swedish immigrants, Gunnar Vingren and Daniel Berg, also associated with Durham, who went to the northern Brazilian state of Pará in 1910, where they founded the Apostolic Faith Mission, registered in 1918 as the Assembly of God. By 2000 the AG was the largest non-Catholic church in Latin America, with over four million affiliates. A second phase of twenty to thirty new Brazilian Pentecostal denominations arose after 1952, the most important being Brazil for Christ Evangelical Pentecostal church, God is Love Pentecostal church and Foursquare Gospel church. After about 1975, a third type of Pentecostal movement began, the largest being the Universal Church of the Kingdom of God (UCKG), a prosperity-oriented movement founded in 1977 in Rio de Janeiro by Edir Machedo. By the early 1990s the UCKG may have been the fastest growing church in Brazil with a thousand churches, well over a million members and operations in over fifty countries.[14]

The countries of Brazil, Chile and Argentina have the biggest Pentecostal churches on the continent, but nearly every other Latin American and Caribbean country has also been affected by this phenomenon, often with the aid of Western missions. Dramatic Pentecostal growth has taken place in Central America, where the largest non-Catholic denomination is the AG. Guatemala has over two million Pentecostals and Charismatics, half of whom are Amerindian Maya.[15] In the Anglophone Caribbean, the Church of God (Cleveland) and the Church of God of Prophecy are the largest Pentecostal

---

13 Willis C. Hoover, *History of the Pentecostal revival in Chile* (Santiago: Imprenta Eben-Ezer, 2000), pp. 18–36, 68–100, 240–7; Burgess and van der Maas, *NID*, pp. 55–7, 770–1; P. Johnstone and J. Mandryk, *Operation World: 21st century edition* (Carlisle: Paternoster, 2001), p. 156.

14 Hollenweger, *The Pentecostals*, pp. 85–92; Harvey Cox, *Fire from heaven: the rise of Pentecostal spirituality and the reshaping of religion in the twenty-first century* (London: Cassell, 1996), pp. 163–8; David Martin, *Tongues of fire: the explosion of Protestantism in Latin America* (Oxford: Blackwell, 1990), p. 66; Mike Berg and Paul Pretiz, *Spontaneous combustion: grass-roots Christianity Latin American style* (Pasadena, CA: William Carey Library, 1996), pp. 101–9; Johnstone and Mandryk, *Operation world*, p. 120.

15 Berg and Pretiz, *Spontaneous combustion*, pp. 41–2, 69, 74–9; Martin, *Tongues of fire*, p. 51.

denominations. Juan Lugo (1890–1984) founded what is now the largest non-Catholic denomination in Puerto Rico, the Pentecostal Church of God of Puerto Rico, which has sent missionaries all over Latin America and to the USA, Spain and Portugal.[16]

European Pentecostalism

Most western European Pentecostal churches have their origins in the revival associated with Thomas B. Barratt (1862–1940), a Methodist pastor in Oslo, Norway who visited New York in 1906 and began writing to Azusa Street. He was baptised in the Spirit and sailed back to Norway a zealous Pentecostal destined to become the founder and prime motivator of classical Pentecostalism in Europe. He was forced to leave the Methodist church and found a fellowship of independent churches known as Pentecostal Revival. The revival in Barratt's Filadelfia church in Oslo was a place of pilgrimage for people from all over Europe. Unlike the hierarchical Pentecostalism that was to develop in North America, Barratt's churches were strictly independent and congregational. From Oslo the Pentecostal movement spread to other parts of Europe and Pentecostals in Scandinavia soon became the biggest churches outside the Lutheran state churches. Lewi Pethrus' (1884–1974) Filadelfia church in Stockholm, Sweden was the largest Pentecostal congregation in the world until the 1960s, with its own extensive mission programme and social activities. Pethrus, a Baptist pastor who became a Pentecostal after visiting Barratt in 1907, was probably the most influential Pentecostal in Europe during his lifetime.[17]

Alexander Boddy (1854–1930), an Anglican vicar in Sunderland, visited Barratt's church and invited him to preach in September 1907 in his parish. This became the most significant early Pentecostal centre in Britain, and annual Whitsun conventions from 1908 to 1914 drew Pentecostals from all over Europe. Boddy edited the influential periodical *Confidence* (1908–26), which reported on Pentecostal revivals all over the world and expounded Pentecostal doctrines. In Belfast in 1915, George Jeffreys founded the Elim Pentecostal church, now the largest Pentecostal denomination in Britain.[18] The Assemblies of God in Great Britain and Ireland emerged in 1924 as a congregational association of autonomous churches. Donald Gee (1891–1966) was its chairman from 1948 until his death in 1966, travelling internationally

16 Berg and Pretiz, *Spontaneous combustion*, pp. 70–3; Allan Anderson, *Introduction*, pp. 79–81.
17 Burgess and van der Maas, *NID*, pp. 80–1, 103–5, 986–7.
18 Hollenweger, *The Pentecostals*, pp. 184–5; Johnstone and Mandryk, *Operation world*, p. 650.

and organising the European Pentecostal conference held in Stockholm in 1939 and the first Pentecostal World Conference (PWC) in Zürich in 1947. He was the first editor of the PWC's periodical *Pentecost* and one of the most influential Pentecostal leaders of his time.[19] After the mass immigration of people from the West Indies to Britain after 1948, African Caribbean Pentecostal churches with links with the Caribbean and the USA were set up and grew remarkably during the sixties. Many new independent churches were formed, resulting in a great variety of churches in this community. Later migrations after 1960 resulted in a number of West African Pentecostal churches being established in Britain and elsewhere in Europe.

Pentecostalism spread from England to France in 1926 and began among the Roma (Gypsy) people in 1952. In France and Spain about a quarter of the Roma population belongs to a Pentecostal church.[20] Portuguese Pentecostalism has its roots in Brazil, from where José Placido da Costa (1869–1965) and José de Mattos (1888–1958) returned to Portugal in 1913 and 1921 respectively as Pentecostal missionaries. Swedish missionaries planted Pentecostalism in Spain in 1923.[21] Italy has the second largest population of Pentecostals in western Europe after Britain. Francescon sent Giacomo Lombardi to Italy from Chicago in 1908, and the Pentecostal Christian Congregations and the Italian Pentecostal Christian church trace their origins to Lombardi.[22]

The Pentecostal movement has been relatively more successful in eastern Europe, where it has grown in the face of severe persecution. During the Soviet years, those Pentecostals that failed to co-operate with state-controlled structures were often imprisoned and exiled. Ivan Voronaev (1886–c.1940) commenced a Russian Pentecostal church in New York and in 1920 established congregations in Bulgaria, Ukraine and Russia. Voronaev's church in Odessa soon had a thousand members, and in 1927 he was appointed president of the Union of Christians of Evangelical Faith. An estimated 80,000 Pentecostals enjoyed the favour of the communist state that had liberated them from Orthodox persecution. But after the passing of anti-religious laws, Voronaev and eight hundred pastors were sent to Siberian concentration camps in 1930, after which Voronaev disappeared and was later presumed dead. The Christians of the Evangelical Faith (Pentecostal) unsuccessfully approached Soviet leaders Khrushchev in 1957 and Brezhnev in 1965 for

---

19 William K. Kay, *Pentecostals in Britain* (Carlisle: Paternoster, 2000), p. 74.
20 Burgess and van der Maas, *NID*, pp. 105–7, 417–18, 683–6, 1027, 1045.
21 Ibid., pp. 208–9, 247; Johnstone and Mandryk, *Operation world*, pp. 529, 583.
22 Burgess and van der Maas, *NID*, pp. 132–41; Cox, *Fire*, pp. 192–5; Hollenweger, *The Pentecostals*, pp. 251; Johnstone and Mandryk, *Operation world*, p. 365.

religious freedom, only realised in 1991. In Ukraine the Evangelical Pentecostal Union is one of the largest Pentecostal denominations in Europe, with some 370,000 members in 2000. By 2000 there were some 400,000 Russian Pentecostals, and in Ukraine 780,000, the highest number of Pentecostals in any European nation. There are over 300,000 Pentecostals in Romania, where the Pentecostal Apostolic Church of God is the largest denomination, founded in 1922 by George Bradin and since 1996 known as the Pentecostal Union. Since the disintegration of communism there has been more freedom for Pentecostals in eastern Europe, but new Pentecostal groups from the west have flooded into former communist countries with evangelistic techniques that have brought opposition from Orthodox churches and national governments.[23]

African Pentecostalism

Possibly 11 per cent of Africa's population in 2000 were 'Charismatic', a significant form of Christianity on the continent. Classical Pentecostals have been operating there since 1907, when missionaries from Azusa Street arrived in Liberia and Angola. The AG in particular had grown to over four million members throughout Africa by 1994. In South Africa in 1908 several independent Pentecostal missionaries arrived in Johannesburg and founded one of South Africa's biggest classical Pentecostal denominations, the Apostolic Faith Mission (AFM) in racially integrated services. But white leaders passed racist laws and kept all significant positions for themselves, contributing to the many schisms that took place. Most classical Pentecostal denominations in South Africa were divided on racial grounds until 1996.[24] Nicholas Bhengu (1909–86) was one of the most influential South African Pentecostals and leader of the 'Back to God' section of the AG. The German evangelist Reinhard Bonnke began his ministry in Lesotho, and has since preached throughout Africa to some of the biggest crowds in Christian history. His Christ for All Nations organisation has been highly effective in promoting Pentecostal practices in Africa. Pentecostal ideas spread from South Africa northwards to surrounding countries mainly through migrant workers who met Pentecostalism in South African mines. The largest Pentecostal church in Zimbabwe, the Zimbabwe Assemblies of God Africa,

23 Hollenweger, *The Pentecostals*, pp. 267–9, 274, 281; Johnstone and Mandryk, *Operation world*, pp. 540, 644; Allan Anderson, *Introduction*, pp. 98–101.
24 Johnstone and Mandryk, *Operation world*, p. 21; Allan Anderson, *Introduction*, pp. 106–10.

popularly known by its acronym ZAOGA, has its roots in both the AFM and Bhengu's AG. The British independent Pentecostal missionary William Burton (1886–1971) worked in the southern Congo from 1915 to 1960, and founded what became the Pentecostal Community of the Congo. In East Africa, most of the numerous African Independent churches place an emphasis on the Holy Spirit as a result of various revival movements. From western Kenya, Pentecostalism spread to Uganda, but because of the ravages of corrupt and oppressive dictatorships and a protracted civil war, Pentecostalism has developed there relatively late, numerous groups arising since 1986.[25]

Pentecostalism has become one of the most prominent Christian movements across west Africa. The Azusa Street missionaries to Liberia in 1907 were African Americans. The four largest classical Pentecostal denominations in Ghana are the Church of Pentecost, the AG, the Apostolic Church of Ghana, and the Christ Apostolic church. All except the AG have origins in the work of a remarkable Ghanaian, Peter Anim (1890–1984), and his Irish contemporary James McKeown (1900–89). In Yorubaland, Nigeria, evangelist Joseph Babalola heard a voice calling him to preach using prayer and 'water of life' (blessed water) which would heal all sicknesses. In 1939, the church that resulted broke with British Pentecostal missionaries, who had objected to the use of blessed water, while the Africans saw the use of medicine by the missionaries as compromising the doctrine of divine healing. The Christ Apostolic church emerged in 1941, the largest *Aladura* ('Prayer') church in Nigeria at the centre of Yoruba society and one of the largest independent churches in Africa with some two million affiliates.[26] Divine healing through the laying on of hands for the sick (and sometimes accompanied by ritual symbols) has always been a prominent part of Pentecostal practice, and this is especially true in Africa.

Pentecostals in Asia, Australia and the Pacific

Within a relatively short time a complex network of Pentecostal missions was established all over India. The AG in India formed a regional council for south India in 1929 and has had independent districts with Indian leadership since 1947. K. E. Abraham (1899–1974) became a Pentecostal in 1923 but

---

25 Burgess and van der Maas, *NID*, pp. 67–74, 150–5, 264–9.
26 Allan Anderson, *Introduction*, pp. 115–21; Johnstone and Mandryk, *Operation world*, pp. 241, 421, 288.

disagreed with missionaries and founded the Indian Pentecostal Church of God. This and the AG are the two largest Pentecostal denominations, with 750,000 affiliates each in 2000. The best known of the Indian healing evangelists is D. G. S. Dhinakaran of Tamilnadu, a member of the Church of South India, whose Jesus Calls Ministry has extensive campaigns with huge crowds.[27]

Myanmar, Thailand, Malaysia and Singapore have vibrant Pentecostal and Charismatic churches, but the greatest Pentecostal expansion in south-east Asia was in Indonesia. Dutch American Pentecostal missionaries arrived in Java in 1922. Over two million Javanese became Christians between 1965 and 1971, during the 'Indonesian Revival', despite heavy persecution from Muslim extremists. By 2000 there were nine to twelve million Pentecostals and charismatics, 4–5 per cent of the total population in a country 80 per cent Muslim.[28] Several Filipino Pentecostal missionaries converted in the USA commenced churches in the Philippines in 1928, where they grew to such an extent that they were regarded as a challenge to the Catholic church. The three largest churches are the Jesus is Lord church founded by Eddie Villanueva in 1978 and the Jesus Miracle Crusade (both Filipino-founded churches), and the AG.[29]

Western Pentecostal missionaries were active in China from 1907. Although there were only some five million Christians in mainland China at the time of the exodus of Westerners in 1949, estimates of membership of unregistered independent Chinese movements in 2000 vary between twenty and seventy-five million. China may now have the largest number of charismatic Christians in Asia, especially in unregistered independent house churches, which have developed in isolation from the rest of Christianity for at least fifty years and despite severe opposition. The True Jesus church founded by Paul Wei in 1917 in Beijing and the Jesus Family founded by Jing Dianying at Mazhuang, Shandong in 1927 are Pentecostal churches, the former Oneness in doctrine. Together with the evangelical Little Flock/ Local Church/Christian Assembly, these churches were banned during the 1950s until the end of the seventies, after which there was rapid growth. By 2000, an estimated 10 per cent of Protestants in China were members of

---

27 Allan Anderson and Edmond Tang (eds.), *Asian and Pentecostal: the charismatic face of Asian Christianity* (Oxford: Regnum, 2005), pp. 224–66; Roger E. Hedlund (ed.), *Christianity is Indian: the emergence of an indigenous community* (Delhi: ISPCK, 2000), pp. 160–1.
28 Anderson and Tang, *Asian and Pentecostal*, pp. 314–53; Johnstone and Mandryk, *Operation world*, p. 339.
29 Johnstone and Mandryk, *Operation world*, p. 521; Anderson and Tang, *Asian and Pentecostal*, pp. 354–416.

the True Jesus church and most Christian groups in central Shandong were of Jesus Family background.[30] There are several independent Japanese Pentecostal churches, including the Spirit of Jesus church founded in 1941 by Jun Marai and probably the largest Pentecostal denomination, the Original Gospel movement, also known as the *Makuya* (Tabernacle) movement, founded in 1948, and the Holy Ekklesia of Jesus, created by Tajeki Otsuki in 1946.[31] In 1932 Mary Rumsey, baptised in the Spirit at Azusa Street, established the first Pentecostal church in Seoul, Korea with Heong Huh. David (formerly Paul) Yonggi Cho (b.1936) and his future mother-in-law Jashil Choi (1915–89) began a small tent church in a Seoul slum area in 1958 and fifteen years later dedicated a 10,000-seat auditorium now called Yoido Full Gospel church (YFGC). Cho became chairman of the World Pentecostal Assemblies of God in 1992, and by 1993 the YFGC reported 700,000 members under 700 pastors, the largest Christian congregation in the world.[32]

The first Pentecostal congregation in Australia, the Good News Hall, was founded by Jeannie ('Mother') Lancaster in 1909. Pentecostal denominations were formed in 1926 when the Apostolic Faith Mission and the Pentecostal Church of Australia were formed, uniting in 1937 to create the AG in Australia, the largest Pentecostal denomination there. There are numerous Pentecostal and Charismatic groupings in Australia, which have also influenced Aotearoa New Zealand. The Pentecostal Church of New Zealand was set up in 1924 after the Australian model, and several schisms ensued. In most of the Pacific Islands Pentecostal and Charismatic Christianity has grown rapidly, especially since the 1970s. The AG is the biggest Pentecostal denomination in the region, but competes with several other movements, including large indigenous ones.[33]

The Charismatic movement

Many observers consider that the Charismatic movement, the practice of Pentecostal phenomena or of spiritual gifts in the 'mainline' Protestant churches, began in the Episcopalian church in the USA in 1960 and in the Roman Catholic church in 1967. But these events were the culmination rather than the commencement of a movement that had already existed for decades.

---

30 Anderson and Tang, *Asian and Pentecostal*, pp. 418–93.
31 Ibid., pp. 494–515; Johnstone and Mandryk, *Operation world*, p. 371.
32 Martin, *Tongues of fire*, pp. 135, 146; Cox, *Fire*, p. 220; Johnstone and Mandryk, *Operation world*, p. 387; Allan Anderson, *Introduction*, pp. 136–9.
33 Burgess and van der Maas, *NID*, pp. 26–9, 99–102, 187–91, 194–7, 221, 271–2; Johnstone and Mandryk, *Operation world*, pp. 83–4, 250, 480, 509–10, 627.

The commencement of Pentecostalism in Europe, the revivals in India, the 'Korean Pentecost' in the Presbyterian and Methodist churches, and the Pentecostal revival among Methodists in Chile at the beginning of the twentieth century were in fact 'charismatic' and ecumenical movements in the 'mainline' churches. Several significant influences prior to 1960 helped change the attitude of older churches to the Pentecostal experience, including the independent healing evangelists who operated independently of classical Pentecostal denominations and through whom Christians outside these denominations were exposed to Pentecostal experience, and the Full Gospel Business Men's Fellowship International (FGBMFI), organised by Demos Shakarian (1913–93) in 1951 with the backing of Oral Roberts, emphasising bringing the Pentecostal experience to laymen and introducing the healing evangelists to them. The South African David du Plessis (1905–87) travelled around the world from 1951 as a spokesperson for Pentecostalism in ecumenical circles and brought many 'mainline' church people into the Pentecostal experience. Several ministers received Spirit baptism in the 'mainline' churches in the 1940s and 1950s and promoted spiritual renewal thereafter. The rector of St Mark's Episcopal church in Van Nuys (suburban Los Angeles), Dennis Bennett (1917–91), and some of his members received Spirit baptism in November 1959. Bennett testified to his experience in a Sunday sermon in April 1960 and was asked to resign. Many regard this event as the beginning of the Charismatic movement. Bennett's story was reported in *Time* and *Newsweek* and charismatics were encouraged to become more public. Bennett was contacted by a sympathetic bishop and appointed rector of a small Episcopal church, St Luke's, Seattle, which grew to be the largest in the diocese and a place to which people came to receive Spirit baptism. Bennett became a national figure and through him other ministers became involved in the Charismatic movement, including Episcopalians, Methodists, Reformed, Baptists, Lutherans and Presbyterians. The Charismatic movement spread during the sixties throughout the USA and Canada. A Lutheran pastor, Larry Christenson (b.1928), from San Pedro, California, who had received Spirit baptism through attending classical Pentecostal meetings, visited Britain and Germany in 1963 and was instrumental in the start of the Charismatic movement there. But charismatics were not universally welcomed in their churches. Resistance often caused them to leave their churches, precipitating the rise of new independent Charismatic churches.[34]

---

34 Hollenweger, *The Pentecostals*, pp. 6–7; Burgess and van der Maas, *NID*, pp. 477–519, 589–93, 653–4, 1024–5; Vinson Synan, *The Holiness-Pentecostal tradition: Charismatic movements in the twentieth century* (Grand Rapids and Cambridge: Eerdmans, 1997), pp. 226–33.

Charismatic experiences in the older churches were encouraged by news reports of charismatic happenings and by hundreds of popular publications – the two most influential of which were probably David Wilkerson's *The cross and the switchblade* (1963) and journalist John Sherrill's *They speak with other tongues* (1964). The *Reader's digest* carried Wilkerson's story around the world and his book was eventually made into a film starring the former pop singer Pat Boone, himself a charismatic. The 'Jesus People' movement was a Charismatic revival movement that began on the Pacific Coast in 1967 among young people, in which thousands of former hippies became Christians through ministries in Christian coffeehouses offering deliverance from drug addiction. The Charismatic movement was further publicised by television broadcasts – particularly those of Oral Roberts and Pat Robertson (1930–), a Southern Baptist minister who resigned in 1987 to contend unsuccessfully for the Republican presidential nomination. Roberts left the Pentecostal Holiness church to join the United Methodist church in 1968 to anchor himself more firmly within the Charismatic movement.[35]

In 1967 the Catholic Charismatic movement began when two lay theology faculty members at Duquesne university in Pittsburgh, Ralph Kiefer and Bill Storey, received Spirit baptism and passed it on to about thirty students at a retreat. It spread from there to the university of Notre Dame, South Bend, Indiana and Michigan State university and included 300,000 people by 1976, spreading internationally into Latin America, Europe and Asia. From 1973 Cardinal Léon-Joseph Suenens (1904–96), primate of Belgium and one of the four moderators of the Second Vatican Council, was acknowledged leader of Catholic charismatics and adviser to the pope on charismatic issues. An important feature of the movement in the early 1970s was the theological reflection made in publications by Catholic scholars, placing the movement firmly within Catholic tradition. The Catholic Charismatic movement spread in Europe to include significant communities in France, Belgium, Italy, Spain, Portugal, Hungary, Czechoslovakia and Poland, and is especially strong in India (perhaps five million) and in the Philippines (perhaps eleven million). In Kerala, India, Father Michael Naikomparambil leads weekly healing and evangelism meetings that draw crowds of 15,000 and hosts conferences of 200,000. The Catholic Charismatic movement of El Shaddai in the Philippines led by layman Mike Velarde is the largest of all these national Charismatic movements with seven million members. By 2000 there were an estimated 120 million Catholic charismatics, some 11 per cent of all Catholics worldwide

---

35 Synan, *Holiness-Pentecostal*, pp. 255–6, 289–90; Burgess and van der Maas, *NID*, pp. 352–5, 1111.

and almost twice the number of classical Pentecostals combined.[36] This remarkable achievement probably stemmed the tide of the exodus from the Catholic church into classical Pentecostalism.

Independent Pentecostalism and the 'Third Wave'

As the Charismatic movement began to decline in the late seventies, a new 'non-denominational' movement with much weaker links with older churches began to emerge, emphasising house groups and 'radical' discipleship, and also known as the 'restoration' movement. Associations of independent churches were formed, soon the fastest-growing Charismatic movements in the English-speaking world, becoming hundreds of independent global networks. In the USA, the 'Fort Lauderdale five' of Charles Simpson (Southern Baptist background), Derek Prince (British Pentecostal), Ern Baxter (Canadian Pentecostal), Bob Mumford (AG) and Don Basham (Disciples of Christ) came together in 1970 to lead a movement known as the 'shepherding' or 'discipleship' movement because of its strong and highly controversial emphasis on submission to 'shepherds' or church leaders. Large numbers of independent charismatic pastors were associated with this group. This movement was subject to serious criticism and created a rift in the Charismatic movement from which it is still recovering, but by 1986 the shepherding movement had effectively ended. The British 'restoration' movement, known at first as the 'house church movement', was a parallel movement that began in the late 1950s to become the largest Charismatic grouping in the UK, so that by 2000 over 400,000 people were affiliated to the 'New churches'.

The 'Word of Faith' movement of the USA, also known as 'positive confession', the 'faith message', the 'prosperity gospel' and the 'health and wealth' movement, is thought to have originated in early Pentecostalism and been influenced by Baptist pastor E. W. Kenyon (1867–1948). Kenyon taught the 'positive confession of the word of God' and a 'law of faith' working by pre-determined divine principles. The development of the movement was stimulated by the teachings of Pentecostal healing evangelists like William Branham and especially Oral Roberts, the FGBMFI, contemporary popular televangelists and the Charismatic movement. Its essence is that health, wealth and success are promised to the one who has faith. By 2000 this was a prominent teaching in many churches globally. Its leading North American

---

36 Burgess and van der Maas, *NID*, pp. 118, 201, 230–1, 286, 450–1, 460–7; Synan, *Holiness-Pentecostal*, pp. 246–52.

exponents have been Kenneth Hagin (1917–2003) of Tulsa, Oklahoma (widely regarded as 'father of the Faith movement') and Kenneth Copeland of Fort Worth, Texas, among many others. Preachers in other parts of the world have propounded a modified form of this teaching to suit their own contexts, and leading exponents include Yonggi Cho, Nigerians Benson Idahosa and David Oyedepo, Ghanaians Nicholas Duncan-Williams and Mensa Otabil, Ulf Ekman of Sweden, Edir Machedo of Brazil, Hector Gimenez of Argentina and South African Ray McCauley, to name some of the more prominent.[37]

In the 1980s the 'Third Wave', following the two 'waves' of the classical Pentecostal movement and the Charismatic movement, was identified particularly with John Wimber (1934–97), whose Vineyard Christian Fellowship in Anaheim, California (commenced in 1977) spearheaded a new emphasis on renewal in the established churches throughout the English-speaking world. A network of five hundred Vineyard churches in the USA had emerged by 1998. Wimber's first visit to Britain in 1982 and his 'power evangelism' that taught the role of 'signs and wonders' (especially healing) as an instrument of church growth was widely accepted by older churches, especially evangelical Anglicans. The churches of Holy Trinity, Brompton and St Andrew's, Chorleywood became centres of the new renewal from the mid-1980s onwards. The 1990s have also been the era of the 'cell church'. Based on the pioneering work of Yonggi Cho, Lawrence Kwang in Singapore and the writings of Ralph Neighbour, Jr, the 'cell church' strategy is widely used in the Pentecostal and Charismatic movements and is particularly effective in maintaining cohesion in 'mega-churches' through its emphasis on the home cell group as the focus of pastoral care, discipleship and evangelism. Since the eighties, large independent Charismatic congregations have sprung up all over the world, particularly in Africa, Latin America and North America. These new churches often form loose associations for co-operation and networking, sometimes internationally. In many parts of Africa, Asia and Latin America they are the fastest-growing section of Christianity, appealing especially to younger, educated, urban people. West Africa, and in particular Nigeria and Ghana, has been the scene of an explosion of a new form of Pentecostalism since the mid-1970s, to such an extent that African Christianity is turning increasingly charismatic. From west Africa this new Pentecostalism has spread rapidly throughout Africa's cities.[38]

---

37 Burgess and van der Maas, *NID*, pp. 484–8, 1060–2; Synan, *Holiness-Pentecostal*, pp. 260–6; Allan Anderson, *Introduction*, pp. 145–60.
38 Paul Gifford, *African Christianity: its public role* (London: Hurst, 1998), pp. 334–9; Johnstone and Mandryk, *Operation world*, pp. 421, 488.

In the mid-1990s two sensational and controversial new revival movements appeared in North America. In January 1994 a phenomenon to be known as the 'Toronto Blessing' emerged in the Toronto Airport Vineyard church in Canada, pastored by John Arnott. The unusual phenomena included 'holy laughter' and attracted worldwide attention as thousands visited Toronto to see and experience the 'revival' for themselves. It was estimated that some 600,000 people had visited the Toronto church by the end of 1995. The phenomena spread to other places in the Western world, especially as ministers who had visited Toronto went back with the 'refreshing' to their own churches. The Toronto church, expelled from the Vineyard Association, became known as the Toronto Airport Christian Fellowship. In June 1995 a second major revival began in an AG church in Brownsville, Pensacola, Florida, known as the 'Pensacola Outpouring' and the 'Brownsville Revival'. This also attracted international interest and by 1997 this more classical Pentecostal revival claimed over one and a half million visitors from all over the world, some 5,000 people at nightly services and 100,000 converts. The revival has also been accompanied by strange manifestations like twitching and jerking, and noisy meetings reminiscent of the classical Pentecostal sub-culture in the USA, with a focus on repentance and forgiveness. Both Toronto and Pensacola have become places for pilgrimage for several new 'revival' movements springing up in various parts of the Western world. But both movements have also experienced rejection and resulted in division.[39]

Pentecostalism in all its multi-faceted variety, including the 'Pentecostal-like' independent churches and the Catholic charismatics, is one of the most significant forms of Christianity in the twentieth century. According to oft-quoted but controversial estimates, there may have been over five hundred million adherents of these movements worldwide in 2000,[40] found in almost every country in the world and spanning all Christian denominations. In less than a hundred years, Pentecostal, Charismatic and associated movements have become a major new force in world Christianity.

39 Burgess and van der Maas, NID, pp. 445–7, 1149–52.
40 D. B. Barrett and T. M. Johnson, 'Annual statistical table on global mission: 2003', International bulletin of missionary research 27:1 (2003), p. 25. This statistic, though widely quoted, is impossible to verify and depends on how 'Pentecostalism' is defined. The majority of those included in this figure are members of independent churches worldwide and charismatics in older churches.

7

Independency in Africa and Asia

ALLAN ANDERSON AND EDMOND TANG

Independency has existed since the early church, but never as prominently as in the twentieth century. Although there are large independent church movements in every continent, in this chapter we concentrate on those movements that have proliferated as a deliberate reaction to the perceived hegemony of Western forms of Christianity in Africa and Asia.

Africa

African Independent churches (AICs) were a major form of Christianity by 2000, consisting of thousands of different movements all over the sub-Sahara. They are living, radical examples of an African Christianity that has consciously rejected Western ecclesiastical models and forms of being Christian. Many place the birth of the modern AIC movement in the Antonian movement founded by a twenty-year-old prophetess, Kimpa Vita, also known as Donna Beatrice, in the recently colonised Kongo kingdom (northern Angola) in 1700. She was arrested in 1706 and burnt to death by command of the Portuguese King Pedro IV and at the request of the Catholic Capuchin missionaries. Her followers were forcefully subdued, although she became a national heroine and martyr, and today is regarded as a prototype of the contemporary African phenomenon of prophecy.[1] The significance of Kimpa Vita and her movement is that not only was it the first recorded AIC movement, but it was also a manifestation of a phenomenon that was to be repeated frequently in Africa.[2]

---

1 Adrian Hastings, *The church in Africa 1450–1950* (Oxford: Clarendon Press, 1994), pp. 104–5; Marie-Louise Martin, *Kimbangu: an African prophet and his church* (Oxford: Blackwell, 1975), pp. 14, 16–17; Allan Anderson, *African reformation: African initiated Christianity in the 20th century* (Trenton, NJ and Asmara, Eritrea: Africa World Press, 2001), pp. 47–51.
2 Hastings, *Church*, p. 219; Marthinus Daneel, *Quest for belonging* (Gweru, Zimbabwe: Mambo Press, 1987), p. 47; Anderson, *African reformation*, pp. 51–3.

Causative factors

Since the beginning of studies on AICs, writers have speculated on what might be the causes of their origin and growth.[3] Africa has witnessed a century of rapid social change, with its accompanying industrialisation and urbanisation, as well as the transition from a colonial to a post-colonial political order. The situation was aggravated in colonial Africa – particularly in South Africa – with the imposition of discriminatory laws that created migratory labour, the loss of land, alienation and impersonal mass housing. This resulted in a sense of oppression, disorientation and marginalisation that left people seeking to form new relationships in smaller social groups where they could belong and regain human dignity.

Secession was not a peculiarly African phenomenon, as AICs were simply continuing what had become commonplace in European Protestantism in the nineteenth century. By 1900, there were already hundreds of new denominations, 'faith missions' and other mission societies in Africa. It is hardly surprising that it should be considered a natural thing for secessions to take place, urged on by mission policies and politics that were highly prejudicial to Africans. African Christians saw a multiplicity of denominations as the norm, and the creation of many new ones was a natural consequence.

The translation of the Bible was often the first literature in an African language, and for many years the primary objective of mission schools was to enable people to read the Bible in their own language. Great authority was thus given to the printed word, and Africans were now able to distinguish between what the missionaries had said (or had not said) and what the Bible said (or did not say). Most AICs became literalist in their interpretation of the Bible. Some felt that missionaries had concealed or at least had misunderstood the truth, particularly when the Bible seemed to support African customs that the missionaries had condemned, like the marriage dowry and polygamy.[4]

There are many different kinds of AIC, from the 'Ethiopian' and 'African' churches that emerged at the end of the nineteenth century to the more prolific 'prophet-healing' and 'Spirit' churches of the early twentieth century, and the most recent 'new Pentecostal' or 'Charismatic' churches that emerged after 1975. Three broad categories of AIC have been identified:

---

3 Daneel, *Quest*, pp. 68–101; Anderson, *African reformation*, pp. 23–67.
4 Hastings, *Church*, p. 527.

1. *Ethiopian and African churches*

AICs which do not claim to be prophetic or to have special manifestations of the Holy Spirit, and which have modelled themselves on the European churches from which they seceded, have been called 'Ethiopian' or 'Ethiopian-type' churches in southern Africa, and 'African' churches in Nigeria. These were usually the first AICs to emerge primarily as political and administrative reactions to European missions, a reaction to the white missions' conquest of African peoples. In southern Africa, the word 'Ethiopian' in the church name is more common and had special significance in these countries more heavily colonised than the rest of Africa. Ethiopia, the only African nation that had successfully resisted European colonialism by defeating Italy in war, is mentioned in the Bible as a nation that 'stretches out her hands to God' (Psalm 68:31). This formed the basis of the 'Ethiopian' ideology that spread in South Africa in the 1890s. Africa had received Christianity before Europe and therefore had a special place in God's plan of salvation. Towards the end of the nineteenth century, 'African' churches in Nigeria and Ghana and 'Ethiopian' type churches in South Africa emerged.[5] The causes of these secessions were the question of ecclesiastical control, often triggered by matters of discipline involving African ministers, their career prospects, and poor race relations within the European-founded churches.[6] Resistance to white authoritarian measures was a common cause of secession. The secessions in South and west Africa were to set a pattern for the next century.[7]

2. *Churches of the Spirit*

The rapidly growing prophet-healing or 'Spiritual' churches – so named because of their emphasis on the Holy Spirit – were to present a more penetrating challenge to older churches than that of the 'African churches' because they questioned the very heart of Western Christianity. In this, they were sometimes aided and abetted by new churches from the North, especially the Pentecostals, whose ideas they borrowed freely yet selectively, but this was a specifically African Christian response. These churches emphasise spiritual power and are the largest and most significant grouping of AICs, although a particularly difficult type to describe, for it includes a vast variety of some of the biggest of all churches in Africa with millions of followers.

5 Ibid., p. 493; J. D. Y. Peel, *Aladura: a religious movement among the Yoruba* (Oxford: Oxford University Press, 1968), pp. 55–6.
6 Hastings, *Church*, p. 498. 7 Anderson, *African reformation*, pp. 10–16.

Some of these churches became members of ecumenical bodies like the different national councils of churches, the continental All Africa Council of Churches and the World Council of Churches. In the eyes of those who consider these councils as offering some measure of respectability, these moves are welcomed and give the AICs legitimacy denied them by European churches and colonial powers for so long. But most AICs are not members of ecumenical bodies and are not clamouring to be so. Their legitimacy hails from a belief in divinely appointed leaders who do not feel a need to seek human recognition, and from their time-tested strengths as major denominations in their own right.[8]

William Wade Harris (1865–1929), a Liberian Grebo, was one of the first and most influential African Christian prophets, preaching in the Ivory Coast and Ghana in 1913. He is believed to have baptised some 120,000 adult Ivorian converts in one year, before being deported by French colonial authorities in 1914, when he returned to Liberia. Thousands of his converts organised themselves into the Harrist church under John Ahui. Severely persecuted by the French colonial administration, the Harrist church in the Ivory Coast was officially constituted only in 1955. Harris' style of ministry became a pattern for many African prophets. There were also many schisms in the Harrisist movement, two of which were led by women. The Deima church of Marie Lalou, which has instituted women as successive leaders since Lalou's death in 1951, has become the second largest AIC in the Ivory Coast.[9]

In Ghana, the first 'Spiritual church' to be formed was the Church of the Twelve Apostles, begun in 1918 by converts of Wade Harris, Grace Tani and Kwesi John Nackabah. Tani was spiritual leader of the church and Nackabah administrative and public leader, a convenient method used by several AICs to overcome traditional male resistance to women's leadership. Jemisemiham Jehu-Appiah (1893–1948), called Akaboha ('king'), founded the Musama Disco Christo church (Army of the Cross of Christ) and established the holy city of Mozano, which Appiah was given by the local chief. The dynastic succession of this church has been a feature of several prominent AICs.

In 1916 the followers of a popular Anglican preacher in the Niger river delta, Garrick Sokari Braide, formed the Christ Army church, the first 'Spiritual church' in Nigeria.[10] The first *Aladura* church, the Eternal Sacred Order of Cherubim and Seraphim Society, was founded by a former

---

8 Ibid., pp. 16–18.   9 Ibid., pp. 75–6.
10 Harold W. Turner, *History of an African Independent church (1) The Church of the Lord (Aladura)* (Oxford: Clarendon Press, 1967), p. 122; Harold W. Turner, *Religious innovation in Africa* (Boston, MA: G. K. Hall, 1979), pp. 138–44.

Anglican, Moses Orimolade Tunolashe, and a fifteen-year-old girl, Abiodun Akinsowon, as a prayer group within Anglicanism until the break in 1928.[11] The movement called themselves *aladura* ('prayer people'), a term that distinguished them from other Christian churches. There were some 300 Cherubim and Seraphim groups in Nigeria in 2000.[12] Another Anglican church leader, Joseph Shadare, formed the Precious Stone Society in 1918, a prayer group to provide spiritual support and healing for victims of the influenza epidemic. In 1922 it left the Anglican church and affiliated first with the US evangelical group Faith Tabernacle, and from 1931 to 1941 with the Apostolic church, a British Pentecostal denomination.[13] After a series of divine visions, former road construction driver Joseph Ayo Babalola (1906–59) began preaching, and the ensuing revival resulted in thousands of people becoming Christians and burning their traditional fetishes. The colonial authorities became disturbed, and Babalola and some of the revival leaders were imprisoned. The movement broke with the Apostolic church in 1939 over the British missionaries' attempt to control the church and their opposition to the use of water in healing prayer.[14] Babalola became general evangelist of the Christ Apostolic church (CAC), constituted in 1941 and soon the largest *Aladura* church in Nigeria.[15] The first president of the CAC became ruler (*olubadan*) of Ibadan, Sir Isaac Akinyele. Babalola died in 1959 and Akinyele in 1964, but by 2000 the church had two million affiliates.[16] Josiah Ositelu, an Anglican schoolteacher involved in the prophetic exposure of witchcraft, was also associated with Shadare and Babalola during the revival, founding the Church of the Lord (*Aladura*) in 1930.[17]

During the 1950s *Aladura* churches spread to Ghana, Liberia and Sierra Leone, through the efforts of travelling Nigerian preachers, and Ghanaian churches in the traditions of *Aladura* seceded.[18] Adejobi was involved in the creation of two ecumenical associations for AICs, the Nigeria Association of Aladura Churches formed in 1968, and the inter-continental Organisation of African Instituted Churches, created in Cairo in 1978, with Adejobi as the first chairman (1978–82).[19]

---

11 Peel, *Aladura*, pp. 59–60.
12 Elizabeth Isichei, *A history of Christianity in Africa* (London: SCM, 1995), p. 282.
13 Turner, *African Independent*, pp. 11–12; Isichei, *History*, p. 280.
14 Turner, *African Independent*, p. 32.   15 Peel, *Aladura*, p. 91.
16 P. Johnstone and J. Mandryk, *Operation world: 21st century edition* (Carlisle: Paternoster, 2001), p. 488.
17 Turner, *African Independent*, pp. 22–5, 49–50.   18 Turner, *Religious innovation*, p. 125.
19 Isichei, *History*, p. 284; Anderson, *African reformation*, pp. 167–90.

Possibly the largest AIC in Africa, with some six million adherents in the Congo in 2000, is the 'Church of Jesus Christ on Earth through the Prophet Simon Kimbangu' (CJCSK), or the Kimbanguist church.[20] Simon Kimbangu (1890–1951), a Baptist preacher, was born in the village of Nkamba in western Congo. On 6 April 1921 (the founding date of the church), he was reported to have miraculous healing powers. His fame spread, and thousands flocked to Nkamba to be healed. In spite of his peaceful message, Belgian authorities repressed the movement and Kimbangu was forced underground. Stories abounded about Kimbangu's miraculous escapes from arrest, until he (following Christ's example) gave himself up voluntarily to the police. On 3 October 1921, after a military trial, Kimbangu was found guilty of sedition and sentenced to death. Pleas for mercy by Baptist missionaries resulted in his sentence being commuted to life imprisonment, after he had received 120 lashes. He was taken to prison in Elizabethville (now Lubumbashi), many hundreds of miles from his home, to be put in solitary confinement until his death thirty years later on 12 October 1951.[21] Kimbangu became a national hero, but the colonial authorities and European missions persecuted Kimbanguists everywhere with imprisonment, exile and restrictions. Deportations actually helped the movement spread across the entire Congo. The Kimbanguists did not organise themselves into a denomination until 1956, when the CJCSK was formally constituted, given official recognition in 1959, six months before independence. The youngest son of Kimbangu, Joseph Diangienda, became head and 'legal representative'. After independence, the church grew rapidly. In 1960 Simon Kimbangu's remains were reinterred at Nkamba. Kimbanguists have founded schools, clinics, agricultural settlements, brickyards and many other successful enterprises. In 1969 the CJCSK was admitted to the World Council of Churches, and was soon afterwards declared by President Mobuto to be one of three recognised churches in the Congo, the largest after the Catholics.[22] Several secessions from the CJCSK occurred during the 1960s, but Mobutu's severe repression and tough laws discouraged these. Diangienda died in 1993 and was succeeded by his older brother Salomon Dialungana Kiangani.

An alternative Kimbanguist movement known as Ngunzism (after the Kikongo *ngunza* or 'prophet'), saw Kimbangu as a black Messiah who would dramatically return from prison and destroy the colonialists with a

20 Johnstone and Mandryk, *Operation world*, p. 198.
21 Martin, *Kimbangu*, pp. 45–51, 57, 61–4.
22 Hastings, *Church*, p. 130; Martin, *Kimbangu*, pp. 105, 107, 110, 128, 158.

holy war.[23] Simon Pierre Mpadi, trained as a Salvation Army officer, founded the Mission of the Blacks in 1939 and was arrested and imprisoned in the same prison as Kimbangu in 1949. André Matswa founded the Amical Balali movement in Congo-Brazzaville, but was imprisoned in 1930, where he remained until his death in 1942. He, like Kimbangu, was transformed into a religious figure, a saviour who would come back to free his people from oppression and restore the old Kongo empire. Mpadi's movement, known as Mpadism or the Khaki movement (after the khaki uniforms worn by his followers) became one of the most influential churches in the Congo. In Angola, several Kimbanguist movements started after the prophet's arrest in 1921.[24]

All AICs in east Africa place an emphasis on the Holy Spirit and have been impacted by various revival movements in the region, especially the African 'Holy Spirit' movement that began around the time of the First World War and the later East African Revival movement. The *Roho* (Spirit) movement commenced in 1912 as a charismatic Anglican movement, and its best-known leader, Alfayo Odongo Mango, is believed to have received the Holy Spirit in 1916. Mango was a Luo Anglican deacon who prophesied the end of colonialism and was expelled from the CMS in 1934. He and several Luo followers were murdered by a mob and his house set alight, but his followers began a vigorous movement emphasising the power of the Spirit, and dressed in white robes. The *Roho* church split in 1941 to form two churches, which together with another Luo Pentecostal church were collectively registered with the Kenyan government in 1957 as the Holy Ghost Church of Kenya.[25] The most prominent of the Spiritual churches at this time was the African Israel Church Nineveh, founded in 1942 by Zakayo Kivuli, a Pentecostal evangelist, among the Luyia in western Kenya. In common with AICs in many other parts of the continent, this church wears white robes, practises constant singing and dancing and Spirit possession, and has a holy place (Nineveh) where the leader was high priest. This church joined the Christian Council of Kenya, as did several other AICs at this time. The largest secessionist church from the Roman Catholic church in Africa is the Legion of Mary (*Maria Legio*), which was founded in 1963 by Catholic Luos in western Kenya, Simeon Ondeto and Gaudencia Aoko, a young woman.[26]

23 Martin, *Kimbangu*, pp. 73, 89.
24 James Grenfell, 'Simâo Toco: an Angolan prophet', *Journal of religion in Africa* 28:2 (1998), 210–26.
25 Cynthia Hoehler-Fatton, *Women of fire and spirit: history, faith and gender in Roho religion in western Kenya* (Oxford: Oxford University Press, 1996), pp. 3–6, 58–64, 96–7.
26 Hastings, *History*, pp. 177–8.

John Alexander Dowie's Zion movement, brought from Chicago in 1902–3, was responsible for a group of 'Zionists' that grew to 5,000 by 1905.[27] The Zionist and Apostolic churches emerged in South Africa after Pentecostal missionaries from the USA established the Apostolic Faith Mission (AFM) in 1908, soon causing estrangement with the African Zionists who followed them. In 1917, Elias Mahlangu founded the Zion Apostolic Church of South Africa. From Mahlangu's church, Edward Motaung (also known as Edward Lion) seceded in 1920 to form the Zion Apostolic Faith Mission (ZAFM). The St John Apostolic Faith Mission was founded in the 1920s by former AFM worker Christina Nku. Engenas Lekganyane's Zion Christian church seceded from the ZAFM in 1925, and is now the largest church in South Africa and one of the largest in Africa.[28] Isaiah Shembe (1869–1935) in about 1903 founded the Nazareth Baptist church or the Nazarites (in Zulu, amaNazaretha), and in 1916 established a 'high place', Ekuphakameni, outside Durban, and a holy mountain, Nhlangakazi, sites for annual festivals in July and January respectively.

AICs in other parts of southern Africa were greatly influenced by developments in South Africa, from where Ethiopian and Zionist ideas spread to Zimbabwe, Swaziland, Lesotho, Botswana, Zambia and Malawi, mainly through migrant workers. Zionist and Apostolic churches soon eclipsed other AICs in size and influence.[29] The largest AIC in Zimbabwe is the African Apostolic Church of Johane Marange (AACJM), founded in 1932, and spreading to many parts of central and southern Africa.[30]

In Kasomo in northern Zambia in 1953 a Bemba Presbyterian woman known as Alice Lenshina founded a new church in 1955 called the Lumpa church. A cathedral was opened in 1958 at Kasomo, and by 1959 there were 100,000 Lumpa members. Members were prohibited from joining political parties, from appearing at secular courts or from sending their children to schools, and the authority of both the government and traditional leaders was also rejected. Violent clashes between Lumpa members and Kenneth Kaunda's United National Independence Party (UNIP) supporters ensued in 1963. Virtual civil war broke out from July to October 1964, and Lenshina announced that the end of the world had come. Over 700 people, mostly

---

27 Allan Anderson, *Zion and Pentecost: the spirituality and experience of Pentecostal and Zionist/Apostolic churches in South Africa* (Pretoria: University of South Africa Press, 2000), p. 20; B. G. M. Sundkler, *Zulu Zion and some Swazi Zionists* (London: Oxford University Press, 1976), pp. 16–28, 46–52.
28 Anderson, *Zion and Pentecost*, pp. 45–6, 61, 65, 72–4; Sundkler, *Zulu Zion*, pp. 50, 55–6.
29 Johnstone and Mandryk, *Operation world*, pp. 117, 603, 689.
30 Marthinus Daneel, *Old and new in southern Shona Independent churches*, vol. 1 (The Hague: Mouton, 1971), pp. 315–38.

Lumpa members, were killed. The Lumpa were defeated, the church banned and Lenshina and her followers imprisoned – two weeks before the independence of Zambia. Many Lumpa members fled to the southern Congo, where a Lumpa branch existed. After the defeat of the UNIP government in 1991, Lumpa followers returned to Zambia but were prevented from returning to Kasomo, where Lenshina's body lies in a tomb in the middle of her ruined cathedral, now a place of pilgrimage.[31]

3. Charismatic churches

The newer Charismatic churches and 'ministries' are of more recent origin, and may be regarded as 'Pentecostal' movements because they too emphasise the power and the gifts of the Holy Spirit. They vary in nature from hundreds of small independent house churches to rapidly growing and large church organisations. Despite their recent origins, some of these churches are already among the largest and most influential denominations in their respective countries, especially in west Africa. There is a strong Western, especially North American, Pentecostal influence in many of these churches both in liturgy and in leadership patterns. They are often seen, particularly by the older AICs, as mounting a sustained attack on traditional African values.[32] As these are more easily described as Pentecostal churches, they will not be examined here.

A religious revolution, an 'African reformation', has been going on in Africa for many years, and Christianity has been irrevocably changed in this process. It no longer makes sense to speak of AICs and Pentecostal churches in Africa as 'sects' and European mission-founded churches as 'mainline'. The reverse might now be more appropriate.[33]

Asia

Independency is a worldwide phenomenon, and is by no means confined to Africa. The rest of this chapter will discuss the phenomenon of Christian Independency in four Asian countries, where it has a long history.

Independent churches in India and Sri Lanka

The great majority of India's Christians are found in south India, where six independent Indian churches of the Mar Thoma tradition (Eastern or 'Syrian'

---

31 Hastings, *History*, pp. 125, 157.   32 Anderson, *African reformation*, pp. 18–20.
33 Ibid., pp. 93–124, 136–9.

Orthodox, also known as the St Thomas Christians) have been in existence at least since the fourth century. According to one estimate, more than half of India's at least 25 million Christians are 'Independents'.[34] Many of these are members of 'Pentecostal' or 'Charismatic' churches founded in the twentieth century, and several significant churches had their origins in the state of Kerala, which is also where India's Thomas Christians are found.[35] The history of Indian Independency is a complicated one. There were important influences encouraging Indian Independency in the early twentieth century, including those of the famous Christian social reformer Pandita Ramabai (1858–1922) and the Christian mystic Sadhu Sundar Singh (1889–1919). Both of these leaders promoted a truly Indian Christianity, in distinction to Western Christianity. Sundar Singh was the inspiration for a focus on the experiential and the ecstatic through his adopting elements of the Hindu *Bhakti* (devotion) tradition, and Ramabai's Mukti church is still active today.[36]

A common thread running through each of these divergent independent churches is a conscious expression of their Indian identity and character. Their faith binds them to fellow believers worldwide, yet their life and witness at home and in the diaspora are indelibly marked by an Indian identity and character. Most of the major independent churches have branches wherever Indians have migrated. The Indian Pentecostal Church of God (750,000), the Christian Assemblies of India (433,000) and the Assemblies (Jehovah Shammah) (250,000) are the biggest independent Indian churches.[37] This latter church was founded by Bakht Singh, raised as a Sikh in the Punjab, in Chennai, in 1941. Bakht Singh knew and was greatly influenced by Sadhu Sundar Singh, and taught a mystical union with and intimate devotion to Christ. His church has its main centre in Hyderabad and its strongest work in Andhra Pradesh. It has no official hierarchical structures or paid clergy, but has established itself through large, annual, national, eight-day conventions called 'holy convocations' and an emphasis on teaching the Bible. There have also been several secessions from this movement,[38] which is 'Brethren' rather than Pentecostal in character. Another important, non-Pentecostal,

---

34 Steven Barrie-Anthony, 'India, religion in contemporary', in J. Gordan Melton and Martin Baumann (eds.), *Religions of the world: a comprehensive encyclopedia of beliefs and practices* (Santa Barbara, CA: ABC-Clio, 2002), vol. II, p. 627.
35 Roger E. Hedlund, *Quest for identity: India's churches of indigenous origin* (Delhi: ISPCK, 2000), p. 80.
36 Ibid., pp. 157–67.
37 Allan Anderson and Edmond Tang (eds.), *Asian and Pentecostal: the charismatic face of Asian Christianity* (Oxford: Regnum, 2005), pp. 215–44; Hedlund, *Quest*, pp. 140–2.
38 Hedlund, *Quest*, pp. 152–6.

independent church is the Laymen's Evangelical Fellowship, founded in Chennai by Nagabakthul Daniel in 1935, also influenced by his acquaintance with the ministry of Sundar Singh, and led by the founder's son Joseph (Joe) Daniel since his father's death in 1953. Considerable emphasis is placed on the exorcism of evil spirits, healing, and confession of sins, and the church is more properly considered a 'Holiness' church.[39]

K. E. Abraham (1899–1974), formerly a Syrian Orthodox schoolteacher and ardent nationalist, was one of the most important influences on the emergence of Indian independent churches. He joined the Pentecostal movement in 1923 and worked with an American missionary, Robert Cook, until 1930. The break with the missionaries revolved around the issue of funding for church buildings, which the missionaries controlled, and the question of Indian leadership. Abraham in his many writings and recorded sermons said that Indians should be the leaders of Indian churches, emphasised the autonomy of the local church and said that foreign missionaries were 'non-biblical and non-apostolic'.[40] After working with the Ceylon Pentecostal Mission for three years, Abraham together with other Indian leaders founded the Indian Pentecostal Church of God (IPCG) in 1934. The new organisation planted its first congregations in Tamilnadu, Andhra Pradesh and Karnataka. It suffered the first of many schisms in 1953, when the Sharon Pentecostal Fellowship church was formed. The IPCG was an important expression of Christian nationalism in India prior to India's independence. It was also an expression of Indian Christianity, using Indian music and instruments only (the most important is the drum) with worshippers barefoot, sitting on the floor of the church, singing loudly with hand-clapping the vernacular songs of Indian Christians.[41]

The origins of Independency in Sri Lanka are closely related to developments in India. Anna Lewini from Denmark arrived in Colombo in 1919 and founded the first Pentecostal church in Sri Lanka, known as Glad Tidings Hall, later Colombo Gospel Tabernacle. The Ceylon Pentecostal Mission (CPM) began as a breakaway group in 1923 led by Alwin R. de Alwis and Pastor Ramankutty Paul, and espoused an ascetic approach to spirituality. Ministers were not to marry and they should wear white. They disdained the use of medicine and gave central importance to the doctrine of the Second Coming of Christ. The CPM also instituted indigenous forms of worship like

39 Ibid., pp. 148–52.
40 Quoted in Roger E. Hedlund (ed.), *Christianity is Indian: the emergence of an indigenous community* (Delhi: ISPCK, 2000), p. 450.
41 Hedlund, *Quest*, pp. 143–8; Hedlund, *Christianity*, pp. 445–58.

seating arrangements on mats, and the use of Indian musical instruments and tunes. But the main reason for its growth seems to have been its ministry of healing.[42] The CPM, despite its name, did not remain confined to Sri Lanka but spread to other countries including south India, the birthplace of Pastor Paul (1881–1945), then to other countries. Pastor Paul returned to India in 1924 to establish this very influential Pentecostal denomination with headquarters in Madras (Chennai), since 1984 known as the Pentecostal Mission. This is a movement where celibacy is encouraged for the increase of spiritual power, and members live together in 'faith homes', communal living quarters where private ownership is banned.[43]

The Philippines

The Philippines is another Asian nation with a long history of Independency, though regarded as a Catholic country since the sixteenth century when colonised by the Spanish. An anti-colonial, nationalist movement within the Catholic church resulted in the formation of the Philippine Independent church in 1902 under its 'supreme bishop' Gregorio Aglipay (1860–1940). The nationalist leader Emilio Aguinaldo revolted against US rule in 1898 and appointed Aglipay to head the Catholic church in the area he controlled. When the archbishop of Manila excommunicated Aglipay, he reorganised his churches as the *Iglesia Filipina Independente* and served as a revolutionary leader. In 1906 he was ordered to turn over the buildings used by the new church to the Roman Catholics. Aglipay's successor, Isebelo de los Reyes, led the church into affiliation with the Episcopal church in the USA in 1948. This is the largest of over a hundred Filipino independent 'Catholic' churches with about 2 million members in 2000, but has been in serious decline in recent years, especially since splits in the 1980s resulted in several new churches, the largest of which was the Philippine Independent Catholic church.[44]

Some movements, such as the Santuala and the Rizalista, incorporate more of traditional religious practices and beliefs. The Iglesia ni Cristo ('Church of Christ'), or Manalistas, had 1.4 million members by 1990. It was founded by Felix Manalo (1886–1963) in 1914. He was born into a Catholic family, but as a young man joined the Methodists, Disciples of Christ, and Seventh-day Adventists in succession. After a revelation he determined to

42 Hedlund, *Quest*, p. 138.
43 Anderson and Tang, *Asian and Pentecostal*, pp. 215–44; Hedlund, *Quest*, pp. 139–40; Hedlund, *Christianity*, pp. 437–44.
44 George W. Harper, 'Philippine tongues of fire? Latin American Pentecostalism and the future of Filipino Christianity', *Journal of Asian mission* 2:2 (2000), p. 238.

start a Filipino church that had no foreign influence.[45] Among its distinctive beliefs are a non-trinitarian view of God, denial of the deity of Christ, salvation only through church membership, and the veneration of its founder as the 'angel from the East' of Revelation 7, the prophet (*sugo*) sent from God to bring the final message. Members may not read or interpret the Bible by themselves, and the church hierarchy has the only right interpretation, as this is the only true church.

The two largest independent Charismatic churches are the Jesus is Lord church (JIL) founded by Bishop Eddie Villanueva in 1978, and the Jesus Miracle Crusade. JIL has a television station and an active socio-political programme. Villanueva was a university professor and a Marxist who became a Christian in 1973 and rose to become the best-known Pentecostal evangelist in the country. His church grew out of Bible studies for students and now is probably the most visible non-Catholic church, using open-air stadiums that seat tens of thousands of people. It is perhaps the only Pentecostal group in the Philippines that owns and runs a school providing complete education from nursery to high school, with plans for a Christian university. Villanueva and JIL publicly endorsed a presidential candidate in the 1998 presidential elections, and Villaneuva was himself a candidate in the 2004 elections. He runs and hosts a weekly television show that tackles current religious, social and political issues.[46] By 1999 there were some 404 JIL congregations in the Philippines and a further 72 among Filipino communities across the globe.[47]

Many new independent denominations have been founded in recent years. They are among the liveliest, most rapidly growing and prominent of the Filipino churches. If present growth rates continue, the Philippines will have a Pentecostal/Charismatic population comprising 10 per cent of the total by 2020, excluding the larger numbers of Catholic charismatics.[48] There has been some discussion among Catholic scholars about the reasons for the growth of these movements. Salazar emphasises the management of resources within the churches themselves, such as member recruitment and socialisation, information dissemination, ample finances, and symbolic and ritual elements as being reasons for their growth. In particular, he mentions the celebratory rituals, healing services, and other practices that resonate with

45 Ann C. Harper, 'The Iglesia Ni Cristo and evangelical Christianity', *Journal of Asian mission* 3:1 (2001), pp. 105–8.
46 Anderson and Tang, *Asian and Pentecostal*, pp. 345–62.
47 George Harper, 'Philippine tongues', pp. 248–50.   48 Ibid., p. 251.

the local culture. He concludes that these elements together 'help contribute to an experience of community, belongingness, hope, and confidence among the members'.[49]

Grassroots Christianity in China

There are many similarities between what we observe in China and other independent churches in Africa and Asia. We are almost promised a readily available explanation of the outburst of activities on the ground – the prevalence of an emotional style of worship, emphasis on healing, opposition to the organised institutional churches and their liberal theology, resistance to any form of state control, as well as certain characteristics too often judged by others as 'sectarian' tendencies, etc. On the other hand, we must be warned against the danger of imposing a ready-made explanation on an indigenous phenomenon. Or is it really indigenous? There is no doubt from scanning both official and visitors' reports that the Christian churches are growing, particularly among Protestants and in the countryside. As early as 1987, in an internal document, the Chinese government identified this phenomenon in rural Henan and called it a 'religious fever'.[50] Since then many explanations have been given, but none of them convincing. The government denied the growth in the beginning, but later acknowledged the existence of the phenomenon. Their explanation is reasonably common-sense: there is still poverty and lack of access to health and education in the rural areas and these contribute to the spread of religion as an escape from the real problems. Another theory propounded by scholars from the state academies is based on the following argument: the growth of religion is a 'rebound effect' from the suppression of religion during the period of the Cultural revolution. When it is allowed, everybody flocks to the formerly forbidden fruit, very much like the current explosion of interest in Western goods as well as Western habits and fashion, including Western ideas. This theory, however, cannot explain the difference between the cities and the countryside, or the difference between religions and between Christian denominations.

The pattern of Christian growth is not uniform: it grows faster in some localities than others. Protestant grassroots groups show clear affinity with so-called evangelical forms and some express clear charismatic tendencies.

49 Robert C. Salazar (ed.), *New religious movements in Asia and the Pacific Islands: implications for church and society* (Manila: De La Salle University, 1994), pp. 190–205.
50 Tony Lambert, *Resurrection of the Chinese church*, 2nd edn (Chicago: OMF, 1994), p. 309 n. 2.

The lack of reliable information that is not 'packaged' either by official bodies or by partisan scholarship, coupled with the difficulties in doing any field research, make it equally impossible to study religion objectively even in this relatively more open period. We are not any closer to a more objective understanding of the situation of Christianity on the ground. Many Christians in China feel empowered by an experience of God – experiences of deep conversion, feelings of inexplicable joy, repentance and forgiveness, etc. These experiences, however, are common to all Christian converts to various degrees (even traditional Catholics), and the list of characteristics can be applied equally to basic ecclesial communities in Latin America and the Philippines.

Sometimes also translated as 'Shouters', the 'Yellers' are a group of Christians that gained a widespread following in China in the 1980s, the first to be criticised by the China Christian Council and then condemned by the government as an 'evil cult' in 1983. They are a group under the leadership of Li Changsou (Witness Lee) that broke away from another independent Christian group, the Little Flock, sometimes called the Assembly Hall, founded by Watchman Nee in the 1920s. In 1949 Li took some of the Little Flock to Taiwan where he took charge of the Assembly Halls there and in south-east Asia. In 1962 he established the church in the USA. In 1967 he started the movement of 'yelling' – a form of public, emotional repentance of sin by loud confession – and his followers took on that name. When China opened up in the late 1970s the group established itself along the south-eastern coast of China and spread to a number of provinces.[51]

Under the influence of Li, followers of the sect consider all other Christian churches heretical, and in China this exclusivist stand led to violent attacks on other Christian groups and attempts to take over churches and meeting points. They were also sent in teams of two or three to other churches where they denounced Three-Self churches as 'whores' and threatened to bring down 'Jericho' with their shouts. These extreme actions led to many divisions in Christian communities and violent clashes. In 1983 the Chinese government banned the group, and many local leaders were sentenced to long periods in prison. However the ban did not stop them from spreading underground.

---

51 See *Tian Feng*, May 1983, pp. 11–12 (official publication of the China Christian Council), and various issues in 1983 of the *Course materials*, used by the correspondence course run by the Nanjing theological seminary. See also various issues of *Bridge*, a magazine published by the Christian Study Centre on Chinese Religion and Culture in Hong Kong and *China study journal*, published in London by the China Desk of Churches Together in Britain and Ireland.

Yellers were already in most of the provinces of China, especially in Zhejiang, Henan, Fujian and Guangdong. Lushan, a small provincial city in Henan, became their stronghold and among a population of just over 100,000 there are tens of thousands of them.[52]

The historical origins of the Yellers are well established. They can be traced to the Little Flock whose leader Watchman Nee was in turn influenced by the Brethren and their holiness stress on the Holy Spirit, as well as by other revivalist movements. One cannot help but speculate that it is this emphasis on the Holy Spirit that has become the source of Li Changshou's theory of the age of the Spirit. The emphasis on the Holy Spirit is not unrelated to the emotional character of the group's worship services, characterised by wailing and crying in order to release the Spirit. That seems to be a major factor in their appeal. In the areas where the Yellers are active there are also conventional groups of Christians, both government sanctioned as well as 'house churches', all of which are conservative and evangelical in nature. It seems that the Yellers are recruiting especially from existing congregations, leading us to believe that their appeal is precisely in their special form of affective expression and fierce independence from other denominations. Can it be that their extreme emotionalism in worship and exclusivist stance fills a spiritual vacuum left by twenty years of harsh oppression and provides the necessary psychological outlet as well as identity through a strong social bond? It is worth noting that many of the sectarian movements also started during a similar period, when organised religions were only slowly responding to the religious needs of the population and there was no doctrinal authority to guide believers in their discernment.

At least two other groups are said to have issued from the Yellers, or at least to have been strongly influenced by them. One of these is the 'Established King' sect, which was also banned by the Chinese government and their leader arrested and executed in 1994. The second, where the link is tenuous and not proven, is the Way of Rebirth, which puts a strong emphasis on the Christian's rebirth in the Spirit.

A sympathetic account of a revival movement in the early 1900s, calling it 'the greatest spiritual movement in the history of missions in China', described how people would confess 'with sobs, shrieks, and groans', falling on their faces, until 'their separate cries were merged and lost in the swelling

---

52 Deng Zhaoming, *The torch of the testimony in China* (Hong Kong: Christian Study Centre on Chinese Religion & Culture Ltd, 1998), p. 220; *China study journal*, April 2002, section K.

tide of general weeping'. The same account noted that 'strange thrills coursed up and down one's body', and that everywhere could be heard 'the agony of the penitent, his groans and cries and voice shaken with sobs'.[53] This account, written eighty years before the Yellers, could very well be a present-day description of their yelling expressions. But Bays is reluctant to associate the revival activities of that time with Pentecostalism. He admits that it is easier to report the phenomenon than to analyse it, but he did relate it to the Welsh and Korean revivals and accepted that the phenomenon resembled early Pentecostal revivals.[54] Bays' prudence is that of an able historian and must be followed by students of present-day Christianity in China. The 'Pentecostal' paradigm is tempting but further research must be done before we can come to any clear conclusions.

As opposed to the case of the Yellers, the Pentecostal nature of the True Jesus church is not in doubt. It is a radically independent and sectarian Chinese church that began in north China in 1917.[55] By 1949 they had established themselves in many parts of China, with over 700 churches and more than 100,000 members. Under the new regime they received harsh treatment. In parts of China, such as Hubei, they were banned and their leaders put in prison, while in others they came under the banner of the Three-Self movement but maintained a certain autonomy. After the Cultural revolution they became active again and gained a strong influence among grassroots Christian groups in Jiangsu, Hubei, Hunan, Zhejiang, Fujian and Shanxi provinces. According to official figures they form over 30 per cent of the Christians in Jiangsu province and out of a total of 150,000 Christians in Hunan over 110,000 belong to their church.

A possible breakaway from the True Jesus church is the Spirit-Spirit Sect (a poor translation of *Ling-ling Jiao*). It was formed around 1985 in Jiangsu by Hua Xuehe and another True Jesus church leader, Li Guiyao. The first 'Spirit' in its name refers to the Holy Spirit, and the second 'Spirit' – a play on Chinese tones – refers to the 'spiritual proof' of the work of the Spirit in the Christian. Members of the group perform 'spirit dances' and spontaneous 'spirit songs'. Like the True Jesus church, it is also exclusivist in character, believing that all the older denominations are 'ineffective' and only by joining the sect can a Christian be saved. It became notorious in the mid-90s when

---

53 Noted by Dr W. Phillips in *Chinese recorder*, September 1908, p. 524. Quoted in Daniel Bays, 'Christian revival in China, 1900–1937', in Edith L. Blumhofer and Randall Balmer (eds.), *Modern Christian revivals* (Chicago: University of Illinois Press, 1993), p. 164.
54 Bays, 'Christian revival', p. 164.
55 Anderson and Tang, *Asian and Pentecostal*, pp. 439–68.

the official seminary in Yunan was closed after an open conflict between the teaching staff who became members of the sect and those who were against. It is now on the list of forbidden 'cults' of the Chinese government.

Besides the True Jesus church there are a number of important Christian groups that can either claim some Pentecostal origins or be described as Pentecostal from their actual belief and practice. These include the Jesus Family, started in 1928, which emphasises spiritual dreams and revelations; the Disciple Faith church that puts great emphasis on the external signs of being filled with the Spirit, such as speaking in tongues, and leading a holy life; and the New Testament church, a recent import from Taiwan. The latter church believes the end times are near, and the church must re-experience the power of the Spirit, as felt by the early disciples. Baptism of the Spirit and the speaking of tongues are obligatory for Christians.[56] The *Fangcheng Pai* church has links with North American Pentecostalism. Even a cursory treatment of independent groups in China reveals the extent of Pentecostal/ charismatic influences among the grassroots Christian communities. Some can be identified as such while others are clearly on the borderline.

All Christian churches in China practise some form of healing, including Three-Self churches. In fact, according to some surveys, 90 per cent of new believers cite healing as a reason for their conversion. This is especially true in the countryside where medical facilities are often inadequate or non-existent. Normal Sunday worship is often interrupted by long periods of prayer for the sick and ends with Christians rushing forward to the altar to kneel in prayer for sick members of the family. In some churches there may be a weekday session devoted to healing. These sessions are not 'healing services' as commonly known outside China. They are simply prayer meetings with some emphasis on praying for the sick. If the leader is known to be blessed with special gifts of the Spirit, then the prayer meeting may emphasise the laying on of hands by the church leader or the sick may be brought to be touched by him or her. There are few structured services, and these 'democratic' prayers of healing are seen to be the duty of Christians – in fact, the main evangelistic witness. If healing is common to all Christian groups, nevertheless it is more prevalent in charismatic Christianity, and when the ritual of healing is incorporated into a Pentecostal type of religious service it also takes on a heightened intensity and meaning. However, study in the field is only beginning.

56 Leung Ka-lung, *The rural churches of mainland China since 1978* (Hong Kong: Alliance Bible Seminary, 1999), pp. 180–1.

To approach the understanding of Chinese Protestant Christianity from the Pentecostal perspective serves several corrective functions. First of all, it shows the inadequacy of the simplistic division of Christians into so-called Three-Self churches and 'house churches'. The difference between them is often said to be political. There is some truth in that since most independent churches resist government interference and control. However, the differences go much deeper than that. If the differences are not strictly 'theological', since both camps subscribe to the same basic tenets of the Protestant creed, nevertheless there is a huge divide in their religious sentiments and the way these are expressed.

Second, it is also clear from the above account that 'house churches' cannot be lumped together as a movement. There are as many common characteristics among all grassroots Christians as there are differences. Some are clearly Pentecostal, others are on the margin, while many are simply of the conservative evangelical type. Some are exclusivist to the extreme and reject the validity of any other group, while others are more conciliatory and willing to work together, including working with Three-Self churches.

Third, in probing the Pentecostal/charismatic undercurrent of grassroots groups we are clearly reminded of the tradition of fierce independence of these groups which had its origin in the anti-missionary and anti-ecumenical period of the 1920s and 1930s.[57] They have a tendency to distrust organised institutions and emphasise fluidity and democratic spontaneity. Any administrative measure to bring them into rigid structures will only end in antagonism and division. Since the 1980s, the official Protestant church has promoted the idea of a post-denominational church in China. It declared that the age of denominations was over. From our description above it is clear that many independent churches still exist after the 1980s. These groups cannot be accused of foreign or missionary domination since they emerged in the earlier part of the last century as anti-foreign and anti-missionary groups. They are also 'Independent' churches with closely knit bonds and identities, a characteristic they also share with similar independent forms of Christianity in other parts of Asia and in Africa. It seems that any plans to create a super, national church or to establish one form of theology are almost doomed to failure from the start.

A final comment relates to the folk-religions. A few Chinese scholars have already observed the parallels between grassroots Christian practices in

---

57 Bays, 'Christian Revival'.

China and the traditional folk-religions.[58] Their organisations are fluid (forming when needed and disappearing when their function is fulfilled, without a professional full-time clergy), holistic (attending to both mind and body), employing predominantly non-verbal forms of expression (chants and ritual dances) and affective/emotional experiences (trances). Of course the Christian symbolism is different, but we should not dismiss too quickly the possibility that there is cross-fertilisation and even movement between the two. There are well-founded reports of folk-religious practices seeping into Christian communities (talismans, exorcisms, worship of ancestral spirits, etc.). Chinese scholars call this the 'folk-religionisation' of Christianity.[59] Pentecostal groups that do not benefit from a clear denominational history are particularly vulnerable to various levels of syncretism.[60]

Clearly, Independency has developed rapidly in Asia. The emergence of this phenomenon raises several issues. First, in the four countries discussed there is the question of relevance in a culture that is used to 'powerful' phenomena in religious life. One of the main reasons for the popularity of Pentecostal and charismatic forms of Christianity is that they provide a more 'powerful' religion than either the Catholic, mainline Protestant, or older independent churches had done, and they address issues relevant to the popular world-view and religious consciousness. Western theologies tend to ignore or minimise the awareness of the spirit world with its destructive, evil and powerful forces that underlie both Asian and African worldviews. Particularly in their practices of healing and deliverance from evil spirits, independent and Pentecostal churches in Asia and elsewhere demonstrate that Christianity has this power, and they appeal to people oppressed by sickness, misfortune and affliction. Just as AICs represent a source of African theology, so independent churches in Asia represent valuable case studies of an Asian theology that may begin to examine hitherto unexplored questions. Most independent churches in Asia are 'orthodox' in theology and have much in common with Western-founded denominations, but they have also taken a stand against all that is seen as foreign, including foreign Pentecostal churches. Roger Hedlund has outlined some of the doctrinal distinctives of Indian independent churches, but warns us against generalising about such diverse movements. Many of these distinctives are

---

58 Gao Shining, 'Twenty-first century Chinese Christianity and the Chinese social process', *China study journal* 15:2/3 (December 2000), 14–18.
59 Ibid., p. 14.   60 Anderson and Tang, *Asian and Pentecostal*, pp. 411–38.

particularly appropriate in India's Hindu context, including 'mysteries' explained from the Bible, meditation as a method of understanding the Bible, and an emphasis on the experiential dimension of 'knowing God' through intense and prolonged prayer.[61] Founders of independent churches in Asia (just as in Africa) are given a special place of veneration after their death. Sometimes the leaders occupy a similar function to the Hindu gurus (and are sometimes called 'Christian gurus'), highly respected by their disciples as authoritative guides and examples who provide daily guidance for living. Hedlund says that there are also a number of 'deviant' ideas among a few Indian churches, such as tritheism and an emphasis on extra-biblical prophecies and 'new revelations'. But the independent church movement demonstrates what Maggay has described as the reason for their growth: 'it connects receptivity to a religion oriented towards power'. She says that 'to incarnate Christianity more genuinely within the context of Filipino culture is to become, not only perhaps more Christian, but also more Filipino'.[62] This is what Independency is all about.

61 Hedlund, *Quest*, pp. 233–53.
62 Melba P. Maggay, 'Towards sensitive engagement with Filipino indigenous consciousness', *International review of mission* 87:346 (1998), pp. 366, 372.

PART II

*

NARRATIVES OF CHANGE

8

The Great War

MICHAEL SNAPE

Introduction

Despite its magnitude as a global event, the First World War has not been well served by historians of Catholic and Protestant Christianity. Although numerous studies have been published on the churches' involvement in the war, they have tended to adopt a relatively narrow national or denominational focus, a tendency which has hampered the identification of connecting themes and which has served to obscure the wider impact of the war on Western Christianity as a whole.

If the coverage of these studies has also been uneven (much has been written on the churches in Great Britain and its dominions, for example, whilst little has been done to address the case of Catholics and Protestants in the Austro-Hungarian empire), these studies have also tended to pursue rather rigid and predictable lines of enquiry. With respect to the French experience of the war, for example, the energy of church historians has only lately been diverted from examining the myths and realities of the nation's 'sacred union' to the impact of the war on the religious habits and beliefs of the French people. In terms of the historiography of the churches and the war in Germany and the English-speaking world, even such modest progress has yet to be made. In Germany's case, scholarly interest has been chiefly devoted to the 'war preaching' and 'war theology' of the Protestant clergy, a preoccupation that has been informed by guilt engendered by the Second World War and by a historical quest to locate the origins of the Third Reich in the temper and culture of Wilhelmine Germany.

Similarly, in Great Britain and the United States, the historiography of Christianity during the war years has been heavily focused on the churches and their leadership and has been strongly influenced by the pacifism of the inter-war and Cold War eras. In Germany, Britain and the United States alike, the churches' wartime attitudes and activities have become the targets of much harsh and self-righteous criticism. In J. A. Moses' words, for example, the spiritual leaders of the belligerent European powers in 1914 did not find themselves opting to support the secular arm because of their history and circumstances but, along with the other leaders of these societies, 'they all succumbed to the intoxication of vulgar nationalism and hurled themselves like the Gadarine swine into the apocalypse of World War I'.[1]

Whilst providing plenty of scope for moralising and recrimination, such tendencies have bedevilled our understanding of the churches' role in the First World War. In particular, what they have obscured is the fundamental fact that the churches interpreted the war and their role within it in the light of their nineteenth-century experiences and outlook, not in the more chastened spirit of later decades of the twentieth. Hence, Germany's Protestant clergy were liable to see the war as the ultimate phase of the divinely guided struggle of the German people against their foreign rivals, a struggle that had commenced with the War of Liberation against Napoleon a century earlier and which had secured a precarious triumph in 1871 with German victory over France and national unification. Likewise, many of the French Catholic clergy construed the war as a divine judgement on the avowedly secular spirit of the Third Republic and as a heaven-sent opportunity to regain for the church a central and defining role in French society. Moreover, it was an early and almost universal expectation among the major churches of the belligerent nations that the idealism and anxieties of war would produce an abundant harvest of souls and a powerful antidote to the secularising tendencies of the modern age. Indeed, if this expectation diminished as the initial optimism of 1914 faded, then other more sophisticated prognoses seemed to gain in credibility as the war intensified. For example, in British and North American Protestantism, the currency of liberal theology and of the Social Gospel enabled the war to be widely interpreted as a means of advancing the kingdom of God on earth, a kingdom whose social, economic and international dimensions demanded the forging of a new spirit of fellowship and sacrifice in the fiery crucible of global war.

The churches and the war

Notwithstanding the profound influence of the history and ideas of the nineteenth century, the overwhelmingly pro-war attitudes of Europe's

---

1 J. A. Moses, 'The British and German churches and the perception of war, 1908–1914', *War and society* 5 (1987), p. 24.

established churches also drew on much deeper historical roots. By dint of being king of Prussia and primate of the Prussian church, Kaiser Wilhelm II was the pre-eminent source of ecclesiastical authority in Protestant Germany, a position which he emphasised upon the outbreak of war by summoning his subjects to prayer. Given the strength of the continuing alliance between throne and altar and their position as *de facto* civil servants in Germany's Protestant states, the Protestant clergy proved themselves worthy successors of their forbears of 1813 and 1870–1. Their bellicose wartime sermons and conspicuous support for the aggressively pro-war 'German Fatherland Party' (founded on 'Sedan Day' 1917) confirmed that 'no sector of the population was more ardent a supporter of the war than the German Protestant churches'.[2] In Great Britain, King George V, as head of the Church of England, called national days of prayer in the time-honoured tradition of his predecessors and, although there existed a somewhat greater practical distance between church and state than in the highly Erastian context of Protestant Germany, the established churches of England and Scotland proved almost equally zealous in their support for the war. Many clergymen of military age shunned even the option of becoming military chaplains in order to enlist as medical orderlies or fighting soldiers.

Ethnic and confessional ties with the old world ensured that the position of the churches in Europe was a significant factor in determining attitudes towards the war among Christians in the United States and in the self-governing dominions of the British empire. Whilst support for American intervention on the side of the Allies was understandably lacking among German-speaking Lutherans in the United States, it was also limited among Catholics of German and Irish extraction – notwithstanding the patriotic stance that was quickly assumed by America's Catholic hierarchy upon the country's declaration of war on Good Friday 1917. Almost by default, grass-roots support for American intervention was at its strongest among the English-speaking Protestant denominations – Episcopalians, Methodists, Congregationalists and Presbyterians. Similarly, in Canada and Australia, denominational and ethnic factors also influenced the churches' position on the war. As in mainland Britain and the United States, the Catholic hierarchy in both dominions generally stood behind the war effort. However, Catholics of French descent in Canada and of Irish descent in Australia proved much less willing than Anglophone Protestants to pursue victory by all necessary

2 R. Chickering, *Imperial Germany and the Great War, 1914–1918* (Cambridge: Cambridge University Press, 1998), p. 127.

means. The implementation of conscription was successfully if controversially resisted by Catholic Ireland and its clergy in 1918 and French Canadian opposition to conscription provoked fatal rioting in Quebec city in March of that year. The question of conscription also exposed deep ethnic and religious divisions in Australia, with the conscription referenda of October 1916 and December 1917 seeing the pro-conscription cause championed and even sacralised by the mainstream Protestant churches, whilst the case against compulsory service found its most controversial advocate in Daniel Mannix, the Irish-born Catholic archbishop of Melbourne.

If the loyalty and commitment of their Catholic minorities could raise some awkward questions in largely Protestant countries, Catholic loyalty could not be taken for granted by the governments of most Catholic belligerents either. Even in Austria-Hungary, where the Catholic church remained on close and comparatively amicable terms with the Habsburgs, Catholic support for the war effort was less than total. Although the higher clergy of the Dual Monarchy tended to remain strongly attached to the historic alliance of the Catholic church and the Habsburg dynasty, many of the Catholic clergy in Bohemia, Slovenia and Croatia were deeply involved in the nationalist movements that were to help precipitate the defeat and dissolution of the empire in the autumn of 1918. In France and Italy, the poisonous legacy of decades of conflict between Catholics and anti-clericals ensured that the anti-clerical governments of Rome's 'bad parishioners' (as Mgr Duchesne, the rector of the French School in Rome, memorably described them)[3] had to keep a watchful eye on Catholic opinion. In France, the bitter religious and political divisions of pre-war French society were famously subsumed in the nation's 'sacred union', whose advent was proclaimed upon the outbreak of war by President Poincaré. Although the image of heroic soldier-priests fighting and dying in their thousands for *la Patrie* made for powerful Catholic propaganda, there were clear limitations to the co-operation and goodwill that existed within the vaunted 'sacred union'. Demands from certain Catholic quarters for the public consecration of French arms to the Sacred Heart in fulfilment of a seventeenth-century prophecy were naturally ignored by President Poincaré, and many anti-clericals greatly resented the spiritual capital that the church was making out of the war. Indeed, the anti-clerical press happily circulated rumours of clerical duplicity and malingering and made much of the equivocal position

---

3 A. Dansette, *Religious history of modern France volume II: under the Third Republic* (Edinburgh: Nelson, 1961), p. 328.

of the pope and of that tendency in Catholic homiletics which (as in the disastrous days of the Franco-Prussian war) depicted the present conflict as a just chastisement of an apostate French nation.

Notwithstanding the many qualifications that must be made with respect to the French experience of the 'sacred union', the situation which obtained in Italy was clearly worse. With relations between the Vatican and the kingdom of Italy still bedevilled by the Roman question, and with the attitude of Italian interventionists and the Vatican towards Austria-Hungary clearly at odds in the months preceding Italy's entry into the war in May 1915, the situation was not propitious for a show of rapprochement between the Catholic church and Italy's liberal establishment. Attempts by more conservative nationalists to recruit Catholic support for intervention in the months prior to Italy's declaration of war made little impression and a significant element of Catholic opinion, particularly among the Italian peasantry, remained doggedly neutralist throughout the war. In their distinct lack of enthusiasm for Italy's treacherous and bungled war of aggression against Austria-Hungary and Germany, many Italian Catholics were in fact fellow travellers with their socialist compatriots. Indeed, the timing of Benedict XV's Peace Note in August 1917, just weeks before the rout of the Italian army at Caporetto, confirmed existing suspicions in anti-clerical quarters that the church was undermining rather than assisting the Italian war effort. Notwithstanding these charges, it was only in the wake of Caporetto (and of the German and Austro-Hungarian advances that followed) that a greater sense of national cohesion emerged in Italy and that Italian Catholics showed any general enthusiasm for a cause which few of them had embraced hitherto.

Given its delicate if not difficult situation in the internal politics of nearly all the major belligerents, it was perhaps only in occupied Belgium that the Catholic church enjoyed the benefits of full identification with the national cause. Here, and despite Benedict XV's reluctance to condemn the German invasion and its attendant atrocities, the spirit of national resistance was embodied in the person of Belgium's primate, Cardinal Mercier, the archbishop of Malines. As early as September 1914, Mercier was involved in a pointed exchange with Cardinal Hartmann of Cologne during the election of Benedict XV and, in the absence of King Albert I and the Belgian government, he went on to resist German policies towards his tormented homeland, most notably the forced deportation of Belgian civilians for work in Germany and the cynical promotion of Flemish nationalism. Although viewed rather warily by the Vatican, Mercier's exploits were naturally acclaimed by the

Allies and their sympathisers. Indeed, such was the wartime celebrity of Cardinal Mercier among the Allies that a recent biographer of Benedict XV has spoken of the presentation of Mercier as 'a kind of "anti-pope" ' in Allied countries.[4] Certainly, his pastoral letter of Christmas 1914 –spiritedly entitled *Patriotism and endurance* – was widely employed in Italy as a means of winning Catholics over to the interventionist cause.

The case of Mercier's pastoral of Christmas 1914 (in which the redoubtable primate declared, 'The religion of Christ makes patriotism a law; there is no perfect Christian who is not a perfect patriot')[5] introduces one of the most fundamental aspects of the churches' wartime role, namely that of 'spiritual mobilisation', as the German biblical scholar Adolf Deissmann described it.[6] Although the later nineteenth century had witnessed the onward march of nationalist movements across Europe and the development of varied forms of nationalist ideology, what must be recognised is that many forms of nationalism, even if not associated with a particular religious tradition, exerted a powerful emotional appeal that was largely derived from the appropriation of religious language and motifs. Even in France and Italy, where the nineteenth century had seen the evolution of aggressively secular forms of nationalism, the vocabulary of secular patriots was often full of religious resonance. If Italian nationalists had long chafed over the predicament of *Italia irredenta*, namely those Italian territories still under Habsburg rule, with the coming of war secular French patriots could trumpet the birth of the *union sacrée* and, during the critical battle of Verdun in 1916, exalt the precarious roadway that linked the fortress city to the rest of France as the *voie sacrée*.

Whilst French Catholics had their own distinctive sense of national iden-tity, one which hinged on their vision of France as 'the eldest daughter of the church' and which was supported by a militant Marianism and by the cults of the Sacred Heart and of St Martin of Tours, in Germany and in Great Britain nationalism was still largely anchored in a strong cultural Protestantism. In the context of war, the language of national election and divine purpose came easily to the lips of Protestant churchmen. In 1915, for example, Bishop John Percival of Hereford, once a rare Anglican opponent of the Boer war, now spoke of Great Britain and its allies as being 'the predestined instruments to

---

4 J. F. Pollard, *The unknown pope: Benedict XV (1914–1922) and the pursuit of peace* (London: Geoffrey Chapman, 1999), p. 95.
5 H. Strachan, *The First World War volume I: to arms* (Oxford: Oxford University Press, 2001), pp. 1117–18.
6 A. J. Hoover, *The gospel of nationalism: German patriotic preaching from Napoleon to Versailles* (Stuttgart: Franz Steiner, 1986), p. 50.

save the Christian civilisation of Europe from being overcome by a brutal and ruthless military paganism'.[7] Likewise, the unprecedented spirit of unity which the outbreak of war had manifested in Germany (a unity that was archetypally expressed by a unanimous Reichstag vote on war credits) was fervently presented as a new Pentecost. As one pastor put it in 1915, 'The apostles of the Reich stood together united on the fourth of August, and the Kaiser gave this unanimity the most appropriate expression: "I see no more parties, I see only Germans!"'[8]

Given their common Augustinian heritage in the field of moral theology, both Catholic and Protestant churchmen in the belligerent nations were quick to vindicate the justice of the national cause by conflicting appeals to just war theory. However, and perhaps inevitably, the scale, intensity and uncertainty of the conflict also fuelled a more hysterical and apocalyptic interpretation of the war. Whereas German religious propagandists tended to play upon the decadence of France, the envy and hypocrisy of Britain and the oriental ignorance and brutality of Russia, Allied religious propaganda acquired a more hysterical edge from a lengthy catalogue of lurid German atrocities against Allied and even neutral civilians. Although German church-men made much of the cruelty of Britain's naval blockade, the cultural treason inherent in deploying heathen colonial troops on the battlefields of Europe, and the heavy-handed treatment of German missions and mission-aries by the Allies in Africa and Asia, this was meagre fare in comparison with Germany's own wartime atrocities, deeds that made for much more colour-ful propaganda in Allied countries. The savage and systematic anti-guerrilla methods employed by the German army during its advance through Belgium and northern France in 1914, Germany's treatment of occupied Belgium, and its strategic use of submarines and zeppelins against civilian targets through-out the war all contributed to Germany's rapid demonisation. Its position was not helped by Germany's first use of poison gas or by its iniquitous alliance with the infidel and genocidal Turks. In Anglophone countries, the identifica-tion of Germany as the apotheosis of evil was assisted by rumours of the crucifixion of a Canadian sergeant near Ypres in 1915 and by the appearance of such moral studies of Wilhelm II as *The beast* and *Is the kaiser 'Lucifer'?* By the time of America's entry into the war, German atrocities had persuaded the American evangelist Billy Sunday that 'if you turn Hell upside down, you will

7 A. Wilkinson, *The Church of England and the First World War* (London: SPCK, 1978), p. 26.
8 A. J. Hoover, *God, Germany, and Britain in the Great War: a study in clerical nationalism* (New York: Praeger, 1989), p. 11.

find "Made in Germany" stamped on the bottom';[9] and, as victory edged closer in 1918, J. R. Day, the chancellor of Syracuse university, announced to his students: 'It would be a blessing if we could turn the beast of Berlin over to God and say, "Lord, inflict violent wrath upon this creature." '[10]

Given the kaiser's close identification with antichrist and Germany's widely perceived descent into paganism and pre-Christian barbarism, the language of holy war flowed spontaneously and quickly in Allied countries, eclipsing more measured talk of a just war and melding with a popular crusading rhetoric whose currency was derived from Turkey's entry into the war and from an atavistic interest in the crusades which was widespread in nineteenth-century Europe. However, the vision of a holy war was by no means confined to the Allies, for among German Protestants this titanic struggle was widely interpreted as yet another irruption of the divine purpose in German history. Taking as his text Romans 8:31 ('If God be for us, who can be against us?') Dr Ernst Dryander, the kaiser's court preacher, averred in a sermon given in Berlin cathedral only hours before Britain entered the war on 4 August 1914 that the German nation fought to preserve 'German faith and German piety' against the uncultured, barbaric and undisciplined masses of the Russian empire and the Third Republic.[11] Likewise, and drawing on the kingdom theology that was so prevalent in liberal Protestantism at this time, Adolf von Harnack declared in 1916 that the nobility of Germany's war aims sanctified the war itself, these aims being to secure Germany's right to wield its beneficent influence on international affairs and thereby promote the kingdom of God on earth.

Historians have almost invariably been repelled by the churches' often fearsome rhetoric of moral mobilisation; in their haste to condemn it many of them have lost sight of its significance as a vital dimension of full-scale war in the historically Christian societies to which it was addressed. Although the nineteenth century is not usually seen as an age of religious wars, since 1792 Europe had seen many bloody and prolonged conflicts which had testified to the continuing power of militant religiosity in mobilising societies for war.

9 J. Nagler, 'Pandora's box: propaganda and war hysteria in the United States during World War I', in R. Chickering and S. Förster (eds.), *Great War, total war: combat and mobilization on the western front, 1914–1918* (Cambridge: Cambridge University Press, 2000), p. 494.

10 R. H. Abrams, *Preachers present arms: the role of the American churches and clergy in World Wars I and II, with some observations on the war in Vietnam* (Scottdale: Herald Press, 1969), p. 104.

11 J. A. Moses, 'State, war, revolution and the German Evangelical church, 1914–18', *Journal of religious history* 17 (1992), p. 52.

Between 1792 and 1815, religion had played a key role in inspiring and sustaining resistance to French Republican and Napoleonic rule in western France, southern Italy, Spain, Portugal, the Tyrol and northern Germany. Moreover, the Carlist wars in Spain, the wars of Italian unification and the Franco-Prussian war had all subsequently demonstrated how religion could still fuel popular resistance, particularly (although not exclusively) in conservative Catholic societies. Nor, indeed, were Anglophone societies immune from these lessons, the American civil war and the more recent Boer war illustrating how militant forms of Protestantism could help keep citizen armies in the field during other wars of appalling destructiveness.

However much the churches in Europe may have lost ground during the nineteenth century, among none of the western belligerents of 1914–18 was Christianity an inconsequential moral force. Although levels of church membership or churchgoing may have been low or in decline in many parts of Europe, and although the Catholic church in particular had suffered in the constitutional reconfiguration of many Catholic societies since the French revolution, only a small minority of Europeans were consistent atheists or secularists. If Christianity still framed the public and personal morality of most of Europe, at a popular level the Christian rites of passage still exercised a wide appeal, even in contexts (such as Protestant, working-class Berlin) where the churches' influence was otherwise weak. In the light of Christianity's broad and continuing appeal, a shared religious identity was an important rallying point in most belligerent societies – particularly when a spirit of national unity was required in the face of an external threat. Significantly, the best illustration of this phenomenon is a negative one, namely the case of Italy, where the state's failure to enlist the firm support of the Catholic church proved a stumbling block throughout most of the war. Moreover, it was also very much apparent in the case of the United States, where the fiercely patriotic consensus of the principal American churches after 6 April 1917 helped to make a geographically and psychologically remote war seem immediate and necessary to a polyglot society which had largely embraced neutrality up to this point. Despite the churches' high-profile role in promoting national cohesion, the relative importance of their contribution to such an elusive quantity as national morale is almost impossible to quantify. Nevertheless, independent studies of German Protestantism and of Canadian Methodism have each concluded that the preaching and activities of the churches provided meaning and support for many during the war. In fact, it has even been alleged that the success of Germany's pastors in disseminating their exalted view of the war helped to sustain the widespread delusion that Germany's spiritual strength would more than offset the huge material superiority of the Allies. Furthermore, it is indicative of the importance of the churches in endorsing and exalting the war effort that the role of the military chaplain acquired a new emphasis in the British, American and even the Italian army, where increasingly their role was seen as motivational as much as ministerial.

In addition to a common and profound ideological commitment to the war, the churches' support for the national war effort could take many practical forms. Besides justifying and popularising the war among their own constituencies, leading clergy and laity were soon engaged in a long-running propaganda war in the international arena. In view of the conspicuous weakness of the pro-Allied lobby at the Vatican on the outbreak of war (of the Allied powers, only Russia and Belgium were represented whereas Prussia, Bavaria and Austria-Hungary each had their own envoys), towards the end of 1914 the British government was persuaded to forsake the policy of centuries by restoring formal diplomatic links with the Holy See, a development that prompted the government of the secular Third Republic to send an unofficial representative of its own. In addition to assisting in the covert propaganda war centred upon the Vatican, French and British Catholics threw themselves into the propaganda war for international Catholic opinion. In France, this work was carried out by the Catholic Committee for Propaganda Abroad, whose published work included *La Guerre allemande et le catholicisme* of April 1915. In Britain, prominent Catholics wrote for the British Catholic Information Society, whose monthly *Letters* were published in several languages and were widely circulated among the Catholic clergy in the United States. Prompted by Matthias Erzberger, co-ordinator of German propaganda in neutral states and the leader of the Catholic Centre Party, German Catholics also joined the fray, refuting the charges of their enemy co-religionists in publications such as *Deutsche Kultur, Katholizismus und Weltkrieg*.

In parallel to this Catholic propaganda war, rival Protestant churchmen also made a bid for neutral – and particularly American – opinion during the early years of the war. Only a week after Britain's declaration of war, Adolf von Harnack lamented to a group of visiting Americans that only Germany and America remained committed to the preservation of Anglo-Saxon *Kultur*, Britain having prostituted itself in order to support its 'Mongolian-Muscovite' nemesis.[12]

---

12 C. E. Bailey, 'The British Protestant theologians in the First World War: Germanophobia unleashed', *Harvard theological review* 77 (1984), p. 201.

More controversially still, at the end of August 1914 Harnack joined with twenty-eight other theologians associated with the German missionary movement in their joint *Appeal to evangelical Christians abroad*, a plea that was aimed at safeguarding German missionary work in Allied possessions and in German colonies abroad. Finally, in October of that year, Harnack and ninety-two other German scholars and theologians issued their 'Appeal to the civilised world' in the *Frankfurter Zeitung*, a manifesto which denied German responsibility for the war and which defended German militarism as an integral facet of the nation's greatness. Whatever their impact may have been on Protestant opinion in neutral countries, their most immediate and significant effect was to emphasise the divisions that had now emerged in the international community of Protestant theological scholarship, all of these initiatives meeting with a spirited public response from churchmen and academics in Britain, a response that was aided and abetted by Britain's propaganda headquarters at Wellington House.

However, the churches' part in the war amounted to much more than moral suasion at home and abroad, their material efforts to relieve (and, in some cases, even increase) its attendant suffering being staggering in scale and variety. In addition to the humanitarian work of the Red Cross, which was closely associated with the churches in many countries, the pope spent 82 million lire on international relief work among civilians and prisoners of war, a level of expenditure that brought the Vatican to the verge of bankruptcy. Besides these activities on the part of international and supranational bodies, among the belligerents vast sums of money were raised and spent by the churches on religious and welfare work among civilians and service personnel. In the United States, for example, the United War Work Campaign, a nine-day national and ecumenical fundraising initiative which commenced, ironically enough, on 11 November 1918, raised the staggering sum of $188 million. In France, the Catholic church threw itself into various *œuvres de guerre*, although not always in the spirit of co-operation with the secular authorities that the *union sacrée* seemed to demand. In Germany, too, the churches devoted themselves to welfare work, with Protestant and Catholic women's charitable organisations joining with their Jewish and secular equivalents in the 'National Women's Service'. However, and as in the case of the *union sacrée*, in wartime Germany the reality of unity often fell short of the conciliatory rhetoric of wartime fellowship, with Catholic army chaplains on the eastern front (where Protestant welfare work had the edge) often being critical and wary of the supposedly *überkonfessionell* soldiers' halls run by their Protestant counterparts.

In addition to providing succour and support for those affected by the war, the churches were also active in directly resourcing it. Clergy in Britain and in the United States joined in exhorting their co-religionists to invest in war loans (in order, as Billy Sunday told his fellow Americans, to help the guns of the US army and navy dig the graves of the Hohenzollerns), and the churches also made financial investments of their own. Between June 1915 and February 1917, six Church of England agencies put a total of £4.5 million into government bonds whilst in Germany the first three of nine successive war loans raised during the course of the war elicited nearly 13 million marks from the Prussian *Landeskirche*. Besides supplying funds, the churches also played a significant role in raising men, especially in Great Britain and Canada (where conscription was only introduced as a last resort) and in Australia, where conscription was successfully resisted until the end of the war. Even in British East Africa, where local labour was essential in pursuing the regional war against Germany, Anglican missionaries were active in recruiting thousands of native porters, some even being formed into units such as the Kikuyu Mission Volunteers. The military potential of the overseas missions was also realised by Catholic missionaries in the eastern reaches of the Belgian Congo, where the White Fathers organised their flocks against anticipated German incursions from across lake Tanganyika. Similarly, in the vast expanses of French West Africa, which the French government increasingly regarded as a reservoir of manpower for the western front and other theatres of war, their confreres proved equally zealous in persuading Christian converts to enlist in French colonial units.

It was the verdict of Alphonse Dupront that, in the intensity and scale of the First World War, 'the West rediscovered the holy war', and also that 'On both sides, it was necessary to claim God.'[13] However, there was more to the religious character of the First World War than exalted inference and patriotic imputation, for in certain theatres of war the conflict very much reflected bitter and historic religious enmities. On the eastern front the clash of arms was characterised by the resurgence of old religious animosities from the outset, with Austria-Hungary seeking a papal blessing for its polyglot and largely Catholic armies as they went forth to do battle against Orthodox Serbia and Russia. Although this blessing was not forthcoming, Pius X was known to sympathise with the Austro-Hungarian case against Serbia, a state whose influence he regarded as a 'corrosive illness' which threatened to infect

---

13 A. Becker and S. Audoin-Rouzeau, *1914–1918: understanding the Great War* (London: Profile Books, 2002), p. 115.

Catholic central Europe.[14] As the war developed, the Russian invasion and occupation of Austro-Hungarian eastern Galicia was marked by the forced conversion of Galician Catholics and by the imprisonment of Catholic priests, schoolteachers and the archbishop of Lemberg – all as part of a crude policy of Russification. Significantly, the Central Powers countered by exploiting the religious grievances of Russia's own ethnic minorities. Following the capture of Warsaw in 1915, the Germans opened a Catholic theological faculty in the city's university and, in the wake of their capture of Riga two years later, they not only restored a Lutheran church order to this part of Latvia but also reconsecrated the Orthodox cathedral for Lutheran worship in April 1918.

If the war on the eastern front often smacked of a religious war, then the same was also true of those theatres of war where the Allies confronted the Turks. Turkey's entry into the war was accompanied by the declaration of a *Jihad* against the Allied powers on 14 November 1914, a declaration that was partly instigated by Germany and which issued from the Ottomans' historical claim to the Sunni caliphate. Hoping to capitalise on the pan-Islamic feeling that Ottoman sultans had recently promoted, the Turkish *fatwah* cited the oppression of Muslims in the French, Russian and British empires and was addressed to Shi'ite as well as to Sunni Muslims. Given that more than half of the world's Muslims lived under Allied rule, the subversive potential of the Ottoman *Jihad* was abundantly clear. During the course of the war, the call to *Jihad* was heard as far afield as the Caucasus and the Congo and it fed militant Islam on India's north-west frontier and on the borders of Egypt and Libya, and even provoked mutinies in predominantly Muslim regiments of Britain's Indian army. However, if the Ottoman empire was prepared to approach the war as a war of religions, then so too were its enemies. Although allusions to a latter-day crusade in the middle east were eschewed by the governments of the Western Allies (who were careful not to alienate Arab nationalists or their own Muslim subjects), these perceptions were certainly very current among Allied journalists and Allied servicemen who fought at Gallipoli and in Palestine and Mesopotamia. Unsurprisingly, the Allied capture of Jerusalem in December 1917 was hailed in the British press as the long-awaited fulfilment of the dream of Richard the Lionheart and was celebrated in Rome with the singing of the *Te Deum* in all of the city's churches. The religious character of the war between Turkey and the Allies

14 D. R. Živojinović, 'Pope Benedict XV's peace efforts (1914–1917)', in R. Bosworth and G. Cresciani (eds.), *Altro polo: a volume of Italian studies* (Sydney: University of Sydney, 1979), p. 73.

was reflected in the fact that Turkey's Christian subjects frequently lent their support to encroaching Allied forces in the northern and southern reaches of the Ottoman empire, a factor that not only fuelled Turkish atrocities against the Armenians but also drove wartime persecution of Nestorian, Jacobite and Maronite Christians in Syria and the Lebanon.

Religion in the war years

If the religious animosities provoked by the war indicate the limited extent of the secularisation of European culture in the nineteenth century, then so too does the religious revival that accompanied it. In Germany, Great Britain and France, the early months of the war were marked by a dramatic resurgence in formal religious observance, with the belligerent nations witnessing greater attendance at church services, higher numbers of communicants and (in the case of France especially) larger pilgrimages, especially to local shrines. The fact that inflated levels of formal religious observance clearly subsided during the course of the war has often been taken as evidence that the religious enthusiasm of the war years was ephemeral, and even as demonstrating that the war was a further secularising influence upon European societies. However, in the context of months and years of deepening conflict that saw the enlistment or conscription of millions of the faithful, the loss of thousands of clergymen to various forms of wartime service and the whole-sale disruption of normal patterns of church life, such conclusions have to be treated with scepticism. Indeed, other indicators would seem to suggest that the religious revival of the early months of the war simply took alternative forms which were less dependent on the provision of regular and formal services. The nature of this situation is reflected in wartime Germany, where, at the same time as they were losing their organ pipes to government requisitions, Protestant churches found that they had to meet an increasing demand for old and familiar hymnody in congregational worship. Moreover, in Hamburg and Berlin the percentage of religious funerals in traditionally non-churchgoing areas rose dramatically throughout the war, climbing from 55.39 per cent in Hamburg in 1913 to 80 per cent in 1918 and from 65.55 per cent in Berlin to 80.53 per cent over the same period.[15]

The religious ferment of the home front can also be discerned in the credence that was widely accorded to sensational claims of divine

---

15 N. Hope, *German and Scandinavian Protestantism 1700–1918* (Oxford: Clarendon Press, 1995), p. 597.

intervention in the war. In France, the timely defeat of the German army outside Paris in September 1914 was widely hailed as the 'miracle of the Marne', a victory that represented for French Catholics positive proof of the Virgin Mary's intercession on behalf of their country. In Britain, the sobering lessons of the first months of the war on the western front were palliated by the story of the angels of Mons, a legend which put a positive gloss on an early British defeat and which was actually inspired by a short piece of fiction in London's *Evening News*. Less famously, and as war-weariness became increasingly evident, further stories circulated in the summer of 1917 as to the appearance of 'angels of peace' above the Thames. Most famously of all, however, the bloody and tumultuous year of 1917 was marked in Portugal by the appearance of the Virgin Mary at Fatima, the visionaries being told to recite the rosary daily 'in order to obtain peace for the world and the end of the war'.[16] Certainly, in Portugal's case, these visions had an enormous impact on domestic politics and helped to legitimise the overthrow of Alfonso Costa's rabidly anti-clerical government by a military coup in December 1917.

Evidence of this religious ferment and of a widely diffused religious revival was also apparent among the belligerent armies. Given the apparent feminisation of European religious life in the nineteenth century, the significance of this widespread return to religion in such overwhelmingly male contexts should not be under-estimated. In the French army, the background of a pre-war Catholic revival and the fear and uncertainties of war contributed to a heightened religious consciousness that was evident throughout the war years. This piety was reflected in the popularity of military saints and putative saints such as St Martin of Tours, St Michael, St Maurice and Joan of Arc, with French soldiers also seeking solace and protection in the new cult of 'Our Lady of the trenches'. Before the introduction of conscription and the battle of the Somme in 1916, an exalted sense of national purpose, a high proportion of churchgoers in its ranks and a natural fear of death or wounding also contributed to a wave of religious revivals in the British army. Naturally, a ubiquitous craving for protection spawned an insatiable and often debased demand for religious paraphernalia among soldiers of all nationalities. Whilst Bibles and prayer books were often carried as amulets in the British and American armies, Protestant soldiers like their Catholic comrades also wore rosaries, scapulars and miraculous medals in addition to a bewildering array of secular talismans. The battlefields of the western front proved fertile

16 N. Perry and L. Echeverria, *Under the heel of Mary* (London: Routledge, 1988), p. 184.

ground for a range of fatalistic discourses (discourses that embraced a spectrum of religious and philosophical positions ranging from hyper-Calvinism through to scientific determinism). They also gave rise to numerous legends relating to the providential survival of wayside calvaries and, in the British and dominion armies at least, to the figure of a 'White Comrade' who tended the wounded in no-man's land. Indeed, these stories could even assume a prophetic character, the 'Golden Virgin' of Albert (a statue which leaned from the dome of the basilica over the battlefields of the Somme for more than three years) prompting numerous variations on the theme of its fall and the end of the war in the British, French and German armies alike.

The vital if highly eclectic religiosity of the war years found vivid and lasting expression in the commemoration of the myriads of war dead. Although some cultural historians have been preoccupied with the growth of spiritualism, seeing in it evidence for the resilience of traditional culture, far more significant in this respect was the enduring ability of Christianity (and perhaps of Catholicism in particular) to accommodate the needs of the bereaved. In Germany the Catholic symbolism of the Pietà was commonly and consciously incorporated into post-war memorials, whilst in Britain a Catholic influence was also discernible in numerous civic memorials based on the wayside calvaries of France and Belgium. The war also led to the growth of prayers for the dead and to reassessments of the theology of purgatory among British Protestants. Two of the more striking coincidences of the war were that it came to an end in November, which is traditionally the month of the Holy Souls in Roman Catholicism, and that the armistice was signed, as French Catholics were not slow to point out, on the feast day of St Martin of Tours. In France, and despite the existence of an alternative secular and Republican idiom, the Catholic church was 'present at all levels of commemoration',[17] ranging from the saying of masses for the dead, through the erection of parish memorials, to the construction of impressive new ossuaries on the old battlefields of the western front. Indeed, in the commemoration of the war as much as in its prosecution, French Catholics and Republicans were at least partly reconciled, with crucifixes often adorning civic memorials and the archbishop of Paris blessing the coffin of the nation's Unknown Soldier. Of course, for those who survived the war, there was much to be thankful for, this gratitude being reflected in the texts of innumerable votive plaques that came to adorn churches across France in particular. Even in Germany,

17 D. J. Sherman, 'Bodies and names: the emergence of commemoration in interwar France', *American historical review* 103 (1998), p. 449.

returning soldiers were often keen to give thanks in tangible form. The Marian shrine of Marpingen was adorned with a new chapel in the early 1930s, due to the efforts of a local veteran who had made a vow at the front that he would build a chapel to the Virgin Mary should he survive the war.

The churches and peace

One of the most significant aspects of the First World War for Western Christianity was the evident failure of the Vatican and of certain suprana-tional Protestant bodies to mobilise the churches against the war. Although the nineteenth century had witnessed a growing personality cult of the papacy in Catholic countries and also the centralisation of institutional power in the hands of the pope (a process that was marked in 1917 by the introduction of a new code of canon law) Pope Benedict XV proved signally incapable of rallying international Catholic support for a negotiated peace. If, following his unexpected death in August 1914, Pius X was portrayed as a tragic casualty of the war, his successor has often been depicted as a martyr for peace. Secretly plotted against by the Italian political establishment, widely accused of active or passive partiality by a host of critics on both sides, and ultimately thwarted in his successive attempts to encourage a negotiated peace, the trials of Benedict XV have paid dividends in the long term, particularly given the anti-war tenor of much of the historiography of the First World War. In his biography of Benedict, for example, John Pollard has claimed that the wartime pontiff had a real claim to greatness, one that rested on the fact that 'his pursuit of peace in all spheres was sincere, committed and courageous'.[18] However, this interpretation of Benedict's role seems unduly influenced by a western European perspective. Although the Holy See was careful in its dealings with the western Allies, this essentially pragmatic policy has to be offset by its solicitude for Austria-Hungary and by its inherent mistrust of Orthodox Russia. If the former was demonstrated in attempts to avert Italian aggression against Austria-Hungary in 1915 (attempts that the Vatican undertook in concert with Germany), then the latter was manifested by a chronic fear that Russia, if victorious, might extend its influence to Constantinople, reinvigorate its Orthodox patriarchate and boost Orthodoxy as a rival to Catholicism in south-east Europe. Indeed, the Vatican's concern for Austria-Hungary and its marked Russophobia were implicit even in the content and timing of Benedict's celebrated Peace Note of August 1917, a note

---

18 Pollard, *The unknown pope*, p. 215.

whose contents were formulated following consultations with the governments of Germany and Austria-Hungary. Significantly, the note outlined a peace settlement based on little more than a return to the *status quo ante bellum*, a formula that would have favoured the beleaguered Dual Monarchy. Moreover, the note was published at a time when Russia was sliding into irrecoverable military defeat, a factor which the note recognised in its advocacy of an independent Poland, a state which would be largely Catholic and which would be mainly carved out of the western reaches of the defeated and defunct Russian empire.

If Christian internationalism in its various forms was subverted and disrupted by the war, then it also demonstrated the inherent weakness of Christian pacifism, whose strongest following among the mainstream churches was to be found among liberal Anglophone Protestants. Superficially at least, in the fateful summer of 1914 the anti-war dynamic seemed strong in these quarters. On a theological level, Christian pacifism had been given an academic underpinning through the recent work of Adolf von Harnack and there was a growing conviction that the churches could and should do more to promote international amity. In this respect, the most significant by-product of the Hague Peace Conference of 1907 had been the inauguration of a high-profile dialogue between the British and German churches against a backdrop of growing Anglo–German tensions. With official bodies in being for promoting friendship between the British and German empires through the churches and with the creation of a Church of England Peace League in 1911, the outlook for Anglo–German relations looked promising. In January 1914, John Clifford, a prominent British Baptist and veteran anti-war campaigner, even felt justified in declaring: 'Militarism belongs to the dark ages; it is not fit for our time. It must go. It is going.'[19] This mood of optimism was shared across the Atlantic, for in the following month the steel magnate Andrew Carnegie, who had given freely towards the peace work of the British and German churches, boosted the burgeoning peace movement among the American churches by bringing the Church Peace Union into being with an endowment of $2 million. Indeed, so fair did the international outlook appear that Carnegie had even specified how these funds should be disposed of 'when peace is fully established, and no more need be done in that cause'.[20] It was, of course, bitterly ironic that an international Protestant

19 A. Wilkinson, *Dissent or conform? War, peace and the English churches, 1900–1945* (London: SCM, 1986), p. 23.
20 Abrams, *Preachers present arms*, p. 9.

peace conference was scheduled to take place in Constance on 3–4 August 1914 and that the main item on the agenda was the creation of a new World Alliance for Promoting International Friendship through the Churches. Moreover, a parallel Catholic peace conference was scheduled to meet at Liège the following week, its principal object being to foster friendly relations between the French and German clergy.

The war, of course, hit this rather sanguine world with the force and suddenness of a whirlwind, dragging into its vortex scholars and churchmen who had played a prominent role in recent Anglo–German exchanges. Even Clifford, who had been a delegate at Constance, was swept up in its wake, the veteran anti-Boer war campaigner taking the platform at recruiting rallies and declaring that the present war was a struggle between 'the forces of freedom and those of slavery'.[21] In the crucible of war, and particularly following the introduction of conscription in Great Britain, the United States and Canada, it became clear that Christian pacifism did not command a strong following among Anglophone Protestants outside of its traditional and relatively small constituency of the Society of Friends and of more marginal sectarian groups such as the Mennonites, Christadelphians, Plymouth Brethren and Jehovah's Witnesses. Among the more sectarian groups, of course, conscientious objection was often inspired by separatist rather than altruistic concerns and their scruples did not necessarily extend to labouring in war-related industries given appropriate conditions of work. Indeed, it was indicative of the ambiguities generated by the war that even the Society of Friends was divided on the question of military service, with many Quakers of military age on both sides of the Atlantic forsaking the traditional witness for peace in order to enlist.

Conclusion

Although it is difficult to judge the overall impact of the First World War upon Western Christianity, some comment is appropriate. Clearly, given its nature as a far-reaching global event that affected numerous Christian traditions, its impact has to be assessed on an international and pan-denominational level. When approached from this perspective, some interesting conclusions arise. Undoubtedly, in political terms the Catholic church seems to have done rather well out of the conflict. First, there was the final humiliation of historic enemies in the East, for not only was the spectre of militant Orthodoxy

---

21 Wilkinson, *Dissent or conform?*, p. 23.

exorcised from eastern Europe but the holy places were delivered from centuries of Turkish control. Additionally, the war helped the situation of the church in many Western countries. If it generated new and important national organisations for American Catholics, it turned Cardinal Mercier into an international symbol of heroic resistance and helped to destroy a viciously anti-clerical regime in Portugal. In France and Italy, and notwithstanding ongoing difficulties, the common experience of war ultimately served to help relations with other anti-clerical governments, easing the admission of Catholic politicians into government and demonstrating the necessity of Catholic support in mobilising the nation for war. Moreover, the defeat and collapse of the central European empires also brought dividends in its wake, not least because the common danger of Bolshevik Russia served to cement alliances with dominant forms of conservative nationalism in newly independent countries, especially in Poland and in Hungary. Furthermore, the collapse of the political and ecclesiastical systems of imperial Germany also benefited the Catholic church and its Centre Party, which were now free to wield greater influence and power in the more egalitarian if unstable context of the Weimar Republic. Finally, the contrasting posture of the church's leadership at the national and international levels had the dual if unforeseen effect of demonstrating (for the benefit of contemporary patriots) that it stood for war and (for the benefit of a more critical posterity) that it also stood for peace. For Protestantism, however, the picture was more mixed. If the displacement of European missionaries gave many African Christians an intoxicating taste of autonomy, for the established Protestant churches of Germany the crushing experience of defeat led to disestablishment and demoralisation, the hitherto inconceivable outcome of the war creating a palpable and dangerous desire for national redemption. Moreover, although the war seems to have fuelled an incipient reaction to liberal optimism in the realm of Protestant theology (a reaction that was to flower in the Barthian Neo-Orthodoxy of the inter-war years), the liberal Protestant spirit clearly endured in the Anglophone world in ambitious plans for social and ecclesiastical reconstruction and in new hopes for the League of Nations and for the World Alliance that had been inaugurated at Constance in August 1914. Finally, and in terms of its significance for popular Christianity, the war had vividly exposed its strength and vitality in advanced and supposedly secular European societies. However, in doing so it had also exposed its perennial eclecticism and its ambivalent and paradoxical relationship with the institutional churches.

The Christian churches and politics in Europe, 1914–1939

MARTIN CONWAY[1]

Any survey of the power and influence of the Christian churches in Europe undertaken in the summer of 1939 would have been largely pessimistic. Be it in the few remaining parliamentary regimes of Europe or the heterogeneous and increasing number of authoritarian, quasi-authoritarian or simply dictatorial regimes that were becoming the new European norm, the influence of the Christian churches, political parties and values appeared to have receded considerably over the twenty-five years since the outbreak of the First World War. Socialism, still rooted in much of Europe in the anti-clerical culture of its nineteenth-century origins, had become a major electoral force and an intermittent party of government in many states. In addition, its fission after the First World War had given rise to a militantly atheist communism which, despite its repeated failure to extend its power in Europe beyond the frontiers of the Soviet Union, had established itself by the 1930s as a durable and, in some areas, important presence in European politics. Undoubtedly the most dramatic trend, however, was the emergence of forms of right-wing politics separate from or even emphatically hostile to Christian ideas. Though elements of this 'dechristianisation' of the political right had been evident since at least the middle decades of the nineteenth century, it acquired emphatic importance after the First World War. Italian Fascism and German-Austrian Nazism were dissimilar and profoundly unstable amalgams of diverse ideological influences, within which Christian ideas, both Catholic and (in the case of Germany) Protestant in origin, had a significant presence. Both, however, had evolved by the 1930s into forms of state power in which a reluctance to challenge directly church power and a courting of Christian opinion went hand in hand with a prevailing

---

1 I gratefully acknowledge the assistance of Iselin Theien, Ben Frommer and Alexis Schwarzenbach with particular points during the preparation of this chapter. I am also indebted to Tom Buchanan and to Hugh McLeod for reading and commenting on a first draft.

attitude among both the governing elite and local officials of hostility towards the organised churches and independent forms of Christian action.

In some respects, such pessimism would have been misplaced. In Britain the absence of explicitly confessional forms of politics, outside of Northern Ireland and lowland Scotland, did not prevent the more discrete but tangible influence of Anglican values within the Conservative Party and of a variety of religious denominations (notably non-conformist Protestant denominations and Catholicism) on the Labour Party. Much the same, in a very different context, could be said of the Irish Free State where the two major political parties (*Fine Gael* and *Fianna Fáil*) accepted the cultural influence of Catholicism over the politics of the new state. In a rather similar way, the semi-authoritarian regimes of Poland, Hungary and, until the *Anschluss* of 1938, Austria had come to accept the advantages of a rapprochement with the Catholic and, in the case of Hungary, Protestant churches. Moreover, in many of the remaining parliamentary regimes of Catholic Europe (Belgium, the Netherlands, Switzerland and, until its demise in 1939, Czechoslovakia), Catholic political parties occupied an influential position in national and local political life. More immediately, the victory of the Nationalist forces in the Spanish civil war in the spring of 1939 brought to an end the secular Republican regime and installed in its place the Francoist dictatorship which, in common with the Salazar regime established in Portugal since the early 1930s, accorded substantial privileges and power to the Catholic church and its affiliated institutions. Similarly, the collapse of the unitary Czechoslovak state in March 1939 enabled an authoritarian Slovak state to be created which, under the leadership of Jozef Tiso, had a strongly Catholic and even clerical character.[2]

Yet, to most Christian Europeans who observed the disjointed but remorseless evolution of their continent from multi-lateral diplomacy to localised conflicts and ultimately generalised war between the early 1930s and the early 1940s, the dominant trend would have appeared to have been towards the marginalisation of Christian values in public and political life. The discrimination and in some cases persecution experienced by the clergy and lay activists in the Soviet Union, Nazi Germany and fascist Italy, as well as the anti-clerical violence that occurred in Republican Spain during the early stages of the civil war in 1936, seemed to mark a further step in the remorseless secularisation of Europe. This,

---

2 Survey histories of Christian politics during this period include T. Buchanan and M. Conway (eds.), *Political Catholicism in Europe 1918–1965* (Oxford: Oxford University Press, 1996); M. Conway, *Catholic politics in Europe* (London and New York: Routledge, 1997); W. Kaiser and H. Wohnout (eds.), *Political Catholicism in Europe 1918–45*, vol. 1 (London and New York: Routledge, 2004).

however, was more profound than a struggle between the churches and their ideological opponents. The institutional and political conflicts surrounding the public role of the churches that developed in many European states during the early decades of the twentieth century indicated the contested borderline that existed between the universal scope and rationalising ambitions of modern state institutions and the peculiar mixture of ecclesiastical hierarchies, lay organisations and social and economic institutions which comprised the Christian churches of twentieth-century Europe. Conflict between church and state in these circumstances was not inevitable; but nor was it easy to avoid. In response to this threat, the Catholic and, more hesitantly, the Protestant churches had stepped into the new arena of mass electoral politics by encouraging the creation of Christian political parties which in the years preceding 1914 had won a number of major electoral victories.[3] After the First World War, however, the golden age of Christian political mobilisation appeared to have passed. The electorates of the confessional parties were eroded as new parties competed for Christian political loyalties and divisions of ideology and social class undermined the ideal of confessional unity. Not only, therefore, by the end of the 1930s was it impossible to pretend that the churches were outside politics; it was also difficult to claim that they were winning inside politics.

Terminus dates, however, are never innocent. If, instead of 1939, one were to choose 1949 or 1959 a rather different picture would emerge. Though the post-war partition of Europe extended Soviet intolerance of church independence and, on occasions, religious practice into the very heart of central Europe, Christian politics rapidly acquired a much more influential position in the remaining territories of non-communist Europe. In the two decades between the collapse of the Third Reich and the socio-political upheavals of the late 1960s and early 1970s, Christian Democrat parties, generally largely Catholic in composition but also in some states inter-confessional in character, enjoyed a substantial political ascendancy at the expense of the secular right and in some cases the left. Their electoral success may have owed less to their Christian ideological inspiration than the parties' leaders were inclined to believe, but their emergence contributed to what one might term a 'recentring' of religion in west European political life at the end of the 1940s. Appeals to Christian values formed part of the spirit of the Cold War age; the ecclesiastical hierarchies, most notably the papacy, acquired an enhanced prominence in public life; and Christian networks of educational, social and welfare organisations

---

3 S. Kalyvas, *The rise of Christian democracy in Europe* (Ithaca and London: Cornell University Press, 1996).

played a major role in the daily lives of many Europeans. Many of the reasons for this Christian and, more especially, Catholic post-war ascendancy lay in the events of the Second World War and their prolonged aftermath. But it also owed much to the ways in which the Christian churches had been changing, both institutionally and intellectually, over the preceding decades. Though the immediate impact of these innovations had been frustrated by the unfavourable circumstances of the time, they enabled Christian parties to burst upon the political stage after 1945 as a self-confident and powerful force.[4]

The period between 1914 and 1939, which forms the subject of this contribution, therefore lacks an obvious unity in the history of Christian politics in twentieth-century Europe. Seen from the perspective of the nineteenth century, it was an era when a distinct Christian presence in European political life appeared to be disintegrating amidst the tumult of economic, ideological and military conflicts. But viewed from the perspective of the post-war decades, it appears as a formative period when Christian movements and organisations gradually succeeded in articulating a modern form of democratic politics that would play a major role in non-communist Europe during the second half of the twentieth century. In truth, of course, both of these interpretations are valid. They are, however, also indicative of the complexity of the inter-relationship between religion and modernisation in twentieth-century Europe. Historians of religious faith have long demonstrated that any simple equation between modernisation and secularisation is misleading. The vast processes of social and economic change that transformed the lives of almost all Europeans within a few generations from the middle of the nineteenth century onwards disrupted the former centrality of the churches and the practice of religion in many areas of European life. Churches lost contact with the populations of new urban communities, public and private institutions usurped many of their social roles, and belief systems emerged that challenged Christian values. At the same time, however, these processes also hastened the creation of more committed communities of believers, encouraged the development of new forms of religious faith and provided the churches with new means of communicating their message. Rather, therefore, than consigning religious faith along with folk costumes and horse-drawn transport to the museum, modernisation in effect initiated a period of competition, both among the Christian denominations and with those other ideologies and movements seeking to win the hearts and minds of twentieth-century Europeans.

4 T. Kselman and J. Buttigieg (eds.), *European Christian democracy: historical legacies and comparative perspectives* (Notre Dame: Notre Dame University Press, 2003).

The diverse outcomes of these processes of modernisation were clearly evident in the different patterns of Christian politics in early and mid twentieth-century Europe. The largely dechristianised character of certain major urban centres, such as Madrid and Barcelona, contrasted with the much more rooted role of confessional organisations in industrial regions of the Netherlands and western Germany. In rural Europe, too, the secular politics of much of southern France and areas of central Italy was very different from the durability of Christian political movements in north-central Spain or German-speaking Switzerland. No attempt to reduce the evolution of Christian politics in Europe to a simple narrative of decline or renewal in this period can therefore do justice to the many variations in levels of religious faith but also of political culture. The constitutional and public status of the Christian churches in European states had evolved over the preceding half-century in highly dissimilar ways. In much of northern Europe the Protestant churches remained closely tied to the political and constitutional order, while in those states of predominantly Catholic Europe where struggles between clerical and anti-clerical forces had been most intense during the latter decades of the nineteenth century state and church confronted each other as mutually suspicious and often antagonistic institutions. These differences were in turn reflected in the varied patterns of Christian political mobilisation. In much of Scandinavia, the emergence of a distinct Christian politics was impeded by the largely uncontested position of the churches within overwhelmingly Protestant societies. In contrast, the fierce church–state struggles in Spain, Portugal and France prior to 1914 had forged a tight bond between religious faith and political commitment. The complex inter-connections between national and religious forms of identity constituted a further source of diversity. In that considerable number of nation-states, notably Finland, Norway, the Baltic States, Poland, Czechoslovakia and Ireland, which gradually achieved full statehood between 1900 and the 1920s, the secular struggle for national independence had often been inseparable from issues of religious and confessional identity. Thus, rejection of the legacies of Catholic Habsburg rule in Bohemia after the First World War lent a Protestant hue to the new Czechoslovak state; while, in Ireland, the difficult emergence of the Irish Free State from British rule and a violent civil war fostered a durable convergence between Catholicism and a certain definition of Irish nationalism.[5]

5 M. Spinka, 'The religious situation in Czechoslovakia', in R. Kerner (ed.), *Czechoslovakia: twenty years of independence* (Berkeley and Los Angeles: University of California Press, 1940), pp. 284–301; D. Keogh, *The Vatican, the bishops and Irish politics 1919–39* (Cambridge: Cambridge University Press, 1986).

Notwithstanding these multiple forms of diversity, the most obvious fault-line in European Christian politics was, however, that between a central band of European states stretching across Europe from the Low Countries to central Europe and northern Italy where Christian parties formed a highly visible element of public life, and those states in northern and southern Europe where an identifiable Christian political tradition was less apparent. In Belgium, the Netherlands, western Germany, Switzerland and Austria, a continuity of Christian politics was evident throughout the first half of the twentieth century, despite the often traumatic changes of regime, and was able to come to fruition in the more settled political circumstances that prevailed after the Second World War. In these territories, the influence of Christian parties was inseparable from a wider process of social 'pillarisation' whereby confessional institutions had assumed a wide range of social and economic roles. The Christian welfare organisations, trade unions, women's organisations and farmers' leagues founded at the end of the nineteenth century occupied a prominent place in national and local life until the religious and social caesurae of the 1960s, and provided an organisational bed-rock upon which the parties could be built.[6] This situation contrasted markedly with those states of Catholic southern Europe, notably Spain, Portugal and Italy, where the past legacies and present reality of the 'culture wars' between clericals and anti-clericals ensured that the position of the church and its affiliated institutions within society was much more contested. Different again were those states, notably republican France and the parliamentary regimes of northern Europe, where the dominance of national and local state institutions marginalised the intermediate role of the churches and also served as a brake on the political mobilisation of Christians within distinct political parties.

In some respects this fault-line followed the frontiers between the unitary structures of Catholicism and the much more diverse and internally differentiated landscape of Protestantism. It was, to put it at its most simplistic, no accident that Christian political mobilisation was most emphatic in the majority Catholic territories of central Europe. The modern development of the hierarchical and increasingly uniform Catholic church from the mid-nineteenth to the mid-twentieth centuries had manifold consequences for the emergence of Catholic political parties held together by their organisational loyalty to the institutions of the church and their shared membership of the

---

6 H. Righart, *De katholieke zuil in Europa* (Meppel: Boom, 1986); P. Luykx, 'The Netherlands', in Buchanan and Conway, *Political Catholicism*, pp. 221–6.

'imagined community' of Catholicism. The factors that facilitated the emergence of Catholic politics were largely absent from Protestantism. Quite apart from the imbalance between the resources of the Catholic church and those of the various Protestant confessions, the more segmented and localised structure of the Protestant churches hindered the emergence of the disciplined political parties essential to success in an era of mass political mobilisation. In Sweden, for example, the important role played by the Free Church movement in the notable parliamentary politics of the pre-1914 era faded away as it was subsumed by the mass politics that followed the constitutional upheavals of 1917–18.[7] The decision of the Free Church movement in Sweden not to transform itself into a political party, in favour of allowing its members to participate as individuals within a variety of political organisations, also indicated the wider temperamental and theological differences between Catholicism and the diverse Lutheran and Calvinist confessions of Europe. While the Catholic church under the leadership of a series of energetic popes emphasised the existence of an all-embracing Catholic worldview, the Protestant confessions predominantly focused their energies on matters of doctrine and internal organisation. This did not exclude political engagement; but it ensured that such political activism tended to be concentrated on particular issues rather than the creation of separate political parties.

The dichotomy between Catholics and Protestants can, however, be overdrawn. The impulses within the vast, and expanding, range of Protestant churches active in Europe in the early twentieth century ranged from the rigorous quietism of certain groups to the highly politicised character of some of the state churches of northern Europe. The example of the (Calvinist) Anti-Revolutionary Party (*Anti-Revolutionaire Partij*) demonstrates the powerful role that a Protestant party could play in the pillarised society of the Netherlands.[8] Moreover, the absence in other European states of explicitly Protestant parties did not signify the neutrality of Protestants on political issues. Protestant minorities in majority Catholic states, such as those in Czechoslovakia and France, maintained a political profile and influence disproportionate to their numbers, and surveys of electoral data in many Protestant states reveal the connection between active membership of a church and support for particular political parties. This 'shadow effect' of Protestantism on European politics was

---

7 S. Lundkvist, 'Popular movements and reforms', in S. Koblik (ed.), *Sweden's development from poverty to affluence 1750–1970* (Minneapolis: University of Minnesota Press, 1975), pp. 180–93.
8 M. Wintle, *Pillars of piety: religion in the Netherlands in the nineteenth century* (Hull: Hull University Press, 1987).

reinforced at times of crisis by more explicit forms of political mobilisation. This was clearly evident in Germany during the 1920s, where the predominantly Lutheran and Prussian-oriented *Landeskirchen* were among the most outspoken opponents of the secular principles of the Weimar Republic, and provided a social and ideological focus for the mobilisation of the anti-republican right.[9]

There was therefore no simple logic to the patterns of Christian political engagement in Europe between 1914 and 1939. Instead, there was a series of overlapping and in some respects contradictory trends, the relative importance of which varied from confession to confession, from time to time and, above all, from place to place. Over and above this irreducible diversity, however, the most important general theme was the embedding of a Christian presence within the socio-political structures of twentieth-century Europe. After the nineteenth-century dialectic of church and state, in which the two rival powers had in turn collaborated, competed and conflicted, the dominant feature of the early and mid-twentieth century was the blurring of the frontiers of church and state. State involvement in religion and, more especially, in the non-religious activities of the churches steadily increased, but so too did Christian engagement, both collective and individual, in the political sphere. This took, as we have seen, highly varied forms, and met with differing degrees of success and failure. The twin outcomes, however, by the middle of the twentieth century (beyond the frontiers of the Soviet Union and its post-1945 sphere of influence) were the establishment of a durable Christian presence in European political life and the consolidation of the churches and their affiliated institutions as important and, often, privileged interlocutors in the increasingly complex interaction between state and society.

Neither of these outcomes was pre-ordained. Nor indeed did either seem likely amidst the often-cacophonous evolution of Europe between 1914 and the chaos of the Second World War. To explore the reasons for the embedding of a Christian presence in twentieth-century politics therefore requires to some extent standing back from the more familiar narratives of inter-war Europe. The complex legacies of the First World War and the emergence of communism and fascism, as well as the economic depression of the early 1930s, all played a more limited role than one might at first sight expect in the evolution of Christian politics. More influential, however, were longer-term processes of political change, which proceeded beneath the noise of war,

9 J. R. C. Wright, *'Above parties': the political attitudes of the German Protestant church leadership 1918–1933* (Oxford: Oxford University Press, 1974), pp. 74–98; R. Steigmann-Gall, *The Holy Reich: Nazi conceptions of Christianity 1919–1945* (Cambridge: Cambridge University Press, 2003), pp. 13–50.

ideological conflict and regime instability. Three factors stand out as having been of particular importance in this process: the vitality of the associational principle among the communities of the various churches; ideological and social changes taking place within European Christianity which reinforced the connection between religious belief and political commitment; and, finally, changes in European politics that created a more favourable context for Christian political action.

Of these three themes, the first perhaps requires the least elucidation. Since at least the mid-nineteenth century one of the most pervasive elements of Christian life in Europe had been the conversion of the rituals of religious observance into a definable community of believers who through their values and choices in daily life demonstrated their affiliation to their religious faith. This transition from the universal ambitions of churches to the consolidation of a smaller sub-community of believers proceeded at different speeds within denominations and areas. Its consequence, however, by the early decades of the twentieth century had been to create a more or less fixed fence between those who formed part of the church (or churches) and those who consciously or tacitly did not. The proportions of the population within and without this frontier varied greatly, from the near-universal religious affiliation in some communities such as the predominantly Catholic southern areas of the Netherlands to the small minorities of church attendees in some areas of central France. Numbers were, however, less important than the sense of commitment that formal or informal membership of the community of believers generated. Around the nodes provided by the churches clustered a wide range of affiliated institutions ranging from schools and welfare organisations to sports clubs and youth groups. This phenomenon of 'pillarisation' whereby European societies became internally sectionalised between sub-communities of Catholics and Protestants as well as non-confessional groupings such as socialists and liberals varied in intensity. It was most marked in some areas of Catholic Europe, such as the Low Countries and western Germany and Austria, but its traces were evident almost everywhere. In the influential formulation of the Swiss historian Urs Altermatt, Catholics constructed a 'ghetto' as a protection for the faithful against the alien values of secular modernity.[10] Yet, though pillarisation was a reaction against modernity, it also became the vehicle whereby Europe's Christian communities entered into the modern world. Through the construction of self-contained Catholic (and, to a

10 U. Altermatt, *Der Weg der Schweizer Katholiken ins Ghetto*, 2nd edn (Zurich: Benziger, 1991).

lesser extent, Protestant) pillarised structures of confessional organisations Europe's Christians were able to have a powerful influence on the social structures of modern Europe.

The political consequences of this process of pillarisation were considerable. The rapid development of Christian parties in many European states during the late nineteenth century owed much to the way that they were able to build their political superstructure on the networks of confessional associations. This remained the case after the First World War. The major Catholic parties of inter-war Europe, notably the Centre Party (*Zentrumspartei*) in Germany, the Christian Social Party (*Christlich-Soziale Partei*) in Austria and the Catholic Party (*Union Catholique Belge–Katholiek Verbond van België*) in Belgium, derived much of their solidity from the way in which they were less freestanding parties than institutions rooted at a local level in the plethora of Catholic associations.[11] There existed, in effect, a differential between the capacity of Catholic, and in some areas Protestant, communities to mobilise quickly and powerfully in the political sphere and that of other political traditions. This was well demonstrated in both Italy and Spain where the rapid expansion of the PPI (*Partito Popolare Italiano*) in the turbulent politics of Italy after the First World War and of the CEDA (*Confederación Espanola de Derechas Autonomas*) during the Second Republic in Spain profited from the organisational frameworks provided by Catholic associational life. The fortress metaphor of the embattled community, used so repeatedly in the electoral literature of Catholic political parties during the inter-war era, was primarily a rhetorical device; but it derived its strength from the sense of confessional solidarity generated by the confessional schools, unions and welfare organisations that structured the lives of many European Catholics.[12]

Nevertheless, in many respects the heyday of these parties had passed by the inter-war years. In some cases, their electoral support remained impressive: for example, the Dutch Catholic Party (*Rooms Katholieke Staatspartij*, RKSP) won the support of an estimated 80–90 per cent of Dutch Catholics in all national elections from 1920 until the 1960s. More typical, however, was the

11 J. Elvert, 'A microcosm of society or a key to a majority in the Reichstag? The Centre Party', E. Gerard, 'Religion, class and language: the Catholic Party in Belgium', and H. Wohnout, 'Middle-class governmental party and secular arm of the Catholic church: the Christian Socials in Austria', in Kaiser and Wohnout, *Political Catholicism*, pp. 48–53, 101–3 and 174–7.

12 L. Rölli-Alkemper, 'Catholics between emancipation and integration: the Conservative People's Party in Switzerland', and M. Conway, 'Catholic Politics or Christian democracy? The evolution of inter-war political Catholicism', in Kaiser and Wohnout, *Political Catholicism*, pp. 65 and 236–41.

gradual but significant decline of the Centre Party (and its Bavarian equivalent, the *Bayerische Volkspartei*) in Germany, which in 1920 had won almost 63 per cent of the Catholic vote, but by November 1932 had declined to 47 per cent.[13] The Catholic parties of the pre-1914 era had been primarily defensive organisations called into existence, often under close clerical control, to rally the faithful in defence of a specific agenda of confessional interests against the threats perceived to be posed by hostile governments and atheist liberalism and socialism. After the First World War, this model of political mobilisation no longer worked so effectively. The clergy, influenced by the new spiritual priorities of the papacy, generally preferred to step back from direct involvement in political life. The laity, too, was more self-confident and less willing to accept clerical direction on political matters. A new generation of lay Catholic and Protestant leaders had come of age who saw political action not so much as the defence of church interests than as an engagement with the political and social issues of the age based on the principles of their Christian faith. This shift in mentality from defensive solidarity to a more wide-ranging political commitment was, however, prejudicial to the principle of unity. As Christian politics went beyond protection of the church and the faithful, so fault-lines of ideology and of socio-economic interest came to disrupt the unity that had been such an imposing feature of the first generation of Christian political mobilisation.

The inter-war era was therefore characterised by a plurality of different and often competing forms of Christian-inspired political organisation. At moments of crisis, most notably in the clerical–anticlerical disputes of the Spanish Second Republic, a large majority of Catholics came together behind a single political organisation, the CEDA.[14] At other times, however, divisions tended to surface in Christian ranks. Thus, in Germany the ambition of the Centre Party to act as the political focus (or *Zentrum*) of all Catholics was undermined by the centrifugal forces released by the First World War and its aftermath. Some Catholics embraced the new republican order while others drew close to the authoritarian ideas advanced by anti-Weimar ideologists of the right. Many rural and small-town Catholics in the south and west joined protest campaigns against the new regime while Catholic trade unionists came together with their Protestant equivalents in a Christian trade-union

13 H. Bakvis, *Catholic power in the Netherlands* (Kingston and Montreal: McGill-Queen's University Press, 1981), p. 2; Conway, *Catholic politics*, p. 36.
14 F. Lannon, *Privilege, persecution and prophecy: the Catholic church in Spain, 1875–1975* (Oxford: Oxford University Press, 1987), pp. 179–97; M. Vincent, 'Spain', in Buchanan and Conway, *Political Catholicism*, pp. 109–16.

confederation (the *Deutscher Gewerkschaftsbund*, DGB).[15] Thus, though the Centre Party survived, and played a major role as a regional and national party of government in the Weimar Republic, its political coherence was increasingly undermined by tensions between its component interest groups. Much the same was true in Protestant ranks. The close ties that had existed between the principal Lutheran and Reformed (i.e., Calvinist) churches and the pre-war German empire rendered them politically homeless in the very different circumstances of the Weimar Republic. Though many rallied initially to the *Deutschnationale Volkspartei* (DNVP) as the principal political organisation of the right, some were drawn more actively into republican politics while many others gravitated towards the anti-republican and nationalist extreme right, including ultimately the NSDAP (*Nationalsozialistische Deutsche Arbeiterpartei*).[16]

It was, however, France that provided the most durable example of this political plurality. Unlike in many other areas of Europe, there had been no dominant Catholic political organisation prior to 1914. This remained the case after the First World War. The pretension of organisations such as the *Fédération Nationale Catholique* (FNC) of the late 1920s to speak for all French Catholics was contradicted by the regional and ideological divisions within Catholic ranks. The legacies of the anti-republicanism of the nineteenth century, though mitigated by the so-called *union sacrée* of Catholics and republicans in the First World War, remained strong and Catholics were prominent in the extreme-right movements and periodicals that flourished in the 1930s. In contrast, however, other Catholics were drawn, like the members of the Protestant minority, into active involvement in the political life of the Third Republic. The pragmatic logic of Catholic associations, such as the trade unionists of the CFTC (*Confédération Française des Travailleurs Chrétiens*), led them to reject the abstentionism of the past in favour of participation in the political and socio-economic institutions of the republic. In addition, for the first time, a party emerged, the PDP (*Parti démocrate populaire*) that accepted the republic and sought to work within it as a Catholic presence. Such putative Christian democracy remained a minority current within Catholic ranks, but its very existence indicated the extent of the political

---

15 K.-E. Lonne, 'Germany', in ibid., pp. 159–67; R. G. Moeller, *German peasants and agrarian politics, 1914–1924: the Rhineland and Westphalia* (Chapel Hill and London: University of North Carolina Press, 1986); W. Patch, *The Christian trade unions in the Weimar Republic 1918–1933: the failure of 'corporate pluralism'* (New Haven and London: Yale University Press, 1985).
16 Wright, *Above parties*, pp. 11–98.

differentiation that had taken place within French Catholicism since the turn of the century.[17]

Political division, contrary to the repeated warnings issued by the clergy, was not, however, a sign of weakness. In many respects, the plurality of Christian political organisations during the inter-war years reflected the intensification of Christian engagement in the political sphere. The multiple crises, international and national, socio-economic and ideological, that swept across Europe after 1914 destroyed much of the Christian abstentionism from politics that had been evident during the nineteenth century. They also accelerated processes of democratisation within Christian, and more especially Catholic, ranks. The egalitarianism of (male) service in the armies of the First World War and the extension of the (male but also in some cases female) electoral franchise that occurred in many states after the war eroded the spirit of deference to social and clerical superiors that had been a strong feature of Catholic political organisations prior to 1914. Christian workers and farmers were not, for the most part, inclined to abandon their Christian commitment, but they were increasingly determined to take their political future into their own hands. The rapid expansion in Christian trade unions, such as the DGB in Germany, the CIL (*Confederazione Italiana dei Lavatori*) in Italy and the CFTC in France, were one indication of the pressure of material grievances but also of the social self-confidence within the Christian working class.[18] So too were the processes of emancipation taking place in the countryside. A consistent theme of politics in much of Europe during the 1920s and 1930s was the grievances of rural populations against urban rulers who appeared neglectful of the problems of foreign competition, over-production, debt and taxation faced by many of Europe's small-scale farmers. Christian political parties, with their strong electoral support in many rural areas, could not remain immune from these pressures. Consequently, confessional farmers' organisations, such as those in Germany and Austria, became more militant in defence of their sectional interests within Christian political

---

17 J. McMillan, 'France', in Buchanan and Conway, *Political Catholicism*, pp. 40–54; J. McMillan, 'Catholicism and nationalism in France: the case of the *Fédération Nationale Catholique, 1924–1939*', in F. Tallett and N. Atkin (eds.), *Catholicism in Britain and France since 1789* (London and Rio Grande: Hambledon, 1996), pp. 151–63; R. Paxton, 'France: the church, the republic and the fascist temptation 1922–1945', in R. J. Wolff and J. K. Hoensch (eds.), *Catholics, the state and the European radical right 1919–1945* (Boulder: Social Science Monographs, 1987), pp. 67–91; J.-C. Delbreil, *Centrisme et démocratie chrétienne en France: le Parti Démocrate Populaire des origines au MRP (1919–1944)* (Paris: Sorbonne, 1990).
18 Patch, *Christian trade unions*; J. Pollard, 'Italy', in Buchanan and Conway, *Political Catholicism*, p. 78.

parties. Moreover, in many rural areas of Europe, new protest movements and parties of the extreme right, which claimed to defend rural interests against the actions of malevolent capitalist forces and unsympathetic urban bureaucrats, challenged Christian parties.

The combined impact of material pressures and electoral competition goes far to explain the more urgent, angry and, on occasions, simply demagogic tone of much Christian politics after the First World War. At the same time, however, it reflected the impact of the second of the three factors identified above: namely, the ways in which social and intellectual changes taking place within Europe's Christian confessions encouraged a more direct connection between religious belief and political commitment. The division between (private) religion and (public) politics, as Christian commentators were often at pains to emphasise, was largely a creation of liberal ideologists of the nineteenth century. It was a distinction that in the late nineteenth century had often served the Christian churches well by establishing a frontier beyond which it was illegitimate for state authorities to step in their efforts to regulate religious matters. But in the much more fluid political circumstances of the inter-war years, it was rejected by many in the expanding ranks of Christian activists, intellectuals and campaigning movements for whom the ambition was no longer to protect religion from politics but to bring religion into politics. The pervasive sense of a 'crisis of civilisation', symbolised by the mass slaughter of the First World War, appeared to demonstrate the bank-ruptcy of the liberal model of society and the need for a distinctively Christian solution. This goal combined a spiritual and a political dimension, or more frequently an admixture of the two. The reconversion of the 'dechristianised' populations of Europe and the ambition of constructing some form of Christian City where the values of the Christian faith would once again predominate co-existed, often rather uneasily, within many Christian organ-isations and minds during the inter-war years. Common to both, however, was a more integral and less compromising mentality. Far from being reconciled to contemporary society, much Christian politics defined itself against the values of liberal society as well as the secular political ideologies, of both left and right, to which it had given rise.

This counter-cultural militancy took different forms within Europe's varied religious cultures. In Lutheran northern Europe, religious missions denounced the manifold sins of the modern world and the complicity of established church leaderships with them. Such revivalist campaigns tended to stop short of explicit political engagement, but in 1938 they did lead to the formation of the Christian People's Party (*Kristelig Folkeparti*, KrF) in Norway, which, from its stronghold in the Lutheran west of the country, brought a new Christian militancy into Norwegian politics.[19] In the Netherlands, too, despite the close bonds that had long existed between mainstream Protestantism and the political order, the (Calvinist) Anti-Revolutionary Party under the leadership of Hendrikus Colijn in the 1930s denounced the perceived social anarchy of contemporary society, as well as the danger posed by the materialist and atheist evils of liberalism, socialism and communism.[20] In the troubled circumstances of inter-war Germany this ideological antipathy towards the structures and ethos of modern society could not fail to take more radical political shape. The alienation initially felt by much of the Protestant clergy and laity from the Weimar Republic as the illegitimate product of national defeat was appeased somewhat by the election of the Protestant Hindenburg as president in 1925. This circumspect engagement of the churches with the republic was, however, rapidly undermined during the political crisis of the early 1930s when many Protestant clergy, and electors, rallied to the 'national opposition' led by the NSDAP.[21]

It was in Catholic ranks that the more militant character of Christianity was most explicit. This owed much to the efforts of the papacy. The modern construction of the pope as the ultimate head of the Catholic church and, at the same time, as the spiritual leader of the international community of Catholic believers had gathered pace since the mid-nineteenth century. It was, however, in the first five decades of the twentieth century that it attained its full expression. Under the determined leadership of Pope Pius XI (1922–39), the papacy strove to impose its unifying principles on the personnel, structures and priorities of Europe's somewhat heterogeneous Catholic cultures. The appointment of reliable figures to key positions of ecclesiastical authority, the conclusion with many European states of treaties (termed concordats) that allowed a greater freedom to Catholic spiritual and educational activities, albeit under papal direction, and the proliferation of organisations such as Catholic Action that reflected the doctrinal and spiritual priorities of the papacy were all components of the construction of an emphatically more Roman Catholicism.[22] At the heart of these actions lay a confident belief in the place of the Catholic church in the modern world. Building on the declarations of his predecessors, notably Pius IX,

19 M. Schwarz-Lausten, *A church history of Denmark* (Aldershot and Burlington: Ashgate, 2002), pp. 278–96; O. Garvik (ed.), *Kristelig Folkeparti. Mellom tro og makt* (Oslo: Cappelen, 1983).
20 E. H. Kossmann, *The Low Countries 1780–1940* (Oxford: Oxford University Press, 1978), pp. 603–6.
21 Wright, *Above parties*, pp. 99–109.
22 M. Agostino, *Le Pape Pie XI et l'opinion publique 1922–1939* (Rome: Ecole Française de Rome, 1991).

Leo XIII and Pius X, Pius XI constructed an all-encompassing Catholic doctrine that extended beyond questions of faith and morality to the economic and political principles of society. In his two most substantial encyclicals, *Quas primas*, issued in 1925, and *Quadragesimo anno*, issued in 1931 to mark the fortieth anniversary of Leo XIII's *Rerum novarum*, Pius presented Catholicism as providing the sole and self-sufficient solution for the ills of the modern world. The role of the church, and of the Catholic laity, was not to compromise with contemporary society but to stand as a bastion of truth within it.[23]

The determination with which Pius XI pursued this vision bore fruit in the remarkable centrality that the papacy attained in European Catholicism during the pontificate of his successor, Pius XII (1939–58). This historic highpoint of the power and prestige of the modern papacy owed, however, at least as much to evolutions in the social and ideological character of Catholicism within many European societies as it did to the self-interested efforts of the papacy. The networks of specifically Catholic educational institutions established since the late nineteenth century, as well as the mass organisations aimed at young people, women and particular socio-economic groups, forged a more self-conscious Catholic laity. Significantly, it was the Catholic activists, both male and female, formed in these milieux who were to the fore in the spiritual movements such as Catholic Action of the 1920s and who often went on to dominate the Catholic political and intellectual movements of the 1930s as well as subsequently occupying many of the leadership positions in the Christian democrat parties established after the Second World War. This generational cohort of younger European Catholics, often from middle-class and intellectual backgrounds, injected a new energy and militancy into inter-war Catholicism. Movements as diverse as *Odrodzenie* (Renaissance) in Poland, *Ateitis* (The Future) in Lithuania, *Esprit* (Spirit) in France and *Christus Rex* (Christ the King) in francophone Belgium were all manifestations of a burgeoning Catholic student and intellectual culture which embraced the uncompromising language and symbolism of the papacy and rejected the more cautious approach of their elders in the established Catholic parties. The Catholic universities were central to this process. Institutions such as Nijmegen in the Netherlands, Leuven in Belgium, Salamanca in Spain and Coimbra in Portugal, as well as Catholic student organisations such as the FUCI (*Federazione Universitari Cattolici Italiani*) in Italy, encouraged the development of a Catholic intelligentsia

---

23 E. Fouilloux, 'Le catholicisme', in J.-M. Mayeur (ed.), *Histoire du Christianisme*, vol. XII (Paris: Desclée-Fayard, 1990), pp. 116–239.

formed in the certainties of neo-Thomist doctrine and unindulgent in their criticism of the modern world.[24]

It was also this generation of younger Catholic activists who set the more militant tone of Catholic politics during the 1930s. The combined impact of the economic depression that followed the Wall Street Crash of 1929 and the rise of extremist political movements of left and right encouraged the emergence of a more radical Catholic politics hostile to both liberal parliamentarism and economic capitalism. The evolution of the Centre Party in the final years of the Weimar Republic towards a tacit rejection of republican democracy, and the twin success in Belgium of the populist and anti-parliamentary Rexist movement led by Léon Degrelle and the extreme-right Flemish nationalist VNV (*Vlaamsch Nationaal Verbond*), were both manifestations of the new mood in Catholic ranks.[25] Its most dramatic manifestations were, however, in Austria and Portugal. These republican and parliamentary states were transformed in the early 1930s into authoritarian regimes under the leadership of Engelbert Dollfuss and António Salazar respectively. Both men came from emphatically Catholic backgrounds and initially enjoyed considerable support from the church hierarchy and from Catholic social and political organisations. In fact, neither regime proved in practice to be as sympathetic to Catholic concerns as their many apologists suggested. Nevertheless, both drew heavily on Catholic symbolism and made much of the papal inspiration which they claimed lay behind their authoritarian political structures and socio-economic corporatist institutions.[26] Catholic support for the regimes of Dollfuss and Salazar, as well as, after 1936, for that of Franco in Spain, was indicative of the authoritarian drift in Catholic politics during the 1930s. Though there remained Christian democrats who sought a rapprochement with the political left, the weight of Catholic

24 M. Przeciszewski, 'L'association catholique de la jeunesse académique, "Odrodzenie" (La Renaissance): aperçu historique', *Revue du nord* 70 (1988), 333–47; V. S. Vardys, *The Catholic church, dissent and nationality in Soviet Lithuania* (Boulder: East European Quarterly, 1978), pp. 21–2; M. Conway, 'Building the Christian type: Catholics and politics in inter-war Francophone Belgium', *Past and present* 128 (1990), 117–51; R. Moro, *La formazione della classe dirigente cattolica* (Bologna: Il Mulino, 1979).

25 R. Morsey, *Der Untergang des politischen Katholizismus: die Zentrumspartei zwischen christlichem Selbstverständnis und 'nationaler Erhebung' 1932–1933* (Stuttgart and Zurich: Belser, 1977); E. Gerard, *De Katholieke Partij in crisis: partijpolitiek leven in België 1918–1940* (Leuven, Kritak, 1985).

26 F. L. Carsten, *Fascist movements in Austria: from Schönerer to Hitler* (London and Beverly Hills: Sage, 1977), pp. 229–48; L. Gellott, 'Defending Catholic interests in the Christian state: the role of Catholic Action in Austria 1933–1938', *The Catholic historical review* 74 (1988), 571–89; T. Gallagher, 'Portugal', in Buchanan and Conway, *Political Catholicism*, pp. 136–43.

political engagement during the 1930s was predominantly on the right, and often on the anti-parliamentary right.[27] This did not equate with support for fascism. Catholic opinion, particularly outside Italy and Germany, was predominantly hostile to the cult of the state and 'brown bolshevism' which they associated with the Fascist and more especially Nazi regimes. Instead, the ambition of many politically engaged Catholics in the 1930s was to create a 'third way' between fascism and liberal democracy. In contrast to the anarchic conflict of liberal societies and the enforced collectivism of communism and fascism, Catholics advocated a new model of society in which the intermediate institutions of family, workplace and local community would be valued. Corporatist institutions, bringing together the representatives of workers and employers, would replace the class conflict of capitalism while the ascendancy of Catholic spiritual values would restore a lost unity to modern society.[28]

It would be wrong to take these vague models of a Catholic social and political 'revolution' at face value. The anti-democratic rhetoric of Catholic militants tended to be more emphatic than their actions. Nevertheless, the radical language of the 1930s was significant for the way in which it demonstrated the evolution that had taken place in Catholic politics from the rather limited confessional agenda of the early years of the century towards a more ambitious political vision. In the short term, this helped to prepare the way for the support that Catholics would give to the wartime authoritarian regimes established in Vichy France, Slovakia and Croatia.[29] In the longer term, however, its more durable legacy was perhaps to be found in the Catholic politics of the post-war decades. The energy and self-confidence of Catholic parties and movements in Italy, Germany, France and the Low Countries from 1945 onwards owed much to short-term influences, notably the engagement of many younger Catholic militants in wartime resistance to fascism and foreign occupation. But, more profoundly, it can be seen as the coming of age of a more activist Catholic engagement with politics that had been prepared over the previous twenty years.

The Christian ascendancy in west European political life after 1945 was not, however, solely the product of changes within the Christian churches. It also reflected how European politics had evolved in ways that were more

---

27 Wolff and Hoensch, *Catholics.*   28 Conway, *Catholic politics*, pp. 60–3.
29 McMillan, 'France', in Buchanan and Conway, *Political Catholicism*, pp. 54–6; S. Alexander, 'Croatia: the Catholic church and clergy 1919–1945', in Wolff and Hoensch, *Catholics*, pp. 31–66; Y. Jelinek, *The parish republic: Hlinka's Slovak People's Party 1939–1945* (New York and London: East European Quarterly, 1976).

accommodating of a distinctly Christian presence. Undoubtedly the most immediately obvious of these changes was the deepening and multiplication of forms of representative politics in the years preceding and following the First World War. The demise of the empires of central Europe and the often-dramatic expansions of the franchise in many west European states did not in themselves create a new culture of democracy. In a number of states, the female majority remained disenfranchised, partly because of its alleged susceptibility to clerical influence. Moreover, the establishment of authoritarian regimes in Hungary, Italy and Spain during the 1920s reversed substantially the gains achieved over the previous years. Nevertheless, the extension of representative politics after the First World War to the new states of central and eastern Europe such as Czechoslovakia, Poland and the Baltic States, as well as its expansion downward into local government and forms of socio-economic organisation, clearly gave a premium to those political groupings best able to transform amorphous groups of supporters into reliable armies of voters.[30] The Christian churches, with their substantial associational structures and mentality of confessional solidarity, were, as we have seen, well equipped to compete in this new world of multiple elections. Christian parties were successful in a number of the initial elections held in the new states of central and eastern Europe, and a similar capacity to mobilise and organise was evident in the success of Christian parties and trade unions in local government and workplace elections in many areas of Europe.

The multi-party character of politics in most inter-war European states also favoured Christian parties. Britain remained almost unique in its evolution towards a largely two-party system. Elsewhere, systems of proportional representation encouraged the development of several major parties, none of which enjoyed an overall majority in elections. This worked to the advantage of Christian parties. Though they could in some circumstances (such as in Belgium and Austria in the 1920s) succeed in becoming the largest single party, they generally had little chance of achieving an absolute majority of the votes. But, as reliable and electorally stable political forces occupying the political centre-ground between the extremes of left and right, the Christian parties were well placed to play an influential role in the subsequent coalition politics. Thus, for example, in the multi-party politics of the

---

30 See, for examples, A. Suppan, 'Catholic people's parties in east central Europe: the Bohemian lands and Slovakia', and L. Kuk, 'A powerful Catholic church, unstable state and authoritarian political regime: the Christian Democratic Party in Poland', in Kaiser and Wohnout, *Political Catholicism*, pp. 223–5, 153–5 and 161; Vardys, *The Catholic church*, pp. 20–36.

Netherlands, Belgium, Czechoslovakia and Germany during the Weimar years, Christian parties were almost indispensable components of national governing coalitions as well as of numerous regional and local administrations.

A second, and subtler, change in the patterns of European politics was the decline in anti-clerical and more especially anti-Catholic politics. The liberal movements which, in the later nineteenth century, had served as the standard-bearers of a militant secularism tended to lose influence after the First World War. At the same time, a slow change took place in socialist attitudes towards religion. Especially in urban areas, the electoral rivalry between socialist and Christian parties was often intense. Nevertheless, beneath the trading of mutual insults, there were also signs of a tentative rapprochement. The hesitant but gradual ideological evolution of many European socialist parties away from the rather two-dimensional Marxism of the Second Internationale allowed for a reassessment of socialist attitudes towards the churches, which was reflected in a softening of the anti-clerical language of the past. Thus, when socialist parties did acquire substantial governmental power, as in Germany immediately after the First World War and in the Scandinavian states during the mid-1930s, Christian fears of legislative attacks on the churches proved to be largely misplaced. Even in France, where a shared loyalty to republican secularism provided one of the glues that held together the alliance of the Radical, Socialist and Communist parties that came to power in the Popular Front government of 1936, there was no return to the church–state conflicts of the pre-1914 era. Only in Spain did the clerical–anticlerical struggle retain its political centrality, as well as its capacity for violence. In the Second Republic, legislation intended to diminish the social influence of the Catholic church was one of the major goals of the parties of the republican left while the Catholic party, the CEDA, rallied to the defence of the church and its affiliated institutions. This conflict was, however, much more than one of parliamentary politics. The position occupied by the church had become one of the defining issues in the broader conflict between the advocates of a modern secular Spain and the defenders of a Catholic and monarchist Spain. In regions such as Catalonia, Extramadura and Andalucia, as well as in the major cities of Madrid and Barcelona, conflicts over church property and the role of the clergy and religious orders in education and welfare were rooted in the structures of daily life. It was this local reality that in large part explained why, after the military uprising against the republic in the summer of 1936, political polarisation was transformed into social violence. Priests and members of religious communities were the focus of violent attacks in some Republican areas, while socialists, communists and anarchists were the targets of repression by the Catholic and Nationalist forces in Francoist Spain.[31]

The abatement, outside Spain, of the clerical–anticlerical wars of previous decades was, however, slow to be reflected in the mentalities of Christian politics. Fears of the threat that ill-intentioned parties and state bureaucrats posed to Christian interests remained an essential element of the glue that forged confessional solidarity. A standard component of the rhetoric of Catholic parties throughout the inter-war period, powerfully reinforced by the guidance regularly issued to the faithful by the clergy prior to national and local elections, was therefore the need to unite against the dangers of atheist liberalism and socialism. Legislative conflicts over technical but often highly emblematic issues such as education reform and the degree of state funding for the clergy, as well as the social undertow of local disputes over the building of new churches, secular funerals and marriages and the holding of religious processions and festivals, helped to keep alive the mentality of clerical–secular conflict, even after it had been emptied of much of its former virulence. Conversely, where such conflicts disappeared or were subsumed by new political issues, Christian politics tended to lose much of its coherence. In the Irish Free State, the division between the republican *Fianna Fáil* party of Eamon De Valera and the more cautious and pro-Catholic *Cumann na nGaedheal* party (subsequently refounded as *Fine Gael*) led by William Cosgrave had been one of the principal legacies of the civil war that had accompanied the acquisition of *de facto* political independence from Britain in 1921. Thus, after the defeat of Cosgrave's government in the elections of 1932 and the formation of a *Fianna Fáil* government headed by De Valera, there was an upsurge in militant Catholic opposition to the new government, notably by the Blue Shirt movement led by Eoin O'Duffy. Subsequently, however, the willingness of the leader of *Fianna Fáil*, Eamon De Valera, to court Catholic opinion, most notably through the privileged position granted to the Catholic church by the constitution of 1937, effectively drained Irish politics of a clerical–anticlerical dimension. The social and cultural distinctions between practising and non-practising Catholics, as well as the Protestant minority, remained; but disputes over the role of the Catholic church largely disappeared from mainstream political debate.[32]

---

31 Lannon, *Privilege, persecution and prophecy*, pp. 198–214; M. Vincent, *Catholicism in the Second Spanish Republic: religion and politics in Salamanca 1930–1936* (Oxford: Oxford University Press, 1996).

32 D. Keogh and F. O'Driscoll, 'Ireland', in Buchanan and Conway, *Political Catholicism*, pp. 285–93.

The Christian solidarity derived from mobilisation against domestic political opponents was reinforced by the more distant threat constituted by the militantly atheist Soviet Union. The revolutionary upheavals in central Europe during the immediate post-war years left a long legacy of fear in Christian ranks, which was subsequently given a new focus by the emergence of the Soviet Union as an influential force in European politics. The construction of small but vocal communist parties, closely tied to the Soviet Union, in most European states, and their participation in the Popular Front movements in France and Spain during the mid-1930s, helped to conjure up the caricatural image of the threat posed to Christian Europe by the Soviet and communist menace. The rather optimistic attempts of communist parties to reach out to progressive Christian opinion during the Popular Front period were rebuffed by all but a tiny minority, while perceived communist dominance of the Republican government in Spain during the civil war was an important element in Catholic support, within and outside Spain, for the Francoist cause.[33] The communists had become in many respects the new incarnations of the Jewish and anti-clerical enemies of previous eras, and when Germany and its allies invaded the Soviet Union in June 1941 the Nazis inevitably presented the military campaign as a Christian crusade against the Soviet antichrist. The war in the east helped to bond Christian opinion within the Third Reich to the Nazi war effort, while elsewhere in Europe the merging of the external struggle against the Soviet Union and the internal conflict with communist-influenced resistance groups tempted some Catholic groups into collaboration with the Nazi forces.[34]

The combination of a decline in the clerical–anticlerical disputes of the past and the resilience of Christian fears of enemies, both old and new, served to hasten the 'normalisation' of Christian politics in many European states. Root-and-branch Christian hostility to the modern political process had been declining since the end of the nineteenth century, but it disappeared almost entirely during the inter-war years. Though some Protestant sects and intransigent Catholic groups continued to reject any engagement with politics, mainstream Christianity had come to embrace not merely the necessity but also the advantages that accrued from participation in the public sphere. As a consequence, Christian politics gradually lost the exceptional or emergency character that had always tended to surround it in the pre-1914 era. Rather than irrupting periodically into the political arena in defence of a cause declared to be above or outside of politics, Christian parties moved tacitly and

---

33 E.g. T. Buchanan, 'Great Britain', in ibid., pp. 268–9.
34 Conway, *Catholic politics*, pp. 84–6.

often unconsciously towards a permanent presence in political life. Their role in local administration and in national coalition governments accustomed them, and their opponents, to regarding parties that claimed an inspiration from Christian principles as a normal element in European politics.

This process was further encouraged by the social evolution of Europe after the First World War. The expansion of the *petite bourgeoisie* of employees, traders and small businessmen, and the internal stratification of the working class between different skill groups, ethnic communities and genders, created a more graduated social landscape in which the nineteenth-century polarisation between proletariat and bourgeoisie was subsumed, or at least complicated, by a multi-polar process of negotiation between variable coalitions of social forces, each of which was also drawn into a closer relationship with the state. This more complex social framework tended to work to the advantage of Christian parties and socio-economic organisations, which were able to pose as the defenders of the interests of particular social constituencies. Christian trade unions, liberated from the paternalist straitjacket of much *fin-de-siècle* social Catholicism, expanded rapidly, especially among those workers neglected by the socialist unions. Similarly, the large Christian women's organisations developed from their spiritual and charitable origins into articulate campaigning organisations for women's interests on social and welfare issues. Above all, Christian organisations proved particularly adept from the end of the nineteenth century onwards in reaching out to new social groups who lacked an obvious home in any of the other political camps. The *kleine luyden* (small people) whom Abraham Kuyper famously sought to recruit for his Anti-Revolutionary Party in the Netherlands were an increasingly prominent presence in Christian ranks in many areas of inter-war Europe.[35] Confessional organisations designed to meet the particular needs of groups such as tenant farmers, small businessmen and white-collar employees performed a wide variety of social roles, including creating purchasing and marketing networks for farmers, organising insurance for the self-employed and distributing welfare benefits to families.

These non-religious but indispensable activities gave the Christian social and political organisations a rootedness in European life that extended beyond the rituals of faith and confessional political loyalty. Political parties were in this sense only the most visible but not necessarily the most important element of a wider process by which the Christian communities gradually took on a wide range of social, economic and cultural roles in many

---

35 Wintle, *Pillars of piety*, pp. 58–61.

European states. Churches, schools, welfare organisations, youth movements, trade unions and the flourishing Christian press were in this respect all elements of the expanding archipelago of Christian institutions that became part of the fabric of civic culture at national and local levels. This process, as we have seen, did not take place in all areas of Europe. But in the central band of territories of Catholic Europe from the Low Countries to north-eastern Italy the pillarised communities of Catholic institutions enveloped much of daily life and served as the principal intermediaries between individuals, families, communities and the wider public and economic world.

It was the all-encompassing character of the Christian institutions that ensured that they were largely resilient to changes of political regime. Neither the more state-oriented democratic culture of the Weimar Republic in Germany in the 1920s, nor the authoritarian regimes established in the inter-war years in, for example, Hungary and Austria, substantially disrupted the social role of the confessional institutions.[36] In contrast, one of the central ambitions of the fascist regime in Italy from the mid-1920s onwards and of the Nazi regime in Germany after 1933 was to bring about a radical reorientation of the relationship between the individual and the national state. For all of their other differences, the fascist and Nazi dictatorships were united by their hostility towards intermediate institutions that stood between the citizen and the ethnic or national community. Both regimes therefore sought with differing degrees of fervour and success to repress, dismantle and subsume confessional institutions and replace them with new organisations tied to the state and single governing party. This goal, however, was complicated and to some extent contradicted by the decision of both regimes to conclude treaties with the papacy that in effect confirmed the withdrawal of the Catholic church from politics while guaranteeing the church a circumscribed institutional independence within the fascist and Nazi regimes. The willingness of the papacy to sign the Lateran Treaties of 1929 and the Reich Concordat of July 1933 reflected the newfound confidence with which the papacy engaged in international diplomacy during the inter-war years; but neither treaty was able to bring to an end the underlying institutional conflict between the regimes and the churches.[37] Throughout the 1930s and the war years, the fascist and Nazi authorities pursued characteristically inconsistent policies of

36 C. Fazekas, 'Collaborating with Horthy: political Catholicism and Christian political organizations in Hungary', in Kaiser and Wohnout, *Political Catholicism*, pp. 204–11; Carsten, *Fascist movements*, pp. 279–80.
37 S. Stehlin, 'The emergence of a new Vatican diplomacy during the Great War and its aftermath, 1914–1929', in P. Kent and J. Pollard (eds.), *Papal diplomacy in the modern age*

intimidation and propagandistic attack, mixed with occasional concessions, which reflected the diversity of attitudes towards the churches within both regimes as well as the fluctuations in policy-making.

Seen in retrospect, the numerous points of institutional conflict between the Fascist and Nazi regimes and the churches could be held to demonstrate the fundamental incompatibility between fascism and Christianity. This would, however, be a misleading simplification. There was a strong ideological dimension to Christian rejection of the cult of the state and of race within Fascist and, more especially, Nazi doctrine that was reflected, for example, in the writings of the Swiss Calvinist theologian Karl Barth and the outspoken letter of Pius XI to German Catholics of 1937, *Mit brennender Sorge*. Christian activists were also prominent in individual and collective acts of dissidence within the Nazi state in Germany, such as those of the Protestant theologian Dietrich Bonhoeffer and the so-called Kreisau Circle. For most Christians within both Germany and Italy, however, their distrust of the anti-clerical temper of Fascist and Nazi propaganda went no further than occasional and cautious acts of collective protest against policies such as the euthanasia programme in Germany which were seen as particularly alien to Christian beliefs. Alongside such instances of divergence, there were also substantial points of ideological convergence and common interest. The engagement of substantial numbers of Protestant laity and clergy in the Nazi cause reflected the deeply rooted aspiration in Protestant ranks for a coming together of religion and nation. Hitler acknowledged and to some extent shared those feelings. The anti-Christian currents within Nazism were largely sidelined, at least until the ascendancy of the SS in the final years of the war, and the regime made frequent recourse to the language and symbolism of a tacitly Protestant but largely deconfessionalised Christianity. In Italy, too, the secular and anti-clerical fascism of the movement's early years gave way to a rather opportunistic courting of Catholic opinion. Despite the conflicts between church and regime that continued after the treaties of 1929, the church and many lay Catholics emphatically supported the nationalist rhetoric and expansionist foreign policy of Mussolini. Especially among those Catholic intellectuals, such as Giovanni Montini (the future Pope Paul VI), who were active in the Catholic student movement, there always remained a circumspect attitude towards the ideas and actions of fascism, but it was only in the wake of the regime's military failures

(Westport, CT and London: Praeger, 1994), pp. 75–85; J. Pollard, *The Vatican and Italian fascism 1929–1932* (Cambridge, Cambridge University Press, 1985); Lönne, 'Germany', in Buchanan and Conway, *Political Catholicism*, pp. 171–3.

from 1940 onwards that the attitudes of most Catholics moved towards a disengagement from fascism.[38]

The more complex reality of relations between Europe's Christian churches and the fascist regimes was therefore one that embraced accommodation and support as well as distrust and opposition. From this uneasy relationship it was, however, the churches that emerged as the eventual victors. Though the Nazi and Fascist revolutions eroded church independence and created a more centralised political culture in both states, they never succeeded in transforming the churches into adjuncts of the regimes. Thus, when Fascist and subsequently Nazi rule collapsed under the stimulus of military defeat, the Christian churches and affiliated organisations emerged as one of the most powerful political and social institutions of the post-fascist era. The Christian Democrats (*Democrazia Cristiana*) in Italy and the CDU (*Christlich-Demokratische Union*) and CSU (*Christlich-Soziale Union*) in the Federal Republic of Germany became the dominant political parties of the post-war era and, in so doing, were able to put a distinctively Christian stamp on the Italian and German states that emerged from the chaos of war. The Italian Republic and the Federal Republic of Germany accorded considerable independence to confessional institutions and organisations and provided a political framework in which Christian, generally Catholic, politicians occupied many of the principal positions of power.[39]

The durability of confessional milieux in Germany and Italy, but also in many other areas of non-communist Europe, during the second half of the twentieth century indicates the broader inter-connection between processes of political modernisation and Christian politics. Accounts of political modernisation in Europe over the span of the decades from the late nineteenth century to the mid-twentieth century have often been written, understandably enough, in terms of the revolutionary changes brought about by industrial growth and the extension of state power which uprooted the individual from pre-existing loyalties and communities. In some states, such as Britain, this took the form of an incremental process of political adaptation, while elsewhere, most notably in Germany, it gave rise to a series of highly dissimilar political regimes. The emphasis laid on the rapidity of change and the disruptive impacts of industrialisation and political revolution risks, however, occluding longer-term

---

38 E. C. Helmreich, *The German churches under Hitler: background, struggle and epilogue* (Detroit: Wayne State University Press, 1979); S. Baranowski, *The Confessing Church, conservative elites and the Nazi state* (Lewiston: Edwin Mellen, 1986); Steigmann-Gall, *Holy Reich* ; Pollard, 'Italy', in Buchanan and Conway, *Political Catholicism*, pp. 82–5.

39 J.-D. Durand, *L'Europe de la démocratie chrétienne* (Brussels: Complexe, 1995).

processes of adaptation and evolution. Foremost among these was the way in which Christian parties and confessional organisations succeeded in inserting themselves within the political institutions, para-statal organisations and socio-economic bodies that by the middle of the twentieth century structured and regulated the lives of Europe's citizens. This success was not universal. In France, the resilience of a political culture of republican secularism hindered the development of a specifically Catholic politics, even as confessional organisations acquired a more prominent role in many spheres of social and economic life. In Britain, the political ascendancy of the Conservative and Labour parties, buttressed by the single-member constituency electoral system, thrust religious politics to the political and geographical margins of national life. In Scandinavia, moreover, the emergence from the 1930s onwards of a dominant social democracy led the state to assume many of the social roles assumed by confessional organisations elsewhere in Europe.

There was therefore no single path to political modernisation in Europe. But in many areas of the truncated western Europe which emerged from the Second World War and which subsequently came together in the institutions of the nascent European Union Christian politics and, more generally, Christian forms of social and political organisation had an influential presence. Christian democrat parties, as well as the panoply of confessional trade unions, women's leagues and youth movements, might have had their origins in a late nineteenth-century reaction against the values of liberal modernity, but during the first half of the twentieth century they became in effect one of the most influential architects of European modernity. In national and local politics, but also more widely in the structures of socio-economic corporatism, education systems and health and welfare provision, Christian institutions were an integral element of the fabric of European states. In turn, this Christian influence was reflected in the political and social order that took shape across non-communist Europe during and after the Second World War. Obeisance to the moral tenets and outward rituals of the Christian faith remained pervasive, even as levels of religious practice waned. The panoply of established, semi-established or simply privileged churches gave European civic culture a durably Christian veneer and marginalised the power and even the visibility of Europe's other faiths. The political structures of a predominantly conservative democracy that combined parliamentary sovereignty with the devolution of many areas of responsibility to para-statal social and economic institutions reflected the imprint of Christian social and political teachings and provided many niches for Christian organisations. None of this was exclusively a Christian achievement; nor, of course, could it entirely arrest or still less reverse the impact of more subterranean processes of cultural, social and economic modernisation. In the political sphere, however, the apparent high road to secularisation evident since the middle decades of the nineteenth century had reached a terminus that in much of western Europe was more advantageous to the Christian churches than their opponents.

Latin America, c.1914–c.1950

CHRISTOPHER ABEL

Around 1914 Latin America was widely understood to be a Catholic continent, and Catholic propagandists depicted it as the beneficiary of sustained
missionary endeavour during the colonial period. This orthodoxy seemed
confirmed by national censuses, which routinely identified over 90 per cent of
the populations of various countries as Catholic. Protestant missionaries,
reaffirming these simplicities, viewed themselves as championing a heroic
struggle against 'Romish domination'. The reality was different: more subtle,
diverse and complex. The spatial impact of the Catholic church was never
uniform, being more pronounced in upland areas of relatively dense settlement than in the more sparsely inhabited lowlands. The social significance of
the Catholic church varied considerably between and within social classes
and ethnic groups. Profound and nominal commitment, indifference, suspicion and unalloyed hostility were all observed. The political influence of
Catholicism varied by nation, region and municipality, according to specific
experiences of regalism, independence and civil war, and the impact of
secularising ideologies. The direction of change in Christianity across Latin
America over the first half of the twentieth century was broadly the same, but
its pace was never uniform. Domestic trends interacted with external influences to produce a richly heterogeneous picture, which often defies general-
isation. Thus the record of the Catholic church in catechisation was patchy, as
was its distribution of institutional resources. The limits to formal Catholic
influence were observed in low rates of church marriage over vast areas. In
many dioceses more effort was invested by the bishops in obstructing
legislation for civil marriage and divorce that interested small minorities
than in assuring effective ratios of clergy to parishioners.

Several challenges confronted the church in Latin America. From c.1870 to
the World Depression (1929–33) progressive insertion of the continent into the
international economy gave rise to new processes – international and internal
migrations, urbanisation and incipient industrialisation – that profoundly

altered the demographic profile, class composition and literacy levels of Latin American populations, and exposed them to new, secular, pressures. How were Catholic leaders to respond to the organisational and pastoral implications of these trends? Catholic leaders had to take regard of pressures from the Vatican, which sought to reverse the legacy of 'Luso-Hispanisation' of the church during the colonial period, to accelerate processes of 'Romanisation', and to transform the language of universalism of the Catholic church into reality. Rome aimed to impose patterns of authority upon a mosaic of secular clergy and religious orders, many with little prior experience of institutional discipline. Countering positivistic cosmopolitanism with Catholic universalism was probably expedient; but the enforcement of norms of obedience, celibacy and the wearing of external vestments at times provoked defections and schism. The religious sincerity of rural majorities was seldom in doubt; but peasant beliefs often consisted of loose and fluid amalgams of Catholicism and Amerindian, African and Iberian 'folk' practices. Attempts to instil Catholic orthodoxies were thwarted both by shortages of clergy and by resistance – overt or concealed – from rural populations determined to conserve local symbols and identities against external interference. Anxious about questions of order, authority and discipline, the personnel of the Catholic church was often inappropriate to the task of negotiating these delicate issues and malleable relationships. Protestantism was beginning to offer alternatives. What inroads would Protestantism make in a continent where its survival depended upon laws of religious tolerance that were not always enforced?

The Catholic church and the liberal state

By 1914 the broad trend in Latin American religious history was away from crisis to the pursuit of accommodations between the liberal state and the Catholic church. Since the inception of modern banking, the church had ceased to be a major creditor and its wealth was rarely an inflammatory issue; indeed, it expanded as an employer of teachers, builders, engravers, glaziers and printworkers. Attempts to apply draconian religious sanctions – excommunication of defiant laypeople, the exercise of control over printing and film, and the burning of 'heretical' books – could give unwanted publicity to the church's critics. Yet particular issues – official harassment of the clergy, divorce reform, sex education and an assault on confessional schools – precipitated eruptions of the church into politics. Remembering the negative consequences of reducing religion to simple maxims, the church was usually careful to maintain an identity separate from the political parties.

The Vatican aimed to diffuse Catholic doctrines and values more effectively by imposing a programme of 'Romanisation'. By 1920 the Catholic church was more formally structured than hitherto. After the Plenary Council for Latin America (1899), a drive to standardise canon law and enforce disciplinary norms was launched. Rome demanded obedience from the bishops, and enjoined obedience to the bishops from the clergy. Nuncios and apostolic delegates alone served as diplomatic representatives before governments, and had the task of reporting to Rome on the condition of each diocese. The alumni of the Pontificio Collegio Latinoamericano in Rome – fifty-two bishops among them in 1925 – figured prominently among exponents of standardising trends. A reinvigorated episcopate commended new cults and revived old devotions in order to harness popular piety; and the range and volume of ecclesiastical publication grew exponentially. Measures aimed at children by Pius X – parish catechism classes, first communions and the reform of Catholic schools – followed logically from the social doctrines that Leo XIII had aimed at adults. The programme of 'Romanisation' was applied only slowly, and its overall achievement was uneven. It had a deep impact upon Argentina and southern Brazil, but little in Cuba and northern Brazil.

Anti-clericalism remained a force in Latin American societies: its scale and tenacity readily under-appreciated, but its significance easily exaggerated, except where governments and lay schoolteachers set out vigorously to instil a formal lay morality. Anti-clericals and clericals kept alive memories of bitter conflicts, and distorted, fictionalised and often decontextualised each other's positions in order to place them in as unfavourable a light as possible. While anti-clericals often misinterpreted the underlying seriousness of the clergy, clericals resorted casually to denunciations of persecution, heresy and 'Jacobinism' rather than answer genuine misgivings. On occasion a 'confessional struggle' could be a convenient diversion from other contentious issues like land reform. By 1920 anti-clericals were arguing that they wanted to restore the true spiritual mission to the church by secularising its temporal functions, and to uphold the proper prophetic role of the clergy by prohibiting its members from holding public office. Certain of these contentions slowly acquired force among senior clergy. Formal separation of church and state in Brazil (1891), Cuba (1902), Uruguay (1909) and Chile (1925) was acknowledged to have strengthened the church. (The opposite was true of Mexico and Colombia.) Some Catholic conservatives spoke wistfully of reversing the 'contagion' of the French revolution and the 'freethinking insurrection' of the independence struggles. Yet liberalism was accommodated where it extended to Catholics those freedoms – to teach, to publish, to speak, to associate – that liberals argued to be essential to the modern state. Diminishing distrust in the 1910s and 1920s foreshadowed a convergence of the populist and corporatist state with the church on the urgency of ameliorative welfare provision between the 1930s and the 1950s.

Recent writing on secularisation has dispelled simplistic schema of the 1960s that saw secularisation as a once-and-for-all process. The broad thrust of socio-economic change favoured secularisation, creating an alluring range of career opportunities – in commerce, law, medicine, engineering and architecture – for ambitious young men. The authoritarian features of Catholicism probably diverted some potential recruits to the clergy from an illiberal to the liberal professions, where more scope for initiative existed, together with better material prospects. Certain professions tended to have an anti-clerical slant, like physicians, critical of the stance of the Vatican on theories of evolution and divine revelation. Yet everyday realities muted differences: anti-clerical physicians were assisted by nurses from the women religious; and advocates of secularisation converged with proponents of Catholic renewal on the need for 'moralising' measures that fostered orderly, sanitary cities, like highhandedness against illegal distilleries and prostitution. Religious institutions and beliefs continued to assuage anxieties caused by bereavements, unemployment, hardship and warfare; to supply an explanation of mysteries where scientific analysis was incomplete or unconvincing; and to play a useful function in education, nursing, hospital management, and assistance to orphans, widows and the 'deserving' indigent. Catholicism and liberalism shared an emphasis upon social harmony, which eased moves towards co-operation, as new challenges, like anarchism and communism, acquired force. By 1930 Catholic elites set their sights on influencing secular institutions from within, seeing this as a more effective strategy for safeguarding Catholic ethics and interests than confrontation.

Starting from the assumption that the heroic missionary incursions of the Iberian colonial period had been permanently successful, the Vatican did not declare Latin America to be a mission zone again until the 1950s. Nor did Latin American dioceses receive external support: they were expected to be self-financing and to generate their own personnel. Since the fiscal autonomy of dioceses was never publicly challenged and questions of distribution were never raised, gaping disparities of income between dioceses grew, as the church enjoyed the benefits of export-led growth in prosperous regions and the poorest remained woefully impoverished. The work of Catholic missions was largely directed at Amerindian tribes inhabiting the Amazon valley and its tributaries. Conservative governments in the Andean republics revived colonial practices of hiring European, usually Spanish, orders to catechise and 'civilise' indigenous groups in 'mission territories' – vast but lightly populated expanses of tropical forest. The state delegated to the male religious extensive powers of policing, justice and public administration, which were open to abuse and hence to political censure. Embarrassed that he learnt of atrocities committed by Peruvian rubber entrepreneurs against the Putumayo Indians only because they were exposed by a British envoy, Sir Roger Casement, Pius X severely reprimanded the Capuchin missions in 1912 for failing to protect their charges from brutality. There was little evidence of a humanitarian idealism in the tradition of Bartolomé de las Casas or of a determined Catholic effort to comprehend Amerindian cultures; indeed, when secular Peruvian *indigenistas* sought to understand indigenous cultures better, they were accused of disparaging Hispanic traditions.

Latin American governments contracted European religious orders for other purposes. The Jesuits, Christian Brothers and Salesians played a valuable part in the education sector; women religious, like the Sisters of Presentation, were imported to raise the quality of nursing care and hospital management. Thus in Colombia the best male religious educators adapted to new demands for the teaching of scientific and commercial subjects and modern languages, as well as to innovations in vocational training, while the weakest over-relied on rote method and punitive discipline. The female orders were accused of placing notions of female propriety above educational standards for girls. Religious orders usually began from a powerful sense of personal vocation and a zealous commitment to a historical mission, which infused their work to positive ends; but some had a rigid, portmanteau view of society, which gave rise to an uncharitable inflexibility, excluded blacks and castigated stigmatised groups like unmarried mothers, alcoholics and vagrants. Communal purpose – care of the sick, teaching, the reception of guests and pilgrims – and a secure but austere living appealed to some idealistic youth; but strict corporate rules that stressed poverty, chastity and obedience discouraged others. Though demonisation of religious orders was less common by 1920 than sixty years before, liberal notions that monasteries were unproductive and that charity encouraged mendacity persisted. Some secular clergy, jealous of the resources and the influence of the religious, argued that structures of authority and funding that were separate from the diocese caused division in the church, and pressed for stringent diocesan inspection to ensure that the religious fulfilled their obligations. Some liberals saw the orders as secretive, subversive forces that conspired to restore a society dominated by corporate privilege and managed exclusive schools that lacked a patriotic commitment to teaching national geography and history.

The Catholic church had an ambivalent relationship with the expanding market economy, and made little effort to influence its character and direction. An adequate explanation for this failure is difficult to find. While referring ritually to doctrines on usury, Catholic leaders were loath to reopen earlier acrimonious debates about church wealth, and were compelled to accept that the church as an investor, borrower, educator and employer benefited from the better material conditions associated with capitalist growth. The bishops understandably acknowledged that debates about economic growth models lay beyond their domain and competence. But on questions of inequality and the maldistribution of the benefits of growth senior Catholics displayed a startling timidity. Absent from campaigns to abolish plantation and urban slavery in Brazil and Cuba, the church did nothing to smoothe the transition of black workers from slave to wage labour, and often to vagabondage. The leadership of campaigns to ameliorate the working and living conditions of workers in new and transformed sectors – railways, public utilities, ports, mines and, from the 1900s, oil wells – was secular. Catholic clergy were often out of touch with artisans and craftsmen threatened by deskilling, like Cuban cigar-workers, and were absent from modern enterprises outside the cities, like the Chilean copper mines and Cuban sugar mills. Because the clergy, like the new professions, often opted to live in the cities, the church was absent from transitions to agrarian capitalism. As *hacendados* became more cost-conscious, and abandoned practices of employing even tame chaplains, the influence of the church waned in many areas of 'historic' rural settlement. Meanwhile, the clergy showed little interest in new frontiers: though essential to national consciousness, Argentine *gauchos* (cowhands) do not feature in ecclesiastical archives.

The Catholic church did not insulate itself from day-to-day reality in one sector, namely factory industry, where some sustained effort was made to implement the social encyclical *Rerum novarum* issued by Leo XIII in 1891 (and restated by Pius XI in *Quadragesimo anno*, 1931). Alarmed by the rise of atheistic ideologies that proclaimed the imperative of class warfare in industrialising Catholic Europe, Leo XIII set out the responsibilities of Catholics in the manufacturing workplace and beyond. The church was to behave as a mediator promoting class collaboration, encouraging employers to recognise the need for an adequate wage for workers that underpinned stable families, and teaching workers to respect authority and family values. Social peace and harmonious industrial relations would be assured by a drive to 'humanise' capital and to 'dignify' labour, thus both mitigating the brutal excesses of an egoistic, unfettered capitalism, and obstructing the propagation of socialism, anarchism, syndicalism and communism. Catholic activists encouraged the formation of workers' circles, which pre-figured experiments with Catholic trade unionism; and nuclei of Catholic industrialists in the cities of São Paulo and Medellín adopted an entrepreneurial paternalism consonant with papal prescriptions. The social encyclicals had an impact beyond the factories and the barrios in which they were located. Urban growth brought in its wake major changes in occupational structures and class composition. New parishes were founded, and new pious groups were established, and older ones relaunched, that were targeted at women, girls, students and workers. But initiatives aimed in the 1920s at 'gaining the working classes for the social kingdom of Jesus Christ' were insufficient to forestall the emergence of radical movements; and Catholics joined other 'nationalists' in scapegoating immigrants from southern Europe. However, Catholic social policies assured the church of an urban base that extended beyond the middle class, and enabled it to project itself as a mouthpiece of wide sectors of the population. Earlier piecemeal charitable activities that seemed anachronistic in complex metropolises like Buenos Aires evolved slowly into more systematic Catholic welfarism.

The final defeat of Spain in 1898 did not sever peninsular ties with the continent; indeed, to an extent they were fortified by new flows of migrants to the Southern Cone and Cuba. The Columbus quatercentenary in 1892 prompted Spanish and Spanish American conservatives to join in proclaiming the spiritual glories of the past and diffusing a critique of Protestant 'materialism' in the United States. Aiming to hold back levelling pressures, social revolution and US influences, Catholic conservatives restated a vision of Spain as God's chosen instrument to preserve spiritual values across the world and to defend a hierarchical, organic order in her former colonies. Some cause for optimism was found by Catholic intellectuals in writings by religiously indifferent thinkers, like José Enrique Rodó, who rejected positivism and utilitarianism, but sought higher humanistic values – ideas which, reshaped, could be placed at the service of a resurgence of Catholic influence.[1] Irritated at the 'spiritual tutelage' that some Spaniards claimed to exercise, various Spanish American Catholics spoke against the *Día de la Raza* – Day of the Race – that commemorated the arrival of Columbus and was

---

1 Fredrick B. Pike, *Hispanismo: Spanish liberals and conservatives and their relations with Spanish America, 1898–1936* (Notre Dame: Louisiana State University Press, 1971).

recommended by the plenary council. As early as 1918 the Day of the Race was denounced as an ethnocentric occasion proclaiming a pride in Spanish exclusivity that was contrary to universalistic Catholic values.

Mexico

Mexico was in many respects a special case. The outbreak of the Mexican revolution in 1910 initiated a period of renewed hostility between clericals, determined to build upon gains made during the dictatorship of President Porfirio Díaz (1876–1910), and anti-clericals, insistent upon implementing the anti-clerical provisions of the 1857 constitution. Two decisions supplied anti-clericals with a rationale for reprisals and, in some parishes, pillaging and desecration of churches: first, the formation of a National Catholic Party in 1912, aiming to 're-Christianise' the state; and, secondly, the endorsement of the ruthless *caudillo* General Victoriano Huerta by Catholic leaders. Anti-clericalism was a core ingredient of the 1917 constitution, a document designed in other respects to unite the warring factions behind a drive to national reconstruction. All education was to be secular; property ownership by the church was prohibited; religious ceremonies were proscribed outside churches and homes; and state legislatures were granted the right to determine the number of clergymen. Specific features of the constitution, notably a minimum family wage, appealed to Catholic reformists, who later claimed that it had first been advocated by a Catholic congress in 1903. Official anti-clericalism prevailed at national level during the 1920s, when secularising elites closed churches and exiled clergy from some states, and fostered a short-lived schismatic church that denied the authority of Rome. In particular, central government provoked the deeply Catholic population of the states of Jalisco and Colima into mounting an armed rebellion led by guerrilla priests and laymen, in defence, as they claimed, of religious freedom. Neither the Vatican nor the archbishop of Mexico City authorised the Cristero revolt, with the consequence that the rebels received no material support from US Catholics. Yet the insurgency was quelled only slowly: a testimony to the determination of the rebels and a consequence of self-sufficiency of the region in cereals.[2] Though defeated, the Cristero rebellion reanimated Mexican Catholicism. At a state level a new, conciliatory, generation of politicians and bishops circumvented the anti-clerical provisions of the 1917 constitution, and prepared for an accommodation. Yet reconciliation was slowed down

---

2 Jean A. Meyer, *The Cristero rebellion: the Mexican people between church and state 1926–1929*, trans. Richard Southern (Cambridge: Cambridge University Press, 1976).

both by anti-clericals, who, denouncing the obstacles posed by Catholics to a transition from laicism to socialism in the education sector, demanded an official campaign of 'defanaticisation', and by clericals, forming a secret lay organisation that campaigned vigorously against 'Jacobin' school-inspectors. Amidst a climate of conspiracy, civil war was rumoured; yet social Catholics worked to restrain reactionaries, and pragmatic revolutionaries to curb anti-clerical excesses. Though President Lázaro Cárdenas (1934–40) is usually credited with the Modus Vivendi of 1937, by which basic proprieties between church and state were restored, recent historiography argues that the ground was prepared at state level. While the ruling party was no longer denounced by the church as atheistic and communist and the church endorsed the decision of the government to nationalise foreign-owned oil wells, tensions persisted. The Holy See approved the opening of a seminary for exiled Mexican ordinands in the United States; and in the early 1940s the Sinarquista movement aimed to revive the uncompromising spirit of the Cristeros. The long-term trend was towards convergence: President Manuel Avila Camacho (1940–6) declared he was a believer, and met with bishops at public ceremonies; and the bishops dismantled the Catholic Students move-ment when it threatened to defy their pragmatism. The beginning of the Cold War presaged a new era, in which the ruling party tolerated a dissenting minority party that represented Catholics and regional interests against secularism and centralism, and a Catholic university was founded.

Brazil

On the transition from the Second Empire to the First Republic in 1889, the Brazilian church was notoriously weak, smothered by an anti-clerical, ration-alist state, which was backed by new professional elites like military engineers who rejected Catholic humanistic culture. Owing to separation of church and state the church began to recover influence under the First Republic: the number of dioceses quintupled between 1889 and 1920, and the number of seminaries rose too; convents were reopened, and new religious orders took shape. The main figure in this revival was Sebastiao Leme de Silveira Cintra, who became archbishop coadjutor of Rio de Janeiro (1921–30) and then cardinal archbishop of Rio (1930–42). Viewing Brazil as an essentially Catholic country, where, paradoxically, the church had little influence in politics, the arts, literature or with the intelligentsia, Leme adopted a pressure-group approach aimed at the 're-Christianisation of Brazil'. This involved fierce opposition to the principle of free enquiry and its advocates like the freemason lodges of Pernambuco and São Paulo. Regaining what Leme considered to be the rightful place of the church involved a long-term strategy with implications for its relationships with the civil and military authorities, as well as for the internal organisation of the church. Two acts in 1931 symbolised a restoration of institutional self-confidence and a partial reconnection of the official church with popular devotion: the building of the statue of Christ on Corvocado Hill in Rio to 'control popular passions'; and the triumphant procession of Our Lady of Aparecida from her shrine to the city of Rio, where, accompanied by one million people and attended by the state authorities, she was proclaimed 'Patroness of Brazil' by Leme.[3] From 1921 Leme gave encouragement to an increasingly dense network of lay associations, notably the JOC (Catholic Youth Workers' movement), which was committed to 'conquering and converting young workers' and stressed the urgency of decent wages, social justice, concern for the poor and limited political participation. Leme also gave his blessing to the Centro Dom Vital which, launched by a prominent layman and former atheist, Jackson de Figuereido, set out to expand church influence among urban intellectuals through a new magazine *A ordem*, which linked the thinking of Jacques Maritain and Georges Bernanos to Brazilian daily life and liturgy. The Brazilian Catholic church specifically singled out anarchism for anathematisation, probably exaggerating the appeal of its vision of restoring the 'peaceful happiness' of primitive societies and the significance of its challenge to church-sanctioned marriage contracts. Catholic leaders were offended that anarchists appropriated some religious language and assumptions, resented anarchist declarations of 'war' against Catholicism as an immoral deviation like alcohol and tobacco, and were angered that anarchists identified the Vatican with London and New York as imperialist capitals that perpetuated private property and subverted principles of justice and social equality. When Catholic leaders set out to weaken anarchist trade unions by founding a Centro Operário Católico for Catholic workers, anarchists accused the church of co-ordinating a reign of terror with the civil authorities and foreign business. Leme ostentatiously demonstrated his support for Catholic unions by officiating at their public masses twice on May Day: in 1929, and again in 1931.

Where did women fit into this picture? Urban expansion revived Catholic fears of a chaotic liberation of social mores and, especially, a dangerous 'emancipation of the modern woman', as the Catholic ideal of the woman as an unworldly domestic recluse became increasingly unrealistic. Catholic publicists debated questions of honour: in particular, the priority of upholding

---

3 L. P. R. Gabaglia, *O Cardeal Leme 1882–1942* (Rio de Janeiro: Livraria José Olympio, 1962).

a conservative view of 'civilisation' that rested upon the maintenance of social differences and of codes of honour that linked patriarchal authority to female restraint and sexual purity. One Brazilian feminist argued for divorce on the grounds that problems for women and families arose from the hypocrisy and despair inherent in indissoluble marriage, and needled the clergy by asking why Catholic beliefs were so shallow that they could not withstand 'matrimonial disillusionment'. In the 1920s the Catholic church, stung by allegations that it was a misogynist institution, went on to the offensive against secular feminists. Arguing that Catholic teachings and the sacrament of marriage elevated women and protected female honour, male Catholic leaders reiterated the teaching of St Augustine of Hippo on the sanctity of virginity, and stressed the principle of *pudor* (honour/shame) as the foundation of public morality. Endorsing the publication of a magazine for women that stressed family life and religious morality, the bishops went on to encourage a militantly anti-feminist organisation among Catholic lay-women, who worked to shore up Catholic marriage, to replace outmoded forms of charity with social assistance, and to mobilise women from 'good families' to embark on systematic tutelage of poor women.

The Catholic church welcomed the incipient business welfarism prac-tised by some industrial entrepreneurs, who, influenced by Fordism and Taylorism, aimed to combine goals of efficiency and productivity with cohesion at the workplace, through modest concessions – shops, canteens and recreational facilities, plus hygienic housing and schooling – that were offered to loyal workers and their families. Following the assertion of Pius XI that the worst scandal of the century was that the church had lost the working class, Catholic leaders hoped that business paternalism would be imbued by an ethos of class co-operation. One textiles entrepreneur in São Paulo tried in the early 1920s to create the image of the mill as an extended Catholic family, where social distances between employer and worker were reduced, but distinctions were nevertheless carefully conserved. He acted as godparent to the children of workers, helped to finance Holy Week commemorations, opened a workplace chapel and sponsored open-air masses on a soccer pitch. Young women workers were encouraged to attend night courses on personal behaviour that were run by nuns, and to compete for the honour of playing the role of Veronica or one of the three Marys in the Good Friday afternoon vigil. However, the priest on the factory payroll was soon sacked for ignoring patronal warnings that workers were insufficiently educated to distinguish the teachings of Leo XIII from those of communism. The limits to the effectiveness of Catholic paternalistic measures were indicated by the reluctance of other industrialists to take them up. Strategies of forming employer confederations that called in police help and blacklisted labour militants probably proved cheaper and more effective in handling an incipient culture of workplace militancy.

The 1930s and 1940s

The crisis of the World Depression (1929–33) had profound consequences for Latin America – hunger, hardship, unemployment, debt. National responses varied considerably; but the overall trend of Latin American states was towards pragmatic experiment, economic intervention and social collectivism. Acknowledging the scale and intensity of the crisis, the Catholic church was better organised than before, and aimed in various countries to complement state welfare initiative. The process of accommodation between state and church was hastened, because the proponents of the economic individualism that the church had condemned most vigorously were forced on to the defensive. Crisis compelled both state and church to retrench and to reappraise fiscal priorities in primary schooling and social welfare provision; and pragmatic deals were struck between Catholic and secular agencies to assure the survival of essential urban social services.

During the trough of the World Depression elements in the upper classes and middle classes panicked, fearful that the swollen ranks of the urban unemployed would form the vanguard of social revolution. Overlooking the problems of crisis-ridden village communities, various bishops exhorted the urban unemployed to return to their rural roots – with little success. But, as the continent slowly recovered from the Depression, so the Catholic church reacquired its moorings, and staged a series of national religious spectacles – eucharistic congresses. The Catholic Church used these to identify itself as a centrepiece of *patria*, to counter liberal accusations that it commanded allegiances that superseded those to the nation, and to reaffirm the role of religion in ordering lives and restraining sensuality. While recoiling from mass society and displaying a revulsion for incipient mass politics and a distaste for racial intermixture, the church was not averse to promoting mass religiosity. During the 1930s and 1940s the church displayed some impressive intellectual ferment and social activism, and enjoyed one little-observed advantage in its dealings with the state: the staffing of the church was more stable and continuous than that of many insecure regimes.

Catholic intellectuals, especially Jesuits, set out to persuade laymen that they should promote political schema in keeping with Catholic priorities of hierarchy, authority, obedience and security. Contending that disorder and instability were inherent in liberal democracies founded upon individualistic and pluralistic principles, the Jesuits advocated corporatist models of state and society, in which intermediary associations would safeguard the individual from overweening state control. They proposed constitutional arrangements by which responsible organic corporations – the military, church, producer and merchant organisations, and guilds (i.e., Catholic unions) would be represented in a national legislative body, together with paterfamilias of mature age. Portugal and Austria were extolled as the archetypes of well-regulated corporatist states, where the *sanas costumbres* (healthy customs) of a deferential peasant society prevailed, and the Catholic church played a full and proper part in political life. In no Latin American country were corporatist ideas implemented in full; but their influence was seen in several, notably during the Brazilian *Estado Nôvo* (1937–45) of President Getúlio Vargas, and the Colombian authoritarian conservatism of President Laureano Gómez (1950–3). Meanwhile, in Argentina the fall of the Radicals in 1930 ushered in over a decade when the influence of Catholics with government grew. Interpreting Argentina more as a nation of displaced Europeans than of Latin Americans, one Catholic faction argued that, with liberalism at bay, the time had come to reverse the consequences of the Enlightenment and the Reformation, and to restore an idealised Middle Ages – hieratic, static and European.[4]

Other Catholic intellectuals recoiled from theocratic yearnings and utopian pipedreams, saw constitutional experiments as mistimed when regime decomposition looked imminent, and looked to practical solutions to immediate problems.

Many Catholic bishops strove to give more effective leadership and organisation to the laity through Catholic Social Action. Countering secular educational initiatives, notably the 'pragmatic' pedagogy of the American New School movement of John Dewey, the church overhauled its networks of primary and secondary schools. It also aimed to expand its influence in secular society by opening Catholic universities that were manned by Catholic clergy and lay professors. Bold in its educational programmes, the church trod more cautiously with Catholic trade unions and peasant organisations for fear that militant laymen or maverick clergy might hijack policy and unleash uncontrollable popular mobilisations. Transmitting an ethos of

---

4 Austen Ivereigh, *Catholicism and politics in Argentina, 1810–1960* (Basingstoke: Macmillan, 1995).

activism carried acknowledged risks. Because the Catholic church lacked the resources to respond to many social problems, its leaders usually welcomed the slow transitions from state public assistance via social insurance to social security that occurred between the 1920s and the 1960s. These seemed to reinforce stable family units and enable households to evolve strategies that combined self-help, philanthropic assistance and public provision. Although the principles behind social security provision seldom ran contrary to Catholic social doctrines, official welfare provision contained one inherent defect: it was targeted at strategic organised groups, in particular the urban constituencies of populist and other regimes. By failing to press emphatically for a clear sequence of moves towards universal provision, the Catholic church opened itself to charges of over-identification with the constituencies of urban-based government, and of favouring organised sectors at the expense of the poor.

Having seen the value to his opponent of religious slogans like 'God, Country and Family' in the Integralist Manifesto of 1930, President Getúlio Vargas of Brazil gave Cardinal Leme new opportunities. Presiding initially over a populist regime in which he attempted to reconcile most organised groups, Vargas, an agnostic, left space for the church to influence socio-political change. The 1934 constitution embodied demands made by the Catholic Electoral League, founded in 1932. Separation of church and state no longer precluded the presence of the name of God in the preamble to the constitution or state subventions for Catholic schools. Catholic family values were upheld by state assistance to large families, the indissolubility of marriage for civil purposes, and the opportunity for parents to opt for religious instruction in state schools. The church was also allowed a presence in the military establishment. The overall strategy of Leme was to modify the 'secularist' complexion of the state, and enter pragmatic alliances with particular groups, like trade unions, on specific issues like Sunday rest-days.

The Brazilian *Estado Nôvo* embodied a corporatist vision of reimposing the social mores and structures that had supposedly existed thirty years before. The church worked energetically to reinstate lessons in religion, traditional discipline and rote learning in public schools, and to enforce differential curricula for girls and boys. The church succeeded in imposing moral censorship of the cinema. And Catholic conservatives played an essential part in reversing feminist gains of the early 1930s – votes for women, female control of family policy, and equal pay and equal access to public employment. The church was identified with conservative priorities of enshrining notions of women's and family honour in legislation. Co-opting Integralist language of purity, piety and the natural roles of each sex, Catholic propagandists looked to social institutions that protected the Brazilian family from 'degradation'. Family values and traditional gender roles ordained by God were reclaimed by funding special programmes for the health of mothers and children from taxes imposed upon single adults and childless married couples. Thus church and state collaborated in the restructuring of patriarchy, the modernisation of gender inequality and the resubordination of women. The late 1930s witnessed the greatest point of church influence in Brazil since independence. From the mid-1940s this was less evident, and the church was over-reliant on state support. Catholic Action withered, trapped in networks of official patronage. Brazilian Catholic Action was built on an inappropriate Italian model – corporate, centralised and authoritarian – which left little scope for diocesan and parochial initiative.

A broader crisis loomed: international warfare. No one could predict that Latin America would be the continent least scarred by warfare between 1914 and 1945. The Spanish civil war had a profound impact upon Hispanic American clergy, the intelligentsia and labour leaders; and the Mexican government of President Lázaro Cárdenas (1934–40) opened its doors generously to Spanish Republican exiles, prompting Catholic fears of a new wave of anti-clericalism. However, the left across Latin America was anxious to avoid violent conflicts that might culminate in a government along Francoist lines; and, while powerful Catholic factions favoured an authoritarian right-wing regime, most Catholic leaders preferred to conciliate secular regimes, none of which caused as much alarm as the Spanish Second Republic. The Second World War gave rise to other anxieties. Concerned that Pan-Americanism might conceal Protestant expansion, Catholic churchmen in Latin America regarded alliances with the United States cautiously. The government of President Franklin Delano Roosevelt propagated a 'good neighbour' policy of hemispheric unity against fascism and Nazism, and welcomed Catholic condemnations of the idolatry, paganism and pseudo-mysticism of Nazism and fascism. Left-leaning New Dealers in Washington feared the potential of Spanish legations as hotbeds of fifth-column activism, which encouraged a climate of subversion among military, ecclesiastical and civilian conservatives. These fears were mostly exaggerated, though one Colombian archbishop was removed to Spain after the exposure of his role in a gun-running network from Buenos Aires that aimed to overthrow a Liberal government. In the early 1940s small circles of right-wing clergy joined with civilian and military conservatives to celebrate Spanish racial pride and to reassert the superiority of Hispanic culture over 'Anglo-Saxon', the Catholic over the Protestant, and the Spanish colonial period over the republican. Given the economic and political weakness of Spain, fantasies of a supranational collectivity of *hispanidad* were dismissed as vapid lyricism by the professional and commercial groups at whom they were aimed.

Protestantism

Protestantism posed a less significant challenge to Catholicism in Latin America than secularising trends, and had fewer adherents than indigenous and black religions. The defeat of Spain in the war of 1898 confirmed US mission leaders in their providential duty to 'arrest the downward trend of degenerate races' that were steeped in 'superstition and paganism' by undertaking an 'evangelical enterprise' which would liberate Cuba, Puerto Rico (and the Philippines) from the 'yoke' of Catholic 'obscurantism', and would instil qualities of honesty, sobriety, thrift and industriousness where these were absent. The modest and paternalistic reformism of the Social Gospel that stressed 'Christianisation' through education, medicine and technology proved consistent with the broad thrust of US policy towards northern Latin America. A missionary impetus from the United States was complemented by a secondary impetus from radical (often provincial) elites in Latin America, especially in Mexico and Guatemala, that had debated from the 1860s whether Catholicism constituted a deadweight on society and whether Protestantism would shape more dynamic, democratic cultures. Certain Protestant missionaries extolled the Baptist millionaire John D. Rockefeller as an exemplary capitalist, whose foundation promoted an ideology of public service, managerial rationalism and 'scientific philanthropy', and was praised by prominent Latin American Catholics.

By the 1920s Protestantism was observed among immigrant German Lutheran congregations in Brazil, Chile and Argentina, and made headway in some frontier zones of Brazil, Mexico and Cuba, where Catholic institutions were notoriously weak. Polemics between Catholics and Protestants thrived upon wilful misrepresentations of the sincerity of the other. For ardent Protestants, Protestantism embodied a set of cultural values – freedom, progress, equality, individual conscience, peace and entrepreneurship – which clashed with those of Catholicism – authority, reaction, hierarchy, organicism and militarism. Catholic conservatives with a teleological view of history contended that the denial of papal authority by Protestants during the Reformation had fomented a sequence of subversive challenges to 'civilised' values. US 'Protestant imperialism' was now added to the Enlightenment, the

French revolution, liberalism, freemasonry, atheism, socialism, anarchism and communism as a source of rebellion against constituted authority. On occasion polemic spilled over into violence, notably in upland Colombia.[5] However, oppression was not the main obstacle to Protestant success. Many Latin Americans interpreted denominational differences – between Methodists, Baptists, Quakers, Presbyterians – as evidence of sectarianism, and were confused by debates within the Protestant churches over the proper balance between education and evangelism. The Pentecostalists were accused of poaching converts from their Protestant rivals; and breakaway fundamentalist missions multiplied in the 1920s following the rift between modernists and fundamentalists in the United States. The overall achievement of Protestantism was limited: in Mexico and Cuba less than 1 per cent of the population was Protestant in 1940 and 1942 respectively. Indeed, by the 1950s Protestants were open to the criticism that they had levelled against Roman Catholicism half a century before: they neglected the countryside.

Perspectives

The position mid-century was ambiguous. By 1950 Catholic leaders were more concerned with influence through lobbying, public ceremonies and pressures exerted by the laity than with formal power. The Catholic church had kept abreast with various needs of sections of the middle class and of organised labour, and its educational institutions were firmly established. Anti-clericalism had declined, but not died; and, in one sense, the church lost by its decline. In periods of intense conflict between church and anti-clericals, church–state relations had been in continuous flux and constantly refashioned; but by 1950 routinised patterns of church–state co-operation posed a threat of stagnation. It seemed that the *estado cartorial* (the paper-shuffling state) had found its natural complement, the paper-shuffling church, with inert structures, little concern for extending its outreach, policies devised from above, a preoccupation with constitutional formalities and social palliatives, and a timidity bordering upon indifference to humanitarian issues and social deprivation.

The problem around 1950 was not a changing tenor of debate, but the absence of debate within the Catholic church, even on limited issues like making marriage more affordable. Paranoid that any relaxation of controls

---

5 Christopher Abel, *Política, iglesia y partidos en Colombia* (Bogotá: FAES/Universidad Nacional de Colombia, 1987).

might open the floodgates to communism, the church refrained from public discussion of rights, whether political, civil, human or social, contenting itself with occasional allusions to an aversion to capitalism. Catholic leaders spoke of the church as a guide to authoritative doctrine, insisted on juridically defined roles, and took comfort from the organisational changes of the past fifty years. The bishops enjoyed a close rapport with certain patronage-ridden regimes; and co-option prevented them from criticising extreme right-wing regimes in Nicaragua and the Dominican Republic. The adoption of a fortress mentality was misplaced in countries where socialism, atheism, freemasonry, Protestantism and communism had few adherents, and where an edifice of religion, tradition and authority was not crumbling. A language of inclusiveness, with membership of the Catholic church open to all repentant sinners, was observed only in the breach. Paradoxically, the Catholic church was most successful when it behaved as a vigorous voluntary association; yet so often it aspired to be a privileged entity. Indeed, it was seldom a self-aware institution that admitted its shortcomings, energetically recruited indigenous and black clergy, or carried its mission confidently to the urban slums and shanty towns. Protestantism, meanwhile, had failed to fill many gaps left by Catholicism.

The conditions for change were manifest: massive population growth, urbanisation, a crisis of vocations, and a better-educated laity. There was little evidence that the Catholic church was ready to confront the changes of the post-1945 period, or, indeed, that the Vatican acknowledged that its largest constituency lay outside Europe. Dom Helder Câmara, whose archdiocese of Recife (Brazil) had more in common with the absolute poverty of sub-Saharan Africa than with the more prosperous regions of Latin America, later recalled of the years around 1950: 'Our job was to preach patience, obedience and the acceptance of suffering in union with Christ. Great virtues, no doubt. But in that context we were simply tools of the authorities.'[6] Preoccupied by the Cold War, Catholic leaders were more concerned with the political containment of Latin American populations than with their basic needs.

6 Dom Helder Câmara, *The conversions of a bishop*, an interview with José de Broucker (London: Collins, 1977), p. 172.

African Christianity: from the world wars to decolonisation

OGBU U. KALU

Introduction

An exciting event occurred in 1969 when the pope visited Uganda. He told his hosts that 'you must have an African Christianity. Indeed, you possess human values and characteristic forms of culture which can rise up to be capable of a richness of expression of its own, and genuinely African.'[1] The audience was stunned, as if he were reversing the story of centuries of European relationship with Africa; as if he were proclaiming release from a relationship that suffocated in favour of one that recognised the pluralistic context of mission. It was as if Europeans finally acknowledged that after many years of missionary presence, an African expression of Christianity had emerged. That speech turned attention from patterns of insertion to modes of appropriation and their consequences, especially as the numbers of Christians in Africa had grown enormously. Perhaps being a musical people, African responses to the pope's declaration could be traced in various liturgical initiatives and musical symbols. It meant that the story of African encounter with the gospel should privilege African initiatives and yet be told in an ecumenical and irenic manner.

But this growth pattern was not so obvious in 1914 when the drums of war summoned Europeans to far-flung trenches. No African was invited to the Edinburgh Conference of 1910. Western missionary interest was in India, Japan and China. Within Africa, missionary presence was characterised by enclavement strategy, social distance and vocational dominance, and interracial relationships were quite strained. Many Africans assumed that the war was a white man's war and wondered why they could not forgive each other. They soon realised that the Anglo-French attacks on

---

1 Gaba Pastoral Letter 7 (1969), 50–1.

German colonies in Africa would implicate over half a million Africans as soldiers and many millions more as hapless porters and fodder. The First World War drastically reshaped the interior of African Christianity. But before the drums of war, the religious landscape was suffused with the din of Ethiopians who gave voice to African discontent and dared to exit from the white man's church to initiate gospel expressions that would be authentically African. By 1914 their relevance was increasingly ebbing, albeit with regional differences; indeed, the period 1914–1939 heard the swan song of Ethiopianism. A number of reasons could be adduced. Among Africans in the diaspora, a broader Pan-African ideology gained prominence. In central Africa, Chilembwe's failed rebellion in 1915 yielded the premier place to Roman Catholics and caused scandal by the murderous and chiliastic turn of Ethiopian spirituality. In South Africa, the politics of the inter-war years, characterised by an intense Afrikaner nationalism, land-grabbing and political engineering, elicited an overtly political response from Africans beyond the ken of religious entrepreneurs. A similar shift from cultural to political nationalism occurred in west Africa as political parties emerged. In eastern Africa, the space may have widened for African agency in the church but white settlers garnered many economic and political dividends in the aftermath. The settlers benefited from the weakness at the home bases of missions. Untoward geopolitical forces, such as rumours of war, wars, economic collapse, political instability and the rise of anti-Christian communist and totalitarian ideologies, were followed by another six-year war. All these affected missionary presence and structures by 1945. Some contemplated massive restructuring and downsizing in recognition of the new-fangled self-confidence of the 'younger churches'.

Ironically, missionary structures showed a high degree of resilience in the inter-war years as 'internationalism' became a new war cry that spurred young university students into the mission fields. Indeed, a process of domesticating the Christian values and hymns intensified between 1919 and 1950. The process was aided by two other factors, namely the outbreak of an ecumenical spirit, detectable in various assemblies of the International Missionary Council, and the formation of national councils of churches. But it was education and its mass appeal that rescued the missionary enterprise and ensured its recovery after the First World War.

Beyond the pursuit of 'white power' or literacy, African Christian initiative could be traced through the choruses of Spiritual churches, whether they were called Zionists, *Aladura* or *Roho*. As Ethiopianism lost its glow, Africans showed a stronger charismatic initiative which spread from urban areas into rural enclaves. The literature has burgeoned as interpretations multiply. It has been suggested that these constitute an African Christian initiative and contribution to world Christianity, with immense creativity on the gospel–culture interface; that they are a poignant reaction to colonial Christianity, or a religion of the oppressed, resembling cargo cults; that they reflect the quest for belonging, safe havens amidst white racism, or an emergent syncretistic spirituality; that they are based on exploitation of the schismatic character of Protestantism; or that they are the religious aspect of a nascent political nationalism, offering succour to displaced peoples amidst increased urbanisation. A few have profiled an indigenous brand of Pentecostalism and a theological response to the missionary gospel, albeit one that privileged *Christus Victor*.

As a pneumatic response to the gospel, the spiritual flares proliferated in the immediate aftermath of the First World War. Was there a connection with the post-war environment? Obviously, the surge was aided by the translation of the message into indigenous languages to renew interest in those elements that the missionary message ignored or muted. They mined the biblical resonance with indigenous worldviews. Their astounding popularity engendered persecution. It should be noted that there were three different types of charismatic responses to the gospel message in these times. Individual prophets burst into the scene and left; these were different from the Spiritual churches that mushroomed as competitors to mission churches. Early Pentecostalism can be traced with growing significance between 1906 and 1945. A spiritual wind in the 1970s gave it more prominence but unknown tongues featured prominently in African Christian spirituality before the decolonisation blues of the 1960s.

By the mid-1950s a tired Europe was compelled by many negative forces to trim sails. Debates abound over the causes and nature of decolonisation: whether it was a dishevelled process, a creative enterprise or a passive revolution. Does the transfer of power or the change of rulers constitute *uhuru*? Missionary attitudes gyrated because the protagonists were products of mission schools: some were opposed, arguing that the 'children' had not sufficiently matured to govern themselves; others were in support; still others devised a new strategy of ministerial formation to train indigenous priests, liaise with prominent laity and waltz with nationalists in the hope of securing the influence cultivated over the years. The music would later turn staccato as one-party states jettisoned colonial constitutions and disengaged themselves from Christian roots. No prophecy in the heady politics of decolonisation could have revealed the trend because missionary bodies pretended to be different from colonial governments; thus, decolonisation in the churches took much longer as the cry for indigenisation turned into strident calls for moratorium. When the General Assembly of the World Council of Churches met in Nairobi in 1975, the choice of venue was as significant as the speech of the pope in Kampala in 1969.

The aim of this chapter is to explore these seven themes that shaped the emergence of an African Christianity during the turbulent years of 1914 to 1975, with an eye on periodisation and regional coverage. It is argued that from the drums of war in 1914, the swan songs of the Ethiopians gave place to the early morning calls of prophets, the gusty choruses of Spiritual churches and the unknown tongues of early Pentecostals. Still, millions of Africans sang Western hymns and psalms of unity. The Second World War finally reconfigured the colonial landscape. Indigenisers boldly insisted on beating African drums in churches. Missionaries adjusted to the changing circumstances, ordained indigenous priests and waltzed with political nationalists before the tune turned staccato. A massive growth of Christianity in Africa ensued in this period and would escalate thereafter, driven by a charismatic wind. The explosion of Christianity in contemporary Africa occurred after the missionary period but it is rooted in the charismatic activity that started in the inter-war years.

Drums of war and the swan song of Ethiopianism, 1914–1939

One dimension of the war environment was the role of rumours and the conflation of rumours with reality to inflame the populace. When the war broke out, it was rumoured among Africans that the rule of the whites was about to end. Colonial officials became quite apprehensive about security, control and the threat of rebellion. Provincial commissioners urged the district officers to keep files on intelligence reports about potential flash points and individuals. This increased the tension between the colonial governments and the communities. On the religious front, it exacerbated the relationship with Ethiopianism, which was perceived as a form of black nationalism with a religious stroke. Its connections with African American missionary enterprise to Africa made it doubly suspicious, spurred on by some confusion with Watch Tower's anti-authoritarian posture. As James Campbell argued for South Africa, 'the concept of Black America retained an imaginative potency among Africans ... Moreover, the African Methodist Episcopal Church remained enmeshed within a system of racial domination in which the very essence of a black-run church could assume profound political significance.'[2] In Malawi, it was rumoured that an invading army of black Americans had arrived at Karonga as messiahs who would make Africans rich, educated and respected.[3] When one of Simon Kimbangu's songs referred to the change of baton and encouraged devotees: 'Be brave, the kingdom is ours. We have it! They, the whites, no longer have it. None of us shall be discouraged,' the Belgian rulers of the Congo perceived treason rather than a theological affirmation.[4] In Zimbabwe the African Orthodox church, which had roots in Marcus Garvey's ideology, elicited negative responses.[5] Some district officers warned about a renaissance of secret societies as an anti-white bonding. Colonial governments dreaded the competition to rational administrative structures by religious power nodes as secret societies and oracles.

Beyond rumours, the war further heightened tension within African communities because it required the services of recruits and porters and gave the local chiefs extraordinary powers to mobilise able-bodied men. In Kenya, some men escaped into the bush to avoid recruitment; others devised the subterfuge of conversion and moved into missionary enclaves/stations in large numbers, to the initial delight of missionaries. Soon all devices collapsed as missionaries themselves were compelled to engage in the affray.[6] The First World War severely disrupted the structure and moral economy of the missionary enterprise in Africa.

The location of the four centres of German colonies implicated all of Africa and determined the number of recruits demanded from various regions: Kenya, Uganda and South Africa supplied over 40,000 soldiers for the Tanzanian front; Zambia, Malawi and Zaire yielded 18,000 for the Namibian, Rwandan and Burundi fronts; and West African countries provided several thousands to serve in Togo and Cameroon. Madagascar mobilised 45,000 men, euphemistically termed 'volunteers', to serve in Europe.[7] But it was the demand for millions of porters (*tenga-tenga*) that disrupted

---

2 James Campbell, 'African American missionaries and the colonial state: the AME church in South Africa', in H. B. Hansen and M. Twaddle (eds.) *Christian missionaries and the state in the third world* (Oxford: James Currey, 2002), p. 234.
3 Ian Linden, *Catholics, peasants, and Chewa resistance in Nyasaland, 1889–1939* (Berkeley: University of California Press, 1974), p. 95.
4 Marie-Louise Martin, *Kimbangu* (Oxford: Blackwell, 1975).
5 Michael O. West, 'Ethiopianism and colonialism: the African Orthodox church in Zimbabwe, 1924–34', in Hansen and Twaddle, *Christian missionaries*, pp. 237–54.
6 A. J. Temu, *British Protestant missions* (London: Longmans, 1972), p. 117.
7 Bengt Sundkler and Christopher Steed, *A history of the church in Africa* (Cambridge: Cambridge University Press, 2000), pp. 610–15.

African communities and missionary work and caused so much suffering. The irony is that it betrayed a gap between the missionary message and ethics, especially as it appeared to compromise missionaries who organised the cruel system and press-ganged potential converts, sometimes employing trickery. As Ian Linden put it:

> As in England, recruiting officers passed through the villages with drums banging and trumpets blaring. If interest in joining the band failed to bring unsuspecting Africans from their huts, promises of huge financial rewards were made. Chiefs welcomed the opportunity to get rid of awkward villagers and would direct army officers to their huts. Africans were tricked and press-ganged into joining a war in which they had no stake or interest.[8]

The bishop of Zanzibar, Frank Weston, organised thousands in Tanzania; J. W. Arthur of the Church of Scotland mission recruited 1,750 Kikuyu members of the Mission Carrier Corps who served nine months in Southern Tanganyika.[9] Many died from poor feeding, arduous trekking and poor medical care. It was a war where more porters died than soldiers. Missionaries (priests and nuns) became soldiers in the transport, supplies and medical units and performed a number of mundane tasks for the governments, leaving parishes without pastoral care. Indigenous people had the unenviable opportunity of carrying on the task. The lice they searched for in their hair just dropped on their feet. Meanwhile, Germans expelled priests from Allied countries and German missionaries were deported or incarcerated in many British and French colonies. The war disrupted the supplies, mail, and funds of missions. At the end, the ecclesiastical map of Africa was redrawn as German missionary societies lost their stations and had to face a harsh inter-war period that left them at the mercy of other European countries. Missionaries learnt to source locally for sustainability, relying more than before on indigenous resources for mission work.

Ethiopians, as cultural and religious nationalists, were muzzled. Thus, when Chilembwe rebelled in 1915, he betrayed the helpless frustration of Africans who were compelled to join a war that did not make sense. An anecdote tells of a befuddled Cameroonian suggesting that whites should shoot whites and blacks shoot fellow blacks during an Anglo–German battle. As Chilembwe watched the massive carnage of Africans, he predicted that after the war, blacks would have little to show for their sufferings and whites

---

8 Linden, *Catholics, peasants and Chewa resistance*, p. 109.
9 Temu, *British Protestant Missions*, p. 118.

would continue to disrespect them; he attacked the nearest white compound. Conjectures abound about this variety of Ethiopianism but it was the swan song of a movement that had its internal varieties but served as a form of African agency designed to regain the initiative on the political and religious fronts and create an African response to the gospel that was unique and not controlled by whites. Linden argues that before the rebellion, the Catholic Montfort fathers at nearby Nguludi respected the dignified Chilembwe who was a role model of African 'elevation'. But his defeat and the Allied victory in the war created a new dispensation that made Chilembwe less than a prophet.

He was right that Africans may have grabbed the wrong end of the stick; he was right that many more Africans would turn to violent rebellion out of frustration. George Shepperson computed seven such cases between 1906, when the last Zulu Bambata rebellion occurred, and 1927.[10] But other Ethiopians pursued a different route and their form of Christianity grew. Regional conditions mattered. In west Africa, the movement grew in the midst of the strong racial antipathy that followed the war. In the 1921 census in Nigeria, the critical mass of the six branches of Ethiopian churches constituted the third largest Christian form. More importantly, missionaries increased in numbers, revamped their structures, and employed education as a tool; Africans responded massively. Ethiopians had to intensify their educational programmes in competition. But neither the Young Kikuyu nor the Harrists, Christ Army church/Garrick Braidists or Native African churches could mobilise enough resources for the cost-intensive enterprise amidst the Great Depression whose effects reverberated into the colonies. Western missions defeated the Ethiopians on this front. But Africans initiated new spiritualities that took on a charismatic character and challenged missionary Christianity.

Catechisms and hymns: the domestication of missionary Christianity, 1919–1945

The end of the war was fraught with ambiguities: Africans tasted a dose of responsibility in the churches and in the survival of the colonial states. But in southern and eastern Africa, the British government felt more grateful to white settlers and rewarded them with enlarged political clout, land and

---

10 George Shepperson, 'Ethiopianism: past and present', in C. G. Baeta (ed.) *Christianity in tropical Africa* (London: Oxford University Press, 1968), p. 253.

labour. The Ex-Soldiers' Settlement Scheme settled many veterans in Kenya with huge acreages of land; they demanded that taxation should be used to pry Africans into a plantation labour force where low wages would keep them vulnerable. Only a few missionary voices, such as J. H. Oldham's, protested against forced labour and heavy taxation. The *kipande* or identity card system was imposed on the indigenous people in 1919 as a reward for being such helpful *tenga-tenga*. Missions turned their attention to education so as to supply settlers 'with trained boys, clerks, artisans and hospital dressers', as an honest Scot admitted.[11]

Soon after the war, missions reorganised, brought back some German-speaking priests and exploited the unsettled circumstances to steal bases and expand. Throughout this period, the 'bush school' became the mascot of missionary presence. Schools were used as a means of evangelisation, rivalry, civilisation, legitimisation of colonial industrial policy, expansion into rural areas and domestication of Christian values. One had to be literate to read the catechism and sing the salvation hymns. School and church shared space and significance. Those who did not attend Sunday school were caned in the school on Mondays. Debate ranged around the curricula, level of education, use of indigenous personnel, governments' roles and the relationship between education and evangelism. Does an emphasis on education detract from the primary goal of leading the people to Christ? Some missionaries resisted the expansion of the school apostolate while others saw it as the means to capture the future generation. Many perceived education as an investment good and objected to the notion of a consumer-good concept whereby Africans would study the classics and suchlike; they hated the pretensions of educated Africans. Curricula should be confined to assisting them to cope within their cultural milieux, acculturate the values of the agents of change, serve as intermediaries between Western and traditional societies and mediate colonial civilising policies and instruments. Industrial missions held much promise. The debate was fierce in the inter-war years as the governments employed grants-in-aid to control the quality through an inspectorate unit. Mission churches colluded with governments against the schools founded by Ethiopians, which were denied accreditation and funding.

Ironies piled up as missions concentrated on teacher training and primary schools. There were only a few secondary and grammar schools until the

11 See Temu, *British Protestant missions*, pp. 117–39.

1940s. Africans instigated much of the expansion: those returning from the war or from mines and plantations urged the presence of schools as a sign of development, the acquisition of white power, a solution to the riddle of the paper that talked, and a coping mechanism for the new times. Communities would build the school and a house for a teacher, carry the luggage, and even put a deposit towards the salary. Missionaries wrote home requesting more personnel because of village delegations demanding schools. Either the war's experiences opened people's eyes to the power of white technology or the onslaught of the years on traditional mores finally took its toll. Or it may be that the new patterns of exploitation weakened primary resistance; for whatever reason, a mass movement to Christianity occurred. The presence of a school and church became an instrument of communal rivalry. Instead of sending their children to a school in a neighbouring village, proud elders would contribute money for their own school. Competing missions exploited inter-communal rivalry while the district officers delimited areas of operation. Rapid expansion compelled the use of half-baked teachers. By the 1940s some indigenous entrepreneurs funded secondary education; sometimes communities would provide the infrastructure while missions supplied the personnel. For the foundation in 1925 of the Dennis Memorial grammar school in Onitsha, Eastern Nigeria, the indigenous people raised most of the funds for the Anglicans. Government policy changed after the Phelps-Stokes Commission Report which showed off the capability of the brilliant Ghanaian, Dr J. K. Aggrey. But its reliance on Booker T. Washington's approach would meet with African criticism that it limited the ranges of African access to education. One effect of the First World War was to open the space for some young Africans to go overseas for the 'golden fleece'. These would become the agitators of the post-1945 era. Already their strident tone could be heard in Nnmadi Azikiwe's brand of journalism in the Gold Coast from 1937. Agitation for university education after the Second World War induced government concern for secondary education.

Other crucial dimensions to the story of the inter-war years include the increasing concern among missions about the employment goals of their pupils, many of whom deserted into government employ; urbanisation grew, with many moral implications; and education for girls became a key concern. The appeal of the gospel must be nuanced because when the gospel spread to the villages and, like the roots of the mustard seed, changed the soil of the communities by contesting their cultures, the encounter of gospel and culture created disquiet. Thus, in spite of mass movement, a spectrum of responses appeared as the guardians of the ancestral calabash struck back in persecutions. Indeed, some of the patrons of church and school did not convert, because it was education that they sought for their progeny. Novelists have captured this mood more accurately.

Native choruses of prophets, Zionists, *Aladura* and *Roho*, 1914–1960

Influenza ravaged Africa from 1918, to add salt to the injury of coping with the rapacious European presence. Some surmise that the epidemic triggered a radical reshaping of the Christian landscape. The story of Zionists in Swaziland characterises the new trends in the continent for the period between the First World War and the bugles of independence. Many missionary bodies operated here from the arrival of the Methodists in 1845, followed by the Anglicans in 1880 and Lutherans in 1887. The country enjoyed a whiff of radical African American presence when the African Methodist Episcopal church (AMEC) came in 1904, and by 1920 the number of organisations had grown to fourteen. With a comity arrangement, the evangelicals shared the land as from 1911. Within three years, a new phenomenon appeared on the religious landscape when Joanna Nxumalo returned from South Africa where she had been working as a teacher and became converted as a Zionist. Others followed and founded their own versions as this fervent variety of evangelicalism grew very rapidly. The League of African Churches bound them together. Apparently a Zionist healed the queen mother and regent, Labotibeni, of some eye ailment in 1914, and after this miracle Zionism became allied with the throne. The theology was gradually adjusted to make the monarch a type of 'King Solomon' and the land, Zion. In this invented history, King Sobhuza II was portrayed as the instrument for reclaiming the rights to the land from colonial settlers. By the 1930s the religious landscape was completely reimagined; missionaries in Swaziland were perceived as the agents of settlers and colonial powers while the Independent churches posed as the instruments with which the Swazi people first expressed their desire for religious and political change. Independency combined religious innovation with protest and the search for social justice and political freedom in evangelical language. The monarchy sealed this view by turning the Easter service into a programme for celebrating the national heritage. The lion and the lamb lay down together to produce a new version of African Zionist evangelicalism.

A number of points need to be examined, namely, the origin, type and nature of Zionism in South Africa, which spread to contiguous areas. It came from Zion City outside Chicago where John Alexander Dowie founded a group, the Christian Catholic Apostolic church, which claimed connection with the Azusa Street Pentecostal movement. In 1908 one of the beneficiaries of Dowie's healing ministry, J. G. Lake, went on a mission to South Africa where he founded the Apostolic Faith mission. When he returned to America in 1913, the leadership fell to a certain P. L. le Roux who left the Dutch Reformed church to found a little chapel at Wakkerstroom (now in the Mpumalanga province), teaching faith healing, baptism in the river Jordan and speaking in tongues. He described his pilgrimage as *crossing to Zion* and the name stuck. The other Africans who joined the AFM soon experienced racial discrimination and opened a number of all-black Apostolic churches. Each group held firmly to the Zion and Apostolic nomenclature. The phenomenon grew rapidly among Africans in the early twentieth century. Daniel Nkonyane replaced le Roux; others such as Paul Mabilitsa and Elias Mhlangu established their Zions. Eduard Lion, a Sotho, took it to Basutoland, Rhodesian workers such as Andreas Shoko and Samuel Mutendi evangelised their homelands, while Engemas Lekganyanes spread it in the Transvaal. Zionism gradually developed new forms that put pressure on analysis. It therefore requires a typology. For instance, Allan Anderson has argued that, from official census data (fraught with bias in the apartheid era), the number of African Independent church groups in South Africa greatly proliferated as follows:[12]

1913	30
1939	600
1955	1,000
1960	2,000
1970	3,000
1990	6,000

Just as in Swaziland, some interpreters of this religious form have focused on the element of protest and schism. Certainly, the issues of alienation of land and culture, political disenfranchisement under settler rule and colonialism, racial discrimination and economic deprivation bred psychological pressure that only a certain religious formation could help to assuage. Zion became a dream for the recovery of alienated land, a place where there will be

---

12 For an attempt to construct a coherent discourse on this form of spirituality, see Allan Anderson, *African Reformation: African Initiated Christianity in the 20th century* (Trenton, NJ: Africa World Press, 2001).

no more tears. The founder's home became a mecca, a powerful ritual: Zion, a place of belonging. Some of the Ethiopian themes could be replayed but with a different conclusion. But the dominant character of this religion was the prominence given to experience (revelation, dreams, visions, prophecy), orality, and the use of indigenous knowledge, symbols and ritual resources. The liturgical revolution was achieved by bringing traditional worship style into the church through song, dance, choruses and indigenous instruments. There was an intentional quest for resonance in biblical symbols and themes. Leaders took on the mantles of prophets and individuals found full participation as members of the household of faith. The African sense of community was recreated and polity ordered along traditional hierarchies. Prophecy, of both individual and predictive type, was supremely important as an instrument for diagnosis and cure in a religion where healing was primary. It is this fact that produced the debate on the relationship between the prophet and the indigenous diviner. Some have argued that the offices merged; others insisted that the *forms* were the same because the prophet was the agent not only of the Holy Spirit but also of the ancestors, but that the *contents* were different and more Christian. Zionists devised a plethora of symbolic healing objects such as sanctified sticks, pieces of wood, cloths, tea (labelled *tea ya bophelo*, tea of life), coffee, copper wires, needles (for removing impure blood), papers of various colors (which would be waved rapidly over a patient's body), smoke, sand, salt, and water, sometimes with alum. The concerns of traditional society over witchcraft and sorcery attacks would usually top the list of complaints. Prophets sometimes provided strips of blue cloth to be worn in a secret place for protection against enemy attacks that might come in the form of lightning.

Among the Spiritual churches, schisms occur frequently as charisma develops and internal differences abound. H. W. Turner, therefore, argued for a strong typology that would distinguish the *vitalistic*, which employed occult practices and esoteric books from Asia, the *nativistic* types that employed a high dosage of indigenous cultus, the *messianic* types in which the leader claims to be a part of the Trinity, and *revivalistic* groups that seek to clothe an African religious form with a Christian veneer; for instance, Godianism.[13] Two broad types, Sunday and sabbath worshippers, each have identical typological characteristics. Certain ethnic groups have patronised

---

13 Harold W. Turner, 'Pagan features in west African Independent churches', *Practical anthropology* 12:4 (1965), 145–51 and 'A typology for African religious movements', *Journal of religion in Africa* 1:1 (1967), 1–32.

them more than others, for instance the Zulu in South Africa, Yoruba in Nigeria and Luo in Kenya, described as *Abaroho*, people of the Spirit (according to a Kenyan census in 1966).

The rise of Spiritual churches in west Africa demonstrates how African appropriation of the spiritual dimension of the gospel took different turns in the vibrant periods 1910–30 and 1930–60. They may have benefited from the prophetic movement that started just before the First World War. The *Aladura* or 'praying people' movement arose during the influenza epidemic of 1918–25, and had more religious than political import. The earliest group, the Cherubim and Seraphim, emerged from a prayer group in the Anglican church that insisted on gathering to pray for and heal victims of the epidemic. Others such as the Church of the Lord Aladura and the Christ Apostolic church followed apace. All over the continent, the nature, direction and pace of Christianity changed from the burst of the prophetic and spiritual revivals. In one place after another a prophetic figure would emerge symbolising a certain form of appropriation. Besides the African Indigenous churches (AICs) four other types emerged during the period. First, a diviner or religious leader within the traditional religion would inexplicably shift base by appropriating some aspects of Christian symbols and message to create a new synthesis, often induced by the pressure of responding to displacement or a threat to traditional roots amidst the expansion of whites. The Zulu prophet Isaiah Shembe (c.1870–1935) testified that 'just after my arrival at Boss Coenraad's home, it came to me to go and pray alone, towards dusk, as the light was failing'.[14] A voice started giving him directions and revelations followed. Many ministries of this nature appeared in the colonial period and formed the backdrop to the Zion, *Aladura* and *Roho* movements.

A second type could be illustrated from west Africa where a prophet would emerge from the ranks of Christians emphasising the pneumatic and ethical components of the gospel to intensify the evangelisation of communities. Sometimes he would pose as an Old Testament prophet sporting a beard, staff, flowing gown and the cross. Wade Harris and Garrick Braide have received the most scholarly attention but there were many others such as Peter Anim and Samson Oppong in the Gold Coast. Certain characteristics distinguished a prophet beyond the beard and emblem, either a cross, staff or bowl with holy water: a prophet was a charismatic figure, stringently opposed to traditional religion and nominalism. They perceived that the

---

14 Robert Papini, 'Carl Faye's transcript of Isaiah Shembe's testimony of his early life and calling', *Journal of religion in Africa* 29:3 (1999), p. 265.

pattern of Christianisation merely replaced one culture with another and hardly attacked the core allegiances. It was as if Africans created a periphery where they dialogued with the missionary message while preserving a core interior or epicentre where traditional allegiances predominated. The prophets focused their ministries on the interior of individual and communal allegiances. Prophets were sometimes precursors of Zionists, exhibiting the same features such as praying and healing. But the prophet was imbued with a message, unwilling to found a church but anxious to save through word and miracles. Many were gifted with the ability to compose choruses. Researchers have retrieved and translated 173 choruses by Garrick Braide, composed in his native Kalabari language.[15] A simple one that his followers used at the beginning of an outreach simply declared, 'Jesus has come and Satan has run away.' As it was repeated many times, the evangelists would pour holy water on shrines that would burst into flames to the consternation and conversion of votaries. Some were educated and others not; they attacked the symbols of traditional religion and nominal Christianity with the same hostility as missionaries, but demonstrated their engagement with signs and wonders. Their attitude to primal worldview declared a power-encounter scenario. Typically, people acclaimed that Braide was 'Elijah II'. Before Braide came on the scene around 1914, Wade Harris, a Grebo, journeyed on foot from Liberia into Ivory Coast and Gold Coast in the years between 1910 and 1914, preaching, performing miracles, and creating an enormous growth for both Roman Catholics and Methodists. He, too, composed many choruses. Churches formed after their ministries. The colonial governments, both British and French, hounded each of the prophets into prison, out of fear of an uncontrolled charisma. Braide was imprisoned on false charges in 1915 and died three years later. Strangely, his movement grew after his death. Similarly, Harris was confined to Cape Palmas where many came to visit and enlist his support. Churches grew in his name.

In a third type, a Christian group linked itself with an international evangelical or Pentecostal denomination because it needed the white support to survive in a hostile colonial terrain where the mission churches deployed civil powers to persecute indigenous initiative. Some indigenous Christians had contacted the Faith Tabernacle and used their literature, but since the latter did mission only through the post office the Faith people turned to the British Apostolic church. The Faith Tabernacle and Apostolic church contacts flowed

---

15 G. O. M. Tasie, *Thoughts and voices of an African church: Christ Army church, Nigeria* (Jos: Connack Nigeria Ltd, 1997).

into early Pentecostalism. For instance, in 1928, a prophet in Yorubaland, Babalola, linked with former members of the Faith Tabernacle to form the Christ Apostolic church. The same group refused membership to another prophet, Joseph Oshitelu, because of his secret names for God and other mystical doctrinal stances. He formed the Church of the Lord Aladura. In Eastern Nigeria, some Faith Tabernacle people spoke in tongues, were kicked out, founded the Church of Jesus Christ in 1934 and invited the Assemblies of God (who had been in Ivory Coast and Dahomey since 1925 and 1928 respectively) to take them over in 1939. It should be added that before denominational brands of Pentecostalism arrived, a number of individual Pentecostal missionaries tried between 1906 and 1912 to establish themselves in various parts of Africa, especially western Kenya, Liberia and South Africa. Thus, classical Pentecostals as well as indigenous ones emerged early in the religious landscape. A similar pattern occurred in the Gold Coast.[16]

Equally intriguing is a fourth type of cycle of charismatic revivals that emerged within mission churches between 1925 and 1935: in 1927, for instance, the Qua Iboe mission among the Ibibio of south-eastern Nigeria enjoyed an outbreak during a weekend retreat. Similarly, a revival occurred among the Quakers in Kaimosi in western Kenya in the same year, characterised by public confessions, fasting, vigils and spiritual emotionalism. When the elders could not restrain them, they were forced out in 1930 and formed the African Church of the Holy Spirit which has since blossomed. Also in the same 1930s, the *Balokole* or 'saved ones' spread rapidly among Anglicans from Rwanda through Uganda and Sudan to Kenya and Tanzania. With a muscular christology and call for repentance, it confronted missionary Christianity and caused much disquiet with its signature tune *Tukutenderaza Yezu* ('We praise you, Jesus, Jesus the Lamb. Your blood has cleansed me, I am grateful, Saviour'). It resembled the Jamaa movement among the Catholics of the Congo. The Congo region was suffused with prophetic or *ngunza* movements. After Simon Kimbangu was deported in 1921 to Elizabethville where he died in 1952, other prophets claimed to be imbued by his spirit in very vibrant political rebellion against the colonial authorities. But the enduring revival in Congo Brazzaville was led by Buana Kibongi from 1947. It started among the Swedish Covenant church during a leadership retreat. Kibongi was a student and was the most affected when the Spirit fell on the group. He grew

---

16 Ogbu U. Kalu, 'Doing mission through the post office: the Naked Faith people of Igboland, 1920–1960', *Neue Zeitschrift für Missionswissenschaft* 54:4 (2000), pp. 263–80. See also John Peel, *Aladura* (London: Oxford University Press, 1968).

to leadership heights and turned the church into the Evangelical Church of the Congo. He succeeded because his vision was the unity of whites and blacks, an ecumenical vision for all churches in Brazzaville, and because the Swedish were already open to the pietistic tradition. His longevity till 1998 ensured that he provided long years of leadership and theological articulation. All these figures established a charismatic spirituality that would define the African response to the gospel: at once conservative, evangelical, with a vibrant liturgy and orality, under a different type of leadership, eschewing the philosophical aridity that characterised Western Christianity and emphasising miracles, visions, dreams and healing.

African drums and decolonisation blues, 1945–1960

The Second World War had an immense impact on Africa: it fuelled the political nationalism that ensured that by the 1960s many African states had emerged, first in north Africa, then among the other French colonies and from 1957 among the British colonies. In each place, the exposure during the war spurred the formation of nationalist movements. The decolonisation process divided the missionaries and the colonial governments. In 1967 T. A. Beetham, secretary of the Conference of Missionary Societies in Great Britain and Ireland, wrote a book that expressed the fear that African Christians might, in the heat of nationalism, resort back to primal religion.[17] The counter by some was that although the process was dishevelled, liquidation of the empire, while providing the new states with constitutions, offered the best protection of British interests. It proceeded from a deliberate calculation of British interests to be protected with constitutions and a conscious initiative to liquidate the empire. This perception may not be too far from the argument that in the politics of containment, decolonisation was an opportunistic response in crisis management. In the course of it, the colonial governments abandoned their intimate enemy, the missionaries. The inescapable conclusion is that decolonisation did not imply a radical change of socio-economic structure. The compromise is explained by Gramsci as *passive revolution*, describing the way that a dominant socio-political group may have to change its way of wielding power if it wants to maintain it. The goal of decolonisation was to return to informal empire where former rulers would retain sufficient economic and technological resources to exercise a powerful influence upon future development; it was a limited transfer of

17 T. A. Beetham, *Christianity and the new Africa* (London: Pall Mall, 1967).

power. Passive revolution has fuelled the modernisation and dependency theories in political analysis of contemporary African pathology. It is the root of the divinity of the market and co-operation between a predatory elite and multi-national companies.

The perspective here is that missionaries shared a similar tactical response to decolonisation, albeit at a great cost, and with resilience and a change of tack. For instance, they abandoned their opposition to modernity, embraced it and sought to channel it towards the hallmarks of liberal theology, reflecting the shift in European culture in the economic boom years between 1960 and 1970 and under the shivers of the Cold War. However, the responses of the missionaries to nationalist insurgence at the twilight of colonialism, in the period 1945–59, differed in quality from the retooling strategies in the immediate aftermath, 1960–75. Vast changes in the political climate of the decade 1966–75 forced enormous changes in the religious landscape. The story goes back to the late 1940s when African nationalist activities rose in crescendo as political parties sprouted from country to country. One explanation is that a younger breed with sharper focus came to the fore, sidelining both traditional rulers and moderates to bask in the fiery sun of mass adulation. Some appeasers such as Albert Luthuli abandoned the ideal of racial co-operation, disillusioned by the racism in the evangelical wing of the South African church. Undoubtedly, missionary responses to nationalism varied during the decade 1945–54 according to individual whims, official or denominational/institutional policies, and regional contexts. A certain shift followed as missionaries, betrayed by both government and protégés, felt powerless to halt the process. Some, in the field, tried to use available facilities to stem the tide by postulating a dichotomy between Christianity and politics. Drama, public debates and lectures were pressed into the effort to warn Christians to eschew politics and seek first the kingdom of God; colonialism, when properly reined, was for the good of Africans. The Moral Re-armament group networked through west Africa to inculcate salient political ethics. Some missionaries such as William Carey, formerly archbishop of Bloemfontein, were indiscreetly hostile, while others such as the irrepressible Michael Scott, the voice of Herero, represented those sympathetic to the African cause. Generally, institutional attitudes varied: those at the home base espoused idealistic positions that showed some sympathy for Africans but were so cautious that these amounted to little. In the field, some were alarmed at the prospect of Marxism or the resurgence of paganism, angry about the ingratitude of the African elite and resolved to contain the damage. Nationalism was portrayed as irreligious and the nationalists as too immature to lead nations to a democratic vision. A Church of Scotland missionary, writing in a house journal in 1947, put it succinctly. Entitled 'Democracy without religion', this article argued that 'a nation does not learn overnight to think of power as servant and not the master of justice. People do not acquire in a single generation that sense of responsibility, that sense of stewardship, that integrity without which corruption and greed will speedily threaten all attempts to run their own affairs.'[18] The period of tutelage had been too short to produce the right moral environment for independence. The cautious mood could be traced in ecumenical political thought from Whitby, Ontario, in 1947, which showcased the term, through partnership with younger churches through Amsterdam's interest in 'The responsible society' in 1948, to Willingen in 1952 when, for once, a strong social concern provided a shift.

Regional differences abounded. West Africa had plenty of mosquitoes and no white settler community; therefore, an indigenisation policy predominated in the mid-1950s. It had three prongs: to waltz with nationalists, to utilise the services of indigenous personnel, and to seek to adapt Christianity to African culture in the belief that the African need was to 'baptise' ingredients of their culture. Many of the priests trained in the early 1950s were in the vanguard. This limited perception of African Christian initiative in religion would be exposed later. Meanwhile, it formed a part of the arsenal for a passive revolution. In other places, the state tried to compromise or directly incorporate the church into the state apparatus. The Belgians in central Africa sought to legitimise their rule with Catholicism. Salazar's concordat of 1940 recognised and funded the Catholic church as the official instrument to promote the national colonial aims of the state in Angola and Mozambique. In both places, the leadership of anti-colonial rule came from the ranks of African evangelicals. In the Congo, the career of Bishop Jean de Hemptinne, vicar apostolic of Katanga, buttressed the loyalist cause. Similarly, the church's manipulation of religion in Rwanda has become the subject of indictment. In Ethiopia the emperor, Haile Selassie, used a revised constitution to rope the Orthodox church into state structures as the *abuna* sat in the council of regency and crown council. In eastern Africa, waltzing with nationalists in Uganda forced the church into the public space and, in the first elections, the Catholic Kiwanuka jostled with the Protestant Obote, celebrating the fruits of years of virulent rivalry and thereby dividing the society. Liberia offered an unenviable model where the state stood on the

---

18 N. M. Bowman, 'Democracy without religion', *Life and work* 28:4 (October 1947), 111. See a longer discussion in Ogbu U. Kalu, *Power, poverty and prayer: the challenges of poverty and pluralism in African Christianity, 1960–1996* (Frankfurt, Peter Lang, 2000), ch. 5.

tripod of Christianity, Masonic Lodge and True Whig Party as the rulers bowed to the three power nodes.

The impact of decolonisation on church groups varied according to certain indices: their size and ecclesiastical organisation, the vertical spread and social quality of their adherents, their inherited pattern of colonial relationship, their theological emphasis and their international relations. It also depended upon the manner of disengagement, the weave of neo-colonial fabric and the dosage of Marxism in the political mix. Any of these could have a positive or negative effect depending on the context. For instance, in the Congo, Mobutu perceived the Christian church (except Kimbanguism) as a danger to be demolished because gods do not brook competition.

The core of the missionary response to the challenge by nationalists to decolonise the African churches depended on the rear-guard actions to retool so as to maintain influence using indigenous personnel and resources. This was the main thrust of the missionary policy of indigenisation. Many different measures were tried: manpower development; internal restructuring through church unity and ecumenism; balancing aid and selfhood in funding so as to cure dependency and nurture stewardship; revisiting cultural policy through adaptation and thereby catalysing a controlled initiative in art and liturgy; realigning the church–state relationship by involving more Christians in politics; encouraging theological reflection; and installing a new model of relationship which uses the idiom of partnership to camouflage paternalism, thus essaying to maintain social services along the old lines. These cumulatively would remedy the after-effects of the excessive control of the past and preserve the core of missionary structures while broadening African participation. These measures constituted a response to the challenges created by the insurgent nationalism of the new African states. This counter-insurgence was aided by a paradigm shift in the ecumenical movement that occurred in Uppsala in 1968. Its delegates raised a new understanding of mission, science and technology, the challenges of modernity, dialogue with other faiths, and justice and race. The support for freedom fighters stirred an internal debate which only began to subside at the WCC assembly in Nairobi in 1975. Similarly, Vatican II, which had only 61 Africans out of 2,500 bishops, was a watershed in redesigning the church's policy in mission and social service. It released African energy in the church as a number of papal pronouncements appeared to speak to *all* Africans (irrespective of denomination) in a new voice. Pope John Paul II's call for inculturation and enrichment released much hope before people realised that curial control and liturgy within Roman rites shortened the ropes. Nonetheless, the renaissance of Christian art left an enduring mark as Father Kevin Carroll in Nigeria, Ethelbert Mveng in Cameroon and John Groeber in southern Africa mentored a number of young artists. Evangelicals did not indulge in the development of Christian art; they used the anti-iconic passages against graven images to insist that God could be better represented by nature. Portraiture and landscapes remained the dominant forms of evangelical art. They were not alone in being wary of the introduction of African traditional motifs into Christian art; some Catholics opposed the new forms of art in the church. But among all Christian groups there was an impressive depth of liturgical renewal in music, dance, the use of native languages, the radicalisation of block rosary (in which approved laymen and -women set up a street altar, by which children of the neighbourhood would be taught the rosary and catechism), and the formation of associations around new liturgical practices as vigils and retreat centres sprang up to the consternation of missionaries.

The details of these strategies will not bear repetition. Suffice it to say that the level of ministerial formation galloped from the 1960s. Theological education had an enormous boost with the formation of regional and continental associations that encouraged theological reflection and the revision of curricula in Bible schools. Many experimented with theological education by extension, while the genesis of the Ecumenical Association of Third World Theologians (EATWOT) brought together many from those regions of the world where the pressing question was 'eat what?' In the rainy season of 1973, the WCC met at Ibadan to explore how to readjust the funding of African churches so as to encourage them to learn the art of giving. When the board of faith and order of the WCC met at Accra in August 1974, there were more ongoing union talks in Africa than in other continents. The leaders of the Church of South India and those from Ceylon toured Africa to provide advice. Except in the case of Zambia, all others collapsed. To use the case of Nigeria as an example, theological and non-theological reasons colluded to thwart the dream. The scions of the faith churches dismissed the constitution of the union as lacking adequate spirituality. Other minor doctrinal matters caused concern but the real weighty issues were personality clashes and rivalries, denominational hostilities that had not healed, competition for the bishoprics and ethnicity. Finally some Methodist congregations took the union committee to court while the civil war (1967–70) scattered the litigants.[19] Studies from eastern Africa have confirmed how the same factors

---

19 O. U. Kalu, *Divided People of God: Church Union Movement in Nigeria: 1876–1996* (New York, NOK Publishers, 1978).

that destabilised African nation-states wreaked havoc in Christian circles. Admittedly, many of these could occur in any other context beyond Africa, but the key difference was that it was felt that church unity was being imposed from the outside.

Waltzing with the nationalists, 1955–1975

The African story in the decade from 1965 to 1975 worked out more clearly the issues raised in the period 1945–60. People increasingly found the missionary version of indigenisation to be unsatisfactory and restrictive. Missionaries themselves admitted that they were not certain that they were ready to relinquish power because of a dearth of responsible indigenous personnel. Yet they witnessed the surge of indigenous Spiritual churches; Christianity was attractive and growing tremendously and the youth were interested in the charismatic spirituality. Perceptive bishops, such as the Roman Catholic bishop Francis Arinze, created official space for charismatic resources to be absorbed into the mission churches. Liturgical experimentation caused disquiet in many places as 'traditionalism' impeded progress. There was also an increase in the roles played by laypeople, both men and women, in the churches. Many reasons are adduced: the increased use of the Bible and the vernacular; the energy released by Vatican II and Uppsala which removed the restriction of yesteryear, enabling the Africanisation of the liturgy; the government takeover of schools and hospitals which jolted the ascendancy of the churches and compelled them to turn to their true calling; the growing competition from the Christian left-wing or African Indigenous churches, which forced changes in liturgy; the deliberate policy of engaging the elite dovetailed with the impact of a new crop of trained clergy and theologians. Attention could also be paid to the power of women's lay associations such as the Mothers' Union/Women's Guild in the churches. The laicisation of the church was particularly significant because the churches wanted their people to use their powers and good offices to act as defenders of the faith. Knighthood orders were designed to attract the political elite. These, in turn, found the church members to be dependable voters. Soon, the laity's social and financial influence became more important in church affairs and decision-making than had been anticipated. From a different angle, African theology was loudly canvassed by the academics and the 'nationalism' of the new theologians harped on the vestiges of missionary structures and the predicaments of an un-indigenised church. New terminologies were canvassed in the quest to name African Christianity; for instance, *contextualisation, traditionalisation, incarnation* and *inculturation.* Africans wanted a new type of church or renewed Body of Christ and a new relationship with the West. While Roman Catholic priests challenged celibacy, their Protestant counterparts wanted to celebrate the eucharist with palm wine or kola-nut. The Bible supplied precedents that proffered continuity and the possibility that the spirituality of primal religion did not always conflict with the canon. There was much ferment in the churches as well as efforts to sabotage the limited indigenisation project from the inside.

Outside the church, the growth of state power in Africa from 1960 was significant in causing political instability, human rights abuse, environmental degradation and economic collapse. New states portrayed their goals in Christian garb in an obvious attempt at appropriation: *national redemption, economic salvation, political justification, national regeneration, sanctity of the state.* Many became one-party states, others praetorian (governing their states as if they were army camps), while some took to Marxism. The churches became alarmed. Out of forty-four sub-Saharan nations fifteen leaned in this direction soon after independence. On a closer look, none was pure Marxist as the Cold War attracted a variety of leftist ideologies from the USSR, China, Cuba, America and Europe. Africans responded with home-grown breeds such as Consciencism, African Socialism, Humanism, Centralised Democracy, and so on. In spite of Ratsiraka's *Red Book* in Madagascar, the churches thrived. The hostility in former Iberian enclaves soon diminished. Renamo, the South African backed guerrillas in Mozambique, flirted with Pentecostals, FNLA, the South African backed guerrillas in Angola, with Baptists, even as peace in the civil war in Mozambique was brokered by lay Catholics of the Communità di Sant' Egidio in Italy. In Angola and Zambia political rhetoric did not hurt the churches as much as bad economic policies and disease. On the whole, the power adventurism of the states forced major changes on the pattern of Christian presence in Africa. All these chickens came to roost in the moratorium debate between 1971 and 1975. African Christianity came of age in the aftermath of the world wars.

The African diaspora in the Caribbean and Europe from pre-emancipation to the present day

ROSWITH GERLOFF

The history of Caribbean Christianity can be divided, with overlaps, into four main periods: the rather monolithic form of Spanish Catholicism from 1492, and of the Church of England from 1620; the arrival of the Evangelicals or non-conformist missionaries, Moravians, Methodists, Baptists, Congregationalists and Presbyterians, from the mid-eighteenth century; the consolidation and growth of various European denominations in the region in uneasy tension with the proliferation of independent black Christian groups and African religions in the post-emancipation era from 1833; and the contest for political, economic and religious independence after 1870, including the shift from British imperial intervention and influence to that from North America, and national independence after 1962. Because the Caribbean has been discussed only briefly in earlier volumes of the series, this chapter will deal with the earlier history in some detail, before focusing on the twentieth century.

Contemporary studies in anthropology and sociology of religion speak of '*religions on the move*', or the process of transmigration and transculturation, as it refers to dynamic, reciprocal, transitory and multi-dimensional creations in shaping a 'poly-contextual world'. This implies that religions have to be regarded as cultural and spiritual phenomena whose 'taken-for granted' essence[1] has resulted from transcultural and transnational processes of mutual influence, interaction and continuous adaptation to new environments, developments and encounters. The emphasis here is on 'a new model of understanding religion which emphasizes process and practitioners over form and content': religions, including different forms of Christianity, respond to ever-changing circumstances and play a role in constructing and

---

1 Klaus Hock, University of Rostock, abstract for an essay on the African Christian diaspora in Europe, January 2002 (unpublished); R. Stephen Warner and Judith G. Wittner (eds.), *Gatherings in diaspora: religious communities and the new immigration* (Philadelphia: Temple University Press, 1998), p. 15.

reconstructing cultural and national identities.[2] The continent of Africa, with its traumatic experience of the transatlantic slave trade as an unprecedented mode of forced exile, and the development of accelerated inter-continental African migration in the context of globalisation in the second half of the twentieth century, is a case in point. Today, the Western world is faced with the arrival of indigenous religions in cross-fertilisation with contextualised Christian interpretations on its own shores. Moreover, it is compelled to acknowledge that these current manifestations are *not new* but have had precursors in a multi-faceted history. Here the Caribbean region between the gulf of Mexico and the Latin American continent, often overlooked in both historical and theological studies which would give credit to its unique experience, is a case in point. For three hundred years these islands were politically, economically and denominationally the 'hunting ground' of the European powers, particularly Spain, England, France, Denmark and the Netherlands. Yet the oppressed communities at the grassroots of diverse islands, both indigenous and imported from Africa and Asia, in resistance and struggle for survival and human dignity, exercised as much influence on the shaping of people's experience, expressions and negotiation of identities as the main European established and non-conformist missions that tried to keep them under social control. Hence the complexity of *contemporary* transmigratory processes must be considered in the light of this past, especially of Western colonial expansion and the Western missionary movement; and vice versa. This turbulent history can be seen as facilitating a worldwide transformation of modern Christianity in the South, not only in the Caribbean, but also in Africa and Asia. Cross-cultural transplantation from either side in the transatlantic cycle, and the capability of Christianity to reinterpret faith in diverse contexts, have forged an understanding in which traditions and activities overlie one another, overlap, blend, create new forms on the margins and therefore challenge the validity of all boundaries, exclusivist doctrines and centres.

The concept 'African diaspora' has become, at least for those once forcibly removed from their homelands, and their descendants, a viable instrument of *empowerment*, based on the biblical imagery of Exodus and the history of endurance, survival and the perseverance of human values. Some European academics question the term because of the historical difference between a

---

2 Carole D. Yawney, 'Introduction to part ɪɪ', in John W. Pulis, *Religion, diaspora, and cultural identity: a reader in the Anglophone Caribbean* (Amsterdam: Gordon and Breach, 1999), p. 185.

past enforced exile and present voluntary migration from Africa, and because the concept can exegetically and linguistically provoke negative connotations of persecution in Jewish history. Yet we give priority to the *self-expression* of blacks who, inspired by liberational biblical stories, for centuries identified with Israel seeking the 'promised land' and developed physical, cultural and spiritual means to resist bondage. For the slaves, in particular with the development of strong Ethiopian ideas in the Caribbean and North America in the eighteenth and nineteenth centuries, the concept 'African diaspora' confirmed *continuity in variations*; it granted them access to alternative interpretations of power and destiny, and could therefore be used as the description of past and present processes. Significantly, African and Caribbean youths on both side of the Atlantic today are increasingly guided by similar concepts and values spelt out in Pan-Africanism and Afrocentricity.

Spanish Catholicism, while enslaving indigenous populations and, after their extinction, the imported Africans, at least did not deny their humanity; it taught them a memorised form of 'main truth' called the *Doctrina Christiana*, and allowed them to be baptised. In contrast, Protestant powers, in a capitalist economy compelled by new technologies of the sugar complex, the cheap supply of labour, and rivalries with trading competitors, treated African slaves as mere chattels and property. Although the imported black population constituted a large majority in all the islands, they were not to be instructed in literacy or the Christian faith or to be baptised. The Church of England as the church of the plantocracy was the dominating Christian body in Barbados from 1625, in Nevis, Antigua and Montserrat from 1634, and in Jamaica from 1655. Clergy and parishioners, intrinsically tied to vested interests, had no desire to address the appalling conditions of the slaves or include them in civil society. Humanitarian efforts, influenced by the Quakers' protest, such as the work of the Society for the Propagation of the Gospel in Foreign Parts (SPG: 1701) proved powerless to change the overall system of subordination and cruelty.[3] The striking feature of the period, however, was 'not the failure of the established church to launch a mission for the slaves, but its failure to make any impact on the lives of the free and white members of colonial society'.[4]

---

3 Arthur Charles Dayfoot, *The shaping of the West Indian church 1492–1962* (Kingston, Jamaica: University of the West Indies Press, 1999), pp. 100, 107–8.
4 Keith Hunter, 'Protestantism and slavery in the British Caribbean', in Armands Lampe (ed.), *Christianity in the Caribbean – essays on church history* (Barbados: University of the West Indies Press, 2001), p. 97.

Against this background of an ecclesiastical life based on the dominance of European thought, rituals and values and the deculturisation and despiritualisation of human beings, there arrived another mission motivated by a personal approach and care for the slaves: the Moravians, from 1732; the African American Baptists from 1783; the Methodists from 1787; the Congregationalists from 1807; and the Presbyterians from 1827. *Coastlands and islands*[5] mentions five strongholds for this Evangelical mission: (1) places entered by planter invitation, made use of by the Moravians; (2) the significance of urban freed slaves, starting points for the Methodists; (3) the significance of slave migration, enforced and voluntary, within the Caribbean; (4) the role played by the army, as in the African American Baptist Liele's escape from America to Jamaica; (5) stations opened by various London-based missionary societies from 1789.[6]

From a Eurocentric perspective, the Caribbean pre-emancipation movement is interpreted as part of those fundamental changes in human politics, economics and philosophy that emerged at the end of the eighteenth century. Eventually, inhuman coercion came to be morally condemned and legally abandoned. However, as Curtin points out, there was a convenient chronological distinction between two separate Acts, that abolishing the slave trade (1807), and that abolishing slavery (Britain: 1833; France: 1848; Cuba and Brazil: 1880).[7] When emancipation came, it brought 'freedom' without equality, 'tolerance' without cultural recognition, religious pluralism without basic human respect. The predominance of European socio-political interests remained guaranteed through the industrial revolution, new developments of technology, food production and international trade. They ensured that the former racist patterns lingered on into the nineteenth and twentieth centuries. 'The antislavery campaign ... went hand in hand with *laissez-faire* capitalism.'[8]

From the perspective of the African diaspora, slaves and emancipated slaves, the story must be told differently. From the outset there was passive and active resistance, often fuelled by religion. Harsh suppression did not produce lasting submission nor quench the spirit of freedom and the hope for

---

5 Francis J. Osborne and G. Johnston, *Coastlands and islands* (Kingston, Jamaica: UTCWI, 1972), p. 46.
6 Robert J. Stewart, *Religion and society in post-emancipation Jamaica* (Knoxville: University of Tennessee Press, 1992), pp. 6–11.
7 Paul Curtin, *Two Jamaicas: the role of ideas in a tropical colony, 1830–1865* (Cambridge, MA: Harvard University Press, 1955), p. 174.
8 David Lowenthal, *West Indian societies* (London: Oxford University Press, 1972), p. 51.

liberation. There were more than fifty major slave revolts in three hundred years, besides the Maroon wars. Without exception they ended in arrests, reprisals and executions. In the midst of inhuman treatment, the Africans held on to their religious worldviews: 'Uprooted from their homeland, they maintained some of their identity and so filled the vacuum to which the church only paid attention in an inadequate way.'[9]

Imagine that the white non-conformist missionaries in opposition to older ecclesiastical traditions would have, if not allied themselves, at least sympathised with non-violent black resistance! Some few indeed did, led by an emphasis on experience, evangelistic zeal, egalitarian beliefs and practical morality.[10] But, primarily, the Evangelical mission concentrated on the personal conversion of the slaves. In an utterly senseless and destructive world, they preached a gospel of salvation sympathetic and meaningful to the conditions and demands of plantation life; they therefore helped the oppressed to arrive at personal integrity and moral conduct. As they did not need 'organised' religion, they turned the converted into effective evangelists for others and spread rapidly. Unwittingly they introduced an inter-cultural interface, if not yet a synthesis, between biblical and African–creole elements. In this way, they posed a serious threat to the establishment and the planters' interests which would later force them to take an unambiguous stand in the anti-slavery campaign. For the time being, their understanding of Christianity referred to one's personal relationship to God, and not at all to civil or political affairs, turning Africans into more useful servants. Absolute neutrality, therefore, in the slavery issue was a matter of necessity in mission policy. When in the ensuing years they themselves became engulfed in conflicts and persecution, they still regarded it as irresponsible to encourage violence and advocated only 'amelioration' of the system brought on by institutional reforms. However, this 'missionary gradualism' on the slavery and injustice issues, the missionaries' ambiguity and ineptitude in engaging in earnest cross-cultural encounters, could not satisfy black Christians. The missionaries 'accepted the blacks abstractly as equal, while rejecting the cultural expressions which defined black life'.[11]

As an outstanding example, we concentrate on the mission, strategies and theology of the Black Baptists who entered Jamaica in 1783 (Trinidad: 1812).[12]

---

9 Johannes Meier, 'The beginnings of the Catholic church in the Caribbean', in Lampe, *Christianity*, p. 49.
10 Dayfoot, *Shaping*, p. 113.
11 Robert J. Stewart, 'Religion in the Anglophone Caribbean', in Pulis, *Religion*, p. 22.
12 See, among others, Horace O. Russell, *Foundations and anticipations: the Jamaica Baptist story 1783–1892* (Columbus, GA: Brentwood Christian Press, 1993).

They recruited the rural and urban masses, became the most critical opponents of the authorities' and planters' attitude and practice towards the slaves, influenced the pre-emancipation as well as post-emancipation periods throughout the nineteenth century, and introduced a Black Theology of liberation and inter-culturation. A key figure is George Liele (or Lile), often called the 'Negro prophet of deliverance'. Born a slave in Virginia, but in 1773 set free by his master to exercise his spiritual gifts, he was ordained and licensed in 1775 to preach and sing salvation to the oppressed. He later escaped to Jamaica, where he obtained the licence to preach and founded the first 'Ethiopian Baptist church' at Kingston racecourse in 1784. Thirty years before the arrival of the British Baptists, he together with other American ex-slaves laid the foundation for overt African expressions of the Christian faith and the 'freedom of the African soul'. They called for support from the Baptist Missionary Society (BMS) in London because of lack of finance, and the need to counteract mounting persecution and tightened legal restrictions (from 1807; Jamaica slave code 1816), and to channel the mission into more orderly Baptist patterns. Missionaries, among them William Knibb, arrived from 1814. They rendered assistance, not oversight. So Liele, who died in 1828, was intentionally and unintentionally instrumental in three essential developments in the Caribbean: (1) the mainly amiable bond between Black Baptists and British Baptists, among whom Knibb would became the most outspoken proponent of the abolitionist movement in the British Parliament in 1833 – a testimony to the conversion of whites to the black freedom cause; (2) the birth of the Native Baptist movement which facilitated a symbiosis of African indigenous and Christian traditions; (3) the preparation of a fertile ground for the political struggle.

As Liele and his co-workers were Protestant missionaries without formal education whose influence spread far beyond the boundaries of their initial preaching, we note the close connection between the Caribbean and African America. Far from being isolated, the continuing influx of black itinerant preachers from the States, the Bahamas, Santo Domingo and the new Republic of Haiti after emancipation reinforced religious and cultural networks and created ever-new patterns of black Christian protest in various national contexts, long before the emergence of Pan-Africanism.

In 1824, London established an episcopate in the region, with one seat in Barbados and the other in Jamaica. After long delays, it was a serious attempt to free the Church of England from dependence on the plantocracy, yet with little success. Neither the SPG nor the young Church Missionary Society could help to promote a 'native church' and replace the expatriate clergy with one trained on the islands. The Methodists recruited initially most converts from among the 'free people of colour' in towns, but also reached white settlers and turned into a church for the mixed-race middle class. By 1824, they had bases all over the Caribbean.[13] Concerned about the violent hostility of the white upper classes, they chose political passivity and pious moderation.

This cannot be said of the Baptists, both black and white. William Knibb typified 'the approach to slavery . . . by the British philanthropists William Wilberforce and Thomas Fowell Buxton' who, in 1823, declared in the Commons that 'slavery was repugnant to the principles of the British Constitution and of the Christian religion', and therefore had to be gradually abolished throughout the British dominions.[14] Emancipation would not have come without this shift in the balance of power in England. But more significant in the process were the Black Baptists; increasingly, white Baptists were at variance with their radical position. Liele's biblical vision of a new society had fostered a social and political consciousness, but its practical application to the continued oppressive reality, progressive aspirations for freedom and socio-political recognition after the abolition of the slave trade, and the merger of Christian values with African religious practices, led to their departure from the official position of the BMS. Many Black Baptists began to hold a dual membership – respectable Christians in the missions, and free native Baptists in the backyards of the island.

The 'Baptist war' broke out after a drought, floods, hunger and epidemics at Montego Bay in Jamaica during the Christmas season of 1831. Initially, it was organised as a non-violent slave strike by Sam Sharpe, a deacon in the Baptist church and a charismatic leader. By interpreting the quest for religious freedom as identical with social freedom, it constituted a new form of both religious and political leadership, an 'organised resistance' to an 'organised repression'.[15] Planned without prior knowledge of the missionaries (but claiming them as allies), it used the network of multiple Baptist congregations who, inspired by the Bible and fervent prayer, took affairs into their own hands. The insurrection ended in martial law and ruthless retaliation against

13 Dale Bisnauth, *History of religions in the Caribbean*, 3rd reprint (Kingston, Jamaica: Kingston Publishers, 1996), pp. 113–14.
14 Noel L. Erskine, 'Prologue: religion in Jamaica', in Winston Arthur Lawson, *Religion and race: African and European roots in conflict – a Jamaican testament*. Research in Religion and Family: Black Perspectives 4 (New York: Peter Lang, 1996), p. xii.
15 Mary Turner, *Slaves and missionaries: the disintegration of Jamaican slave society 1787–1834* (Urbana: University of Illinois Press, 1982), p. 163.

the rebels, but also against the white Evangelicals accused of collaboration. Sharpe was publicly hanged in May 1832. Missionaries were unsuccessfully charged with treason; some left the island. Eventually, European Christians were compelled to take an unambiguous stand. Never again would they work on concessions to slavery and undisputed rights to property. The 'Colonial Church Union', the planters' violent response, short-lived as it was, tried to rid the island of the Baptists' presence and incited the mob against Nonconformist chapels;[16] however, in the changing social climate, it was outlawed by the authorities. In August 1833, the British Parliament passed the Emancipation Act. The aims and strategies of the revolt 'pushed Jamaica into the revolutionary mainstream of the time, the struggle for individual liberty sanctioned by law. They made the first step on the long, devious road to universal suffrage and national independence.'[17]

The resistance of Christian black and free coloured converts before emancipation warranted its continuance into the nineteenth and twentieth centuries. The first of August 1834 was without exception celebrated as the 'Day of Jubilee' (Lev. 25).[18] By then half of the Jamaican ex-slave population pronounced themselves Methodists, Baptists, Moravians or Presbyterians. They understood Christianity as protecting basic liberty and equality. The missionary churches seemed to offer them self-respect, 'respectability based on British non-conformist models',[19] much-needed education, assistance in accessing land, and upward social mobility. Since previous conflicts between the denominations had given way to some kind of mutual acquiescence and co-operation, even Anglicans were now accepted as the church able to bestow propriety and political influence on the black and mixed-race middle class. They all expanded. However, when the euphoria had passed, the majority discovered that socio-politically and economically they were not set free; and the assumed inter-cultural partnership between black and white missions was not to take place. Hope began to fade and gave way to disillusionment. After the period of 'apprenticeship' (1834–8), perceived by Africans as half-slavery, the plantation owners carried on with their usual techniques in order to keep control of the labour force. The import of indentured labour from the Indian

---

16 See Shirley C. Gordon, *God Almighty, make me free: Christianity in pre-emancipation Jamaica* (Burton Sankeralli: Trinidad and Tobago CCC, 1994), pp. 101–2.

17 Turner, *Slaves and missionaries*, p. 164.

18 Horace O. Russell, 'Understandings and interpretations of scripture in eighteenth- and nineteenth-century Jamaica', in Hemchand Gossai and Nathaniel Samuel Murrell (eds.), *Religion, culture and tradition in the Caribbean* (London and Basingstoke: Macmillan, 2000), p. 104.

19 Gordon, *God Almighty, make me free*, p. 119.

sub-continent because of the labour shortage, voluntary migration within and between regions, and schemes developed by the British and French for continued (partly coerced) migration from West Africa, all facilitated further exploitation, but also aided more adaptability among shifting populations, granting them access to new, even revolutionary, ideas.

Between 1840 and 1870, the European missions embarked on humanitarian projects and established schools (helped by parliamentary and other educational grants) and founded theological training colleges (Anglicans: Codrington, 1830; Baptists: Calabar, 1843). They also went to Africa. However, except the Baptists, they dismally failed to develop an indigenous leadership. When, in 1853, the black priest Robert Gordon applied to enter the Anglican ministry in his homeland Jamaica, the bishop urged him to work in Africa.[20] Only vigilant supervision, strict moral discipline, and preaching an 'undefiled' Christian gospel would free blacks from 'pagan' rituals and 'superstitions' and thus prevent church life and theology from becoming syncretistic. Missionaries were eager to 'ameliorate' the conditions of the underclass faced with impoverishment, natural disasters and diseases, but they ignored other forces and remedies at work. Racism, based on colour of skin, cultural superiority and social status, was even to intensify in the second half of the century.

Only the Baptists, particularly native Baptists, followed a different direction. 'Native Baptist', according to Turner, is the generic term for a proliferation of groups in which blacks 'developed religious forms, more or less Christian in content, that reflected their needs more closely than the orthodox churches, black or white'.[21] Led by congregational, non-hierarchical principles, and gathered in hundreds of 'free villages', they developed a local leadership of African 'mammies' and 'daddies', applied a 'class-ticket and leader' system which augmented independent membership, and expressed themselves in often unorthodox styles. Recent studies from 1990 such as those by Stewart, Gordon, Segal, Lawson, Austin-Broos and others[22] have thrown light on this lasting legacy surviving to the present. This concurs with the debate, from the mid-twentieth century, about the retention of African elements anywhere in the diaspora, or what Aleyne has called an 'African continuum in variations'.[23] It confirms two conflicting cosmologies, two cultures, two theologies, one European and one African, in mutual encounter or inter-cultural interplay which, ever refreshed by ongoing contacts with

---

20 Stewart, *Religion and society*, pp. 96–105.   21 Turner, *Slaves and missionaries*, p. 58.
22 See bibliography.
23 Mervyn Aleyne, *Roots of Jamaican culture* (London: Pluto Press, 1998); cp. the American anthropologists Zora Neale Hurston and Melville J. Herskovits.

Africa, introduced a process of cross-fertilisation, allowed for a creative synthesis of different traditions, and made syncretisation in various degrees inevitable.[24] Curtin, for the years 1830–65, coined the term 'two Jamaicas': Native Baptists had become 'another religion competing with the Christianity of the European missionaries'.[25]

Two examples may suffice. One is the existence of *Myal*, a Jamaican version of organised African worship, the first documented African–creole religion.[26] It provided protection against *Obeah*, witchcraft or evil spirits, safeguarded African 'rites of passage', and functioned as a source for medical and healing practices. The other is the Native Baptist interpretation of *sin as sorcery*, 'categorized as the destructive, alienating, and self-centred pre-occupation of anti-social people'.[27] With a sense for reality, black Christians understood sin as evils that interrupted the community, including slavery, injustice, greed, immorality, and double standards manifest in the prevailing system. People would be liberated by conversion, cleansed through baptism, and redeemed by salvation in Christ.

Here we draw a brief comparison between Native Baptist theology and the 'black roots' of Pentecostalism as well as traits in the African Indigenous churches (AICs) in the early years of the twentieth century. Pentecostalism and AICs also emerged among the poor and migrants seeking a better life. Common elements, akin to those in oral cultures, can be described thus: a spirituality of belonging and kinship in hostile and violent societies; worship as a 'feel-good' event and celebration of life, involving each and every one as participants; the incorporation of music, dance, dreams and visions and other ecstatic phenomena[28] into communal life; a personal commitment to moral standards and 'holiness'; a healing ministry which responds to the physical as well as the social needs of people; evangelism understood as embracing the whole person, not dichotomising between the material and spiritual, and empowering to break down barriers of race, gender, class and culture; theology done at the grassroots, full of vibrancy and giving meaning to daily life; the development of networks of mutual support between leaders, con-gregations and prayer meetings; and a strong eschatological expectation of

24 Erskine, 'Prologue', in Lawson, *Religion and race*, pp. x–xi.
25 Paul Curtin, *Two Jamaicas: the role of ideas in a tropical colony, 1830–1865* (Cambridge, MA: Harvard University Press, 1955), p. 34.
26 Lawson, *Religion and race*, p. 25; cp. Stewart, *Religion and society*, p. 196.
27 Lawson, *Religion and race*, p. 28.
28 Turner, *Slaves and missionaries*, p. 57, even refers to 'sects where the spirit spoke in tongues'.

freedom and justice in the kingdom of God, carrying an inherent political potential. Even the fact that black leaders there and then were branded as 'self-styled'[29] found a parallel in the biased reception of Pentecostal pastors by Europe's church and secular authorities a hundred years later. From a Western point of view they still had no legitimacy.

In 1842 the Jamaican Baptist Association became independent from the BMS, opened Calabar college as a training centre for indigenous ministers, and founded the Jamaica Baptist Missionary Society. Following the trends of the time, they started mission in Africa. However, black membership, discontented with a missionary stance operating on double standards, decreased. After Knibb's death in 1845, Edward B. Underhill, secretary of the BMS, can be regarded as 'the last progressive English Baptist voice on Jamaican problems'.[30] The early forties saw a revival of Myalism as resistance to further Western Christianisation. So the erupting Great Revival of 1860–1 came as a surprise. It introduced a process that can be described as a first symbiosis between Christian and African elements. It began among the Moravians, spread to Methodists and Baptists, and was inspired by African-creole enthusiasts as much as by white participants. Wilmore calls it the force of folk-religion which asserted itself 'to keep body and soul together against every destructive element of the universe – in other words the power to be, the power to survive'.[31] Influenced by the Great Awakenings in America and Britain, its dramatic impact sprang from the emotional and physical commitment of African Christians. Conversions to the Christian faith, renunciation of sin, prayer, healing and bodily manifestations were constitutive. Hence Evangelicals, who first welcomed the revival, began to fear the 'violent spirit' that possessed the worshippers, in contrast to a spirit of 'inner peace and joy', similar to the 'conflict paradigm' apparent in the Azusa Street revival in 1906. Too little oral research has yet been conducted on the Jamaica revival; written reports stem from white-only sources.[32] However, the event seems to fall in line with similar 'outpourings of the Spirit' with 'signs and miracles' (Acts 2:11) in Africa, Asia and Latin America *before* Azusa Street, only less publicised.[33] In

---

29 Stewart, *Religion and society*, p. 128.   30 Ibid., p. 24.
31 Gayraud S. Wilmore, *Black religion and black radicalism*, 2nd edn (Maryknoll, NY: Orbis, 1983), p. 226.
32 Diane Austin-Broos, *Jamaica genesis: religion and the politics of moral orders* (Chicago: University of Chicago Press, 1997), p. 57, quotes W. J. Gardner (1873): 'The sword of the Spirit has penetrated a multitude of souls, convinced them of sin, and forced them to cry for mercy.'
33 See, e.g., Tirunelveli (1860–5), Travancore (1873–81), and the Mukti mission (1905–7) in India; or the early beginnings of AICs around the turn of the nineteenth to twentieth centuries.

the Caribbean, it sparked off a Christian renewal, led to a superabundance of Bibles,[34] and became the watershed for a great proliferation of African religions in various degrees of syncretisation. It marked the region as deeply religious and established emancipatory ideas and biblical imagery as guiding principles in political and social development: 'a hermeneutic of Scripture incarnate in Caribbean history'.[35]

This was brought out in the Morant Bay rebellion of 1865, a milestone on the road to change, independence and black nationalism. It also illustrates the alienation between native and orthodox Baptists. The key protesters integrated spiritual and cultural values as tools for social protest and political liberation. George William Gordon, a coloured landowner in St Thomas and a member of an independent Baptist congregation, entered politics and attacked the governor, Edward J. Eyre, over human rights, social justice and land distribution. Paul Bogle, a free African and Baptist deacon, supported Gordon, and in October 1865 led a march to the Morant Bay court house in protest against the central government. Violence erupted between the demonstrators and officials. Troops and warships were brought in; several hundred blacks, including children and pregnant women, died; the unrest was brutally quelled. Both Gordon and Bogle were arrested, tried by martial law and executed. In modern Jamaica they are honoured as national heroes. Governor Eyre was recalled, yet the incident stirred up a hot debate about the correctness of his actions. The 'Jamaica question', with its associated fears of another 'Indian mutiny' or return to 'barbarism', influenced the pseudo-scientific racial theories that so horribly influenced the twentieth century. Jamaica became a crown colony.

By the end of the nineteenth century, the surviving elements of African culture had become embodied in a great variety of African-creole religions, some opposed to Christianity, staying relatively intact outside the influence of Western missions; others blending African worldviews with Christian interpretations, potent in finding ways of adapting to new life conditions in new social contexts: Convince, Kumina and Pocomania in Jamaica, Shango and Rada in Trinidad, Voodoo in Haiti, Santeria in Cuba, and the Jordanites in Guyana. Genuinely Christian creations such as the Spiritual Baptists in Trinidad, Grenada and St Vincent, and the Revivalists in Jamaica, would have an impact on Caribbean migration to Europe.

---

34 Austin-Broos, *Jamaica genesis*, p. 59.
35 Leslie R. James, 'Text and rhetoric of change: Bible and decolonisation in post World War II Caribbean political discourse', in Gossai and Murrell, *Religion, culture and tradition*, p. 147.

From 1870, with the disestablishment of the Church of England, the American ascendancy in the region, and the arrival of a new missionary wave of American evangelism, Caribbean societies changed. Less than one-third of the population were Anglicans, often in dual membership. Only in Barbados did the Church of England remain the undisputed authority, 'little England', manifest in later migration patterns. The Anglican province of the West Indies, established in 1893, never stemmed the tide of further proliferation of Christian and non-Christian groups, including Hinduism and Islam in the southern regions. It remained 'the white man's church', defined by race and class, and – in tune with Methodists and Moravians – did not support indigenous leadership. European Christian denominations undoubtedly contributed to continued social and racial stratification. For the period between the late nineteenth century and independence in 1962, we observe four streams in the struggle for self-determination: political campaigns; the religious quest for freedom; the liberational philosophy of Garveyism and Pan-Africanism; and the Pentecostal explosion.

Socio-economically, World War I disrupted the European beet sugar production, so there was a slight recovery of the cane sugar economy after 1919. However, economic hardships between the two world wars made workers vulnerable, caused popular unrest, and threw up trade unions and national labour movements such as those organised by Manley and Bustamante in Jamaica and Eric Williams in Trinidad. Sustained development became discussed merely in terms of international relationships and dependency on the 'advanced' 'first world' economies: 'The end of slavery had been followed by the constraints of colonial rule, and the end of colonial rule had been followed by a democracy of floating disillusionment.'[36]

The religious quest for freedom can be observed in the emerging revivalism which carried redemptionism into the streets and backyards of Jamaica. 'Zion revival', desiring to heal self and community, became a blending of central Christian elements with specific African-creole notions. Its healing ministries, 'though abhorrent to the missionaries', drew on biblical practice.[37] My research on the early Pentecostal Apostolic movement in St Ann, Jamaica discovered inherent revivalist elements such as gifts of healing, dreams and visions, spirit possession, secret languages or 'unknown tongues', songs and dance, prophecy, and baptism by immersion in the

36 Ronald Segal, *The black diaspora* (London and Boston: Faber&Faber, 1995), p. 185.
37 Austin-Broos, *Jamaica genesis*, pp. 62, 79.

sea.[38] In the 1970s, there were congregations with revivalist features in England, now absorbed by Pentecostalism. Differently, the Spiritual Baptists, a synthesis between Christianity and Yoruba religion in competition with the Pentecostals, still have large congregations in London. All these movements, including the messianic actions of Alexander Bedward, the father of revivalism, abandoned organised religion and gave fresh, even unusual, articulations to biblical practice, autonomy 'in the Spirit', and faith in human salvation.

By the turn of the century, new evangelical missions arrived, the Salvation Army, Sabbatarians, and Holiness churches. The Salvation Army in Jamaica under Raglan Phillips turned into the 'Light Brigade', and after his death into the International City mission, a renowned Jamaican Pentecostal church under two women bishops with outposts in North America, the Bahamas and, later, Britain.[39] The Seventh-day Adventists, a white American denomination, established in the Caribbean from 1903, transmuted over the years into a genuinely 'third world' movement, based on the prophetess Ellen G. White's anti-racist position, health and educational activities and eschatological teachings, with far-reaching consequences for British Adventism from the 1950s: Black Adventists in Britain foster a theology of empowerment, community- and lay-orientation, and an understanding of evangelism as including social care. The Holiness movements, especially the Wesleyan Holiness church and Pilgrims in Barbados, also came to Britain; theirs, too, was an anti-slavery tradition of working with the poor, non-hierarchical structures and the emancipation of women.

A theologically motivated philosophy of political liberation developed in Garveyism. Here we observe a similar development as in South Africa where the AICs included 'Spiritual churches' (Zionists) and Ethiopian churches. Marcus Garvey, born in Jamaica in 1887, reared in the Wesleyan Methodist tradition but deeply influenced by Roman Catholicism, was widely travelled. After work in Costa Rica, Panama and Ecuador, he came to London in 1912 and became introduced to Pan-Africanism. In 1914 he returned to Jamaica and organised the Universal Negro Improvement Association with the aim of uniting all Africans in the diaspora 'into one great body' of self-government. His black nationalism had a precursor in the 'black theology of missionary emigrationism and racial destiny'[40] of Pan-Africanists such as Edward Wilmot

---

38 Roswith Gerloff, *A plea for British Black Theologies: the black church movement in Britain in its transatlantic cultural and theological interaction*, International history of Christianity 77 (Frankfurt am Main: Peter Lang, 1992), vol. 1 pp. 153–6, drawing on Martha W. Beckwith's work in 1929.

39 Austin-Broos, *Jamaica genesis*, pp. 87–91.   40 Wilmore, *Black religion*, pp. 109, 116.

Blyden, also a Jamaican, who with others in African America had established a firm connection between the African 'homeland' and the African diaspora. Garvey's influence on the cultural and political scene in the Caribbean cannot be over-estimated, but also religiously he cultivated a biblical vision. Under his auspices, George Alexander McGuire from Antigua founded the African Orthodox church (with an impact on Uganda and Kenya). Importantly, the Rastafari movement in Jamaica from the 1930s began to hail him as one of their foremost prophets. When by 1973 their maxim '*Africa for the Africans*' had been internalised as the 'kingdom within', Rastafarians also migrated to Europe and invited the Ethiopian Orthodox church, one of the oldest African Christian churches, to England and the Caribbean. The movement strongly influenced the young British African Caribbean generations and continues to challenge black Pentecostal theology. Many black youths now cross over to the Nation of Islam.

The worldwide Pentecostal explosion has long been overlooked as non-respectable by academic theology both in Europe and in the Caribbean; and the advent of Pentecostalism in the Caribbean has often been interpreted as a white American importation, insignificant for politics and development. Nothing could be further from the truth. In the wake of the Baptist withdrawal, states Austin-Broos, 'the lower classes were in need of a powerful organisation that would promote re-vitalization of their lives'.[41] My research on the black church movement in Britain from 1973 marked out Pentecostalism, together with Adventism, as the most powerful force in Caribbean Christian migration. Such findings accord with recent studies on the Pentecostal/Charismatic churches in Asia, Africa and Latin America.[42] In 1980, Wedenoja interpreted Jamaican Pentecostalism as a positive force for coping with the radical social and cultural changes after independence: 'techno-economic development, urbanization, increasing affluence and social mobility, new expectations for social progress, expansion of the middle class, more democratic politics and materialism'.[43] World War II had put an end to European domination and forced Britain to dismantle a vast empire, 'to facilitate the genesis of new nations from the colonial womb'.[44] Black Pentecostalism can be seen as an integral part of these

---

41 Austin-Broos, *Jamaica genesis*, p. 79.
42 The author is researching this development, with reference to anthropological, socio-logical and theological studies of the 1990s on the movement in the two-thirds world.
43 W. A. Wedenoja, 'Modernization and the Pentecostal movement in Jamaica', in Stephen D. Glazier (ed.), *Perspectives on Pentecostalism: case studies from the Caribbean and Latin America* (New York and London: University Press of America, 1980), p. 42.
44 James, 'Text and rhetoric', in Gossai and Murrell, *Religion, culture and tradition*, p. 144.

indigenous struggles to defy and transcend, under widening horizons, former hegemonial powers.

Most Caribbean immigrants to Britain after 1948, ironically, saw themselves as 'children of the motherland': British citizens who had fought fascism in the army, and were now invited by London Transport, the Restaurants' Association and the National Health Service to help rebuild the national economy. This process, caused by unemployment and disasters in the West Indies, was accelerated by the McCarran-Walter Act which closed doors to America. From the outset, though, the new arrivals underwent a culture shock, facing racial discrimination in housing, labour, education and also churches. Pentecostals responded to this experience of rejection by offering people a 'spiritual home', self-respect, life in 'holy' discipline, confidence, and overall protection. Sunday worship became a joyful party before the Lord – a celebration of blessings amidst the hardships during the week. Blacks in the established denominations joined independent groups or held dual membership. Essentially, they knew they were part of an expanding movement, kept alive by constant traffic across the Atlantic, and counter to English monoculturalism. They created a symbolic space in which the 'saints' could find an identity, different from the one historically imposed by British society as derived not from particularity but a common humanity.[45] So black Pentecostal theology in Britain was never simply an offshoot of American evangelicalism, but a genuine Caribbean creation which had weathered the storms of time.

The main organisations in modern Britain are the trinitarian Churches of God of white American provenance (begun in Jamaica in 1918) and the Church of God in Christ, the largest African American Pentecostal church, with work from 1952. The Pentecostal Oneness (Apostolic) movement followed from 1955 (as did the AICs in the 1960s). Caribbean evangelists and bishops[46] were held in high esteem. Garfield T. Haywood, a friend of W. J. Seymour and a giant among the early African American Pentecostal leaders, was remembered as having visited Jamaica in 1931 – a living memory of Azusa Street. Similarly to Caribbean Pentecostals who needed initial recognition from the States, those in England were also at first closely connected with headquarters there. Soon, however, the process of adaptation

45 Roswith Gerloff, '"Africa as laboratory of the world": the African Christian diaspora in Europe as challenge to mission and ecumenical relations', in *Mission is crossing frontiers* (Pietermaritzburg: Cluster, 2003), p. 371.
46 E.g., Melvina and George White (Jamaica), or Bishop Randolph A. Carr (Nevis); see Gerloff, *Plea*, pp. 130–4, 168–74; Austin-Broos, *Jamaica genesis*, pp. 109–14.

to new contexts set in, with congregations desiring autonomy and others separating on racial or gender grounds. Again in a way comparable to Jamaica, where, for example, the Pentecostal Apostolic movement had to free itself from the white supremacy of its American branches,[47] black Pentecostals in England also began to contest white American dominance, a still unfinished task. Generally, only those already fully indigenised 'at home' succeeded in consolidating work in Britain. At present, some leaders in the New Testament Church of God (still governed from Cleveland, Tennessee) are attempting to overcome the still inherent racism in favour of true 'internationalisation' of the organisation. Black majority churches all over Britain – some organised in councils of churches, some interacting with the British bodies – include, besides those already mentioned, the oldest African Methodists, Anglo-Catholic Pentecostals, a great variety of AICs (from Nigeria and Ghana), and the growing African Charismatic churches, part of the 'third wave' of world-wide Pentecostalism in the context of globalisation from 1980.

Bridge-building between African and Caribbean Christians leaves much to be desired. The African Caribbean Evangelical Alliance, sadly repeating history, regards many AICs as too steeped in African traditional religion. Though radical black scholars utilise the African heritage in Caribbean history and theology, they seem to avoid getting involved with contemporary Africans. Dialogue between the English churches and the African diaspora, such as that promoted by the Birmingham-based Centre for Black and White Christian Partnership from 1978, has not progressed as hoped, as culturally and theologically white churches have stayed within their domain, and black churches have begun to imitate Western denominationalism. From the 1980s, there is a growing number of both Anglophone and Francophone African churches on the European continent, mainly of the new charismatic type. Sufficient interaction between Caribbean and African churches across national and language barriers of European countries, such as that initiated by the recently founded Council of Christian Communities of an African Approach, is still in an embryonic state.

---

47 Gerloff, *Plea*, pp. 121–3, 187.

13

Christianity in the United States during the inter-war years

COLLEEN McDANNELL

The period between the end of World War I and the beginning of World War II was a critical time for the development of a religiously pluralistic United States.[1] With more people living in the cities than in the countryside, urban culture began to overshadow agricultural life. Earlier generations of foreign-born Americans – many of whom were Catholics – now had children who were voting and assuming positions of power in the government, economy and education. Disputes over the nature of the scriptures and the place of Christians in the modern world fragmented the Protestant community into 'fundamentalists' and 'modernists'. Other Christians established their own church communities based on religious innovations such as speaking in tongues or sanctification. Additional diversification occurred as Dust Bowl migrants carried their evangelical ways to the west and African Americans left the rural south for the urban north. The economic and social insecurities of the Depression encouraged both intense devotional practices that focused on the miraculous *and* creative combinations of politics with faith. All leaders, including religious ones, took advantage of new forms of communication, especially radio, to spread their messages. While certain forms of Protestantism would decline in the twenties and thirties, for the most part Christianity in the United States was varied and flourishing.

Post-war abundance

Following war, the United States experienced an unprecedented period of abundance. Unemployment fell to around 5 per cent, worker productivity and salaries increased, the government set up protective tariffs to prop up American business, and the stock market flourished. 'We're in the money', a popular tune,

---

1 While the Canadian story at times parallels that of its southern neighbour, it has too many unique elements to be covered here.

summarised it all. Christian congregations also indulged in this apparent economic prosperity. Between 1916 and 1926 moderate and liberal Protestant congregations expanded their physical plants, broadened their services and increased their staffs. The value of churches doubled and money spent on new buildings went from $60 million in 1921 to an astonishing $284 million by 1926. The clergy developed programmes that required larger staffs and bigger payrolls. In the cities, Protestant churches acted as social centres with recreational facilities and meeting rooms. More effort was put into the religious education of children, with a commensurate growth in Sunday schools and the invention of 'vacation Bible schools' for summertime instruction. Church growth paralleled business growth as ministers attempted to maintain positions of prominence in their communities. And, like businesses, congregations took on more debts as their operational costs rose.

Mainstream Congregationalists, Presbyterians, Unitarians, Episcopalians, Baptists and Methodists were attracted to models of Christianity that legitimated the growing business community. In 1925 a former advertising executive, Bruce Barton, published *The man nobody knows*, a book that boldly cast Jesus as a salesman, and this bestseller sold 750,000 copies in its first two years. Those who went to church appeared content with an otherworldly, genteel Protestantism that reinforced existing social norms. The religious spirit that had driven many Progressive Era reformers to struggle for changes in labour laws, women's rights, prisons, housing and diet had waned. While the Social Gospel movement of the pre-war years continued as Christian socialism, it seemed trapped in a world of seminary professors.

It was also increasingly acceptable for certain kinds of Americans to stop going to church. By the twenties the growing secular fields of social work, education and government service offered individuals who hoped to change society an opportunity to do so without insisting on religious commitments. Social science researchers pushed reformers to look at larger cultural problems rather than focusing on individual moral behaviour. Anthropologists like Franz Boas stressed the unique character of all societies, not merely Christian ones. Sigmund Freud's psychological models were popularised and rhetoric about the 'unconscious' came to challenge ideas about 'the soul'. The rise of mass entertainment and sports, along with the legitimisation of leisure activities on Sunday, provided acceptable ways for Americans to spend their free time. Intellectuals debated the ideas of Marx and some workers looked towards socialism rather than Christianity to end their labour miseries. While it had always been acceptable for men of certain classes, especially young men, not to be involved in a religious organisation, by the twenties many more Americans counted themselves among the 'unchurched'. The fragmentation of Protestantism and Judaism in the early twentieth century both diversified religious observance and opened up a space for quiet absence from religious practices.

The spread of secular modernism appeared to be temporarily halted in 1920 when the Volstead Act effectively outlawed the selling of wine, beer and spirits in the United States. Prohibition was a political and cultural victory of Protestant ministers and their female supporters. Like the anti-slavery movement and even the women's rights movement, Prohibition was energised by moral concerns and often organised through Christian churches. Reformers contended that the consumption of alcohol, like slavery, reduced people to the condition of animals and threatened the sanctity of the family. Women in particular charged that drink led to poverty, desertion, wife and child abuse, promiscuity and disease. Prohibition was one of many efforts that attempted to equate American identity with Protestant culture. Some Catholic leaders and middle-class parishioners did promote voluntary temperance, but Prohibition had little support. While a few ethnic Protestants, like the writer and Lutheran H. L. Mencken, bemoaned the pretensions of native-born Methodists, for the most part Prohibition was the triumph of rural and small-town Protestants over urban Catholics.

The failure of the Volstead Act to end drinking underlined the erosion of clerical control over the behaviour of ordinary men and women. Bootlegging and illegal drinking, rather than becoming unacceptable moral vices, were common activities that were often celebrated in movies and dime novels. Police accepted bribes, politicians looked the other way, organised crime flourished, and speakeasies proliferated. By 1929 there were an estimated 32,000 of them in New York City alone. Flappers, jazz and Hollywood celebrities all could be marshalled by Protestant critics as evidence of their declining influence over values.

Federal Prohibition ended in 1933, and Protestant moral authority was never re-established in America's urban centres. As early as the first decade after the First World War, Catholics had become a political and cultural force. Decades of Protestant proselytising among immigrant Irish, Italians, Slavs and Poles had not altered the fact that city-dwelling Christians were Roman Catholic Christians. It was in the parish that immigrants learned how to navigate between faith, American nationalism and ethnic identity. Since the turn of the century, urban 'national parishes' had been established to address the spiritual and corporeal needs of specific ethnic groups. Nuns and priests of a particular nationality, who understood the culture of their parishioners, staffed such parishes.

By 1915, for instance, the archdiocese of Chicago had over 200 well-defined national parishes for sixteen different groups – St Joseph's (1900) was for Lithuanians, St John the Baptist (1909) was one of nine Slovak parishes, St Florian (1905) was one of many Polish parishes. Each parish took pride in their church and school, seeing the visible growth of Catholic institutions as evidence of both their right to be in America and their religious superiority. German, French and Polish parishes in particular insisted that children study their families' languages, in spite of national trends to establish English as the language of instruction. While changes in canon law in 1918 mandated that territorial parishes be the Catholic norm, national parishes continued and as late as 1930 55 per cent of Chicago's Catholics attended national parishes.

Catholic leaders spoke out against the nativist tendencies of the period and workers supported their parishes because they met their spiritual and physical needs. Priests acted as employment counsellors, negotiated with factory owners on behalf of workers, and raised funds for elaborate churches. Nuns and sisters taught in schools, nursed in Catholic hospitals, and staffed orphanages. The abundance of post-war America encouraged 'bricks and mortar' Catholicism. Parishes boasted about their stained glass windows and imported marble altars. The number of Catholic schools doubled between 1916 and 1926. Catholic sisters were admired for maintaining good high schools for both Catholic and Protestant girls. Women religious often provided the only educational opportunities for children in rural areas. Vocations to religious orders were strong because immigrant children saw church professions as a way to improve their spiritual and social standing.

When parishes did not meet the needs of the congregation, the laity actively protested. In 1920 the police were called out in Providence, Rhode Island, to prevent Italian American women from forcibly removing their pastor, the Revd Domenico Belliotti, from Holy Ghost church. Belliotti was a member of the Scalabrini Fathers, a northern Italian order, and the southern Italian laypeople of Holy Ghost thought he and his order were materialistic snobs who dismissed their patron saints and feast days. Conflicts within and between ethnic groups occurred often in large urban centres, and bishops, often Irish or of Irish descent, tried to negotiate between conflicting Catholic cultures.

A spiritual depression?

The seemingly endless abundance of the post-war United States was not apparent in rural areas. During World War I, American farmers had expanded their production to meet the demands of a world at war. More fields were ploughed with tractors purchased on credit. With the cessation of hostilities, the world market for American farm products shrank. High tariffs, while good for American businessmen and factory workers, meant that foodstuffs could not be profitably sold in Europe. Agricultural prices fell, and farmers could not afford to reduce their debts or pay their employees. Within ten years after 1919, the agricultural share of the national income plummeted from 25 per cent to 10 per cent. Even if rural Protestant and Catholic congregations had wanted to modernise their physical plants, the regional economy would have made this difficult to accomplish.

With the fall of the stock market in 1929, the economic crisis spread into every aspect of American life. By 1933 25 per cent of the workforce was unemployed and industry had ground to a halt. No one could afford to buy what was being produced. Seventy per cent of American families were living on less than the recognised minimum standard of living. Clergy stopped building churches and congregations found themselves in debt. For moderate and liberal Protestant denominations, the change in the economic climate was devastating. Philanthropists stopped giving money for large projects, publishing houses found it impossible to meet their pay rolls, and missionaries were called back home. Progressive, liberal Protestantism seemed incapable of explaining why people were suffering so. The alliance between business and faith that had gone unchallenged ten years earlier was now condemned. Protestant ministers and theologians regretted that the *material* abundance of the twenties had not produced a *spiritual* abundance. The weakness of white, theologically moderate, churches both before and after the Crash led one historian to define the period between 1925 and 1935 as 'the American Religious Depression'.[2]

One Protestant response to the tensions of the thirties was to articulate a more realistic response to the social and religious failings of the age. In *Moral man and immoral society* (1932) and *An interpretation of Christian ethics* (1935), Reinhold Niebuhr argued that Christians had over-identified with the secular culture of modernism. A former pastor who became a professor at Union theological seminary in New York, Niebuhr called for a prophetic faith to stand against the sentimentality of liberal Protestantism and the pessimism of Christian orthodoxy. Full justice, he argued, could never be achieved by humanity, and the tragic sense of life must be acknowledged. During the thirties, Reinhold Niebuhr was only one of many theologians – including his

2 Robert T. Handy, 'The American religious depression, 1925–1935', *Church history* 24 (1960), 3–16.

brother Richard, Paul Tillich, Walter Lowrie, William Pauck and Walter Marshall Horton – who promoted Christian realism as an alternative to the optimism of American Protestantism.

Other Protestants worked to strengthen their churches through denominational mergers and ecumenical activities. As ethnic Protestants became Americanised, and fewer children spoke their parents' language, distinctive 'national' churches became harder to maintain. For instance, in 1930 three independent German Lutheran synods united to form the American Lutheran church, which later joined with two Norwegian and one Swedish group to form the American Lutheran Conference. Methodist bodies that had earlier split over slavery merged in 1939 along with the Methodist Protestant church. The new denomination, however, did not unite with any of the all-black communions such as the African Methodist Episcopal church. In 1931 modernist Protestants formed the Federal Council of Churches to promote their common interests. The National Conference of Christians and Jews (1928) brought together Protestants and Jews.

Such mergers and associations did not heal the increasingly contentious and fragmented nature of American Protestantism. During the first part of the century, as biblical criticism took hold in seminaries, certain clergy refused to alter their belief in the inerrancy of the Bible. The pamphlet 'The fundamentals' (1914) summarised their theological beliefs and gave a name to their movement. New worship patterns emerged, and believers understood them to be inspired by the Holy Spirit as at Pentecost. 'Pentecostals', who stressed the religious enthusiasm of the early church, spoke in unusual languages, danced holy dances, healed the sick, and prophesied.

Fundamentalist and Pentecostal Christians rejected the progressive optimism of the era and the 'Jesus the businessman' images of the gospel of wealth. They refused to participate in the agitation for women's suffrage and preferred Victorian sex roles for men and women. Academics like J. Gresham Machen provided intellectual leadership and theological credibility. By 1929 Machen had left the Presbyterian Princeton seminary and had accused modern liberalism of belonging to a totally different class of religion from Christianity. While northern Baptists could count on such liberal luminaries as Walter Rauschenbusch, Henry Emerson Fosdick and Shailer Mathews to justify the modernist position, they could not keep conservatives from tearing apart their annual meetings by violent debates. Conservatives formed new denominations, like the Assemblies of God, while pushing existing denominations to the right.

The public humiliation of fundamentalism during the infamous Scopes trial (1925) succeeded only in giving modernists a false sense of cultural victory. The trial of science teacher John Scopes, accused of teaching evolutionary theory, brought writers and political celebrities to Dayton, Tennessee. Northern reporters delighted in portraying southerners as country bumpkins as the country listened to a religious drama being played out on their radios. While Scopes would be found guilty, it was a Pyrrhic victory. The defence attorney, Clarence Darrow, had shown that prosecuting attorney and Progressive Era reformer William Jennings Bryant had no understanding of modern biology or theology. Fundamentalism was treated as if it had died, killed by its own refusal to accept the inevitable march of progress.

Fundamentalism, however, was far more embedded in the religious fabric of the United States than modernists recognised. Southerners continued to pass anti-evolution laws – Mississippi in 1926 and Arkansas in 1927. Rather than develop a theology to counter modernism, conservatives increased their evangelisation efforts. They established educational and para-church organisations that articulated their own religious opinions. Conservatives did not reject education but, rather, sent their children to their own institutions. By 1930 there were approximately fifty non-denominational Bible schools in major cities training lay workers, Sunday school leaders and foreign missionaries. A network of Bible conferences offered a mix of piety and recreation during the summer months. Conservative denominations started companies like 'The Gospel Trumpet' that not only published church materials but also sold Christian material culture. Unemployed workers found they could earn a living peddling Bibles, lamps sporting Jesus' picture, Christian greeting cards, and pious motto art. Foreign missionary activity increased. The conservative *Sunday school times* listed forty-nine mission agencies in 1931 with the number increasing to seventy-six by 1941. While liberal Protestant missionaries increasingly preferred humanitarian activities to promoting religion, conservatives remained overseas preaching the gospel even during the dark years of the Depression.

As with the revival traditions of the nineteenth century, conservatives were attracted by emotional preaching and good singing that stressed the reality of sin and the importance of conversion and repentance. Sermons were directed towards the everyday problems of average men and women, and preachers did not have to have seminary degrees to get their points across. Healing figured prominently. Conservatives established, maintained and dismantled churches with a degree of flexibility unknown in more established denominations. While critics condemned the supposedly anti-modern orientation of conservatives, their stress on institution building, creating worship styles that utilised modern music, and encouraging organisational flexibility, made these new communities more adaptable to change.

Women were particularly attracted to conservative churches where sex roles were well defined, men were told not to drink, and services could be highly emotional. In Pentecostal denominations, women typically outnumbered men two to one. In such churches women could preach and heal. A few women rose to positions of prominence among conservative Protestants. Alma White founded the Pillar of Fire church in Denver, Colorado, buying land in 1922 and finishing building her 'temple' in 1935. Her radio station, KPOF, began broadcasting in 1928 and still provides Denver with Christian music and news. Aimee Semple McPherson, who was raised in a Salvation Army family in Canada, travelled in 1918 with her mother by car to California. By 1923 she had started her own denomination, the Four-square Gospel church, and opened her $1.5 million 'temple' in Los Angeles. A religious celebrity, she mounted elaborated theatrical productions which were fictionalised in Frank Capra's 1931 movie *Miracle woman*.

The spiritual depression of the inter-war years was not apparent in the membership statistics of many religious communities. Between 1926 and 1940 Southern Baptists grew by 1.5 million. Membership in the Assemblies of God increased fourfold during the same period. Another Pentecostal community, the Church of the Nazarene, went from 63,558 congregants to 165,532. These denominations drew from the former 'frontier' faiths like Methodism, which by the 1920s had lost much of its revivalist spirit. From 1926 to 1936 membership in the Methodist Protestant church declined by over 22 per cent. One contemporary observer, the sociologist Robert Lynd, noticed the increase in 'marginal groups' in 'Middletown' (Muncie, Indiana), but paid them scant attention.[3] He referred to them as 'primitive sects' and failed to see the significance of comments such as: 'my church has grown from 40 to 200 during the past four or five years as it is one of only two churches of our denomination and draws working people from all over the city'.[4] Mormons in the western states also made converts with a 25 per cent increase in membership between 1926 and 1936. While some Christians left their churches and became fully secular, many more forged different ways of being religious.

---

3 Robert S. Lynd and Helen Merrell Lynd, *Middletown in transition: a study in cultural conflicts* (New York: Harcourt, Brace, and Co., 1937), p. 297.
4 Ibid., p. 301.

Internal migrations and religious diversity

The inter-war years brought a shift in where Americans lived. Even before the Depression, white agricultural workers from the southern states travelled westwards and blacks travelled northward in order to find a better life for themselves and their children. Then in 1930 a drought struck the country with Arkansas being the hardest hit. The drought continued, and in 1933 farm prices hit rock bottom. The natural disaster of the drought aggravated the ecological disaster that had been caused by decades of over-farming. Winds created dust storms and blew the topsoil away. Four million people packed up a few possessions and moved. Eventually, 23 per cent of people born in Oklahoma, Texas, Arkansas and Missouri would leave their homes and settle in the west. A quarter of the migrants settled permanently in California while others stayed in Arizona, New Mexico, Oregon and Washington. Life in the west was also difficult. California farmers had a history of exploiting itinerate Mexican labourers. Native-born, white, 'Oakies' and 'Arkies' did not fare much better. Established Californians resented the newcomers who were poor and dirty and different. With their insistence on the literal truth of the Bible, their pious language and their unfashionable clothes, migrants felt like outsiders and few in the west tried to overcome those feelings.

These 'Dust Bowl migrants' would permanently alter the religious landscape of the west. They brought with them forms of southern, rural Protestantism. By the mid-thirties, a group of Southern Baptist ministers decided that the influx of migrants demanded a change in Baptist response. They rejected the Southern Baptist Convention's agreement with the Northern Baptists not to establish churches in the region and began missionary activities in the west. Since it was common in the south for men – and even women – to be part-time preachers and full-time farmers, migrants easily established small non-denominational fundamentalist and Pentecostal congregations. Leaders set up prayer circles and devised plans for building churches. Photographs from the period show migrants preaching in garages, holding Sunday school in tent camps for their children, singing hymns, praying before community meetings, driving 'gospel trucks', and building simple wooden churches. Just as in Oklahoma, Arkansas, Texas and Missouri, religion and music became the means by which poor people described their current plight and expressed their hope for a better future. Few migrants gave up religion, as did Jim Casy, the preacher from John Steinbeck's *The grapes of wrath*. Country music and country faith were established in the fertile central valley and, as the children of the migrants spread out, they established conservative Christianity throughout southern California.

Just as white farmers moved to California to find work, so black farmers moved to the cities of the midwest and east. The early twentieth century saw the nadir of race relations in the United States. Although black male southerners had voted after the civil war, by the late nineteenth century most had been legally disenfranchised. In 1896 the Supreme Court declared that racial segregation did not contradict the rights guaranteed by the constitution, thus encouraging separate schools, hospitals, swimming pools and even water fountains for the two races. Violence was common and between 1900 and 1914 over 1,000 African Americans had been lynched. African Americans in the south were exceedingly impoverished sharecroppers and tenant farmers. Even before the Dust Bowl and the Depression, they would find life in the countryside unbearable.

Between 1900 and 1930 more than 1.2 million African Americans left the south and settled in cities like Chicago, Detroit, New York, Philadelphia, Boston and Washington, DC. As with white migrants who moved west, and foreign immigrants who before the war had flocked to American cities, African Americans travelled to find work. For many ministers in the south, this 'Great Migration' was a threat to the cohesiveness of black religious culture. They feared that urban temptations would lure Christians away from the church. Migrants, however, imagined the move from the south to the north as paralleling the biblical Exodus from Egypt to Zion and the march from slavery into freedom. Like white southerners, black southerners possessed an enduring faith. When they arrived in the cities, they looked for churches filled with other African American sojourners.

African Americans built and refurbished churches in segregated neighbourhoods. In Chicago, Olivet Baptist church would become the largest Protestant congregation – black or white – of the 1920s. By 1930 Pilgrim Baptist, also on Chicago's all-black South Side, was one of the nation's ten largest churches. Its congregation managed to liquidate its $150,000 debt during the Depression. While it was known locally for its classical music presentations, it also was the home of Thomas A. Dorsey who developed the new musical form of gospel music. Gospel music used modern instruments and rhythms to articulate feelings of displacement as well as to assert the Christian promise of redemption. Neither Chicago or any other northern city was the promised land, but for many African Americans the church continued to provide hope for survival in a sinful and racist society.

While Methodist and Baptist churches flourished in the urban north, less traditional communities were also established. Marcus Garvey's Universal Negro Improvement Association (UNIA) provided an explanation for American racism and a ritual system for connecting together believers. Garvey, who was born in Jamaica in 1887, came to New York in 1916. He directed his message at Africans living throughout the world, telling them to struggle for self-empowerment, legal justice and economic opportunity. Garvey believed that only if the former slaves could return to Africa would they be able to be fully self-sufficient. Garvey revelled in the pageantry of ceremony. In 1921 he began the African Orthodox church, although he permitted UNIA members to subscribe to any faith. Blacks, he insisted, would not progress spiritually or politically unless they worshipped a black God. Garvey was attacked by the government, convicted of mail fraud, and sent to jail in 1923, but his movement gained considerable prominence among African Americans. The UNIA proclaimed on a popular level what many black leaders were saying more cautiously – that white racist society was intrinsically evil and that it was only through black initiatives, or even separatism, that freedom could ever be achieved.

George Baker was one of the many southern blacks who left an impoverished life in Georgia for the promise of hope in the north. By 1933 he had claimed the name of 'Father Divine' and was connecting concepts of health and positive thinking to socialism and racial integration. Like Marcus Garvey, Father Divine laid out an involved regime of religious practices for his followers and, like Garvey, he was attacked by whites for altering acceptable race relations. The UNIA and Father Divine's Peace mission gained public attention and numerous adherents, especially in the large cities of the east coast. As with many African Americans, they were constructing new rituals of spiritual and physical renewal as well as rethinking their place in a changing world.

Migration to the cities enabled African Americans to be exposed to a variety of religious traditions. On the South Side of Chicago, for example, some African Americans chose to join Episcopal or Catholic churches. As European immigrants prospered, they left the decaying cities for the surrounding suburbs. African Americans moved into these 'changing' areas, often buying 'used' churches and synagogues for their own worship needs. Episcopalian and Catholic bishops, however, preferred to establish new black parishes rather than sell their buildings to Protestant newcomers. In 1928 the Episcopal bishop of Chicago, Charles Palmerton Anderson, assigned an African American, Samuel J. Martin, to a church in a black neighbourhood. St Edmund's thus became one of two Episcopal churches in Chicago made up exclusively of African Americans. Father Martin not only maintained a building built by white people during a far more financially flush time, he converted low-church southern migrants to high-church Episcopal ways. Within ten years his congregation grew from 150 black communicants to

800 members. In addition to being respected for his ritually correct and elegant liturgies, Father Martin helped his parishioners find decent housing and provided for their families when they lost their jobs.

The Catholic decade

Roman Catholicism also appealed to African Americans who moved northward and urban Catholic dioceses saw an increase in black participation. Catholic bishops established racially segregated parishes that continued the tradition of ethnic 'national' parishes. At the same time they contributed towards institutionalising white racism because African Americans could *only* be members of all-black parishes. Some Catholic religious orders specialised in ministry to non-Catholic minority groups, such as African Americans, and these nuns came to staff their parochial schools. Non-Catholic black parents often looked to these new parishes to provide educational alternatives for their children. Over time, African Americans converted to Catholicism.

Two segregated black parishes in Chicago grew dramatically during the inter-war years. In 1920 white priests at Corpus Christi church baptised twenty-one adult African Americans, and by 1935 that number had increased to 131 and then in 1938 to 322. In 1923, when St Elizabeth's congregation was still bi-racial but its schools segregated, Mercy Sisters taught 168 white children and Blessed Sacrament Sisters taught 281 black children. Three years later, after a declaration that St Elizabeth's parish would only serve black Catholics, the number of black children enrolled in its parochial school increased to 505. By 1943 the Sisters of the Blessed Sacrament were teaching 908 elementary students at St Elizabeth's and ran the only Catholic high school in Chicago that accepted African American students.

Although the overall percentage of African American Catholics was small, the appeal of Catholicism for the dispossessed reflected the new position of Catholics in the nation. African Americans were attracted to parish life, at least initially, because of the social services it offered. By the thirties, working-class Catholics supported a vast array of schools, orphanages, hospitals and seminaries. They were also politically established in local and state governments. The nomination in 1928 of Alfred E. Smith as the Democratic presidential candidate drew attention to the fact that Catholics living in east coast cities now held considerable federal electoral power. Al Smith, the governor of the state of New York, was the first Catholic presidential candidate.

The presidential candidate Herbert Hoover (a Quaker) soundly beat the Catholic Al Smith by winning forty of forty-eight states. Hoover's support of

Prohibition permitted him to secure the votes of southern Protestants, enabling him to become the first Republican presidential candidate since Reconstruction to make important inroads in that soundly Democratic region. Hoover even beat Smith in his home state of New York. However, New York City, as well as every other large urban centre, went for Al Smith. While in the previous 1924 presidential election Republicans had won the country's twelve largest cities, four years later they could win none of them. Democrats realised that city people would vote for a candidate who believed differently from the Protestant clergy.

By 1932, with the Depression wrenching the American economy, the Democratic candidate had not only the attention of city dwellers but the votes of farmers and factory workers who were being crushed by Hoover's inability to address the nation's economic problems. Roosevelt won the election and immediately set about repealing Prohibition. His victory also brought about enormous changes in the makeup of the federal government and its relationship to average Americans. Roosevelt knew that his supporters were not members of the Protestant establishment. Indeed, when polled shortly after Roosevelt's landslide re-election in 1936, 70 per cent of Protestant clergymen said they were *still* against the New Deal. One way the president acknowledged his supporters was by bringing Catholics and Jews in unprecedented numbers into his administration. Of the 196 federal judges whom the president appointed, fifty-one were Catholic. During the previous three administrations, only eight Catholics out of 214 had been appointed. The president appointed two Catholics, James A. Farley and Thomas J. Walsh, as postmaster general and attorney general respectively. Catholics were no longer excluded from the federal government and their political strength was felt across the nation.

Within the Catholic church, the inter-war years saw a focus on lay piety. A new emphasis on eucharistic devotion and frequent confession brought more people to mass, even if congregational membership remained constant. In 1919, for instance, one Oregon parish reported 330 yearly communions. By 1923 this number had increased to 14,400. Religious orders ran lay retreats, and by the end of the decade more than fifty-five retreat houses were operating in the United States. As with Protestant churches, more attention was being paid to children. During the thirties a large-scale catechetical movement succeeded in bringing children into Catholic summer-vacation schools and adults into discussion clubs. The Catholic Youth Organization (CYO), founded by a Chicago priest, Bernard J. Sheil, stressed the importance of both physical and spiritual growth. It quickly became popular in parishes across the country.

More Catholics were now being better educated in the dynamics of ritual practices. Novenas, nine-day series of prayers, were promoted in parishes. During the the thirties over 35 million Catholics attended novenas and at some churches as many as 70,000 attended services each week. Priests offered to enrol people in devotional societies and in return for their donations sent the new members medals and holy cards. When the seemingly unending economic instability of the Depression caused individual failure, intense family suffering and neighbourhood decline, Catholics utilised their tradition's healing strategies. Women especially used the idioms of Catholic prayer to negotiate their way amid the conflicting expectations of their immigrant communities and the changing American society.

Accompanying a rise in lay piety was a renewed interest in Catholic ethics and social justice. Just before the 1932 election, Father James Cox of Pittsburgh, Pennsylvania, organised and led what was then the largest protest march on Washington in American history. Forty per cent of workers in Pittsburgh were unemployed and Cox intended to draw attention to the needs of suffering workers and the inadequate Hoover presidency. President Roosevelt's social initiatives, summarised in his 'New Deal' for the American people, resonated well with the pro-labour papal encyclicals *Rerum novarum* (1891) and *Quadragesimo anno* (1931). Two priests committed to Catholic visions of social justice, John A. Ryan and Francis J. Haas, sat on governmental committees that administered the New Deal. On a more radical level, in 1931 Dorothy Day and Peter Maurin founded the Catholic Worker movement, which demanded both personal involvement in the plight of the poor and the reconfiguration of capitalism. By 1942 thirty-two 'Houses of Hospitality' and twelve farms were caring for the victims of the Depression and providing models of Christian living. A Russian emigrée, Catherine de Hueck Doherty, during the late thirties founded a series of 'Friendship Houses' in Toronto, New York and Chicago which provided direct assistance and neighbourhood education to the inner-city poor. A charismatic speaker, she promoted inter-racial justice in a period when the sham of the Scottsboro Boys trial (1931), in which a group of young African Americans were wrongly convicted of rape, filled the newspapers.

Christianity over the airwaves

For both Catholics and Protestants, new forms of technology stimulated personal piety and promulgated various visions of a Christian future. Although movies were made to strengthen devotion and Hollywood promoted the biblical epic, it was radio that became a new evangelising tool. By 1925 there were at least sixty-three church-owned radio broadcasting stations across the United States. With the Depression, however, many individual churches had to sell their equipment and air rights. Rather than see the elimination of religion from the airwaves, the major commercial broadcasting networks of NBC and ABC decided to provide free time to representatives of Protestant, Catholic and Jewish communities. In consultation with liberal Protestants, the networks agreed that religious broadcasting should be non-denominational, avoid controversial or doctrinal matters, and stress ecumenical ideals. In 1934 the Federal Council of Churches assumed the responsibility for network Protestant broadcasting, to the consternation of conservative groups. On their 'national radio pulpit' NBC presented sermons by theologically moderate clergy. NBC also broadcasted the 'Message of Israel' and the 'Catholic hour'. Bishop Fulton J. Sheen in 1930 began his media career on the 'Catholic hour', attracting a listening audience of 7 million and receiving 6,000 letters per day.

Groups whose religious messages did not conform to network standards had to purchase on-the-air time or struggle to maintain their own broadcasting systems. In 1926 a fundamentalist, Bob Shuler, installed a radio station in the tower of his church and sent his message out across Los Angeles. His sensationalist exposés of political corruption eventually provoked the Federal Radio Commission in 1931 to terminate his right to broadcast. Less controversial was the preaching of Walter A. Maier during the 'Lutheran hour'. Belonging to the conservative Missouri synod, Maier preached in English rather than German, and in 1938 listeners sent over 125,000 letters responding to his programmes. Other ministers presented music, healing and testimonials on the radio. Elder Lucy Smith, the founder of All Nations Pentecostal church and an important African American healer in Chicago, broadcast her inter-racial healing services. People often listened in merely to hear her gospel choir sing. Radio ministries were essential to evangelists, and Aimee Semple McPherson broke with the sermon model of preaching by designing dramatic re-enactments of biblical and moral tales. Her radio congregations could not see her flashy costumes and elaborate stage sets but she did encourage them to participate by kneeling in prayer next to their radios and placing their hands on the receiver in order to be healed. Americans who never entered a church or who had doubts about religion could tune in to Christianity through the radio.

Father Charles E. Coughlin, with the approval of his local bishop, also bought radio time to promote his notions of Catholic piety and economic reform. Although at first a Roosevelt supporter, Coughlin would eventually use the airwaves to promote his own schemes of ending the Depression. Included in his rhetoric were attacks on the Jews. By 1936 Coughlin claimed 1.6 million active supporters and many more listeners. He employed 150 clerks to take care of his mail and count the money sent to his Shrine of the Little Flower located outside Detroit, Michigan. Coughlin's entry into politics, his vicious criticism of Roosevelt, and his praise of the Nazis would eventually end his popularity as America entered the Second World War. Coughlin and others utilised radio as older evangelists had used newspapers and outdoor amphitheatres to spread their ideas.

Coughlin was not unique in his use of the radio to spread his conflation of politics, economics and religion. The airwaves were filled with expressions of hatred clothed in Christian sentiments. Gerald B. Winrod founded the Defenders of the Christian Faith, and in 1938 entered the Republican primary as a candidate for the United States Senate from Kansas. His anti-Jewish, anti-Catholic and anti-black vitriol combined pre-millennial fundamentalism with political populism. Gerald L. K. Smith was a Disciples of Christ minister who joined with the governor of Louisiana, Huey Long, to promote his 'Share-Our-Wealth' programme. William D. Pelley, the son of a Methodist preacher, hoped to establish a Christian (fundamentalist Protestant) state where Jews would be disenfranchised and confined to the equivalent of an American ghetto. Unlike Winrod and Smith who stayed close to their fundamentalist roots, Pelley's message also included theosophy, astrology and spiritualism. While these individuals were extreme in their hatred, anti-immigrant and racist sentiments were voiced frequently during the inter-war years and helped legitimise immigration restrictions, encourage the rise of the Ku Klux Klan, and establish limits on the number of Jews in private colleges and universities.

For those who thought of themselves as Christians, the inter-war years in the United States were decades of innovation and diversity. Some tried to minimise this religious flourishing by creating a stable picture of a tripartite nation made up of Protestants, Catholics and Jews. Others ignored the religious creativity of the period entirely by focusing on secular trends. The reality, however, was quite the opposite.

14
Christian churches in Australia, New Zealand and the Pacific, 1914–1970

KATHARINE MASSAM

Overview: practical Christianity

The stars of the Southern Cross define the night sky across the vast and varied region of Australasia and the Pacific. Legend and science concur that this constellation was last seen above the northern horizon near Jerusalem at the time of the crucifixion of Jesus. When European explorers rediscovered the four points in the southern sky in the sixteenth century, they recognised a banner of faith; but they also saw, and perhaps more clearly, an accurate astronomical clock by which to take new scientific measurements. A practical, rational, spirit has always rested alongside the readings of Christian faith in this region. By the end of the twentieth century, even though the Southern Cross was a popular civic and church emblem, any claims of Christendom translated south were clearly out of place. For the settler societies of Australia and New Zealand, church and state had always had separate and frequently competing cultures. And even in those Pacific Island groups where the missionary message had merged strongly with local authority, denominational variety pointed away from established churches towards ecumenical goals.

The practical demands of church life have dominated expressions of Christianity through the region, overshadowing any emphasis on intellectual exploration or prayerful contemplation for its own sake. Although mystics and visionaries have played a role in most traditions, it has generally been a hidden one, accidental to the life of the institution. Holiness was understood as the core of Christian life, but was most respected when it meant a capacity to relate widely to ordinary people, to respond sensitively to material needs, or to lead effectively without fuss or self-promotion. Scholarship was acknowledged early as a dimension of Christian ministry, but was valued most when it made for lively preaching and the plain interpretation of complex questions, or had clear application to administrative problems. The demands of church building, religious instruction of children, and the promotion of the moral life of the community have generally taken precedence over prophetic reflection on the gospel or academic investigation of its demands. Richly textured as it is, the pattern of Christian life and the experience of Christian churches in the region has been marked by response to immediate need and circumstance, forging a practical and activist Christian identity in the process.

A geographic rather than a cultural or social region, Australasia and the Pacific stretches roughly 16,000 km east to west and 10,000 km north to south. Defined by ocean, it encompasses both the island-continent Australia and the coral atolls of Kiribati only hundreds of metres wide. It runs from sandy limestone plains and giant karri forests, through sharp eucalyptus scrub, snow-capped mountains and hot mud springs, to dense forest, tropical highlands and palm-fringed beaches. In 1914, it included the settler societies of nearly 5 million Australians and 1 million New Zealanders, and ranged across some 1,500 language communities in the Pacific islands. These were linked by traditions of influence and dependence within the region itself, and colonial histories. Together, they took the total population of the region to an estimated 10 million people at the beginning of the century. By the end of the 1960s, numbers had almost doubled across the region to approach 19 million.[1]

Three encounters with church: conversion, translation, missions

Churchgoers, always a minority in New Zealand or Australia, although commonly a majority in the Pacific, gathered on Sundays in whitewashed weatherboard and iron chapels on isolated mission stations, stately stone cathedrals in modern cities, makeshift halls in country towns, and brick 'war memorial' churches in new suburbs. They sought God in Christian traditions that varied as widely as any other dimension of the territory. But in general they built on three distinct experiences: a missionary and conversion heritage in the Pacific islands; the denominational traditions imported and translated

---

1 For discussion of census data see Ian Breward, *A history of the churches in Australasia* (Oxford and New York: Oxford University Press, 2000); Allan Davidson and Peter Lineham, *Transplanted Christianity: documents illustrating aspects of New Zealand church history* 3rd edn (Palmerston North: Department of History, Massey University, 1995); K. R. Howe, Robert C. Kiste and Brij V. Lal (eds.), *Tides of history: the Pacific Islands in the twentieth century* (St Leonards, NSW: Allen and Unwin, 1994).

by European settlers in Australia and New Zealand; and the mission past of Aboriginal Australia and of the Maori in New Zealand. In each of these three broad patterns, the style of Christianity that resulted was not so much 'innovative' as a distinct mix of denominations, each consciously modelled on 'home', but relating to new circumstances.

Initially in the Pacific it was not so much a denominational mix at all, but a map divided by spheres of missionary influence. In the eastern and central Pacific, where hierarchical Polynesian societies had followed their monarchs into Christianity, the Congregationalism of the London Missionary Society, Methodism from Britain and Australia, and Catholicism from France were well established in the nineteenth century. In the western Pacific, the flatter and smaller social groups of Melanesia converted village by village in a slower process that burgeoned in the 1950s. Missionary numbers boomed after the Second World War, growing from 1,700 in 1930 to 4,500 in 1960.[2]

In Australia and New Zealand, European settlers claimed, but generally sat lightly to, denominational traditions from Britain and Ireland. Growing from colonies founded by combinations of the British crown, English business enterprise, and efforts to regularise European fringe-dwellers, neither country ever had an established church. Nevertheless, the Church of England was the largest denomination through the period in both countries, positioned as both the church with most social influence and the default category for nominal Christians. Denominational proportions were consistent through the period. In New Zealand, Presbyterians were the second largest group, followed by Roman Catholics with roughly half as many adherents, just ahead of the Methodists. In a significant difference in the mix in Australia, Catholics were the second largest denomination and Presbyterian or 'Reformed' shared equal numbers with the Methodists. Throughout, smaller denominations hoped the division of church and state would assist them, and individual congregations did flourish, but expansion was consistently difficult without centralised co-ordination. Deep sectarian suspicion divided denominations, and separated Catholics from all others, until wartime co-operation, the foundation of the World Council of Churches, and then the sea-changes of the Second Vatican Council gave permission for contact and then co-operation. In both countries the proportion of respondents who declared themselves Christian

2 Charles Forman, *The Island churches of the South Pacific: emergence in the twentieth century* (Maryknoll, NY: Orbis, 1982).

dropped through the period, but remained over 85 per cent in each country. The biggest increase was in the numbers choosing not to state their religion.[3]

Within the settler societies, Aboriginal Australians and the Maori in New Zealand had contrasting but related experiences of Christianity. For Australian Aborigines the encounter was predominantly through missions and welfare outreach; the Maori experience included separate denominational structures and independent Ratana and Ringatu churches. But contact between European and indigenous Christians was almost never on equal terms. Christian institutions were at one and the same time a buffer against the colonising power, and its agents. Belief in the equality of all under God moderated the worst biological determinism, but racist assumptions remained powerful. Throughout the twentieth century, indigenous activists took strong Christian convictions into their fight for justice. They were supported by individuals and small networks within the Christian communities, but as institutions the churches were silent and uncomprehending. From the 1960s, however, as movements advocating self-determination gained political ground, churches began to acknowledge the significance of traditional cultures, and to hear the grief and anger that 'assimilationist' mission policies had wrought. In wrestling with how to respond, churches faced a question that also applied in the Pacific and to settler Christianity itself: was the Christianity of the region simply derivative of the European churches of origin, or could faith take root in the local environment and cultures to become a particular expression of the wider tradition?

The Pacific: mission and conversion churches move 'beyond the reef'

From the seventeenth century, Christianity was diffused through the Pacific, carried predominantly by local evangelists who heard the story from European missionaries and made it their own. At first glance, Pacific Christianity can look like an extension of Western denominational patterns. But viewed more closely, it is the amalgam of Pacific and Christian identity, in which Christianity was fused into local structures in post-conversion local churches, that demands most attention. The years from 1914 to 1960 fall into two distinct periods: a missionary phase up to 1942 when the region was

---

3 Davidson and Lineham, *Transplanted Christianity*, pp. 178, 183–5, 250–2, 314–15; W. W. Phillips, 'Religion' in Wray Vamplew (ed.), *Australians: historical statistics* (Broadway, NSW: Fairfax, Syme & Weldon, 1987), pp. 421–7.

engulfed by the Second World War, and then a period of related but separate patterns in the Pacific's three geo-cultural regions: Polynesia, Micronesia and Melanesia.

By 1914 most of the communities in Polynesia and Micronesia, in the central and eastern Pacific, had adopted the missionaries' message and thought of themselves as 'Christian'. In the inter-war years church life had generally settled into a colonial enterprise. The missionary stance, in which pagan beliefs were contested and Pacific identities recast in Christian terms, was widely adopted, although Islanders wryly caricatured some customs. The most persuasive Pacific missionaries were themselves Pacific men and women. Some perceptive Europeans aimed to create an indigenous church and fostered strong local leadership, but mostly the missions were run on paternalist lines. An outstanding few, such as Maurice Leenhardt in New Caledonia, appreciated the significance and value of the Islanders' worldview as a valid starting place for theological reflection. It was sometimes missionary women who forged strong links with the people through the women and girls, and mediated most sensitively between cultures.

At the same time, in Melanesia in the western Pacific, north-east of Australia, the coastal missions were still extending inland with frontier enthusiasm. In New Guinea in particular the missions 'boomed' as air travel made contact with the populous highlands more possible. After the Second World War, Christian missionaries from established churches and new evangelical societies rushed from around the globe to make contact with the 'remotest peoples'.

For the older churches across the region, war in the Pacific from 1942 to 1945 was also a turning point. The war brought intense suffering through the region, and shattered any illusions of Pacific isolation. Foreign missionaries were evacuated, executed or interned, and tens of thousands of local men conscripted to assist the one million troops in the region. Shocking brutality rivalled any stories of the pagan past and stripped the gloss off Christianity and 'civilisation' elsewhere. With missionary leaders gone, and no church structures beyond the disrupted villages, Pacific Christianity emerged as self-reliant under local leadership. Congregations continued to meet where they could, and local Christians were among the hundreds killed and martyred. In the wake of the distress, Islanders and sympathetic missionaries were increasingly confident of the need to work towards self-government in churches. The move was often in the lead of political independence. The corresponding interest in finding a 'Pacific way' in worship and new respect for local theology also echoed post-colonial concerns.

The question of how churches and missions should respond to the post-war world was at the heart of an ecumenical conference of Protestant churches at Malua in Western Samoa in April 1961. Sessions were allocated to ministry, evangelism, the gospel in a changing context, young people and family, each being addressed by a speaker from the Pacific and a 'consultant'. The speeches stressed the importance of working together, and the disturbing realities of change.[4] It led to the foundation of the Pacific Conference of Churches in 1966. Catholic support for indigenous leadership and ecumenical work was buoyed by the Second Vatican Council, and they joined the PCC in 1976. The theme of the 1961 conference, 'Beyond the reef', hinted at new horizons. It also suggested there was more for the wider church to see, as Island Christians not only reflected the missionary church back to the institutional centres, but also offered a complex model of religious adaptation and change.

Australia and New Zealand: private faith in public life?

As the fading of colonial assumptions prompted new movements in the Pacific churches, so secularisation shifted the relationship between Christianity and the world in twentieth-century Australia and New Zealand. As the proportion of regular churchgoers slid to under 40 per cent in all denominations, more from indifference than hostility, members struggled to maintain a place for churches as relevant social institutions, and to find new ways to engage the surrounding culture and speak to the changing context. The main weight of devotional life, charitable work, and other 'domestic' dimensions of church life, even including attendance, was carried by women through the period. As one Australian man observed to researchers in the 1940s: 'I don't go to church much, although I send along my contributions, you know. The wife and youngsters go, but it's the only day I've got free, and I must say I like to be out in the open air.'[5] But men were leaders and decision-makers in the public life of the church, both internally and especially at the intersections of church and state. Barriers to the participation of women in church structures began to

---

4 International Missionary Council, *Beyond the reef: records of the Conference of Churches and Missions in the Pacific, Malua theological college, Western Samoa, 22 April–4 May 1961* (London: International Missionary Council, 1961).

5 A. J. Macintyre and J. J. Macintyre, *Country towns in Victoria: a social survey* (Carlton, Vic.: Melbourne University Press, 1944), p. 22.

fall in this period. The ordination of Winifried Kiek, as a Congregational minister in South Australia in 1927, was an important first, but few other women were ordained before 1970. Some sections of the church insisted women's ministry could not be formalised through ordination, but all churches relied on the labour and talents of their women members.

If religion was women's work, but churches and the state men's responsibility, there were defining links in time of war. In both the First and Second World Wars, faith was more visible and 'masculine' as national days of prayer marked the progress of fighting, and church and political leaders spoke in biblical terms assuming a 'civic Protestantism'. The reputation of the Australian and New Zealand Army Corps (ANZAC) became a marker of national identity in both countries. This soldierly tradition had entwined early but uncomfortably with Christianity around themes of self-sacrifice and loving remembrance. The commemorations of ANZAC Day that began in 1916 encompass values that are sufficiently solemn, and widespread enough, to be cited as 'civil religion'.[6] Although individuals held more nuanced positions, and Catholics led by Archbishop Mannix were prominent in two Australian campaigns against conscription, the Australasian churches were powerful advocates of the nationalism that fuelled the cause of the war. But in keeping with a cultural suspicion of pomp, the most widely known war-hero was the larrikan 'man with the donkey', an anti-authoritarian stretcher-bearer who rescued his mates.

In the inter-war years, Christian churches attempted a return to 'business as usual', expanding networks of schools and churches among grieving, radicalised or disillusioned constituents, even as they wrestled with the possibility that faith might not be relevant to social solutions. The loss from the churches of so many men to death or indifference caused anxious comment, especially when the competing attractions of the beach or sport broke through a heritage of Protestant Sabbatarianism and began to take young people away from Sunday activities. The promotion of the 'Social Gospel' encouraged a vision of Christian society. Methodists in New Zealand adopted a 'Social creed' in 1922, the Baptist minister Joseph Archer became president of the Labour Party of New Zealand in 1928, and in Australia Ernest Burgmann, later Anglican bishop of Goulbourn, urged the church to take seriously the twin engines of human life: love and hunger. Although devotion to 'Christ the worker' grew in some Catholic associations, Catholicism regarded socialism with suspicion. Catholic Action groups of women as

---

6 K. S. Inglis, *Sacred places: war memorials in the Australian landscape* (Carlton, Vic.: Miegunyah Press at Melbourne University Press, 1999), p. 471.

well as men were founded from 1931 in response to Vatican encouragement for the reform of the working world, but moved firmly to the political right, especially as events of the Spanish civil war became known from 1936. Churches developed sub-structures of belonging to incorporate all family members in particular cohorts, making provision at the margins for the unmarried adults, especially women. Some of these groups were sectarian or denominational 'clubs', others were catechetical and formational as well as social. These groups reached beyond local church boundaries, and national gatherings in particular gave a sense of 'critical mass' for believers.

Church members were also increasingly aware of and involved in international networks of co-operation. In contrast to the nationalism of the war years, churches promoted an understanding of 'universal humanity' in the 1920s and 1930s, fuelled particularly by university-based groups. These were tiny – a reflection of the small retention rate beyond the school-leaving age of fourteen – but vibrant in a church population where theology was barred from the universities. The Student Christian Movement (SCM) in particular drew Australians and New Zealanders into ecumenical and international relationships. It fostered a theologically 'comprehensive' Christianity among graduates, supporting a mainline Protestant spirit characterised by biblical study, social concern and ecumenical practice. It also nurtured a significant proportion of the mainstream Protestant leadership through to the 1970s. The origins of the Uniting church in Australia, founded to incorporate the Methodist, Presbyterian and Congregational traditions in 1977, can be traced clearly to more than sixty years of discussion and commitment to the gospel ideal of church union among key leaders formed by the SCM. The evangelical Inter-Varsity Fellowship split from the SCM in 1930, concerned to defend the Bible and traditional doctrine against liberal and modernist attacks. It flourished especially in Sydney where the Anglican church set a powerful low-church tone. Within Catholicism the achievement of a separate school system left little energy to expand beyond the tight catechetical link of primary school and parish church, but nevertheless the network of Catholic university groups held its first national gathering in 1934. The national conferences and international links of the student church groups inspired several generations of future leaders with wider visions of Christian life.

When war broke out in Europe in 1939, both governments committed troops promptly. Pacifism was again a rare stance among Christians, but the churches were more knowing about the complexities of war, and discussion of building a new peace in post-war reconstruction was under way by 1942. When the war ended with the bombing of Hiroshima the sense of religious crisis did not abate. The Cold War was understood in churches as a conflict between good and evil, between the Christian West and the Communist East.

Hope that a religious cure could be found for social ills and the causes of war was strong. Post-war churches were buoyant as suburbs expanded around cities, and standards of living and leisure time rose. The mainstream press affirmed Christian faith as part of a moral society, linked to democracy, security and happy homes. Public campaigns underlined the connection both across and within denominations. On 11 November 1951 all Australian newspapers published a 'Call to the people of Australia', signed by church leaders and chief justices, urging higher moral standards in response to the danger of the Cold War. The same anxieties marked rallies that explicitly urged Christian commitment or demonstrated denominational loyalty. Between 1953 and 1957 a prominent Australian Methodist minister, Alan Walker, preached a 'Mission to the nation', visiting dockyards and red-light districts, avoiding church venues and filling town halls. The international Rosary Crusade, led by the Irish American priest Father Patrick Peyton, reached New Zealand and Australia in 1953. Its famous campaign slogan urged Catholics to remember that 'the family that prays together, stays together'. Over 90 per cent of churchgoing Catholics committed themselves to pray daily against the prospect of a third world war and the rise of 'atheistic materialism'.[7] The same themes of personal holiness to safeguard family and society also dominated the largest religious rallies of the period: the Billy Graham crusade of 1959. Graham used modern marketing and media to preach a conservative, personal, faith. Backed by intense preparation in thousands of prayer groups, evangelical Christians believed the community was on the cusp of 'genuine revival'.[8] Graham returned in 1968, but between his visits the Beatles had toured 'down under'. Like Graham, they found the crowds more fervent than any elsewhere. But the social upheaval of massed Beatlemaniacs, especially young women, breaking public barricades and screaming in the streets in 1964, made a cultural gulf visible. Popularity and propriety had split, old certainties had ended.

Music was one of the touchstones as churches confronted questions of the relationship between religion and culture with new starkness. The metrical psalms of Presbyterians, Gregorian chant of Catholics, the hymnody of Luther and the Wesleys, did not go well with guitar. Whether rock music,

---

7 Katharine Massam, *Sacred threads: Catholic spirituality in Australia 1922–1962* (Sydney: University of New South Wales Press, 1996), p. 106.

8 Stuart Piggin, *Evangelical Christianity in Australia: Spirit, word and world* (Melbourne: Oxford University Press, 1996).

or folk music, or protest songs of the secular radio, were appropriate for public worship in the churches pointed to theological questions that would replace the Catholic–Protestant divide. By 1970 it was not denominational labels but other indicators that named powerful realities for Christians. Evangelical, charismatic, or activist Christians from various denominations found they could co-operate with each other and forge links more comfortably across rather than within traditional groupings. Under the stars of the Southern Cross a new transdenominational sectarianism pivoted on contrasting assumptions about the gospel and how it should be lived in the world. For Christians in the region the deepest question would concern the relationship of faith and culture: whether the world should or can be converted into the church, whether the church should accommodate its message to the values of the world, or whether the signs of the times speak in more subtle language altogether.

Catholicism and Protestantism in the Second World War in Europe

ANDREW CHANDLER

The Italian city of Pisa was no stranger to violence, war, disease or revolution. In its turn, the twentieth century brought it democracy, wars abroad, revolution, dictatorship and then war at home. By 1944 the dictatorship of Mussolini had given way before a coup at home, invasion by Allied forces in the south of the country, and an occupation by his German allies moving from the north to meet this advance. Pisa itself was now garrisoned by German forces. On the night of 17 June 1944 British bombers attacked it. Incendiaries fell in rapid succession on the central medieval piazza and soon fires had broken out there. In the mayhem, sections of one of the treasures of the Piazza Miracoli, the great mural by the Master of the Black Death which had for centuries adorned the walls of the ancient graveyard, were engulfed in flames. Much of it was lost for ever.

The mural was a work of the fourteenth century. It offered a colossal depiction of all the social orders of medieval Italy, crowds of men and women, the beautiful and gracious and the mean and humble, the clergy and the bishops, the nobility, the clergy, the artisans and the poor, all caught up together in a grotesque reflection on death and judgement, damnation and salvation. Such a picture might well have appeared remote and barbarous only a generation before, but in the inferno of the Second World War it spoke now with a terrible new life, even as it was consumed. For here the orders and authorities of civil life, church life and secular, are broken up and divided, and then reconfigured – often quite against our own expectations – in the new eternal order. The man who is justified at the Last Judgement may be a labourer of no worldly account, and the man tarnished by sin and damned might prove to be a prince or a bishop.

Medieval Christian theology was fascinated by dialectic, by the arrangement and confrontation of propositions that might march against each other to victory or defeat. It was such an insistence which placed Eck against Luther five centuries before and which, in turn, yielded with inexorable power the new division of Catholics and Protestants against each other. At the outset of the twenty-first century we still turn to the tragic drama of the Second World War in a spirit of campaigns, in which the word and works of a pope himself, the bishops, the clergy and the vast crowds of the faithful – even the church entirely and Christianity itself – are to be judged and consigned either to heaven or hell. The air is still filled with justifications, accusations, exonerations, apologies, damnations and canonisations. For the period has not yet turned cold in our minds. And yet we are still left holding only fragments. Within this dense fabric of public and secret, personal and corporate life, inhabited by institutions and bureaucracies and individuals and families, all practising and owning a Christian faith as best they could, lay many contradictory words and acts, many quite different responses to the debacle. It is difficult to find a common form for such complexity; hard even to measure what we encounter. We are left to reflect on how little we know about it all, about the private decisions of conscience, the secret conversations within authorities, orders, families, congregations, which must have occurred in every life and every community.

The incapacity of prophecy and the determination to survive

That Christianity survived the Second World War is the first thing that we should not simply take for granted. To a Catholic observer, the government of Germany was widely judged abroad to be a power whose totalitarian government and ideology were manifestly opposed to Christianity, one which had broken its promises to protect the claims of religion and had increasingly persecuted believers. Its ally, the Italian state, had also broken its pledges against the church. The democracies were of a different order, with a government in Britain which was historically Protestant but in almost all respects now effectively secular. The government of France was tolerant, but still leaning back on to its anti-clerical traditions and certainly no particular ally of the Catholic faith. Then there stood against all this the power of the Soviet Union, which avowed the extinction of religion itself, which had taken its part in the destruction of Poland at the outset of the conflict and pursued an aggressive course in the Baltic, and which bore the weight of the European war after the German invasion of the summer of 1941. In short, Christians entered this new war in an already deep-rooted state of doubt.

Church leaders of both traditions owned a responsibility to judge what was just and unjust. Protestantism, after all, was a faith of the Word and of the sermon. Catholicism could present itself to the world as a construction of authority, in which those of high position must guide the faithful with encyclicals and statements. But both now found that what they had offered most confidently to the world was the most fragile task of all. For who is to pay the price of such words and such authority? How do churches negotiate with such political powers, when they move with such relentless, unpitying force against ordinary men and women of the faith? If there is protest, will it bring change – or simply sufferings far worse upon the heads of the oppressed? Subsequent generations have struggled quite to grasp how real was this fear in the mind of those who bore official responsibilities in the churches in 1939. For those who lived beyond the borders of occupying forces it was often enfeebling. For those who faced enemies in their own societies, it was simply debilitating.

Given such vast and insuperable realities as these, those who led the churches were determined that the faith must somehow be preserved, in the churches that were still standing, in the sacraments that were still administered to the faithful, in the prayers and hearts of congregations still living. This committed them to a course of discretion, calculation and manoeuvre which seemed to their critics to run the risk of betraying prophetic power and even justice, as people of all backgrounds recognised it and hoped to hear it. For them the fundamental question was not merely the exposition of justice to a fallen world, but a more basic one: how could the church actually inhabit this terrible new paradigm? For the preservation of the faith was the task of the church, and in a world in turmoil its commission was to survive.

Historians have often been tempted to see whether churches criticised the political order or sympathised, whether they collaborated or resisted. But the essential concern of many Christian leaders, be they Catholic or Protestant, was rather to uphold the integrity of the church on its own terms, to maintain its own narrative of salvation. It was to see that the sacraments were still offered to the faithful; that sacred words were still said and rituals enacted as they had been for generations. This was a different language and a distinct identity. It was often said that the church lived in the world but was not of the world. The abstraction may not appear helpful, and it certainly begs many questions. But it does speak of a perceived duality, a division, a marking of boundaries. The Protestant and Catholic churches were not institutions, and not simply popular movements. They were both. Under pressure it was natural that they should mark out such boundaries as firmly as they could, and turn inwards within them. But the greater the pressure the more hesitations and doubts within them accumulate. Contradictions break out. It would be too much to expect churches of any description to present a coherent form. Centres, where they have been constructed, do not hold; things fall apart. The bishop of one diocese understands his situation and views his responsibilities differently from that of another; a priest who pursues a particular course finds his fellow clergy supportive or critical. Laity risk the disapproval of their priests in committing acts which to them still bear the mark of a Christian conscience at work. But there are also times when the divisions break up, and bishops, clergy and laity manage to reconfigure their relationships in new forms, sometimes more sensitive and outward-looking in composition, character and purpose. In Germany one might think of the dissenting Kreisau Circle, which gathered around the two figures of Helmuth James von Moltke and Peter Yorck von Wartenburg.[1] This remarkable group, which set itself the task of mapping a course for their country once war was over, embraced three Jesuits, there secretly to report to a bishop, a Protestant pastor who was acting independently, and others, some religious, others agnostic.

The justification of war

When war broke out between Germany, Poland, France and Britain at the beginning of September 1939 church people widely owned a responsibility to judge the justice of the course on which their respective governments were set. At the same time, they were at once represented in the conflict, for the forces of all countries were attended by chaplains who worked to guide and sustain those who must set off for battle. But it was a very different thing to do this in a free country from a dictatorship. In Britain the news of the declaration of the war coincided with the Sunday morning services and was often reported to congregations by their priests or ministers during the course of them. Most saw this war to be necessary and unavoidable. Even from pacifists there was no concerted campaign of criticism. All arguments were exhausted; war appeared unavoidable because Hitler would not have peace.[2] They went to war with justice blowing into their sails not because of what Hitler did at home – though they knew these things well – but because German forces continued to break its pledges and to cross international borders. Moreover, feeling was not high against the German people themselves. They were seen to be tyrannised. This could not be their

---

1 See Ger van Roon, *Neuordnung im Widerstand: der Kreisauer Kreis innerhalb der deutschen Widerstandsbewegung* (Munich: Oldenbourg Verlag, 1967).
2 See Alan Wilkinson, *Dissent or conform? War, peace and the English churches 1900–45* (London: SCM, 1986), pp. 232–51.

war. There was also some determination to see that the church held to its own, independent, line. For a bishop like George Bell of Chichester it was not enough to support the decision for war. It must be justly fought. The church was not 'the State's spiritual auxiliary'.[3] When British opinion turned increasingly against the German people Bell would deny that all Germans must themselves be unjust because of the crimes committed in war by a government over which they had no control. In time, too, Bell would criticise publicly the British government for its policy of obliteration bombing. In these things he was, however, often an isolated figure.

What of Germany? Here the churches had to weigh up the political realities of their own situation before they could utter a judgement of their own. The Catholic areas had never been the heartland of National Socialism. Now the Catholic authorities were more than ever aware of their vulnerability. The agreement of 1933 had bought only a little time and grace. In 1937 Pope Pius XI had delivered an exasperated encyclical against the German government, cataloguing its betrayals of that agreement.[4] As for the Protestants, they had for six years been engaged in a tenacious conflict among themselves for the integrity of the church and its gospel. Most had quietly embraced a new, corporate, state church, which was broadly an ally of the political state. A minority movement, which enjoyed some political patronage, favoured an integration of National Socialism and Protestant Christianity. A significant and determined minority had held out against it, while they voiced insistently their loyalty to the state, and were in no way a movement of resistance against it. In September 1938 a statement had been released by the leaders of this dissenting minority, the Confessing Church, which would in other societies have seemed innocuous enough, expressing the mood of the continent at that time for peace and not for war. But to those in the state who needed only a slender excuse to move against them it was an invitation to retribution. A new wave of repression left a deep mark.[5] They would not venture into these waters again.

For most Catholic and Protestant clergy the very fact of the war was reason enough to pledge their support, not explicitly to their own government

---

3 See G. K. A. Bell, 'The church's function in wartime' (1939), reproduced in G. K. A. Bell, *The church and humanity 1939–1946* (London: Longman, 1946), pp. 22–31.
4 This was 'Mit brennender Sorge'. The full text is reproduced in Simon Hirt (ed.), *Mit brennender Sorge* (Freiburg im Breisgau, 1946), pp. 1–24.
5 See Ernst Christian Helmreich, *The German churches under Hitler: background, struggle and epilogue* (Detroit: Wayne State University Press, 1979), pp. 230–2.

and its policies, but to the German people in this time of need as they looked across their borders – wherever they might be – and into the eyes of committed and powerful enemies who sought the defeat of their country. This language of solidarity with a people circumvented a more intricate measuring of political questions and became a characteristic of Christian discourse across Europe. It became the expression of pastoral love, but not of explicit political association.

The Vatican and Geneva: Christian internationalism and the dilemmas of neutrality

The Vatican was a state, however small, and in time of war a state must have a policy. But, more than this, the concordat signed by the Vatican and the state of Italy in 1929 required the papacy to be neutral in times of conflict. Pragmatically, there was every reason to direct Pius XII towards an official avowal of neutrality in this new war in 1939. He faced now a unique and demanding combination of realities: on the one hand the pope was master of the smallest state in Europe, if not the world, with a Swiss guard who were essentially an ornamental police force. But then he was the Vicar of Christ, the supreme head of the Catholic faithful across all the continents of the world. For decades Catholic people of many countries had suffered penalties and indignities for the loyalty which they owed to the pope. Now Catholics were living in all the conflicting nations and it was the task of a pope to show that he favoured none among them, whatever the respective policies of their governments.

But neutrality was more than a premise. It was a policy that must be constructed, and it would be seen that in its applications and calculations the pain of it would be found. In the Great War Benedict XV had worked away beneath the brittle surface of national diplomatic life to mediate, to prod, and to work for amelioration and justice. In September 1939, too, it could be seen that if a pope could not mobilise forces to weigh in the balance of the powers, he could exploit the powers of discretion that still existed beneath them. Between September 1939 and the summer of 1941 Pius XII found that such diplomacy favoured the policy of neutrality.[6] Thereafter it was

---

6 See Frank J. Coppa, *The modern papacy since 1789* (London: Longman, 1998), pp. 185–97. But also Harold Deutsch, *The conspiracy against Hitler in the twilight war: an account of the German anti-Nazi plot from September 1939 to May 1940 and the role of Pope Pius XII* (London: Andre Deutsch, 1968).

demanded by the new reality of the war against the Soviet Union and the reckoning of the new terrors: how could he condemn Germany without condemning the Soviet Union? To a growing number of critics this state of neutrality soon looked more like a moral incarceration than a premise for active leadership.

But evidently the choice for neutrality was useful not only to Catholics. By 1939 the Protestant ecumenical movement had reached a stage whereby a number of bodies, by now busy for decades in uniting Protestant traditions and giving them a common voice in the world, had coalesced, and it was widely recognised that the institutional home of this movement was Geneva. The symbolism of Geneva was obvious: it had also been the seat of the Red Cross and the League of Nations. And if ecumenical Protestantism was not a state, its officers bustled about a neutral country whose participation in the war was confined to funding the protagonists and, naturally, sustaining the conflict with its essential oils.

The two great engines of Protestant ecumenism, Life and Work and Faith and Order, were now on the brink of a momentous amalgamation under the name of the World Council of Churches. In 1939 the name was even common currency, but its full, provisional, title was, more cautiously, the World Council of Churches in the Process of Formation. Here the authorities of the churches maintained representatives to keep the ecumenical debate alive even though the outbreak of war effectively ended all direct contacts between them. Here, too, a quiet, purposeful, diplomacy was pursued. Many of these strands gathered around one man, Visser 't Hooft. He was a confident, assertive Dutchman who showed a particular interest in the secret work of Germans who were even now working against their own government in search of peace. To them, he was a rigorous, questioning, but sympathetic host. He saw Geneva as a safe house for various secret diplomatic sorties, and one for various networks to meet as they threaded their perilous way across the borders of the continent. More than this, it offered an alternative, supranational grammar of action in a belligerent world of closed borders. For Visser 't Hooft this was not simply a conflict of nations, but a war of ideologies which placed some Germans in as profound a state of opposition to their government as were those in other states who fought against it.[7] This made him an ally of Bishop Bell in England.

7 See W. A. Visser 't Hooft, *Memoirs* (London: SCM, 1973), pp. 113–64.

The experience of occupation

Whatever over-arching structures of authority had been created around them, the everyday experiences of Protestants and Catholics were above all defined by their experiences within their own local and national societies. In western Europe German invasions had been successfully accomplished by the end of the summer of 1940. The Low Countries, Denmark, Norway and France were then to remain for almost five years occupied countries. These were lightning wars, over in a matter of weeks. In the east the German borders extended from Poland and then, with western Europe defeated, deeper into the Soviet Union from 1941 to 1944, when Soviet forces blunted them and began, at appalling cost, to turn them back towards the German heartland. Accordingly, for most Catholics and Protestants the experience of war was not like that of the Great War, one of attrition between front lines maintained by hundreds of thousands of conscripted troops. It was, instead, one of occupation. Each national experience was unique, but a distinction may be drawn between the occupied countries of eastern Europe and those of western Europe. The eastern front was, from the beginning, a war without reservation, compunction or humanity, fought with almost no regard to international convention. The realities of occupation were those of wholesale deportation, dispossessions, incarceration and unhesitating mass murder. The German occupation of western Europe was brutal and horrifying. But it was founded upon different ideological perceptions which allowed some pragmatic accommodation. To be sure, the violent methods of confiscations, imprisonment, reprisals and deportations were applied with increasing severity and consistency. But they were applied less often, less arbitrarily and on a lesser scale.

Historians of occupied Europe have found archbishops and bishops, superintendents and synods of both churches voicing loyalty and compliance to the occupying powers of the day. Then, they turned inwards: if there were protests they were likely to be in defence of religious youth organisations or schools. This can rather easily be represented simply as a defence of interests rather than an appeal to principles of justice, and, in truth, it has not won much admiration from later generations, searching for evidence of prophetic courage. But it would be wrong to find it utterly at odds with a contrary mood of criticism, opposition and even resistance. For, in seeking to preserve an integral identity whose roots were not those of the prevailing powers, and whose language and ways of being were distinctive and different, Christian churches maintained a parallel reality and an ethical and spiritual resource upon which men and women could draw in their own way: the church could still be a sovereign space, in which there might still be some freedom of thought and action. Within this caveat emerged all kinds of patterns of interaction with the world of political society, patterns which involved church people of every position and degree: from enthusiastic collaboration to dissent and even resistance. In a totalitarian society, or one threatened by intimidation and force, the possibilities offered by such a presence acquired a particular weight and reality. People who had rarely found much in Christianity to concern them now turned to it with a new seriousness.

Poland

In the autumn of 1939 the German government occupied the western and central portions of Poland: Poznania, Polish Pomerania and Silesia in the west, together with central and southern parts of the country, were inhabited by 9 million Poles and 600,000 Germans; the second, the Government General, the central portion embracing Warsaw, Cracow and Lublin, was inhabited by 12 million Poles. In the first area occupation led virtually at once to mass confiscations and deportations eastwards. From the Government General deportations of labour into Germany itself followed.

In the first sphere lay the archdiocese of Gniezno and Poznan, the oldest in the Polish church. The primate of Poland, Cardinal Hlond, dispatched two reports to the Vatican listing in meticulous detail the character and scale of the onslaught that followed. The Gestapo shut down the archdiocesan curia of Gniezno; the vicar-general was confined to his home while the records of the archdiocesan offices were investigated. The curia's finances were simply expropriated. The metropolitan chapter was scattered; the basilica – only recently restored and furnished – was shut by the police. The seminary was occupied by soldiers; a general had moved into the archbishop's palace. The canons were evicted; retired priests had been turned out of their hostels. The convent of Gniezno was emptied and converted into a detention centre for Jews. The church of the Holy Trinity there was profaned and its contents carried off. Priests who ventured into their pulpits were simply hauled away. Hlond listed the names of ten priests who had been shot, one who had been beaten to death, one who had died in forced labour, two who had died in prison, and another who had been the victim of a bomb. Many more, he added, were in prison where they suffered horribly. Of those who had been deported he knew nothing. Others were in concentration camps. Some had gone to ground to continue their work as best they could. Priests were a common sight in labour gangs on the roads and bridges, in the fields, on coal trucks, 'and even engaged in demolishing the synagogues'. Families were arrested as they left church. Priests in every parish disappeared; half of the parishes of Gniezno had no clergy left at all. At Bydgoszcz sermons could still be heard, but in German, and a prayer for Hitler was added after mass. And yet when the churches opened people poured inside, for baptism, confession, communion. Marriages were proscribed outright. In the schools religious education was suppressed and crucifixes were removed. Catholic associations of all kinds were shut down. Iconoclasm was regularly reported; desecrations, profanation, expropriation, expulsion, deportation. Women's orders were seen to be particularly severely attacked.[8]

The same was occurring in Poznan, the home of Catholic Action in Poland; here too newspapers were abolished, printing houses suppressed, academic institutes shut. There were firing squads in public squares. The 'entire leading class' had been dispossessed and exiled from the Government General; only labourers and servants were left undisturbed. In Poznan deportations were summary and brutal; every night between 500 and 1,500 people disappeared: 'no one even dares undress, for the time allowed to leave has recently been reduced to a few minutes'. Many were separated and taken away to Germany; boys old enough to work, attractive girls too. Those who remained were sent on to the Government General in cattle wagons, and this was now a region largely bombed and demolished, a countryside stripped bare, already heavily over-populated. Hlond wrote, 'All this spells extermination, extermination conceived with the malice of the devil and carried out with unparalleled brutality.'[9]

These things were not kept quiet. A report by the former manager of the Catholic press agency in Warsaw, now chaplain to the president of the Polish representative in London, Mgr Kaczynski, was published in Rome. When German papers fabricated reports of what was occurring in Poland they were repudiated firmly – they were, said Kaczynski, forging and lying to the world, assuming 'the credulity of mankind and its talent for frequently forgetting'.[10]

---

8 *The persecution of the Catholic church in German-occupied Poland: reports presented by H. E. Cardinal Hlond, primate of Poland, to Pope Pius XII, Vatican broadcasts and other reliable evidence*, preface by Cardinal Hinsley (London: Burns Oates, 1941). First report, 6 January 1940, pp. 3–11.
9 Ibid., pp. 12–19.
10 Ibid., report of Mgr Sigismund Kaczynski, manager of the Polish Catholic press agency, pp. 87–100.

A communiqué was broadcast on Vatican radio to the United States on 21–2 January 1940, before being repeated, in modified versions, in German, Spanish, Portuguese and other languages: 'It is no longer a secret that His Holiness has been profoundly pained by reports lately received at the Vatican, and all too completely confirmed, on the martyr's fate reserved once more for his dear Poland, in whose inevitable resurrection he continues to count with such confidence.'[11]

France

By this time France, too, had fallen and was also divided into regions: the occupied zone to the north, including Paris, governed by German authorities; the Vichy area to the south, ruled by a sympathetic and compliant puppet state which almost at once took the names of the town from which it was governed, Vichy, and its president, the retired General Pétain; and a small Italian zone in the south-east.

French Catholics were left to reflect in their own particular ways on the catastrophe that had destroyed their nation in only six weeks, and the drama lent itself to vivid arguments about the character of all they had affirmed before defeat. The collapse of France was the collapse, after all, of a particular state, the Third Republic, whose politicians had viewed the power of Catholicism with distaste. Since 1870 the presence of the church in the civil life of the nation had been purposefully curtailed, driven from the law courts and the schools, in a society which had witnessed a climbing divorce rate and a decline in the birth rate. French republicanism had little exerted itself to overcome an old anti-clericalism, a suspicion of religion altogether. Like Christians in Germany who looked upon social democracy and found little encouragement for their participation, French Catholics struggled to find a place for themselves in French republicanism. Some pronounced that the defeat of France was a judgement upon their nation. It was a call to return to God. And within this call the Vichy state stood with a smile of welcome and an open door to the corridors of authority. Some bishops even grumbled that it had stolen their own tunes, with the new rhetoric of family, work, service, contrition and sacrifice. Meanwhile, for the first time in decades Catholic bishops were courted by the politicians. For the men of Vichy the appeal of an entente was obvious: this essentially collaborationist state was weak from the start and never better than rickety, and it needed to build a defensible moral

---

11 Communiqué intended for America and broadcast on the night of 21/2 January 1940, ibid., p. 115.

credibility. The church was arguably the most prominent public institution and popular movement left remaining in the country. To attach Christianity to Vichy was to strain towards public viability and moral legitimacy. Not that a man like Pétain was much concerned with the church otherwise; and not that Vichy was a clericalising state. What was offered now to the church was given to accommodate, not out of conviction.

To these overtures many of the bishops appeared to respond. They could not embrace defeat, but neither could they turn back the clock. It was widely agreed that the Vichy state was legal, and Christians owed to the properly constituted authorities a due obedience. In November 1940 Cardinal Gerlier welcomed Pétain to Lyon with the pronouncement, 'Pétain is France, and France, today, is Pétain.'[12] On 15 January 1941 a further gathering of cardinals and archbishops affirmed their loyalty to the state with rather more reserve, stepping discreetly from reference to the 'legitimate power' to the 'established power'.[13] Reciprocal gestures followed nicely and neatly. Religious education reappeared in the state schools (it had disappeared in 1882). Religious orders banished at the turn of the century were allowed back.

The difference between this occupation and that of doomed Poland was perhaps expressed in the fate of church bells. In Poland they had been silenced, taken away, melted down. In Nantes, the German forces at first worried that the ringing of church bells might issue a call to arms, but this was soon relaxed, in time for the feast of St Anne, who was Brittany's patron saint. And where there had been wholesale extinguishing of public religion in Poland, now in France there was some confusion. The Germans agreed that processions might be allowed if they were 'purely religious'. This inevitably provoked uncertainty, for what did that mean? In some parishes priests found themselves arrested for doing what priests in neighbouring parishes did unhindered. Meanwhile, Catholic youth movements were banned, more because they were youth movements than because they were Catholic. But they were sometimes turned into sports clubs, and when lines of young men and women raced off across the countryside on bicycles it was difficult to be sure if this was something religious or 'more than religious'. Sometimes such enterprises were prohibited, sometimes they

---

12 See Julian Jackson, *France: the dark years 1940–1944* (Oxford: Oxford University Press, 2000), p. 268.
13 Ibid.

were permitted. This confusion – or manipulation – of religious expression and activity did not only exist between secular authorities and churches, but also within the churches themselves. The bishop of Angers told his clergy that they must be religious and moral, not political. In 1941 he banned a Mothers' Day service because, it was later explained, of an accident of translation.[14]

The bishops were largely obedient, but it would be a mistake to generalise too confidently. If the bishop of Angers was compliant, the bishop of Nantes was obtuse. When the latter received a request from the local *Kommandatur* for use of the cathedral by his soldiers for a service he refused permission, for this service would be a Protestant one, and a scandal in such a place. A bishop, after all, could be expected to know a religious question when it was proposed. But by the time this was going on the cathedrals at Tours and Bourges had already been used for such services.[15] In Paris Archbishop Suhard was particularly agreeable to the German forces and served on the *Conseil national*. Priests served in ten departmental committees; 200 others worked at commune and canton level.[16]

But time, too, brought changes in attitudes. The occupation bit harder. Within these broad affirmations of loyalty a certain amount of independent life managed to breathe for itself. Soon variations and even contradictions across the fabric of French Catholicism were not difficult to discern. The clergy were more clearly a voice of popular unhappiness. Some had early in the occupation committed themselves to active participation in all manner of illegal schemes, sometimes with the silent, nodding connivance of their superiors, sometimes in the teeth of their censure. The dean of St Martins' cathedral in Tours, Canon Robin, who had once served as an army chaplain and had been for a little while a prisoner of war, offered shelter to escaping prisoners of war. In time, this help was extended to Jews and resistance fighters as well, and an escape line stretched silently from St Martin's out through Captain Morel of the Tours gendarmerie and to the Abbé Lacour, the curé of Athée, and Fr Lhermitte of Esvres-sur-Loire, and then Abbé Péan who was curé of Drache. This proved a costly enterprise. Robin survived and would become bishop of Blois. Morel was deported and executed. Lacour and Lhermitte were also deported to Germany where they disappeared. Péan was arrested in February 1944 and was tortured and murdered by the Gestapo in Tours itself.[17] Criticism was

---

14 See Robert Gildea, *Marianne in Chains: in search of the German occupation 1940–45* (London: Macmillan, 2002), pp. 211–13.
15 Ibid.   16 See Jackson, *France*, p. 269.
17 See Gildea, *Marianne in chains*, pp. 215–16.

heard insistently in the orders: in the words of the Dominican Jean Maydieu and the Jesuits Gaston Fessard, Pierre Chaillet and Stanislas Fumet. In them some have observed the roots of Catholic resistance.

Norway

German forces occupied Norway suddenly on 9 April 1940. While there already existed in the country a sympathetic political movement in the Nasjonal Samlung, it was barely more than a fringe organisation of only around 43,000 members, and was something too weak on which to build an effective collaborationist government. The Norwegians were overwhelmingly hostile to the new powers and, with their own king and government in exile, frequently turned to the state church to frame a critical response. That it did so with a measure of coherence and vitality was in no small measure owed to the bishop of Oslo, Eivind Berggrav.

Berggrav was a specialist in political ethics and, before the war, had learnt a good deal from the fate of fellow Protestants in Germany. Meanwhile, his own position in the church was senior by virtue of the fact that the bishop of Oslo chaired the annual conference of bishops. He was also an active ecumenist with friends across many traditions and many borders. On the outbreak of war he had undertaken a good deal of busy diplomacy to see if a negotiated settlement might yet be secured. If this won few admirers and was, in any case, soon cast aside by the force of political and military circumstance, in the occupation of his own country Berggrav found a more durable role, one in which he combined closely the duty of the church to maintain its independence from unjust government and its equal responsibility to seek justice for humanity. The tools of such a trade he found all about him. He saw that the Augsburg Confession offered him ample ground for refining a new political theology. His Luther was one who preached the duty of disobedience. Berggrav also exploited the possibilities offered by official structures. If the National Socialist church department was soon issuing directives from one side, Berggrav's new council, the Kristent Samrad, was soon ready to launch its ripostes back again. When the head of the collaborationist government, Vidkun Quisling, set himself up as *summus episcopus* and precipitated a crisis of loyalty across the church, and when this was followed by further tensions over youth organisations, almost 800 pastors (93 per cent of the whole) cut their connection with the state altogether and the bishops followed suit. On Easter Day 1942 they pronounced from their pulpits that they would no longer enjoy any official status or income, or perform any official duties. They would become instead a folk-church.

This movement was not uncontested within the church itself. About sixty pastors continued to maintain the state church, but they received little congregational support. And if they criticised those who had resigned for simply creating a 'Berggrav church', by then it could be seen that Berggrav himself was not much in control of these events, for he was confined by police in his house for the rest of the occupation – not a severe incarceration, and one that he turned to his advantage by writing a succession of books, all of them very much to the point.[18] By the time German forces disappeared from Norway on 8 May 1945 about 130 pastors had, at some time, been arrested. But none died and Berggrav, too, survived.

The deportations of the Jews of Europe

The churches of occupied Europe often raised protests against the deportations of young men for labour in Germany itself. But more has come to be written of their reaction to the persecution of the Jews by the new German authorities.

The plight of Jews living under the Hitler regime had been widely known outside Germany itself almost as soon as Hitler came to power in January 1933. Within months it had also been widely deplored by Christians across western Europe and in the United States.[19] If the various attempts to respond to the refugee crisis before the autumn and winter of 1938 were poorly co-ordinated and, in the eyes of their promoters, shamefully inadequate, it would be a mistake to see in this evidence simply of an inability to acknowledge clearly what the persecution meant and how a Christian might condemn it. Now, from the autumn of 1941, the Christians of occupied Europe confronted the mass deportations of Jewish families within their own cities and towns.

Even so, the receiving, verifying and interpreting of information appears to have been as complicated a business for church authorities as it was for governments. In 1941–2 many of them were still in the business of assessing the reports that were coming their way. While a number of historians have

---

18 See Torleiv Austad, 'Eivind Berggrav and the Church of Norway's resistance against Nazism, 1940–1945', *Mid-stream: an ecumenical journal*, 26:1 (1987), 51–61 and 'Der Widerstand der Kirche gegen den nationalsozialistischen Staat in Norwegen 1940–1945', *Kirchliche Zeitgeschichte*, 1:1 (1988), 79–94. But Austad and Arne Hassing are soon to publish a two-volume study. I would like to thank Torleiv Austad for help with the section on Norway.

19 See Johan M. Snoek, *The grey book: a collection of protests against anti-semitism and the persecution of Jews issued by non-Roman Catholic churches and church leaders during Hitler's rule* (Assen: Van Gorcam & Comp, 1969).

argued that the Vatican knew a great deal about what was occurring, in 1942 it does not appear to have been better off than any other government or authority.[20] Officials saw reason to hesitate. Visser 't Hooft later remembered that at Geneva they had first received 'rather mysterious messages using Hebrew words so as to conceal their meaning from the censors and their interpretation was difficult'. But by the end of 1942 the fragments were assuming a clear overall form. But this was, even now, beyond the credulity of responsible people. Visser 't Hooft, again, later recalled that information appeared 'ineffective' because it seemed, simply, 'improbable': 'I must confess that it took several months before the information received entered fully into my consciousness.' It did, not when he read a report, but when he met a Swiss businessman who told him of a business trip to Russia on which he had himself been invited by German officers to witness a mass killing. Visser 't Hooft resolved to do what he could to precipitate a clear governmental response, but he found it immensely difficult to make headway. A new aide-memoire written jointly by the secretariat of the World Council of Churches and the World Jewish Congress simply disappeared into the offices of international bureaucracy without visible effect.[21]

The German churches were unable to orchestrate a response. There is a great gulf fixed between the formal words of men occupying responsible office, like Dibelius, Koch, Wurm and Marahrens, and the exasperation of others like Dietrich Bonhoeffer, Wilhelm von Pechmann and Marga Meusel. On paper they did not share a basic vocabulary; in life they converged with awkwardness and embarrassment. These stray enterprises do not emerge in a clear, obvious form. Instead, we are left with a purposeful accumulation of memoranda, *Gutachten* ('expert opinions') and public statements, emanating from a variety of sources, many of them corporate, synodical or, in other senses, institutional. Church leaders who have cited them as evidence of opposition to the persecution have often claimed too much for them. Some scholars have, in their turn, pointed to the compromises, the failures, silences

---

20 See Owen Chadwick, 'The pope and the Jews in 1942', in W. J. Sheils (ed.), *Persecution and toleration*, Studies in Church History 21 (Oxford: Blackwell, 1984); also his *Britain and the Vatican during the Second World War* (Cambridge: Cambridge University Press, 1986), p. 1. There is now a vast amount of material on Pius XII and the 'Final Solution'. One of the latest attempts to identify specifically the character of his response is Sandra Zuccotti, *Under his very windows: the Vatican and the Holocaust in Italy* (Yale: Yale University Press, 2001). But this is a controversy which will endure for many years yet.

21 Visser 't Hooft, *Memoirs*, pp. 165–72. But for a discussion of the ecumenical response at Geneva and beyond see, too, Armin Boyens, *Kirchenkampf und Ökumene 1939–45: Darstellungen und Dokumentation unter besonderer Berücksichtigung der Quellen des Ökumenischen Rates der Kirchen* (Munich: Chr. Kaiser Verlag, 1973), pp. 100–51.

and betrayals that occur within such sources. For them, gallant protests are seen to be the work of individual voices, sinking unheeded in an ocean of religious anti-semitism, prevarication, delusion and avoidance.

Institutions of authority may claim a representative power, but the careful historian cannot accept that premise uncritically. To be sure, official words may inspire both official and unofficial acts, but they still find their meaning primarily in the diplomacy and the politics of corporate systems, and it is not often easy to know what impression they leave on a broader, inhabited landscape. However grand their claims, how does one connect such statements to everyday experience? But we are still clutching at straws and inherit only fragments and glimpses: of the envelope of ration vouchers secretly passed to a rabbi in an unobserved moment on a Berlin street; the sixty-one private homes in Württemberg where Jews were hidden throughout the war.[22]

A discreet but effective relief and refugee agency led by Pastor Grüber in Berlin had been shut down by the Gestapo in December 1940. Grüber would survive the war, but his partner Dr Sylten was within weeks in the concentration camp at Dachau and was later killed there. When Jews were ordered to wear a yellow star observers noted incidents of sympathy. Bishops Wienken and Berning attempted to secure the concession that Jewish Catholics might be allowed to put aside their yellow stars when in church. Even this was rejected. The deportations from Germany began on 15 October 1941. The National Socialist *Deutsche Christen* alone voiced their support for these new measures. Berning found them harsh and again pressed for ameliorations, and this time was reassured. But these were soon seen to count for nothing. In November 1941 a corporate statement by bishops protesting against compulsory divorce of Jews was sapped by an inserted qualification observing 'harmful Jewish influences upon German culture and national interests' by their chairman, Archbishop Bertram. By February 1943 Christians living in mixed marriages were also deported. The Catholic bishops were discreetly dividing their sympathies between Bertram and the bishop of Eichstätt, Preysing, who, like Saliège in France, was a lawyer by training, and who had pressed for a harder line against the Hitler regime from its beginning. Now Preysing urged clear words about 'the Jews generally'.[23] Beside this there were the vehement words of the anti-semitic Archbishop Gröber. Then

---

22 See Wolfgang Gerlach, *And the witnesses were silent: the Confessing Church and the persecution of the Jews*, trans. and ed. Victoria Barnett (Lincoln and London 2000), pp. 161–2.

23 See Guenter Lewy, *The Catholic church and Nazi Germany* (London: Weidenfeld & Nicolson, 1964), p. 290.

there was the provost of Berlin, Lichtenberg, who prayed daily for the Jews until he was arrested in October 1941. In interrogations he replied that the measures were at odds with moral law, inverted the customary understanding of the injunction of Romans 13 to justify his opposition, and asked to be deported with those who were be taken away. Released from prison in October 1943 he was transported at once by the Gestapo to Dachau, but died during the journey.[24]

Bishops, clergy and laity interwove densely. Gertrud Luckner of Caritas worked from Freiburg to get Jews across into Switzerland. She, too, was arrested in November 1943 and taken to a concentration camp. There was a loud and very public protest by wives at Rosenstrasse, in a mainly Jewish district of Berlin, and their husbands were released. It was a striking episode, and some remark that it showed what could be done. But it was singular.[25]

The remaining bodies of the Confessing Church could muster nothing until 1943, and what then occurred, after much debate, was an anonymous statement written by a number of laity to their bishop, but also to Bishop Wurm at Württemberg. On 12 March 1943 Wurm himself wrote to the church ministry that these measures had 'for a long time been depressing many circles in our nation, particularly the Christian ones'. Fearful that foreign governments might make much of dissent within Germany, church people had kept their counsel. But they could not continue to be silent. Wurm pressed on with two further letters in July and December 1943, and these were both sent to the government ministries and distributed secretly across parishes. Wurm did not mince his words: he spoke of a policy of 'persecution and destruction' which worked 'without legal conviction', deploring the treatment in particular of those who were in Christian marriages. He declared, 'Such purposes like the extermination measures already taken against the other non-aryans, stand in the strongest possible opposition to the commandments of God and destroy the foundation of all our Western thought and life, in particular our fundamental belief in the God-given right to human existence and human dignity.'[26] In October 1943 the Prussian synod of the Confessing Church sent out a pastoral letter denying that the state possessed the right to kill, except criminals or enemies in wartime: 'The murdering of men solely because they are members of a foreign race, or

---

24 See Beate Ruhm von Oppen, *Religion and resistance* (Princeton: Princeton University Press, 1971), pp. 39–49.
25 Nathan Stoltzfus, *Resistance of the heart: inter-marriage and the Rosenstrasse protest in Nazi Germany* (New York: W. W. Norton, 1996).
26 See Gerlach, *And the witnesses were silent*, pp. 198–205.

because they are old, or mentally ill, or the relatives of a criminal, cannot be considered as carrying out the authority entrusted to the State by God.'[27]

In France, the response of the churches to the great persecution was similarly, and inevitably, disjointed. When French Jews were ordered to wear the yellow star there was evidence of public sympathy. The Jewish census of 1941, which laid the administrative foundation for deportation, was accepted. Church leaders were increasingly given to allowing the principles of such actions, but pleading that charity be shown in practice. When the first deportations from Paris began in July 1942 public opinion rose against it. The bishops were divided. The bishops of Marseille and Grenoble approved of the policy and said so. Most preferred to keep their silence. Archbishop Gerlier of Lyon, a lawyer, an authoritarian who admired Franco and now approved warmly of Pétain, also enjoyed a number of cordial connections with Jewish officials. Gerlier allowed the case for economic anti-semitism, but he would not accept a racial argument. On 23 August Archbishop Saliège read a new pastoral letter from the pulpit of Toulouse cathedral. The Jews, he declared, were their brothers. Though forbidden by the prefect, these words were read out in every church in the diocese. Five bishops in the southern zone had protested. Thirty more did not. More significant was the fact that no bishops in the occupied zone protested either publicly or privately. Most conceded that there was a Jewish 'problem', but Saliège and Théas would not allow for that either.[28]

On 29 October Suhard and Gerlier met Pétain in Vichy. The conference marked a decline in interest in the persecution amid a profusion of declarations of loyalty. Certainly, some concessions to the church itself followed – new grants to the Institut Catholique and other institutions of higher education. There were some, too, for Protestant theological faculties. From now the deportations would lack the scale and drama of the first ones that summer. Gerlier either did not know how to press his case once he had stated it openly, or lacked the power of persistence, or the inclination. Most likely he sensed that the issue had gone off the boil. At all events, he was not going to risk the new entente over it.

It is difficult to measure what these salvoes achieved. Saliège's words spread widely and caused excitement, being published by resistance journals, distributed by Catholic book stores, and carried across country by teams of cyclists. Further afield, they were broadcast by the BBC and voiced as far

27 Ibid., pp. 198–214.   28 See Jackson, *France*, pp. 375–6.

away as New York. Resistance movements evidently took more notice of the persecution thereafter. It was enough, however, to encourage more fusillades from the Catholic press, particularly from the vocal journal *Témoignage chrétien*. A number of religious orders grew active. The nuns of Notre-Dame-de-Sion in Paris arranged the shelter of around 450 children in family homes; in Lyon nuns of the same order were soon busy forging identity papers. Fr Pierre Marie-Benoît, a Capuchin friar in Marseille, managed to transfer about 30,000 Jews to the Italian zone after November 1942, and got another 4,000 across the border to Switzerland. *Amitié Chrétienne*, run by two Catholic priests, Chaillet and Glasburg, dispersed as many as they could in religious houses and amongst sympathetic Catholic families. But such enterprises could not last long. In the spring of 1943 the Gestapo raided the offices of *Amitié Chrétienne* and Chaillet himself was forced into hiding.[29]

In France the Protestant congregations were strikingly vigorous on behalf of the persecuted. Protestants there had long sensed their vulnerability in a society in which Catholicism was such a dominant power, and they were often quick to recognise their responsibilities to other minorities. In March 1941 Marc Boegner – who also served on Vichy's *Conseil national* – wrote to Darlan and to the Grand Rabbi, Israel Lévi. The letters were published. It is likely, too, that it was Boegner who pressed Gerlier to make his own protests when the deportations began that summer. The Protestant organisation CIMADE, under Madeleine Barot and J. Delpech, set to work with a will to hide and rescue Jews. Perhaps still more striking were the Protestants who lived in little straggled communities in the Cévennes region: they had been there for generations, even from the sixteenth century. Persecution was etched into their history and their identity. In time they were receiving migrating Jews even from eastern Europe. In communities like Le Chambon and Saint-Germaine-de-Calberto those who held positions of local responsibility, such as schoolteachers, pastors and civil servants, showed what a small, sympathetic, civil society could manage in the face of orchestrated intimidation and persistent intrusion. By the end of the war the 3,000 people of Le Chambon had hidden 5,000 Jews.[30]

In the Netherlands the church authorities sought to throw all that they could against the deportations. The combined representatives of the

29 Ibid., pp. 374–7.
30 See Michael R. Marrus and Robert O. Paxton, *Vichy France and the Jews* (New York: Basic Books, 1981), pp. 203–8. See, too, Philip Hallie, *Lest innocent blood be shed* (London, 1979).

Protestant churches there sent a protest against the dismissal of Jewish officials on 24 October 1940 and it was read from the pulpits. A further proclamation followed three days later. Twenty to thirty thousand copies of a pamphlet, 'Almost too late', were soon distributed across the country secretly. The General Synod of the Dutch Reformed Church had published a pastoral letter concerning the Jews in September 1941. In July 1942 Catholic bishops meeting with Protestant leaders sent a telegram to the *Reichskommissar* protesting against the deportations and warning that they were prepared to oppose them publicly. This secured an offer: for their silence the Germans would release all Jews who had converted to Christianity before 1941. The archbishop of Utrecht, Johannes de Jong, could not accept this distinction; the Protestants were inclined to do so. De Jong at once published a pastoral letter for all Jews and retaliation followed.[31] All Catholic non-Aryans were deported, among them the convert Edith Stein. The Vatican took note, bleakly.

In Britain and the United States protest was open. On 17 December 1941 the British government made a public statement in Parliament. The archbishop of York added his own furious declamation in the House of Lords.[32] When it was perceived that too little was being done the archbishop of Canterbury fulminated in the House of Lords in March 1943 and asked the government to allow group visas in order to ensure the rescue of as many Jews as possible.[33] This intervention was encouraged by Visser 't Hooft but it secured very little. A new Council of Christians and Jews pressed the government to do more while seeking to establish a durable foundation for the ongoing relationship between their two faiths. Meanwhile, there was patient, ongoing work to support the Jews who had reached British shores.

The legacy of the Second World War

In the wake of the war many observers perceived that this age of totalitarianism and conflict had actually invigorated the churches. Before the war it was often heard that German Christianity had found a new urgency in the witness of the Confessing movement; during the war it was said that Dutch

---

31 All these are collected together in W. A. Visser 't Hooft, *The struggle of the Dutch church for the maintenance of the commandments of God in the life of the state* (New York, 1945).

32 *Hansard*, the debates of the House of Lords, fifth series, no. 125, cols. 486–7 (9 December 1942).

33 Ibid., fifth series, no. 126, col. 811 (23 March 1943).

Christianity, too, had recovered its sense of social identity and commitment. Some of this energy found its way into the ecumenical enterprise, and the new confidence which brought to life the World Council of Churches three years later. Western Protestantism may well have been better placed to sense vindication and embrace the future in a western Europe which had been returned to democracy. But that fear of communism which had haunted the Christian imagination since 1917 was now translated by the result of the conflict into a new reckoning with a dreaded reality, for communism was now at their door. Christians in Poland, Hungary, Czechoslovakia and the eastern zone of Germany must now inhabit a new paradigm, a new imposition, carrying with it all the weight of a more-than-ever powerful Soviet Union.

In this sense, many of the debates that had characterised the lives of Protestants and Catholics between 1939 and 1945 did not end with the destruction of National Socialist Germany. They assumed new forms. At the same time, the experience of the Second World War became to them a defining experience in a continuing culture of self-justification, something to which they turned and returned. For if Christianity had survived it was important to show that it had done so with integrity. In this context, the names and experiences that they drew from the maelstrom made new and striking contributions to their own self-understanding. Some names were pressed into the background; others emerged from the general reflection with new vitality. The theological imagination of both Protestantism and Catholicism was in many respects an altered one: within two decades Christianity in that era had been defined not by the names of its authorities, but by the new departures of a young German pastor like Dietrich Bonhoeffer, who had become fatally embroiled in the world of political resistance, had written words of astonishing freshness and vision in his prison cells and been executed only days before the end of the conflict;[34] or in the mystical, purposeful intellectualism of the young French woman Simone Weil, who, like Bonhoeffer, had chosen to leave the safety of the United States and return to Europe to face danger and even death.[35] Both Bonhoeffer and Weil shared an intense commitment to inhabit the world freely and openly, and sensed that a place within a church of orthodoxies and authorities

---

34 Dietrich Bonhoeffer, *Letters and papers from prison*, enlarged edn (London: SCM, 1972). But see, too, the even larger new German edition of *Widerstand und Ergebung* (Gütersloh: Christian Kaiser Verlag, 1998).
35 See David McLellan, *Simone Weil: utopian pessimist* (London: Macmillan, 1983).

must be both restrictive and painfully separated from the hectic, onward rush of humanity in which they sought to immerse themselves. And in the sense that both their lives and works proved an exposition of this disturbing dilemma, they left Christians of future generations, and historians no less, with a note of warning.

16

The Cold War, the hegemony of the United States and the golden age of Christian democracy

DIANNE KIRBY

Christianity and Cold War

The concept of the Cold War as one of history's great religious wars, a global conflict between the god-fearing and the godless, derives from the fact that ideology, based on and informed by religious beliefs and values, was central in shaping both perceptions of and responses to the USSR. From a Western religio-political perspective, Marxist atheism was the Achilles' heel of Soviet communism, which was portrayed as a fanatical pseudo-religion that only a superior spiritual force could resist. The provision of an ideological rationale based on Christianity to justify political actions in the international arena was a continuation of the struggle against Hitler's New Order, in which Christianity and ideas of social justice had been called into play.

Containment was an ideological call to arms. Britain and America attempted to construct a 'Western' doctrine with universal appeal. Beset with difficulties, not least how to reconcile left-leaning Europeans with an America moving rapidly to the right, the project was seen as a blatant propaganda contrivance and poorly received. Asked to write a 'credo' for Cold War liberalism, Isaiah Berlin responded: 'I do not think that the answer to communism is a counter-faith, equally fervent, militant, etc.; to begin with, nothing is less likely to create a "faith" than perpetual reiteration of the fact that we are looking for one, must find one, are lost without one.'[1] The historian Daniel Boorstin was sceptical about the 'un-American demand for a philosophy of democracy' to use 'as a weapon against Russia and a prop for our own institutions'.[2]

Anti-communism came to serve the required purpose. The religious roots of popular anti-communism helped it assume doctrinal status, legitimated by

---

1 M. Ignatieff, *Isaiah Berlin: a life* (London: Henry Holt, 1998), p. 200.
2 D. J. Boorstin, *The genius of American politics* (Chicago: University of Chicago Press, 1953), pp. 184–9.

the potency of religious themes, symbols and metaphors in public discourse. Christianity and democracy were placed at the core of anti-communism. It became a unifying force that reminded Europe and America of their shared fundamental beliefs and basic values, their common history and interests. The defence of Western civilisation and Christianity became anti-communism's central rhetorical device, reinforcing the two fundamental contentions on which anti-communism rested: that communism was a supreme and unqualified evil, and that its purpose was world domination.

The appeal to religious sentiment was motivated by more than propaganda: religious faith could inoculate people against the 'virus' of communist ideas and inspire them to resist communist rule. It was seen as a means of turning against communism the very masses to which it theoretically should most appeal.

For America, 'God's country', the Cold War became a Christian enterprise, a crusade against the forces of evil. The defeat of Nazi tyranny strengthened the view of America as an anointed nation, with a unique mission born of its righteousness. As president of a world power with a spiritually provincial people, Harry Truman used religion to persuade Americans to abandon isolationism, embrace internationalism, accept world leadership and roll back communism. Although Truman was invoking a universal tradition of harnessing the power of religion to the policy goals of the state, it was conditioned by the special religious character of American culture and had profound implications for the home front and international relations.

Western church leaders were united in calling for a post-war world based on sacred rights, natural law, moral order and belief in God and Christian values. There was little unity, however, in defining what such terms meant or how they were to be achieved. There appeared an assumption that, confronted by the need to rebuild the world, shared belief in the fatherhood of God and the brotherhood of man could lead to joint or parallel actions.

Following the Depression and two global conflicts, churchmen, aware of their own culpability as well as systemic failures, saw the war's end as an opportunity for Christianity to reclaim a place in the popular mind and to exercise a decisive influence on policy and behaviour. The excesses of capitalism and communism had already confronted the churches in localised and national contexts: religious persecution in the USSR and structural inequalities in the capitalist world, both industrialised and colonised. The churches had offered little in the way of substantive solutions beyond the requirement that nations should return to God. However, amid the chaos of war-torn Europe, despite significant collaboration and quietism, the churches remained the only organised bodies that consistently and successfully resisted the National-Socialist *Weltanschauung*. In many cases the clergy and the bishops of the various churches had become leaders, trusted by their people.

Church leaders engaged meaningfully in post-war planning. The victorious Allies, unwilling to relinquish any power, declined to include them in peace negotiations. Still, wartime experience had shown that the combination of state and spiritual power was helpful in ensuring successful social, economic and political outcomes. Even the USSR recognised the benefits to be gained from closer church–state relations. The savage persecution of the Russian Orthodox church by the Soviet regime meant that by 1940 it was on the verge of institutional elimination in Russia. The most church leaders could have hoped for was survival. By 1946 it had the power to become involved in Soviet foreign policy objectives, largely derived from its wartime co-operation with the state. The Soviet regime elected to use the patriarchal church and recognised its need to re-establish its power throughout Russia. The relationship was mutually beneficial, although far from a partnership of equals.

State support of the church was owing to both domestic and foreign policy considerations. The strengthening of the Russian Orthodox church outside Russia was primarily to facilitate its assertion of political control over the liberated territories, challenge Catholic power and destroy indigenous nationalist movements. Allowed to play a missionary role, it became complicit in aiding the Soviet government's destruction of the Uniate church, made possible by a convergence of interest, reflected also in their joint attacks on the underground churches. Members of the underground churches avoided participation in Soviet society and the patriarchal Orthodox church. The Moscow patriarchate and the Soviet state, therefore, had a joint interest in their eradication. In essence, the Soviets were able to manipulate the church's concern for self-preservation to help ensure the survival of their regime.[3]

In addition, Stalin hoped that religion might be one means of bridging the gulf that remained between him and his allies. Soviet generals and local communist leaders honoured Greek Orthodox clergy in the Balkans and courted Roman Catholic clergy in Poland. Stalin, albeit by maladroit means, attempted a reconciliation with the pope in the spring of 1944.[4] To no avail: Pius XII remained the locus of ideological opposition to communism in western Europe in the immediate post-war period. Indeed, as the great power alliance

---

3 A. Dickinson, 'Domestic and foreign policy considerations and the origins of post-war Soviet church–state relations, 1941–46', in D. Kirby (ed.), *Religion and the Cold War* (Basingstoke: Palgrave-Macmillan, 2003), pp. 23–36.
4 I. Deutscher, *Stalin* (Harmondsworth: Penguin, 1972), pp. 506–7.

disintegrated in the war's aftermath, the US moved closer to the Vatican as it grew more hostile toward the USSR. A widely publicised letter exchange between president and pope in August 1947 seemingly precluded negotiation with the USSR, which both presented as the incarnation of evil.[5]

US–Vatican relations

Mutual interest lay at the heart of the US–Vatican alliance against the USSR. Both shared a deep fear of the potential of Soviet communism to undermine their global positions. The USSR emerged from World War II held in high popular esteem. People admired 'Uncle Joe', the victorious Red Army and the communist role in resistance movements. Above all, communism spoke to the poor, the oppressed and the downtrodden. The swing to the right in post-war America was greatly at odds with the political climate in western Europe where many viewed capitalism as a failed system. In Europe a return to the pre-war status quo was unthinkable. People were looking for alternatives and the USSR had one to offer.

The Vatican feared that the crucible of war might merge the Orthodox conception of a messianic Russia with the Marxist conception of a messianic proletariat, effecting a fusion of ideas the consequences of which would be incalculable. America feared its way of life would be compromised in a world in which the dominance of free markets and capitalism was threatened. Both wanted the Soviet experiment to fail. 'Liberation' was implicit in the policy of containment formulated during the Truman era.

'The Vatican hierarchy had been preparing for the *dopo-fascismo* (the post-fascist era) for a long time' and had been seeking a relationship with the US from well before the war.[6] Cardinal Pacelli, the future Pius XII, visited America in 1936, warning that the greatest threat to the future was the USSR and that a time would come when all the churches would need to combine in order to resist and defeat atheistic communism.[7] Pacelli and his counsel impressed Myron C. Taylor, a former president of US Steel. Subsequently appointed by Presidents Roosevelt and Truman as their personal representative to the pope, Taylor was instrumental in persuading Truman of the value of US–Vatican relations. The Vatican's worldwide moral and spiritual authority helped endorse

---

5 D. Kirby, 'Truman's holy alliance: the president, the pope and the origins of the Cold War', *Borderlines: studies in American culture* 4 (1997), 1–17.
6 J. Pollard, 'The Vatican, Italy and the Cold War', in Kirby, *Religion*, p. 106.
7 'Meeting with Protestant clergymen', 20 October 1947, Myron C. Taylor papers, Harry Truman library.

US leadership of the free world while demonising Soviet influence, mobilised Catholics to defeat communists in electoral contests, and provided intelligence material at a time when US intelligence services were in their infancy.[8]

The first test of the alliance was in Italy, of strategic importance and containing the largest communist party in western Europe. The Vatican and the US became the arbiters of Italy's fate in the immediate post-war period. The US State Department was deeply impressed by Roman Catholic resistance to the spread of communism at every level of Italian life. The election and referendum of 2 June 1946 saw the monarchy deposed and a republican government established under the Christian Democratic Party, referred to by Taylor as the 'party of the Church'. Despite Vatican reservations about the new Catholic party, Christian Democratic success significantly enhanced the Holy See's political standing.[9] It was further enhanced by the 1947 Truman–Pius XII letter exchange, a joint attack on the USSR which acknowledged the pope as a central figure in the Western alliance.

The 1948 Italian national election was approached by the US as an East–West contest. The role of the CIA has received considerable attention. One estimate suggests it spent $10 million to ensure a Christian Democrat victory.[10] However, while the electoral defeat of the Italian left has been attributed to and accepted by the CIA, it was Truman's personal representative at the Vatican, Myron Taylor, who was most instrumental in securing the necessary funding. Urged by Pius XII to encourage US intervention 'to avert a Communist take-over', Taylor considered US money would be the solution. Funds came, on Taylor's recommendation to Truman, from the US treasury. Secretary John Snyder, a Missouri associate of the president, met Taylor several times in Rome. The treasury provided $30 million, most of which was distributed clandestinely by the US embassy, for the financing of all parties 'opposed to Stalin'.[11]

The product of a process of history reaching back through the centuries, Christian democracy came into its own in the post-war period. It was defined in

---

8 Kirby, 'Holy alliance'.
9 J. Pollard, 'Italy', in Tom Buchanan and Martin Conway (eds.), *Political Catholicism in Europe 1918–1965* (Oxford: Clarendon Press, 1996), p. 87.
10 C. Simpson, *Blowback: America's recruitment of Nazis and its effects on the Cold War* (New York: Weidenfeld, 1988), p. 92. How much funding the infant CIA would have had at this time is questionable.
11 William E. W. Gowen to author, 18 May 2000, 7 August 2004. Gowen served as an officer investigator with the 428th (US Army) Counter Intelligence Corps unit headquartered in Rome less than two blocks from Taylor's offices. His father, Franklin C. Gowen, was Taylor's assistant, serving from August 1944. Gowen met Snyder during his first visit to Rome in 1947.

1957 by Michael Fogarty as 'that aspect of the ecumenical or catholic movement in modern Christianity which is concerned with the application of Christian principles in the areas of political, economic, and social life for which the Christian laity has independent responsibility'.[12] Christian democracy enjoyed considerable electoral success in France, Italy, Germany and Belgium, helped by the demise of pre-war parties of the right, which had been discredited by their involvement with fascism and authoritarianism. While left-wing opponents accused them of relying on erstwhile votes of fascists, Christian democracy offered policies that responded to the demands for social and political change.

The leading Italian Christian democrat, Don Luigi Sturzo, had, notably, spent 1940–6 in America, writing about Christian democracy and conversing with the OSS, predecessor to the CIA.[13] Sturzo's successor, Alcide De Gasperi, sought American support for himself and his party.[14] Both considered good relations with the Vatican crucial if Christian democracy was to be successful.[15] The CIA and the US embassy in Rome supported Luigi Gedda, the Vatican official who created a lay organisation of Catholic activists to defeat the communists.

Vatican mobilisation of Catholic Action, supplemented by covert US funding and Truman's overt threat that a communist Italy would not be a recipient of Marshall aid, ensured a Christian democrat victory, with 48 per cent of the vote.[16] It was a resounding demonstration of what a combination of spiritual and economic power could achieve. It also confirmed Taylor's conviction, which he impressed upon Truman, that what the US had been able to achieve in Italy with Vatican help, it could achieve elsewhere because the great issue of the future was Christianity and democracy versus communism.[17] Truman responded by transforming the pope's idea into a presidential project that extended to all religions.[18] Taylor was entrusted with a mission to marshal the Christian forces into a united front against communism and in support of

---

12 M. Fogarty, *Christian democracy in western Europe, 1820–1953* (London: Routledge, 1957), p. 435.

13 US Office of Strategic Services, Foreign Nationalities Branch, confidential memorandum of conversation (6 September 1943), Italian anti-fascist file, IT 810. Thanks to Charles Gallagher for this reference.

14 J. E. Miller, *The US and Italy, 1940–1950* (London: University of North Carolina Press, 1986), p. 217.

15 Pollard, 'Italy', p. 84.

16 R. J. Aldrich, 'OSS, CIA and European unity', *Diplomacy and statecraft* 8 (1977), 186–227. CIA support for Gedda increased when he claimed to have persuaded the pope to support Western union.

17 Kirby, 'Holy alliance', pp. 1–17. The Vatican ceased combat and silently began to tolerate democracy only in 1918, with official acceptance not arriving until Pius XII's 1944 Christmas address.

18 H. S. Truman, *Mr. Citizen* (New York: Popular Library, 1961), p. 119.

Truman's foreign policy. The endeavour eventually floundered on that other, older, cold war, between Catholic and Protestant, exacerbating already dismal relations. But Truman bequeathed a powerful legacy, culminating in the alliance between Ronald Reagan and John Paul II that contributed to the collapse of the Soviet regime and the demise of communism.[19]

Truman met key American Protestant leaders in 1947. His purpose was to convince them of the value of his relationship with the pope and secure their active support. However, 'the working alliance between the world's two great anti-communist forces, the US and the Vatican, made the spiritual children of Martin Luther uneasy'.[20] Truman nonetheless felt sufficiently assured of their support to dispatch Taylor to Geneva to bring the World Council of Churches (WCC) then in formation, the institutional expression of the ecumenical movement, into his plan.

Across the Atlantic, responding to the emphasis that their foremost ally was placing on the religious dimension of the Cold War, the British foreign office took decisive steps to bring its own church leaders into line. The foreign secretary, Ernest Bevin, presented 'the threat to Western civilisation' to the Cabinet in March 1948.[21] Bevin painted a harrowing picture of Soviet activities, including world domination: 'physical control of the Eurasian land mass and eventual control of the whole World Island is what the Politburo is aiming at – no less a thing than that'. He suggested steps should be taken to associate Britain's churches with government policy, and American ambitions, for a united western Europe.[22]

Foreign office strategy to promote Western union included a study of its 'spiritual aspects', intended to present the basic division between the Western democracies and the totalitarian states as a conflict between Christianity and communism. An external consultant objected that the argument was fundamentally flawed, pointing to Spain where good relations existed between Franco and the Catholic hierarchy. He argued that the USSR illustrated how once revolutionary government becomes established its conflict with religion as a stalwart of the status quo can cease.[23] The analysis was rejected in preference for the theory of totalitarianism that raised the question of the structural similarities between

---

19 P. Michel, *Politics and religion in eastern Europe* (Cambridge: Polity Press, 1991).
20 R. S. Ellwood, *The fifties spiritual marketplace: American religion in a decade of conflict* (New Jersey: Rutgers University Press, 1997), p. 52.
21 D. Kirby, 'Divinely sanctioned', *Journal of contemporary history* 35 (2000), 385–412.
22 P. M. Coupland, 'British Christians and European integration', *The historian* 78 (Summer 2003), 33–8.
23 Kirby, 'Divinely sanctioned'.

National Socialism and Stalinism. The totalitarianism approach provided a useful taxonomy of repressive regimes that justified the Western switch from one enemy to another. Hitler's attempted mobilisation of religion, as part of his 'crusade' against the USSR, was ignored.[24]

Pressure at the highest level was exerted on churchmen to support Cold War policies. Christian opinion, however, was as diverse and divided about communism and the USSR as was secular, with a minority appreciative of its 'Christ-like' qualities. Nor were Christians necessarily supportive of capitalism or an anti-communist 'crusade' against the USSR. The diversity and range of Christian views were illustrated in the deliberations of three major church conferences held in the consequential Cold War year, 1948: the Lambeth conference, a meeting of the worldwide Anglican communion held in London; the inaugural assembly of the WCC in Amsterdam; and the Moscow conference called by the Russian patriarch for Orthodox leaders.

The Anglican and Orthodox communions essentially supported their respective blocs. The WCC, with participants from both blocs, called for a 'third way'. Ecumenists feared adverse consequences for the welfare of the Eastern bloc churches, and for their relationships with them, should Western churches identify with the West. The WCC's attempt to transcend the Cold War conflict was repudiated by the Vatican when, on 11 February 1949, the pope delivered an exhortation on 'atheism' to the Catholic episcopate which identified the Christian cause with that of the West.

Christianity and communism

The Soviet answer to the West's 'crusade' was the peace movement. Nuclear weapons and peace were inevitably contested ground in the Cold War.[25] When the Soviet representative, Andrei Vyshinsky, made his simple proposal for disarmament to the United Nations, Western leaders feared that the Soviets had won a propaganda 'coup'. The 'Soviet-inspired' peace movement was officially organised in 1949 and was endorsed from the beginning by religious leaders in the Eastern bloc who appealed for support from their Western counterparts. At the convocation of the World Congress of the Partisans for Peace, held in April 1949 in Paris, it was clear that the USSR was disturbed by the prospect of a Christian front, and for good reasons. The

24 D. Kirby, 'Anglican–Orthodox relations and the religious rehabilitation of the Soviet regime during the Second World War', *Revue d'histoire ecclésiastique* 96 (2001), 101–23.
25 D. Kirby, 'The Church of England and the Cold War nuclear debate', *Twentieth century British history* 4 (1993), 250–83.

Soviet bloc was made up of deeply religious peoples, including significant Catholic populations, for which there were historical connections between faith and national identity. Eastern Christianity was divided, as it was in the West. The prospect that it could be united in an ecumenism of suffering or struggle was deeply worrying for the Soviets.

The peace movement contrived to present a positive image of Soviet intentions, to cast the West as warmongering and provide a moral cause for collective religious action that would help protect rather than threaten the communist regimes. Although indicted as a sinister ploy intended to weaken the West, it struck a visceral chord in a world still scarred by the horror of war and apprehensive about nuclear weapons. The peace movement appealed directly to Western Christians through a prism of religious and moral arguments that advocated co-existence, repudiated the Iron Curtain and claimed ideological differences could reside peacefully in one world.

Western propaganda sought to discredit peace appeals as deriving from communist coercion or 'communist stooges'. But many supporters had credentials and reputations that were not easily dismissed. Bishop Albert Bereczky of the Hungarian Reformed church, well respected in ecumenical circles, 'had become the most outspoken representative of those leaders in the Eastern European churches who were attempting to find a modus vivendi with the communist regime and who defended their policy on theological grounds'.

Bereczky came from a pietistic background, but had come to the conclusion that by their lack of concern for social justice the churches themselves were to be blamed for the fact that the social revolution had been carried out by the communist movement. The WCC secretary, Visser 't Hooft, recognised that 'he was certainly not a mere opportunist who had adapted his outlook to the new political environment. He was passionately, almost fanatically, convinced that he had the prophetic mission to proclaim that, through the communist revolution, the churches were called to make a complete break with their past and that they should take a fundamentally positive attitude to the new communist order.'[26]

The argument that Christianity and communism were incompatible was intended to render suspect Christians who subscribed to the tenets of communism and ensure no more succumbed. It was enforced on the Catholic faithful in July 1949 when the Sacred Congregation of the Holy Office excommunicated, *ipso facto*, communists and those who aided and abetted

---

26 Visser 't Hooft, W. *Memoirs* (London: SCM, 1973), pp. 220–1.

communism. As no such measures had been taken against fascists or Nazis, it was a remarkable indication of the extent to which the Vatican wanted to prevent Christian–communist co-operation, keeping the former in opposition to the latter.

Western propaganda's focus on communist persecution of religion had the same motivation, and it buttressed the proposition that communism was ideologically driven to conquer the world and eradicate religion. This sequence of deductions could not be applied to other perpetrators, and it was elsewhere disregarded – especially in cases of persecution of one religion by another, as in Spain, or in the homeland of the Vatican, where 'Catholic power at the national level was effectively replicated at the level of local government, creating a repressive atmosphere for both political and religious minorities'.[27]

When the USSR had been a 'friend', toleration, even understanding, had been extended to Soviet attitudes that would later be labelled religious persecution. During the war, the British representative to the Vatican warned Pius XII that he should not expect the USSR to allow the Roman Catholic church free rein and he must not regard the restrictions imposed upon it as religious persecution. He also insisted that if a country supported its own national church and discouraged the Catholic faith, it could not be interpreted as fostering atheism.[28]

In May 1946, America interceded with Yugoslavia against the death sentences on four Sisters of Charity, suggesting a new approach was emerging. One month later Archbishop Stepinac, the foremost Catholic bishop in Croatia, was found guilty of collaborating with the wartime occupation Ustashi regime. The Vatican claimed that it marked 'the "first phase" in a systematic reign of terror to be meted out against the Catholic Church in Yugoslavia'. America and Britain remained silent.

The Anglo–American allies were unwilling to support the papal absolution granted Stepinac for a number of reasons, including his possible guilt. The Nuremberg trials naturally constrained displays of Anglo–American sympathy for former collaborators. With clear-cut examples of religious persecution in Spain under a remaining Axis leader, to indict Tito and not Franco would be a gift to Soviet propaganda. To indict Spain as well would displease the Vatican, with which America was developing a special relationship that included valuable intelligence coming from the nuncio in Yugoslavia.

---

27 Pollard, 'Italy', p. 88.
28 D. Kirby, 'The Church of England and the Cold War, 1945–56', PhD dissertation, University of Hull, 1991, p. 331.

Once Stalin publicly expelled Tito's Yugoslavia from the Cominform, providing an opportunity to 'penetrate and disunite the Soviet bloc', there was even less likelihood of America championing Stepinac. The US had used religious liberty as an indicator for international threat since the 1930s; so resolution of the Stepinac case would ease US–Yugoslav relations. Tito, however, was prepared to forego millions of dollars of US aid rather than release the archbishop. Unwilling to relinquish their new Yugoslav policy, the US minimised the Stepinac affair. A personal appeal from Pius XII to Truman did not stop the 25 million Export-Import Bank credit, granted by the US to Yugoslavia in September 1949.[29]

Religious persecution

A significant change followed the arrest and trial of Cardinal Mindszenty in Hungary, which saw communist persecution of religion elevated to the forefront of anti-communist propaganda. The trial was widely publicised and indicted by leading Western churchmen and statesmen, arousing popular outrage. Yet prior to the breakdown in East–West relations, Western diplomats regarded Mindszenty with contempt and their dispatches testified to the subversive nature of his activities. Mindszenty's behaviour so outraged the British that representations were made to the Vatican to constrain activities that were judged as damaging and provocative.[30]

Visser 't Hooft regarded with alarm the West's 'political obsession' with religious persecution. In a highly confidential memorandum, he repudiated the claim that communism sought the abolition of the churches and the destruction of Christianity. He feared that the treatment accorded the Mindszenty case, along with that of the Bulgarian pastors, had allowed communist propaganda to portray church leaders as reactionaries. His fears proved unfounded. The concept of suffering Christians behind the Iron Curtain aroused strong feelings, transforming Roman Catholicism into a persecuted religion and the champion of oppressed Christianity.[31]

Religious persecution became a staple of anti-communist propaganda, kept to the forefront of public consciousness, not least through the popular medium of film.[32] It was increasingly used during the 1950s despite Eastern

---

29 C. Gallagher, 'The US and the Vatican in Yugoslavia, 1945–50', in Kirby, *Religion*, pp. 118–44.
30 Kirby, 'Cold War', pp. 337–8.   31 Ibid., p. 375.
32 T. Shaw, 'Martyrs, miracles and Martians': religion and Cold War cinematic propaganda in the 1950s', in Kirby, *Religion*, pp. 211–31.

bloc churches reaching a state of accommodation with their communist governments.[33] The image of persecuted Christians aroused fear and loathing, undermining defenders of the new regimes and helping discredit peace activists in both East and West. It reinforced the concept of 'evil' communism and contributed to the emergence of 'lesser evilism': the justification for Western misdeeds in the name of 'containment', often repressive, violent, illegal and immoral actions, usually undertaken in third world venues.

The US was the propaganda master in the Cold War, in terms of both effort and resources spent, not least in the sphere of religion. Religion was integral to Western attempts to promote disaffection and instability in the USSR without recourse to direct military action. The funding and use of religion for political purposes is partially concealed in the murky world of intelligence activities. Enough is known to appreciate that the churches were subject to the same sort of infiltration and manipulation as that accorded other influential bodies, students, intellectuals, artists, scientists, trade unionists and so forth. Early covert action relied on private organisations, making it notoriously difficult to document, especially in the case of Christianity with a plethora of poor churches and worthy causes. Apart, of course, from the most obvious instances, such as American business contributions to the Holy See's Sacred Congregation for the Oriental Church, which trained priests for underground missionary activities in communist countries.[34]

America supported Russian Orthodox dissidents and exiles and, most importantly, the Ecumenical patriarchate in Constantinople, all potential rivals and counter-influences to the Moscow patriarch. In 1949 the CIA established the National Committee for a Free Europe as a front to mobilise dissent by exploiting eastern Europe's spiritual and moral resources. Religious belief was an important basis for American faith in the liberation of Russia. The existence of a wide gulf separating the peoples of Russia from their Kremlin masters was a cardinal tenet of US propagandists. Walter Bedell Smith, ambassador to the USSR from 1946 to 1949, believed religious faith could be used against the regime. Under his directorship, 1950–3, the CIA began funding propaganda organisations that sought to rouse religious feeling against communist governments. Under the leadership of the like-minded Edward W. Barrett, the US Information Service placed increased emphasis in their programmes on 'the great appeal of godliness versus godlessness'. Voice

---

33 Accommodation did not mean the absence of repression, as Premier Khrushchev's anti-religious campaigns between 1959 and 1964 demonstrated.
34 S. Lucas, *Freedom's war* (Manchester: Manchester University Press, 1999).

of America broadcasts repeatedly attacked Soviet tyranny as hostile to religion, denounced Stalin as a pseudo-God and claimed that the Russian people crowded into churches despite all the persecution and peril.[35]

Religious revival

Certainly some policy-makers used religion cynically and pragmatically, but for many their actions and convictions were more than simply a 'realist' response to the Soviet threat. Religious ideas were enshrined in the crucial 1950 Cold War document NSC 68, which demanded a change in the nature of the Soviet system.[36] Notably, it referred to defeating the fanatic faith of communism by mobilising a 'spiritual counter-force'. It advocated missionary tactics, embraced by the State Department and the CIA. Fought on two fronts, at home as well as abroad, the Cold War helped produce the 'age of anxiety' that gave rise to neo-religious movements centred on individual expression and personal development. 'Harmonial' religion was perhaps best represented by Norman Vincent Peale with his two bestsellers: *A guide to confident living* (1948) and *The power of positive thinking* (1952). While his critics indicted the image of Christianity Pealeism conveyed, it was in the long American church tradition of preoccupation with wealth and well-being in this life as much as in the next.

By the time Eisenhower took office in 1953, opinion polls, the consumption of religious books, films, TV and radio programmes, all indicated an increase in religious behaviour. Contemporaries questioned whether the quantitative increase represented a qualitative change in the nation's religious life.[37] Critics charged that it was superficial and lacked theological depth, that it minimised doctrine and dogma in order to make Christianity more comfortable, practical and usable. Intellectuals expressed disdain for its convenient infatuation with capitalism and 'Americanism' and its emphasis on personal happiness and success rather than the larger theological issues.[38]

The Cold War exacerbated the popular patriotism and civic religion that marked the post-war revival. Politicians joined churchmen in calling for a revival. The latter subsequently worried about the instrumentalisation of

---

35 D. S. Foglesong, 'Roots of "liberation": American images of the future Russia in the early Cold War, 1948–1953', *International history review* 21 (March 1999), p. 61.

36 E. R. May (ed.) *American Cold War strategy: interpreting NSC 68* (Boston, MA: Palgrave-Macmillan, 1993), pp. 29–30.

37 W. L. Miller, *Piety along the Potomac* (Boston, MA: Houghton Mifflin, 1964).

38 Ellwood, *Fifties spiritual marketplace*, pp. 10–11.

religion and the way in which the American way of life was assigned the status of religion.[39] A variety of groups promoted civic religion. 'Religion in American Life' stressed 'the importance of all religious institutions as the foundations of American life'. 'Spiritual Mobilisation' identified American religion with anti-communism and the defence of free enterprise capitalism.[40] The Foundation for Religious Action in the Social and Civil Order was established in 1953. One of its promoters was Elton Trueblood, the US Information Service's chief of religious policy. It had two major aims: 'to stress the importance of religious truth in the preservation and development of genuine democracy; and to unite all believers in God in the struggle between the free world and atheistic Communism, which aims to destroy both religion and liberty'.[41]

Religion and Americanism were brought together in a consensus that personal religious faith reflected proper patriotic commitment. Eisenhower, who only joined a church on becoming president, declared in 1955 that 'Recognition of the Supreme Being is the first, the most basic, expression of Americanism. Without God, there could be no American form of government, nor an American way of life.'[42] In 1954, the phrase 'under God' was added to the pledge of allegiance and Congress required all US coins and paper currency to bear the slogan 'In God We Trust'. Two years later that became the official US motto without a dissenting voice in House or Senate.

In this same period a 'Christian amendment' to the constitution was easily defeated. In line with Truman's vision, 'Adhesional religious symbolism was what Congress wanted, not invidious distinctions among the God-fearing.'[43] The same sentiment permeated the Supreme Court, which in 1931 used the word *Christian* to describe the nation. By 1952 it was using the term *religious*: 'We are a religious people whose institutions presuppose a Supreme Being.' The Manichaean imagery of the Cold War and the distinction drawn between the godly US and the godless USSR affirmed the value of religion more than of any particular form.[44] Eisenhower symbolised the generalised religiosity and patriotic moralism characteristic of America's revival, crystallised in his 1954

---

39 W. Herberg, *Protestant, Catholic, Jew: an essay in American religious sociology* (Garden City: Doubleday, 1955).

40 M. E. Marty, *Modern American religion: under God indivisible, 1941–1960*, 3 vols. (Chicago: University of Chicago Press, 1996), p. 291.

41 M. Silk, *Spiritual politics: religion and America since World War II* (New York: Simon & Schuster, 1988), pp. 96–7.

42 *New York herald tribune*, 21 February 1955.   43 Silk, *Spiritual politics*, p. 107.

44 M. S. Sherry, *In the shadow of war: the United States since the 1930s* (New Haven: Yale University Press, 1995).

declaration: 'Our government makes no sense unless it is founded on a deeply felt religious faith – and I don't care what it is.'[45]

The demographics of the revival lay in the post-war baby boom and internal migration. Significant developments only indirectly related to the Cold War affected American Christianity, not least Catholic–Protestant tensions and the burgeoning Civil Rights movement. The Cold War was not perceived by all Christians in the same way or given the same emphasis by all mainstream religious leaders. But it imposed a ubiquitous context that created much of the impetus and the rhetoric for dealing with other issues, the Civil Rights movement in particular.

If religion was the USSR's Achilles' heel, racism was America's. Soviet propaganda highlighted the abysmal treatment accorded black Americans, particularly damaging to America's image in the developing world. The super-power battle for hearts and minds to some extent empowered churches in the communist regimes and African Americans in the Civil Rights movement, but it also made them objects of suspicion. The Cold War was a double-edged sword that required careful handling. Wisdom dictated that church leaders in the USSR at least pay lip-service to the commonality between socialism and Christianity, while Martin Luther King's Southern *Christian* Leadership Conference deliberately inserted 'Christian' into their name to deflect charges of subversion.[46]

Features of the American revival were discernible across the Atlantic, where Christians were also susceptible to Cold War images of light and darkness, good and evil. A study of British clergy in the fifties suggests that the significance of the Cold War as a cosmic struggle between good and evil should not be under-estimated. The communist threat also offered, as in the US, a culturally acceptable scapegoat against which clergy attempted to reforge the waning connection between religious duty, social participation and national identity.[47] At the end of the Eisenhower administration, Reinhold Niebuhr, America's pre-eminent religious intellectual, declared that the West had been successfully inoculated against communism 'by the historical dynamism of the Judaeo-Christian tradition'.[48] However, America's

---

45 *Christian century* 71 (1954).
46 A. Fairclough, 'Was Martin Luther King a Marxist?', *History workshop journal* 15 (Spring 1983), 117–25.
47 I. Jones, 'The clergy, the Cold War and the mission of the local church; England ca. 1945–60', in Kirby, *Religion*, pp. 188–99.
48 Silk, *Spiritual Politics*, p. 107.

appropriation of that tradition to facilitate its Cold War policies, especially the cultivation of popular perceptions about US moral leadership and benign use of power, meant that Christian values were increasingly represented in secular forms. It reflected a process of assimilation and translation of a religious system of values into secular ethics. Such a process accords with Van Kersbergen's view of secularisation as representing 'the condensation or transference of religious morality into secular ethics. Secularisation may be looked upon as comprising a transformation of religious contents into worldly substance.'[49] The same process was discernible in the 1950s in the electoral success of Christian democracy, a post-war phenomenon that remained a significant force in European politics for the rest of the century. It was to prove a more effective ally for America than had the churches.

Christian democracy

By 1950 the Christian community was divided and damaged by the East–West conflict. The Korean war forced the WCC to acknowledge that its ecumenical aspirations could not be realised if it succumbed to Cold War pressures. When the second WCC assembly was held at Evanston in August 1954, it seemed that a major world religious presence was being symbolically brought into alignment with the US. President Eisenhower opened the session, calling faith 'the mightiest force that man has at his command'.[50] Communism was repeatedly condemned. Yet the presence of Christian delegates from communist countries seated alongside their Western colleagues was evidence that the two worlds could conceivably engage in peaceful dialogue. Moreover, conversations were then taking place that would bring the Russian Orthodox church, along with most other Eastern bloc churches, into the WCC fellowship in the 1960s.[51]

In the 1950s, the Vatican was confronted with the unreliability of its American ally and the fact that its own hierarchies were prepared to work out a *modus vivendi* with their communist governments.[52] Sensitive to charges of warmongering and indictments of US–Vatican relations amidst an increase in European anti-Americanism, Pius XII inclined towards neutralism. The

49 S. Kalyvas, *The rise of Christian democracy in Europe* (Ithaca: Cornell University Press, 1996), p. 261.
50 Silk, *Spiritual Politics*, p. 131.
51 Visser 't Hooft, *Has the ecumenical movement a future?* (Belfast: Christian Journals Limited, 1974), p. 23.
52 P. Kent, 'The lonely Cold War of Pope Pius XII', in Kirby, *Religion*, pp. 67–76.

development of the hydrogen bomb, followed by the death of Stalin, moved the pope toward co-existence, prompted further by the proliferation of nuclear weapons and the apparent readiness of the Americans to use them, as indicated by their policy of 'massive retaliation'. By the end of 1955 the pope was warning the West about its indiscriminate opposition to any form of co-existence and indicating to the communist bloc his readiness to engage in dialogue. Positive responses from the USSR led to a shift from the Vatican's alliance with the West toward non-alignment in order to reach an accommodation with the Soviet system. The seeds were sown for Christian–Marxist engagement in the 1960s, as well as John XXIII's *aggiornamento* and Paul VI's *Ostpolitik*.[53]

The international Christian community had proved a disappointing ally for America, failing to unite against the USSR and too often critical of capitalism and America's growing stockpile of nuclear weapons. This was not a problem on the home front where indigenous churches, with support from Cold Warrior celebrity priests, such as Billy Graham, Fulton Sheen and Cardinal Spellman, helped maintain the consensus. The National Council of Churches of Christ, for example, was voted into existence in the US in 1950 to confront communism, materialism and secularism. In addition, America's key political institutions embody priestly functions, the presidency above all. Truman and Eisenhower instinctively appealed to the messianic character of the American people, effecting a fusion of political and spiritual leadership.

Outside America, Christian democracy was proving a far more effective ally than the churches. For Protestant America, speculating that the pope was manipulating US foreign policy to help him build up a Catholic western Europe, Christian democracy was certainly preferable to the Vatican.[54] Although predominantly a Catholic movement, Christian democracy contained mixed and Protestant parties. Moreover, its distinctive political principles matched those of America's own mainstream political parties. In addition to commitments to human rights and liberal democracy, the key concepts for understanding Christian democracy belong equally to the Republican and Democrat parties: integration, compromise, accommodation and pluralism. All are distinguished by their attempts to integrate and reconcile a plurality of societal groups, often with opposing interests.

Christian democrats, rejecting the tenets of nineteenth-century liberalism, accepted the necessity for the state to protect the weak in society and to guide

---

53 F. J. Coppa, 'Pope Pius XII and the Cold War: the post-war confrontation between Catholicism and communism', in Kirby, *Religion*, pp. 50–66.
54 *New York Times*, 7 March 1954, IV, 3.

the economy. At the same time, they held important convictions that endeared them to the USA, most importantly 'that private property constitutes an inviolable right, that communism is an abhorrent movement, and that the state should be confined and carefully watched in terms of its interventionist zeal'.[55] In the Cold War climate of the late 1940s and early 1950s, Christian democrats opted for the Atlantic alliance and what seemed to be its essential corollary, a united western Europe.[56] By the 1950s they were established as parties of government, devoted to a Cold War political agenda of capitalist economics and defence of western Europe against the USSR.

Rather than presenting themselves as the defenders in the political sphere of the Catholic church, the new parties consciously stressed their independence from clerical guidance and declared their wish to win the support of all voters regardless of their social or confessional background. For all protestations of their autonomy, the parties benefited considerably from the church's instructions to the faithful to vote Christian democrat. In order to be seen as viable, independent political parties rather than political arms of the church, party leaders sought to construct a distinct political identity. Consequently, Christian democracy reinterpreted the meaning of religion for politics and society.

The construction of a Christian democratic identity was achieved through a radical reinterpretation of Catholicism that challenged the church's monopoly in defining the relationship between religion and politics. 'In a process of symbolic appropriation, confessional party leaders reinterpreted Catholicism as an increasingly abstract and moral concept, controlled and mediated by them rather than the church.' Concepts such as Christian, moral, religious inspiration, values of Christian civilisation, even humanism, replaced Catholic doctrine and the interests of the church as the foundation of the parties' ideology and programme. These concepts were as vague as the doctrine of the Catholic church was detailed and specific. The French Catholic thinker Jacques Maritain identified the 'so-called Christian parties' as the reason behind the total destruction of any hope for truly Christian policies.[57]

Confessional parties never discarded religion. It defined their identity and guaranteed their unity, confirming Van Kersbergen's argument that

---

55 K. Van Kersbergen, 'The distinctiveness of Christian democracy', in D. Hanley (ed.), *Christian democracy in Europe: a comparative perspective* (London: Pinter, 1994), p. 33.
56 R. E. M. Irving, *The Christian Democratic Parties of western Europe* (London: Allen & Unwin, 1979), p. 242.
57 Kalyvas, *Christian democracy*, pp. 244–5.

'secularisation might be a threat to the churches or to organised religion in general, but it is neither imperatively a danger for Christian values nor necessarily an obstacle to the enduring attractiveness of the Christian Democratic alternative'.[58]

Conclusion

The impact of the Cold War on Christianity and the churches is complex and contentious. Religion on both sides of the Atlantic was turned into a vehicle of general political appeal. The adjustment of religious idealism to worldly affairs and interests led to weakening popular ties with the churches, but strengthened popular adherence to their moral and religious values. The emergence of the practising non-believer in both the US and USSR suggested a corrupted Christianity with a diminished and trivialised mission. Certainly there was the survival, in the face of relentless modernisation and secularisation, of implicitly Christian, tolerant and compassionate societies. Yet Christendom was turned into an arena where competing ideologies vied for influence, encouraging inter-necine conflict between progressive and reactionary church elements. Churchmen, from prelates in their palaces to missionaries in the field, were employed as agents and informants. Western-sponsored religious dissent and disaffection in the Eastern bloc rebounded with the advent of Liberation Theology in South America, where left-sympathising priests discovered the god-fearing could be as ruthless as the godless.[59]

America today is the greatest power the world has seen and one of its most religious nations. Despite secular modernity, America appropriated religion to help construct a Cold War 'other' to provide a serviceable enemy. The nation with the soul of a church demonstrated, like the Romans before them, the continuing potency of combining economic and military strength with spiritual power. A noted American historian once observed: 'The tragedy of American diplomacy is not that it is evil, but that it denies and subverts American ideas and ideals.'[60] It can perhaps equally be claimed that the moral ambiguities, unanticipated consequences, paradoxes and ironies of the Cold War meant that the tragedy of ecclesiastical diplomacy was its denial and subversion of Christian ideas and ideals.

58 Van Kersbergen, 'Christian democracy', p. 45.
59 P. Lernoux, *People of God: the struggle for world Catholicism* (New York: Penguin, 1989).
60 W. A. Williams, *The tragedy of American diplomacy* (New York: W. W. Norton, 1972), p. 291.

The religious ferment of the sixties

MICHAEL WALSH

On 5 March 1967, twenty-six-year-old Kevin Ranaghan, a devout Roman Catholic, was 'baptised in the Spirit'. He was attending, during the spring vacation, a religious gathering at Duquesne university, which had appropriately been founded in 1878 as the Pittsburgh College of the Holy Ghost. Ranaghan, who had recently completed his doctoral studies in liturgy at the university of Notre Dame and was newly married, began speaking in tongues. The following year there was a meeting of 150 Catholic Pentecostals (or 'Catholic charismatics', as they preferred to be called) at the university of Notre Dame; in 1969, the year Kevin and Dorothy Ranaghan published their study *Catholic Pentecostals*,[1] there were some 500 at a similar gathering. In 1974 at least 30,000 attended a conference at Notre Dame and the following year 10,000 made their way to an international gathering in Rome where they were greeted by Pope Paul VI.

In 1976 the Netherlands-based think tank *cum* information service, Pro Mundi Vita (PMV), presided over by the Jesuit sociologist Jan Kerkhofs, published a bulletin, reproduced in book form the following year, which examined the phenomenon in detail.[2] PMV suggested a number of factors which had encouraged the birth and growth of the Charismatic movement within Catholicism: increased contact with Protestants, including prayer in common; the fact that Pentecostalism had, at least in the USA, become a phenomenon *within* the mainline Protestant churches rather than driving Pentecostals into separate churches; the impact of the Cursillo movement of the 1950s which had introduced participants to a more emotional style of Catholicism; theological confusion, liturgical reforms 'which had awakened spiritual appetites they did not satisfy', and a renewed theology of the Holy Spirit in the church at large.[3]

---

1 New York: Paulist, 1969.
2 Pro Mundi Vita Bulletin no. 60; J. Kerkhofs (ed.), *Catholic Pentecostals now, 1967–1977* (Canfield, OH: Alba Books, 1997).
3 Kerkhofs, *Catholic Pentecostals now*, p. 11.

As will later be seen, the theological confusion of the 1960s was not limited to Catholicism, just as the general turmoil of the 1960s was not limited to churches and churchgoers, but Roman Catholicism was by far the largest of the Christian churches, outnumbering all the rest put together,[4] and the impact of changes in Catholicism consequently became that much more visible. The emergence of the Catholic Charismatic movement may have been a benign outcome of the general unrest; church authorities could hardly have regarded other outcomes quite so equably. The recruitment of nuns in the United States of America, for example, reached a peak in 1965, by which date there were almost 180,000 sisters in the many religious orders working in the USA. Five years later, at the end of the decade, the number had dropped by 20,000. The decline in new recruits was equally marked: in the second half of the decade less than 9,000 joined the sisterhoods, compared to more than twice that number in the first half. And more were leaving: twice as many in 1965 as in 1960, and three times as many in 1970 as in 1965. There was similar evidence of turmoil elsewhere. In France, for example, in the first half of the 1960s the number of French priests resigning their ministry was running at something like forty a year; in 1972 225 resigned, roughly the same number as new clergy entering the profession. These were the figures for the diocesan clergy. A similar proportion was leaving the religious orders.

There were other signs of disenchantment with official Catholicism. Dissident, even schismatic, groups promptly emerged, taking their stand on a whole variety of issues, but especially perhaps liturgical ones, against changes imposed from Rome.[5]

Other Christian denominations, as already remarked, were not immune from the ferment. It descended upon the Church of England in March 1963 in the form of a slim paperback published by SCM Press and entitled *Honest to God*. Its author, Dr John Robinson, had been appointed suffragan bishop of Woolwich in south London in 1959. He came to public notice when the following year he appeared in the witness box to defend D. H. Lawrence's novel *Lady Chatterley's lover* from charges of obscenity. But Robinson had

---

4 This was certainly true in the 1960s; subsequently the inroads of Protestant, and especially Pentecostalist, churches into Catholic hegemony in Latin America may have slightly altered the statistics.

5 These groups have been much studied. Cf., for example, Mary Jo Weaver and R. Scott Appleby (eds.), *Being right* (Bloomington: Indiana University Press, 1995) and Michael W. Cuneo, *The smoke of Satan* (New York and Oxford: Oxford University Press, 1997). There is a briefer but wider survey in Michael J. Walsh, 'The conservative reaction', in Adrian Hastings (ed.), *Modern Catholicism* (London: SPCK; New York: Oxford University Press, 1991), pp. 283–8.

been, and was later to return to being, an academic, well versed in the writings of Bultmann, Tillich and, perhaps especially, Dietrich Bonhoeffer. In *Honest to God* he drew upon these largely to reveal the unsatisfactory imagery which Christian theologians had commonly used to talk about God.

The book caught the popular imagination, undoubtedly helped by the lengthy excerpt from it which appeared in the Sunday *Observer* newspaper. Within a very short time over 250,000 copies had been printed, and translations were in progress into several European languages, and also into Japanese. It had stirred up, *Time* magazine commented, 'the Church of England's loudest row for years'.[6] It was widely reviewed – including by Rudolf Bultmann himself. It was given air time on the BBC; the archbishop of Canterbury criticised it in his address to the Convocation of Clergy; the philosopher Alasdair McIntyre declared Robinson to be an atheist and the Dominican Herbert McCabe, soon afterwards to create a furore of his own (see below), was surprisingly hostile. David Edwards himself, the book's publisher, writing in the sociological journal *New society* for 30 May 1963, thought the controversy was evidence of a 'new stirring in English Christianity'. But the stirring, if such it was, fairly swiftly settled itself again. Robinson, having served his pastoral term, returned to academia and wrote important but, in the light of *Honest to God*, remarkably conservative studies of the New Testament.

Stirrings in Roman Catholicism lasted rather longer. As Clifford Geertz has commented, nothing alters quite like the unalterable,[7] and 'fortress Catholicism', as it was often called, had seemed, at least to the unhistorical eye, steadfastly unchangeable. This was particularly so under the pontificate of Pope Pius XII,[8] whose austere figure and penchant for oracular pronouncements had seemed to many Catholics the ideal of what a pontiff should be. And then, in the conclave of 1958, the cardinals elected the roly-poly figure of Angelo Giuseppe Roncalli, a long-time member of the papal diplomatic service – including a fraught period as nuncio in Paris at the end of World War II – before becoming patriarch of Venice. He took the title John XXIII.

A Roman Catholic council

The election of a pope who smiled at the camera rather than staring into the middle distance as if enthralled by a vision of the Virgin (with which, it was

---

6 Quoted by David Edwards, the publisher of *Honest to God*, in his collection *The Honest to God debate* (London: SCM, 1963), p. 8.
7 Quoted in Cuneo, *The Smoke of Satan*, p. 14.
8 At least, as perceived. In fact Pius XII had begun modest liturgical reforms.

popularly believed, Pius XII had been blessed) was swiftly overshadowed by the summoning of what became the Second Vatican Council. The historian Edward Norman is, perhaps typically, dismissive of the council's long-term effects, believing that what happened subsequently to the Roman Catholic, and other, churches would have happened anyway.[9] There is, however, no denying the impact which the council had at the time upon Catholicism, and indeed upon much of worldwide Christianity. Though it lasted only for four, relatively short, sessions between 1962 and 1965 it was the dominant religious feature of the decade, and perhaps of the rest of the twentieth century. It was an updating, an *aggiornamento* as Pope John termed it, of Catholicism.

Whether the outcome was quite what John intended is unclear. The problem of the council's origins is confounded because there are contradictory versions given at different times by the pope himself. To compound the problem, the first version to become public, in an address to pilgrims from his old patriarchal see of Venice on 8 May 1962, is almost certainly the least reliable.[10] It seems, however, that this council, widely regarded as a reforming one, was in fact suggested to Roncalli on the night before his election by two of the most conservative of Italian cardinals. Ernesto Ruffini (1888–1967) was archbishop of Palermo from 1945, and the following year had been created cardinal in Pius XII's first consistory. Alfredo Ottaviani (1890–1979) had been elevated to the purple in the same consistory, Pius XII's second, in January 1953, as Roncalli himself. He had spent his early years in the secretariat of state, but from 1935 in the Holy Office of which he became pro secretary in 1953, and secretary in 1959.

The two, Ruffini and Ottaviani, had proposed a general council to Pope Pius XII in 1948. They wanted one, they said, because of the doctrinal errors which were inflicting harm upon the faithful, because canon law needed to be brought up to date (they used the term *aggiornamento*), because Catholics had to be united against communism, and because, they argued, it could be an occasion for the definition of the dogma of the Assumption of Mary. In the end Pius XII did not choose the conciliar route. It was in any case a common view in the church that, after the definition of papal primacy and infallibility at the Vatican Council of 1869–70, councils were unnecessary. Some at least of the supposed heresies Pius attacked in his 1950 encyclical *Humani generis*, and in the same year he proclaimed the Assumption of Our Lady to be a truth

---

9 'An outsider's evaluation', in Hastings, *Modern Catholicism*, pp. 457–62.
10 The various accounts are discussed in Peter Hebblethwaite, *John XXIII: pope of the council* (London: Geoffrey Chapman, 1984), pp. 312–19.

of faith to be held by the whole church. Nevertheless, Pius had made tentative moves in the direction of a council, and handed the planning over to Ottaviani's Holy Office.

Whether Roncalli had himself ever considered the possibility of calling a council before Ruffini and Ottaviani had a word in his ear on the evening of 27 October 1958 we do not know. After that date he thought about it quite often, and possibly made up his mind on the night of 8 January 1959 though he was later to give the impression that the notion had come to him on 20 January 1959 in conversation with Domenico Tardini (1888–1961), whom he had made secretary of state in November 1958 and created cardinal a month later. The formal announcement came to an extraordinary consistory of just seventeen cardinals gathered on 25 January in the basilica of St Paul-without-the-walls for a service to mark the end of the octave of prayer for Christian unity. The news, Pope John recorded, was greeted with 'a devout and impressive silence'.[11]

It was not only the council that was announced that day. The pope, who took very seriously his pastoral responsibilities as bishop of Rome, said he would summon a Roman synod. And he accepted the Ruffini–Ottaviani suggestion that an *aggiornamento* of canon law was required. The synod, it should be said, met, and proved to be of little but symbolic significance; the updating of the code was indeed put in train, but lasted well into the pontificate of John Paul II.[12] The council met three and a half years later – after a remarkably short time for preparation, but then John was feeling his age, and was eager to get it under way. It is questionable, however, whether the council which took place was the council the pope had mind when he first spoke of it to the cardinals.

The occasion chosen for the announcement was, as has been remarked, a gathering to mark the end of the church unity octave. There was in Pope John's address an especial appeal to non-Roman Catholics. It was, he said, 'a renewed invitation to our brothers of the separated Christian Churches to share with us in this banquet of grace and brotherhood'. The words sounded remarkably like an invitation to take part in the council. The official version of what he said had a rather different emphasis. The renewed invitation was 'to the faithful of separated communities likewise to follow us, in good will, in this search for unity and grace'. The term 'churches' had disappeared, and the apparent invitation to take part was played down: the

---

11 Quoted from Xavier Rynne [F. X. Murphy], *Vatican Council II* (New York: Orbis, 1999), p. 4.
12 The new code of canon law for the Western church came into effect on 27 November 1983.

non-RCs were to follow the papacy in the search for unity, rather than join in as seemingly equal partners. But the context, and the pope's words, suggest that one of his chief aims for the council was Christian unity.

It was all too much for the Vatican's semi-official newspaper, *Osservatore Romano*, which only mentioned the calling of the council on an inside page, and made the pope's standard condemnation of communism its lead story. *Civiltà Cattolica*, the Jesuit journal which is censored by the secretariat of state, managed to avoid mentioning the council for a whole year. In New York Cardinal Spellman, who had taken part in the conclave which elected Roncalli, complained that he had first heard about the council from the press, and then said he thought the pope had been pushed into it. In Milan, the first reaction of Giovanni Battista Montini, whom John had created a cardinal but who, because of his hitherto more modest rank of archbishop, had not been at the conclave, was to say that the pope did not realise what a hornets' nest he was stirring up. As a long-time member of the papal curia, the newly created Cardinal Montini may well have been aware of the plans made under Pius XII, and been nervous of the outcome. Once the die was cast, however, he committed himself fully to the council.

Conciliar conflicts

The preparations for the council revealed the battle-lines in the Vatican, particularly between the new-created Secretariat for Promoting Christian Unity (SPCU) under Cardinal Augustine Bea, SJ and the Theological Commission presided over by Ottaviani. The two committees clashed over the preparatory document for the council on the sources of revelation. Bea was a scripture scholar, and had been for many years rector of the Jesuit-run Pontifical Biblical Institute. The Biblical Institute, and implicitly Bea himself, were attacked in an article in the journal of the Lateran university, *Divinitas*, by a professor at the Lateran. If this was an attempt to undermine Bea, it backfired. Pope John let it be known how much he disapproved of the article, and had the rector of the Biblical Institute appointed to the Theological Commission.

The history of the council, which opened on 11 October 1962 and closed on 8 December 1965, is complex, and I do not intend to discuss it here.[13] The pre-conciliar conflicts between the 'old' Vatican, represented by Ottaviani,

---

13 There is appearing what will clearly be the standard history in five volumes: Giuseppe Alberigo and Joseph A. Komonchak (eds.), *History of Vatican II* (Maryknoll, NY: Orbis; Leuven: Peeters, 1995–).

and the new, represented by Bea, immediately resurfaced. Ottaviani's attempts to present lists of prelates to be elected to the conciliar working-parties was frustrated by Cardinal Liénart of Lille, one of the council's presidents, when he proposed that the council fathers put off voting for a week. It was an apparently small, but in the long term very significant, victory for the bishops of the church over the Vatican curia. Not only did it assert the authority of the council fathers over the church bureaucracy, discussions about whom to elect brought together bishops in national, or language, groups and helped them to get to know one another. When the council opened there were relatively few national conferences of bishops.

The council as it proceeded undoubtedly raised great hopes, as well as sowing much confusion, among Catholics. The Constitution on the Church, *Lumen gentium*, with its emphasis first on the whole church as 'the people' of God, and then on the doctrine of 'collegiality' (the doctrine that all bishops of the church, as a 'college', shared responsibility for the governance of the church, and not just for their own dioceses), raised the expectation that authority would in future be much more diffuse and not solely associated, as it was in Catholics' minds, with the papacy and the Vatican curia. It was also expected that the doctrine of collegiality would be applied, *mutatis mutandis*, to structures at every level in the church, down to the parish.

Perhaps paradoxically, the document of Vatican II which was afterwards to cause the most turmoil in the church because of its espousal of the use in worship of the vernacular rather than (at least in the Western church) Latin, *Sacrosanctum concilium*, on the liturgy, managed to make its way through the council relatively easily. It was far otherwise with what many outsiders would have regarded as a fairly innocuous document, the Declaration on Religious Liberty.

Religious tolerance or religious liberty?

When the council was announced, Willem Visser 't Hooft, general secretary of the Geneva-based World Council of Churches (WCC) since its foundation in 1948, was at best ambiguous. As we have seen, Pope John first cast the council in the context of church unity. And it was, after all, called by some 'an ecumenical council'. It is debatable whether the term, as applied to Vatican II, is entirely appropriate.[14] But certainly it was confusing to those who were

14 Cf. Norman P. Tanner, *The councils of the church: a short history* (New York: Crossroad, 2001), pp. 3–4, and *passim*.

accustomed to using the term 'ecumenical' in the context of inter-church relations. Futhermore Visser't Hooft was not entirely happy that the Roman Catholic church should suddenly appear centre stage in the world of ecumenism, particularly after the hostility that it had shown in the first half of the twentieth century. Those who had been working in the ecumenical vineyard from the first hour, he said in a broadcast in May 1964, had not looked kindly upon those who had arrived at the eleventh hour.[15]

There was, moreover, a particular grievance. In August 1959 the central committee of the WCC met at Rhodes. It was the first time the committee had met within the confines of the Orthodox world, and they were particularly concerned to make it possible for the autocephalous Orthodox churches behind the Iron Curtain to join the WCC. There were Vatican officials present, not as observers because the curia was not yet prepared to tolerate this, but as 'journalists'. In the margins of the conference, however, these journalists engaged in discussions with the Orthodox: Rome had, of course, always believed that reunion with the Orthodox would be easier to achieve than with churches of the Reform.

When Visser 't Hooft learned of these talks he was furious. He had suspected, ever since the announcement of the council, that Rome would attempt to steal the ecumenical initiative from Geneva. He had, nonetheless, formally welcomed the announcement and had expressed the hope that ecumenism would be a major feature of its deliberations. By the time of the 'incident of Rhodes', however, the 'reunion' aspect of the council had receded. In his first encyclical, *Ad Petri cathedram*, of 29 June 1959, Pope John made it clear that the chief aim of the council was the renewal of the Roman Catholic church. He had also invited the non-Roman Catholics 'to seek and enter into that unity for which Jesus Christ prayed'. At this point John's understanding of church unity was that of submission to Rome, an approach naturally unacceptable to the WCC.

In addition to the general welcome he had accorded to the council on 23 March 1959, Visser 't Hooft expressed a hope not just that church unity would be high on the agenda, but that the council would address the difficult – for Roman Catholics – issue of religious freedom.[16] In June 1960 Pope John XXIII set up a Secretariat for Promoting Christian Unity (SPCU), mentioned

---

15 Quoted in J. Grootaers, *Actes et acteurs à Vatican II* (Leuven: Leuven University Press / Peeters, 1998), p. 487.
16 Cf Giuseppe Alberigo and Joseph A. Komonchak (eds.), *History of Vatican II, volume I: announcing and preparing Vatican II: toward a new era in Catholicism* (Maryknoll, NY: Orbis; Leuven: Peeters, 1995), p. 29.

above. Johannes Willebrands, who had been involved in the 'incident of Rhodes', was its secretary. At its first plenary meeting religious freedom was indeed put on its agenda.

The Theological Commission also produced a a draft: 'The duties of a Catholic state with regard to religion'. As Joseph Komonchak has pointed out, this was basically a text prepared in 1958 by the Holy Office.[17] According to this document it was a government's duty to give the Catholic church complete freedom and prevent the spread of false doctrines. Obviously, this obligation applied to states which were Catholic: in all others complete religious freedom was expected. Error, it was argued, has no rights, but might have to be tolerated.

Religious freedom appeared first of all as chapter nine of the draft schema on the church. Possibly no document of the Second Vatican Council was more contentious than that which eventually became *Dignitatis humanae*. It is possible that had Paul VI not been going to the United Nations[18] the schema would have been lost entirely: Paul needed it as a central theme of his address. A Spanish curial cardinal, Arcadio Larraona, prefect of the Congregation of Rites, wrote to Paul VI in the name of a group of Spanish bishops trying to prevent religious freedom being voted upon. Many Latin Americans and some Italians sympathised with the Spanish contingent. There had been an effort on the part of the document's opponents to have it removed entirely from the agenda of the council, and only the efforts of the US bishops kept it there.[19] They turned to the American Jesuit John Courtney Murray.

Murray had long been concerned about church–state relations in the USA, and especially about the issue of religious freedom. It had arisen in ecumenical circles, but criticism of the Roman Catholic attitude had come most vigorously from Paul Blanshard, whose *American freedom and Catholic power* had achieved considerable success, running to several editions. Moreover, though in the US presidential election of 8 November 1960 the Democratic Party candidate, Senator John F. Kennedy, defeated the Republican choice, Richard Nixon, it had been a close-run thing. The Kennedy White House has been accorded almost mythic status, and Nixon is remembered only for his

---

17 Joseph A. Komonchak, '"The crisis in church–state relationships in the U.S.A.": a recently discovered text by John Courtney Murray', *The review of politics* 61 (1999), 675–714.

18 The pope mentioned it when he addressed the United Nations on 4 October 1965. For Paul VI's intervention, cf. Peter Hebblethwaite, *Paul VI: the first modern pope* (London: HarperCollins, 1993), pp. 417–20.

19 I have discussed this in 'The thorny question of religious freedom', in Austen Ivereigh (ed.), *Journey unfinished* (London: Continuum, 2003), pp. 134–48.

ignominious retirement from office, but the margin between the two had been narrow. And one of the factors in the campaign, militating against Kennedy, was his Roman Catholicism, the campaign against the election of a Roman Catholic being led by the Episcopal bishop of California, James Pike, himself a former Roman Catholic, and the apostle of the power of positive thinking and Dutch Reformed minister, Norman Vincent Peale. The US Catholic bishops were determined to use the council to improve the perception of Catholicism as an intolerant dictatorship.

Courtney Murray was not present at the opening of the council. He had, he claimed, been 'disinvited' as a *peritus* or expert theologian at the insistence of the papal representative in Washington, Archbishop Egidio Vagnozzi, because, presumably, he had already fallen foul of the Holy Office.[20] When it seemed that the document on religious liberty might fail entirely or be unsatisfactory, Cardinal Spellman insisted Murray go to Rome. He was made a *peritus* at the beginning of April 1963. By that time a text on religious freedom had been written, though it was not yet approved as suitable to be put before the conciliar fathers. It was still part of the schema on the church, becoming a separate declaration a year later.

Opponents of the declaration argued that it was directly contrary to the teaching of the church in the nineteenth century – a statement it was impossible to deny – and that pope after pope had warned the faithful against religious freedom, and freedom of thought and expression in general. Its supporters were divided between those, many of them French, who wanted the arguments to be based on theological and scriptural grounds, and those (like Murray) who based their arguments on political philosophy and the natural law.[21]

When the council was over the Spanish bishops were faced with the task, not just of implementing the church's new stance on religious liberty, but of formally breaking with the Franco regime. In the week of 13 September 1971 there was a meeting in Madrid to seal the fate of national Catholicism. One of those responsible for drawing up the document on church–state relations commented: 'Never did I dream that a gathering of priests and bishops in Spain would pronounce so clearly on the need for the Church

---

20 Cf. Joseph A. Komonchak, 'The silencing of John Courtney Murray', in A. Melloni, D. Menozzi, G. Ruggieri and M. Toschi (eds.), *Cristianesimo nella storia: saggi in onore di Giuseppe Alberigo* (Bologna: Il Mulino, 1996), pp. 657–702.

21 A useful discussion of the conciliar debates can be found in Herminio Rico, *John Paul II and the legacy of 'Dignitatis humanae'* (Washington: Georgetown University Press, 2002), pp. 27–103.

to be independent of the State.' The end of the integralist state, however, did not come easily. There was an attempt, orchestrated in Rome by some members of Opus Dei and at least one conservative-minded Spanish Jesuit, to undermine the conclusions of what had become known as the *Asamblea Conjunta*. The attempt, which ostensibly came from the Congregation for the Clergy, presided over by the American Cardinal John Wright, backfired, and served only to strengthen the position of the reforming archbishop of Madrid, Cardinal Enrique y Tarancón.[22] It seemed as if, even in the heartland of the confessional state, the battle for religious freedom had been won.

The World Council

But under Eugene Carson Blake, who in 1966 had replaced Visser 't Hooft as general secretary on the latter's retirement, the WCC showed itself less interested in theological issues and much more concerned about social problems. Blake, an American Presbyterian minister, had a long personal involvement in such issues. As president, and then member, of the National Council for the Churches of Christ, he was a leading protagonist in the Civil Rights movement in the USA, and in 1963 had been imprisoned for leading an anti-segregation march. He was also an outspoken critic of the Vietnam war. The Civil Rights movement in the USA, though not expressly Christian, had numbered a good many clergy among its leaders, most notably, of course, Martin Luther King, assassinated in Memphis, Tennessee in April 1968, and Jesse Jackson. The anti-Vietnam protests similarly involved clergy, of whom the best known were the Berrigan brothers, Dan and Philip, the former a Jesuit priest, the latter a Josephite. Daniel Berrigan was a co-founder, with Rabbi Abraham Heschel and the Lutheran pastor (though he later became a Roman Catholic) Richard John Neuhaus, of Clergy Concerned About Vietnam. Berrigan's superiors were at first alarmed by his anti-war activities and in 1965 sent him off to Mexico. He went obediently, but so widespread was the protest, including an advertisement in the *New York times* that December, that the Jesuit authorities brought him back. The Berrigan brothers' campaign caught the imagination of many anti-war groups in Christian denominations across the States, and gave rise to a spate of burning of draft cards, or of splattering them with blood. The Catholic hierarchy at first kept

---

22 Cf. Michael J. Walsh, 'Spain on the move', *The month* (June 1972), 163ff.

their distance from such activities, but in 1968 issued a pastoral letter calling for selective conscientious objection.

It was against a background of such unrest among Christian groups, as well as, and especially, the student riots in Paris, that the Uppsala General Assembly of the WCC took place. It is perhaps not surprising, therefore, that the WCC was becoming politically radicalised.

The theme of the assembly was 'Behold, I make all things new' (Rev. 21:5). Though economic and social issues had always been part of the agenda of the WCC, concern for such issues was at its height in the years before the assembly. The venerable Life and Work movement had become the WCC's Department on Church and Society. The department had in 1965 launched a worldwide consultation on 'Common Christian responsibility towards areas of rapid social change', and the consultation had produced a number of reports with titles such as 'Africa in transition' or, more tellingly perhaps, 'Christianity in the Asian revolution'. At the 1966 conference mounted by the department in Geneva on 'Christians in the technical and social revolution of our time' half the delegates were from the developing world. There was much talk not just of 'revolution' but of the 'theology of revolution'.

The themes of the Geneva conference were revisited in Uppsala. Three of its six working sections, 'World economic and social development', 'Towards justice and peace in international affairs' and 'Towards new styles of living', dealt with social issues. Racism was high on the agenda, especially after an electrifying address by the black American novelist James Baldwin. The theme was given added urgency by the death of Martin Luther King, who had been invited to deliver the sermon at the opening service.

At the assembly the Roman Catholic economist Barbara Ward, a member of the Pontifical Council for Justice and Peace with which the WCC established a joint committee (SODEPAX), called for a 'wealth tax' on the richer nations of 1 per cent of their gross national product to aid the developing world, a campaign then taken up by the WCC. But the more radical initiatives of the World Council came after the assembly proper. The central committee met in Canterbury in 1969. It had before it the report of an International Consultation on Racism, a consultation which had been inspired in part by the race riots in London's Notting Hill in the late summer of 1958. The consultation itself had been disrupted by demonstrations by Black Power leaders. Despite the financially precarious situation in the WCC itself, the central committee voted to set aside $150,000 a year for five years to be distributed among oppressed peoples, and among the organisations that supported them. When in 1970 the first recipients of these grants were announced there was widespread controversy. The recipients included liberation movements in several African countries, some of which were banned organisations engaged in guerrilla warfare against white-dominated governments. The WCC grants were not supposed to be used for military purposes but, as the vociferous critics of the WCC's policy speedily pointed out, the WCC funds released monies for armaments that might otherwise have had to be spent on humanitarian projects, thereby indirectly financing the armed struggle.

The fourth assembly itself had also been marked by disruption, in this instance arising from the youth contingent of 150 which had been invited and of whom 127 eventually arrived. They clearly chafed at the restrictions placed upon their participation in the assembly proper. A considerable subsidy, Carson Blake rather tartly remarked, had been set aside for their travel costs and 'entertainment',[23] but clearly they were unhappy. Their interventions received from the 704 delegates representing 235 member churches a distinctly mixed reception.

The assembly's agenda was not wholly devoted to social issues. The other sections encompassed 'The Holy Spirit and the Catholicity of the church', 'Renewal in mission' and 'Worship'. Fr (later Cardinal) Roberto Tucci, then editor of Civiltà Cattolica, gave an address at the assembly which seemed to foresee the entry of the Roman Catholic church into full membership of the World Council: it was in fact from that year a member of the Faith and Order Commission with twelve representatives. Visser 't Hooft was not so sanguine. Paul VI was already reining in over-enthusiastic RC ecumenists under the pretext of preserving unity within his own church, and Visser 't Hooft was aware of the difficulties that lay in the path of the entry of Rome into the WCC. Papal primacy was one, the sheer problem of numbers another. It was unthinkable that the Roman Catholic church would enter as a single entity, given its size. But the entry of individual bishops' conferences would likewise be unacceptable – if they were to act together they would be a dominant force within the WCC. And how would other WCC members react, Visser 't Hooft wondered, when the Vatican started censoring its theologians?[24] There were, said Pope Paul when he visited the WCC in Geneva in 1969, practical problems as well as theological ones.

23 Eugene Carson Blake, 'Uppsala and afterwards', in Harold E. Fey (ed.), The ecumenical advance: a history of the Ecumenical movement, volume 2, 1948–1968 (London: SPCK, 1970), pp. 411–45, esp. pp. 416–17.
24 Cf. Grootaers, Actes et acteurs, pp. 494–5.

It was for the radical social issues rather than for the theological ones that the Uppsala conference was chiefly to be remembered. As Neil Middleton wrote in the introduction to a book published at the time of the assembly:[25]

> In a world where new ideas and new forces are moving so fast, where immense developments of every kind are taking place, the role of teacher can only be one of encouragement along paths dimly seen. For this role the churches have already been discredited by their consistent tendency to remain on the political and social right. The pusillanimous conservatism of largely bourgeois churches has no place in the new world.

The WCC seemed to have taken that message on board. Politics, the Harvard theologian Harvey Cox wrote in his influential book *The secular city*, published in 1965,[26] has replaced metaphysics as the new language of theology.

Despite Cox's suggestion that Christians copy Jewish practice and stop, at least for a time, using the name of God, his thesis, that the world should be allowed to be secular, was hardly radical. Indeed, the much more radical 'God is dead' theologians – the term was invented by a *Time* magazine cover[27] rather than being coined by themselves – were criticised by Cox in his book, among them Thomas Altizer, William Hamilton and Paul van Buren. The 'death of God' theologians scarcely constituted a school or movement, and the vogue, though excitedly embraced at the time by many, Catholics[28] as well as Protestants, had what Cox was later to describe as 'an unusually short half-life'.[29] Though these theologians had little in common they agreed – with Cox – that secularisation was to be welcomed. For Gabriel Vahanian the 'death of God' was simply a cultural fact; for others secularisation was to be welcomed because it cleared away the superstitions of medieval religion.

---

25 Neil Middleton, *The language of Christian revolution* (London: Sheed and Ward, 1968), p. 4. The lectures contained in the book had been delivered in 1966 in New York at a college under the direction of an order of nuns.

26 New York: Macmillan. Cox wrote this book while teaching at Andover Newton theological seminary, and after spending a year lecturing in Berlin just after the Berlin Wall had been erected. It was fairly slim volume, intended as a book for students rather than the seminal work that it became.

27 Issue of 8 April 1966.

28 Including the future neo-conservative Michael Novak, cf. *Belief and unbelief* (New York: Macmillan, 1965), *A theology for radical politics* (New York: Herder and Herder, 1969) and *The experience of nothingness* (New York: Harper and Row, 1970).

29 Harvey Cox, 'The secular city twenty-five years later', *Christian century* 107 (1990), 1025–9.

Supping with the devil

Despite the obvious nod in his direction, the teaching of these theologians owed little to the philosophy of Nietzsche. Far more significant in Christian thought and – particularly – action during the 1960s were the writings of Karl Marx. The implacable hostility that Pope Pius XII had displayed towards communism was considerably moderated under his successor. Pope John XXIII's encyclical *Mater et magistra* of 1961 showed itself more sympathetic to the left than many found palatable. In the *National review*, edited by the conservative Catholic columnist William Buckley Jr, an editorial famously said 'Mater si, magistra no'.[30] Two years later *Pacem in terris* insisted:

> It is perfectly legitimate to make a clear distinction between a false philosophy of the nature, origin and purpose of men and the world, and economic, social, cultural and political undertakings, even when such undertakings draw their origin and inspiration from that philosophy ... who can deny the possible existence of good and commendable elements in these undertakings, elements which do indeed conform to the dictates of right reason, and are an expression of man's lawful aspirations?[31]

This came after the Cuban missile crisis of October 1962, when Pope John had made an appeal for peace so as to allow the Russians to open talks with the Americans without losing face.[32] Under the aegis of the *Paulusgesellschaft* a series of meetings was held, though they did not survive the Russian invasion of Czechoslovakia in 1968. But the USSR's brutal suppression of the Dubček regime did not deter other Christians from demonstrating far left-wing sympathies which, certainly in the case of Roman Catholics, would have been unthinkable in the 1940s or 1950s. In France the Young Christian Workers movement came into conflict with the hierarchy over its political stance but had, by the mid-1970s, committed itself to socialism. In Italy the Catholic trade union organisation had become so left-wing that, in 1971, chaplains were withdrawn. In Britain in 1964 *Slant*, a bi-monthly journal, began to appear. It was the mouthpiece for a small group of young Catholic (largely Cambridge) students with links in particular to the Dominicans, and professed itself committed to socialist revolution. It survived until 1970. In Chile, in 1970, over two hundred people, three-quarters of them priests or

---

30 'Mother yes, teacher no'. The encyclical was shaped by the need for an *apertura a sinistra*, an 'opening to the left' approved by the church, if the Christian Democrat Party was going to retain power in Italy.
31 § v – the individual paragraphs are not numbered.
32 For this curious story, see Hebblethwaite, *John XXIII*, pp. 445–8.

nuns, met to found Christians for Socialism, a movement which quickly spread to Europe. Also in Latin America theologians were using the tools of Marxist analysis, even if they did not embrace the philosophical materialism that underpinned the social theory. In 1968 Gustavo Gutiérrez, then a chaplain to university students in Lima, delivered an address 'Towards a theology of liberation'. His book *A theology of liberation: history, politics and salvation* appeared in Peru in 1971. He thus launched what was the most unsettling, and at the same time most popular, theological movement in the last quarter of the twentieth century, but its worldwide repercussions fall outside the chronological limits of this chapter.

It was perhaps in Germany that socialism, Christian and otherwise, was most closely linked to student unrest, socialism especially as mediated through the revisionist Marxism of Ernst Bloch (1885–1977). Bloch, a member of the German Communist Party since the 1920s, nonetheless travelled widely in Europe and the United States – indeed much of his major work, *Das Prinzip Hoffnung, The principle of hope*, was mainly written during World War II while he was in the United States. In 1948 he returned to (East) Germany to teach at the university of Leipzig, but his version of Marxism, together with his criticism of the East German state, led to his expulsion from the (East) Berlin Academy of Sciences in 1961, the year he took up an appointment at the university of Tübingen. Here he had considerable influence, not least upon the evangelical theologian Jürgen Moltmann, whose *Theology of hope* appeared in German in 1964 and went into six printings in the next two years: the English edition appeared in 1967. More significantly, however, Bloch was regarded as the inspiration for the radical student movement in Germany of 1968 – one activist sprayed the title 'Ernst Bloch university' over a nameplate for the university of Tübingen.

One professor recently arrived, fresh from his stint as a *peritus* at Vatican II, was (the future cardinal and pope) Joseph Ratzinger. In his own account it was not so much student protest that disturbed him as the hostility of junior members of the faculty. But he was also upset by the attempt by radical students to take over the university chaplaincy and turn it into a centre of left-wing politics. Hans Küng, a colleague of Ratzinger's on the theology faculty, was also shaken by the events of 1968 despite his more left-wing views, but he remained at the university.[33] Ratzinger himself departed, however, to take up a teaching post in the much less prestigious, and newly founded, university of

33 Hans Küng, *My struggle for freedom* (New York and London: Continuum, 2003), pp. 457–9.

Regensburg. It marked for him a step to the more conservative stance with which he subsequently became identified. He went on to assist in 1972 in the publication of the periodical *Communio*, a counterpoint to the much more radical *Concilium*, despite the fact that in 1964 he had agreed to serve on the editorial board of the latter journal. As John Allen has pointed out, many of the founding fathers of *Communio* were raised to the cardinalate by Pope John Paul II.[34]

Pope Paul and contraception

But the publication on 29 June 1968 of Paul VI's encyclical *Humanae vitae* forbidding Catholics from the use of artificial means of contraception also played its part in Ratzinger's decision – or rather, the public reaction to the encyclical did so. Perhaps no event during the 1960s caused so much turmoil within the Catholic church, or gave rise to more column inches in newspapers outside it. Clearly the ban on contraception was a cause of considerable concern among Catholics, particularly in an era when traditional sexual conventions were being widely challenged – or simply flouted.[35] Expectations that there would be a change had been high, fed by books such as *The time has come* by the American gynaecologist John Rock, and John Noonan's *Contraception: a history of its treatment by the Catholic theologians and canonists*. Both Rock and Noonan were practising Catholics, neither of them a radical. Rock argued that the contraceptive pill was compatible with church-approved methods of natural birth regulation, while Noonan's history demonstrated that what was thought to have been a traditional teaching from time immemorial was nothing of the sort.[36] Contraception was not debated at Vatican II. Instead Pope John set up a commission of six members to investigate the ban.[37]

In April 1966 it was revealed that the four most conservative theologians were finding it difficult to demonstrate that contraception was intrinsically evil. The pope let it be known that, whatever the outcome of the commission, Catholics still had for now to abide by the traditional teaching. This played its

---

34 John L. Allen, *Cardinal Ratzinger* (New York and London: Continuum, 2000), p. 91.
35 Cf. Michael Novak, *The experience of marriage* (New York: Macmillan, 1964) or, far more entertainingly, David Lodge, *The British Museum is falling down* (London: Gibbon and MacKee, 1965).
36 John Rock, *The time has come* (New York: Knopf, 1963); John Noonan, *Contraception* (Cambridge, MA: Harvard University Press, 1965).
37 For the history of the commission, see Robert Blair Kaiser, *The encyclical that never was* (London: Sheed and Ward, 1987).

part in the decision, taken later that year, by one of Britain's better-known Catholic theologians to leave the church. Charles Davis, at the time a lecturer at the Jesuit-run Heythrop college in Oxfordshire (though he was a diocesan priest), and editor of the monthly *Clergy review*, gave his reasons at a press conference in December, and at greater length in an article in *The observer* (syndicated throughout the USA and Canada) on 1 January 1967. As he said at his press conference,

> For me Christian commitment is inseparable from concern for truth and concern for people. I do not find either of these represented by the official Church. There is concern for authority at the expense of truth, and I am constantly saddened by instances of the damage done to persons by the workings of an impersonal and unfree system. Further, I do not think that the claim the Church makes as an institution rests upon any adequate biblical and historical basis. The Church in its existing form seems to me to be a pseudo-political structure from the past.[38]

The controversy about the church claimed another victim when the Dominican priest and editor of *New Blackfriars*, Herbert McCabe, wrote in a sympathetic editorial for February 1967 that the church was 'quite plainly corrupt'. McCabe was removed from the editorship, though such was the outcry that he was fairly soon given his job back.

Two months later the *National Catholic reporter* in the USA and the *Tablet* in England both published what came to be called 'the majority report' of the birth control commission: it was in fact the final report, and had been signed by most of its members – sixty of the sixty-four theologians and nine of the fifteen cardinals. In London Cardinal Heenan, the archbishop of Westminster and certainly no radical, who had been one of the two vice-presidents, prepared people for a change in the church's teaching. Which made the negative impact of *Humanae vitae* all the greater, even though it had been launched in the height of the summer.

There were protests across Europe and the United States, led mainly by priests and religious. Many clergy were suspended from their duties, forbidden to say mass in public, or to preach. Some left the priesthood, some left the church. In the diocese of Washington DC no less than twenty-five of the clergy were sacked by their bishop. The clear and open hostility to the papal ruling, and the fact, which soon became obvious, that despite initial soul-searching many, if not most, Catholic married couples disobeyed *Humanae*

---

38 Charles Davis, *A question of conscience* (London: Hodder and Stoughton, 1967), p. 16.

vitae and continued to use contraception without much of a qualm, contributed to Ratzinger's decision to leave his high-profile post. The decision put him on a path which led, eventually, to the cardinalate, and the office of prefect of the Vatican's Sacred Congregation for the Doctrine of the Faith, the Church's doctrinal watchdog.

As the decade ended the controversy over birth control rumbled on. The most lasting impact of *Humanae vitae* was a diminution of papal authority. Pope Paul VI, apparently not wanting to put his authority on the line ever again, never wrote another encyclical.

18

The crisis of Christianity in the West: entering a post-Christian era?

HUGH McLEOD

In 1996 Terence Murphy concluded a history of Canadian Christianity by declaring that 'the concept of "Christendom" – that is of a society where Christianity and culture are essentially integrated, is gone for ever in Canada'. He went on to claim: 'The defining reality of contemporary Canadian society is pluralism, which includes not only cultural, racial and religious diversity, but also the recognition of tolerance and of differing beliefs and customs as a basic societal value.' In 1956, when 61 per cent of the population said they had attended a place of worship during the preceding week, Canada had ranked among the most strongly churchgoing of Western countries. By 1990 this figure had dropped to 23 per cent.[1] This was still higher than in many European countries. But it was hardly surprising that Canadians were conscious of having entered a new era in their history.

In Britain churchgoing had never been as high, even at the peak of the Victorian religious boom, as in Canada, and by 1990 the weekly attendance rate was around 10 per cent. Callum Brown, in a much-discussed book published in 2001, felt able to adopt a more apocalyptic tone. He began:

> This book is about the death of Christian Britain – the demise of the nation's core religious and moral identity ... It took several centuries ... to convert Britain to Christianity, but it has taken less than forty years for the country to forsake it. For a thousand years, Christianity penetrated deeply into the lives of the people ... Then really quite suddenly in 1963, something very profound ruptured the character of the nation and its people, sending organised Christianity on a downward spiral to the margins of social significance.[2]

---

1 Terence Murphy and Roberto Perin (eds.), *A concise history of Christianity in Canada* (Don Mills ONT: Oxford University Press, 1996), p. 369; Reginald W. Bibby, *Fragmented gods* (Toronto: Stoddart, 1990), p. 17.
2 Callum G. Brown, *The death of Christian Britain: understanding secularisation 1800–2000* (London: Routledge, 2001), p. 1.

323

Symptoms of Christian decline

Brown sees the 'irrelevance' of what the churches have been saying as both a cause and a consequence of their decline. Murphy, on the other hand, sees secularisation as having some positive effects, since it has enabled the churches to move from a 'legitimating' to a 'prophetic' role, and he is approving of the stands they have taken on aboriginal rights and other social justice issues in the 1980s and 1990s.[3] In most respects, however, the symptoms of Christian decline noted by observers in Britain, in Canada, and in many other countries are much the same. They include the weakening of orthodox belief and diminishing rates of observance among Christians; the growing numbers of those belonging to non-Christian religions or to no religion; and the declining influence of Christianity and the churches on morality, politics and the law. More generally, Brown argues that until the 1960s there was a Christian culture in Britain, which strongly influenced the ways of thinking and behaving even of those who never went to church, but that this has now disappeared.

Statistics compiled by pollsters, by governments and by the churches themselves during the last forty years have provided a mass of evidence for the decline of Christianity and the churches. For instance, the erosion of the Christian identity of a large part of the population is reflected in the declining number of couples marrying in church and of babies being baptised. Taking the example of baptisms, every west European country other than Ireland, and possibly Sweden (where the figures are incomplete), has seen a decline since the 1960s, though the extent of this decline varies greatly. In Italy where 99 per cent of babies born in 1970 were baptised as Catholics, the figure was still 92 per cent in 2000. But in Spain the drop was from 99 per cent to 79 per cent, and in France from 78 per cent to 51 per cent. In England, Anglican baptisms fell from 47 per cent in 1970 to 29 per cent in 1988, though figures for the Catholics and free churches are not available. In Switzerland 95 per cent of babies were baptised either as Catholics or as Protestants in 1970, but 65 per cent in 2000.[4]

In 2000 Christianity was still by far the largest religion in western Europe, North America and Australasia, but in all these regions of the world there had been a considerable increase during the last four decades of the millennium in the numbers of those belonging to other religions or to none at all. In 1999 the

---

3 Ibid., p. 191; Murphy and Perin, *Concise history*, pp. 361–9.

4 Alfred Dittgen, 'Évolution des rites religieux dans l'Europe contemporaine. Statistiques et contextes', *Annales de démographie historique* 2 (2003), 111–29; Robin Gill, *The myth of the empty church* (London: SPCK, 1993), p. 218.

number of those with no religion was highest in the Netherlands (54 per cent), France (43 per cent) and Belgium (37 per cent). Elsewhere the figures were generally between 10 and 20 per cent.[5] Of course, the numbers with no religion were even higher in some of the formerly communist countries and regions of eastern Europe. (See map 18.1.) France had by far the largest number of Muslims – possibly as many as 8 per cent. England and Wales with 3 per cent was more typical. Less quantifiable, but equally significant, was the growth of 'new age' beliefs or of what Heelas and Woodhead, in a major new study of religion and 'spirituality' in the north-west of England, have called 'the holistic milieu'. While the numbers actively involved may still be relatively small, Heelas and Woodhead argue that ideas emanating from this milieu have had a pervasive cultural influence, reflected in the media, in the large 'Mind, Body, Spirit' sections in bookshops, in the products sold in high street shops, and most importantly in attitudes to health and sickness.[6] According to this view, Western societies may not be 'secular', but their beliefs and practices are becoming much less recognisably Christian.

There has been some weakening of Christian belief, though much less than the decline of practice. It is difficult to say how great this decline has been, because of the paucity of information from periods earlier than the 1960s, but there has certainly been a downward trend in the period since then. For instance, a particularly thorough study of opinion poll data in Scotland showed that 85 per cent had professed belief in God in 1976, but 73 per cent in 1997. On the other hand various polls which asked if Jesus was the Son of God, a belief professed by 69 per cent in 1981, found fluctuations in the responses, but no clear trend.[7] In a group of European countries where 74 per cent of those questioned had said in 1981 that they believed in God, the proportion was 68 per cent in 1999, and it was 60 per cent for those aged between eighteen and twenty-nine. Belief in life after death remained unchanged at 43 per cent, but this was partly because of increasing belief in reincarnation.[8]

The social and political influence of Christianity is a lot harder to measure than church attendance – and those who want to emphasise present-day

5 Yves Lambert, 'New Christianity, indifference and diffused spirituality', in Hugh McLeod and Werner Ustorf (eds.), *The decline of Christendom in western Europe, 1750–2000* (Cambridge: Cambridge University Press, 2003), p. 71.
6 Paul Heelas and Linda Woodhead, *The spiritual revolution* (Oxford: Blackwell, 2004).
7 Clive Field, 'The haemorrhage of faith? Opinion polls as sources for religious practices, beliefs and attitudes in Scotland since the 1970s', *Journal of contemporary religion* 16 (2001), p. 164.
8 Lambert, 'New Christianity', pp. 71–2.

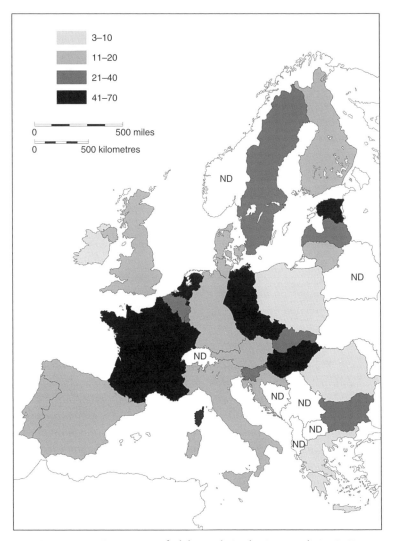

Map 18.1 Europe 1999: Percentages of adult population having no religion in European countries (ND = No Data)

secularisation often do so by exaggerating the influence that the churches exercised in earlier times. One area, however, where the influence of the churches has clearly weakened since the 1960s is that of sexual morality. The teaching of both Protestants and Catholics that sex is only morally right within heterosexual marriage, which retained considerable authority up to about 1960, has come to be increasingly rejected or ignored since that time. Indeed, many of the Protestant churches have been forced to rethink their approach to sexual ethics. Similarly the Catholic church's condemnation of artificial contraception is widely ignored even by otherwise devout Catholics. During the 1960s and 1970s there was a widespread liberalisation of laws relating to abortion, divorce and homosexuality. These changes were especially contentious in Catholic countries, and the Irish Republic, the most strongly Catholic of Western countries, continues to ban abortion.

The Christian Democratic parties which dominated much of western Europe in the 1940s and 1950s are no longer so formidable. In particular, the Italian party collapsed in the 1990s after more than forty years in power. Until the 1960s religion was the biggest influence on voting in many parts of Europe, but since then there has been a decline in the political significance both of religion and of class, which had been the other key factor. There are still correlations between religious affiliation and political choice, but with fewer people being religiously active, and fewer concentrations of people with the same religious convictions in the same place, the impact of these religious–political correlations is much less. In the United States, however, religion continues to be an important influence on voting.[9]

The 1960s

I have referred several times to the 1960s, and it is clear that this decade marks in some important respects a turning point in Western religious history. The later sixties, especially, saw a sharp drop in churchgoing, a growing interest in Eastern alternatives to Christianity, and, in some countries, declining participation in the Christian rites of passage. However, historians and sociologists are deeply divided as to how the religious developments in that decade should be interpreted and explained. The older view, of which Alan Gilbert is an eloquent representative, is that secularisation has a very long history, and that the 1960s mark only the culmination of a process which had been developing over decades or even over centuries.[10] Gilbert focuses mainly on the impact of industrialisation and urbanisation in the nineteenth century. The sociologist Steve Bruce links secularisation to the individualism

9 Barry A. Kosmin and Seymour P. Lachman, *One nation under God: religion in contemporary American society* (New York: Crown, 1993), pp. 182–6.
10 Alan D. Gilbert, *The making of post-Christian Britain* (London: Longman, 1980).

stemming from the Reformation.[11] Others have highlighted the significance of the Enlightenment, the French revolution, the rise of science or the complex of economic, social and political changes that came about in the years around 1900. Theories of long-term secularisation in Western societies are numerous, but they are often incompatible one with another.

The time was therefore ripe in the 1990s for a new approach. It came from a group of historians, including Callum Brown in Britain, Olaf Blaschke in Germany, Peter van Rooden in the Netherlands and Patrick Pasture in Belgium.[12] Largely independently, they each came to the conclusion that theories of long-term secularisation had grossly under-estimated the importance of religion in Western societies in the nineteenth century and the first half of the twentieth. The real crisis, they argued, came only in the 1960s, and it was then that the secularisation of Western societies began in earnest. Callum Brown, for instance, accepted that churchgoing was dropping in Britain at least from the 1890s. But he argued that Christian 'discourse' remained dominant until around 1960, shaping individual life-narratives, inculcating a sense of sin and guilt, imposing notions of respectability and, in particular, defining what it meant to be a woman. Brown and Pasture both contend that women had a central role in the religious life of Western societies between about 1800 and 1960, forming the majority of churchgoers and members of religious organisations, keeping their menfolk from straying too far from the norms of belief and behaviour prescribed by the church, and passing on the faith to the next generation. For a century and a half the church had depended on the piety and activism of laywomen, and when in the 1960s women started leaving the church in large numbers, the structure collapsed.

Brown and Pasture are right to suggest that the older histories seriously exaggerated the extent of secularisation in the nineteenth century and the first half of the twentieth. However, they go to the opposite extreme by over-stating the dominance of Christianity in this period. The 1960s certainly mark the beginning of a more radical phase of dechristianisation in Western societies. However, this would not have been possible without the antecedent history of the alienation from the church of significant sections of the

11 Steve Bruce, *Religion in the modern world: from cathedrals to cults* (Oxford: Oxford University Press, 1995).
12 Brown, *Death*; Olaf Blaschke (ed.), *Konfessionen im Konflikt: Deutschland zwischen 1800 und 1970: ein zweites konfessionelles Zeitalter* (Göttingen: Vandenhoeck und Ruprecht, 2001); Peter van Rooden, 'Long-term religious developments in the Netherlands, c.1750–2000', in McLeod and Ustorf (eds.), *Christendom*, pp. 113–29; Patrick Pasture, 'Christendom and the legacy of the sixties: between the secular city and the age of Aquarius', *Revue d'histoire ecclésiastique* 99 (2004), pp. 88–116.

population, which had begun in the eighteenth century. The extent to which this happened in the nineteenth and early twentieth centuries varied greatly from country to country, and between different social classes. The Western world in 1960 was highly variegated religiously. In some countries, such as France, there were huge regional differences. What was new about the 1960s and 1970s was the fact that the decline in Christian practice affected all social classes, women as well as men, the country as well as the town, and nearly all regions.

The 1960s were unquestionably a critical decade and one of the achievements of historians like Brown and Pasture has been to make this clear. The older evolutionary approaches to the history of secularisation focused too much on causes and not enough on processes, with the result that the significance of specific periods and events was often overlooked. For instance, Gilbert makes no mention of the fact that the 1940s and 1950s saw an upturn in religious involvement in Britain, as in most Western countries.[13] In the United States these were known as the years of the 'religious revival', reaching a peak in 1957, when 49 per cent of those questioned claimed to have attended church during the preceding week.[14] This period also saw a church-building boom. In many European countries this was made necessary by wartime bomb-damage. In the United States, Canada and Australia, it was linked with suburbanisation. Whether the money came from church taxes, as in Germany and Scandinavia, or from private giving, the many new structures helped to fuel the religious optimism of these years.

In 1960 Christian commentators in the United States, as in other countries, were still inclined to take a relatively favourable view of the situation. But changes were under way which would during the next fifteen years transform the religious landscape. I will mention four examples: the rise in the number of Muslims, Hindus, Buddhists, and those belonging to other non-Christian religions; the decline in churchgoing and other forms of religious practice by Christians; the growing number of professed atheists and agnostics or others with no religion; and legislation intended to mark a shift from a professedly Christian to a pluralist society.

The growth of non-Christian religions

The growth of Islam, and other non-Christian faiths, was initially a result of immigration. In the 1950s and 1960s the booming economies of northern and

---

13 Brown, *Death*, pp. 170–5; David Hilliard, 'The religious crisis of the 1960s: the experience of the Australian churches', *Journal of religious history* 21 (1997), p. 211.
14 Robert Wuthnow, *Experimentation in American religion: the new mysticisms and their implications for the churches* (Berkeley: University of California Press, 1978), pp. 130–1.

north-western Europe attracted migrant workers from colonies or former colonies in Asia and Africa, from Turkey and from southern Europe. By the 1970s they were being joined by smaller numbers of refugees from war and from political or religious persecution, ranging from Soviet Jews and Vietnamese Catholics to Chilean socialists and communists, and from Christians in various middle eastern countries to Sri Lankan Hindus. The result was a great mixing of religions in countries which had previously been dominated by one, or maybe two, branches of Christianity. Catholic France saw a huge influx of Muslims from north Africa. Lutheran Sweden now for the first time was home to significant numbers of Catholics and Assyrian Orthodox, as well as Muslims. In Britain the new diversity was reflected not only in the conversion of redundant inner-city churches to Pentecostal or Greek Orthodox places of worship, but also in the growing number of mosques, Hindu temples and Sikh gurdwaras in London, Birmingham, Leicester and other cities. This transformation came a little later in the United States, Canada and Australia, but, following a large immigration in the 1990s, 5 per cent of Canadians and 1.5 per cent of Americans were Muslim, Hindu, Buddhist or Sikh in 2001.[15]

However, by the later 1960s 'Eastern religion' was in fashion, especially on university campuses and in the 'counter-culture'. The most conspicuous exemplars were the Beatles – perhaps the most universally familiar symbols of the decade. In 1967 they announced that they had become disciples of the Maharishi Mahesh Yogi and were travelling to India in search of enlightenment. In the United States Zen Buddhism attracted a big following among campus radicals. A survey at Berkeley in the early 1970s found that the students whom the authors termed 'mystics', defined by such things as interest in yoga, Zen or transcendental meditation, were those most likely to be involved in the counter-culture with its political radicalism, experimentation with drugs and sex, and preference for communal living.[16]

The decline in churchgoing

Many people who had experienced the counter-culture in the sixties continued their taste for religious experimentation: what was 'far out' in the sixties had become 'mainstream' by the nineties. In the United States, it is said that the so-called 'baby-boomer' generation, born between 1946 and 1964, is

15 www12.statcan.ca; www.gc.cuny.edu/studies/key_findings/htm, accessed 28 September 2004.
16 Wuthnow, *Experimenation*, pp. 156–7.

still marked by a religious culture based on exploration and personal choice. 'While religion is seen as something which locks you up and encloses you, spirituality liberates and encourages expression.'[17] From the sixties, the terms 'spiritual' and 'spirituality' began to be used in a new sense to indicate ways of relating to the sacred which were partly or wholly detached from traditional Christianity. One important aspect of this, according to the American sociologist Robert Wuthnow, was a move away from a spirituality based on 'dwelling' towards one based on 'seeking'. The 1980s and 1990s in the United States saw a rising interest in the 'inner self'. Popular psychology books rediscovered terms like 'the soul', and 'care of the soul' became a major concern. This included self-acceptance, and indeed a fair amount of selfishness, combined with a sacralisation of everyday life. As well as seeing a great interest in native American spiritualities, this was also a big time for spirit guides, channelling, encounters with angels and near-death experiences.[18] In Britain:

> Spirituality ... has become a kind of buzzword of the age ... 'I'm trying to cultivate my spiritual side,' people say; or 'I'm learning to connect with my spirituality' ... The spiritual search, what ever that may mean – and it means myriad things to different people – has become a dominant feature of twentieth-century life.[19]

In the United States regular Gallup polls make it possible to trace the decline in churchgoing year by year. In 1957, 49 per cent of those questioned claimed to have been to church during the preceding week; by 1972, after more than a decade of gradual decline, the figure had dropped to 40 per cent. The really big change, however, was in the habits of the younger generation. In 1957, churchgoing by those aged twenty-one to twenty-nine was marginally above the national average, and indeed generational differences were slight. By 1972, young people, 28 per cent of whom said they had been to church in the previous week, were far below the national average.[20] In fact, recently published evidence suggests that the drop in churchgoing in the later 1960s and early 1970s, especially among Catholics, was more rapid than the

17 David A. Roozen, Jackson W. Carroll and Wade C. Roof, 'La génération née après-guerre et la religion instituée: un aperçu sur 50 ans de changement religieux aux Etats Unis', *Archives des sciences sociales de la religion* 83 (1993), pp. 41–3.
18 Robert Wuthnow, *After heaven: spirituality in America since the 1950s* (Berkeley: University of California Press, 1998), ch. 6.
19 M. Brown, *The spiritual tourist* (London, 1998), as quoted by Steven Sutcliffe and Marion Bowman (eds.), *Beyond new age: exploring alternative spirituality* (Edinburgh: Edinburgh University Press, 2000), p. 8.
20 Wuthnow, *Experimentation*, pp. 117–23, 130–1.

Gallup poll data revealed. Surveys in which respondents kept diaries of their activities during the previous week found that the proportion who mentioned having attended a church service fell between 1965–6 and 1975 from 42 per cent to 27 per cent. The disparity seems to be due to the unwillingness of many people to admit to an interviewer that they did not attend church as regularly as they felt they ought to.[21]

Although fewer statistics are available, it is clear that in the later 1950s and early 1960s churchgoing was already falling among Protestants in Canada and Britain.[22] But, in the later sixties and early seventies, the decline was much more rapid and general, and in some communities formerly noted for high levels of churchgoing it took catastrophic proportions. For instance, the proportion of Dutch Catholics attending church on a given Sunday was still in 1965 a very impressive 64 per cent; by 1975 the figure had already dropped to 31 per cent. Where churchgoing was already relatively low, the changes in these years were less dramatic, but still very significant. In France the proportion of the population attending mass on a given Sunday fell from 23 per cent to 17 per cent between 1966 and 1972. Meanwhile, Protestant churches were suffering heavy membership losses. For instance, in the Australian state of Victoria the Anglican, Presbyterian and Methodist churches each lost about a third of their members between 1961 and 1976. In England the proportion of teenagers confirmed into the Anglican church fell by a half between 1956 and 1976.[23]

The growth of atheism and agnosticism

Until the mid-sixties few people in Western countries were prepared to write on a census form or tell a pollster that they had no religion – except in the Netherlands, where already in 1960, 18 per cent of the population declared themselves without religion. In the new atmosphere of the later sixties and early seventies many of those whose religious doubts had previously been a private matter felt free to 'come out'. In Australia, fewer than 1 per cent said they had no religion at the time of the 1966 census; by 1976, 8 per cent of the population did so. These years also saw a growth of atheism and agnosticism, especially among the young and those involved in the counter-culture. *Time*

---

21 Stanley Presser and Linda Stinson, 'Data collection and social desirability bias in self-reported religious attendance', *American sociological review* 63 (1998), 137–45.
22 Brown, *Death*, pp. 188–92; Bibby, *Fragmented gods*, pp. 15–17.
23 Jan Kerkhofs (ed.), *Europe without priests?* (London: SCM, 1995), p. 11; Gérard Cholvy and Yves-Marie Hilaire, *Histoire religieuse de la France contemporaine, 1930–1988* (Toulouse: Privat, 1988), p. 434; Hilliard, 'Crisis', p. 226; Brown, *Death*, p. 191.

magazine was remarkably quick to recognise the way that the wind was blowing. Its famous 'Is God dead?' issue came out on Good Friday, 1966. Student radicals, often strongly influenced by Marxism, were inclined to treat religion as an irrelevance, though Daniel Cohn-Bendit, the most famous leader of the Paris students in 1968, claimed that in abolishing 'hierarchy', 'bureaucracy' and all 'control of information and knowledge', it was necessary to get rid of 'the Judaeo-Christian ethic'. In the Women's Liberation movement of the 1970s, attacks on religion moved nearer to the top of the agenda, as the Christian and Jewish religions were seen as the most influential legitimators of patriarchy.

Religion, morality and the law

These years brought changes from above, as well as below. The Second World War had often been seen as a battle for 'Christian civilisation' against the 'pagan' Nazis. During and immediately after the war there was a widespread assumption that the Christian foundations of Western societies needed to be strengthened and that the laws should reflect Christian morality. Thus, for instance, religious education in schools and the starting of the school day with an act of worship were first made compulsory in England and Wales in 1944. In West Germany the abolition of capital punishment went hand in hand with stringent laws against abortion – both measures being seen as a reaffirmation of the sanctity of life after the horrors of the Nazi period. The extent to which and the ways in which the laws were given a Christian basis differed according to whether a country was predominantly Catholic or Protestant, how powerful these churches were, and whether church and state were formally separated. However, even in France, the country that had taken the principle of separation furthest, Christian influences on the nation's laws remained significant. These influences were seen most clearly in laws relating to sex, marriage and the family. So, for instance, some predominantly Catholic countries, such as Italy, Ireland and Spain, prohibited divorce, and many countries, both Catholic and Protestant, placed strict limits on the circumstances in which divorce was allowed. Some Catholic countries also restricted or outlawed the sale of contraceptives. Most countries prohibited abortion except where the life of the mother was endangered. Many banned the practice of male homosexuality. Censorship of books, films and the theatre was widespread. Protestant countries tended to be less strict in the regulation of sex and marriage, but more severe in their discouragement of drinking and gambling and promotion of Sunday observance. State broadcasting systems, and indeed many independent broadcasting systems, were biased in favour of Christianity, and specifically what they saw as 'mainstream' versions of Christianity.

In the 1960s and 1970s most of these laws came under attack, and in some countries the role of religion in radio and television also changed. Secularists, naturally resentful of the power exercised by religion and the churches, were often among the leaders of the campaigns to change these laws. But secularists were seldom powerful enough to effect such changes single-handed. They needed allies, and plenty of these were to be found. Powerful campaigns could be mounted by interested groups on specific issues – for instance by feminists in favour of liberalising abortion laws. More generally, elite opinion in the 1960s, as reflected in the views of legislators, judges, newspaper editors, academics and many theologians and church leaders, was strongly influenced by principles of individual human rights, the importance of maintaining a 'private' sphere in which the state had no right to intervene, and the need for equity between sections of the population with different moral and religious convictions. Many of these ideas were contained in Britain's Wolfenden Report of 1957, which, in a famous phrase, recommended the legalisation of homosexual activities by 'consenting adults in private', though these recommendations only became law in 1967. Sir John Wolfenden did not approve of homosexuality, any more than did the archbishop of Canterbury, Geoffrey Fisher, who joined many other church leaders in supporting the commission's report; but they no longer thought it should be suppressed by law.[24]

Among the legislators of this period, the most consistent advocate of such views was the Canadian Liberal minister of justice, and later prime minister, Pierre Trudeau, a liberal Catholic, whose ideas had been formed in opposition to what he saw as the over-powerful church in his native Quebec. In 1967 he introduced a comprehensive set of legal reforms covering divorce, homosexuality, abortion, contraception and lotteries, in a bid to 'get the state out of the nation's bedrooms'. In more decorous language, he told members of Parliament:

> We are now living in a social climate in which people are beginning to realize, perhaps for the first time in the history of this country, that we are not entitled to impose the concepts which belong to a sacred society upon a civil or profane society. The concepts of the civil society in which we live are

24 G. I. T. Machin, *Churches and social issues in twentieth-century Britain* (Oxford: Oxford University Press, 1998), pp. 156–8.

pluralistic, and I think this parliament realizes that it would be a mistake for us to try to legislate into this society concepts which belong to a theological or sacred order.[25]

These changes were supported by the largest Protestant churches, though opposed by many evangelicals. The Catholic church accepted most of the package, but strongly opposed the legalisation of abortion. This remains the most contentious of the changes enacted in this period. The official Catholic view, shared by many evangelicals, is that abortion is simply murder, and that the kinds of compromise that have been agreed on other issues are therefore impossible. In such countries as France, Belgium and Italy, abortion legislation was pushed through against strong Catholic opposition. In the United States, the Supreme Court ruled in 1973 that the abortion laws which many states had already passed were constitutional. While few would now advocate going back on any of the other liberalising measures of the sixties and seventies, this issue remains highly contentious, and a potential vote-winner for the Republicans who have emerged as the party more likely to deliver 'pro-life' legislation. Meanwhile the Democrats have become completely identified with the 'pro-choice' cause.

The 1960s also saw a revolution in British television. In 1948 the then director of the British Broadcasting Corporation, Sir William Haley, had referred to Britons as 'citizens of a Christian country', and affirmed that 'the BBC – an institution set up by the State – bases its policy upon a positive attitude towards Christian values'. While tentative steps were taken in the fifties towards giving humanists a voice on radio, the major changes came with the appointment of Sir Hugh Greene as director-general in 1960. He identified the BBC with the new mood of irreverence and questioning of authority figures and established institutions. The pioneering satirical programme *That was the week that was* (1962–3) included some mild humour at the expense of the churches, as well as more acidic attacks on politicians – though more pointed criticism of religion came with *Monty Python's flying circus* (1969–75). Greene also relaxed the restrictions on nudity and swearing, and provided a platform for critics of conventional sexual morality. He soon became the chief target for the evangelical vigilante Mary Whitehouse, who launched her career as champion of conservative Christianity with a campaign to 'Clean Up TV'. Lord Reith, its first director-general, was to claim

25 George Egerton, 'Trudeau, God and the Canadian constitution', in David Lyon and Marguerite van Die (eds.), *Rethinking church, state and modernity: Canada between Europe and America* (Toronto: Toronto University Press, 2000), p. 96.

shortly before his death in 1975 that the BBC had become 'the leader of agnosticism and immorality among young people particularly'. In fact, the BBC under Greene continued to devote a considerable amount of time to religious broadcasting, both of a popular and of a more intellectual kind. This was in keeping with the contemporary ethos of pluralism and free debate, as well as the understanding the BBC then had of its public responsibility.[26]

Why were the sixties so explosive?

In most of the Western world the years 1960–75 saw two major changes in the ways in which Christian rituals and knowledge of Christianity had been embedded into the rhythms of daily life. First, large numbers of people lost the habit of regularly going to church services. Secondly, there was a break in the process by which Christianity was passed on to the younger generation – partly because of the decline of Sunday schools and of catechism and confirmation classes, partly because fewer parents were teaching their children prayers, telling them Bible stories, and decorating the walls with crucifixes and pictures of saints or of biblical scenes. Two surveys of students at Sheffield university in northern England illustrate the rapidity of these changes. In 1961, no fewer than 94 per cent of students claimed to have had some kind of religious upbringing; in 1972 this figure had dropped slightly to 88 per cent; but by 1985 it had already dropped to 51 per cent.[27] This suggests that the period of most rapid change was the later sixties and seventies. Of course this 'religious upbringing' was probably limited in many cases to the sending of children to Sunday school. However, there is a significant change from the situation in the 1950s where Christianity was an inescapable, if often relatively small, part of the whole environment within which children grew up, to the situation that was increasingly common by the 1980s, where it might be hardly ever encountered except in religious education lessons at school. A survey in 1990–1, which included all age-groups, found that the proportion saying they had a religious upbringing was still very high in Ireland (94 per cent) and Italy (93 per cent), but was significantly lower elsewhere. It was 80 per cent in the United States, 71 per cent in France and

---

26 Asa Briggs, 'Christ and the media', in Eileen Barker, Karel Dobbelaere and James Beckford (eds.), *Secularization, rationalism and sectarianism* (Oxford: Oxford University Press, 1993), pp. 267–86.

27 David Bebbington, 'The secularization of British universities since the mid-nineteenth century', in George M. Marsden and Bradley J. Longfield (eds.), *The secularization of the academy* (New York: Oxford University Press, 1992), p. 268.

the Netherlands, 59 per cent in Britain, 43 per cent in Denmark, and 31 per cent in Sweden – a figure only slightly higher than those for Estonia and Belarus.[28]

So there is no doubt that the sixties were a time of decisive change. But no single factor is sufficient to explain this. This decade was so religiously explosive because of the coming together of five currents of change that were initially independent of one another, but increasingly inter-mingled:

(1) the drive, especially by those who had been economically deprived, to enjoy the new prosperity, with the many material benefits and the enhanced leisure possibilities that it offered;
(2) the desire, especially by middle-class youth, to experiment in sex and drugs, and to reject all puritanical restraints, together with the work ethic, both of which seemed redundant in an age of abundance;
(3) women's search for greater freedom and self-fulfilment, especially through more satisfying work and greater financial independence;
(4) the theological radicalisation that began in the early sixties;
(5) the political radicalisation of the middle and later sixties.

The unprecedented prosperity enjoyed in most of the Western world from the later 1950s was a pre-condition for the many far-reaching social and cultural changes of that time. The impact of these changes was most dramatic in the rural 'Christendoms' of western France, Flanders, north-eastern Italy or Quebec. For instance, Yves Lambert in his classic study of the Breton village of Limerzel showed how within a very short period this relatively self-contained and highly traditional community was brought into the cultural orbit of the secularised metropolis. Television came in 1958 and at about the same time newspapers and magazines published in Paris became more easily available. Cars made a difference: they offered the possibility of spending Sunday visiting relatives living at a distance or going to the seaside. So did the decline in agricultural employment: those working in industry or services were more open to outside influences. The proportion of adults who went regularly to mass was still 92 per cent in 1958, but by 1975 it had dropped to 55 per cent.[29]

More generally the prosperity of these years interacted with other social changes to provide a catalyst for the emergence of new lifestyles and values. Better homes, with cars and television sets, promoted a family-centred life,

28 Mattei Dogan, 'The decline of religious beliefs in western Europe', *International social science journal* 143 (1995), p. 411.
29 Yves Lambert, *Dieu change en Bretagne* (Paris: Editions du Cerf, 1985), pp. 237–55.

weakening community ties and the communal institutions that had flourished in periods of relative scarcity. It is no coincidence that membership of political parties was declining at the same time as membership of churches. Expanding leisure opportunities diminished the importance of churches as community centres and Sunday meeting places. Meanwhile, easier credit facilities reduced the need for 'respectability' – often a major motive for churchgoing for those otherwise uninterested in religion. A study of working-class families in the north-west of England, noting the decline in churchgoing in the 1960s, commented that 'few seemed to have experienced a crisis of faith or a dispute with the Church – both situations which had been in evidence earlier in the century. Instead respondents speak of being too busy creating a home to go to church, having other things to do.'[30] And full employment took away a major source of anxiety and made risk-taking easier to contemplate. Here was one reason why the student generation of the sixties and early seventies was readier than any before or since to risk expulsion or failure in examinations.

The invention of the contraceptive pill, available in the United States in 1960 and in Europe in 1961, removed another major form of risk. It was also a key element in the changes in women's aspirations and identity in this period. The Women's Liberation movement started in the United States at the end of the sixties and reached Europe at the start of the seventies. But it was preceded by several important developments: rising participation of married women in the labour market from the 1950s, and, from around the middle of the sixties, declining fertility of married women and rising sexual activity among unmarried women. The implications of all this for religion are not entirely clear. The antipathy to religion of many seventies feminists is well known, but it is clear that the fall in women's religious activity had already started in the sixties. When women gave up going to church it was often for the same reasons that men gave up. But there may be some more specifically female factors. One is that the 'sexual revolution' of the sixties may have had a bigger impact on the religious ties of young women in as much as pre-marital sex, especially if marriage was not intended, involved a bigger act of rebellion by women than by men. The other is that the increasing involvement of married women in paid work simply left less time for taking children to church, teaching them prayers, and the other tasks that had long been seen as part of being a good mother.

30 Elizabeth Roberts, *Women and families: an oral history, 1940–1970* (Oxford: Blackwell, 1995), p. 16.

The sixties were a time not only of broad social changes but of dramatic and often traumatic events. So far as church life was concerned, no event was bigger than the Second Vatican Council. In the course of the more than three years that the council fathers met in Rome, large sections of the laity, and even more of the clergy, became keenly involved in following and trying to influence the debates in Rome.[31] Progressive and conservative pressure-groups were formed and as the council ended in 1965 hopes were high that the church was going to be transformed. Big changes did follow, but they were never enough to satisfy those who had been radicalised by the council. *Humanae vitae* came in 1968 as a shattering blow, both because of the nature of the decision taken by the pope, and because of the manner in which it had been taken, in apparent disregard of all the ideas of 'collegiality' that had come from the council. Across the world, about 3,000 priests decided to quit during 1969.[32]

In the Protestant churches there was no one event that had a similar impact. However, the radicalisation of theology in the sixties had far-reaching consequences. The most revered Protestant theologian in the sixties was Dietrich Bonhoeffer and the most influential concept was his 'religionless Christianity', popularised by such writers as John Robinson and Harvey Cox. The message as understood by many clergy and members of student Christian groups was that action in 'the world' was what matters.[33] Already in the mid-sixties, ministers were abandoning parochial ministry to get involved in apparently more relevant forms of campaigning or work with oppressed groups. As the political temperature reached boiling point in 1968, student Christian organisations were torn apart, as many members decided that working for the revolution was the top priority and everything else was an irrelevant sideshow.[34] In the words of Camilo Torres, the rebel priest who had been killed by the Colombian military in 1966, 'The Christian who is not a revolutionary is in a state of mortal sin.'

Most of the trends established in the sixties continued in subsequent decades, with the exception that the political radicalism of those years sub-sided in the seventies and was submerged by a growing tide of conservatism, sometimes tinged with nationalism or racism, in the eighties. Two important new developments which affected the religious situation were first the gay

31 J. A. Coleman, *The evolution of Dutch Catholicism, 1958–1974* (Berkeley: University of California Press, 1978).
32 Michael Gaine, 'The state of the priesthood', in Adrian Hastings (ed.), *Modern Catholicism: Vatican II and after* (London: SPCK, 1991), pp. 246–54.
33 Hilliard, 'Crisis', pp. 212–14, 221–2.
34 Adrian Hastings, *A history of English Christianity, 1920–2000* (London: Collins, 2001), p. 549; Cholvy and Hilaire, *Histoire religieuse*, pp. 345–52.

and lesbian liberation movement, and second a series of scandals concerning various forms of 'abuse' by clergy which began to surface around 1990. Homosexuality had become the most controversial and divisive issue facing the churches at the end of the century, and it is discussed elsewhere in this volume. But something needs to be said about the 'abuse' scandals. These have been of two kinds. The most numerous and the widest in their impact have been cases where Catholic priests have been accused of sexually abusing boys. Allegations of this kind were rare before the 1980s, or at least they seldom came into the public domain. But since that time they have been numerous and have occurred in many different countries. A considerable number of priests or former priests have received jail sentences. The result has been a collapse of confidence in the clergy, especially in countries such as Ireland where their prestige was high. To make matters worse, it emerged that where the diocesan authorities were aware of the allegations, they had often tried to cover up the offences by simply transferring the priest to another parish or diocese. Tensions between the hierarchy and aggrieved Catholic laity have become especially acute in the United States, where several dioceses face financial crisis or even bankruptcy as a result of legal claims. The senior American bishop, Cardinal Law of Boston, resigned in 2002 following allegations that he had covered up crimes by priests in his diocese. According to one estimate, 4 per cent of all the Catholic priests who served in the United States between 1950 and 2003 have been accused of sexual abuse.[35] The other kinds of 'abuse' accusations concern mistreatment of inmates in church-run institutions, such as homes for former prostitutes, run by nuns in Ireland, or boarding-schools for indigenous children in Canada and Australia. The most important examples have been in Canada, where the schools have been accused of imposing harsh discipline, and especially of making children ashamed of their ancestral culture. The Anglican church in Canada claims that it is threatened with bankruptcy because of legal actions by former pupils in these schools.[36]

Conclusion

The question of whether the West is 'post-Christian' is partly a matter of perspective. In western Europe, Christians lamenting the decline in their

35 www.boston.com/globe/spotlight/abuse/stories5/021704_study.htm, accessed 2 August 2004.
36 www.shannon.thunderbird.com/residential_schools.htm, accessed 2 August 2004.

numbers and influence and secularists eagerly looking forward to a godless future could agree that a new era had dawned, whether for good or for ill. A visitor from another planet – or indeed from a Muslim or a communist-ruled country – would have found the signs of Christianity all too visible.

These signs were most evident in the United States which, in the 1970s, had begun to diverge from the rest of the Western world. The post-war 'religious revival', though its leading centre was the United States, had also reached most other Western countries. The religious crisis of the 1960s was as much a crisis in the United States as anywhere else. But the decline in churchgoing and church membership slowed down considerably in that country in the later 1970s and early 1980s, while continuing with little interruption elsewhere. There seem to have been several reasons for this stabilisation of religious practice. First, the later 1970s and 1980s saw a return to the church by a significant minority of those 'baby-boomers' who had left in the sixties and early seventies but who, when they became parents, wanted to give their children a religious upbringing.[37] The extent of this 'return' should not be exaggerated, but it seems to have been a much more frequent occurrence in the United States than in Europe. Second, the trend towards political conservatism that was common to many Western societies in this period was associated with religious conservatism in the United States in a way that did not happen elsewhere.[38] Third, the 1970s and 1980s were a period of resurgence for the south, the most religiously conservative region of the nation, marked by population growth, booming economies and rising levels of education. This does not mean that the United States is, as the European media likes to claim, a nation dominated by religious conservatives. Rather, it is a pluralist society, where both religious conservatives and religious liberals have been better able to withstand the secularising trends than in Europe, but where secularists also have a powerful voice, and many people are more or less neutral. The unique degree of diversity in the United States has made it much easier for distinctive regional, ethnic and denominational cultures to flourish than in the more centralised and homogeneous societies of Europe. As an example of the big regional differences, the proportion of Americans (and also of Canadians) saying they had no religion was far above average in the west, while remaining low in the American south and in the Canadian maritime provinces. (See maps 18.2 and 18.3.) American free enterprise has allowed a multiplicity of universities and colleges, TV and radio

---

37 Roozen, Carroll and Roof, 'Génération', p. 39.
38 Kosmin and Lachman, *One nation*, pp. 178–82.

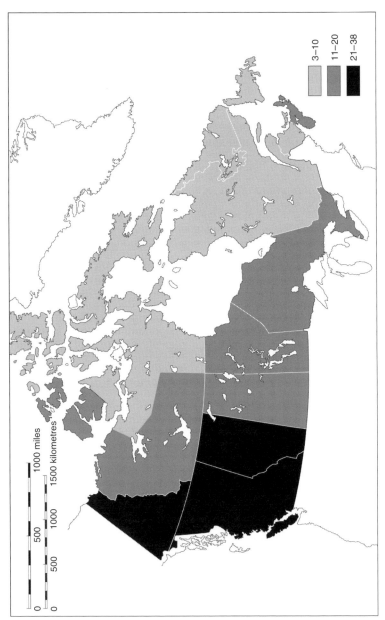

Map 18.2 Canada 2001: Percentage of population in each province having no religion

3–10
11–20
21–38

1000 miles

1500 kilometres

0   500   1000

0   500   1000

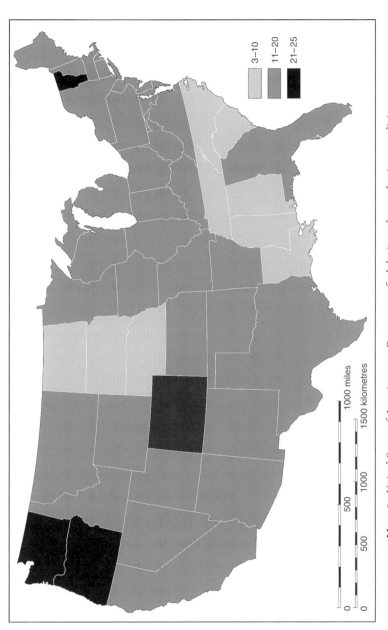

	3–10
	11–20
	21–25

0   500   1000   1000 miles

0   500   1000   1500 kilometres

Map 18.3 United States of America 2001: Percentage of adults in each state having no religion

stations to proliferate, offering the consumer a huge choice so far as their ideological and religious ethos is concerned.[39] In the later 1980s and early 1990s, churchgoing in the United States was again declining, albeit gradually. Although the decline had been greater in most European countries than in the United States, the trend was in the same direction.[40] And while Christians in North America were more likely than those in Europe to be actively involved in their churches, the numbers of declared secularists were by 2001 similar to the numbers in many European countries. So, for instance, the proportions of Americans, Canadians and Britons saying they had no religion were almost identical – 14 per cent, 16 per cent and 15 per cent respectively.

Even if we concentrate on western Europe, there are reasons for doubting that the 'post-Christian era' had yet arrived at the end of the twentieth century. First, the great majority of people still claimed to be Christians. The situation admittedly differed considerably from country to country. For instance, a survey in 1999 found that 89 per cent of those questioned in the Irish Republic claimed to be either Catholic or Protestant, 88 per cent in Denmark, 85 per cent in Portugal, 84 per cent in Finland and 81 per cent in Italy. In the United States in 2001, 77 per cent said they were Christian.[41] England and Wales were more or less average, and the census of 2001 provides highly detailed figures concerning the patterns of religious affiliation in those countries:[42] 71.8 per cent were Christian, 5.8 per cent belonged to other religions, 14.8 per cent had no religion, and 7.7 per cent gave no answer. Among the other religions, Muslims were by far the most numerous, followed by Hindus, Sikhs, Jews and Buddhists. Christians were most numerous in working-class areas in the north, especially in those with a strong Catholic presence, and in suburban and rural districts. They were weakest in inner-city districts, where Muslims, Hindus and Sikhs were numerous, but the numbers with no religion were low. They were also relatively weak in some southern cities with large populations of students and young professionals, in the north London strongholds of the intelligentsia, and in some of the old industrial districts of south Wales, in all of which the proportion with no religion was above average. Among the larger towns and cities the

---

39 Bruce, *Religion in the modern world*, pp. 141–3.
40 Presser and Stinson, 'Religious attendance'.
41 Lambert, 'New Christianity', p. 71; www.gc.cuny.edu/studies/key_findings/htm, accessed 28 September 2004.
42 www.statistics.gov.uk/census2001, accessed 10 March 2004.

proportion with no religion was highest in Norwich (27.8 per cent) and lowest in Sunderland (9.6 per cent).

Second, while the Christianity of many individuals may be largely nominal, the role of Christianity and the churches in public institutions in most Western countries remains very considerable. The separation between church and state is most clearly defined in France, though even there state subsidies to Catholic schools were introduced in 1959. Some countries including Denmark, Finland and England still have a state or established church. (Finland has two: the Lutheran and the Orthodox.) In most other Western countries, there has been a formal separation of church and state, but all sorts of ties between the state and the Christian churches exist and are fairly generally accepted.[43] In Germany, Italy, Spain and the Scandinavian countries the church tax system places the churches in a very favourable financial situation. In Belgium the state pays the salaries of the Catholic clergy. State funding of chaplaincies in the armed forces, hospitals and prisons is more or less universal – though most countries now also fund Jewish and Muslim chaplaincies, and some such as Belgium also provide humanist chaplains. Most countries provide religious teaching in state schools, though the content and approach adopted vary considerably as between, for instance, Italy and most German states, where it is confessional, Sweden where it is required to be neutral, and England and Wales where knowledge of the various world religions is emphasised. Many countries, including Britain, France, Belgium and the Netherlands, have considerable numbers of state-subsidised or state-funded religious schools. In Germany and Belgium the church has a key role in the welfare system, managing many hospitals and orphanages and employing a large proportion of social workers.

Third, Christianity and the churches continue to have a wide-ranging role in many areas of social provision and public debate. This is most conspicuous in the United States. In the 1960s the churches played a key role in the Civil Rights movement. Since the 1970s, conservative Protestants have played an important part in organising opposition to the Equal Rights Amendment, which aimed to outlaw discrimination on the grounds of gender, and in campaigning on a wide range of other 'family' issues. In many states the so-called 'religious right' has acquired a dominant influence within the local Republican Party. While provoking widespread hostility, they have succeeded in changing the rules of public discourse to the extent that professions

---

43 This section is based on Gerhard Robbers (ed.), *State and church in the European Union* (Baden-Baden: Nomos, 1996).

of piety are compulsory for would-be American presidents and desirable for those seeking lesser office. The 1996 edition of the *Almanac of American politics* revealed that out of 585 state governors and members of Congress only four were bold enough to declare that they had no religion.

Few European countries require professions of piety from their legislators, and one may assume that those who do make such professions are sincere in doing so. On the other hand, relatively few leading politicians are declared unbelievers – though in Australia two prime ministers in the 1970s and 1980s, Gough Whitlam and Bob Hawke, were professed agnostics. As religion has become less important as an influence on voting, it has been easier for politicians simply to leave religious considerations out of account. However, churches have seldom been inclined to retire to the 'private sphere'. A conspicuous example of this refusal was the long-running battle between the British churches and Margaret Thatcher's government in the 1980s, culminating in the Church of England's damning report, *Faith in the city* (1985). The main issues were poverty, welfare and unemployment. The churches argued that Thatcher's policies were unjust and divisive, since they had made the rich richer and the poor poorer, and had increased the polarisation between the prosperous south and the deprived north. Thatcher responded that in the long run everyone would benefit from the emergence of an 'enterprise culture' and the elimination of the 'dependency culture'. Differences also arose in many other areas, including immigration, foreign and defence policy, education and local government. How far these criticisms undermined Thatcher's legitimacy and contributed to her fall in 1990 is open to question. Cynics would point out that those who deplored Thatcher's claim that 'there is no such thing as society, only individuals and families' often continued to support her in the secrecy of the voting-booth. Two points are notable, however. First, Thatcher presumably did feel that her legitimacy was being undermined, since she felt required to answer her religious critics in her famous 'Sermon on the Mound' (so-called because it was delivered to the General Assembly of the Church of Scotland, which meets on The Mound, a street in Edinburgh). Second, her successor, John Major, did direct additional funds at the inner cities, and tried to promote co-operation with the various religious groups active there through an Inner Cities Religious Council.

At the same time as these high-profile interventions on public issues, independent church agencies have continued to play a major part in certain areas of social provision. This is particularly so in the field of immigration and asylum, where the bleak situation of asylum-seekers and other immigrants from Africa and Asia would be even worse but for church initiatives.[44] Clergy have spoken out against racism and exclusionist asylum policies, and have warned against voting for far-right parties. At a more practical level, churches have supported numerous schemes to assist asylum-seekers and in some cases church people have hidden them in their homes.

It is premature to speak of a 'post-Christian era' in view of the major social role which the Christian churches still play throughout the Western world. However, their foundations are certainly being undermined by the severe decline in active membership that most have suffered, especially during the last forty years. Particularly serious is the failure to recruit young people in significant numbers. Both clergy and active laity include a heavy over-representation of the middle-aged and the old. Unless ways of addressing this deficit can be found very soon, more serious difficulties lie not very far in the future.

---

44 For the example of France, see Kay Chadwick, 'Accueillir l'étranger: immigration, integration and the French Catholic church', in Kay Chadwick (ed.), Catholicism, politics and society in twentieth-century France (Liverpool: Liverpool University Press, 2000), pp. 175–96.

19

The revolutions in eastern Europe and the beginnings of the post-communist era

PHILIP WALTERS

Catholic and Protestant churches under communism: communist policies and the response of the churches

Introduction

Communist rule was established in eastern Europe in the second half of the 1940s, and came to an end in 1989. Communist policy towards religion, and the response of the churches, varied widely in eastern Europe both geographically and over time.

One factor influencing the experience of Christians was their relative strength within the various countries. In some countries (Poland, Slovakia, Slovenia, Croatia, Lithuania) the historical close identification between the nation and the Catholic church continued. In East Germany, which lacked a distinctive national identity, the Protestant church was the predominant denomination. Other countries, particularly some of those straddling or bordering the 'fault-line' between Western and Eastern Christianity, remained religiously mixed. Hungary was Catholic, Reformed and Lutheran. In the Transylvanian part of Romania there was a large Reformed and Lutheran presence. Particularly strong in Transylvania, but also present elsewhere in the region, were Eastern-rite Catholics. Further south in the Balkans, the majority religion remained Orthodoxy, but in Albania Catholicism as well as Islam was important.

For political rather than purely ideological reasons the Eastern-rite Catholics were declared illegal throughout communist eastern Europe. (The largest Eastern-rite church to suffer this fate was the Ukrainian Catholic church in the Soviet Union, dissolved in 1946.) The only country, however, in which the theoretical communist ideological goal of the disappearance of all religion was said to have been achieved was Albania, where from 1967 it became illegal to manifest a religious faith in any way.

Elsewhere, state and church had to co-exist.

Constitutional guarantees of religious freedom were usually interpreted by the communist authorities to extend only to the individual's right to believe and to worship. In most of the countries concerned it was the aim of the authorities to exclude the churches and Christians as far as possible from the public sphere, to limit their involvement in social work and education and to keep them out of politics, except as tame spokesmen, especially on the international stage, on the subject of 'peace' and the officially promulgated desire of the socialist states to promote it worldwide. (The Prague-based Christian Peace Conference was prominent in this context.) In almost all countries active believers could expect to face discrimination in education and employment; atheist propaganda was prominent in the public space.

Outside Albania, Czechoslovakia saw the most consistent and sustained application of a repressive policy. In order to ensure that Catholic clergy were of the right compliant kind, and to limit their numbers, the state required them to be licensed; the state also paid their salaries. In the early 1980s over one-third of Catholic parishes had no priest (two-thirds in the Prague diocese), and government approval required for the appointment of bishops meant that eight of the thirteen Catholic dioceses were vacant. The state sponsored a pro-regime organisation of Catholic priests, Pacem in Terris. (One of the purposes of the pope's ban on priests' political involvement in 1982 was to undermine the effectiveness of this and similar organisations in eastern Europe.)

At the opposite end of the spectrum, in Yugoslavia from the mid-1960s there was mutual tolerance and recognition between the Catholic church and the state. Religious orders and charitable organisations were allowed to function, the state did not interfere with the seminaries, and large religious assemblies were held. Here too, however, there was constant tension as a result of conflicting aspirations by the two sides. As elsewhere, the secular authorities wanted 'freedom of religion' interpreted in a private sense, and constantly attempted to restrict the church's educational and publishing activities, to refuse it the right to engage in social issues, and to deny it access to radio and television. The Yugoslav authorities also feared that the traditional close identification of the various religions with specific nationalities in Yugoslavia might lead to trouble. Meanwhile the Catholic church, through its identification with the Croat and Slovene nations, its growing association with human rights, and a real concern to involve itself in social issues, persisted in its efforts to expand its legitimate areas of activity.

A combination of 'discretion' and 'valour' frequently characterised church life under communism. Religious leaders would enter into various forms of compromise with the secular authorities; religious dissidents would criticise their leaders for being too compliant. Sometimes this tension could be turned by church leaders to their advantage, enabling them to maintain their churches as a visible presence in society by persuading the authorities that an easing of pressure on religious bodies would prevent believers from joining 'underground' churches and thus slipping out of state control altogether. They constantly had to beware, however, of allowing the secular authorities a chance to operate 'divide and rule' policies. In Poland, for example, internal church conflicts over the Second Vatican Council were deliberately muted by the over-riding need for unity.[1]

East Germany

A milestone in the history of East Germany was when the Protestant church in the GDR split from the united German church in 1969. Shortly afterwards the church determined to be a 'church in socialism'. In the words of Bishop Schönherr in 1972, 'The socialist state will not be able to do without the co-operation of its Christian citizens in the long run.'[2]

This did not involve the development of a new theology. Right from the start the church's stance was seen as 'critical solidarity' with the regime. In March 1978 a meeting of church leaders with party leader Erich Honecker, on the church's initiative, resulted in the state's reluctant acceptance of the church's position and its role in public life. The church leaders particularly associated with this stance, such as Heino Falcke, Werner Krusche and Albrecht Schönherr, had no illusions about current realities in the GDR, and were no collaborators. As Schönherr realistically observed, church–state relations were as good as Christians found them to be in their everyday life.[3] The Protestant church leaders did believe, however, that the socialist system was capable of improvement.[4]

The church was involved in a wide range of charitable and other social activity, with its own network of hospitals, old people's homes, orphanages,

---

1 Michael P. Hornsby-Smith, 'The Catholic church in central and eastern Europe: the view from western Europe', in Irena Borowik and Grzegorz Babiński (eds.), *New religious phenomena in central and eastern Europe* (Kraków: Nomos, 1997), p. 136.

2 'Conversation between the Evangelischer Pressedienst (EPD) and the chairman of the Federation of the Evangelical Churches in the German Democratic Republic (GDR), Bishop D. Albrecht Schönherr', *Ecumenical press service* (Geneva), 11/39, 20 April 1972, p. 4, cited in Roger Williamson, 'East Germany: the Federation of Protestant Churches', *Religion in communist lands* 9 (1981), 19.

3 Arvan Gordon, 'The church and change in the GDR', *Religion in communist lands* 18 (1990), p. 145; Paul Oestreicher, 'Christian pluralism in a monolithic state: the churches of East Germany 1945–1990, *Religion, state & society* 21 (1993), p. 271.

4 For a first-hand account of the development of 'critical solidarity' see Bishop Schönherr, 'Church and state in the GDR', *Religion in communist lands* 19 (1991), 197–206.

kindergartens, schools and the like. It published newspapers and had access to radio and television; there were clergy training facilities and even theological faculties in some universities. One cause of tension with the state was over the secular communist youth dedication ceremony, the *Jugendweihe*, and whether the church ought to withhold confirmation from those who had gone through with it. Others were the question of alternatives to military service for Christian conscientious objectors and the church's objection to pre-military education for children. Christians were generally excluded from the more responsible jobs.

One factor influencing the government of the GDR to maintain a good relationship with the Protestant church was that both the Protestant church and the much smaller Catholic church continued throughout the life of the GDR to receive large-scale financial and material support from their counterparts in the West. The state benefited from this: the Western churches, for example, financed some 10 per cent of the GDR's health services, traditionally run by Catholic and Protestant religious communities.

Poland

A pattern of church–state relations evolved in Poland which was different from that in any of the other eastern European countries. Here not only was the identification of the leading church with the nation bolstered under communism (as in Lithuania and some other countries), but the church came to embody a real alternative to the official ideological system. In contrast to the situation in East Germany, however, this ever more apparent reality was still accompanied by efforts on the part of the authorities to exclude the church from social and political life, despite facts such as that the Catholic University of Lublin continued to function throughout the communist period as the only Christian university between the Elbe and the Pacific. The fact was that the Catholic church in Poland was eventually seen to have more legitimacy than the regime itself. This was central to the role of the Polish church in the demise of communism in eastern Europe.

The role of the Catholic and Protestant churches in overcoming communism

Introduction

The year 1989 saw the sudden and unexpected collapse of communist regimes throughout eastern and central Europe as the leaders were wrongfooted and the opposition fortified by the reforms of the Soviet leader Mikhail Gorbachev (1985–91). 'Round table' meetings between government and Solidarity representatives in Poland from February led to partially free elections in June which produced an anti-communist landslide; the first non-communist government in eastern Europe since 1948 was formed in Poland in August. Hungary had by now started demolishing its border fences with the West, and East Germans were among those who were choosing this path to emigration in increasing numbers. Widespread demonstrations in East Germany led to the collapse of the government and the opening of the Berlin Wall in November. The Czechoslovak government resigned in November. In Romania the Ceauşescu regime was toppled in December. In 1990 democratisation began in Bulgaria, Yugoslavia and Albania. The two German states were reunified in October 1990. Meanwhile in the Soviet Union opposition to rule from Moscow had been spearheaded by the Baltic states, and the end of the Soviet empire came with the dissolution of the Soviet Union in December 1991.

Religion was just one of the factors involved in the end of communism in eastern Europe. It played its part in several inter-related ways.

As Patrick Michel observes, during the communist period religion 'was established in a potential triple role as vector of disalienation (at the level of the individual), of detotalisation (at the level of society) and of desovietisation (at the level of the nation)'.[5] He emphasises that this role was a potential one, and that the churches had to take positive steps if they were actually to play it.

At the level of the individual, religious ideas in their broad sense helped to form an ethical alternative to the communist system. The general concern of all critics of the system was that citizens should 'live in truth'. By the early 1980s secular and religious activists were increasingly speaking a common language; they grew to respect each other and work together. Thus it was, for example, that Czech Catholic activists and Protestant pastors could involve themselves with Charter 77, which had started out as a secular human rights movement.

At the level of society, the churches were the only public institutions that were not initiated and organised by the Communist Party; by permitting, however reluctantly, the existence of the churches the communist authorities showed that their societies were 'post-totalitarian' and that by implication an alternative could exist. There was also a practical aspect to this reality: churches usually possessed the only physical public spaces that were not in

---

5 Patrick Michel, 'Religious renewal or political deficiency: religion and democracy in central Europe', *Religion, state & society* 20 (1992), p. 339; Patrick Michel, *Politics and religion in eastern Europe: Catholicism in Hungary, Poland and Czechoslovakia* (Cambridge: Polity Press, 1991), pp. 1–2 .

the gift of the state, and fringe groups of various kinds were often able to make use of them for meetings and other activities, using the church as a protective umbrella.

At the level of the nation, the churches in several eastern European countries helped preserve the identity of particular nations in the face of Sovietisation or its local equivalent. In the Soviet Union the most prolific *samizdat* (literally 'self-published': unofficial and *de facto* illegal) publication was *The chronicle of the Lithuanian Catholic church* (1972–88) which recounted in great detail not only the persecution of the church but general infringements of citizens' human, cultural and national rights. In Ukraine the Ukrainian Catholic church, declared illegal in 1946, was relegalised by Gorbachev in 1989, and immediately revealed its strength when western Ukrainians identified themselves with it *en masse* in the context of their aspiration for political and cultural self-expression. In Romania the events leading to the overthrow of Ceauşescu in 1989 were sparked by spontaneous efforts by the (Hungarian) congregation of the Hungarian Reformed pastor László Tökés, and soon by local citizens, to defend him against attempts by the secret police to evict him from his church in Timişoara.

It is important to note that the great majority of churches in communist-governed countries positively resisted any temptation to adapt themselves theologically to the Marxist-Leninist worldview and its social and political programmes. As noted above, even in East Germany the Protestant churches' understanding of the concept of the 'church in socialism' involved no tinkering with theology. The one exception to this general rule was provided by Hungary, where under János Kádár there was a relatively high standard of living and relatively high levels of individual freedom. Here the Lutheran and Reformed churches evolved a so-called 'theology of diakonia' (Lutheran) or 'theology of service' (Reformed) which sought to place the idea of the church's service to the world in the context of building socialism and the pursuit of 'peace'. Critics of this theology maintained that it replaced the redemptive element with exclusively humanitarian themes, that the concept of suffering was absent, and that the end result was that the Communist Party determined what kind of good works were appropriate for the church. In the 1980s there was growing opinion in world church circles that the theology of diakonia should be treated as a heresy, like the theology of apartheid.[6]

---

6 See 'The Hungarian Lutheran church and the "theology of diaconia"', *Religion in communist lands* 12 (1984), 130–48; Joseph Pungur, 'Doing theology in Hungary: liberation or adaptation', *Religion, state & society* 21 (1993), 71–85.

Poland

It was in Poland that Stalin (posthumously) received an answer to his question 'How many divisions has the pope?'

By the mid-1970s there was an established tradition of resistance to communist rule in Poland amongst intellectuals and the working classes alike, and by the end of the decade both groups were identifying with the Catholic church. The church did not initiate the opposition, but the latter saw the church as championing the same national and human values, and came to regard the church as the only moral authority in Poland.

The whole movement was then given new impetus by the election of Archbishop Karol Wojtyła of Kraków in 1978 as the first Polish pope. Soviet archives reveal that the election of John Paul II caused alarm verging on panic in the Kremlin.[7]

By the time of the election of John Paul II communism had become thoroughly discredited as an ideology in eastern Europe; but the pope maintained that the positive ideals it claimed to represent – social justice, participation, the dignity of work – were from now on to be interpreted in a Christian way. Successive popes had found that communism could not be intimidated by confrontation (Pius XII), or mitigated by co-operation (John XXIII), or appeased by diplomacy (Paul VI); John Paul II understood that it could be undermined by the power of values.[8] The new pope combined an ostensible readiness to accept the communist system with a form of subversion: an assertion of the church's right to speak to its flock about God and affirm the dignity of every individual.

The pope's first visit to Poland took place in 1979. The Polish authorities knew that it was unrealistic to try to prevent it. They attempted to reduce public fervour, ironically even promising complete live television coverage of the visit in order to keep people off the streets. Speaking directly to the people as individuals, the pope urged them, 'Never lose your spiritual freedom.'[9]

From this time the balance of power between church and state shifted. It was becoming clear that in Poland the Catholic church had greater legitimacy than the state.

---

7 Felix Corley, 'Soviet reaction to the election of Pope John Paul II', Religion, state & society 22 (1994), p. 40.
8 Jonathan Luxmoore and Jolanta Babiuch, The Vatican and the red flag (London and New York: Geoffrey Chapman, 1999), pp. 299–300.
9 Alexander Tomsky, 'John Paul II in Poland: pilgrim of the Holy Spirit', Religion in communist lands 7 (1979), p. 164.

The Solidarity free trade union was organised in 1980. An important part of Solidarity's programme was showing that the communist system and its spokesmen systematically falsified reality. Another salient feature was the demand that, just as systematically, religion should be introduced into public life. The Western public was astonished to watch striking Polish workers kneeling in the mud to pray and crowds assembling under banners saying 'We Want God'.

The head of the Catholic church in Poland from 1948 to 1981, Cardinal Stefan Wyszyński, was a clever politician. While standing firm on matters of fundamental importance he was prepared to be flexible on tactics. During the Polish Spring of 1980–1 he cautioned Solidarity on a number of occasions against trying to gain too much too soon and so jeopardising what had already been achieved. His successor Cardinal Józef Glemp followed the same policy during the period of martial law (December 1981 to July 1983), and though this approach brought criticism from more militant union activists, it helped pave the way for the political change in Poland inaugurated in early 1989.

East Germany

As noted above, the one area in which the communist authorities in eastern Europe regularly expected the churches to be vocal was in speaking out in favour of 'peace'. In the GDR in the 1980s a larger peace movement began to develop, going beyond simple protest against the arms race to assert the concept that peace and human rights were intimately inter-related.

The Protestant church chose to embrace this development, in the context of the so-called 'conciliar movement' (initiated by the World Council of Churches) for justice, peace and ecological responsibility. Pastors and parishes began to organise peace seminars and peace services. Annual *Friedensdekaden* ('ten days for peace') and *Kirchentage* (church festivals lasting three or four days with tens of thousands of participants) included meetings on peace, the environment and issues of social concern. From the mid-1980s the emblem 'Swords into Ploughshares', modelled on the sculpture donated by the Soviet Union to the United Nations in 1961, became increasingly associated with church members, although its use was initially banned by the authorities.

By the middle of the 1980s many of these church groups had expanded their programme to include human rights issues. Meanwhile a whole range of citizens' groups concerned with such issues as peace, the environment, human rights, Women's Liberation and even the question of political change were springing up. The members of these groups were not necessarily

Christians, but the churches had the only public buildings where they could legally meet. There was some conflict within the churches as congregations found their premises used by a 'rainbow coalition'. Church leaders sought to establish ground rules within which churches and groups should operate, but in practice most churches continued to provide an umbrella under which this nascent civil society could function. Growing tension between the church leadership and some local groups of churchgoers came to a head in 1987 with the formation of a new group called *Kirche von Unten* ('Church from Below') which while claiming to be part of the Protestant church dispensed with all leadership and rules. A *modus vivendi* between the two was eventually worked out; but by now the church as a whole was under increasing pressure from the state. In November the environmental library at the East Berlin Zionskirche was raided and four of the staff arrested. It was clear that 'the church in socialism' could no longer operate in the traditional way. From now on the Protestant church in Germany formed part of the opposition to the East German regime.

Problems and challenges facing the churches in the post-communist period

Conflicting assumptions in church resistance to communism

The encounter between the churches and communism entailed some basically conflicting assumptions for the churches which were not apparent at the time but soon became manifest in the post-communist era and began to affect the churches' attempts to find their place in a pluralist environment. These conflicting assumptions affected all three 'vectors', identified above, along which the churches had potential influence in the communist period: the individual, the social and the national (all three now including the possibility of political involvement).

One set of conflicting assumptions concerned two very different understandings of communism. The first saw communism as the ultimate offspring of the Enlightenment. In this understanding the fall of communism represented the victory of the church over modernity. This was an influential perception in the Catholic churches in Poland and in some other eastern European countries (as well as in the Orthodox churches). The second, by contrast, saw communism as a failed attempt to create a surrogate religious faith in a secular age, to 'sacralise' politics. It would probably be true to say that this was the prevailing perception in the Protestant church in the GDR and in some other Protestant circles in eastern Europe.

At the individual level, it soon became clear that a basic question needed to be asked about any religious believer who had resisted the communist system: had he or she done so because that system was *atheist* or because it was *totalitarian*? An individual in the former category would in the post-communist period tend to be defensive of the 'truth', conservative, triumphalist, intolerant of innovations in the spiritual sphere. An individual in the latter category, by contrast, would now very likely be found in the camp promoting democratisation, pluralism and freedom of conscience for all. In post-communist eastern Europe (as in the former Soviet Union), it was thus no longer clear that Christian values could broadly be identified with the values of those professing a secular human rights agenda.

At the socio-political level, the first understanding of communism led to the aspiration to reinstrumentalise religion for socio-political goals. The second understanding, by contrast, saw the primary function of religion in the transition from communism as being to compel politics once again to desacralise itself and limit itself to its proper sphere and meanwhile to encourage the growth of a pluralist political environment and a pluralist civil society.

A second set of conflicting assumptions arose from the fact that in resisting communism, the churches in eastern Europe were in many cases actually doing something different from what they thought they were doing. Even if they were opposing their own conception of totality to that which the official system was attempting to impose, they were in fact promoting pluralism. The consequences of this are perhaps most obvious in those churches which continue to identify themselves with particular nationalities and which champion national self-determination. For many of them it continues to be hard to realise that self-determination in the post-communist context means self-determination for other national and religious groups alongside one's own.

All these tensions were probably exacerbated by what some have called the 'post-totalitarian mentality'. This includes, on the one hand, a tendency to expect solutions from strong leaders rather than from personal initiative, and, on the other hand, a tendency for the individual to dramatise himself or herself as the measure of all things. These contradictory elements tended to encourage polarisation amongst those who were faced with the message the churches were trying to bring. Some eagerly embraced the Christian message as a new set of truths to be adhered to as unquestioningly as the old communist ideology; others were sceptical and suspicious of any attempt to replace the old compulsory truths with a new set, however different in content it might be.

After the end of communism, then, the churches in eastern Europe were facing a range of challenges. Some of these were specific to the legacy of communism; some were shared with the churches in western Europe and the wider world.

Great expectations versus loss of symbolic prestige

After the end of communism the churches in eastern Europe were paradoxically at the same time reinforced and weakened. They now had the opportunity to involve themselves in all areas of public life, and great hopes were placed on them. At the same time, however, they lost the sense of uniqueness they had had under communism. The moment was widely referred to in church circles as a *kairos*: a time that is both challenging and dangerous, requiring discernment if opportunities are to be used correctly.

In the immediate post-communist period the churches were widely seen, especially by the new governments in eastern Europe, as the only source of energy and expertise for social and moral regeneration, and they were expected to be central to the process. This task was to prove far from straightforward, partly because it was not clear that the newly liberated populations at large were necessarily going to be receptive to church teachings. 'We are free to speak now,' said one East German pastor, 'but nobody is listening.'[10] Pastors and church activists in the former GDR felt themselves let down, as though they had simply been used by others as a vehicle to ride to freedom. They were unsure of the mandate and future direction of the church.

At the same time, there was the danger for the churches that they would be increasingly perceived as protective of the interests of their own members as opposed to those of society as a whole. In Poland the early 1990s saw denunciations of the 'black totalitarianism' of the Catholic church, which had allegedly replaced the 'red' variety, coming not only from organisations protesting against the new anti-abortion laws, which had had the strong backing of the church, but, more widely, from average Poles resenting massive church influence in the media and schools. Sixty per cent of respondents in an opinion poll in May 1991 said that the influence of the church was 'too great'.[11] In some countries the resumption of the churches' involvement in education was not achieved without opposition from liberal and left-wing political circles. Nevertheless, citizens of most eastern European countries

---

10 Beth Cantrell and Ute Kemp, 'The role of the Protestant church in eastern Germany: some personal experiences and reflections', *Religion, state & society* 21 (1993), p. 284.
11 Michel, 'Religious renewal', p. 342.

(except eastern Germany, the Czech Republic and Slovenia) continued throughout the 1990s to trust the churches more than other political and social institutions.[12]

Lack of property, resources and experience

Most of the churches in the countries concerned were structurally crippled and restricted in the range of their possible activities by communist governments. As a result most of them lacked property, resources and experience, especially when compared with their counterparts in the West. In 1989 Dean Modris Plate of the Latvian Lutheran church said that his church lacked experience in the social work it was now able to undertake, and needed training in mission work as well. 'If we can unite with the national revival, by uniting the people's renewal with true Christianity, then I shall be satisfied. The question is – can we manage it?'[13] There was a widespread shortage of clergy. In 1995 40 per cent of Hungary's Catholic parishes were still without priests; in the Czech Republic the ratio of one Catholic priest to 5,600 church members compared to the European average of one to 1,295.[14] The process of returning church buildings was soon under way, but was not without its problems. In Hungary, when the Catholic church was given its property back in line with the law of 10 July 1991, appeals for charity and generosity came from the political world, and there was a certain decrease in public confidence in the church.

A problem specific to Germany was the reuniting of the Protestant church in the former GDR with its sister-church in western Germany; the latter was soon perceived to have swamped the former and its identity, and eastern German church activists complained that the church had become 'top-down' rather than 'roots-up'.

Lack of exposure to world developments; conservatism and authoritarianism

There was a general tendency throughout communist eastern Europe for church members (laity, clergy and hierarchs alike) to be more traditionalist

---

12 Miklós Tomka, 'Religious change in east-central Europe', in Irena Borowik and Miklós Tomka (eds.), *Religion and social change in post-communist Europe* (Kraków: Nomos, 2001), p. 21.
13 Marite Sapiets, 'The Baltic churches and the national revival', *Religion in communist lands* 18 (1990), p. 168.
14 Jonathan Luxmoore, 'Eastern Europe, 1995: a review of religious life in Bulgaria, Romania, Hungary, Slovakia, the Czech Republic and Poland', *Religion, state & society* 24 (1996), pp. 361–2.

and conservative than their western European counterparts (though of course liberal individuals and groups were certainly to be found). This tendency became explicit in the post-communist period, particularly in the churches that saw themselves as 'traditional' or 'historic'. East–West disagreement arose over such issues as the ordination of women, homosexuality and abortion. Part of the reason is that during the communist period the churches in eastern Europe had no systematic exposure to developments in world Christianity since the Second World War, such as the Second Vatican Council, the ecumenical movement, the growth of black churches, and new theologies (liberation, feminist). In the post-communist period there was widespread concern at the influx of liberal ideas. Churchgoers in formerly communist countries saw these as symptoms of Western secularism, which in its effects already looked disturbingly similar to the previous secularism of communism.

Christians in eastern Europe had also come to view with suspicion many apparently progressive concepts which had been tainted as a result of their appropriation by the communists: not only words such as 'peace' and 'democracy', but such purely ecclesiastical concepts as 'ecumenism', which was seen as the international activity leading church people had to engage in under communism in order to prove to the world at large that their churches at home enjoyed religious liberty.

In many countries the repressive policies of the communist government succeeded in encouraging the churches to retain an authoritarian structure. Partly this was to prevent internal schism, which could have been exploited by the authorities; partly it was that bishops acted as 'lightning conductors' in order to protect their flock. In many churches an instinctive authoritarianism continued in the post-communist period, with lower clergy denied initiative and laypeople denied any role in reconstructing the churches and their societies.

Divisions, distrust, overcoming the past

Immediately after the end of communism it became clear that a problem for the churches (and for society as a whole) would be to achieve reconciliation between two groups now divided by bitterness and distrust: those who had 'compromised' or 'collaborated' with the secular authorities and those who had 'resisted' and had been persecuted or discriminated against as a result. The reputation the East German Protestant church had built up during the 1980s was deeply compromised by revelations from the files of the Stasi, the East German secret police, in the early 1990s that clergy and church activists had been involved extensively in various forms of contact with the Stasi; the revelations involved a good deal of personal tragedy as individuals realised that these included people they had trusted intimately.

The challenges of pluralism

In their weakened state, the churches in post-communist eastern Europe were suddenly confronted with all the challenges of pluralism and secularisation, and forced to place themselves in an increasingly complex environment.

Levels of religiosity varied widely in eastern Europe both before and during the communist period. Poland and Slovakia were highly religious; the Czech Republic and East Germany were heavily secularised. In communist times the phenomenon of the 'practising non-believer' had been common – someone who attended church in order to demonstrate his or her dissent from the official ideology – and this had tended to distort the 'true' picture. The general picture in eastern Europe after the end of communism combined a sense of a (potential or actual) religious 'revival' with a decline in religious practice (Poland remained an exception).[15] The question increasingly being asked by sociologists of religion after the end of communism was whether patterns of religious observance in eastern and western Europe would come to resemble each other, with an increase in the east of what Grace Davie has identified as 'believing without belonging':[16] possessing a religious faith without allegiance to any specific denomination.

At the same time, a religious 'marketplace' was suddenly opened up. As soon as communism came to an end, missionary work again became possible in eastern Europe. Rivalry and recrimination often arose between denominations that considered themselves 'traditional' and those that were perceived as 'new', with the former accusing the latter of 'sheep-stealing'.

A general lack of resources and infrastructure explained the dismay with which many of the indigenous churches throughout central and eastern Europe reacted to the sudden influx of all kinds of foreign missions and sects. Many of these evangelistic organisations had huge financial and technical resources which could not be matched by the indigenous churches, and were quite happy to use the promise of material rewards or English lessons to attract converts. This kind of approach did nothing to allay the suspicions of

---

15 On the complex question of the revival of religious faith and denominational affiliation in post-communist eastern Europe and its significance see Tomka, 'Religious change'.

16 Grace Davie, *Religion in Britain since 1945: believing without belonging* (Oxford: Blackwell, 1994).

indigenous churches that such 'sects' were simply the aggressive tools of Western secular materialist interests operating under the guise of religion.

Ecumenism and inter-denominational relations

As noted above, in communist times 'ecumenism' was something that church leaders were expected to engage in at the international level but not at home. This still had repercussions in the post-communist period. One specific cause of tension between denominations was the restoration of church property. In communist times the state authorities often favoured one church over another and handed over to it buildings belonging to another denomination, so that in post-communist times the issue of rival claims to the same property arose. In Romania, for example, the 'favoured' Orthodox church received over 2,500 churches belonging to the Eastern-rite Catholic church when the latter was delegalised in 1948. From 1989 the two churches were wrangling over their return. By 1998 the Eastern-rite Catholics had received fewer than 100 churches.[17]

There were, however, encouraging ecumenical initiatives throughout post-communist eastern Europe. Orthodox and Protestant Christians were conspicuous among 70,000 who attended a December 1999 youth meeting of the ecumenical Taizé community in Warsaw. In 2000 the Catholic Council of European Bishops' Conferences under the presidency of a Czech cardinal, Miloslav Vlk, pledged itself in Prague to stepping up 'practical and thematic cooperation' with non-Catholic denominations.[18] In the same year the Catholic church in Poland agreed to a joint recognition of baptisms with the country's seven largest minority churches. Again in 2000, in the Czech Republic Catholic representatives attended the consecration of the Hussite church's first woman bishop, while the pope voiced 'great regret' over the martyrdom of the fifteenth-century Czech reformer Jan Hus.[19]

Legislation

The introduction of new legislation on religion in eastern Europe was a process marked by a tension between the inclination to grant complete religious freedom and the growing perception of a need to place greater restrictions on 'non-traditional' religions or unrestricted missionary activity. There was a tendency for churches that regarded themselves as 'traditional' to favour increased restrictions and for minority churches to favour the

---

17 Jonathan Luxmoore, 'Eastern Europe, 1997–2000: a review of church life', *Religion, state & society* 29 (2001), p. 319.
18 Ibid., p. 328.   19 Ibid., p. 327.

extension of freedom. In most of the countries of the region religious organ-isations were soon being required to gain official 'registration'; this would sometimes be a formality, but would sometimes have negative implications for minority faiths or for denominations claiming the same name as another. With a new law on religion passed in 2002 Belarus became the first country in post-communist Europe to make all unregistered religious activity illegal.

A question that affected the whole of Europe from the mid-1990s was how to head off the danger posed by certain 'cults' or 'sects' perceived to be acting in an anti-social or dangerous manner. Legislation designed specifically for this purpose was passed, mostly in EU member countries. The outcome by the early 2000s was that legislation on religion and its actual application in some former communist countries, for example the Baltic states, could be compared favourably from the religious freedom perspective with legislation in some Western states (France, Austria, Greece).[20]

Relation with politics

In the immediate post-communist period Christian Democratic parties were widely revived and did well at the polls. They tended to rally social forces and interest groups which continued to desire a direct relationship with the church (normally the Catholic church). In Germany, the Christian Democratic Party (CDU) included a number of prominent Protestant pastors. The East German election of March 1990 produced a government with four Protestant pastors in the cabinet; some two dozen members of the 400-member Parliament had theological qualifications; most of them were pastors.

Generally speaking, however, the close involvement of the churches with politics tended to decline. German pastors in the early 1990s seem to have been increasingly of the view that their priority should be social work and witness, and that the CDU did not represent the interests the church ought to be pursuing.

In Poland the Catholic church eventually perceived that it might be ill advised to maintain the high political profile it had initially adopted. In 1995 the Catholic Lech Wałęsa was defeated in the Polish presidential elections and the neo-communists thus gained control of presidency, government and Parliament. Heavy-handed church support for Wałęsa ironically gave the neo-communists the image of the more progressive and modernising party.

---

20 Simon Barnett, 'Religious freedom and the European Convention on Human Rights: the case of the Baltic states', *Religion, state & society* 29 (2001), 91–100; Philip Walters, 'Editorial', ibid., 77–8.

After the election the Catholic leader Cardinal Józef Glemp said, 'We should admit that we have fewer true Catholics than the statistics show.'[21] In 1999 a synod of the Catholic church in Poland warned priests to avoid politics as part of its effort to bring church practices into line with the Second Vatican Council. It said that the church did not 'identify with any party' and that no party had 'a right to represent it'. However, it called on lay Catholics to be generally active politically, and defended the right of priests and bishops to set out 'Catholic criteria' for public life.[22]

Nationalism

In the 1970s and 1980s nationalism was not yet charged with all the negative baggage it acquired during the 1990s: rather, it was a vehicle for the expression of the desire for personal and communal freedom. Pope John Paul II was happy to speak in the context of the close identification of the Polish people and the Catholic church. After the end of communism, however, his vision of a new non-ideological solidarity faded somewhat as new ideologies (notably liberalism and nationalism) gained ground, and he found it necessary to sound warning notes about tendencies to deify the nation. In Lithuania during the last years of Soviet power the Catholic church was in a strong position as perhaps the main repository of the national heritage, reinforced by respect for its own past resistance to Soviet persecution. In June 1989 Cardinal Sladkevičius said that 'the well-being of believers can best be achieved in an independent Lithuania'.[23] However, at that time the hierarchy began distancing itself from a nationalism detached from Christian moral values.

The question of how far the wars between the various national groups in former Yugoslavia in the early 1990s could be called 'religious' was much debated. Some argued that what was involved was an 'instrumentalisation'[24] of religion for non-religious purposes, and saw this as a symptom of the ideological vacuum in eastern Europe, where nationalist and right-wing groups were frequently justifying their programmes in religious language. In some parts of eastern Europe anti-semitism re-emerged as a social phenomenon. In 1999 Polish police and army units had to intervene to remove over 300 crosses from the former Auschwitz concentration camp, installed by

---

21 Luxmoore, 'Eastern Europe, 1995', p. 358.
22 Luxmoore, 'Eastern Europe, 1997–2000', p. 325.
23 Sapiets, 'The Baltic churches', p. 161.
24 See for example Patrick Michel, 'Religion, communism, and democracy in central Europe: the Polish case', in William H. Swatos, Jr (ed.), *Politics and religion in central and eastern Europe: traditions and transitions* (Westport, CT: Praeger, 1994), p. 125.

Catholic nationalists in protest against exclusive Jewish claims to the site. The fact that the number of Jews in Poland after the Second World War was negligible did not stop the routine appearance of anti-semitic graffiti in some Polish cities after 1989.

The market economy and the European Union

Citizens of communist countries placed great reliance on 'the market' as a mechanism for solving all problems, moral and spiritual as well as social. The capitalist economy duly arrived, with unmitigated speed and in a particularly virulent form. Widespread disillusionment was the result. 'The market' in post-communist eastern Europe too often seemed to combine the worst features of the old system (corruption, nepotism) with a whole range of new unwelcome features (lack of job security, inflation, physical danger for the ordinary citizen). Many citizens throughout eastern Europe, especially the older generation, looked back nostalgically to the old days.

Perspectives of this kind coloured debate in the eastern European churches on the question of accession to the European Union. In Poland a nationalist Catholic newspaper which reflected the views of perhaps 12 per cent of the population warned in 1998 against a 'wave of garbage, a post-modernist, liberal slush of pseudo-values – this is what Europe is offering us today'; 'this is all too high a price for being together with the West'.[25] In the late 1990s, however, delegations of bishops from Poland, the Czech Republic and Hungary visited Brussels and returned fully convinced that the EU was the way for the future. Generally speaking Catholic and Protestant leaders and clergy were by now in favour of accession, as was the leadership of the Romanian Orthodox church. Church approval gave a significant boost to the campaign to mobilise public support in these countries. Opponents of accession to the EU were generally in a minority in the churches.

The attitude of the churches to the EU reflected the fact that new church leaders in eastern Europe were increasingly orientated towards the West. Eastern European churches were by now better represented in European consultative bodies: more had joined the World Council of Churches, and eastern Europeans comprised half of the thirty-four Catholic bishops' conferences. There was expansion of local contacts and assistance: hundreds of Polish priests, for example, were working in western Europe, and eastern European Christians were very involved in producing the *Charta oecumenica* issued by the Conference of European Churches in 2001.

---

25 Luxmoore, 'Eastern Europe, 1997–2000', p. 315.

20

The transformation of Latin American Christianity, c.1950–2000

EDWARD L. CLEARY

Christianity in Latin America was about to undergo momentous changes in 1950. On the surface, though, few indications of change showed themselves to observers. Rather, historians and social scientists tended to depict Latin America as dominated by the presence of the Catholic church throughout the region. The church had few challengers. Protestants were few in numbers, relatively the same percentage range as Catholics in Scandinavia and England. African and indigenous religions were practised mostly on the margins of society. The small numbers of Marxists, even in Cuba, did not appear to pose the same threat to Christianity that communists caused in China and eastern Europe.

The Catholic church was in a privileged and only marginally threatened position. However, internal weaknesses and external threats would soon become apparent. In the following sections, three developments will be examined: first, how did awareness of institutional weakness become clear to sectors of the church? Second, how did region-wide social change facilitate new religious choices and changes? Lastly, challengers to Catholicism and Catholic responses will be discussed.

Institutional weakness and response

Great disparities existed in the practice of Catholicism in Latin America. In Mexico and Colombia very high percentages attended church weekly. In Cuba, by contrast, only handfuls attended mass on Sundays. In many countries the Catholic church appeared as weak, even moribund. Throughout the region the church could be described as otherworldly in emphasis, without much regard for social justice.

A small revitalising sector among the laity existed. As militant Christians they saw themselves as different from other Catholics. At a landmark Latin American conference a key group of these activists, Catholic Actionists, gathered in 1953 at Chimbote, Peru. They described Latin American Catholics as only nominally Catholic, with an appalling minimum of religious instruction. Furthermore, Latin American Catholicism consisted of a traditional set of pious customs, a superficial substitute for the demands of the Spirit and dictates of the gospel. The Latin American Catholic church, they concluded, needed a profound revitalisation.

The Vatican had reached the same conclusion earlier. In the late 1940s priests who were young, progressive and closely tied to the laity were selected by Rome to become bishops. Some studied in Europe or were deeply influenced by Christian democracy and the European Catholic revival, exemplified by Jacques Maritain. Helder Câmara illustrated the change marked by these prelates. A bishop by his thirties, Câmara proved a great success in pulling bishops together to form the Brazilian Bishops' Conference (CNBB, *Conferência Nacional dos Bispos do Brasil*) in 1952.

Throughout the 1950s and 1960s the Vatican added at a great rate new dioceses and young bishops with modern ideas to head them. The Vatican also encouraged the sending of hundreds of missionaries from Europe, Canada and the United States. They contributed significantly to a religious revitalisation. The church, transnational by nature, expanded its national and international linkages, structures and activities within Latin America and the larger world. These organisational structures would prove to be crucial for the communication of theological and pastoral innovations that would follow.

Creating a Latin American Bishops' Conference (CELAM) proved to be a key organisational innovation. The Vatican, through the Italian Archbishop Antonio Samoré, encouraged Latin American bishops to form CELAM. The bishops established a general secretariat in Bogotá in September 1955. Contrary to previous emphases in Latin America on stressing traditional piety and individual charity, CELAM leadership began to emphasise concern for political and social issues affecting the lower classes and a much broader participation of lay Catholics in the church and in public life.

By the late 1950s the church had become acutely aware of threats to its religious and ideological hegemony. In January 1959 Cuba fell to communist rule and the majority of priests and sisters were expelled or left the island when the Cuban government nationalised their institutions. Similar threats were seen in Guatemala and the Dominican Republic where civil wars and US interventions resulted from alleged Marxist threats. Protestants began to fill in the spaces where priests were sparse. To meet the challenges that Protestantism and Marxism posed, the Holy See requested that 10 per cent of the abundant number of priests and religious women then available in Europe, Canada and the United States be sent to Latin America. Thousands made their way there. Church offices and religious congregations in Europe, Canada and the United States sent hundreds of millions in aid money to bolster the Latin American church from the 1960s to the present.

The foundation was laid for the Latin American church to absorb the great transforming event of the Second Vatican Council (1962–5). Some 600 Latin American bishops attended the four-year process. They largely went as learners, known to European and US observers as 'the church of silence'. At the council a number of Latin American bishops employed as their advisers their more recently educated clergy or active laity who were in touch with progressive European theology and the movements that dominated the council discussions.

During the Vatican Council Latin American bishops in Rome met among themselves and agreed that a special conference should take place back on their own soil to continue the renewal efforts of Vatican II. Most important for the transition from the ideas of Vatican II to applying them to Latin America were the young theologians, many of them European trained. These Latin Americans, at first a handful and then fifty or more, formed the core group who were charged with writing the basic documents of the all-important Medellín Conference (1968).

Turning point

Of all the regions of the world, Latin America was the only one to apply systematically the themes contained in the documents of Vatican II to their region. This bold effort at Medellín gained the attention of the Catholic and Christian world. Asian and African bishops and their intellectual centres began not so much to copy Latin America, as to try out what grew to become contextual theology. In Latin America it was more commonly identified as Liberation Theology.

In contrast to traditional piety, Liberation Theology emphasised roles that religion should play in society, especially focusing on societal structures that helped or hindered the lives of the poor. This theology undergirded several of the important documents of the Latin American bishops' Medellín Conference (1968), especially those treating the themes of justice and peace.[1] This rather abrupt change in direction from traditional to modernising

---

1 Latin American Bishops' Conference, *The church in the present-day transformation of Latin America in the light of the council* (Bogotá: Latin American Bishops' Conference, 1970).

by the bishops caused rejoicing in progressive sectors, caution in conservative ones and surprise among religious competitors.

Liberation Theology was not by any means the only renovating ideology for the Latin American church emerging from Vatican II or from other sources. Charismatic Catholicism, in contrast to North Atlantic countries, grew steadily from the 1970s in Latin America. In Brazil in the late 1990s as many as two million attended services conducted by Padre Marcelo Rossi in the São Paulo area. Communitarian theologies within newer lay movements, such as Focolari and Schoenstatt, also gained acceptance. Chilean bishops came to emphasise a theology of communion. Liberation Theology continued through affirmations of its major points in church documents and through the lives of millions of Christians working within social movements. However, by 2000, the theology had evolved in such a way that it flourished more in its derivatives, such as Indian theology and women's theology.

Another innovation that followed in the wake of Vatican II had a peculiarly Latin American character, the base ecclesial communities (BECs). The fundamental motivation for their creation and their acceptance was religious. Bible study among Catholics became common. The very large urban or rural parishes embraced tens of thousands of persons or hundreds of kilometres. Latin American pastors and parishioners, feeling the need to read, discuss and apply the Bible to their lives, formed groups of neighbours, mostly adults, into discussion and prayer groups. Probably several million Latin Americans took part in these groups for a number of years. Many members, but by no means all, used the groups as a base for social and political involvement. These communities served as the catalyst for millions of Latin Americans to become involved in new social movements, such as the Movement of the Landless (MST) in Brazil and the peace organisations in Central America.

In the wake of Vatican II and the Medellín Conference millions of Catholics began reading the Bible and attending classes in the new orientations that the church had proposed in the documents of the two meetings. The retreat movement, embodied especially in the Cursillos de Cristiandad (Short Courses in Christianity), emphasised personal growth and service to the church. In place of nominal Catholicism, Cursillo lay leaders and their priest-chaplains emphasised an evangelical change of heart.

Turmoil and conflicts also took place over who spoke for the church, what were the prerogatives of the laity within the church and what roles the institutional church should play in society. For a brief period from the late 1960s through the early 1970s, some activist priests organised groups such as Golconda in Colombia and Priests for the Third World in Argentina to pressurise bishops to make rapid changes in the church. Debates about the proper direction of these modernising efforts continued in two General Conferences of the Latin American Bishops (CELAM) at Puebla (1979) and Santo Domingo (1992), and, for the most part, both conferences affirmed and consolidated what had been declared at the Medellín Conference.

Political and social environments affecting religion

During the 1950s and thereafter Latin American society was reshaped by processes that increasingly impinged on communities and individuals. Technologies that facilitated industrialisation; rail, air, and highway systems; telephone and digital communication; transistor radios and television all deeply affected Latin America, changing virtually all spaces in which men and women lived. Latin America shifted within a few decades from being primarily agricultural and rural to being urban and industrial and, even more, oriented to the service sector.

These changes were visible and increasingly taken for granted. What was not as perceptible were the changes produced in individuals and institutions within Latin America. On the personal level, what the sociologist Max Weber foresaw came true. Migration was forced on many because of the lack of opportunity to farm at home or the attraction of a putative better life in towns and cities. Thereby many Latin Americans became free of the ties to their families and local institutions that held them in a particular social space with generally traditional arrangements. By moving they became, in Weber's terms, masterless slaves. Whereas they had lived as indigenous or peasant, practising Catholic or indigenous religion without choosing their ethnic or religious identity, they were now free. Whatever status they would have would be acquired rather than inherited.

In the 1950s and 1960s, people left farms or villages and went to cities, breaking loose from the social control of family and neighbours and exercising freedom of choice. Most migrants to cities continued to believe in God but some chose what appeared to them to be more attractive forms of religion than Catholicism. To remain Catholic, as the majority did, often meant a conscious choice, implying a conversion to deeper commitment to faith and religion.

From the 1970s the same social forces increasingly affected persons living in villages and open country. Popular media – millions of $10 transistor radios, mimeographed newsletters and other common media, often in indigenous languages – appeared in rural populations with messages that differed from the ones that traditional cultures communicated. Thus messages from religions competing with Catholicism and with one another reached the peoples living in remote areas. A massive change within religion and culture was taking place under these influences.

These social changes also brought new political claims, failed economic policies, grassroots political demands and increasing unrest. Especially during the 1960s and 1970s, but continuing much later in places like Chile, the military took over government and imposed authoritarian rule. In Chile, Brazil and elsewhere the churches (Catholic and historical Protestant) found themselves as the main social institution not under military control and became the 'voice of the voiceless', offering a measure of human rights protection and advocacy. Archbishop Oscar Romero of San Salvador became the symbol of the thousands killed, tortured or imprisoned from 1964 to 1990.

Catholic and historical Protestant churches, sometimes joined by Pentecostal groups, also took a leadership role in the transition from military rule to peace. As Samuel Huntington and others have noted, Latin American churches played a key role in the third wave of democratisation in the world. As mentioned, Christians formed a major part of the social movements that undergirded the peace processes in Central America and hundreds of human rights groups in Latin America. Transnational efforts of Lutherans and Catholics at Oslo and other meetings helped to bring agreements that ended armed strife in Central America in 1996.

After the conflicts, the churches in several countries took part in establishing the historical record about the human rights abuses that occurred under military rule. The World Council of Churches and the Catholic church in Brazil were the instruments by which a million pages of evidence were gathered and issued in summary form as *Nunca mais* (1985). The Catholic church of Guatemala city published its report of the historical records of abuses by guerrillas and government forces during Guatemala's civil war. Two days later, the president of the archdiocesan commission, Bishop Juan Gerardi Conedera, was murdered. Human rights activity continued to grow after military rule in most countries, fuelled in part by religious motivations.

While revitalisation efforts affected sectors of the Catholic church, many Catholics remained on the margins of organised religion. Some were repelled by the changes in Catholicism. In a word, very large numbers of Latin American Catholics were indifferent practitioners of organised religion. Pentecostalism changed that for millions of Latin Americans. So, too, to a lesser degree did other religious groups enliven the religious scene in Latin America. By the end of the millennium Latin America was experiencing a great Christian and religious revival.

Catholic transformation

After David Martin published *Tongues of fire: the explosion of Pentecostalism in Latin America* and David Stoll wrote his *Is Latin America turning Protestant?*[2] in 1990, major print media issued many articles, with increasingly negative assessments of the Catholic church. One might presume that the Catholic church was greatly diminished. While the church did lose millions of indifferent members, the effects of its own reform are noteworthy, for, in effect, a religious revival had been taking place in Latin America, in which the Catholic church shared abundantly. The numbers of Latin Americans entering the priesthood and religious life, the quality of laity participating in the church, and the reformed orientation of the church shown in the Medellín and Puebla documents demonstrated a vitality that was exemplary, worthy of global leadership.

Several factors, occurring as a convergence, led to this revival. Large numbers of missionaries not only increased the workforce but encouraged modern pastoral practices in which lay leaders played key roles. Younger Latin American bishops, especially in Brazil and Chile, assumed leadership not only within their own countries but also within the Latin American Bishops' Conference. Numerous lay movements, including Catholic Action and the Cursillos de Cristiandad, brought hundreds of thousands of lay persons into active roles within the church.

For the first time in the last hundred years the Latin American church had gained fundamental strength. It had built the three foundation blocks it needed: an expanded clergy with mostly national priests, a large corps of recruits in training for the priesthood and a catechised and active laity. The church had especially lacked a laity well educated in religion and its social implications. In providing adult education and building a sense of community, and by making Bibles available to millions, the church produced a core group of committed Catholic parents. They, in turn, fostered among their children large increases in vocations to the priesthood and religious life (61,000 priests and 128,000 sisters in 2000).

By 2000 the number of priests had increased over 70 per cent in forty years. This stands in marked contrast to the well-publicised decline in the United States and Europe. In Mexico alone the number of priests more than doubled from 5,834 to 13,173.[3] There and in most of Latin America the increases in the

2 David Martin, *Tongues of fire: the explosion of Protestantism in Latin America* (Oxford: Blackwell, 1990); David Stoll, *Is Latin America turning Protestant? The politics of evangelical growth* (Berkeley: University of California Press, 1990).
3 Statistics on the Catholic church are available in the annual editions of *Annuarium statisticum ecclesiae* (Vatican City: Typis Polyglottis Vaticanis).

priesthood came mainly from Latin Americans and not from the presence of foreign missionaries.

Thus the replacement rate for priests within Latin America has been the most favourable it has been in decades. One should note, however, that disparity between countries in the number of seminarians per 10,000 Catholics ranges from 1.12 in Colombia to less than 0.3 in Honduras and Cuba. Foreign missionary presence is notably declining. Figures on foreign origins are seldom kept in Latin America. However, sociologists have been able to track the trend in Chile. Every indicator shows a similar trend else-where. In Chile during 1965 slightly more than half (51 per cent) of priests were foreigners.[4] By 1996 the percentage of foreigners had dropped to 29 per cent. A few foreign missionaries became Chilean citizens but the great majority of replacements came from young Chileans entering the priesthood. Priests under forty years old formed a very large sector in Chile, in contrast to the United States and Europe.[5]

These gains contrasted sharply with the situation at mid-century, since the church had declined badly in the nineteenth and early twentieth centuries. In 1965 only four countries (Mexico, Colombia, Argentina and Ecuador) had at least 60 per cent native-born clergy. One was hard-pressed to find native clergy in countries like Panama with 83 per cent foreign clergy or Guatemala with 81 per cent foreign priests.[6] Some Latin Americans felt overwhelmed by foreign clergy. Bolivia had 75 per cent of its clergy supplied by foreigners in the 1960s. During that era Bolivian researchers conducted one of the few systematic studies of the priesthood in Latin America. The researchers, Jaime Ponce García and Oscar Uzín Fernández, concluded: 'Given the enormously high percentage of foreigners ... many ask themselves if a Bolivian church really exists.'[7]

The full range of effects of foreign missionaries would be too lengthy an assessment here. But profound political divisions should be noted. Foreign clergy tended to be more progressive and the national clergy more conser-vative on important national issues at crucial times. Philip Williams carefully portrayed these cleavages among Nicaraguan clergy during the Sandinist

---

4 Pro Mundi Vita Institute, *PMV special note* (Brussels: Pro Mundi Vita Institute) 15 (October 1970), p. 3.
5 For Chile, *Datos estadísticos 1996: clero secular, congregaciones religiosas, sacramentación en Chile* (Santiago: Oficina Sociología Religiosa, 1997).
6 *PMV special note*, p. 3.
7 Jaime Ponce García and Oscar Uzín Fernández, *El clero de Bolivia* (Cuernavaca, Mexico: CIDOC (Centro Intercultural de Documentación), 1970), p. 59.

Table 20.1

	Catholic church in Latin America Growth in seminarians		
	1972	2000	% increase
Argentina	306	2,003	555
Bolivia	49	697	1,322
Brazil	939	8,831	840
Chile	111	680	513
Colombia	738	4,679	534
Ecuador	92	795	764
Paraguay	63	363	476
Peru	190	1,700	795
Uruguay	25	86	244
Venezuela	120	1,128	840
Mexico	2,264	7,059	212
Costa Rica	61	318	421
El Salvador	34	391	1,050
Guatemala	69	366	430
Honduras	16	128	700
Nicaragua	45	263	484
Panama	22	135	514
Cuba	49	105	114
Dominican Republic	51	516	912
Haiti	41	362	783
Puerto Rico	49	96	96

Sources: Annuarium statisticum ecclesiae (Vatican City: Typis Polyglottis Vaticanis, 2001) and *Catholic almanac 1975*.

years.[8] In other places, such as the Caribbean, tensions were chronic between native and foreign clergy.

The trend toward much greater numbers of Latin American seminarians indicated a high replacement rate for priests, a key statistic for the Catholic church.[9] The percentage of increase astounded observers who remember the small and mostly empty seminary buildings of the 1960s (see table 20.1).

---

8 Philip Williams, 'The limits of religious influence: the progressive church in Nicaragua', in Edward L. Cleary and Hannah Stewart-Gambino (eds.), *Conflict and competition: the Latin American church in a changing environment* (Boulder and London: Lynne Rienner, 1992).

9 'Seminarians' here means students in post-secondary education, studying philosophy (two years) or theology (four years).

Also in contrast to the United States, religious women in Latin America increased their numbers, although in more modest percentages than those of seminarians. Nonetheless, they represented more than 128,000 important pastoral workers. A number of them worked in slums and remote regions, as part of the church's emphasis on serving the poor. Some of them acted as leaders of what were called priestless parishes. Many of them preached and ministered in a variety of ways, beyond their traditional roles as teachers or nurses.

Among the laity the revitalisation process, including education in contemporary Christianity and emphasis on interior growth, resulted in lay movements. They were the principal instruments for changes from popular Catholicism and fiestas to active participation in modern worship services and in social outreach from the parishes.

The most telling indicator of changes in the Latin American Catholic church's laity is the office of catechist. If Latinamericanisation of the church is a key goal, catechists have become the major instrument. In the 1950s native and foreign priests, for the most part ignorant of Indian languages, utilised catechists largely as translators of the myriad languages. The catechist movement also greatly spread to non-indigenous areas. After decades of educating catechists in orthodox Christianity, as contrasted to popular Catholicism, catechists became more than lay educators. They were vernacular intellectuals, interpreters of Christianity within Latin America. Their numbers were impressive. In 2000 more than one million lay Catholics served as catechists, in effect acting as non-ordained ministers. Not only their numbers but their valour (they bore the brunt of repression in Central America) were noteworthy.

Religious challengers

Ancient religions of Latin America and the Catholic church

In contrast to Pentecostals and many Protestant groups in Latin America, the Catholic church has been in contact with indigenous and African-based religion for centuries. These sets of religions have been part of the religious resurgence in the region. While African religions found acceptance among middle-class Brazilians and spread to white, mulatto and mestizo practitioners in Uruguay and Argentina, Indian religion gained the most regional attention, in part because Indians greatly outnumbered those who identified themselves as Afro-Latin American or black.

As the fifth centenary of Columbus' first journey to America (1992) was being planned, indigenous movements rebelled. Just when many presumed that the Latin American Indians were either assimilated into national society or were quiescent politically, indigenous movements burst into public consciousness. Ecuador's Indians stormed into the National Congress building in 1990. Bolivia's tropical Indians marched 700 miles across the country in 1990 to make their political demands plain in La Paz. In the most publicised event, Zapatistas rose up in Chiapas on 1 January 1994 to protest against the enactment on that date of the North American free trade agreement that Mexico had signed with Canada and the United States.

These movements, as with the Civil Rights movement in the United States, were fuelled in large part by churches, in this case, by Catholic and some Protestant ones. Indigenous movements would not have arisen as quickly as they did or in the form that they did without the transnational help of missionaries and anthropologists. This was remarkable, in part, because after World War II, when colonialism and its companion, racism, were being challenged, churches were singled out for blame for the subservient status of Latin American Indians. In fact, at a 1971 conference at Barbados (sponsored by the World Council of Churches) that proved to be a benchmark, anthropologists had accused churches, along with governments and international agencies, of cultural imperialism.

Whatever the past record of Spanish and Portuguese missionaries in dealing with indigenous peoples, foreign missionaries of the late twentieth century and key Catholic bishops and Protestant leaders within indigenous regions responded extensively to the perceived need to aid tribal leaders in organising to pressurise governments for their rights and privileges as full citizens. By the 1970s and 1980s not only were the indigenous organising regionally and nationally, they were also creating a transnational Indian rights movement. Missionaries and anthropologists aided substantially in facilitating its creation. Political scientists and anthropologists noted the critical role that Liberation Theology played in establishing indigenous movements. So, too, they publicised the heroic efforts of bishops, such as Samuel Ruiz of Chiapas, who retired at the end of the century after more than thirty years of efforts to respect native cultures and to support non-violent indigenous activism.

Behind this political activism that grew through the 1990s was a change in policy of the Catholic and historical Protestant churches. Indigenous policies of the Catholic church, mirrored in some Protestant ones, can be summed up in four phases: reclaim the region through an infusion of resources; incorporate indigenous within the church; educate in Catholic orthodoxy and in Catholic reformed religion; create an indigenous church.

To reclaim regions where priests became scarce for a long time following Spanish and Portuguese withdrawal after 1810, priests, sisters, and lay volunteers largely from Europe and the United States moved in large numbers in the 1960s to serve the Indian populations. To incorporate indigenous more closely within the church, missionaries began the long process of learning languages, of listening and adapting the Christian message and worship to native cultures, and of taking up vigorous defence of Indians against outside economic interests. To educate in Catholic orthodoxy and reform, missionaries created hundreds of informal educational centres and formal schooling opportunities. Among non-Catholic groups, the Adventist schools around lake Titicaca were especially prominent in educating Indian leaders.

More important, though, was the increasing reliance on catechists in the Catholic church. They became a key instrument in drawing the indigenous people closer to the church. They served as what Andrew Orta calls 'indigenous intellectuals', bridging the gap between a Eurocentric church and native understanding. To create an indigenous church, Catholic and Protestant groups promoted greater use of indigenous languages, helped to recover cultural memory, and stimulated alliances with other Indian groups.

The commitment of the Catholic church to creating an indigenous church could be seen in the heavy investment of talent and resources in creating indigenous study centres and in elaborating Indian theology. While these centres were found in Mexico, Ecuador and Guatemala, they flourished most prominently in Peru and Bolivia. Foreign missionaries were key to stimulating study of indigenous cultures. However, they were most intent on fostering indigenous theologians. Eleazar López (Mexico), Domingo Llanque Chana (Peru) and Nicanor Sarmiento (Bolivia) were among the promising indigenous theologians to appear by the end of the millennium.

Regard for indigenous culture and thought provided the solid footing for indigenous identity needed to confront the state about indigenous rights, to establish status within the churches, and to overcome subordinate position within society. Four Interamerican Indian Theology meetings showed evidence of not only an emerging indigenous theology but also a theology that is ecumenical.

African-based religions

African-based religions did not have the number of followers to match the forty million indigenous of Latin America. These spiritist or Afro religions used to be found almost exclusively in Brazil, Haiti, and small pockets in Cuba and elsewhere. Brazil's last census (2000) showed slightly fewer than three million persons who identified themselves primarily as followers of three African-based religious families. These numbers masked an unknown but not small number of Brazilians who at times practise Afro religion while maintaining their chief identity as Christian. This covert practice was especially true of Pentecostals and neo-Pentecostals who practised these spiritist or Afro religions at times but whose leaders, portraying African religions as diabolic, expelled those with divided loyalties. In the 1980s it became clear that African-based religions were gaining greater acceptance among the middle class and white populations.

On a continuum of more or less Africanicity in content or practice, Candomblé was strongest, Umbanda much less, and spiritism almost off the continuum, being European in origin with Brazilian roots and some African inspiration. In the 2000 census 140,000 Brazilians identified themselves as practitioners of Candomblé and 430,000 as members of Umbanda temples. Both groups had declining numbers from previous estimates. The third religion, spiritism, inspired by Allen Kardec and modified in Brazil, had 2.3 million followers, according to the same census. Its numbers were growing. Spiritism laid claim to being based in science and philosophy and appeared to appeal to Brazilians living in a world of scientific ideas and modern business. Observers of African-based religion, such as David Hess, pointed to the phenomenon of belief in spirits in Brazil that reached through sectors of Brazilian society and continued to give strength and hope.

A related issue, the strengthening of ties of Christian churches with blacks in Brazil, surfaced more strongly in the latter part of the twentieth century. Seventy-one per cent of self-identified blacks listed themselves as Catholic and 9 per cent as Pentecostals in a national survey reported in 1994. Black activist movements made some progress in Brazil but spurted, failed and reorganised. At first, groups turned their backs on Christianity and emphasised Brazilian versions of African religions as a major source of their identity. Later, both Catholic and Protestant black movements were created, with the Catholic initiative being wider than the Protestant initiative.

African-based religions made their way increasingly from Brazil to urban centres in Uruguay and Argentina, beginning in the 1950s. By the 1990s some 1,000 African-based religious temples had been created in the greater Buenos Aires metropolitan area. Despite most members being Argentine, the majority of Argentines appeared not to be ready for religious diversity. In the late 1980s and 1990s practitioners of Umbanda were accused of practising animal sacrifice and black magic, and were even rumoured to have sacrificed a child. Umbandistas defended their religion not as Brazilian but as African and part of Latin America's heritage.

After Jean-Claude Duvalier, Haiti's leader, was toppled from power in 1986, *Vodou* functioned more openly. This was part of the long evolution of the lifting of the veil of secrecy that obscured the practice of Haiti's main African-based religion. The religion was part of the hidden cultural life adhered to by Haitian blacks to survive as slaves. The religion survived despite anti-superstitious campaigns in 1896, 1913 and 1941. By the 1950s *Vodou* was a living religion for masses of Haitians living in rural areas and, to a degree, in towns and cities. Its relation to the upper classes has been more tentative.

By the end of the century *Vodou* priests and followers were practising without government denunciation. *Vodou* is a generic African-based religion with an underlying unity, unlike the black religions of Brazil, although diversity of practices are evident among its practitioners. It had limited institutional structures, and existed without central spokespersons, seminaries or formal schooling. This made dialogue with Christian bodies virtually impossible.

Pentecostal and other contemporary religious groups

By the mid-twentieth century Protestant churches had gained a small but well-established presence in Latin America. With about 5 per cent of the Latin American population, the Protestant sector was probably evenly divided among historical Protestants and Pentecostals. The historical Protestants and inter-denominational missionary churches were becoming more accepted in Catholic Latin America through establishing first-rate American and British secondary schools that trained students in English and led to higher education overseas. Middle-class Latin American students, some Protestant but mostly Catholic, who attended these schools often went on to prominent positions in public life.

These churches drew into their membership talented young men and women, who increasingly furnished Latin American leadership for their churches. Several of them were thrust on to the world stage. Orlando Costas became head of the World Council of Churches; José Míguez Bonino developed into a major liberation theologian; and Samuel Escobar and others assumed leadership in missionary theology.

Latin Americans thus furnished the intellectual leadership necessary for Latin American Protestantism to assume its own identity apart from foreign parent churches. This leadership found a home in several seminaries spread through Latin America, such as the Evangelical seminary in Puerto Rico, the Instituto Superior de Estudios Teológicos (ISEDET) in Buenos Aires and the Department of Ecumenical Investigations at the National university in San José, Costa Rica. These religious studies centres were co-operative efforts of various Protestant denominations and included Roman Catholic students, as well as a few Catholic faculty. From these academic quarters, theologians such as Míguez, Elsa Tamez and others published works that increasingly gained world attention.

Despite this increased institutional consolidation and intellectual vigour, by far the greatest religious growth of the latter half of the century occurred in Pentecostalism, a largely twentieth-century variant of Protestantism. Historical Protestants lost large numbers of their members, especially to Pentecostalism. Nonetheless historical Protestant leaders remained important voices in Latin America at the end of the millennium.

One should understand that the Latin American version of Pentecostalism started within Latin America and was not carried there by missionaries. Pentecost-like events occurred in Chile, Brazil and Central America. Missionaries from Sweden, Italy and the United States were present at these events but Latin Americans were far greater in number at the inception of the Pentecostal movement. They quickly assumed most of the pastoral responsibilities for spreading the movement. Unlike mainstream Protestantism, Pentecostalism grew largely on the margins of society, so much so that some who studied the movement referred to it as a 'haven for the masses'. By the 1960s a small number of social scientists took note of the movement. Foreign social scientists, Christian Lalive d'Epinay and Emilio Willems, published pioneering studies, now largely supplanted by more sophisticated analyses from Latin American academics.[10] Nonetheless important aspects of Pentecostalism, such as retention rates and the role of women, lacked comprehensive research.

One foreign anthropologist's views from mid-century remained prescient. Eugene A. Nida pointed out the indigenous character of Latin American Pentecostalism.[11] Unlike historical Protestantism, born in the European Reformation, or unlike religions, such as Adventism, Jehovah's Witnesses, and Mormonism, created in the United States, Pentecostalism assumed from the beginning a Latin American character. It was *criollo* whereas the other

10 Noteworthy in this regard were the efforts of social scientists of religion of the Southern Cone region who met regularly and issued periodical bulletins.
11 Eugene A. Nida, 'The relationship of social structure to the problems of evangelism in Latin America', *Practical anthropology* 5 (1958), 101–23.

religious groups were not. Latin Americans with little theological education took over as pastors. They learned on the job, proving themselves by probity of life and success in extending the movement through drawing in members. Responsibility for church growth also fell to all church members who drew and kept new members through a warm welcome, shared tasks, and the promise of divine healing and miracles. While some groups, such as the Assemblies of God and Church of God (Cleveland, Tennessee), had fairly strong organisational unity, many Pentecostal congregations remained independent. The unifying spirit behind the amoeba-like growth was a belief that an occurrence like that mentioned in Acts 2 on the Day of Pentecost was taking place in their midst and was an experience available to all believers.

Another strain of Christianity, neo-Pentecostalism, appeared in the 1970s and 1980s and gained many followers. Neo-Pentecostalism looked like a variant of Pentecostalism in its emphasis on the Holy Spirit but it also emphasised that true believers could expect wealth and good health from faith in God and the practice of their religion. As with the Elim church in Guatemala, this strain often had connections to groups in the United States. However, Latin American neo-Pentecostal churches were more like borrowers and adapters than franchises of North America. Several of the more prominent churches of this type, for example those in Guatemala and especially the Church of the Universal Kingdom of Bishop Edir Machedo of Brazil, were Latin American based, middle-class in membership or aspiration and more politically active than the earlier and more numerous classical Pentecostals. Edir Machedo and the former Guatemalan general and president Efraín Ríos Montt thrust themselves, along with some followers, into national politics, in marked contrast to the more quiescent Pentecostals.

By 2000 Pentecostals and neo-Pentecostals – often bunched together for census purposes, to the chagrin of older Pentecostals – had achieved a remarkable place in Latin American society. Protestants accounted for about 50 million Latin Americans, with Pentecostals comprising generally 75 to 90 per cent of Protestants, depending on the country. The magnitude of growth in Latin America was illustrated by what took place in Brazil between 1990 and 2000 when the number of Protestants (mostly Pentecostal ones) doubled from 13 to 26 million. Thus half of Latin American Protestants were in Brazil, accounting for about 15 per cent of the population. In terms of national percentage, the highest, 25 per cent, was in Guatemala.[12] While

---

12 The Guatemalan percentages were highly contested until the 2000 census and numerous Gallup polls in the 1990s.

Pentecostals and other Protestants could be found throughout Latin America, their presence in some countries remained small.

Two aspects of Pentecostalism became apparent only in the 1990s. Studies first in Chile and later in Central America and Mexico revealed that large numbers of Protestants, most of them presumably Pentecostals, were not very observant. Less than half attended church weekly even though Pentecostal pastors and congregations emphasised much more frequent attendance. Second, the apostasy rate among Pentecostals appeared to be very high. Kurt Bowen found that 68 per cent of those baptised in Protestant churches in Mexico in the 1980s had left by 1990. Hence, while they entered Pentecostal churches, very large numbers left after a few years. Bowen and others attribute the high drop-out rate to the perfectionist character of Pentecostalism. Nevertheless, the 2000 Mexican census showed a small percentage increase in Protestants in the ten years from 1990 to 2000.

Thus at the millennium a relatively new category of 'no religion' had grown from insignificance (1 to 2 per cent) to 12 per cent in Guatemala, 8 per cent in Chile and 7 per cent in Brazil. In the state of Río de Janeiro, more than 15 per cent, some 2.2 million Brazilians, list themselves as having no religion. However, belief in God continues at a very high rate. About 99 per cent of Brazilians and the vast majority of Latin Americans persisted in their faith in God.

Religion and politics

Persons from the sector of non-religiously affiliated joined Protestants and other non-Catholic groups in political conflicts with the Catholic church. With their growth in numbers, Protestant and Pentecostal groups increasingly entered the political arena in the late 1980s and 1990s. Largely quiescent politically prior to that time, Protestants in such countries as Chile, Guatemala and Brazil felt that they had an assured place in society and became more assertive in the public sphere. One of their targets was the privilege enjoyed by the Catholic church and the effective legal restrictions placed on other churches in some countries. The privileges of the Catholic church were fewer than those enjoyed by the state churches of Great Britain and Scandinavia but nonetheless rankled some Protestants.

Both Pentecostals and the religiously non-affiliated exerted pressures on lawmakers. Three issues were of special concern: the vestiges of Catholic privilege that existed in law, the explicit mention of Catholicism in national constitutions and the teaching of Catholic doctrine and morals in public schools.[13] In a few countries Protestants argued that they had secondary legal status and were required to register as civic associations not churches.

While a formal dialogue between classical Pentecostals, including some from Latin American countries, and the Vatican took place for twenty-five years, little dialogue occurred in Latin America between Catholics and Pentecostals at the end of the millennium. On the other hand, creative dialogue between Catholics and historical Protestants did take place, especially in the 1970s, following a worldwide pattern. Nonetheless, the vast majority of Latin American Pentecostals shunned ecumenical dialogue and Catholic bishops did not have dialogue with Pentecostals as a high priority. Aside from grassroots ecumenism, especially through inter-marriage, the day-by-day realities of Catholic and non-Catholic relations were determined in politics. The conflicts were kept within tolerable limits of national democratic arenas that have grown since the 1980s.

Conclusion: new expressions of Christianity and missionary impulses

The Latin American Christianity that celebrated the end of the millennium acquired a lustre that it had only in promise at mid-century. A great number of Christians not only practised their faith with the fervour of converts but also entered a variety of churches to do so. Not only did the twentieth century's fastest-growing sector of Christianity, Pentecostalism, become a familiar face of Latin American religion, but Catholicism also found new expressions of its faith and worship in Afro and Indian theology and practice.

One of the vaguest of dreams for Latin America among Protestants and even less formulated among Catholics in 1950 was the sending of Latin American missionaries to other regions. For many this would be the surest test of the vitality of Christianity: a missionary movement that became increasingly strong in the latter twentieth century. At the millennium Protestant missionary scholars pointed with justifiable satisfaction to large numbers of Protestant missionaries – no one knows the exact numbers – to other countries, including North Atlantic ones. Likewise, Catholic missiologists estimated that some 5,000 Latin American priests, sisters and lay persons

---

13 Brian H. Smith, 'Pentecostalism and Catholicism in contemporary Latin America', paper prepared with support of National Endowment for the Humanities, September 1996, p. 53.

went as missionaries to other regions. It was no longer an oddity that a Bolivian Aymara Indian priest served as a pastor in Labrador, Canada, or that he was a promising theologian within the new stream of *teología india* (Indian theology). The transnational character of Christianity was again affirmed.

Religion and racism: struggles around segregation, 'Jim Crow' and apartheid

STEVE DE GRUCHY

Alongside the rise and fall of Nazism, the twentieth century bears witness to two other significant settings in which the Christian faith responded to racist policies and practices in both honourable and dishonourable fashion: the Republic of South Africa and the United States of America. In terms of the sheer scope of events, each of these settings deserves, and has certainly received, its own attention. Furthermore, there are some key differences between them which make comparisons difficult and which would suggest they be treated separately; differences to do with the experience of plantation slavery, the diversity of tribal languages, the white-to-black demographic ratio, traditional land settlement patterns, and constitutional circumstances and provisions. Yet there are two very important themes that link these histories together.

First we must acknowledge that the economic forces behind the system of slavery, which provided the foundation for racism and segregation in the USA, namely European capitalist expansion, are the same forces that drove the European colonisation of southern Africa and laid the foundation for the system of *apartheid* (separateness). In both cases Africa was dehumanised and destroyed on the altar of *Christian* Europe. Whilst much of this background falls outside the time frame of this volume, we would do well to recognise this as providing for the fundamental coherence between the black experience in Africa and the black experience in America.

Furthermore, the dehumanisation of Africans for the benefit of Europeans did not only lay the foundation for the economic power of the latter, but at a psychological level it led to the development of ideological and religious justifications for racism. Prior to this, Europe seems to have held a non-racist view of Africans, as the legends surrounding Prester John in Ethiopia, Mansa Musa of Mali and the fabled city of Timbuktu suggest. To justify the enslavement and disenfranchisement of Africans *whilst at the same time* proclaiming a universalist position on Christian salvation or national citizenship, a range of religious, political and cultural ideas were required to literally dehumanise people with black skins and demote them to the category of non-human.[1] The emergence of this ideology, *and* its unrelenting contestation by many including Christians in both the USA and South Africa, provide the second key theme that unites the two countries.

The Christian struggle against racism in the USA

It is helpful to see the Christian struggle against racism, segregation and 'Jim Crow' laws in the USA in the period under review in three distinct phases. By drawing attention to the dominant focus of Christian energy against racism we can characterise these phases as *cultural resistance* (to 1955), *public struggle* (1955–66) and *ideological critique* (from 1966). There are, of course, always dangers in such periodisation, and we would do well to recognise that certain trajectories of cultural, political and ecclesial opposition to racism flow throughout this century, linking events together in a way that defies neat analytical boxes.[2]

Phase one: cultural resistance (to 1955)

The period of reconstruction immediately following the American civil war was, in retrospect, a brief interlude between the evils of slavery and segregation. The enforcing of the fourteenth and fifteenth amendments (1868 and 1870) granting civil and voting rights to African Americans throughout the old Confederacy by the troops of the Union constituted the high-water mark for non-racism in the country, but also pointed to its precariousness. From the moment the troops were withdrawn in 1877, racism re-emerged triumphant, and became institutionally and psychologically entrenched throughout much of the country. Legislation was directed at Chinese immigrants and Native Americans, and doctrines of racial superiority enabled the USA to become a colonial power in the Caribbean and Pacific, colonising eight million people of colour. The Supreme Court undermined African American voting rights by allowing individual states to apply means tests and poll taxes, and laid the legal basis for segregation and an obese number of

---

1 See George Fredrickson's argument about the emergence of racism in *Racism: a short history* (Princeton: Princeton University Press, 2002), pp. 68f. See also Forrest G. Wood, *The arrogance of faith: Christianity and race in America from the colonial era to the twentieth century* (New York: Alfred A. Knopf, 1990).

2 See John Hope Franklin and Alfred A. Moss, Jr, *From slavery to freedom: a history of Negro Americans*, 6th edn (New York: McGraw-Hill, 1988).

'Jim Crow' laws[3] in the 'separate but equal' ruling of the *Plessy v. Ferguson* case of 1896. In this context, it is not difficult to appreciate the political, social and economic vulnerability which characterised the lives of African Americans at the turn of the twentieth century, and which was ritually inscribed upon their bodies through the lynching of more than a thousand people between 1900 and 1915.[4]

African Americans were indeed victims of the unrivalled power of white supremacy. But that is only half the story – for they were also agents of survival and resistance. That agency operated both underground and above ground, in hidden and public transcripts (James Scott). Hidden from the (white) public eye, 'from sundown to sunup' (Dwight Hopkins),[5] was an infinite number of gestures, songs, prayers, caricatures, and other artistic creations that constituted the affirmation of black humanity, and the concomitant denial of dehumanisation. Below ground, then, throughout the first half of the twentieth century a culture of resistance was growing, one that would provide the wells from which the Civil Rights movement would drink in the 1950s and 1960s, and which would both shape the vision for that movement and sustain it and its leaders in the driest moments. Crucially, that culture was with a few important exceptions nurtured in the black church.

The African American church had been an important role-player in the struggle against slavery, often providing leadership, information networks and physical assistance to fugitives making use of the 'underground railroad'. Yet in the period after reconstruction it stepped back from this overt engagement in bettering the socio-economic and political life of African Americans, followed the advice of Booker T. Washington towards accommodation, conciliation and gradualism, and became a bastion of religious fundamentalism and otherworldliness (with some notable exceptions). However, the involvement of African American Christians in the Civil Rights movement, and their willingness to make sacrifices because of their faith, did not appear from nowhere. It drew from the strength of this cultural resistance which had been honed, ironically, in the segregated freedom of the African American

---

3 In 1916 the eleven southern states spent an average of $10.32 per white public-school student compared to $2.89 for black students. In the 1920s there was one hospital bed for every 139 whites and one for every 1,941 blacks. See Harvard Sitkoff, *The struggle for black equality, 1954–1992*, rev. edn (New York: Hill and Wang, 1981, 1993), p. 6.

4 See ibid., pp. 4–6, for a description.

5 Dwight N. Hopkins, *Down, up and over: slave religion and Black Theology* (Minneapolis: Augsburg Fortress, 2000), p. 108.

church. James Cone, in reference to the sources that shaped Martin Luther King Jr, notes that 'the Church was a haven, a place where blacks could be free of white folks, free of Jim Crow, free of everything that demeaned and humiliated them'.[6]

Second phase: public struggle (1955–66)

Owing to the 'otherworldliness' of the African American church, the task of African American political resistance was taken up by secular organisations in the first half of the twentieth century. The most famous of these was the National Association for the Advancement of Colored People (NAACP), established in 1909. The crucial task undertaken by the organisation was its 'judicially based assault on the legal structures of separate-but-equal',[7] which reached a climax in the Supreme Court victory in the *Brown v. Board of Education* trial in May 1954.

Whilst this 'assault' was taking place, a range of socio-economic and political factors in the first half of the century, including massive black migration to the north, had raised the political profile and militancy of African Americans. Adam Clayton Powell had illustrated the power of organised protest in Harlem in the inter-war years, the Congress of Racial Equality (CORE) was established in 1942 with a view to challenging 'Jim Crow' laws by non-violent direct action, and the March-on-Washington Committee led by A. Philip Randolph sought to become a mass protest movement that would pressurise the Federal government. Yet there were many black voices opposed to such militancy, and the growth of the American economy and the massive increase of civilian jobs created during and after the Second World War created the impression, shared by many in the churches, that with time segregation would pass away.

All of this changed when Rosa Parks was arrested for refusing to give up her seat to a white person on the bus in Montgomery, Alabama on 1 December 1955. 'Somewhere in the universe a gear in the machinery had shifted',[8] and the Civil Rights movement began, producing in a short thirteen-year burst one of the more visible and intense moments of Christian political resistance in the twentieth century, under the leadership of the Revd Martin Luther King Jr and the Southern Christian Leadership Conference (SCLC), which

---

6 James H. Cone. *Martin & Malcolm & America: a dream or a nightmare* (Maryknoll, NY: Orbis, 1991), p. 25.

7 Vincent Harding, 'We the people: the long journey toward a more perfect union', in C. Carson et al. (eds.), *The eyes on the prize: civil rights reader* (New York: Penguin, 1991) p. 17.

8 Elridge Cleaver, publicist of the Black Panthers, quoted in Sitkoff, *Black equality*, p. 38.

was established by nearly one hundred black clergy in New Orleans in February 1957. The black churches brought key assets to the movement, including communication networks, independent black leadership, mass membership and a place to gather and find solace and courage. Drawing on the long tradition of cultural resistance 'they gave the movement a language understood by all, expressed in biblical oratory and hymns, to battle against racial oppression; and they bestowed religious sanction on that battle'.[9]

The story of the Civil Rights movement from the bus boycott of Montgomery in December 1955 to the assassination of Martin Luther King Jr in Memphis on 4 April 1968 is a wonderful story about the courage and commitment of people of faith in the face of horrendous odds and dehumanising power, with some notable victories.[10] These include the undermining of 'Jim Crow' laws throughout the south by non-violent direct action led by the SCLC and the Student Nonviolent Coordinating Committee (SNCC), culminating in the desegregation of Birmingham, Alabama; the March on Washington in 1963 by a quarter of a million people to hear King's 'I have a dream' speech followed by the passing of the Civil Rights Act in early 1964; the struggle for voter registration in the south (especially Mississippi), culminating in the march from Selma to Montgomery in 1965 which led to the passing of the Voting Rights Act in August of that year, and which turned out, in retrospect, to be the high water-mark for the movement; and the struggles, after 1966, to deal with the issues of poverty, the war in Vietnam, the urban black crisis of the north, and the emergence of the Black Power movement.

Seven key themes that bear reflection emerge from this story. (1) Segregation and the political apparatus that kept it in place had destroyed the *pride and dignity* of African Americans in the south. The movement gave that back by affirming the humanity of black Americans and by giving them a role to play in their own freedom struggle. (2) Because of this affirmation of humanity, *non-violence* was initially a principle of the movement, and then later an important strategy. The movement relied upon the outrageously crass and violent reaction from the white leadership to engender moral persuasive force. It was a strategy that came under sustained critique by some, and which was challenged by the Deacons for Defense, armed black Christians who patrolled many of the non-violent marches. (3) Whilst some characterised non-violence as passive, any reading of the story would dispel

9 Sitkoff, *Black equality*, p. 57.
10 For the full story of the SCLC see the incredibly rich text by David J. Garrow, *Bearing the cross: Martin Luther King, Jr., and the Southern Christian Leadership Conference* (New York: William Morrow, 1986).

such a judgement. The *active witness* of the Christian faith in the public square, and the suffering it brought upon those who bore witness, is a highpoint in the twentieth-century proclamation of the gospel.

(4) This witness of black Christians created a *crisis of credibility* for white Christians and church leaders. There were some who were avowedly racist, but most were silently complicit in institutional racism and indifferent to the suffering of those in the Civil Rights movement.[11] There were some courageous white Christians who participated fully in the struggle, and some church leaders took a prophetic stance, such as the Roman Catholic Archbishop William Cody of New Orleans who excommunicated several Catholics who were members of the Ku Klux Klan in 1962. (5) This *non-racial* character of the movement was a key issue around which black leaders struggled. Whilst there was never a huge involvement of whites, a few played important roles in the movement and a small number were murdered for their effort. There was an important symbolic power in this, and yet the question was often asked by African Americans, 'How can we possess the land if we can't even possess our movement?'

(6) The struggle between trusting *the institutions of the USA* and civil disobedience is an important sub-text to the story. Throughout the struggle there was a constant conflict between holding America to the 'self-evident truths' it professed, such as the equality of all citizens, and despairing at the fundamental flaws in the American system. (7) Finally, the *in-fighting* and conflicts over principles, strategies, funding and leadership between and within the many organisations in the movement often played right into the hands of the very racists they were seeking to overthrow, and after the death of King led to the end of the movement and the high-profile public struggle of the black churches.

Third phase: ideological critique (from 1966)

A few days after the signing of the Voting Rights Act in 1965 the Watts suburb of Los Angeles exploded into a violent race riot. It was the first, but not the last, of such riots to hit the cities of the north over the next few years. These riots signalled many things, but at heart they were a political outpouring of rising African American expectations and anger, profoundly captured in the slogan 'Black Power'. This energy drew together a range of experiences including those of the northern urban African American poor who had seen no direct benefit to their lives from the decade of the Civil Rights movement; a growing

11 See Wood, *Arrogance of faith.*

disenchantment with the entire political system of the USA as symbolised by the war in Vietnam; the rallying call of the black nationalist movement, epitomised by the writing and speeches of Malcolm X who had been assassinated in February of that year; and the battered and bereaved student activists of SNCC and CORE who had seen so little progress for their sacrificial actions and who began to voice their rejection of non-violence and reconciliation in favour of Black Power, most dramatically on the 'Meredith March Against Fear' from Memphis, Tennessee to Jackson, Mississippi in June 1966.

Drawing on the energy of both the Civil Rights movement and the *kairos* moment[12] of black power, and reaching back into the resources of the cultural resistance of African American religion, the overtly Christian challenge to racism moved to a mode of ideological critique in what became known as Black Theology.[13] The criticism of the racist state became a criticism of the racist church. The reasons for this are not hard to find. If Malcolm X was right about the conditions of black alienation in the USA, and if advocates of 'Black Power' were correct in their rejection of Christianity as 'white-folks religion', if the SCLC and other Christian bodies could not provide leadership in the face of the riots of 1966, 1967 and 1968; then the fundamental question facing young black urban ministers concerned the relevance of the gospel and the church in the context of the black struggle. For advocates of Black Theology that meant a radical ecclesial critique, akin to the Barmen Declaration of the Confessing Church in Germany.[14]

The first overt expression of what became known as Black Theology grew out of a consultation in Harlem in July 1966, just days after the 'Black Power' controversy engulfed the movement. The statement by an *ad hoc* committee, soon to become the National Conference of Black Churchmen (NCBC), indicated a clear theological break with King and the SCLC as it affirmed the validity of Black Power as a tool with which to engage the leaders of America, white churchmen, Negro citizens and the mass media. Through its

---

12 In the light of the South African story dealt with below, it is interesting that Wilmore used this term in an address given at the tenth anniversary of the NCBC in 1981. Quoted in James Cone, *For my people: Black Theology and the black church* (Maryknoll, NY: Orbis, 1984), p. 17.

13 For insights into the development of Black Theology see Cone, *For my people*; James H. Cone, *Speaking the truth: ecumenism, liberation and Black Theology* (Grand Rapids: Eerdmans, 1986), pp. 83–110; Gayraud S. Wilmore, 'A revolution unfulfilled but not invalidated', a critical reflection in James H. Cone, *A Black Theology of liberation*, twentieth anniversary edn (Maryknoll, NY: Orbis, 1990), pp. 145–63; Gayraud S. Wilmore and James H. Cone (eds.), *Black Theology: a documentary history, 1966–1979* (Maryknoll, NY: Orbis, 1979); Dwight N. Hopkins, *Black Theology USA and South Africa: politics, culture and liberation* (Maryknoll, NY: Orbis, 1989).

14 See the comment by Cone, *For my people*, p. 20.

theological commission led by Gayraud S. Wilmore the NCBC began to provide the necessary leadership to the black churches trying to come to terms with their role in racist America after the assassination of King in April 1968. James Cone was not part of the NCBC at this stage, but the publication of his books, *Black Theology and Black Power* (1969), and *A Black Theology of liberation* (1970) brought a scholarly depth to the movement and catapulted both Cone and Black Theology into a wider arena.

There is no doubt that Black Theology sought to affirm political resistance to the racist state and to support the myriads of such actions that were mushrooming throughout the country. Yet in itself it was a movement that focused on the church and its theology, and this is where the primary energy of organisations like the NCBC and theologians like Cone was focused. On the surface the main target was the ethical failings of the white racist church, but there was a much deeper critique, namely that the theology of the white church was deficient, could no longer be called Christian, and was therefore a heresy. Whilst a *status confessionis* was never proclaimed (unlike in the South Africa, as we shall see), Cone is clear that the heretical nature of white Christianity was the issue at stake.[15]

At the same time, by implication, Black Theology addressed the black church with a word of critique and inspiration. In helping it live up to the task to which it was called, Black Theology sought to go beyond just the negative critique of white religion, to the more constructive project of building a 'theology of the black poor'.[16] This has not been an easy or successful task. Twenty-five years after the publication of Cone's *Black Theology of liberation*, Wilmore writes of an 'unfulfilled revolution' and points to the demise of the NCBC and the 'creeping deradicalization of many black Christians'.[17] At the end of the century, the vision of Du Bois, King and countless other Christians remains as a continuing challenge for black and white Christians in the richest and most powerful country on the globe.

The Christian struggle against racism in South Africa

As we move to consider the Christian response to racism in South Africa we need to pause and consider three key elements that distinguish this setting from the one we have just been exploring, and provide a wider framework for

---

15 Cone, *Speaking the truth*, p. 110.   16 Ibid.
17 Wilmore, 'A revolution unfulfilled', p. 152.

what follows. First, whereas in the USA neither black nor white can lay prior claim to the land, this is not the case in South Africa. Here it is clear that because black people are the hosts and white people are the uninvited guests, the struggle around race is deeply entwined with the struggle around the land. Second, the fact that South Africa was an extremely active mission field as well as a home for a vibrant settler church has rooted the tension of mission church/settler church, black church/white church, and therefore issues of racism, into the very meaning of what it means to be church in South Africa.[18]

Third, the formal separation of church and state in the USA was never part of the South African experience, and indeed South Africa from 1910 to 1990 prided itself on being a Christian country. This meant that, unlike in the USA, a fully fledged theological justification for racism came to have profound political consequences. These three factors signal that the history of the church in South Africa *is* fundamentally the history of the relationship between Christianity and racism in the country, and, furthermore, that this history is so deeply woven into the wider story of South Africa that the field we must cover in this section is extremely wide. Once again, whilst recognising the limitations of periodisation, we shall explore the story in three phases, namely, *diverse opposition* (to 1960), *ideological critique* (1961–82) and *liberating praxis* (from 1983), aware that key aspects of the struggle against racism flow throughout the whole period under review.

First phase: diverse opposition (to 1960)

The twentieth century in South Africa began in the midst of a civil war between Britain and her colonial subjects, and the *Boers* (farmers) of the Afrikaner republics of the Orange Free State and Transvaal. Black people played an important part in the war, but their interests were of little concern to the major protagonists, a point that was made clear when, just eight years after the cessation of hostilities, the Union of South Africa was created by Britain without any regard to the citizenship rights of the five million Africans within it borders. The Boer republics lost the war but won the peace as their avowedly racist policies became the policies of the new country, and segregation was adopted as the national political framework. This cocktail of Boer racism and British arrogance was deadly for black Africans, and the 1913 and

---

18 For an analysis of these foundational tensions in South African church history see John W. de Gruchy with Steve de Gruchy, *The church struggle in South Africa* revd 3rd edn (London: SCM and Minneapolis: Fortress, 2004).

1936 Land Acts sealed their political and economic disinheritance from the land of their ancestors long before the advent of the official policy of apartheid in 1948. Within this context, three strands of diverse opposition to racism emerge within the Christian churches.

(1) The leadership of the *English-speaking churches*[19] was, in the main, cautious and hesitant in its opposition to racism, ensuring that the churches were, in Cochrane's estimation, 'servants of power'.[20] Up to 1960, white clergy and the financial power of the white laity made sure that the official voice of the church promoted 'trusteeship', in which it was understood that white Christians were to raise up black converts to an appropriate level of civilisation, before they could be integrated into the wider society. As it became more and more obvious that this would not be allowed by the state, especially after 1948, this opened the possibilities for a different approach.

(2) *Black members* of these 'English-speaking' churches played a crucial role in the emergence of the African nationalist opposition to segregation and racism. At the founding of what became the African National Congress (ANC) in 1912, two clergymen, the Revd John Dube and the Revd Walter Rubusana, were elected president and honorary president respectively, an illustration of the role that black Christians educated in mission schools would play in the organisation. Indeed, a who's who of ANC leadership down the years, including Chief Albert Luthuli, D. D. T. Jabavu, Dr James Moroka, Dr A. B. Xuma and Prof. Z. K. Matthews serves to remind us that for this organisation 'the strongest and most consistent influence in the early twentieth century was the vision and hope that were rooted in postmillennial Christianity'.[21] As people who had received both 'Christianity and civilisation' from the missionaries, this leadership sought, in the tradition of the 'Social Gospel', to challenge racism and change the system so that they could become citizens in the land of their birth.[22] However, as the realisation of these hopes became less and less likely, a more radical leadership emerged in the nationalist struggle, one that would challenge Christianity's own relationship to racism.

---

19 This clumsy but widely used name refers to churches whose settler and mission origins lie in the English-speaking world.

20 See James Cochrane, *Servants of power: the role of the English-speaking churches 1903–1930* (Johannesburg: Ravan Press, 1987).

21 Wallace G. Mills, 'Millennial Christianity, British imperialism and African nationalism', in Richard Elphick and Rodney Davenport (eds.), *Christianity in South Africa: a political, social and cultural history* (Cape Town: David Philip, 1997), p. 346.

22 See Richard Elphick, 'The benevolent empire and the Social Gospel: missionaries and South African Christians in the age of segregation', in ibid., 347–69.

(3) The *African indigenous churches (AICs)* which grew tremendously in this period were, in their very existence, a conscious mode of Christian opposition to racism. The so-called *Ethiopian* churches were led by mission-educated, black professionals who held to the 'orthodox' beliefs and practices of Western Christianity, but who rejected the paternalism of its white leadership in favour of African nationalism. They were in essence 'a religious and cultural protest against the process of subordination'.[23] The so-called *Zionist* churches broke away from American Pentecostal parent bodies, also as a reaction to white paternalism, infusing what they inherited with elements of African culture. They created the space in which dislocated Africans in both the rural and urban areas resisted the racism implicit in the dominant European culture. A strong apocalyptic element sometimes boiled over into direct political resistance with tragic results, as in the Bulhoek massacre of 1922.

Phase two: ideological critique (1961–1982)

Notwithstanding this diverse Christian opposition to racism in the first half of the twentieth century, it is also important to recognise that on the other hand the Afrikaans Reformed churches[24] were calling for greater institutional segregation. The policy of apartheid had its origins in the Dutch Reformed church (DRC), dating back to a synod resolution of 1857, which allowed for congregations to be racially divided owing to the 'weakness' of racist whites.[25] Over time, what was an allowance became a policy, and the church itself divided into four racially defined denominations (white, 'coloured', black and Indian). By the 1930s, the memory of the sufferings of the Anglo–Boer war and the pressures of cheap black labour amidst the poverty of the Great Depression led the Afrikaner *volk* (people/nation) to consciously organise itself. Many of its leaders studied in Germany in the inter-war years, and were inspired by the visions of racial purity and divine vocation that gave rise to Hitler's Nazism. Afrikaans emerged as a discrete language, the National Party became the political voice of the *volk*, and Christian nationalism was adopted as the ideological vision for God's chosen people on the tip of the pagan African continent.

---

23 James Cochrane, 'Christianity during a period of "national consolidation"', in J. W. Hofmeyer and Gerald J. Pillay (eds.), *A history of Christianity in South Africa*, vol. I (Pretoria: Haum Tertiary, 1994), p. 213.
24 There are three Afrikaans-speaking Reformed churches, the largest being the Nederduitse Gereformeerde kerk (NGK) or Dutch Reformed church (DRC). The other two are the Gereformeerde kerk and the Hervormde kerk.
25 See the range of essays in John W. de Gruchy and Charles Villa-Vicencio, (eds.), *Apartheid is a heresy* (Cape Town: David Philip, 1983).

Given the neo-Calvinist orientation of Christian nationalism, the Bible was a key pillar of apartheid. The story of the tower of Babel became a hermeneutical tool with which to unlock God's providence in the world, namely, the punishment of those who seek unity and the ordaining of separate *volke* (people/nations) as an 'order of creation'. The Old Testament promotion of Jewish purity was also invoked, as well as a particular reading of the Great Commission of Matthew 28, 'Go therefore and make disciples of all *nations*'. Armed with this biblical support for apartheid and a powerful self-belief in its divine destiny the *volk* came to power in the 1948 election. Over the next ten years the National Party enshrined this vision in law with such legislation as the Population Registration Act (1950), the Group Areas Act (1950) and the Bantu Education Act (1953).

In the face of this racial onslaught and sensing that the years of mild protest had achieved nothing, the ANC, energised by the formation of the youth league, now embarked on the 'defiance campaign' aimed at challenging the state in overt political protest. The state responded with arrests, treason trials, repressive legislation and police action, most notoriously at Sharpeville on 21 March 1960. This massacre was a turning point in the history of South Africa. The ANC and the recently formed Pan African Congress (PAC) were 'banned' along with some of their leaders, others such as Nelson Mandela and Robert Sobukwe were arrested and sentenced to lengthy jail terms, and yet others went into exile to launch the armed struggle.[26] The Sharpeville massacre also pushed the church out of its rather limp-wristed opposition to apartheid, forced it to focus on its own theological shortcomings, and led it to engage in over two decades of in-depth ideological critique of Christian nationalism, apartheid and racism.

Given the Christian justification of apartheid, this had to do with the very future of Christianity in South Africa. In much the same way that Black Power had challenged ministers and theologians in the USA, so black Christians were called to account for their faith. Why had the church not put an end to apartheid? Were the Afrikaans Reformed theologians correct about separation? Was Christianity inherently racist? Two lines of the Christian ideological critique of racism emerged, in dialogue with each other, and found a climax in the declaration that apartheid is a heresy. These were the Confessing Church movement and Black Theology.

---

26 See Mokgethi Motlhabi, *The theory and practice of black resistance to apartheid: a socio-ethical analysis* (Johannesburg: Skotaville, 1985).

Soon after Sharpeville, all the South African churches – including the Dutch Reformed Church (DRC) – were invited to a consultation at Cottesloe by the World Council of Churches (WCC). The DRC delegates supported the relatively mild resolutions criticising apartheid, but they were rejected by their own church leadership, which then withdrew from the WCC. Beyers Naudé, one of the delegates and a leading DRC minister, refused to recant and was ultimately expelled from the church. Together with some like-minded colleagues and supporters he established in 1963 the Christian Institute (CI), which became the key non-racial Christian body seeking to articulate the rejection of apartheid.[27] The similarities to the 'Confessing Church' in the struggle against Hitler's Nazism were consciously explored.

This energy, combined with newfound ecumenical commitment in the reconstitution of the South African Council of Churches (SACC), led to the *Message to the people of South Africa* in 1968, a joint project of the CI and the SACC. The *Message* has been criticised for being too liberal and too long, but the key contribution it made was to identify the task of ideological critique as fundamental for the church. Apartheid was wrong, so the *Message* asserted, not just because it was a bad political system, but because it was a 'false gospel', and inherently anti-Christian given that the heart of the gospel was reconciliation. The *Message* led to the Study Project on Christianity in Apartheid Society (SPRO-CAS I), and the Special Programme for Christian Action in Society (SPRO-CAS II), two remarkable efforts at harnessing the creative energies of a range of scholars in economics, politics and law in charting just what some of the alternatives to apartheid could be.

In exploring the alternatives to apartheid, the CI had come into contact with a number of black Christians, student leaders and ministers who were engaged in their own ideological critique of both apartheid and the theology that gave it birth. Fuelled by the insights and passion of Steve Biko and his promotion of Black Consciousness, and inspired by the works of James Cone, Christians in the University Christian Movement (UCM) began to reflect on and write about Black Theology in the South African context in a series of conferences held around the country during 1971. Biko himself called on black Christians 'to take upon themselves the duty of saving Christianity by adopting Black theology's approach'.[28]

---

27 See Peter Walshe, *Church versus state in South Africa* (Maryknoll, NY: Orbis, 1983).
28 Steve Biko, 'Black Consciousness and the quest for a true humanity', in Mokgethi Motlhabi (ed.), *Essays on Black Theology* (Johannesburg: Black Theology Project of UCM, 1972). After it was banned, the book was republished as Basil Moore (ed.), *The challenge of Black Theology in South Africa* (Atlanta: John Knox, 1973).

At the heart of this expression of Black Theology was an affirmation of the humanity and dignity of black South Africans, and the call for solidarity in the struggle against racism. The power of the ideological critique was such that the first book published on the subject was banned, as were many of the key individuals involved in the movement, including Steve Biko, Barney Pityana and Sabela Ntwasa. Within the Afrikaans Reformed church family, albeit the 'coloured' daughter church, the work of Allan Boesak was of obvious ideological significance. The WCC's Programme to Combat Racism (PCR) both drew on this work, and contributed to debates about racism, power and revolutionary violence.

Within this context, the stakes in the ideological struggle were raised. In 1977 the Lutheran World Federation, through the influence of Dr Manus Buthelezi, one of the leading South African promoters of Black Theology, proclaimed a *status confessionis*. In 1980, delegates to a SACC consultation on racism spoke of the need to establish a black Confessing Church, and out of this the Alliance of Black Reformed Christians (ABRECSA) emerged, drawing together the two strands of Black Theology and the Confessing Church. The climax of the ideological critique was its vindication by the World Alliance of Reformed Churches, which declared in 1982 that 'apartheid is a sin, and its theological justification a heresy'. With its formalisation in the Belhar Confession of 1986 no one, least of all Reformed Christians, could claim a theological justification for racism.[29] The ideological struggle had been won.

Third phase: liberatory praxis (from 1982)

From the labour strikes in Durban in 1973, through the Soweto rebellion in 1976, to the ongoing armed resistance in the cities of South Africa, black South Africans – including many Christians, as the PCR had rightly confirmed – were making their rejection of apartheid clear. Christians began, as an act of witness, to be engaged in civil disobedience, conscientious objection, and the fostering of international pressure through the academic boycott and economic sanctions. The state reacted with tremendous power, killing hundreds, including Steve Biko, detaining and torturing many, banning organisations and enacting draconian security legislation.

By 1982, as local and global opposition grew, so the regime sought to reform apartheid. But this too was rejected by the majority of the population, now rallying to the banner of the United Democratic Front (UDF) in which

29 See G. D. Cloete and D. J. Smit, *A moment of truth: the confession of the Dutch Reformed mission church 1982* (Grand Rapids: Eerdmans, 1984).

Christians played a prominent role as members, leaders and patrons. The SACC, under the successive leadership of Desmond Tutu, Frank Chikane and Beyers Naudé, became a key leader of both Christian and popular resistance to the regime. Thus, whilst it is correct to say that the churches as a whole were 'trapped in apartheid' (Villa-Vicencio),[30] a growing number of black clergy, laity and Christian students, with a handful of whites, were at the forefront of the mass action against apartheid – and were many of the victims of the State of Emergency.

Out of this context, drawing on the faith and liberating praxis of such Christians, and helping to articulate and legitimate that praxis, the *Kairos document* was published (1985). It was a powerful theological statement against apartheid and the security state, but also against the failure of the institutional church to be engaged in the struggle for justice: 'The time has come. The moment of truth has arrived. South Africa has been plunged into a crisis . . . It is the *Kairos*, or moment of truth not only for apartheid but also for the Church and all other faiths and religions.'[31] The *Kairos document* was a watershed. No longer was the struggle against racism to be fought out in resolutions and statements, but in programmes of action – such as the Standing for the Truth campaign of the SACC (1988) with its specific proposals such as acts of non-collaboration and symbolic actions of protest.[32] And as more and more leaders of the United Democratic Front were detained, church leaders became important figureheads in the public protests against the regime.

By the end of the 1980s, a multitude of pressures caused the apartheid regime to collapse, and, in February 1990, to un-ban the major resistance organisations, and to release political prisoners such as Nelson Mandela. In the euphoria of this incredible change, all the churches in the country, including the Dutch Reformed church, gathered for a consultation at Rustenburg in November of that year – thirty years after Cottesloe – and declared apartheid a sin and committed themselves to the reconstruction of the country. The four years of transition after February 1990 were full of tears, anxiety and frustration. The churches were called upon to play an extraordinary role in peace-keeping, relationship building and political monitoring. To what extent the success of the 1994 elections could be attributed to

30 See Charles Villa-Vicencio, *Trapped in apartheid* (Cape Town: David Philip, 1988).
31 The Kairos Theologians, *The Kairos document: challenge to the church*, revd 2nd edn (Johannesburg: Skotaville, 1986).
32 J. C. (Hannes) Adonis, 'Christianity in South Africa since 1948', in Hofmeyer and Pillay, *Christianity in South Africa*, p. 294.

the prayers and involvement of millions of Christians in South Africa, and further afield, will never be known, but there was never any doubt that the memory of many ancestors in the faith was honoured in the 'miracle' of those days.

Beyond racism?

We began this chapter by reflecting on two themes that unite the racial situation in the USA and in South Africa, namely the economic forces of colonialism and capitalism, and the promotion and contestation of theories of white supremacy. Mindful of the terrain we have covered it is chastening to note that whereas in both situations the struggle against ideological and religiously supported racism was to a large extent successful, the economic structures that created and benefited from such racism have by and large been left unchanged.

Certainly apartheid and 'Jim Crow', like slavery, have come to an end; certainly South Africa has a non-racial and democratic government in place; and certainly the legal and political circumstances of African Americans are vastly different from those in the 1930s – and yet the social circumstances of so many black South Africans and African Americans remain characterised by all the signs of exclusion: unemployment, hunger, disease and illiteracy. The economic power of the north Atlantic elite continues – as in the days of colonialism and slavery – to dictate the fortunes of the lives of Africans at home and in the diaspora. Both settings enable us to acknowledge that the Christian struggle against racism is at heart a struggle against *unfreedom* (Amartya Sen) in all its forms. Indeed, for Christians to transcend the legacy of racism requires of the church in the twenty-first century an unflinching commitment to the future of Africa, and a refusal to allow the children of Africa wherever they may be living to become second-class citizens of globalised apartheid, and the 'Jim Crow' laws of the global economic order.

22

Post-colonial Christianity in Africa

DAVID MAXWELL

Introduction: setting the scene

The 1950s and 1960s witnessed nationalist movements bringing the majority of sub-Saharan Africa to political independence. The Portuguese colonies and Rhodesia stemmed the process for a decade or longer but by 1994 and the fall of apartheid in South Africa the entire African continent was under black majority rule. Many observers in the 1960s would not have rated the prospects of the mission-derived churches particularly highly. At worst the mission churches had appeared implicated in colonialism, at best their stance had been ambiguous. Most missionaries feared that a successful nationalism would promote either a revived paganism or communism, or both, and hence shunned it. They had schooled the first generation of African nationalist leaders and helped create a modernising African elite but as agents of cultural imperialism had simultaneously disparaged African culture. Nationalists had sought to remedy this by seizing control of missionary education at independence. And given that schools were so central to missionary strategy it seemed likely that mission churches would decline in the new African states. If anything Christianity's future looked brightest with the so-called African Independent churches (AICs).

Yet Christianity's African future turned out to be far from bleak. Since independence the growth in Christian adherence has been phenomenal. (For the strength of Christianity in different countries, see map 22.1.) Whereas the total number of African Christians stood at approximately 75 million in 1965, by 2000 it had risen to approximately 351 million. Within these figures Catholic adherence had increased from 34 million to 175 million and Protestant numbers had risen from 21 million to 110 million. Although by 2000 Independents could

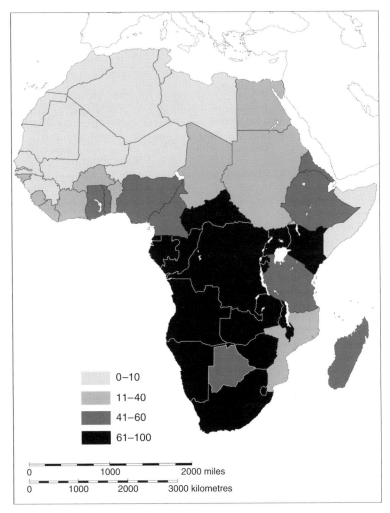

Map 22.1 Africa 2001: Christians as percentage of population in each country

boast 34 million members they represented less than one-tenth of all African Christians.[1]

This numerical growth has led to remarkable changes within global Christianity over the last four decades, making Africa a dynamic presence in its

1 The remainder was made up of 'Orthodox-Coptics'. All the normal caveats about this sort of statistical analysis apply. The figures should be taken as merely illustrative of trends. Bengt Sundkler and Christopher Steed, *A history of the church in Africa* (Cambridge: Cambridge University Press, 2000), p. 906.

new heartland in the South. The case of the worldwide Anglican communion is instructive of Christianity's southward shift. At the 1998 Lambeth Conference, the highest consultative body of the church, 224 of the 735 bishops were from Africa, compared with only 139 from the United Kingdom. At the time of the conference there were 17 million baptised Anglicans in Nigeria compared with 2.8 million in the United States.[2] More recently the *Sunday Times* reported, 'The average Anglican [in the world] is a 24 year old African woman.'[3] In the Roman Catholic church a similar picture emerges. In 1999, there were 18 million official baptisms: of these, 8 million took place in Central and South America, 3 million were in Africa, and 37 per cent of the African baptisms were of adults.[4]

The rise of African Christianity has not just shifted the centre of global Christianity but also radically altered its denominational and theological appearance. Today vast numbers of the latest generation of African Christians describe themselves as 'born again'. They comprise a diverse coalition of evangelicals, charismatics and Pentecostals, who share a belief in the infallibility of scripture and, more importantly, stress the centrality of a 'born-again' experience. Given that the charismatic and Pentecostal strands in the African born-again movement are very much in the ascendant, a third defining characteristic grows increasingly important, namely that of possessing the 'gifts of the Spirit': divine healing, glossolalia, exorcism and prophecy.

Africa's contemporary Christian landscape looks very different from a century ago when the historic mission churches – Catholic, Anglican, Methodist, Baptist and Lutheran – dominated the scene.[5] And it barely resembles the ecclesiastical scene of just three decades ago when African Independent churches *appeared* to be the dynamic element.[6] The explosion of born-again Christianity is difficult to quantify in that it cuts across the historic denominations as well as creating new ones. However, a few examples help illustrate recent trends. By the mid-1990s the Church of Pentecost was probably Ghana's largest Protestant church and a survey of Kenya's capital, Nairobi, revealed that the Assemblies of God was the fastest-growing church with an annual growth rate of 38 per cent. The Zimbabwe Assemblies of God is second only to the country's Catholic church in terms of numbers of

---

2 Dana Robert, 'Shifting southward: global Christianity since 1945', *International bulletin of missionary research* 24:2 (2000), p. 53.
3 *Sunday Times* (London), 15 March 2001.
4 Philip Jenkins, *The next Christendom: the coming of global Christianity* (New York: Oxford University Press, 2002).
5 A. Hastings, *The church in Africa 1450–1950* (Oxford: Clarendon Press, 1994).
6 A. Hastings, *A history of African Christianity, 1950–1975* (Cambridge: Cambridge University Press, 1979).

adherents. And in Uganda both the Glad Tidings church, which is charismatic in orientation, and the more Pentecostal Full Gospel church claim over 700 assemblies, making them key players in the nation's Christian scene. Indeed, in states such as Ghana, Kenya, South Africa, Uganda, Zambia and Zimbabwe born-agains are so numerous and their leaders so influential that they are just as 'mainstream', or 'established', as Anglicans or Catholics.[7]

Given the sheer size and diversity of Africa, the differences in imperial policy, the extraordinary range of missionary organisations that entered the continent, and the diversity of societies and cultures they encountered, contemporary patterns of Christian adherence are complex. For example, in Zambia, the British-derived, but now German-supported, New Apostolic church is the third largest in the country, boasting a membership of 793,934 in 1996,[8] and the Zambian population of Jehovah's Witnesses, 300,000, gives it a 'higher proportion of JWs than any country other than a few Pacific micro-states'. Likewise, while 60 per cent of Ghanaians claim to be Christian and born-again religion has captured popular culture, as many as 50 per cent of Cameroonians remain staunchly traditionalist and born-again Christianity is yet to take off. Even the fault-lines that run between the colonial heritages are now often quite fuzzy. The religious pluralism of British colonial policy diluted Protestant predominance in many of its former colonies. And anti-clerical governments in France and Portugal gave Protestantism a good foothold in some former Lusophone and Francophone states.[9]

Nevertheless it is possible to identify significant patterns in Africa's recent Christian history. In the four decades or more since the beginning of decolonisation African states have experienced a number of political transitions and economic shifts. The churches have responded to these developments but also helped shape them. While they played, at most, a limited role in anti-colonial struggles they were profoundly challenged by the exigencies of the newly independent regimes. One-party government or military rule usually arrived quickly. These autocratic regimes sometimes followed ethnic or regional conflict, even civil war, but the broader economic situation was a crucial determinant. African leaders soon discovered that they had few economic resources at their disposal and prospects of development diminished further with the world oil crisis. The continent's public debts

---

7 D. Maxwell, *African gifts of the Spirit: Pentecostalism and the rise of a Zimbabwean transnational religious movement* (Oxford: James Currey, forthcoming).
8 Paul Gifford, *African Christianity: its public role* (London: Hurst & Co., 1998).
9 Paul Freston, *Evangelicals and politics in Asia, Africa and Latin America* (Cambridge: Cambridge University Press, 2001), p. 107.

quadrupled between 1970 and 1976 as the majority of states lacked oil resources and were forced to import at prices that had increased six times. Responding to popular disillusionment at the slow pace of change, nationalist parties consolidated their positions by continuing a process begun in nationalist struggles, that of subsuming civil society. Trade unions, foreign companies, leaders of traditional churches and other concentrations of independent power were destroyed or incorporated.

Autocratic regimes prevailed until the end of the 1980s when a combination of forces led to their demise. The collapse of the Berlin Wall and the end of the Cold War deprived states of Western or Eastern benefactors and of legitimating models of communist dictatorship. Moreover, events in eastern Europe inspired a revived and resurgent civil society to challenge near bankrupt regimes. A 'second democratic revolution' ensued as more than half of sub-Saharan African states made political reforms and moved toward multi-party democracy. In this revolution the churches played a leading role. Sadly, however, the political transformation begun at the end of the 1980s was shortlived. In a new world dominated by America the new regimes had to embrace neo-liberal economics of trade liberalisation, privatisation and diminished state provision in the form of structural adjustment programmes ordained by the World Bank and International Monetary Fund. While such policies benefited a minority of African businessmen working for international companies they stifled local enterprise, boosted unemployment, and led to new levels of poverty, crime and violence. Worse still, many of the newly elected leaders of multi-party regimes were 'born-again' politicians from the previous generation of politicians. Their conversions to democracy proved to be superficial and they were barely distinguishable from their predecessors. Soon they learnt how to stay in power by dividing opposition parties and manipulating elections and constitutions while satisfying international pressure. Their governments became *de facto* one-party regimes. Thus from the mid-1990s Africa's churches have been involved in a third democratic revolution. This revolution is against 'presidential third termism' – the tendency of leaders to cling to office. It is a struggle for incorrupt 'transparency' and the development of electoral institutions, and a struggle for a democratic political culture.[10] Only through such a revolution can African states begin to reconnect with the needs and aspirations of their citizens.

10 T. Ranger, 'Introduction', in T. Ranger (ed.), *Evangelical Christianity and democracy in Africa* (Oxford: Oxford University Press, forthcoming).

Survival and revival: the first two decades

At independence the historic mission churches were in a weak position relative to the new African states. Relations were animated by a concern on the part of church leaders to give the state the benefit of the doubt and irritability on the part of the state if church leaders did or said anything even vaguely political. While there had been some notable exceptions, many white missionaries had tacitly accepted the colonial land grab and settler racism, or at the very least made use of the broader structures of imperial rule. Now they could easily be cast as meddling neo-colonialists. Black clerics faced other disadvantages. In Protestant churches the standards of clerical training fell far short of those in mission schools, which had trained black elites in the colonial period. Poorly educated Protestant clergy felt themselves to be at distinct disadvantage when dealing with a sophisticated post-colonial leadership. African Catholic priests did have an extensive seminary education but they were few and far between in the 1960s.[11] There were some outstanding African church leaders such as Cardinal Malula of Zaire, Bishop Jean Zoa of Cameroon and Archbishop Janani Luwum of Uganda. A man such as one of these acted as 'the only alternative personality with national significance to that of the current president'.[12] But as Luwum's murder in 1977 by Idi Amin showed, they were initially exposed with few African clergy to support them and no organised base in the laity.

Some of the worst church–state clashes occurred in those regimes that had adopted Marxism-Leninism as official ideology. In 1977, a year after seizing power in Ethiopia, Menghistu Haile Mariam launched his National Democratic Revolutionary Programme with Soviet and Cuban assistance. He began with the expatriate churches, expropriating their lands and property. Then he turned his attention to the Orthodox church. Archbishops were arrested, imprisoned or dismissed and many of the church's books and liturgical objects were seized. Monasteries were infiltrated with *agents-provocateurs* to humiliate and subvert the monks, and key sacred sites were turned into museums. A similar process of the nationalisation of church schools and hospitals began in Mozambique in 1975 following the victory of Frelimo. Over the next four years United Methodist church membership declined by 40 per cent. Even church leaders with strong nationalist sympathies could come unstuck in regimes that adopted scientific socialism.

11 Kevin Ward, 'Africa', in A. Hastings (ed.), *A world history of Christianity* (London: Cassell, 1999), p. 227.
12 Hastings, *History of African Christianity*, p. 263.

Church schools in the eastern region of Ghana were also nationalised in 1959 under Kwame Nkrumah's African socialism. But clerics were equally disquieted by the cult of personality he promoted. It appeared to them as if he actively encouraged the idea that he was the messiah and redeemer. In 1961 his birthplace was turned into a national shrine. The church was also disturbed by the oath of allegiance sworn by his party's youth wing, the Young Pioneers. The Anglican bishop of Accra, the Rt Revd Richard Roseveare, was dismissed after claiming that the youth movement ignored 'the existence and claims of almighty God'.[13] More extreme still were the excesses of the 'authenticity campaign' of President Mobutu of Zaire. Crucifixes in schools and hospitals were replaced by the image of the new messiah, Mobutu. Biblical names were to be changed for genuine African names and Christmas Day was declared a working day.[14] In 1971 the Catholic Louvanium university was nationalised, and so were schools and seminaries.

Nevertheless, to paraphrase Adrian Hastings, the mission churches were sturdy ships, which weathered the storms of independence remarkably well.[15] By the late 1980s they had become a forceful presence in African states. The first reason for this was a steady growth in church adherence throughout the period, a growth stemming from both external and internal sources. The widely publicised call for a missionary moratorium mooted by leading African Christian thinkers in the early 1970s raised important questions about dependency, but on the whole many churches ignored it. Throughout the post-colonial period the Catholic church witnessed remarkable growth, expanding into new regions well beyond former French, Belgian and Portuguese colonies. Traditional fields of missionary Catholic recruitment such as Ireland, France and Holland declined but more than 1,000 new missionaries from Poland filled the gap. Many of these went to Tanzania or Kenya where Catholic growth was prolific. Between 1961 and the 1990s Catholic numbers in the former increased by 419 per cent, while Kenya's Catholic population jumped to 2.5 million in the same period.[16]

There was also a new Protestant missionary impetus, for the most part driven by North Americans. It was predominantly a movement of born-again missionaries, evangelicals, charismatics and Pentecostals, reflecting denominational shifts in American Christianity.[17] Its effects were most vividly seen in

---

13 Sundkler and Steed, *The church in Africa*, pp. 945–6.
14 Hastings, *History of African Christianity*, pp. 191–3.   15 Ibid., p. 224.
16 Jenkins, *The next Christendom*, p. 58; Sundkler and Steed, *The church in Africa*, p. 1001.
17 Paul Gifford, 'Some recent developments in African Christianity', *African affairs* 93:373 (1994), 513–34.

the crusading activities of Billy Graham and Oral Roberts, and more recently the likes of Benny Hinn, Kenneth Hagin and John Avanzini. But probably more significant in the long term was the work of para-church bodies such as Women's Aglow, the Full Gospel Business Men's Fellowship International and the Haggai Institute, which promoted inter-denominationalism. Although the movement 'took off' in the 1980s important groundwork had been done by older Pentecostal missions such as the American and British Assemblies of God and the Pentecostal Assemblies of Canada. It also drew force from broader inter-denominational evangelical ministries such as Scripture Union, Campus Crusade and the Navigators, which targeted Africans in secondary and higher education, as this sector rapidly expanded in the 1960s to meet the needs of newly independent states.[18]

This US born-again impetus, which was particularly strong in the more hospitable environments of former settler colonies like Kenya and Zimbabwe, was matched by a local impetus. African Pentecostals like Ezekiel Guti, leader of the Zimbabwe Assemblies of God Africa, broke away from missionary movements to found their own churches, retaining part of the original name in their new organisations. And African elites, who came into contact with the born-again movement in higher education, began ministries in cities amongst the educated middle classes, forming movements like the Redeemed Christian church in Nigeria. The growing momentum of Pentecostalism caused others to leave mainline churches to found new movements, as was the case with Mensa Otabil, who left the Anglican church to found the Ghana-based International Central Gospel church in 1984.[19]

Indeed most of the Christian expansion within old or new churches was African initiated and African led, as it always had been. There were noteworthy formal initiatives within the historic mission churches. Within Catholicism, Bugandan missionaries started work in Burkino Faso and Zairian Sisters moved amongst the Nyamwezi in Tanzania. And within Protestantism, the English-speaking Anglican church found its way into French-speaking Shaba (Katanga) Zaire and the Lutheran church of Ovambo-Kavango, Namibia, pioneered churches in Senegal. But most of the expansion was the low-level face-to-face kind. The range of locations expanded to include the township and the black middle-class suburb, alongside the village. And enhanced communication and social mobility swelled the ranks of the proselytisers from labour migrants, catechists and evangelists to include nurses, teachers and civil servants on

---

18 Maxwell, *African gifts*.
19 On Ghana see Gifford, *African Christianity*, ch. 3.

placement, returning students, often accompanied by their Christian Union or Scripture Union brethren, and urban churches on 'crusade' determined to establish rural branches. Church planting also occurred indirectly through the enormous transnational traffic in refugees, particularly in the Horn of Africa. Even the trials and persecutions visited upon the church by hostile regimes sometimes brought unexpected blessings, speeding up indigenisation and self-reliance. When the Meghistu regime fell in 1991 a vast and vital underground church survived it. Perhaps the only major constraint on Christian expansion in Africa is Islam. In Sudan there has long been conflict between the Arabic-speaking Muslim north and the black Christian/animist population in the south, but the conflict erupted in the 1980s when the government attempted to impose Sharia law.

Christian–Muslim conflict was also a key element in the Nigerian civil war. The secession of the eastern region, which declared itself the Republic of Biafra in May 1967, followed a series of massacres of Christian Igbo living in the Muslim north. Hundreds of thousands fled back to their eastern homeland, abandoning their livelihoods in the belief that an Islamic *Jihad* (holy war) had begun. In the ensuing three years of conflict approximately one million people died. Tensions between Nigeria's Christian south and Muslim north still pertain, periodically tipping over into violence.[20] Relations with Islam are one of the key issues facing the African church in the twenty-first century.

Given that since the beginning of the missionary enterprise the bulk of African churches had been founded and led by African pastors, catechists and evangelists far from missionary eyes, Christianity already was 'popular' or 'vernacular' at independence. Nevertheless, churches defused the nationalist slur that they were culturally alien through more *formal* acts of Africanisation. The process of liturgical innovation and the training and promotion of African clergy was led by the Protestant churches. At times clerical offices were multiplied or invented for good measure, as in the case of the Methodist church of Nigeria. But soon the Catholic church took the lead, catalysed by the deliberations and proclamations of the Second Vatican Council with which African independence so neatly coincided. In many African states the Africanisation of Catholic clergy was rapid and far-reaching. In 1965 less than a quarter of bishops in Tanzania were African; by 1996 Africans headed all the twenty-nine dioceses. Another Catholic initiative was the founding of base

---

20 Cyril Imo, 'Evangelicals, Muslims and democracy: with particular reference to the declaration of Sharia in northern Nigeria', in Terence Ranger (ed.), *Evangelical Christianity and democracy in Africa* (Oxford: Oxford University Press, forthcoming).

communities in cities such as Kinshasa, Lilongwe and Nairobi where priests were particularly stretched. Led by lay animators with a formal training, these Catholic communities were less overtly political than those in Latin America, focused instead on the regular distribution of the eucharist and the grounding of the faithful in the teachings of the church. As such they mirrored the myriad village Christian communities founded by African Christians since the beginning of the missionary encounter.[21]

Where the process of Africanisation has been most profound is in female vocations. In 1989 members of female religious orders outnumbered their male counterparts by at least five times. Given the importance African cultures attach to motherhood this feminine aspect of Catholicism represents a strong break with the African past. Indeed, the enterprise of Africanisation has not been without incident and ironic results. In Zimbabwe well-intentioned missionary priests often reacted with horror at the Lourdes grottoes, medals and scapulars, and Latin masses introduced by their fore-bears, not grasping the extent to which they had become popular. Transported from rural Ireland to rural Zimbabwe this peasant Catholicism not only had great instrumental effect but had also become deeply incorpo-rated into the devotions of the faithful. Although it did not look like proper inculturation it was nevertheless central to the identity of peasant farmers, who carried it with them as they were evicted to make way for white settlers.[22] Other 'top-down' programmes of inculturation met with equal resistance from the unimpressed recipients. The modern efflorescence of Marian apparitions across the continent has been attributed to the vacuum left by the curtailing of popular devotional practices.[23] Similarly, the *Maria Legio*, a Kenyan movement of independent Catholicism with its own bishops, cardinals and pope, and Latin phrases in the mass, emerged at exactly the same time as Roman Catholics abandoned Latin for the vernacular. In such contexts *indigenous* or *local* is not interpreted by the recipients of inculturation as a reflection of their aspiration but as *marginality*.

The most controversial case of Africanisation concerned the Zambian Catholic Archbishop Emmanuel Milingo who responded to a popularly perceived crisis of spirit possession with a ministry of exorcism and healing.

---

21 On the notion of popular or village Christianity see Hastings, *History of African Christianity* and *The church in Africa*.

22 D. Maxwell, *Christians and chiefs in Zimbabwe: a social history of the Hwesa people c.1870s–1990s* (Edinburgh: International African Library, 1999), ch. 3.

23 Elizabeth Isichei, *A history of Christianity in Africa: from antiquity to the present* (London: SPCK, 1995), p. 328.

Many of his colleagues, particularly the large expatriate Catholic missionary community, were not convinced that his response was authentic and pressurised the Vatican for his removal, which came in 1982. Their confusion stemmed from a model of Africanisation that understood the process only as one of incorporation. It was a model informed by an African theology that drew its inspiration from cultural nationalism, rather than an empirically based historical anthropology of popular Christianity. This theology, epitomised by the work of John Mbiti, was a theology of authenticity in continuity, depicting African traditional religion as 'basically consonant with Christianity' by emphasising in particular pre-Christian African monotheism.[24] Along with his emphasis on pre-Christian belief in God Mbiti also asserted that African religion conceived of no future tense and claimed no founders, prophets or converts. African religion corresponded with African society, and every member of African society was born into its religion.[25] Although more historically minded scholars conclusively disproved all of these propositions, Mbiti's work appealed to the homogenising instincts of nationalist politicians and intellectuals. It was read widely within seminaries and religious studies departments in African universities, recycled endlessly by first-generation African theologians. However, as Mbiti and his colleagues were increasingly domiciled in the West, so their theology grew more irrelevant, obsessed with the affronts of cultural imperialism while ordinary Africans struggled with weightier issues of corruption, poverty and political violence.

On the other hand Milingo, along with Independent church members and Pentecostals, stood in another tradition of cyclical societal cleansing which Africanised Christianity through the exclusion of traditional religious components by exorcism, demonisation and the destruction of polluted objects.[26] In their emphasis on personal security these types of popular Christianity represent both practical and highly successful forms of inculturation.

The historic mission churches made a more straightforward contribution to 'development', the *raison d'être* of independent African states. Here continuities with colonial states proved useful. Mission churches had actively participated in programmes of modernisation and were keen to maintain or rework that role after independence, especially in states where they had lost control of education. Often adopting the same language and priorities of development as the states themselves, many churches 'NGOised', expanding their activities into

---

24 Ward, 'Africa', p. 232.
25 John Mbiti, *African religions and philosophy* (New York: Praeger, 1969).
26 Maxwell, *Christians and chiefs*, ch. 3.

water and power provision, primary and secondary healthcare, the promotion of female self-sufficiency and care for the environment. Even where they lost formal control of education the desire to expand provision through church schools left mission bodies with enormous influence over African youth. There was a similar pattern of church engagement with development across the continent. After independence the National Christian Council of Kenya (NCCK) moved much closer to the state, using its connections with overseas donors to finance development projects such as 'village polytechnics' which provided practical training for peasant farmers. In Zaire in the period 1969–80 the Catholic church registered approximately 2,300 development projects. In Kivu region the bishop established himself as 'something of a modern chief', co-ordinating the construction of a hydroelectric dam and an airport financed by the locally produced coffee, cattle and gold.[27]

The centrality of development to post-colonial states helps explain the declining political influence of African Independent churches. If the new regimes initially loved the church only for its body then the AICs had far less to offer than the well-endowed historic mission churches. Independent church leaders addressed issues of personal security, ministering to their faithful through healing, exorcism and prayer. They initially had little to offer in the way of 'modernising development'. Indeed, their relations with many post-colonial states opened in a precarious, even deadly, manner. Togo banned thirty churches, Kenya legislated against peripheral religious move-ments, and the state-controlled press in Zimbabwe made 'sects' a constant object of criticism for their failure to participate in programmes of primary healthcare. But the most significant clash was between the Lumpa church of Alice Lenshina and Zambia's ruling United National Independence Party (UNIP). Soon after independence the Lumpa came to believe that the Second Coming was drawing near, and increasingly withdrew from the world into separate villages. Their need for land led to conflict with Bemba chiefs and fighting broke out in which 700 were killed. Alice and her husband, Petros, were imprisoned, where they remained until their deaths in 1972 and 1978 respectively. Perverse as it may at first appear AICs came into conflict with post-colonial states because they ignored them. The newly independent African state was 'jealous of its authority and ... fearful of threats to its monopoly over the means of persuasion and coercion, and the function of prescribing national policy'. Its attempts to consolidate power were 'often

---

27 Sundkler and Steed, *The church in Africa*, p. 967.

legitimised in terms of development – a commitment towards economic and social goals . . .'. Thus when sects and small-scale religious groupings refused to participate in modernisation, they were striking at the hegemonic ideology of the state, questioning where 'the locus of moral authority' lay.[28]

There were important exceptions to this rule, mainly among the larger movements such as the Kimbanguists in Zaire, the Harrisists in west Africa and Zion Christian church (ZCC) in South Africa. Such movements 'aged' quickly and under a second generation of more formally educated but less charismatic leaders they bureaucratised, standardising and modernising rules and practices. As such they came to look more and more like the historic mission churches. Under the idiosyncratic Mobutu the Kimbanguist church found great favour, becoming in 1971 one of the three official religious bodies in Zaire along with the Roman Catholic church and the Church of Christ (a forced association of all the other Protestant bodies). Two years earlier it had been admitted to the World Council of Churches. Moreover, movements such as the ZCC and Fambizano, the ecumenical organisation of AICs in Zimbabwe, did embrace 'development', participating in educational and agricultural work. Such organisations often played up their supposed 'authentic' credentials to appeal to Western donors keen to protect 'indigenous cultures'. One of the pioneers of the Fambizano movement was the former Dutch Reformed church missionary Martinus Daneel. Since the 1970s Protestant missionaries have been behind some particularly creative initiatives to help Independents, again breaking down the divide between the two camps.

On the whole, though, the bulk of the smaller fluid AICs remain peripheral to the business of African states. Although they were co-opted into the narrative of anti-colonial 'resistance history' by the first generation of professional African historians, they have turned out to be rather less 'independent' and less 'political' than once imagined.[29] Recent research shows that such movements arose out of an ambience of revivalist and counter-establishment Christianity within the Western missionary enterprise. It also shows that many of these highly sectarian movements have shunned not just colonial states, but all states, as the case of the Watch Tower movement in central Africa powerfully illustrates.[30]

---

28 S. Cross, 'Independent churches and independent states: Jehovah's Witnesses in east and central Africa', in E. Fashole-Luke, R. Gray, A. Hastings and G. Tasie (eds.), *Christianity in independent Africa* (London: Rex Collings, 1978), pp. 312–13.

29 On the changing understanding of the 'political' significance of AICs see T. Ranger, 'Religious movements and politics in sub-Saharan Africa', *African studies review* 29:2 (1986), 1–69.

30 For the best introduction to AICs see Hastings, *The church in Africa*, ch. 11. On Watch Tower see Cross, 'Independent churches'.

Finally, the mission background of many of the first generation of African leaders not only added a significant Christian content to development programmes but also gave them a greater intellectual sympathy with the historic churches rather than the AICs. Julius Nyerere's socialist programme of *ujamaa* – collectivisation – in Tanzania owed much to his Catholicism. Kenneth Kaunda's Presbyterian heritage shaped his brand of humanism for Zambia. And the ex-Methodist minister cum first president, Canaan Banana, developed an explicit theology of development for Zimbabwe. More importantly, this ideological innovation illustrated the extent that Christianity had constituted the elements of a moral discourse upon which political legitimacy could be based. Nkrumah's version of African socialism, drawing from Marxism-Leninism, found little sympathy in Ghana but his use of Christian imagery – 'Seek ye first the political kingdom' – resonated widely amongst friend and foe alike. Christian ideas had captured the African imagination, providing a potent a set of values upon which leaders could draw. But these values they also shared with their citizens and as such they provided a yardstick by which they could be judged. This yardstick became particularly important in Africa's second democratic revolution at the end of the 1980s.

Church and state in the second democratic revolution

As African states faded, or at the very least lost the respect of their citizens, the fortunes of the churches advanced. The numbers of adherents had multiplied, and their bureaucracies, both more complex and more far reaching, were filled with a better-trained African clergy. In Francophone Africa in particular a new generation of African Catholic scholars such as Jean Marc Ela and Fabien Eboussi Boulaga began to articulate a very different theology from their predecessors. Moved by the worsening condition of the poor they were as willing to speak out against the rottenness of African bureaucracies as they were to condemn the West for its neo-colonialism.[31] And as Western donors grew ever more suspicious of states so they looked to the churches as conduits of aid. Churches appeared to be even-handed and efficient institutions able to provide services in health and education where states were failing. By the late 1980s Mobutu was forced to return previously nationalised schools to churches which were far more capable of running them. In

31 Jean-Marc Ela, *African Cry* (Maryknoll, NY: Orbis, 1986); F. Eboussi Boulaga, *Christianity without fetishes* (Maryknoll, NY: Orbis, 1984).

Mozambique religious and secular NGOs were so powerful relative to the state that they called the shots in development strategy. 'The relatively human and moderate autocracy of the early post-independence regimes had given way to excesses which it needed no theological sophistication to denounce.'[32] The churches had largely 'outlived their connection with colonialism' and were ready to enter the fray.

When in the late 1980s Francophone countries began national constitutional conferences Catholic bishops were often appointed to chair them. In Zaire, Mgr Laurent Monsengwo Pansiya was elected in 1991 to preside over the national conference, which sought to halt the country's slide into anarchy. In Benin, Mgr Isidore de Sousa, archbishop of Cotonou, became the highest authority in the land, when as chairman of the High Council of the Republic he oversaw the transition of the country to multi-party elections.

In many other states the churches' entry into the public sphere was equally high profile. In Anglophone countries prophetic criticism was often led by a combination of church councils and historically powerful denominations. In Kenya the most articulate criticism of President Moi came from individual Anglican bishops whose sermons were full of 'Old Testament prophetic fire'. John Lonsdale describes how 'King Rehoboam, who threatened Israel with whips and scorpions, or the Emperor Darius who enacted a decree of which he soon repented but could not amend, have both been taken to typify the ruler of a one-party state who consults no one'. In the face of threats on his life, the most prominent bishop, David Gitari, 'persisted in asking awkward questions, why there was "no Naboth to say No" to corrupt land seizures'.[33] Anglican bishops drew much support from the NCCK, which increasingly drew back from its partnership with the state. In Zambia the historic mission churches had less influence and born-again Christianity played a key role in the events leading to Kaunda's downfall. The president's philosophy of humanism and his exploration of 'demonic' Indian spirituality were significant factors in his delegitimation by the powerful Evangelical Fellowship of Zambia. Realising the political clout of Zambian born-agains, Kaunda's successor, Frederick Chiluba, emphasised his personal evangelical credentials, a sign of things to come.

Finally, the church was involved in peace-making. A civil war, stoked by Rhodesia and then South Africa, had raged in Mozambique since independence,

32 Ranger, 'Introduction'.
33 John Lonsdale, 'Kikuyu Christianities: a history of intimate diversity', in David Maxwell (ed.) with Ingrid Lawrie, *Christianity and the African imagination: essays in honour of Adrian Hastings* (Leiden: Brill, 2002), pp. 189–90.

in which the counter-revolutionary MNR (Mozambique National Resistance) had exploited Frelimo's opposition to organised religion. Desperate for allies, President Machel reached out to the churches in 1982 and offered them a new role. His successor Joaquim Chissano allowed their influence to grow further, giving the Catholic church clout to organise peace talks in Rome beginning in July 1990. A general peace accord, brokered by the Vatican, was finally signed in October 1992. In the making of both peace and new constitutions the historic churches had come to show that they had considerable political influence. In many instances they had come to be the most important social institutions in the country beside the state itself. They possessed vast numbers of adherents, who easily exceeded those in political parties, they were staffed by highly motivated and able clergy and laity, and they had nation-wide structures which could rapidly disseminate ideas and information. Beyond this they had external links to the Vatican, Lambeth Palace and the World Council of Churches, which provided a vital counter-balance to local state pressure. These structures, which had given them great advantages in denouncing dictatorial regimes and reconciling warring parties, play a more ambivalent role in Africa's third revolution for a democratic culture.

The churches in the frontline: violence and poverty and presidential third termism

The end of the Cold War did not bring about a cessation of external intervention in Africa, but rather a change in its nature. The economic ideology of privatisation spread across the continent in the 1990s, inaugurating a new era. Western-dominated international institutions insisted that government revenue be used first and foremost to pay overseas debts, and elevated private initiative over public responsibility. Unemployment mushroomed as the contraction of the state reduced the number of public-sector jobs. The removal of protective tariffs on imports through trade liberalisation led to the decline of local manufacturing industries and added further to the army of jobless, while the growing shortage of foreign currency limited the growth of new private enterprise. A fast-growing population aggravated these hardships. In the face of land shortage and hopes for something better, young people migrated to towns and cities in a new wave of urbanisation. But not every African state was a weak state. Those such as Zimbabwe retained a good deal of ability to coerce citizens, its ruling clique acting in a violent and corrupt manner to remain in power in the face of a loss of popular support. Across the continent leaders and their retainers manipulated national and party constitutions to stay in office.

It was clear that Africa needed another more profound revolution to create a sustainable democratic culture. And given the growing resources and influence of the church it had a pivotal role to play. But as Terence Ranger observes the historic churches were now at a distinct disadvantage. 'Hierarchy and authority had given them great advantage in denouncing dictatorial regimes ... they were an obstacle to a genuine manifestation of democratic practice.'[34] Moreover, as well as being examples of bad practice hierarchical structures were rapidly drawn into the politics of patronage, clientalism and corporatism, with bishops becoming just as compromised as secular politicians.[35] Zimbabwe provides a prime example. As President Mugabe grew increasingly unpopular in the late 1990s so his struggle to remain in power became ever more desperate. Apart from widespread electoral fraud he embarked on a series of illegal land seizures led by war veterans and militarised youth. The Anglican cathedral located beside the Zimbabwean parliament symbolised in colonial times the close relation between church and state. The newly elected bishop of Harare, Nobert Kunonga, actively renewed that alliance, throwing himself uncritically behind the ruling party's land reform programme. In January 2002 Kunonga declared that Mugabe, who has boasted of having degrees in violence, was more Christian than himself. It was left to the Catholic church to fulfil the prophetic role and speak up for the victims of violence and repression as it had done against the racist settler regime of Ian Smith. In November 2002 Archbishop Pious Ncube delivered the Denis Hurley lecture in Durban. In it he described the Zimbabwean government as 'fascists', relying on 'lies, propaganda, the twisting of facts, half truths, downright untruths and gross misinformation'.

But Rwanda, the scene of the genocide of two million Tutsi and moderate Hutu in 1994, provides the most disturbing example of the chameleon character of Christianity, its capacity for both good and evil. During the genocide 'more Rwandese citizens died in churches and parishes than anywhere else'. Moreover, 'killers paused during massacres to pray at the altar'. A number of clergy and church employees lured people into churches knowing that they would be killed, turned over Tutsi to be killed, or actively participated in the death squads. The regional leader of the Seventh-day Adventist church, Elziphan Ntakirutimana, was eventually extradited to the

---

34 Ranger, 'Introduction'.
35 L. Sanneh, 'A resurgent church in a troubled continent: review essay of Bengt Sundkler's *History of the church in Africa*', *International bulletin of missionary research* 25:3 (2001), p. 115.

International Criminal Tribunal in Arusha for his part in the killings.[36] Conversely, church leaders had been involved in peace-making and the transition to multi-partyism in 1992. And many died heroically while attempting to stop the violence. Of the 200 African priests who have died violent deaths in the forty years prior to 1996, 103 were from Rwanda and stood against the genocide.[37] Rwanda was an extreme example, a country dogged by strongly ethnicised politics, over-population, land shortage, and unstable neighbours who have allied with and armed successive alienated segments of Rwandan society. Yet to all intents and purposes Rwanda is a highly 'Christian' country. The vast majority of the perpetrators of the crimes of the genocide had been baptised and had some sort of Christian formation. Equally telling was the pastoral letter issued by the chair of the Catholic Bishops Conference in 1991, which accused the Catholic church of being a 'giant with feet of clay', unwilling to use its power for good or reform its own structures. More than any other case Rwanda points to the need to renew Africa's dominant political culture.

It is at this juncture that the born-again movement needs to be considered. Its numbers have mushroomed in a context of state contraction, neo-liberal economics, poverty and growing political turmoil. The character of some of the larger transnational organisations within the movement points to its growing appeal and its social and political function. It has embraced media technologies, particularly the electronic media and religious broadcasting, with great zeal. It has a tendency to produce oligarchic church governments, often comprising the leader's extended family and friends. It has adopted the faith gospel, drawing from the teachings of Oral Roberts, T. L Osborn, Kenneth Hagin and Kenneth Copeland to argue that material success is a sign of faith and of God's blessing. Its leaders are particularly susceptible to the tools and some of the values of modernity, especially the values of liberal capitalism. And it casts itself as inter-denominational and global in character.

The electronic media has been key to the movement's expansion. In the 'worship stores' the religious consumer can buy gospel songs on audiocassettes and CDs, and videotaped recordings of sermons and conventions, or the latest religious film such as the recent Nigerian productions *Living in bondage*, *Out of bounds* and *Endtime*. In Zimbabwe the local television chart show, *Mutinhimira weMimhanzi/Ezomgido*, regularly features gospel music alongside more secular

---

36 Timothy Longman, 'Church politics and the genocide in Rwanda', *Journal of religion in Africa* 31:2 (2001), 163–86.
37 Ward, 'Africa', p. 230.

sounds. Performers such as Zecks Manatsa, Mahendere Brothers and Vebati VeJehovah are thus just as mainstream as the famous Bundu Boys. And the gospel videos, depicting singing and dancing or more vivid scenes of deliverance or crowds symbolically 'stepping on Satan', are just as compelling as secular alternatives. The electronic media is a vital tool in proselytism but it has also helped born-agains capture popular culture. All of this is very important in a continent where approximately half the population is below the age of fifteen.

But these young Christians have been none too impressed with the authoritarian leaders who more often than not have formed marriages of convenience with politicians. Having been cold-shouldered for so long, evangelical and Pentecostal leaders have engaged with secular leaders for respectability and public recognition, as well as access to the state media. And politicians desperate for new sources of legitimisation in this post-socialist, post-nationalist age have sought to secure a born-again mandate and to make use of the growing born-again constituency. The Kenyan president Daniel arap Moi was a prime example. In February 1992, while the Anglican leader, Archbishop Gitari, and the NCCK pressured for multi-party elections, Moi's ally, the leader of the Gospel Redeemed church, told listeners in a televised sermon: 'In heaven it is just like Kenya has been for many years. There is only one party – and God never makes a mistake ... President Moi has been appointed by God to lead the country ... We have freedom of worship, we can pray and sing in any way we want. What else do we need?'[38]

However, at the level of the local gathering the disciplined believer does participate in a democratic culture of pragmatism and competition. Local level financial accountability is assured as tithes and offerings are recorded with mathematical accuracy. In pre-service Bible studies scripture is discussed in an atmosphere conducive to debate and mutual respect. And elections for the posts of deacons and elders are conducted with great scrupulousness. Women and youth participate fully in assembly leadership, given opportunity to do so through the multiplication of roles within a hierarchy. They are subsequently encouraged to seek greater responsibility in their careers and public life.[39] Moreover, although born-again churches have been accused of spiritualising worldly problems it does not take too much imagination to grasp the politically destabilising potential of their standard spiritual injunctions. Refrains such as 'Fear God not man', or the assertion of first loyalty to a Holy Nation where status and citizenship are redefined, can, as David Martin

---

38 Paul Gifford, 'Bishops for reform', *Tablet*, 30 May 1992, pp. 672–4.
39 Maxwell, *African gifts*.

suggests, 'divest systems of authority of their justification and turn law into a matter of inward judgement and sincerity, rather than external observance'.[40] The potentially reforming effects of born-again culture on politics will only be manifest in the *longue durée*.[41] However, as Martin suggests, it is in the cultural sphere that the significance of this Protestant movement lies.

In sociological terms the born-again movement is much more concerned with social reproduction, the promotion and maintenance of families. Here the sheer range of responses should be noted. At one end of the spectrum the emphasis on unfettered accumulation that characterises the American-derived faith gospel legitimates the lifestyles of those African elites who, through connection with international business or NGOs, have prospered under neo-liberalism. At the other, the emphasis on honesty, sobriety, self-discipline, individualisation, breaking free from the curse of one's ancestors and performing acts of traditional commensality at least offers the vast swathes of mobile poor the greatest chance of survival in an insecure and fluid labour market. Thus, beyond the urban mega-churches, in the townships and rural locations the faith gospel has a different meaning. Here Pentecostals seek security rather than prosperity, looking to their leaders for protection against angry spirits and witchcraft and the provision of fertility, healing, work and stable marriages. And personal security explains the abiding influence of Pentecostalism's cousins, the AICs. These movements, with a strong emphasis on prayer, exorcism and healing, remain vital to millions who live on the margins of African societies. Here, however, it is important not to make too gross a distinction between churches emphasising gifts of the Spirit and others. As Hastings pointed out long ago, prayer not politics remains the primary focus of *all* churches and there are many commonalties between their popular forms.[42]

The inter-denominational and global aspirations of African born-agains also shed light on their needs and the ability of their states to supply them. Their transnational religious identities, enacted in international conventions where the halls are decked out in international flags, and imaged in the electronic and printed media, point to a loss of faith in the ability of their states to bring about meaningful change. They also point to a desire to be part of something big, part of something that counts. More than that, international contacts offer the possibility of much-needed resources, employment

---

40 D. Martin, *Pentecostalism: the world is their parish* (Oxford: Blackwell, 2001), p. 12.
41 Gifford, *African Christianity*, p. 348.
42 Hastings, *History of African Christianity*, pp. 265, 273.

and scholarships abroad. But these same aspirations are also found in the historic mission churches, in their continued openness to missionaries and religious NGOs; in their resistance to imposed inculturation; and in, for example, the hundreds of thousands who turned out to greet John Paul II during papal visits in 1980 and 1995.

Viewed from another perspective international links foster what Paul Gifford calls 'ecclesiastical externality', which disempowers African Christians, making them dependent on the American Bible Belt, or for that matter Rome or Lambeth.[43] African autonomy is often challenged by this externality but the results of international engagement are not always clear cut. African Christian leaders can often choose and manipulate overseas patrons or use external funding to build up networks of local patronage and control the boundaries of their movements. And the messages of a Western-dominated religious media are often localised by the armies of evangelists, catechists and pastors who run African churches. These foot soldiers have little or no specialised training, speak the same language as their flocks, share their perspectives and are dependent on them for their maintenance. Hence, they are open to local agendas and vulnerable to capture from below.

Furthermore, cultural flows move in more than one direction. The African vision has extended beyond the continent. Clergy from the historic churches participate in Western mission through diocesan twinning programmes, while highflying African born-again executives like Ezekiel Guti or Nevers Mumba travel US and European preaching and healing circuits, often visiting 'international' branches of their movements founded by their diaspora. Many of these African Christians consider themselves missionaries. They seek to remoralise secular Western societies and save them from the supposed apostasy of liberal Christianity. Their arrival in the West signals not only the centrality of Africa to global Christianity but also the fact that its missionary impetus has come full circle.

---

43 Gifford, *African Christianity*, pp. 44–7, 148–9.

23

South Asia, 1911–2003

CHANDRA MALLAMPALLI

Christians of south Asia have always consisted of many 'communities', distinguished according to region, language, caste and church tradition. Some are products of relatively recent conversions, while others belong to older, more established, traditions. During the twentieth century, socio-political changes related to Indian nationalism, constitutional reforms and caste politics prompted new forms of theological reflection and new avenues for public engagement. Rather than remaining within their niches, different classes of Christians considered how best to stake their claims within an evolving public domain and inscribe a more collective Christian identity upon the canvass of nationhood. Could an 'Indian Christian community' be attuned to local, nationalistic and international developments at the same time, or would these different sites of engagement remain in constant tension with each other? Challenges concerning the status of Christians within the Indian nation presented themselves poignantly during the decades preceding independence (1947) and continue to this day.

The Indian church

Indian Christianity consists of three principal branches: Syrian (or Thomas) Christian, Roman Catholic and Protestant.[1] During the colonial period, Christians belonging to the oldest church of India, the Thomas Christians, were mostly concentrated within the princely state of Travancore, or what is now Kerala. Significant numbers of Thomas Christians also resided within the Malabar district of British south India. They traced their origins to the apostle Thomas, who allegedly came to India and converted a number of

---

1 Much of the data appearing in this article was collected in 1998–9, and has been published in *Christians and public life in colonial south India, 1863–1937* (London: RoutledgeCurzon, 2004).

Brahmins along the Coromandel coast near Mylapore.[2] Thomas Christians professed Brahmin status and adopted many customs of high-ranking groups of the caste system. Over the centuries, they have avoided efforts to propagate their religion for fear of compromising such status. During the nineteenth and twentieth centuries, however, a more reformed branch, the Mar Thoma, propagated their faith among lower-ranking groups. The outlook of the Mar Thoma was more populist and evangelical than their more exclusive Orthodox Syrian and Jacobite counterparts.

The Christian tradition in Kerala is significant because it illustrates, perhaps more than any other, the deeply rooted history of Christianity within the subcontinent. Pre-dating the arrival of Islam, British rule, Protestant missions, and even movements within modern Hinduism, the history of the Thomas Christians undermines any attempt to portray Christianity as a purely 'colonial' or 'foreign' religion. Such stereotypes circulated during the Indian independence movement and, since the early 1980s, have resurfaced amid the rise of an aggressive Hindu nationalism.

Origins of Roman Catholicism in India can be traced back to the arrival of the Portuguese, who established a colony at Goa toward the end of the fifteenth century. Under the firm backing of both the Portuguese crown and the papacy (who had granted their missionaries the official patronage or *padroado*), Jesuit missionaries established bases in the coastal regions of Goa and Malabar. These missionaries eventually oversaw the conversion of more than 15,000 low-caste fishermen, coming from the Mukkuva and Parava castes. The Jesuit Francis Xavier was said to have founded forty-five churches in Travancore state, primarily among these two caste groups. The Madurai mission, started by the Jesuit Robert de Nobili, established other Catholic communities within south Indian districts such as Ramnad, Padukottai, Mysore, Trichinopoly and Tanjore, and Arcot.

During the early twentieth century, Catholic bishops in India were recruited primarily from France and Italy and, as such, tended to be more attentive to the priorities of the Vatican than to developments within Indian localities. From 1901 to 1920, all priests in Bengal, Tamil Nadu and Andhra were recruits from outside India. By 1933, only 3 per cent of priests in Tamil Nadu were Indian.[3] The laity consisted of a mixture of educated urban

---

2 See A. M. Mundadan, *History of Christianity in India, volume I: From the beginning up to the middle of the sixteenth century* (Bangalore: Theological Publications in India, 1984), p. 21.

3 François Houtart and Geneviève Lemercinier, *Size and structures of the Catholic church in India: indigenization of an exogenous religious institution in a society in transition* (Leuven: Université Catholique de Louvain, 1982), p. 100.

professionals, shoreline fisherman communities (such as in Goa and Malabar), and village labourers from lower castes. Lay professionals, such as Catholic lawyers, members of the legislative assembly (MLAs), scholars, often served as mediators by helping to interpret teachings of the hierarchy to various sections of the laity.

Protestant movements within India flourished primarily during the colonial period. Their legacy is associated not only with involvement in education and translation, but also with the phenomenon of so-called 'mass movements' of conversion (even though Catholic mass movements had occurred much earlier). Several notable Protestant mass movements occurred in north India toward the end of the nineteenth century. During the 1870s the Chuhras, a low-ranking community of sweepers, leatherworkers and agricultural labourers, began converting *en masse* to Christianity. As a result of their conversion, the Indian Christian population in the Punjab rose from 3,912 in 1881 to 395,629 in 1931.[4] Other mass movements in north India include the conversion of the Mazhabi Sikhs and of the Bhangis and Chamars in Uttar Pradesh. While indigenous agents were most often the ones who led mass movements, Methodist, Anglican and Presbyterian missions were involved in these north Indian movements.

Baptists and Presbyterians played a significant role in the conversion of Naga, Mizo, Manipurean and Assamese tribal peoples of north-east India. Today tribal populations of north-east India are predominantly Christian. Since independence, they have been embroiled in cycles of inter-ethnic conflict and conflict with the government of India over demands for regional autonomy.

A large-scale conversion movement in south India occurred among the Nadars (who were previously known as Shanars, and had worked as toddy drawers) of Tirunelveli. As a result of their conversion, the Nadars enhanced their social and economic status dramatically. From the middle of the nineteenth century, the London Missionary Society (LMS) conducted its work within the so-called 'Tamil field' of south India. Under the influence of the LMS, large numbers of persons from Dalit (formerly called 'untouchable') castes, such as the so-called conch shell and green bangle pariahs and Chuklas of Erode, and from Criminal Tribes such as the Kuruvars of Salem, became Christian. Under the auspices of the Church Missionary Society (CMS) and the Society for the Propagation of the Gospel (SPG), Dalit groups such as the Chakkiliyans, Pallans and Shanars of Tinnevelly and Tajore also converted.

---

4 John C. B. Webster, *The Dalit Christians: a history* (New Delhi: ISPCK, 1996), p. 39.

Christians of Sri Lanka (formerly Ceylon) were similarly divided along lines of ethnicity, caste and church tradition. In 1543, Franciscan friars had received permission of the Sinhalese king to conduct their operations within this predominantly Buddhist island kingdom. Jesuit, Dominican and Augustinian orders shortly followed the Franciscans, facilitating the conversion of both Tamil- and Sinhalese-speaking peoples to Catholicism. Backed by the colonial state, Dutch Reformed missionaries had also been active in making converts during the mid-seventeenth century. British rule during the nineteenth century brought many of the same missionary organisations that were active in south India. For the most part, conversion to Christianity had occurred among the Karava fisherman caste and other low-ranking groups. As in India, Christians in Sri Lanka (never exceeding 8 per cent of the total population) learned to thrive within a multi-ethnic and multi-religious society comprising of Muslims, Hindus, Buddhists and persons of varying caste and linguistic affiliations.

Movements toward integration

This sketch of south Asia's Christians shows how particularities of caste, region, language and tradition are ongoing realities of Christian experience and have not been in any sense displaced by a monolithic church. The diversity of Indian Christianity reflects Indian diversity. During the twentieth century, however, socio-political processes of integration that contributed to the crafting of an Indian nation also contributed to the knitting together of various strands of Indian Christianity. These processes made use of print media, conference networks and an emerging politics of representation. Protestant and Catholic elites interacted with the wider Christian world even as they negotiated their relationship to Indian nationalist aspirations for home rule.

Within Indian Protestant circles, a growing spirit of ecumenism coupled with a desire for a genuinely 'Indian' church led to the formation of the Church of South India (CSI). Throughout the nineteenth century, a spirit of co-operation between various denominations and mission societies had been nurtured by a number of factors. Among them were limited resources in the field, conflicts over spheres of influence, and an urgent need for churches to accommodate local converts from wide-ranging caste and denominational backgrounds.

In order to address such concerns, mission societies in India had established regular conferences to discuss their common objectives. In 1900, the South

Indian Missionary Conference in Madras drew nearly 150 missionaries representing forty-five missionary organisations. Among these were the London Missionary Society, Church Missionary Society, American Baptist Mission, and Society for the Propagation of the Gospel. Subsequently, missionaries in the main Christian centres of south India, Madras and Bangalore, organised themselves into missionary conferences. Organisations such as the Christian Literature Society, the YMCA and the Christian Endeavor Convention, along with the leadership of Madras Christian college, were instrumental in bringing European and Indian church leaders together in dialogue. The World Missionary Conference at Edinburgh in 1910 and another consultation in Jerusalem in 1928 inspired further co-operation between churches, old and new, for purposes of church unity and evangelisation.[5]

This climate of ecumenical dialogue helped prepare the way for the formal union of churches in 1947 embodied in the Church of South India (CSI). The CSI united the Anglican dioceses of India, Myanmar (Burma) and Ceylon (Sri Lanka) with the Methodist Church of South India and the South Indian United Church (SIUC). The SIUC itself was established in 1908 and included Presbyterian, Reformed and Congregational churches. Informed and inspired by the CSI example, the Church of North India (CNI) was established in 1972.

During the inter-war period, the YMCA, with its extensive network throughout India, became an important training centre for Indian Protestant leadership. Among the eminent Indian Christians who passed through its ranks were Samuel Satthianadhan, a professor of logic and moral philosophy at Presidency college in Madras, and V. S. Azariah, who became the first Indian secretary of the YMCA and helped establish the National Missionary Council (which changed its name to the 'National Christian Council of India' (NCCI) in 1921). Azariah, the first Indian bishop of the Anglican church, was among the most noteworthy figures of the early twentieth-century church. His career illustrates the complex location of Indian Christians at the interstices of local, national and ecumenical developments.[6]

K. T. Paul, a Presbyterian, became secretary of the YMCA after Azariah. Paul established vital links with missionaries toward the formation of

---

5 Bengt Sundkler, *Church of South India: the movement towards union, 1900–1947* (London: Lutterworth Press, 1954), pp. 23–36.
6 See Susan Billington Harper, *In the shadow of the Mahatma: Bishop V. S. Azariah and the travails of Christianity in British India* (Grand Rapids: Eerdmans; Richmond, Surrey: Curzon Press, 2000).

co-operative credit societies for the uplift of the rural poor.[7] Paul, in 1931, was also the Christian delegate to the joint committee of the Houses of Parliament, the agency assigned to address electoral reforms for religious communities. S. K. Datta succeeded Paul as general secretary and eventually became president of the Indian YMCA. Datta served as the Protestant representative at the second round table conference in 1932 in London.

Rising political consciousness, often described in missionary reports as a time of 'awakening' or 'unrest', marked the turn of the twentieth century in India. This climate was shaped to no small extent by the growing outcry for Indian home rule and the response of the British *raj* to nationalist agitation. Into the 1920s and 1930s, Mohandas K. Gandhi led Indians in a campaign of non-violent civil disobedience against British rule. An important aspect of Gandhian nationalism was *swadeshi*, a doctrine of economic, political and cultural self-reliance. Gandhi portrayed Christianity as a foreign import. He criticised missionaries for encouraging 'material' rather than 'spiritual' motives for conversion. He also saw Christian conversion as a process that engendered hostility toward Indian culture, a form of denationalisation.

Protestant elites often responded to the *swadeshi* movement by stressing the need to 'Indianise' Christianity. For some, this involved efforts to make the church more 'Hindu' or Sanskritic in its liturgy, hymnody and architecture. For others, Indianisation called for higher representation of Indians within the ranks of Christian institutions. At a time when the British *raj* itself was implementing policies of devolution, which increased Indian representation within every branch of government, ecumenical circles stressed the need to implement the ideas of the former CMS secretary, Henry Venn. Known today as the father of the 'indigenous church' principle, Venn advocated the rapid transfer of influence and responsibility for church administration into indigenous hands.

In 1938, a group of Indian Protestant intellectuals published *Rethinking Christianity in India*, which among other things took objection to Western denominational distinctions.[8] According to the theologian V. Chakkarai, the south Indian union scheme addressed Western denominational illnesses more than it did Indian realities. Another 'rethinker', P. Chenchiah, contended that debates over church union were steeped in Western ecclesiastical history and irrelevant to the masses of illiterate Indian laypersons far

---

7 H. A. Popely, *K. T. Paul, Christian leader* (Calcutta: Y.M.C.A. Publishing House, 1938), pp. 53–69.
8 G. V. Job, et al., *Rethinking Christianity in India* (Madras: A. N. Sudarisanam, 1938).

removed from that history. Inspired by Neo-Orthodox theological trends in the West, the Rethinking Group downplayed the church as a visible, dogmatic institution, drawing attention instead to its 'inner core' of spirituality that suited the Indian ethos.

Roman Catholics in India shared many of the concerns of Protestants during this period of political unrest, but did everything possible to differentiate themselves from Protestants. During the early twentieth century, print media nurtured among Indian Catholics a growing self-consciousness and sense of public commitment. Catholic newspapers and societies were established to articulate and defend 'Catholic interests' amidst rising Hindu nationalism. Early on, the Catholic Association of South India (also known as the Catholic Indian Association – CIA) served to bring grievances of the Catholic community to the attention of the government. These grievances included matters relating to religious education, the employment of Catholics in government services, the question of communal electorates, and the right to observe various Catholic holidays.

In 1919 the Catholic Truth Society established a branch in Trichinopoly. Its purpose was to define religious and moral positions on various issues and to 'assist Catholics in counteracting prejudices against religion'.[9] In 1930 the Catholic Truth Propagation League added its voice, establishing numerous libraries and reading rooms aimed at promoting a more literate and publicly conscious Catholic laity. As Catholics came to terms with their status as members of a minority community, both within India and within other national contexts, they sought out new ways to exercise influence. Occasionally, activities of the laity sparked conflicts with the hierarchy over the parameters of legitimate social and political involvement. The need for a united Catholic voice on public matters culminated in 1944 in the establishment of the Catholic Bishops' Conference of India (CBCI). Its aim is to 'facilitate common action of the hierarchy' in matters affecting the common interests of Indian Catholics.[10]

Catholic newspapers of the 1920s and 1930s reflected both international and local factors that were shaping Indian Catholic identity. Newspapers were established in order to equip an emerging class of lay scholars, lawyers, MLA's, and other professionals to wield influence on behalf of the Indian Catholic community at large. One purpose of Catholic media was to establish

---

9 *The Catholic laymen's directory of India* (Mangalore: C. J. Varkey, 1933), pp. 48, 164.
10 *The Catholic directory of India for the year of our Lord 1969* (New Delhi: St. Paul Publishers, 1969), p. 6.

a 'Catholic point of view' regarding developments in social, religious and political spheres. In so doing, Catholic media drew lines of distinction between 'us' and 'them'. Common international enemies included socialism, communism, capitalism, Nazism and freemasonry. Domestically, Catholic media occasionally attacked the Neo-Hindu and Self Respect (an anti-Brahmin movement inspired by communism, launched in south India during the 1920s) movements for the falsity of their religious ideas. But by far the greatest enemy created by the Catholic press was Protestantism.

The Bombay *Examiner*, for instance, often criticised Protestant compromises with 'modernism', with Sanskritic religion, and with secular nationhood. Catholic media nurtured an Indian Catholic identity by differentiating Catholicism from both Hinduism and Protestantism. As newspapers upheld Catholicism as the guardian of the one, true, ancient, faith, they chided Anglicans for adopting weak moral positions on birth control, marriage and divorce at the 1930 Lambeth Conference. The Catholic press also cited the *Laymen's report on Christian missions* as an example of Protestant compromises with religious pluralism.[11]

The *Laymen's report*, drafted by a group of American theologians, criticised Christian exclusiveness as a basis for missionary activity and advocated a spirit of co-operation between Christians and adherents of other religious traditions.[12] Protestant missionaries had opposed the report just as much if not more than Catholics. Catholic elites nevertheless portrayed the report as illustrative of a pervasive trend among Protestants toward liberalism. In a similar vein, Catholics criticised Indian Protestants for their tendency to identify themselves with Sanskritic culture, in their efforts to appear 'more Indian'.

Early twentieth-century Catholic media also instructed Catholics on the meaning of 'Catholic Action'. The origins of this policy lay in concerted attempts of the hierarchy to prescribe legitimate parameters for social and religious activities of Catholic laity. Such attempts became particularly significant as Catholics, pressurised by socio-political conditions within various national contexts, explored various political means of improving their lot. As defined by Pope Pius XI, Catholic Action essentially referred to a role to be played by the laity in the apostolic mission of the church, by defending Catholic faith and morals and engaging in social action under the authority

---

11 'Why Protestant missions must fail', *Examiner* 3 December 1932, p. 534.
12 W. E. Hocking, *Rethinking missions: a laymen's inquiry after one hundred years* (New York: Harper & Bros., 1932).

of the hierarchy. Party politics challenged the integrity of Catholic Action by creating a potential conflict between the authority of a given political party and that of the hierarchy. They also raised the likelihood of creating disagreements between Catholics themselves over political issues.

From 1909 on, constitutional reforms were reshaping Indian politics. These reforms admitted greater numbers of Indians to the legislative councils in the provinces and at the centre. They also introduced separate electorates based on religion and caste, which allowed members of a 'minority community' to elect their own representatives to provincial councils. When implemented in south India, these new rules of the game catalysed new forms of political mobilisation. Muslims, non-Brahmins, Christians and other minorities now had to consider how to maximise their influence based on the size of their constituencies and the number of seats assigned to them within provincial councils.

A major issue debated among Christian elites was the policy of separate electorates (whereby Christians would elect their own representatives to legislative assemblies). This debate raised the larger issue of whether Christians should define themselves as an all-India political community as Muslims and Hindus had done. By 1930, it was the conviction of Protestant leaders such as V. S. Azariah, K. T. Paul, V. Chakkarai and S. K. Datta that Christians would best integrate themselves into national life if they did not cast themselves as a separate political entity. Such leaders felt that a separate 'Christian electorate' would further alienate them from national culture and amount to a form of 'compulsory segregation'.[13] Furthermore, it would compromise both the spiritual and the culturally diverse character of the Indian church.

By contrast, Roman Catholic spokespersons such as A. T. Pannirselvam, an attorney, landowner and former district board member from Tanjore, stridently advocated communal electorates in order to secure Catholic interests. To Catholics of his persuasion, communal identities constituted the very fabric of Indian society. Not to participate in the enterprise of group politics was to be marginal to public life.[14] Other Catholic notables, however, were more nationalistic in their outlook. In 1916 Joseph Baptista, a Catholic barrister from Bombay, became president of the Indian Home Rule League. Baptista, a friend of the extremist leader B. G. Tilak, had recommended that Indians use their participation in the First World War as a

---

13 Mallampalli, *Christians and public life*, p. 2.   14 Ibid.

platform on which to demand home rule.[15] Like Baptista, other Bombay Catholics supported Indian nationalism and opposed the policy of separate electorates for Christians.

It was not as if political activism was limited to British India. Within the princely state of Travancore, where large numbers of Syrian Christians resided, a vibrant 'communal' politics emerged. Low-caste Ezhavas agitated for greater numbers of government jobs and higher rates of admission into village and district schools. G. P. Pillai, an English-educated activist from the Nair community, spoke on behalf of the Ezhavas. Pillai also mobilised numerous communities within Travancore to oppose the state's preferential treatment toward Tamil Brahmins, 'outsiders' who had occupied disproportionate numbers of government posts within Travancore. Numerous Christian groups in Travancore formed political organisations to secure their group interests. Among these were the Catholic Congress, the Latin Christian *Mahajana Sabha*, the Kerala Christian Service League, and the South Travancore Indian Christian Association.[16]

During the 1920s and 1930s, constitutional reforms in Sri Lanka drew Christians, to a greater degree than in India, into the political process, even amid a growing Buddhist revival movement. Christians possessed the English education needed for participation in district boards, legislative councils and professional services.[17] Though more prominent at the national than at regional or district levels, Christian representation often exceeded their actual strength in numbers. Gradually, however, Hindu and Buddhist representation in the legislature also increased. A rising group of Sinhala Buddhist propagandists began to insist on reclaiming their 'rightful place' as the majority while curbing the influence of Christian and Tamil minorities. Such protective sentiments would continue after 1948 when Sri Lanka gained its independence. In the interest of reforming an educational system that favoured Christian schools – now seen as 'alien institutions of privilege' – the government nationalised education. This resulted in the steady marginalisation of Christian influence within Sri Lankan society.[18]

15 George Thomas, *Christian Indians and Indian nationalism, 1885–1950: an interpretation in historical and theological perspectives* (Frankfurt: Peter Lang, 1979), p. 160.
16 George Mathew, *Communal road to a secular Kerala* (New Delhi: Concept Publishing Co., 1989), p. 92.
17 S. Arasaratnam, 'Christians of Ceylon and nationalist politics', in G. A. Oddie (ed.), *Religion in south Asia* (New Delhi: Manohar, 1991), p. 238.
18 Ibid., pp. 246–7.

These developments illustrate how integrative processes of the early twentieth century drew Christian communities into dynamic encounter with each other and with representative voices of newly emerging nationalities. For various classes of Christians, the cost of 'belonging' to India was conceived in terms of supporting the nationalist movement, refashioning the church's cultural complexion, or entering the arena of competitive group politics. Regardless of the strategy adopted, Christians were challenged to reconcile their local, regional and national selves with their membership in the universal church.

The church in independent India

Indian independence in 1947 was accompanied by the trauma of partition, the division of the sub-continent into Muslim-majority Pakistan and Hindu-majority India. This event resulted in a massive resettlement of religious communities, an orgy of communal bloodshed and anarchy. Out of this trauma, new understandings of the relationship between religion and nationality were born. Pakistan became an Islamic state and India came to be regarded as a 'secular' one. Secularism in the Indian context, however, did not imply hostility toward religion or a strict separation of church and state, but a commitment to the development of many religions. Jawaharlal Nehru, India's first prime minister, conceived of India as a 'composite nation' consisting of many religions and ethnicities. This diversity, in his view, enriched the nation and partook of a common Indian ethos.[19] Ever since independence, India's Congress Party, headed by Nehru and his descendants, has presented itself as the chief guardian of the country's secular values.

The status of Christians within this new composite nation has from the very outset been coloured by questions concerning national commitment. In spite of their significant institutional presence – an impressive network of schools, hospitals, orphanages and other social services – Christians have numbered less than 3 per cent of the country's total population and have often been treated with suspicion. The bulk of this suspicion has been tied to the issue of conversion. Do Christian institutions channel Western funds for purposes of conversion, or do they strictly serve humanitarian purposes? In spite of constitutional protection of the right to 'profess, practise and propagate' religion (article 25), government officials have scrutinised so-called

19 Jawaharlal Nehru, *Discovery of India* (New Delhi: Oxford University Press, 1985), p. 62.

'proselytising' activities of missionaries among Dalit (formerly called 'untouchable') and tribal peoples.

In April 1954, the government of the north Indian state of Madhya Pradesh announced its intention to sponsor an official inquiry into missionary activities. Bhawani Shankar Niyogi, a retired chief justice, headed the inquiry. Accompanying him was a committee that was almost entirely Hindu. The Niyogi Commission, as it came to be called, investigated the legitimacy of the methods and motives of conversion within Madhya Pradesh, which had long been a centre of Hindu nationalist activity.

The commission reviewed a wide range of published tracts, periodicals and books relating to Christian missions and conducted extensive interviews throughout the state.[20] The commission was met with heated opposition from Catholics who saw the inquiry as a threat to their religious freedom. The two-volume report charged that Christian institutions were in fact using foreign funding and humanitarian services to 'induce' conversion among the poor.[21] Among its recommendations was a constitutional amendment that would restrict religious freedom to Indian citizens and laws that would impose controls upon the methods and motives behind conversion. Since the publication of the report, four states have enacted laws that prohibit conversion by 'force, fraud or inducement'.

Such developments notwithstanding, Christians enjoyed a high degree of religious freedom in India during the Nehruvian era. In fact, for nearly five decades following independence, Roman Catholic, Protestant and Syrian Christian congregations flourished on Indian soil with little or no overt hostility from the government or non-state organisations. Furthermore, as the church hierarchies became more and more Indianised, the church displayed a greater sense of solidarity with other sections of Indian society.

Following the Second Vatican Ecumenical Council (1962–5), Roman Catholics adopted a much more irenic posture toward other religions and placed a stronger emphasis upon the role of the laity in the mission of the church. Liberation Theology provided Indian Catholics with a new framework for addressing the needs of oppressed Dalit and tribal communities. Indian Protestant congregations reflected theological differences between liberal and

---

20 For an excellent discussion of the findings of the Niyogi Commission and other debates on conversion, see Sebastian Kim, *In search of identity: debates on religious conversion in India* (New Delhi: Oxford University Press, 2003), pp. 63–9.

21 See *Report of the Christian Missionary Activities Enquiry Committee, Madhya Pradesh, 1956* (Nagpur: Government of Madhya Pradesh, 1956), vol. I, pp. 96–101. See also vol. II, part A, pp. 80–4.

conservative that are to be found in Western denominations. Bangalore, Chennai, Serampore, Pune and Trivandrum hosted important centres for theological training and ministry. In an effort to free themselves from dependence upon foreign missionary resources, both the CBCI and the NCCI have adopted policies that stress indigenous principles of church growth.

The vast majority of Christians in independent India came from members of Dalit, tribal and other economically backward communities. During the colonial period, Dalits were designated 'untouchables' because they engaged in occupations that made them ritually 'polluted' or unclean. No section of the Indian Christian population has suffered greater degrees of abuse and discrimination than Dalit Christians. Not only has their experience of caste discrimination persisted in their lives as Christians, but their status as Christians has also precluded them from receiving state assistance.[22] To this day, the government of India offers assistance in the form of educational and employment quotas to 'Scheduled Castes' (SCs), but denies such assistance to those Dalits who have converted to Christianity. Having left Hinduism, they no longer qualify for assistance aimed at rectifying the historical abuses of Hinduism.[23]

During the 1980s, the secular, socialist, consensus of the Nehruvian era began to wither. Growing emphasis upon India as a Hindu rather than a secular nation increased prejudice and hostility toward Muslim and Christian minorities. The Hindu nationalist Bharatiya Janata Party (BJP) challenged the nearly fifty-year reign of the Congress Party. Its ideology of *Hindutva* (or 'Hindu-ness'), far from representing a return to tradition, employed technologies of mass media (including state-sponsored television), political propaganda and electioneering, and new sources of wealth generated by India's liberalising economy. The BJP grew in strength by kindling fear of 'the outsider' among the nation's growing Hindu middle class. In December 1992, a coalition of Hindu organisations congregated in the north Indian city of Ayodhya and demolished a famous Muslim structure, the Babri Masjid. They alleged the mosque had been built upon the ruins of a temple to their god, Rama. This event ignited the worst riots between Hindus and Muslims since partition and signalled an imminent threat to India's commitment to secularism.

---

22 Webster, *The Dalit Christians*, offers an excellent account of the plight of Dalit Christians since the late colonial period.

23 The presidential order of 1950, which denies SC status to non-Hindus, was amended twice: In 1956 to include Dalit converts to Sikhism and in 1990 to include Dalit converts to Buddhism. In spite of persistent protest by Dalit Christians, they have to this day been denied SC status. See Mallampalli, *Christians and public life*, chs. VIII and IX.

During the late 1990s, militant Hindu organisations diverted their hostility away from Muslims, their usual targets, and launched a campaign of violence against India's Christian minority. Christian missionaries, they claimed, were using foreign funds to induce the ignorant poor to leave the Hindu fold and convert to Christianity, a 'foreign religion'.

As such tirades against Christians intensified, attacks against church congregations and clergy became more and more extreme. During the late 1990s, Indian news media and human rights groups drew attention to churches being destroyed, nuns assaulted or raped, priests hacked to death, and social relief organisations solemnly warned not to engage in 'conversions'. Such events occurred in places such as Gujarat, Bihar, Orissa and Madhya Pradesh amid allegations of indifference or complicity by state officials. In December 1998, the same year in which the BJP had finally come to power, a spate of attacks against tribal Christians in the Dangs district of the north-western state of Gujarat drew the attention of major political parties and national forums. Rather than sympathising primarily with victims, Prime Minister Atal Behari Vajpayee called for a 'national debate on conversions'.[24]

These attacks reflect the precarious position of Christians within an evolving India. They find themselves situated amid currents of the twenty-first century while still confronting prejudices of the late colonial period. They belong to an era being shaped by satellite television, corporate power, hysteria over cricket, transnational ties to diaspora communities, and an ongoing conflict with Pakistan over Kashmir. But ghosts of the past remain. Having endured centuries of oppression, Christians from Dalit, tribal and other backward communities continue to seek dignity within the church and Indian society at large. They do so as an aggressive campaign to make India 'Hindu' calls the very idea of an 'Indian Christian' into question. While finding their place within a nation in transition, Christians draw upon a very rich and complex heritage.

---

24 Manas Dasgupta, 'Prime minister calls for national debate on conversions', *The Hindu*, 11 January 1999.

24

Christianity in south-east Asia, 1914–2000[1]

JOHN ROXBOROGH

Introduction

In the course of the twentieth century, Christianity in south-east Asia moved out of the passing shadow of Western colonialism to assert itself as a non-Western Asian religion. In cultures that take spirituality for granted and where poverty, social need and religious diversity are daily facts of life, Christians are discovering the antiquity of their history in the region, but are also part of its stories of colonialism, modernisation, nationalism, independence, nation-building and globalisation. Some groups have been persecuted when their faith or ethnic group provided a religious or economic threat. Both colonial rulers and independent nations encouraged Christian mission when it represented education, social skills, development and the pacification of areas where political control was weak. If missionaries and expatriate workers from other cultures often mediated the transmission of Christianity during the colonial era, the long-term development of south-east Asian Christianity fundamentally relates to its ability to connect with personal and community religious needs and social aspirations. A test of its strength in the twenty-first century may also be its ability not only to engage with its own context, but to challenge traditional centres of Christian authority and power around the globe.

---

1 This chapter includes some material previously published in John Roxborogh, 'Südostasien', in Karl Müller and Werner Ustorf (eds.), *Einleitung in die Missionsgeschichte: Tradition, Situation und Dynamik des Christentums* (Stuttgart: Kohlhammer, 1995), pp. 143–58, and John Roxborogh, 'Contextualisation and re-contextualisation: regional patterns in the history of southeast Asian Christianity', *Asia journal of theology* 9:1 (1995), 30–46.

From 1900 to 1990 Christianity in south-east Asia increased from some 10 per cent of the population to over 20 per cent.[2] Estimates for 2000 suggest that the largest numbers were in the Philippines (68 million), Indonesia (28 million), Vietnam (5.9 million) and Myanmar (3.8 million). By then there were an estimated 1.8 million Christians in Malaysia, 1.4 million (though informal sources suggest about half this number) in Thailand, 820,000 in East Timor, 440,000 in Singapore, 120,000 in Cambodia, 113,000 in Laos, and 25,000 in Brunei. The countries with the highest proportion were East Timor (92 per cent) and the Philippines (90 per cent), followed by Indonesia (13 per cent) and Singapore (12 per cent). Myanmar, Malaysia and Vietnam had about 8 per cent, Thailand and Laos 2 per cent, and Cambodia 1 per cent.

As well as being the majority religion of the Philippines, Christianity is often concentrated in particular areas, as in parts of Indonesia where in 1991, in addition to East Timor which was over 90 per cent Catholic, two provincial units were more than 80 per cent Protestant and Catholic, and a quarter of them more than 20 per cent.[3] Christians are over a third of the population in east Malaysia and Christianity is integral to the identity of significant tribal groups including Chin,[4] Karen,[5] and Lahu[6] in Myanmar and northern Thailand, and the Karo Batak in Sumatra,[7] and important to others such as the Tagal in Sabah.[8] Christians are found in significant numbers among the professions in Singapore. Perceptions of what these concentrations represent affect community relationships, but Christians enjoy relative freedom in most of the region except Brunei, Laos, Vietnam and Myanmar. Conflict

---

2 Statistical observations derived from figures in David B. Barrett, *World Christian ency-clopedia*, 2nd edn (New York: Oxford University Press, 2001). On the basis of Barrett's estimates, in 2000 the proportion of Christians among the total population of south-east Asia was 21.3%.

3 Estimates included: Irian Jaya 64% Protestant, 21% Catholic; West Kalimantan 19% Catholic, 9% Protestant; Maluku 4% Catholic, 41% Protestant; north Sulawesi 3% Catholic, 28% Protestant; east Nusa Tenggara 54% Catholic, 28% Protestant. *Religious affiliation by provincial-level unit* (1991 (accessed 23 January 2004)); available from http://www.indonesiaphoto.com/article247.html

4 H. Sakhong Lian, *Religion and politics among the Chin people in Burma (1896–1949)*, Studia missionalia Upsaliensia 80 (Uppsala: Uppsala University, 2000).

5 'Anatomy of a betrayal: the Karens of Burma', ch. 3 in Clive J. Christie, *A modern history of southeast Asia: decolonization, nationalism and separatism* (London: Tauris, 1996), pp. 53–80.

6 Anthony R. Walker, *Merit and the millennium: routine and crisis in the ritual lives of the Lahu people*, Studies in sociology and social anthropology (New Delhi: Hindustan Pub. Corp., 2003).

7 Simon Rae, *Breath becomes the wind: old and new in Karo religion* (Dunedin, NZ: University of Otago Press, 1994).

8 A. Sue Russell, *Conversion, identity, and power: the impact of Christianity on power relationships and social exchanges* (Lanham, MD: University Press of America, 1999).

with some Muslim groups has developed in central Sulawesi and eastern Indonesia since the mid-1990s.

By 1914 the current political map of the region had been largely drawn by the colonial powers: the French in Indo-China (Vietnam, Laos and Cambodia), the Dutch in the Netherlands East Indies (Indonesia), the British in Burma (Myanmar), the Straits Settlements and Malaya, Sarawak, north Borneo (Malaysia and Singapore), and Brunei, and the Americans who followed the Spanish in the Philippines. Although some sense of regional identity can at times be found earlier, and its acceptance is reflected in the formation of the Association of South East Asian Nations in 1967,[9] the term 'south-east Asia' itself only arose during World War II.

Located between India, China and the Pacific, over centuries this main-land, peninsular and island region was influenced by Hinduism, Theravada Buddhism and Islam from India, and Taoism, Confucianism and Mahayana Buddhism from China. Like other cultural flows, Christianity crossed bound-aries of geography, culture, political power and language as it contributed to the commonalities and diversity of the region.

From the sixteenth to the early nineteenth century Malacca provided a regional base for Christian mission, a role which transferred to Singapore from 1819. Trade routes enabled churches, missionaries and colporteurs with Bibles to cross borders scarcely without thinking. Christian groups moved between north-east India and Myanmar; Thailand and south China; and along the Mekong river through Laos, Vietnam and Cambodia. The porous boundary lines across the islands of Borneo and Papua remain transparent to local Christians. Migration from south India and China included Christians as families, clan groups and communities, not just individuals.

Movements of locally initiated mission still ebb and flow across the region today. Missionaries from Malaysia work among slum dwellers in Cambodia. On Sundays Filipino maids flood streets and Catholic services in Singapore and Kuala Lumpur. Indonesian plantation workers in Malaysia are sometimes discovered to include Christians, and missionary-minded Singaporean churches take charge of congregations in Thailand. The Christian Conference of Asia and the Federation of Asian Bishops' Conferences contri-bute to the development of regional relationships and awareness of local cultural and social agendas.

---

9 By 1997 the Association of Southeast Asian Nations, ASEAN, included Brunei Darussalam, Cambodia, Indonesia, Laos, Malaysia, Myanmar, the Philippines, Singapore, Thailand and Vietnam.

Christianity in Asia[10] has often held an uncertain place in historiography understandably preoccupied with nationalism, independence, nation-building and globalisation. It is easily seen as an epiphenomenon, or, if significant, an embarrassment to Westerners and a source of ammunition for nationalists. It appears compromised by European culture and Western ambition, and may be perceived as lacking the apparent authenticities of Islam, Buddhism and primal folk-religion. Nevertheless, the development of local institutions, indigenous leadership and contextual liturgies and theologies provides a parallel to the colonialism to independence story. Christianity as destroyer and preserver of culture is a many-sided discourse. Local initiatives meant people also received and shaped Christian faith for their own reasons,[11] and local cultural and religious values and leadership styles prove resilient.

Christian literature may reflect popular apologetics and devotional concerns, but some sociologists and anthropologists also offer telling analyses of Christianity's place in the complex matrices of social change,[12] including its effect on the role of women and the growth of democratic values. South-east Asian Christians trapped between powerful competing visions of the political and cultural shape of an authentic future, including traditional, nationalist, communist and Western, faced difficult decisions. Biographical studies provide not only testimonies to personal faith and theological formation,[13] but also evidence of leadership, risky political involvement, and sometimes tragic consequences.[14] They show Christians concerned for modernisation, as well as nationalism and independence, and involved in media, tertiary education and the military, as well as the care of the marginalised, drug addicts, child prostitutes, and others the forces of nation-building find difficult to accommodate. These stories can only increase in importance.

10 Scott Sunquist, *A dictionary of Asian Christianity* (Grand Rapids: Eerdmans, 2001).
11 For example, Karel A. Steenbrink, 'The rehabilitation of the indigenous: a survey of recent research on the history of Christianity in Indonesia', *Exchange. Journal of missiological and ecumenical research* 22 (1993), 250–63.
12 For example, Lorraine V. Aragon, *Fields of the Lord: animism, Christian minorities, and state development in Indonesia* (Honolulu: University of Hawai'i Press, 2000). See also Charles F. Keyes, 'Being Protestant Christians in southeast Asian worlds', *Journal of southeast Asian studies* 27 (1996), and other articles from a symposium on Protestants and Tradition in South-east Asia in the same issue of the *Journal of southeast asian studies*.
13 John C. England (ed.), *Asian Christian theologies: a research guide to authors, movements, sources*, vol. II, *Southeast Asia* (Maryknoll, NY: Orbis ISPCK/Claretian Publishers, 2003).
14 For example, Gerry van Klinken, *Minorities, modernity and the emerging nation: Christians in Indonesia, a biographical approach* (Leiden: KITLV Press, 2003); Frances S. Adeney, *Christian women in Indonesia: a narrative study of gender and religion*, *Women and religion* (Syracuse, NY: Syracuse University Press, 2003).

South-east Asia experienced Christianity as Portuguese and Spanish Catholicism from the sixteenth century, then as Dutch Reformed, Anglican, American Baptist and American Methodist, French Catholic, English Presbyterian, German, Swedish and American Lutheran, Australasian Evangelical, and Pentecostal churches in many forms. Pastors came from India and China and, during World War II, from Japan. While not without indigenous movements such as the Cao Dai in Vietnam or indigenous churches such as the Iglesia Ni Christo in the Philippines, it has nothing like their proliferation in Africa, or even the western Pacific. The dynamics of asserting local control, and maintaining traditional religious goals, can nevertheless be seen at work in other ways. Javanese mysticism, Filipino folk spirituality, and Chinese popular religion bring openness to non-material realities, but have difficulty with exclusive claims. Traditional spirits can form the substance of folk Catholicism and their placation the object of unsuspecting Protestant rituals. While syncretism is usually seen as a heresy to be rejected, and may certainly be evidence of a confusion of loyalties, it may also be considered intrinsic to conversion in a real context. South-east Asian Christians are not alone in their uncertainty about the points at which they should be incarnate in their cultures and those at which they should seek to transform and transcend them. It is not always clear whether the interests of the church are best served by continuity with national identity or by a differentiated way of life. Christians are also caught in situations of war and civil unrest over which they may have little control. Many factors precipitate communal conflict, including the globalisation of religiously sanctioned violence, the vulnerability of moderate groups to extremists, weaknesses in political authority, and local tensions which may be ethnic or economic before they become religious.

The cultural and economic globalisation of the 1990s reinforced international music and managerial styles in some churches, particularly Pentecostal, yet south-east Asian Christianity still reflects regional cultural values, including Confucian respect for authority and the family, and local ethnic and cultural diversity. Christian faith for some is a faith of tradition, a mark of identity shared with ancestors through generations, but it is also still perceived as a religion of progress even when progress is now differently defined. In a religious society, the future may not avoid conflict, but it may also depend less on cultural authenticity than on Christianity's sustaining an ability to address the religious needs of its people.

1914–1942: colonial religion, modernisation and nationalism

By 1914 Christianity was a significant presence in south-east Asia, albeit still associated with colonial and other foreign influences. It was the religion of the majority of Filipinos, many Vietnamese, some Chinese, Indian and Western migrants, some tribal groups in Sumatra, Myanmar and East Borneo, and enclaves in Ambon and East Timor. It was the faith of significant families in distinct communities such as the Straits Chinese in Singapore, Melaka and Penang. It was also seen, however inaccurately, as the faith of the British, the Dutch, the French and the Americans as nations. Thailand alone was independent of foreign rule, but there as elsewhere economic and political issues usually outweighed religious if not cultural considerations. Few governments could resist using missionary activity for their own ends when pressed. Colonialism provided an ambiguous umbrella of greed, guilt, exploitation, idealism and obligation. If even at its best its collective personality could not easily avoid being patronising, it also brought social change which was not all bad, and provided windows into a wider and more hopeful world. Many individuals made the interests of the people of south-east Asia their life's work. In its late phase colonialism also provided infrastructures that facilitated communication, movement and mission and a demand for medical and educational services which churches with international contacts were often the only institutions capable of providing. Plantations and shipping companies brought resources that changed the economic face of the region. Garrison churches and military chaplains added to the range of Christians among expatriate workers who contributed to the evolving churches and their place in society.

In the Philippines Spanish rule had produced the only 'Christian' country in Asia, a Catholic vision many Americans after 1898 hoped to turn Protestant. In Indo-China French political interference had provided openings for Catholicism. In the Dutch East Indies the century began with a spiritually and theologically inspired ethical policy determined to atone for brutality and exploitation. The policy facilitated rapid improvements in education, sometimes empowering local churches as a result, but it also bred its own reaction and demise. The British in Myanmar and Malaysia facilitated the presence of denominations and missions from several nationalities. Protestants arrived in the Philippines with the Americans and were gradually admitted to Vietnam. Thailand's Buddhist heartlands were unyieldingly tolerant but permitted Christian work among tribal groups in the north and Muslims in the south.

The Edinburgh Missionary Conference of 1910 had voices from China and India, though not from south-east Asia, but John Mott visited Rangoon and Singapore in 1912 to co-ordinate regional mission plans. His subsequent visits in the region in the 1920s led to the formation of Christian councils in Thailand, the Philippines, Burma and, two decades later, Malaysia.

World War I reduced mission staffing and placed the few German missions in the region into other hands. In the 1920s and 1930s missionary interest rebuilt, though the Depression affected numbers and resources. Questions of co-operation between Protestant groups at least, and the need for positive action to separate church from colonial state and to become less Eurocentric in polity, theology and leadership were felt. Beginnings were made with the ordination of local clergy, but power lay in expatriate hands and institutions. Moves toward comity and union began soon after Protestant missionaries arrived in the Philippines, but the forces of fragmentation were also strong. There were unions in Thailand and the Philippines in the 1930s and the beginnings of co-operation in Malaya. In 1938, apart from Indo-China most countries in south-east Asia were well represented at the Madras meeting of the International Missionary Council. This provided an important forum for ideas about unity and indigenisation, if also a theology that made inter-religious dialogue and open discussion about what was actually involved in indigenisation difficult.

The period of high colonialism prior to World War II was more significant for associating Christianity with education, medicine, economic progress and democratic ideals than for its links with the Western powers that would one day depart, as a few were beginning to foresee. It also demonstrated that, whatever the progress of the faith among those of tribal backgrounds, and Chinese folk-religion, adherents of Islam and Buddhism were much less likely to convert. Missionary experience among members of other world faiths sometimes brought greater understanding and respect, but theological discussion of their place in the purposes of God was soon overtaken by the pressing realities of international conflict. South-east Asia found itself a major theatre of war which provided a shared experience of invasion by another Asian country. The experience also provided its designation and the beginnings of a new sense of identity within Asia and the world.

1942–1975: conflict and independence

The Japanese period of 1942 to 1945 forced issues of local church leadership and independence which had long been talked about but not always acted on.

The churches suffered loss of life, property and records, and Christians shared in the chaos, uncertainty and deprivation of the times. Missionaries left or were interned. Christians in the Japanese administration sometimes encouraged local believers and Japanese clergy were sent to assist. Some church synods and councils were allowed to meet. In Malaya the Chinese Conference of the Methodist Church declared independence from the American mission.

The occupation demonstrated the ability of the churches to survive without European leadership, but the cost was high. The common experience of suffering was chastening and unifying.

The next two decades brought political independence throughout the region. In Indonesia, independence was declared in August 1945, though the Republic was not firmly established until 1950. Christians found themselves on all sides of the struggle between independence movements, federalist pressures, communist groups, and the Dutch who sought to reimpose their rule. In Malaya, the communist 'Emergency' from 1948 delayed independence till 1957. Sabah and Sarawak joined Malaysia in 1963 along with Singapore. Singapore left Malaysia in 1965 to become an independent republic. Brunei's full independence was not realised until 1983. Myanmar became independent in 1948. In Vietnam, nationalist forces declared independence early, but the struggle with the French lasted until 1953–4 when independence was also granted to Laos and Kampuchea. The struggles of West Papua / Irian Jaya, and East Timor, lay in the future.

Where independence involved armed conflict, it was mostly in Indonesia that Christians played an active part, despite some being on the wrong side of the struggle. In Vietnam Christians were not well represented among groups whose nationalism was most clearly developed. Often in this period it was difficult for Christians 'to convince their fellow compatriots that they too were patriots'.[15]

In Malaya racial groups that were finely balanced numerically found some benefit in having outside rulers, but the question now was not if the British would leave, but what then would be the basis of citizenship. Britain miscalculated Malay fears about finding themselves a minority in their own country. Christians in Malaya were Chinese and Indians whose fears were that as migrants or descendants from migrants they would be excluded. Independence was seen as a Malay, and therefore Muslim rather than

15 Thomas C. Fox, *Pentecost in Asia: a new way of being church* (Maryknoll, NY: Orbis, 2002), p. 13.

Christian, issue. China claimed overseas Chinese for its own, and for many Chinese their identity was still rooted in China. Many were uncertain whether or not their residence overseas would be permanent. Even after the communist revolution in China, in the 1950s many south-east Asian Chinese were still coming to terms with where their future lay. This was no less difficult for those who were Christian, many of whose churches had drawn leadership from China. In Malaya and Singapore, and probably elsewhere, they had the added burden that their faith did not easily link them either to their land of residence, or to the country of their ancestors. People spoke of an 'Asian revolution',[16] not just a Chinese one. It was a time of opportunity as churches and missions organised for a different world. Christianity's and the West's perceived 'loss' of China added to the threat, as did conflict in Korea, the partition of Vietnam, the fragility of Burma, and the Emergency in Malaya. The situation in China forced the relocation of funds and missioners overseas and many looked to south-east Asia, including the China Inland Mission, shortly renamed Overseas [from China] Missionary Fellowship. OMF was to have a significant, enduring role in supporting Evangelical movements and theological education in the Philippines, Cambodia, Thailand, Indonesia, Malaysia and Singapore.

By the 1950s, the community nature of much of south-east Asian Christianity was becoming apparent. Christians reflected the concerns of their ethnic dialect and clan communities. The fragility of those communities made it difficult to be far-sighted enough to speak out in support of wider interests, let alone those of people of other faiths. It was among expatriate, rather than indigenous, church leadership in Malaya that religious freedom was a major issue as independence approached.[17] The Malay community did not want a secular state or the possible threat of pressure to convert. Chinese and Indian communities wanted security for their future in the new Malaysia, and needed to acknowledge the needs and sensitivities of Muslims.

The communist victory in China, the experience of the Korean war, the Emergency in Malaya from 1948 to 1960, and the growing conflict in Vietnam made communism a powerful concern throughout the region in the 1950s and 1960s. Although communists were defeated in Malaya, and discredited and suppressed in Indonesia, their victory in Indo-China and their ability to

---

16 Rajah Bhushanam Manikam, *Christianity and the Asian revolution* (Madras: Christian Literature Society, 1955).

17 John Roxborogh, 'Ministry to all the people? The Anglican church in Malaysia', in W. J. Shiels and Diana Wood (eds.), *The ministry: clerical and lay*, Studies in Church History (Oxford: Blackwell, 1989).

exploit social injustice made it difficult for Christians in some situations, as in Malaya and Singapore, to address similar issues, and reinforced sensitivities through to the end of the Cold War and beyond.

During World War II, communist guerrillas in Malaya had been supported by the British. In 1948 they turned against the British with a campaign of terror. The resultant Emergency led to the creation of 'new villages' of resettled rural Chinese and an invitation to ex-China missionaries to work in them. A desire to stop communism in general as well as to deal with the matter in hand motivated some, especially from American agencies, but British missionaries generally were cautious about the terms on which they would come. Nevertheless they did. In the 1950s the greatest influx of missionaries in Malaysian history contributed to church growth and provided a major focus of activity for the council of churches. The diversity of agencies also led to denominational fragmentation.

In Indonesia the Communist Party was active from the 1920s, and even attracted some Christians, but after the failed coup in September 1965 such association become unthinkable. The post-coup turmoil of the late 1960s and the 'New Order' government encouraged religious identification which led to phenomenal church growth. Tribal groups could not opt for animism and frequently chose Protestant or Catholic. Christian conversion was also one way of distancing oneself from the taint of communism. For Chinese, subjected to renewed pressure and the forced assimilation of their culture, Christianity also offered a new identity. In Java evangelistic bands spread revival. Between 1933 and 1971 the proportion of Christians in Indonesia as a whole increased from 2.8 per cent to 7.5 per cent and in central Java the increase was from 0.1 per cent to 2.1 per cent, mostly Javanese not just Chinese.[18]

In Vietnam, Japanese defeat provided the opportunity to declare independence. However, initial Catholic support was overtaken by mistrust, misdeeds, and the French sympathies of many Catholics. At partition in 1954, given the opportunity to migrate north or south, about 1,400,000 Catholics in the north, including 60 per cent of the bishops, 70 per cent of the clergy and 40 per cent of the laity, went south. Those who remained took time to regain credibility through sharing in the suffering as conflict and civil war developed.

In South Vietnam the migrants attracted international Catholic aid, but the regime was doomed. When Saigon fell in April 1975 no local bishop left his

---

18 M. C. Ricklefs, *A history of modern Indonesia since c. 1200* (Basingstoke: Palgrave, 2001), p. 355.

diocese. Catholics have had their difficulties relating to the regime, but not as much as Protestants. Vietnamese communism is changing, and international contact improving, but the human rights and religious freedom issues, especially for minority tribal groups, remain serious.

1975–1989: nation-building and social justice

Political independence intensified questions of ecclesiastical and theological independence and new governments were not slow to restrict or expel overseas church workers. It did not immediately follow from political freedom that churches were in complete charge of their own affairs and free from dependency on outside funding, personnel, or even direction. There were questions of international and local loyalties, but Catholics after Vatican II were active in seeking more positive links between ethnic groups among their members and into their wider communities.[19] In some cases, as with the Anglican church in relationship to Malaysia and Singapore, the parent church was more willing to let go than the local leadership was prepared to be on their own, particularly if it meant having an archbishop from a neighbouring country.

Latin American Liberation Theology inspired contextualisation and an active social agenda, but its communist taint and the differences in context and temperament relative to south-east Asia were important. There was a common experience of poverty and corruption, but, with the exception of the Philippines, Christians were a minority faith in religious societies, not a majority faith in countries where the Catholic church felt threatened by Protestant growth. An immediate need was to establish the means of intra-regional communication. When Paul VI visited Manila in November 1970, Asian bishops got his backing for a Federation of Asian Bishops' Conferences with a collegial focus on ethical, cultural and justice issues. An emphasis on communication rather than power helped navigate local rivalries and Roman sensitivities. Bishops' Institutes for Social Action and for Interreligious Affairs were developed which had the effect of growing regional identity as well as radically updating the leadership's critical understanding of their environment. In Malaysia a 'priestless August'[20] in 1976 was used to work through the implications of *aggiornamento* by entrusting the church to the laity while

---

19 Fox, *Pentecost in Asia*.
20 Maureen K. C. Chew, *The journey of the Catholic church in Malaysia, 1511–1996* (Kuala Lumpur: Catholic Research Centre, 2000), p. 254.

priests and bishops on retreat sought a common mind on the future of the church.

Christianity as a unifying force in racially diverse states is a possibility, but finding ways of expressing that unity remains a challenge. Churches have experimented with various ways of accepting diversity and affirming unity within themselves with language-based conferences, dioceses or congregations. Given that denominational form is foreign in origin it is not surprising that geographical and ethnic identity is often stronger than denominational.

Church union had some early success in Thailand and the Philippines, driven by both theological principles and strategic considerations, but after independence in many places it no longer had much attraction. Although the 'wider ecumenism' of inter-religious dialogue is fruitful in theory, communal sensitivities can make it difficult to realise in practice. The Malaysian government is ambivalent about Christian use of the national language, in part out of a desire to protect Malays from Christian influence. This can, however, also isolate Christians from national life and culture. As violence between Muslim and Christian communities has developed in a number of areas in Indonesia, the parties behind the conflict are not those likely to be available or interested in dialogue.

Important expressions of identity are art and architecture. Thai, Filipino and Balinese Christians appear more comfortable about encouraging the use of local, including regional, art in the service of Christ, but there are some exceptions. In Malaysia what is Malaysian is often perceived as Islamic. If that may or may not create problems for Christians, Muslims in particular usually prefer the lines of demarcation to be clear.

The Christian Conference of Asia (CCA) displays an ethos shaped by the political experiences of South Korea, Taiwan and the Philippines where churches have been in confrontation with their governments over civil rights issues. Their social critique was to an extent vindicated by the scope and success of Filipino Christian support for the overthrow of the Marcos regime in 1986, but is not universally applicable. In Malaysia, Singapore and Indonesia, not to mention Myanmar, Cambodia, Laos and Vietnam, church–state relations have to be more circumspect.

Internal and international ecumenism followed the YMCA and student movements in providing important avenues for developing local leadership and for shifting the balance of overseas church relations towards the more multi-lateral. National councils of churches and their evangelical counterparts have developed as significant organisations in most places, sometimes connected also with Catholics. Their effectiveness is not unrelated to the need to provide a common voice in dealing with governments whose religious sympathies lie elsewhere.

The Association of Theological Education for South East Asia and the Asian Theological Association have by their publications and the process of accreditation of theological schools provided a means for the improvement of standards and local ownership of ministerial formation. Contextual theology is accepted widely across the theological spectrum,[21] but has some way to go at a parish level. While the Protestant Church of Bali successfully related Christian faith to traditional culture, including architecture,[22] the lack of symbolic boundaries with other faiths could prove problematic, and in the 1990s the attractions of Western youth culture often became stronger than that of their historic Balinese traditions.

1990–2000: globalisation and identity

In trade, media culture and religion south-east Asia has been a recipient of the flows of globalisation in the era of colonialism. In the past decade the term has been a vague reference for all that places local cultures under threat. Yet south-east Asian countries and their Christians have also been resistant to those flows. Cultural identity is of enormous importance to south-east Asian governments, and the place of Christianity within that identity is not always secure. The influence of Western culture and its forms of Christianity may be wide, but they do not necessarily run deep. Singapore is indicative of wider patterns. It may appear to have left its rural and animist roots far behind, but its familiarity and congeniality to Western tourists, businesspeople and missionaries is deceptive. Spirit and ancestral shrines in high-technology business premises and the growth of an Asian Pentecostalism[23] are parallel indications of a pervasive supernaturalist worldview. The values of the society are not those of the West. There is also ample south-east Asian evidence that secularisation theses need to talk about the modification of religion in the face of science, modernisation and technology, not its demise.

In less than a century Christianity in south-east Asia doubled in size, took control of its own affairs and destiny, and grew to fiercely maintain an

---

21 England, *Asian Christian theologies*.
22 Douglas G. McKenzie and I. Wayan Mastra, *The mango tree church: the story of the Protestant Christian church in Bali* (Brisbane: Boolarong Publications, 1988).
23 Yung Hwa, 'Endued with power: the Pentecostal-Charismatic renewal and the Asian church in the twenty-first century', *Asian journal of Pentecostal Studies* 6 (2003), 63–82.

orthodox identity with an Asian face. South-east Asian Christian leaders are willing to take on the principalities and powers of the Western churches in areas where they feel the old churches have lost their way. If they are willing to be challenged in return, it may indeed be an indication of the strength of the church in the region, one that now asserts itself as champion of a universal faith.

East Asia

RICHARD FOX YOUNG

Some two-thirds of the way into *A history of Christian missions in China*, Yale historian Kenneth Scott Latourette's great opus of 1929, a work of massive erudition, readers are invited to join the author in a mind's-eye tour of the Christian educational institutions flourishing in China on the eve of World War I. Latourette starts in the south at Canton (Guangzhou) with Lingnan university, an American Presbyterian institution, and works his way to the north, ending with Shantung (Shandong) Christian university in Tsinan (Jinan), a venture involving American and Canadian Presbyterians, English Baptists and Anglicans. Had Latourette been looking ahead to the 1920s, the premier institution of all, Yenching (Yanjing) university in Peking (Beijing), an even bolder ecumenical, multi-national endeavour, could have been included. Latourette's reverie takes up eight pages; as founders are eulogised, expenditures noted, and graduates enumerated, considerable pride is evinced.[1] Christian institutions, in Latourette's view, were the accelerators of far-reaching changes already occurring as the Qing dynasty (1644–1912) receded into antiquity and the 'new' China of the Republican era (1912–49) dawned.

Latourette stops with China; had he gone beyond it to Japan and Korea in 1914, readers would have been treated to a similar panoply of missionary institutions. Japan, two years into the Taisho era (1912–25), had been ushered out of isolation into the frenzy of modernisation in the Meiji era (1868–1912) by networks of Christian schools stretching from Hokkaido to Honshu to Kyushu. Korea, too, already under Japanese occupation (1910), had its own extensive array of missionary institutions, from P'yongyang to Seoul, founded in the final years of the tottering Choson dynasty (1598–1910). Only Taiwan, formerly a Qing province and now a Japanese colony (1895), had no

---

1 Kenneth Scott Latourette, *A history of Christian missions in China* (New York: Russell and Russell, 1929), pp. 627–34.

stellar Christian institutions of higher education; its missionaries, however, were hardly remiss in offering quality education at lower levels. Virtually all such flagship institutions were Protestant; in due course, Catholics would follow suit, impressively. Collectively, Christian schools would go on to become formidable cogs in the machinery of elitist higher education throughout east Asia. Except, of course, in the People's Republic of China (PRC) and the Democratic People's Republic of Korea (DPRK). Their halls, however, remain hallowed to Europeans and North Americans nostalgic for a past when the action in east Asia most worth watching seemed to be occurring in institutions such as these.[2]

Whether China, Japan, Korea and Taiwan were to be 'saved' by Social Gospel projects of which the schools were emblematic, or by traditional change-of-heart evangelistic methods, all such endeavours, in a deep-time perspective, represented only the latest phase of Christianity's involvements with east Asia. In China, Christianity dates back some 1,350 years; in Japan 450; in Taiwan 350; and in Korea 250. Time and again, institutions of all sorts – churches, monasteries, almshouses, hospitals, schools – have flourished and vanished. On the eve of World War I, Christianity's infrastructure was enviably vigorous and already venerable. Institutionally, however, all such structures were dangerously vulnerable; as so often is the case, larger historical events shaped the outcome of Christianity's subsequent development. Those events having been precipitated by Japan's militaristic ambitions, a history of Christianity in east Asia properly starts with Japan before 1945 and ends with Japan after 1945.

Future trends remain unpredictable, but the gradual subsidence of the cataclysmic forces Japan unleashed allows the shape and contour of Christianity in the twentieth century to be discerned in ways that were not so readily apparent to earlier observers. Understandably, Latourette himself was too heavily invested in the missionary endeavour, too affected by the travails of China, to achieve historiographical distance. The problem, however, was primarily conceptual: Christianity, in his view, radiated outward from a Euro-American centre and employed a Western template to replicate itself. It caught his eye most often when it was missionary-initiated.

One must admit – if transmission outweighs appropriation – that much was swept away. In cross-cultural contexts, however, the gospel is not only

---

2 See Deke Erh (ed.), *Hallowed halls: Protestant colleges in old China* (New York: United Board for Christian Higher Education in Asia, 1998), for a collection of 'then and now' photographs documenting the same institutions Latourette extolled (n. 1).

adopted but adapted. What happens on the margins beyond the established churches (schools, etc.) of Euro-American origin is also worth watching. In this perspective, Christianity in east Asia, a complex of diverse forms, was remarkably resilient; it is so today, and robust as well, with the exception of Christianity in the DPRK. Even there, it may perhaps be hardier than statistical evidence suggests. Overall, Christianity in east Asia registered notable, if uneven, statistical gains from 1900 to 2000. In China, the Christian cohort in 1900 was 0.4 per cent and 7.1 per cent in 2000 in the PRC; in Japan, 1 per cent and 2.9 per cent respectively; in Korea, 0.4 per cent (North) and 0.5 per cent (South), compared with 2.1 per cent in today's DPRK and 39.9 per cent in the Republic of Korea (ROK); and in Taiwan under Japanese occupation 0.3 per cent, as opposed to 6.3 per cent in today's Republic of China (ROC).[3]

Japan, Korea and Taiwan before 1945

Taisho era Japanese Christianity, now in its second generation and no longer buoyed by the blandishments of the West, had already weathered storms of criticism over its allegedly unnationalistic tendencies. Slowly but surely, Christianity was being absorbed into the 'body politic' (*kokutai*) by the architects of State Shinto, Japan's emperor-based civil religion. It was, however, a first-generation Protestant, Uchimura Kanzo (1861–1930), who became emblematic of Christian non-conformity. Like many of his contemporaries, Uchimura hailed from the samurai class, Japan's most literate, which had been disenfranchised by Meiji era reforms and was searching for new identities. In the Bible, Uchimura discovered his. An individualist whose beliefs were sharply profiled, Uchimura committed an unpardonable act of *lèse majesté* in 1891 by declining to bow deeply before the scroll of the imperial rescript on education in the elite Tokyo school where he taught. Believing the ritual idolatrous, Uchimura performed a less-than-full bow and thereby tainted all Christians with the stigma of disloyalty.

A debate ensued: 'In effect,' Carol Gluck argues, 'Christians in the early nineties served the ideologues as metaphorical foreigners in whose alien

---

3 David Barrett et al. (eds.), *World Christian encyclopedia* (Oxford: Oxford University Press, 2001), pp. 191 (PRC), 412 (Japan), 558, 682 (DPRK/ROK), 723 (ROC). Needless to say, 'religiometrics' is a controversial science; statistics vary considerably, especially where the PRC is concerned; and definitions of 'conversion' affect the counting of 'Christians', which in east Asia is complicated by the phenomenon of multiple religious affiliation ('adhesion' versus 'conversion').

reflection the silhouette of patriotism emerged.'[4] To prevent seeds of subversion from being broadcast among Japan's youth in mission schools, the state began to monitor religious education. By 1912, the worst seemed to be over; along with Shintoists and Buddhists, Christians were being invited to participate in officially mandated 'Three Religions Conferences' to mobilise religious resources on behalf of Japan's 'Imperial Way'.

The *lèse majesté* incident provoked a process that eventuated in a politically domesticated Christianity; for Uchimura, however, it was a spur to his quest for an authentically 'Japanese' Christianity beyond the pale of the Euro-American churches being established by the more than sixty missionary societies in the country at the time. Although Japanese Christians were attaining a prominence in the established churches (Kagawa Toyohiko, 1888–1960, renowned for his socially engaged faith, was already working in the Kobe slums), Uchimura affords better evidence than many of his contemporaries of how the gospel was being appropriated by reading the Bible – an instrument of inculturation greater than any other – through Japanese eyes.

Though Methodist initially, Uchimura's years in America (including several at Amherst) had brought him into contact with Quakers and Congregationalists. Declaring himself averse to the standard labels – 'I have as much right to call my Christianity Japanese as thousands of Christians in [Kentucky's] Cumberland Valley have the right to call their Christianity by the name of the valley they live in'[5] – Uchimura's particularism became suspect along with his patriotism. Rhetoric like this, however, was *ex post facto*; the movement Uchimura initiated had been called Non-church Christianity since 1901. Though Non-church Christianity nowadays resembles a denomination more than Uchimura might like, it remains essentially a deritualised, desacralised community of studious Bible readers. Until 1945, Uchimura's most ardent disciples were found in the faculty of law at Tokyo Imperial university.

Other Christians, of course, were likewise reading the Bible through Japanese eyes. In contrast to the intellectuality of Non-church Christianity, which emulated European standards of Enlightenment rationality and exemplified a model of 'top-down' inculturation, Japanese who were inculturating Christianity from 'the bottom up' felt more affinity for Japanese

---

4 Carol Gluck, *Japan's modern myths: ideology in the late Meiji period* (Princeton: Princeton University Press, 1985), pp. 134–5.
5 Cited in Mark R. Mullins, *Christianity made in Japan: a study of indigenous movements* (Honolulu: University of Hawai'i Press, 1998), p. 37.

folk-religiosity and Pentecostalism, which had been growing in the interstices between the established churches since the early 1900s. Influences like these, no matter how contrastive, were also congruent. While Christians such as Uchimura, imbued with Bushido (samurai) traditions, were prejudiced against vernacular piety, others were predisposed toward it and saw in the Bible a world like their own, populated by spirits, malign, benign and (between the two) ancestral.

One such Christian was Murai Jun (1897–1962). Raised in one of the established churches and involved for a time with the Japan mission of the Assemblies of God, Murai founded a community of his own in 1937, the Spirit of Jesus church, to address his followers' soteriological anxieties about the ancestors by developing a rite of vicarious baptism. Instead of turning from the ancestors, as the more prevalent forms of Christianity did, Murai turned the ancestors toward Christ. Although never large, such churches prolifer-ated; by 1945, five more had been initiated.[6]

For their part, Euro-American churches were being turned, implacably, toward the emperor; even though Japanese were filling positions of authority within them, they remained un-Japanese in their structures. Up to 1945, this was the dominant fact of Christian life. After the transition from Taisho to Showa (1926–89; the reign of Hirohito), the rites of civil religion became especially onerous. The religion of politics and the politics of religion became so amorphous that even the National Christian Council (1922) proved an ineffectual buffer between its members and the organs of State Shinto. Christians felt constrained; protest, however, was sporadic.

In 1932, when Catholic students at Tokyo's Sophia university declined to participate in compulsory observances on behalf of the war dead at Yasukuni Shrine, old suspicions about Christian disloyalty were reignited. For some Catholics, however, qualms of conscience were allayed in 1936 when the Vatican declared State Shinto a civil affair. Such resistance as Protestants evinced was tepid compared with that of German Confessing Church Christians; invidious, post-war comparisons with Nazi Party 'Deutsche Christen' have been unavoidable. With the amalgamation of thirty-four previously autonomous denominations into the United Church of Christ in Japan (UCCJ) by government dictate in 1940–1, the process of political domestication became complete.

---

6 On all varieties of Japanese-initiated Christianity before and after 1945, Mullins, ibid., is unsurpassed.

Likewise for Korea and Taiwan, the dominant fact of Christian life up to 1945 was the same unrelenting pressure that turned Japan's churches into unofficial state auxiliaries (Japan's Holiness and Adventist churches, Jehovah's Witnesses, and Non-church Christianity were less compliant). In virtually every other respect, the dynamics of Christian dissent in the colonies differed diametrically from Japan. Since Korea and Taiwan were the victims of odious occupation policies, which included compulsory participation in Shrine Shinto and restrictions on the vernaculars (worship had to be conducted in Japanese), Christians who voiced the people's aspirations for independence and took a public stand for it were perceived as patriots. While Christian nationalism did not precipitate Christianity's post-war growth, which was notably brisk in the ROK, neither was it a hindrance that many of the most resolute resisters came from the established churches of Euro-American origin.

More often than not, the resisting churches were Protestant, even though it was a Catholic nationalist, An Chung-gun (1879–1910), who assassinated Ito Hirobumi (1909), architect of Korea's annexation, shouting '"Long live Korea" in the language of his church – Latin' as he fired the shot.[7] Catholicism in Korea, still burdened with a foreign hierarchy and still largely a rural phenomenon, was reluctant to engage Japan in open confrontation, having endured harrowing domestic persecution under the late Choson dynasty. Protestantism, almost from its inception in the 1880s more urban, more self-supporting, more self-governing, and more self-propagating than Catholicism, was always until the post-war era more active in the burgeoning movement of Korean nationalism.

Protestantism's Koreanisation began with the Great Awakening of 1907 in P'yongyang. The revival was one that stirred the churches institutionally as well as spiritually; withdrawal from worldly affairs had no part in it. That same year, Presbyterians united; virtually all denominations, whether Presbyterian or Methodist or otherwise, were quick to become financially independent of foreign benefactors and – more gradually – of missionary oversight. As Korean nationalism gained momentum, fuelled by the churches' dynamism, Euro-American missionary leaders remained sympathetic by-standers; pro-Japanese factions could even be found among them.

---

7 Don Baker, 'From pottery to politics: the transformation of Korean Catholicism', in Lewis R. Lancaster and Richard K. Payne (eds.), *Religion and society in contemporary Korea* Korea research monograph 24 (Berkeley and Los Angeles: University of California Press, 1997), pp. 144–5.

When Woodrow Wilson's Declaration of Self-Determination (1918) encouraged colonised peoples the world over to anticipate sweeping global changes, thirty-three Korean activists, almost half of them Protestant, gathered in Seoul in 1919 to declare publicly their determination to win Korea's release from Japanese bondage. Retribution was swift. Despite the peaceful character of the demonstrations, large numbers of Protestants (and a few Catholics) were arrested, tried and imprisoned. Such an alarming revelation of anti-occupation sentiment forced Japan to temporarily ameliorate its more dehumanising policies. In the 1930s, however, when military conflict loomed on the horizon, colonial authorities clamped down again and the rites of State Shinto were stridently enforced. Pressure on Christian schools increased incrementally: 'There must be a bow toward the East,' wrote one missionary, 'toward the Emperor's palace in Tokyo.'

> Then the school was ordered to bow ... toward the [Ise] Shrine [dedicated to Amaterasu, progenitrix of the Imperial clan]. Then the school was ordered to attend a ceremony at the Shrine [Yasukuni's colonial counterpart in Seoul], but standing on a lower terrace than the terrace of the main Shrine itself. Then they were ordered to stand in front of the actual Shrine, [etc., etc.][8]

Resistance came at formidable cost; Presbyterians balked but capitulated – the last to do so – in 1938 at their general assembly, orchestrated by the Japanese. In a futile gesture of denial in the face of imminent defeat, all Korean and Taiwanese denominations were absorbed into the United Church of Christ in Japan, just months before World War II ended.

China before 1945–9

'The missionaries came as spiritual reformers,' John King Fairbank observed, 'soon found that material improvements were equally necessary, and in the end helped to foment the great revolution. Yet as foreigners, they could take no part in it, much less bring it to a finish. Instead, it finished them.'[9] Although astute, the observation deflects attention from the indigenous appropriation of the gospel to its missionary transmission. If Euro-American Christianity was the genuine article, all was lost on 1 October 1949 when Mao Zedong founded the PRC. Since the 1980s, however, an out-of-sight,

---

8 Allen D. Clark, *History of the Korean church* (New York: Friendship Press, 1961), p. 197.
9 John K. Fairbank (ed.), *The missionary enterprise in China and America* (Cambridge, MA: Harvard University Press, 1974), p. 2.

Chinese-initiated, Christianity has come to light, which remained alive throughout the chaotic years of the early communist era. Fairbank was certainly right in one respect: Christian missions of the 'Social Gospel' variety did fare poorly in revolutionary China. To appreciate how right he was, the changes initiated by Sun Yat-sen (Sun Zhongshan; 1866–1925) and others who toppled the Qing dynasty and inaugurated the Republic need to be tracked.

Although tumultuous, this was initially a period of promise for the churches. Sun, who had converted to Christianity while in exile and was given to exhorting the Chinese people to embrace *Shangdi* (one of God's Chinese names), enshrined the principle of religious liberty in the Republican constitution. Under the Qing, such liberty had always been grudgingly conceded. That guarantee was soon rescinded when Sun was ousted by Yuan Shikai (1859–1916), a former Qing official who declared himself emperor in 1916 and attempted to reconstitute Confucianism as the state religion. Yuan's conduct provoked country-wide outrage, in part because Christian education had eroded the 'Confucian consensus' that enabled imperial China to survive for more than two millennia.

Whatever false hope lulled the Euro-American establishment into thinking China was being 'saved' by Christian institutions was laid to rest by a demonstration on 4 May 1919 when students, many of them educated by missionaries, protested in Beijing's Tiananmen square against the Versailles treaty, which awarded German enclaves in Shandong to Japan. Almost overnight, provocations like this, also perpetrated by Western nations, transformed China's vast, urban, student sub-culture into a nationalist movement opposed to the revival of Confucianism, which was deemed impotent in the face of foreign aggression. Proponents of the ensuing New Culture movement (1919–27) envisioned a 'new' China different from the 'old'. In 1921–2, a recrudescence of anti-Christian sentiment was evident again; this time round, nationalist intellectuals argued, against missionary claims to the contrary, that China did not need to be Christian to be 'new'.

In this climate, to consort with the Euro-American establishment was to put a blot on one's patriotism; being a Christian became a liability, not an asset (unlike in Korea), even though that establishment was undergoing considerable change. In 1922, for instance, the National Christian Council was created; in 1927, several Protestant denominations united to form the sizeable Church of Christ in China; around the same time, Catholics had their first Chinese bishops. The helm, however, was not surrendered easily; most missionaries remained paternalistic – and in charge. Whether encouraged by their Euro-American counterparts or not, Chinese theologians of the renowned institutions dedicated themselves to the task of inculturation. Creative scholarship was being done in a Chinese way in response to Chinese criticism of Christianity's un-Chinese character.

A founder of Beijing's Furen university, Joseph Ma (Ma Xiangbo; 1840–1939), who hailed from a Catholic family of the seventeenth century, lobbied magisterially for a fundamental rapport between Christianity and Confucianism. A Protestant theologian, Wu Leichuan (1870–1944) of Yanjing, likewise found an affinity between Jesus and the sages of antiquity. More so than Ma, Wu dialogued with socialists. For this he was severely criticised by T. C. Chao (Zhao Zichen; 1888–1979), a Yanjing colleague said to be China's foremost theologian. While each had the integrity to swim against the current, the inculturational model they exemplified was the 'top-down' variety, rather more backward- than forward-looking.

As in Japan, inculturation from 'the bottom up' occurred outside the churches of Euro-American origin. While anti-clerical Chinese disillusioned with missionary paternalism sometimes founded their own congregations out of pique, and while principled conservatives like Wang Mingdao (1900–91) of Beijing's Christian Tabernacle sometimes turned their backs on the established churches because of their Social Gospel theologies, the prevalent form of independency was Chinese-initiated Christianity. China, too, had individuals predisposed toward the vernacular traditions of popular piety who read the Bible through Chinese eyes. It did not hurt, of course, that their understanding of it had been influenced by Pentecostalists, China's less memorialised missionaries (active in the country since the early 1900s). Their orientation to the spirit world concurred with that of China's as neatly as with Japan's.

Chinese-initiated Christianity is well represented by a community of obscure origins, the True Jesus church, founded by a former Presbyterian, Zhang Bin of Shandong. Around 1916, Zhang was instructed in a revelation to worship on the sabbath and separate himself from Christians who didn't. Although an Adventist hybrid, the True Jesus church was predominantly Pentecostal; the 'True Jesus' of its name was the Jesus of 'Unitarian' Pentecostalism. While the usual signs of Spirit-filled experience were evident in Zhang's community (tongues, miracles, exorcisms), the template it used to replicate itself included distinctively Chinese innovations: face-down, full-immersion baptism and sacramental foot-washing. By 1919, True Jesus evangelists were operating beyond Shandong; in the 1920s they reached Japan where Murai Jun came into contact with them. In the 900+ pages of Latourette's monumental history the True Jesus church is mentioned once; being more attuned to the gospel's transmission than its appropriation,

Latourette brushed it off as an aberration: 'it [has] begun to wane'. Still, by 1945, Chinese-initiated Christianity collectively accounted for a quarter of China's one million Protestants.[10]

China after 1945–9

After Sun's death (1925), Euro-American Christianity continued to pin its hopes on the Guomindang (GMD). Sun's successor, Chiang Kai-shek (Jiang Jieshi; 1888–1975) had declared himself a Methodist in 1930; even though the GMD had an anti-foreign, anti-Christian 'left wing', the Chinese Communist Party (CCP) looked vastly worse. China's Christians, dislocated and disheartened by relentless Japanese military incursions, doggedly did their best to 'save' China through dialogue between the warring factions of the much-frayed GMD/CCP United Front. The YMCA, arguably the most Chinese of all Christian institutions, campaigned for a national consensus on peace. Conditions, however, were not conducive to Christian intervention.

Guo Moruo (1892–1978), a disillusioned Christian writer who allied himself with the CCP, captured the ethos of opposition in a satirical story about a political commissar invited to address a YMCA rally in Hankou, recently liberated from a warlord in a crucial victory for the United Front's Northern Expedition (1926–7). The commissar, who is the narrator, recalls the event, which began with a bombastic speech by the YMCA's Chinese director:

> The Northern Expedition . . . has defeated the northern warlords. And whose disciples are the Northern Expedition's commanders? They are the disciples of Sun Yatsen. Whose disciple was he? He was the disciple of Our Lord Jesus. Thus it is that all who believe in Our Lord Jesus win final victory; the victory of the Northern Expedition is his victory.

The commissar, who knew his Bible, tells how he responded:

> We Chinese were really more Christian than any Christians. It was harder for a rich man to enter the kingdom of heaven than for a camel to go through the eye of a needle. How did we Chinese make out on this? We had got rid of all our earthly wealth long ago . . . We Chinese were now as thin as a thread, and even if the heavenly gates were no bigger than the eye of a needle, we were fully qualified for entry.

10 On all forms of Chinese-initiated Christianity before and after 1945, the work of Daniel H. Bays is unsurpassed. On the True Jesus church, see 'Indigenous Protestant churches in China, 1900–1937: a Pentecostal case study', in Steven Kaplan (ed.), *Indigenous responses to Western Christianity* (New York: New York University Press, 1995), pp. 124–43.

Then to the YMCA's director:

> I said that as a Chinese and a believer in Christianity he was a double
> Christian and possibly more Christian than Christ. However, I was sorry
> for him for being stuck in Hankow like Jesus nailed to the cross, unable to use
> his divine powers. He should really have gone to London, Paris, New York,
> or Tokyo to make those camels shrink till they were thin enough to go
> through the needle's eye.[11]

In his own way, Guo was saying what Fairbank said: Euro-American
Christianity didn't finish the revolution, the revolution finished it.

Ironically, it was a YMCA official, Y. T. Wu (Wu Yaozong; 1893–1979), who
emerged in the aftermath of Japan's defeat to become the foremost proponent of Chinese Christianity's alignment with the CCP. As in Guo Moruo's
story, one hears in Wu's 'Christian Manifesto' of 1950, approved in advance
by Premier Zhou Enlai, the mantra of deforeignisation. With this declaration,
an umbrella organisation called the Three Self Patriotic movement (TSPM)
came into existence. Along with the resurrected China Christian Council
(CCC), actually a complex of councils from the local to the national, the
TSPM/CCC assumed the position it still holds as a semi-autonomous agency
that regulates the affairs of China's Protestants in accordance with the
principles of self-support, self-government and self-propagation. Though
hardly new to Protestants, who held them in high regard before the CCP
even existed, such principles encapsulate the patriotism the TSPM/CCC
was designed to engender among Christians whose Euro-American denominational identity had become a liability. Although its leaders nowadays refer
to the TSPM/CCC as a 'church in formation', one also hears of 'post-
denominationalism' (referring to the fact that members come from a broad
but defunct denominational spectrum).

In the 1952–6 period, however, the TSPM/CCC idiom was more of being a
'movement' than a 'church'. Theological conservatives who were constitu-
tionally separatist – Wang Mingdao being the prime example, even though he
was already famously anti-foreign in the early Republican era – were pressurised to subordinate themselves to TSPM/CCC authority. Many who
resisted suffered humiliation and imprisonment. Wang, for one, capitulated
(1956), confessing himself a counter-revolutionary, and then abruptly
recanted. Though acclaimed for his integrity by the TSPM/CCC's numerous

11 Kuo Mo-jo [Guo Moruo], 'Double Performance', trans. W. J. F. Jenner and Gladys
Yang, in W. J. F. Jenner (ed.), *Modern Chinese short stories* (Oxford: Oxford University
Press, 1936), pp. 68–74.

international critics, Wang was again imprisoned (1959–79). Like many Chinese institutions during the Cultural revolution and its aftermath (1966–76), the TSPM/CCC hardly functioned; even Y. T. Wu, publicly humiliated by the Red Guards, fell into disrepute.

Following the Cold War thaw, the rise to power of reformer Deng Xiaoping and other dramatic developments of the 1970s, the TSPM/CCC revitalised itself in the early 1980s under K. H. Ting (Ding Guangxun; b. 1915). As of 2002, the TSPM/CCC claimed 15 million members (a twenty-fold increase from 1949). Outside the TSPM/CCC umbrella one finds the unofficial, Chinese-initiated, 'house church' population, which first began to increase phenomenally in the 1980s in rural areas where collective farming was discontinued; later, it spread to regions where foreign investment was particularly heavy. How one correlates the growth in 'house church' Protestantism to socio-economic change remains unclear, as does the population affected, estimated to exceed that of the TSPM/CCC by several magnitudes (without official figures, all estimates remain unverifiable). Relations between the two Protestantisms can be adversarial because the TSPM/CCC considers itself responsible for identifying 'heresies' that might provoke social unrest; relations, however, can also be symbiotic because 'house churches' that grow need TSPM/CCC endorsement to acquire better facilities. TSPM/CCC is thus both an efferent and afferent force in the life of Chinese Protestants.

While the TSPM/CCC nowadays advocates more boldly for its members' religious rights and those of the 'house churches' being drawn toward it, its attitude toward churches and sectarian associations considered 'deviant' can be inquisitorial. In 2002, for instance, TSPM/CCC spokespersons travelled abroad to explain the government's crackdown on the religiously eclectic Falun Gong community. When the TSPM/CCC functions as an unofficial prosecutor – even though the TSPM/CCC is itself the representative of a minority religion – and refuses to defend the rights of another minority religion, questions naturally arise. And, when 'deviance' is defined more politically than theologically – as, for instance, in being anti-TSPM/CCC – one wonders whether the 'new' China really differs from the 'old'. The Qing and earlier dynasties likewise arrogated the power to regulate religion – and suppress it. In Hong Kong, since 1997 a special administrative territory of the PRC, Protestants voice anxiety, wondering whether Christian schools will be nationalised and whether denominational identities will be submerged in the post-denominational TSPM/CCC ethos.

The Catholic experience in China after Mao established the PRC was similar to the Protestant in that relentless pressure was applied to the church to turn it toward the state, the ultimate arbiter of religious affairs. The similarities, however, stop there. In the early 1950s, a Catholic counterpart to the TSPM/CCC was created, the Chinese Patriotic Association (CPA), which consecrates bishops of its own. On grounds of canon law, the Vatican staunchly opposes the CPA. 'Self-propagation', which might imply autonomy in doctrine, has been an especially prickly issue. Worse yet, bishops consecrated without Vatican approval are technically schismatics, being out of communion with Rome. This was the position assumed by Pope Pius XII in the 1952 encyclical, *Ad Sinarum gentes*; since then, the Vatican has never wavered. As a result, Catholics are divided into pro-Rome, pro-CCP factions.

While a number of CCP-approved Chinese bishops are reported to be secretly reconciled with Rome, that remains uncertain; likewise uncertain is the exact number of bishops detained for being pro-Rome, anywhere from thirty to fifty in 2002. That same year, the Vatican estimated that two-thirds of China's 12 million Catholics worship 'underground'. When the Tiananmen pro-democracy demonstrations of 1989 were crushed, Catholics came under rigorous scrutiny, the role of religion in the collapse of the Soviet bloc being to the CCP only too evident. One of the most recent altercations occurred in 2000 when the Vatican canonised 120 Chinese martyrs, who, in Beijing's view, were 'imperialist lackeys'. Relations remain strained, despite a public admission by Pope John Paul II in 2001, when the Jesuit Matteo Ricci's arrival in Beijing in 1601 was being commemorated, that the church had made 'mistakes' in China. When Chinese Catholicism does emerge from the shadows of that history, in all likelihood it will be a non-vernacular Catholicism; its bishops, some of them imprisoned before Vatican II, will have considerable catching up to do. When that day will arrive – and how – remains unpredictable, given the Vatican's oppositional stance toward the CPA, which the CCP perceives as a frontal attack upon its hegemonic prerogatives. As in Hong Kong, Macanese Catholics, now under PRC jurisdiction after 450 years of Portuguese administration, likewise wonder whether the CPA model is the one to which they too will eventually be conformed.

Taiwan, Korea and Japan after 1945

In 1949, when the defeat of Chiang Kai-shek's GMD induced an exodus of mainlanders, including Protestants and Catholics, to seek refuge in Taiwan, the island's churches were better prepared to handle the influx institutionally than linguistically. The Taiwan Presbyterian church (TPC), founded by

British and Canadian missionaries before the 1895 annexation and always thereafter the island's largest denomination, had benefited from Japanese occupation restrictions, which prevented the entry of other missionaries until the mid-1920s. More significantly, by 1945 the TPC had overcome the paternalism that plagued Presbyterianism on the mainland and was well on its way to achieving the 'Three Self' success formula. TPC congregations mainly consisted of Taiwanese on the plains and ethnolinguistic (tribal) peoples on the mountains.

At a time when mainlander refugees were in dire need of medical services and education, the TPC's infrastructure was already there. Presbyterians consequently experienced considerable growth, only to reach a plateau in the 1960s when Taiwan's economy picked up speed and mainlanders began to patronise state institutions, perceived as being more accessible to the general public. That public being more mixed than before 1945–9 and now dominated linguistically by Mandarin-speakers, the TPC found itself in competition with denominations that shifted from the mainland to Taiwan. In particular, the American Southern Baptist Convention grew to become a sizeable rival, along with a plethora of smaller churches serviced by missionaries deported from the PRC.

'[The TPC] began as a mission-connected body,' writes Murray Rubinstein, 'and, after the war, began to assume the difficult role of a spiritual conscience confronting tyranny, as the voice of the oppressed Taiwanese minority in a GMD- and mainlander-governed Taiwan.'[12] Tensions between the TPC and the GMD became acute in 1966 when the World Council of Churches called for the PRC's admission to the United Nations. The TPC being committed to open dialogue on the reunification issue, relations again worsened in 1979 when the United States adopted its 'one China' doctrine, to which the GMD was opposed.

In contrast to the TPC, the Catholic church, which is able in the ROC to be the institution it never could be in the PRC – a church in full communion with Rome – has been, and is, more pro-GMD. Primarily mainlander and Mandarin-speaking, the church is not yet Taiwanese in language or composition. Though the church in Taiwan is notable for being the one most directly affected by the Vatican's 1939 rescission of the ban on ancestral practices (a result of the early eighteenth-century 'Chinese Rites' controversy), 'top-down' inculturational innovations (simulacra for Confucian funerary rituals, etc.)

---

12 Murray A. Rubinstein, *The Protestant community of modern Taiwan: mission, seminary, and church* (Armonk, NY and London: M. E. Sharpe, 1991), p. 154.

have proved less effective than the 'bottom-up' innovations of the True Jesus church. Now Taiwan's third-largest Protestant denomination, the True Jesus church flourishes on the island – despite Latourette's prediction – and oversees its worldwide mission activities from Taichung.

In Korea, the occupation-initiated United Church of Christ immediately dissolved upon Japan's surrender in 1945. Protestant churches, reconstituted as Presbyterian or Methodist (the prevalent pre-war denominations), sprang back to life but with less amity than before: accusations of complicity in Shrine Shinto were hurled back and forth, some pastors having collaborated when others resisted. Controversy simmered, Christians divided, and the Koryu church separated from the Presbyterians (1951), followed by others with grievances over 'liberalism'. While other denominations likewise splintered, none was so dominated by independency as the Presbyterian, which is today a convoluted cluster of four major blocs and dozens of contending factions.

In the aftermath of war, however, political divisions over-rode the others. United for centuries and culturally homogenous, Korea was bifurcated in 1945 into separate spheres of influence, Soviet and American, along the 38th parallel, pending the outcome of UN-mandated elections. In the North, Christians agitated for political liberalisation; all such activism was thwarted by Kim Il Sung's single-party ideology. Either out of rectitude or rigidity, Christians boycotted the first elections, scheduled for a Sunday in 1946. Coercion followed provocation; pastors were pressurised to join a federation of Protestants not unlike China's TSPM/CCC. Non-conformists fled to the South after Syngman Rhee (Yi Sungman) was elected president of the ROK and Kim Il Sung the premier of the PDRK, both in 1948.

When the Korean war broke out in 1950, a great exodus commenced, shifting Christianity's centre of gravity, Protestant and Catholic, from P'yongyang in the North, Korea's 'old' Jerusalem, to Seoul in the South, the 'new' Jerusalem. Massive migration, coupled with dramatic post-war growth, produced astonishing demographic results: the ratio of Christians to other Koreans in 2000 was perhaps as high as 1·2.5, all but a negligible percentage below the 38th parallel. Being the 'new' Jerusalem has entailed a 'burden' upon Christians for the DPRK and the world at large, much of which has yet to witness phenomenal growth like Korea's. Koreans have long been missionally active (starting with Manchuria in the 1910s), so much so that the worldwide evangelistic projects of some churches manifest a 'chosen people' syndrome. And while the Christianity of the DPRK is statistically moribund, it had already moved to the South where it replicated itself according to a P'yongyang template. It is a theologically conservative, staunchly anti-communist

Christianity that flourishes in congregations with memories of a past glory and a hope that the glory might still return with reunification.

In the DPRK itself, Christianity is largely vestigial; in the 1980s, however, inter-church contact was re-established with the help of European interme-diaries. Since then, several Catholic and Protestant 'showcase' churches have been opened in P'yongyang. A 'house church' movement also exists, but on a smaller scale than China's (statistical estimates are sheer guesswork). Premier Kim Jong Il's reactivation of nuclear armaments projects in 2003, an action that provoked international criticism, may mean that contact with DPRK Christians may become increasingly difficult.

To many Christians, a more immediate threat than the DPRK was the ROK itself. Even though Christian political participation in the First Republic (1948–60) was prominent and more than a few Protestants (and some Catholics) held high office, the period beginning in 1948 with Syngman Rhee (a Methodist) and ending in 1992 with Roh Tae Woo (No T'ae-u) was one of severe constraint on Christian political dissent. Such dissent had a corollary in Minjung, a 'bottom-up' theology which emerged from the people's experience of dislocation, exploitation and oppression.

These years also coincided with the emergence of a revitalised Catholicism, which grew at a rate only slightly slower than Protestantism's. The combi-nation of a shift in Catholicism's centre of gravity, the migration of laity from the countryside to urban centres, and Koreanisation of the hierarchy brought the church out of isolation and made it a more dynamic force in the 1960s than it had been under Euro-American bishops. Korea's Catholicism is a Vatican II Catholicism, vernacular and politically interventionist. Seoul's city-centre Myongdong cathedral became the symbol of resistance and the scene of student-led demonstrations, which rocked regime after regime until Kim Young Sam, a former dissident, was elected in 1992, ending nearly fifty years of authoritarian rule.

Outside the established churches, Korean-initiated Christianity burgeoned into a likewise formidable array of independent Pentecostal churches, denominations in and of themselves because of sheer size. While Seoul's Yoido Full Gospel, a mega-church of gargantuan proportions (900,000+) with 700 ministers (many of whom are women) and 50,000 neighbourhood 'cells' in 2000, may not be typical, some of its emphases are emblematic. Its most distinctive features are the same ones that appear elsewhere in east Asia whenever the Bible is read through a Pentecostal lens and without Euro-American blinkers. To Yoido's founder, Paul Yonggi Cho, the biblical rationale for traditional ancestral rites (*chesa*) is the commandment to honour one's parents. While rationales of that sort have been around since Matteo Ricci, Christian simulacra have been considerably de-Confucianised; they are conducted, for instance, only on behalf of one's immediate progenitors. While such rituals, technically speaking, are not 'ancestral' (if they were, earlier generations would be included), the 'bottom-up' model of inculturation has been widely applied in all churches, Korean-initiated and Euro-American. Mourning rituals and food offerings on memorial days are but a few of the more widespread simulacra.

Inculturational innovations go beyond 'great tradition' Confucianism to include the 'little tradition' of vernacular folk-religion, which flourishes in the 'prayer mountain' (*kidowan*) phenomenon. At these retreat centres, which many churches have, the 'new' maladies of Korean life, which resemble the 'old' in many respects, are treated prayerfully by modern Christian 'shamans' (*shimnyong puhunghoe*) who see to the spiritual needs and physical ills of urban parishioners. Instead of directly voicing the grievances of the dead against the living, Christian 'shamans' are perceived as mediums of the Holy Spirit. More than any other 'bottom-up' variety of inculturated Christianity, this one readily transcends cultural boundaries and moves beyond Korea to east Asia more widely.

While Japan is a neighbour affected by imported 'shamanised' Christianity and some of the action most worth watching is Korean-initiated, established churches have not been slack in exorcising the ghosts of 'Imperial Way' Christianity. Upon Japan's surrender, the UCCJ fragmented but did not dissolve; Anglicans, Baptists and Lutherans were among those who left, for the same reasons that Korean Protestants left the UCCJ's colonial counterpart. Unlike in Korea, however, Presbyterians, Congregationalists and others remained, believing the UCCJ had been providentially blessed with a unity that no amount of ecumenical goodwill would ever achieve. Under the Allied occupation (1945–52), 'worshipping the West' was again evident as State Shinto was disestablished and the Showa emperor (Hirohito) desacralised. The UCCJ along with all churches enjoyed a degree of growth they have not seen since, the present rate being lacklustre compared with Korea's.

During the frenetic period of post-war reconstruction, the NCCJ quietly reflected on its complicity in violating the religious rights of conquered peoples; in 1967, its Confession of War Responsibility was announced. The Anglican Church of Japan followed suit in 1996: '[The church] confesses to God and apologizes to the people in Asia and the Pacific that we did not admit our fault immediately after the end of the war, were unaware of our responsibility for the past 50 years, and have not actively called for reconciliation and compensation until today.'[13] State-initiated confessions, unlike the churches', appear equivocal and inept.

In post-war Japan, Christianity has become notably contrarian; its most emblematic 'grassroots' non-conformist is the NCCJ's Nakaya Yasuko, a rural parishioner. Nakaya discovered that her husband, a member of the self-defence forces who died in an accident in 1968, had been posthumously apotheosised in a shrine for the war dead by state officials without her permission, which she, as a Christian, would have withheld. Filing suit in 1973, Nakaya pursued the case to the Supreme Court; in 1988, it was dismissed on grounds that enshrinement is not unconstitutional unless promotion of Shinto is the state's intent. 'Intent' being virtually undemonstrable when the state is involved, decisions like this, in the view of Japan's neighbours, augur the return of a Japan they know only too well as an aggressor.

> When we say 'Hiroshima,'
> do people answer, gently,
> 'Ah, Hiroshima'?

The question is Kurihara Sadako's (b. 1913), not a Christian herself but a peace-activist and poet who survived the atomic bombing of her city in 1945. She continues:

> Say 'Hiroshima,' and hear 'Pearl Harbor.'
> Say 'Hiroshima,' and hear 'Rape of Nanjing.'
> Say 'Hiroshima,' and hear of women and children in Manila
> thrown into trenches, doused with gasoline,
> and burned alive.
> Say 'Hiroshima,'
> and hear echoes of blood and fire . . .
> That we may say 'Hiroshima,'
> And hear in reply, gently,
> 'Ah, Hiroshima,'
> we first must
> wash the blood
> off our own hands.[14]

While the 'old' and 'new' Japan are not the same, Japan's continuing transformation may depend in no small measure on poetry like this and the pluck of Christian non-conformists.

13 'Statement of war responsibility of Nippon Sei Ko Kai: 49th Regular General Synod excerpt from May 23, 1996', *Anglican and Episcopal history* 65 (1996), p. 490.
14 Sadako Kurihara, *Black eggs: poems of Kurihara Sadako*, trans. Richard H. Minear (Ann Arbor: Center for Japanese Studies, University of Michigan, 1994), pp. 226–7.

PART III

★

SOCIAL AND CULTURAL IMPACT

26

Liturgy

BRYAN D. SPINKS

Writing in 1960 the American Episcopal liturgical scholar, Massey Shepherd, accurately stated, 'There is no individual who is competent to give sufficient account of the liturgical renewal of our times.'[1] The twentieth century has witnessed little short of a revolution in terms of worship texts and practices in most Western churches and in those third world churches that were the product of Western missionary movements. From the Roman Catholic church, to Presbyterian and Disciples of Christ, we find new prayer books and texts for public worship; alongside this there have been movements, such as in Korea, Africa and India, to indigenise or inculturate worship, making it less Euro- or north Atlantic-centred, and reflecting something of the religious temperament of the local culture. Some of this work has been the sophisticated product of committees of experts, drawing on a wide knowledge of historical forms of worship. Often the end results in different churches were very similar in shape and content, showing the common assumptions and conclusions of the liturgical movement and ecumenical movement. Some have been more spontaneous, often without a clearly thought out and articulated theology. These latter fall mainly into three categories: the seeker services; the praise and worship movement; and the contemporary worship music industry.[2] It is unlikely that all the endeavours in different churches by different individuals can ever be fully documented. The result, however, is that the face of public worship in the churches at the end of the twentieth century is very different from what it was in 1900. This article will be mainly concerned with the Roman Catholic, Anglican and Reformed churches.

---

1 Massey H. Shepherd, *The liturgical renewal of the church* (New York: Oxford University Press, 1960), p. 21.
2 For this taxonomy, see Robb Redman, *The great worship awakening: sharing a new song in the postmodern church* (San Francisco: Jossey-Bass, 2002).

The Roman Catholic church

The liturgical movement is the name given to a movement within the Roman Catholic church for renewal of liturgical life in the church. At first it was simply concerned that the laity should be taught to pray the liturgy – mainly the mass – rather than recite their own private devotions while the public worship of the church was left to the priest. Later it would develop to become a movement for liturgical reform. Although some have argued that the movement had its origins with Dom Prosper Guéranger and the abbey of Solesmes in the nineteenth century, Bernard Botte has argued that its real birth was at a conference at Malines in 1909 with a paper given by Dom Lambert Beauduin, a Benedictine monk from the abbey of Mont César, Leuven, Belgium.[3] He had entered the monastery in 1905 after some years working as what today would be termed an industrial chaplain. Drawing on that experience, Beauduin argued that the liturgy should be the prayer of the people, and be the basis of piety and spirituality. However, in the course of time Christian piety had become divorced from the public liturgy. The way forward was to help the laity understand the meaning of the (Latin) texts. Beyond this, he argued that the liturgical renewal was necessary for the renewal of society which had become too individualistic. His views were set out in more clarity in *La piété de l'eglise* in 1914. He also began two journals, *La vie liturgique* which gave translations of the text of the mass for each month, and *Questions liturgiques* which contained papers of a more technical nature aimed at the clergy.[4]

The year 1914 also marked a similar concern in Germany with Abbot Ildephonse Herwegen at a Holy Week conference. Herwegen was abbot from 1913 to 1946, and under his leadership the abbey of Maria Laach became a centre for the liturgical movement in Germany. In *Kirche und Seele* (1928) Herwegen argued that Christianity is not essentially a doctrine but a life, the life of Christ in the baptised. He criticised subjective individualism, which he traced to the Middle Ages. Another product of Maria Laach was Dom Odo Casel, whose *Das christliche Kultmysterium* became an influential work for the liturgical movement. Casel argued for a threefold mysterium – God in himself, God in Christ and his saving work, and God in the cult (the liturgy) in which the saving mystery is rendered present to the believers.

3 Bernard Botte, *From silence to participation* (Washington: Pastoral Press, 1988).
4 For fuller details, see John Fenwick and Bryan D. Spinks, *Worship in transition: the liturgical movement in the twentieth century* (Edinburgh: T&T Clark, 1995).

In Austria the movement centred on the abbey of Klosterneuberg and Pius Parsch, whose main contribution was to emphasise the importance of the Bible readings in worship, and to stress the connection between the liturgy and salvation history in scripture. In the USA the movement centred on the abbey of St John's Collegeville in Minnesota, led by Dom Virgil Michel with encouragement from Abbot Alcuin Deutsch. Virgil Michel began the journal *Orate fratres*, later to be renamed *Worship*, and in his own writings he stressed the link between the corporate liturgy and social justice.

It became clear to many of the pioneers of the movement that Latin was a stumbling block to the full realisation of their goals. Hand in hand with the pastoral movement there developed a steady scholarly research into the history and development of liturgies, East and West, some of which raised questions about the current Catholic rites and practices. Books such as Joseph Jungmann's *Missarum solemnia* (1949; ET *The mass of the Roman rite*, New York, 1951–2) provided studies of the origin of the Roman rite with implications for reform. Yet it was clear that the movement could only achieve its goals if there was some official encouragement. Such endorsement was set forth in the encyclical *Mediator Dei* (1947), which has been hailed as the Magna Carta of the liturgical movement. Though firing warning shots across some of the more radical bows of the movement, Pius XII paid homage to the renewal coming from the Benedictines, and gave encouragement to more active participation and understanding by the laity. The document noted that the liturgy consists of divine and human elements, and the latter does and may change. Some modest changes did take place in the 1950s, such as a simplification of the calendar and the restoration of the Holy Week services. During the 1950s a number of liturgical congresses were held at which liturgical experts began to explore possible avenues of revision of more fundamental liturgical rites, though these became more restrained when dignitaries attended.

With the calling of the Second Vatican Council by Pope John XXIII, the Roman Catholic church braced itself for *aggiornamento* in order to face life in the modern world, which would include a complete revision of the liturgical rites and styles of celebration, though John XXIII did not live to see the results. It was left to his successor, Paul VI, to approve and promulgate the *Constitution on the sacred liturgy* on 4 December 1963. This document stressed that the faithful should take part in the liturgy intelligently, actively and fruitfully, and in order for this to be achieved a number of changes were to be made. The liturgy was to be in the vernacular, duplications and redundancies removed, scripture and preaching were to be central, and the divine office should be reformed in such a manner as to enable the laity to take part and use it. It also stated that liturgy must be adapted to the particular genius and traditions of different peoples, and that in mission fields traditional music may be used. It also stated that buildings must be designed so that the faithful may actively participate. The necessary work was given into the hands of a consilium, consisting of cardinals and bishops, together with consultors – liturgical scholars who could carry out the actual work. The consultors were assigned particular areas or rites on which to work. The procedure was that once certain texts had been agreed they appeared in a Latin *editio typica*, and it was for national bishops' conferences to undertake the task of translation. In the order of mass, the old single Roman canon of the mass (prayer of consecration) was slightly revised, but augmented by three new prayers which included an epiklesis (request for the Holy Spirit to come upon the bread and wine) in deference to the Eastern tradition. The form for Christian Initiation of Adults provides staged rites over a period of time, acknowledging growth in faith from enquiry to instruction, to actual baptism, and these rites have been patterned after those of the fourth century. This new rite has been particularly influential on many other Western churches.

The *Constitution on the sacred liturgy* had allowed for local adaptation, subject to approval from Rome. In terms of new texts, approval has not always been easy to obtain. Some aspects of A *mass for India* in 1974 were given approval – mainly Indian gestures and ceremonial – but the eucharistic prayer, which used terminology and religious concepts from the various religions found in India, was rejected. A new prayer composed in Italian by the Swiss Synod was approved, as was an Aboriginal prayer. The Zaire mass was eventually authorised, though Pope John Paul II declined to use it when he visited Zaire. However, it would seem that it has been the English-speaking world that has been regarded with the most suspicion by the Congregation for Divine Worship and Discipline for the Sacraments. Although John McHugh of Ushaw college, Durham, circulated a paper making a plea for regional forms of English, it has been the case that, with few exceptions, the English-speaking Catholic world has been required to have common forms, regardless of whether it is British English, American English or Australian English. For this purpose the International Commission on English in the Liturgy (ICEL) was formed, having its headquarters in Washington. As other English-speaking, non-Catholic, churches thought it expedient that, where possible, any text used in common such as the creed should be a common text, the International Consultation on English Texts (ICET) came into being, and was invited to use the facilities of ICEL. It has sometimes appeared that Rome has been suspicious of the domination by a perceived liberalism of the American church, and infiltration of Protestant agendas by ICET. Whether this perception is correct or not, the ICEL eucharistic prayer was rejected by Rome. ICEL felt that the original ICEL translations of the sacramentary were hasty, departed from the original Latin text, and had a terse style, and so from 1981 to 1998 a new English sacramentary was prepared, which included some new collects which echo the lectionary readings. The whole project has so far stalled in Rome, where the collects have been criticised (though comparable Italian ones were authorised in 1983), as also some of the inclusive language that is used. Almost coinciding with the issue of *Liturgiam authenticam* (April 2001; seen by many Catholics as a conservative, reactionary document) ICEL was reorganised, downsized, and withdrawn from ICET. It would seem to those outside the Vatican that from the mid-1980s a more conservative interpretation of the liturgical implications of the *Constitution on the sacred liturgy* has come to prevail.

It is perhaps the visual aspect of worship that to many seems to have been the greatest change. The old eastward-facing mass, with priest in fiddle-back chasuble with his back to the congregation, whispering the rite at a baroque altar more resembling a cluttered sideboard than an altar table, with six candles, has given way to a nave altar, westward facing, little clutter, and the adoption of more graceful gothic-style chasubles. While in large churches these changes have been carried out without loss of a sense of dignity, in smaller churches an air of informality and ill-prepared, off-the-cuff explanations of parts of the liturgy, with amateur guitar music, has appalled many Catholic laity. It is perhaps no wonder that there have been groups that have called for a return, if not to the Tridentine forms and ritual, at least to a more dignified style of celebration.

Though the term 'liturgical movement' was coined amongst Roman Catholics, its characteristics and fruits have not been confined to that church. Other churches faced some similar pastoral challenges to those of the Roman Catholic church, and had parallel stirrings for renewal of the church through its worship, and, within Protestant traditions, a renewed importance attached to the frequent celebration of the eucharist. The WCC Montreal 1963 report on worship could be seen as a counterpart to the *Constitution on the sacred liturgy*. Indeed, the increased ecumenical activity that flowed from Vatican II, together with the WCC interest in worship, led to greater exchange between liturgical scholars, with the shared wisdom of the academy. This resulted in considerable cross-fertilisation of ideas and goals. This can be illustrated by reference to the liturgical development within Anglicanism and some Reformed churches.

Anglicanism

Since the Reformation Anglicans had a vernacular liturgy in theory accessible to the laity, but in England it had not been revised since 1662, and elsewhere in the worldwide Anglican communion most other Anglican churches (e.g., the Protestant Episcopal Church of the United States of America [ECUSA]) had not strayed far from the 1662 language and format in their revisions. The Tractarian and Anglo-Catholic revival of the nineteenth century had resulted in some clergy using Catholic ceremonial and liturgical forms, while a great many more wished for enrichment and more flexibility to the services. Anglo-Catholic churches put the eucharist as the central worship service of the church, but churches influenced by Christian socialism also began to pioneer a parish communion as the main Sunday service. A round of liturgical revision took place around 1928, with new prayer books in Scotland, South Africa, the USA and England, though the English book was twice presented to Parliament and twice rejected, and thus never became a lawful replacement for the 1662 prayer book. However, in the 1930s the insights of the Roman Catholic movement were being mediated to the Church of England by such exponents as Henry de Candole (1895–1971) and Gabriel Hebert (1886–1963). De Candole's *The church's offering: a brief study of eucharistic worship* and *The sacraments and the church: a study in the corporate nature of Christianity*, (1935), and Hebert's *Liturgy and society* (1935) are all classic English expressions of the earlier continental concepts and writings. A series of essays entitled *The parish communion* was published in 1937. They advocated the eucharist as the main service on a Sunday, with active participation of the laity. The bread and wine of the eucharist represent the whole substance of our lives, all our joys, sorrows, plans for the future, our hopes and fears.

Progress was interrupted by the Second World War. However, in 1947 a meeting between Henry de Candole, Kenneth Packard and Patrick McLaughlin led to the founding of Parish and People, which was dedicated to promoting and disseminating the concepts of the liturgical movement. In the USA, Dean William Palmer Ladd of the Berkeley divinity school in New Haven, CT was an enthusiast for the liturgical movement, and read the material as mediated by Virgil Michel and *Orate fratres* at St John's Collegeville. He invited Gabriel Hebert over to spend some time at Berkeley divinity school. Ladd's *Prayer book interleaves* remains the classic American Anglican expression of the aims of the liturgical movement. Ladd was also in touch with and encouraging the studies of Massey Shepherd, who would become one of the leading liturgical scholars and exponents of the liturgical movement for the Episcopal church. In that church the counterpart to Parish and People was called Associated Parishes, and Shepherd played a large part in its founding and work.

An important stimulus in Anglican thinking was Dom Gregory Dix's large work, *The shape of the liturgy* (1945). Dix argued that the actions of Jesus at the Last Supper had been universally reduced by the early church to four actions: taking, giving thanks, breaking and communion. The latter part of the book traced how the earliest strata of the liturgy were overlaid by medieval growth, which Dix regarded as distortion, and how Thomas Cranmer in the English prayer book failed to express clearly the fourfold shape of the eucharist. This fourfold shape, though actually based on misinterpretations of material, has established itself as a fundamental structural item of many of the more recent Anglican eucharistic liturgies.

One of the first fruits of this new liturgical awareness was, ironically, the liturgy of the Church of South India (1950). Itself an amalgamation of Methodist, Reformed and Anglican traditions, together with the Basel mission, it was not immediately admitted into full communion with the Anglican communion. The new liturgy that was produced for this church, a key drafter being Leslie Brown, was the first to break from the Cranmerian mould. The liturgy of the word was capable of standing as a separate service in its own right. The confession and absolution came at the beginning of the service. It included the exchange of peace. There was emphasis on congregational participation. The eucharistic prayer (prayer of consecration) gave thanks for the mighty acts of God in salvation history, and was nearer to the structure of those of the fourth and fifth centuries than to Cranmer's version in its 1662 format. This new liturgy would be an encouragement to the rest of the Anglican world.

ECUSA had a standing liturgical commission, which was refused permission to draft a new liturgy in 1947, but was allowed to produce 'prayer book studies' as teaching and discussion material, and by the 1960s these began to emerge as trial services, spurred on by the new work emerging from Rome. In an ecumenical atmosphere a new prayer book was drafted which would replace that of 1928. This new book was published in 1976, and formally adopted in 1979.

The Church of England had appointed a liturgical commission in 1954. Its members, in conjunction with Leslie Brown and Massey Shepherd, prepared papers for the Lambeth Conference of 1958, as a guide for the communion. It encouraged the reintroduction of an Old Testament reading and psalm in the communion service, and suggested that eucharistic prayers should give thanks for the whole of the mighty works of God. However, as various provinces, spurred on by south India and more indirectly Vatican II, appointed commissions to undertake liturgical revision, it was feared that what held the Anglican communion together – namely Books of Common Prayer still showing the Cranmerian root – would fly apart as provinces acted independently. In order to try to lay down common guidelines, a 'pan-Anglican' document was issued in 1965 and another in 1969. More recently a body known as the International Anglican Liturgical Consultation has met every two to four years, bringing together scholars and represent-atives of provincial liturgical commissions for the exchange of ideas, and to formulate statements giving some guidance to the communion on possible principles and revision needs. In the Church of England, after experimental rites in pamphlet form (Series 1, 2 and 3) a new prayer book, entitled *The alternative service book*, appeared in 1980. The American book of 1976/9 was influential on the Canadian *Book of alternative services* 1985. Ireland produced a new book in 1984; Australia produced one in 1978 and another in 1995; South Africa produced a new book in 1982, and included a eucharistic prayer from the Roman Catholic missal; New Zealand produced one in 1989. Kenya had new services in the 1990s, but only printed them as a whole in 2002.

Just as some had lamented the passing of Latin in the Roman Catholic church, so too some who appreciated the language of the old prayer book were outraged by the modern language versions, indicting them for poor, unpoetic, language. But this debate was overtaken in the 1980s by the whole question of inclusive language – of people, and of God. This was particularly canvassed in North America and Australia, though with less vehemence in England. The result has been moves to be inclusive by toning down the use of male metaphors and pronouns, and, in some provinces, by the deliberate use of feminine terms for God. This is reflected in some degree in *A New Zealand prayer book* (1989), and in the ECUSA supplementary texts using 'expansive language', where again masculine terms for God are muted, and feminine imagery for God is employed. In the Church of England the Liturgical Commission began a new round of revisions, beginning in 1986 and gaining momentum in the 1990s, with the 1980 book being replaced by *Common worship 2000*. The latter is much larger in its provisions for flexibility, and uses inclusive language for people, but stops short of using any non-biblical feminine imagery in association with God. This in part reflects the cultural differences between, for example, the USA and Great Britain, and is not limited to Anglicanism. Stemming from feminist theology, it seems to be mainly a preoccupation of the more liberal English-speaking Euro-churches and centres on the relationship between grammatical gender and biological gender. In many languages this 'problem' simply does not exist, and appears to many as 'English-speaking parochialism'.

Alongside these new services has been new ceremonial. Often the white cassock alb has been adopted as a neutral vestment, worn with a stole by the priest. Reordering of churches has resulted in anything from a nave altar to the removal of pews and their replacement by chairs for flexibility. The presentation of services has tended to be more informal than in earlier in the century.

However, alongside official revision has gone unofficial, and at times irregular, worship, usually found in Anglican churches of the more Evangelical tradition. Here the altar table has sometimes been removed, and the nave used as a stage, housing a band for contemporary music, with extemporary forms of prayer in place of authorised forms, and the abandonment of any vesture beyond the clerical collar. This great variety is something that has been endemic to Anglicanism since the Reformation, and thus styles vary from a sung eucharist with choir and fully vested clergy in a cathedral, to an informal praise service without any traditional Anglican liturgical trappings.

The Reformed tradition

A similar tale can be told of the worldwide Reformed church. For example, in the French-speaking Swiss Reformed and Reformed Church of France, Richard Paquier was a leading ecumenist and liturgist. Under the auspices of *Eglise et liturgie*, Paquier helped author a liturgy that went back beyond the Calvinist roots of these churches to the liturgies of the early centuries. The liturgy that resulted was published in 1931, and revised in 1952. This 'private' venture influenced the Genevan liturgy of 1945, as well as the Reformed Church of France liturgy of 1963, J.-D. Benoit playing an important role in the latter. A new liturgy for the *Eglise Reformée de France* was published in 1996. In Switzerland the insights of Paquier were given strong support from J. Leehardt and J.-J. Von Allmen, and some of the fruits were seen in the Jura liturgy of 1955, the Vaud liturgy of 1963 and the 1979 liturgy for French-speaking Switzerland. In the German Reformed churches the *Kirchenbuch* of 1983 represents a blending of traditionally Reformed orders in keeping with the 1563 Palatinate liturgy together with newer orders reflecting the ecumenical consensus, and drawing on the patterns of the fourth and fifth centuries. The Dutch Reformed church brought out a new liturgy in 1955, having had scholars in the forefront of the liturgical movement. Thereafter the movement in the Dutch church seemed to stagnate until recently when amalgamation with the Dutch Lutheran church has resulted in a new *Dienstboek* in 1998. The Presbyterian church in the USA published a *Book of common worship* in 1906, which was revised in 1946. The latter was based on Anglican models. However, the impact of Neo-Orthodoxy and then the insights of the liturgical movement meant that by 1957, when the General Assembly began considering revision, a rather different model and theology were being considered. As Horace Allen explained, 'its work had to be done in the midst of swirling and often uncertain liturgical upheaval throughout the Western churches, Catholic and Protestant, led, astonishingly enough, by the Church of Rome'.[5] Thus when the *Worshipbook* of 1970 was published, it had modern English, a basic structure of word and sacrament (with an ante-communion option) rather than imitation Anglican morning prayer and sermon, and a lectionary based on that of Vatican II. The *Worshipbook* was a precursor to the 1993 *Book of common worship*, giving the American Presbyterians rites based on the classic rites of the fourth and fifth century, but thoroughly modern, with restored rites and ceremonies, such as the Holy Week services and the use of oil for anointing in baptism. The eucharist is presented as the normative Sunday worship, though often it is celebrated only once a month. Many Presbyterian clergy wear the cassock alb and stole in place of the traditional Geneva gown, and altars are adorned with candles, and banners used to give colour to the once austere interior of Reformed church buildings. In Scotland the 1940 *Book of common order* was revised in 1979, but this was regarded as unsatisfactory. Some supplementary texts were published, but a new book was published in 1994 entitled *Common order*. This book draws on the insights of the liturgical movement and makes the eucharist central. It also draws on Celtic prayer tradition.[6]

New trends, different styles, other churches

Generally speaking, it is possible to speak of a Euro–North American liturg-ical movement, by which the Roman Catholic and mainline Protestant churches have renewed their worship by authoring modern rites suitable for the times, but inspired by earlier forms of the fourth and fifth centuries. But a number of other factors and trends may be noted.

---

5 Bryan D. Spinks and Iain R. Torrance (eds.), *To glorify God: essays on modern Reformed worship* (Edinburgh: T&T Clark, 1991), p. 18.
6 Ibid.

First, coming out of the ecumenical movement, there have been a number of amalgamations of churches, resulting in the need for a liturgy which draws on the traditions of the amalgamating churches, but which also gives the new church its new identity. The Uniting church in Australia is one such example, the Methodist scholar Robert Gribben playing a key role in its composition. The union of the Dutch Reformed and Lutheran churches in Holland is another example.

Second is the continued quest for inculturation. In Korea, for example, there are experiments with incorporating Shinto customs, suitably Christianised, such as in the Minjung community.[7] The Zaire mass includes ceremonial dancing at the entrance of the clergy and assistants, prayer for the saints and ancestors at the beginning of the service, dancing and presentation of foods as gifts alongside the bread and wine of communion, and use of ritual gestures of reverence and celebration that are traditionally African. It has its own eucharistic prayer that echoes traditional African themes of thanksgiving, including for the river Zaire.

Third, particularly in North America, though the model tends to be part of globalisation, is the worship in mega-churches called seeker services. These tend to be a blend of modern pop music, contemporary Christian music and choruses, with 'down to earth' talks (rather than 'sermons') on practical things in life, and minimum use of traditional Christian worship formulae. These services are aimed at the non-churched middle class, and are modelled on entertainment and sales techniques, the most famous being those at the Willow Creek church near Chicago. While attracting huge numbers, they require considerable financial backing, and the limited number of 'seekers' who become fully committed suggests that many prefer to be entertained weekly without further commitment and demands.

Fourth, living alongside and quite independent of the major churches have been the newer Pentecostal and Holiness churches. The cultural and social implications of these churches suggest that in some ways they are a result of the exclusiveness and middle-class cultural assumptions of many mainstream churches. These churches have antecedents in nineteenth-century frontier revivalism in America, where itinerant preachers would hold outdoor camp meetings, at which the fervour of preaching would result in rapturous dancing, singing and ecstatic shouting.

---

7 Dong-sun Kim, *The bread for today and the bread for tomorrow* (New York: Peter Lang, 2001).

The Pentecostal and Holiness movements, which were a twentieth-century development from this earlier frontier religion, tend to centre worship on singing hymns and spiritual songs, testimony, preaching, an 'altar call' to respond to the conviction of sin, and being freed by the gospel message. Often ecstasy gives rise to speaking in tongues. The laying on of hands for healing is another important element. Many of these churches have grown rapidly, and those such as the Assemblies of God are concerned with mission to the unchurched, both home and abroad. Contemporary Christian music with music bands and choirs are important elements in their worship. But equally there are Holiness heirs to the 'High Calvinist Primitive Baptists' who believed in predestination to a point that they regarded all outreach and mission as a waste of time. Such groups exist in the Appalachians, practising a closed communion, with worship centred on singing, and preaching in a particular style and rhythm of breathing. And amongst these groups are the serpent handlers, or churches 'with signs following'. Dating from c. 1910 with George Went Hensley, these small sects worship for anything up to three or four hours, with singing, speaking in tongues, extemporaneous prayer, handling venomous snakes, drinking (and surviving) poison, and anointing with oil for healing – all regarded as signs of being 'anointed by the Spirit'. They remain a curiosity as the twenty-first century and the age of global Christianity begins; yet in some ways they stand as a protest against the sophistication and professionalism of the modern, and now post-modern, world, and are the very antithesis of the high-tech seeker services. They are also a reminder that the liturgical movement of the mainstream churches has never touched some areas of Christian life and worship.

The 'other'

I

RELATIONS BETWEEN CHRISTIANS AND JEWS, 1914–2000

DANIEL R. LANGTON

It is something of an under-statement to describe 1914 to 2000 as a significant period for Jewish–Christian relations. Two key events included the destruction of European Jewry during the Nazi Holocaust of 1933–45 and the establishment of the state of Israel in 1948. These had profound implications for modern Jewish identity and also posed powerful challenges to the Christian churches in terms of traditional attitudes and theology. Ultimately, the scope and content of any survey of Christian interaction with the Jewish other in the twentieth century are determined by these events.

One problem that must be addressed from the outset relates to the boundaries of the interaction. It is important to recognise the fragmented nature of the Jewish community in the modern world, just as for the Christian community. Ultra-Orthodox, Orthodox, Conservative, Reform, Liberal and Progressive, Reconstructionist, and a wide range of secular Jews are among some of the groups that comprise the Jewish 'community' that has emerged since the Enlightenment. In contrast to a common view of Christianity as being religiously or theologically defined, Jewish identity is more complex and can be expressed in ways that are often regarded as non-religious. One way, Zionism, the movement for the establishment and maintenance of a Jewish state, is in many of its forms entirely unreligious, even anti-religious. Again, a large proportion of the six million Jewish victims of the Holocaust did not, in fact, regard themselves religiously as Jews, but rather as secularists or as assimilated Christians of Jewish descent. It seems necessary, despite the dangers inherent, to speak of Jewish culture in the widest possible sense. Having said that, the explicitly religious dimensions of Jewish–Christian interaction during this period will be the primary focus here.

The Nazi Holocaust, the systematic, state-sponsored persecution and murder of approximately six million Jews together with many millions of others, was perpetrated by Germans and their collaborators at all levels of society and throughout many Christian countries. It raises a number of profound questions for humankind in general, but this should not detract from the specific problems that it poses for Christianity. Few historians today would support the so-called 'rhetoric of continuity', the claim to trace a direct path from the 'teaching of contempt'[1] and the hostility that emerged between early followers of Jesus and other Jews in the first century, to the racial, pseudo-scientific, eliminationist, anti-semitism of the twentieth. Nevertheless, Christian anti-Judaism, while not a sufficient cause, was surely a necessary one. Despite the anti-religious tendencies of the Third Reich, Nazi propagandists were quick to tap into a rich vein of anti-semitism that lay close to the surface of European Christian culture. Thus the Munich 1936 edition of Martin Luther's selected works included his virulent polemic 'On the Jews and their lies' (1543).[2] Such materials reinforced racist propaganda and made it possible for an ostensibly Christian society to turn a blind eye to the treatment of the Jews. Those who professed a Christian faith could be found among death camp staff and mobile killing squads as well as among the bureaucrats and technocrats who administered the process of liquidation. Peasants throughout eastern Europe acquiesced in the confiscation of Jewish property and justified the treatment of the Jews as punishment for the ancient crime of deicide.

At the institutional level, the Roman Catholic church has been criticised for its 'silence' and for the inadequacy of its diplomatic efforts during the Holocaust. Eugenio Pacelli, the future Pius XII (1939–58), implemented a concordat or treaty with the Nazis only six months after they came to power. It gave international credence to the Nazi regime and seriously undermined Christian resistance by pledging non-interference in political matters. During Pius XII's papacy, a fear of the godless Bolsheviks and a determination to maintain a general policy of neutrality for the sake of its followers and for diplomatic reasons compromised the position of the Vatican with regard to

---

1 Jules Isaac, *The teaching of contempt: Christian roots of anti-semitism*, trans. Helen Weaver (New York: Holt, Reinhart and Winston, 1964).
2 H. H. Borcherdt and Georg Merz (eds.), *Martin Luther: ausgewählte Werke* (Munich: 1934–8), vol. III, pp. 61–228. The 1922 and 1948 editions did not include this treatise.

the Nazi treatment of the Jews. In his 1942 Christmas message, Pius XII refrained from explicitly mentioning either the Nazis or the Jews, although he spoke of 'hundreds of thousands of persons who, without any fault on their part, sometimes only because of their nationality or race, have been consigned to death or to a slow decline'. Claims that the church secured the lives of thousands of Jews through diplomatic channels and by hiding large numbers in monasteries are contentious, although towards the end of the war Pius XII did encourage church representatives in Germany and Hungary to provide humanitarian assistance to Nazi victims.

Protestantism under the Nazi regime was complicated by the establishment in 1933 of the German Evangelical church, a federation of Lutheran, Reformed and United territorial churches. A right-wing faction, the German Christians' Faith movement, gained control. In addition to suggesting that the Old Testament and Paul's epistles should be expunged from the canon on the grounds of their Jewishness, the 'German Christians' supported the doctrine of Aryan racial supremacy. Opposition arose in the shape of the Pastors' Emergency League, founded by the Lutheran Martin Niemöller, and in May 1934 the synod of Barmen established the Confessing Church, with the Lutheran Dietrich Bonhoeffer among its leading pastors. Despite some successes in opposing the 'German Christians' and Nazis, such as the role they played along with others in pressuring the government in 1941 to find alternatives to the euthanasia programme for the mentally ill and disabled, the leadership of the Confessing Church was fragmented – and ambiguous in its attitude towards the Jews. Niemöller was imprisoned from 1937 until the end of the war and Bonhoeffer was arrested in 1943 and executed in 1945. The Nazis were able to take full advantage of lack of unity and internal conflicts within the Protestant church. Those few Protestant leaders who protested against the treatment of the Jews often did so despite a theologically negative attitude to Judaism. Thus at the same time as teaching that Christians should not persecute the Jews, Bonhoeffer and Niemöller both explicitly maintained that the suffering of the Jews was punishment from God for the ancient rejection and murder of his Son, and looked forward to the conversion of Israel.[3]

After the death and destruction of the Holocaust, the birth of the modern state of Israel in 1948 represents the second most significant development in Jewish–Christian relations in the twentieth century. The very concept of a

---

3 Dietrich Bonhoeffer, *No rusty swords: letters, lectures and notes 1928–1936*, ed. and trans. Edwin Robertson (London: Collins, 1965), pp. 225–6; Martin Niemoeller, *Here stand I!*, trans. Jane Lymburn (Chicago and New York: Willett, Clark & Co., 1937), p. 195.

Jewish state represents a challenge to traditional Christian and Muslim theologies. The Jews were represented for many centuries as adherents of a superseded religion and murderers of God. In punishment for their stubborn perversity, they were exiled from their land, denuded of political power, condemned to wander the earth. Despite this, philosemitic traditions have co-existed in Christian thought and the modern Zionist project has therefore met with a range of Christian responses.

The term 'Christian Zionists' covers a wide spectrum of groups with a variety of perspectives, from biblical literalists who regarded the return of the exiles to Israel as a stage in the divine plan that heralds the return of Christ, to liberal thinkers whose pronounced ecumenicalism and internalisation of the lessons of the Holocaust led them to unconditional support for Israeli state policy. In the sense of a romanticised, mythologised view of the Jewish people, Christian Zionism was an important influence in the period in question. An example of this was the role that religion played in the proclamation of the Balfour Declaration in 1917.[4] This document made public the British government's support for 'the establishment in Palestine of a national home for the Jewish people'. There were a number of British statesmen, including Arthur Balfour and Prime Minister Lloyd George, whose familiarity with scripture encouraged them to see their support of Zionism as fulfilment of a historical mission. To them the announcement that signalled the intent to return the land to the ancient people of Israel, an announcement made just as British forces were poised to capture Jerusalem from the Ottoman Turks, appealed as a grand symbolic gesture of historic justice. It would be simplistic to regard the declaration solely or even mainly in terms of religious agendas. Nevertheless, the intersection of religion and politics at this point cannot be ignored in any account of why Britain set aside the interests of the Arab inhabitants of the land, who made up around 90 per cent of the population (10 per cent of whom were Arab Christians). In his own account, the Zionist leader Chaim Weizmann concluded that British statesmen 'believed in the Bible, that to them the return of the Jewish people to Palestine was a reality, so that we Zionists represented to them a great tradition for which they had an enormous respect'.[5] In the second half of the twentieth century, Christian Zionists were popular with successive Israeli governments in so far as they

---

4 The declaration took the form of an open letter from Arthur Balfour to Lord Rothschild, 2 November 1917.
5 Chaim Weizmann, *Trial and error: the autobiography of Chaim Weizmann* (London: Hamish Hamilton, 1949), p. 200.

publicly supported government policies and channelled funds and Jewish immigrants from Russia and eastern European countries to Israel.

The Roman Catholic church took a more hostile stance towards Zionism and the Jewish state. In 1904 Pope Pius X had informed Theodor Herzl, the father of political Zionism:

> We cannot prevent the Jews from going to Jerusalem, but we could never sanction it. The ground of Jerusalem . . . has been sanctified by the life of Christ. As head of the Church I cannot answer you otherwise. The Jews have not recognized our Lord, therefore we cannot recognize the Jewish people . . . [T]o support the Jews in the acquisition of the Holy Places, that we cannot do.[6]

In December 1917 the Allies captured Jerusalem and, despite Vatican concerns over Protestant control, Pope Benedict XV could speak in 1919 of 'the rejoicing of all good men' that the holy places had been freed from 'the domination of infidels' and had 'finally returned into the hands of Christians'.[7] The possibility of Jewish control provoked a different reaction, however. In discussions of the 1947 UN partition plans, the Vatican supported the idea of the internationalisation of Jerusalem, and after the 1967 Six Day war it lobbied for the international status of Christian holy places. The Vatican refused to recognise the new state after its establishment in 1948 and continued this refusal even when Pope Paul VI spent a day in Israel in 1967. The traditional position softened under Pope John Paul II, who in 1980 spoke publicly of Israel and of the right of the Jewish people to a homeland. Formal recognition of the state of Israel by the Church of Rome came in December 1993.

Arguably, the rapprochement of Jews and Christians and the development of inter-faith relations at an international level had at least as much to do with the emergence of the state, confounding Christian traditional attitudes to the Jews, as it did with guilt relating to the Holocaust and the 'teaching of contempt'. From 1922 until 1948 the British had attempted to implement the League of Nations mandate for Palestine. This had involved the facilitation of Jewish immigration, Jewish settlement, and self-governing institutions, whilst preserving the civil rights of all the inhabitants of Palestine. Despite its formal internationalist credentials, the mandatory power had been ostensibly Christian, the first such administration there since the crusades. However, Christian political domination over Jews ended with the

6 Theodor Herzl, *The complete diaries of Theodor Herzl*, ed. Raphael Patai, trans. Harry Zohn (New York and London: The Herzl Press, 1960), vol. IV, pp. 1602–3.
7 Speech to the College of Cardinals, cited in H. Eugene Bovis, *The Jerusalem question, 1917–1968* (Stanford: Hoover Institution Press, 1971), pp. 6–7.

UN recognition of Israel. The military victories of the Israeli War of Independence (1948) and the Six Day war (1967) against multiple Arab armies were impressive and unexpected. In contradiction to the negative images of the Jew as stateless, weak and parasitical, the modern Israeli state proved itself militarily and diplomatically effective, culturally vibrant and self-confident. The 1967 war was also significant because, to many Jewish observers, the churches had failed for the second time to speak out against the threat of Jewish annihilation. The embryonic inter-faith dialogue was shaken but eventually regained its balance, resulting in an increased comprehension among Christians as to the significance of Israel for the Jew. In addition to the theological challenges, the new state also posed new practical dilemmas. Following the Holocaust, Christians were faced with the delicate issue of how to approach the power-relations between Israelis and Palestinians. Steering a course between the claims of social justice and allegations of anti-semitic bias proved difficult.

It is against the background of the Holocaust that a number of controversial episodes in recent Jewish–Christian history can best be understood. All reflect a Jewish fear of the 'Christianisation of the Holocaust', that is, a perceived tendency of the church to emphasise Christian victimhood and heroism in such a way as to undermine the uniqueness of the Jewish experience. From the 1970s, US and western European Jewish communal institutions became fiercely protective of the memory of those murdered members of the Jewish people who, in contrast to other groups and largely without external support, had been targeted by the Nazis for total elimination. The counter-reaction by some Christians was to condemn what was regarded as the Jewish claim to a monopoly on suffering. On occasion, such criticisms were coloured by anti-semitic undertones.

The announcement in 1984 of a proposal to build a Carmelite monastery at the concentration camp Auschwitz brought about an inter-communal crisis. Jewish groups argued that the Christian contemplative and commemorative project was in fact an appropriation of the archetypal symbol of Jewish suffering during the *Shoah*. A decade of acrimony and bitter polemic followed, reaching its nadir in 1989 when an American rabbi led a group of protesters on an assault on the camp in prison dress, denouncing those who apprehended him as Nazi anti-semites, and a Polish cardinal publicly warned the Jews not to abuse their power over the media of many countries by making impossible demands. Matters appeared to be resolved in 1993 when the nuns left the old convent, following the direct intervention of the Polish bishops' conference and a letter from the pope, but controversy was reignited in 1998–9 when a Catholic extremist supervised the planting of a 'forest of crosses' on the same site. Charges of misappropriation were similarly made in relation to the beatification (1987) and canonisation (1998) of Sister Theresa Benedicta of the Cross, a Carmelite nun who was killed at Auschwitz in 1942. Jewish groups protested because Sister Theresa, a convert to Catholicism, had been born Edith Stein and was murdered at Auschwitz as a Jew. More generally, the beatification of individuals whose attitude towards the Jews was suspect provoked much criticism. The canonisation in 1982 of Maximilian Kolbe, a priest who bravely saved the life of another prisoner at Auschwitz by taking the condemned man's place in 1941, was problematic in that Kolbe's pre-war activities had included the editorship of a magazine which had included anti-semitic material. Proposals to beatify Pius XII likewise caused considerable consternation among those who interpreted the record of his wartime papacy negatively. Jewish groups were also angered by the meeting of Pope John Paul II with the Austrian president Kurt Waldheim in 1987, after allegations were made associating Waldheim with Nazi war-crimes.

Other areas of Jewish–Christian conflict in the twentieth century derive from more ancient quarrels. Attitudes towards conversion is one example, attitudes towards Jewish Christians another.

From a Jewish perspective, conversion to Christianity represents the betrayal of one's culture, traditions and heritage, but attitudes towards the apostate have been complex as the celebrated case of Brother Daniel showed. A Polish Jewish Zionist, Oswald Rufeisen was active during the Second World War as a resistance fighter. He infiltrated the German police and used his position to warn the local Jewish community of plans against them, saving around 150 lives. Following his capture and escape, he took refuge in a Carmelite monastery and in 1942 was converted to Christianity. Even after joining the order in 1945 and taking the name Daniel, Rufeisen maintained a Jewish self-identity and in 1962 he applied for citizenship in Israel under the Law of Return. In their rulings, the judges were sympathetic to Rufeisen, admiring of his wartime record, and recognised that he was a Jew according to Jewish religious law (*halakhah*). Ultimately, however, it was regarded as too profound a break with the past for Rufeisen to be granted citizenship as a Jew under the Law of Return. The so-called lachrymose history of the Jews remains a significant influence in the modern Jewish psyche, a powerful factor in determining Jewish identity in the Jewish state.

The issue of Jewish Christianity was also fraught. While 'Hebrew Christians' in the nineteenth century tended to affiliate closely with non-Jewish churches, the 1970s saw the emergence of 'Messianic Jewish' groups that distanced themselves from gentile Christianity. Moshe Rosen, a Hebrew Christian missionary who had become critical of the influence of 'gentilisation' upon Jewish believers in Jesus and who was concerned to emphasise Jewish ethnic identity, established a San Francisco-based evangelical group which became known as 'Jews for Jesus' and which aimed its message at both gentile Christians and Jews throughout America. For many within the wider Jewish community, Jews for Jesus came to represent Messianic Judaism *per se*, largely as a result of their high profile and often confrontational witnessing on college campuses and at airports. Ironically, opposition to such groups unified an often-fragmented Jewish community. Incidents such as those in 1980, when the Jewish Defence League removed a *Torah* scroll from a Los Angeles messianic congregation and picketed their synagogue, indicated the strength of feeling. The Jewish press was unanimous in its condemnation of what were regarded as deceptive Christian conversionary tactics and the misappropriation of Jewish religious symbols. Christian leaders involved in inter-faith dialogue were also critical, recognising the offence caused to Jews and disturbed themselves by what they perceived as the misrepresentation of Christianity. One prominent exception to the general rule was the Reform rabbi Dan Cohn-Sherbok, whose study *Messianic Judaism* (2000) concluded that Messianic Judaism could be regarded as a legitimate expression of Judaism since it was no more radical than was the rejection of a supernatural God by Reconstructionist Jews and since many of its adherents were in fact more observant than many Reform Jews.[8]

The intense reaction and suspicion generated by apostasy is useful in understanding Jewish reticence regarding inter-faith dialogue. A key obstacle is the perception of many Jews that 'dialogue' equates to a more subtle continuation of a traditional policy of mission. The German Jewish philosopher and theologian Martin Buber (1878–1965), in his seminal *Ich und Du (I and thou*, 1922), distinguished between two kinds of interaction: *I–it* monologues, where the partners were unequal and regarded each other as resources, and *I–thou* dialogues, where the partners' attitudes were characterised by mutuality, openness, directness and presentness. The key to religious dialogue was, he suggested, acknowledgement of the mystery of the other's faith-reality. 'We are not in a position to appraise the meaning of their confession because we do not know it from within as we know ourselves from within.'[9] Such an

8 Dan Cohn-Sherbok, *Messianic Judaism* (London and New York: Continuum, 2000).
9 Martin Buber in Stuttgart, January 1933, cited in Fritz A. Rothschild (ed.), *Jewish perspectives on Christianity* (New York: Crossroad, 1990), p. 134.

attitude precluded the possibility of true dialogue being conducted with any missionary objective in mind. Buber's influence among Jews in this context was limited, but among Christian (especially Protestant) thinkers his views had a profound impact. Many characteristics of his model for dialogue were later adopted by inter-faith groups such as the Council of Christians and Jews, which was established in Britain in 1942 to counter anti-semitism and to cultivate mutual understanding. Certainly, Buber contributed to a shift in intellectual climate so that, following the Holocaust and the establishment of Israel, it was possible for statements to be issued by a range of Protestant denominations recommending a cessation of attempts to convert Jews.

Twentieth-century official church pronouncements represent a remarkable development, a tectonic shift, in the intellectual history of Jewish–Christian relations, although the limited readership of such documents should always be borne in mind. As early as 1947, an inter-denominational statement was issued in Seelisberg which condemned Christian teaching that inculcated anti-semitism and also unwarranted or coercive Christian mission. Later Protestant statements typically reflected a non-triumphalist attitude and were respectful of post-biblical Judaism, recommending a reassessment of traditional church teachings such as deicide, and emphasising the Jewish roots of the Christian religion. The Synod of the Evangelical Church of the Rhineland (1980) was a particularly striking example. It accepted 'Christian co-responsibility and guilt for the Holocaust', it recognised Jewish self-definition, Israel's permanent election, and the state of Israel, it rejected supersessionist teaching, and, crucially, it was explicit in condemning conversion of the Jews. 'We believe that in their respective calling Jews and Christians are witnesses of God before the world and before each other. Therefore we are convinced that the Church may not express its witness towards the Jewish people as it does its mission to the peoples of the world.' Such documents encouraged Jews to engage more robustly with Christian institutions that continued to maintain a missionary stance. An international chorus of disapproval met a US Baptist statement issued in 1996, which stated, '[W]e direct our energies and resources toward the proclamation of the gospel to the Jewish people.' For the Jewish community, however, greatest interest was directed towards the pronouncements of the Vatican; for many, the pope's authority over the largest body of Christians on earth was regarded as absolute and of critical significance for future relations. Thus the Catholic church's decision in 1959 to remove from its Good Friday liturgy the term 'perfidious' as a derogatory reference to the Jews was greeted positively. In *Nostra aetate* (*In our time*, 1965) it expressed its wish 'to foster and recommend ... mutual understanding and respect' and argued that '[a]lthough the Church is the new people of God, the Jews should not be presented as repudiated or cursed by God, as if such views followed from the holy scriptures'. This and other documents that followed tended to be well received by Jewish groups who, nevertheless, made their expectations of further progress clear. The 1998 publication of 'We remember: a reflection on the Shoah', however, met with considerable criticism. While welcoming any attempt to address the subject of the Holocaust and the record of the church during that period, critics disapproved of the defence made for Pius XII and the emphasis on Catholic heroism, and of the apparent distinction between the 'the errors and failures . . . [of the] sons and daughters of the Church' and the culpability of the church itself.

The changes in attitude of the Christian churches were related to some extent to developments in scholarship. In the nineteenth and early twentieth centuries a number of Jewish writers, including the German Reform rabbi Abraham Geiger and the co-founder of Anglo-Liberal Judaism Claude Montefiore, argued that Christian scholarship had severely misrepresented Judaism in both the ancient and the modern periods, and that Jesus should be regarded as a Jew of one sort or another (e.g., a Pharisee, or a prophet in an age of law).[10] Their works were neglected. Jewish scholarship was taken more seriously within the world of biblical and New Testament studies after the Second World War. Partly this was due to the influence of a few American and English Christian scholars, such as the Presbyterian George Foot Moore and the Unitarian Robert Travers-Herford, who were highly critical of previous Christian (especially German) representations of 'late Judaism' and the Pharisees.[11] Partly it was due to contributions of American and European Jewish scholars who, having successfully entered the academy, sought to confront some of the Christian assumptions underlying it. Partly it was due to the uninhibited writings of Jewish historians living in the land of Israel, such as Joseph Klausner and David Flusser for whom Jesus, as a Jew, was a part of the Jewish national heritage.[12] Whatever the reason, the impact of the so-called 'Jewish reclamation of Jesus' and related developments helped bring

10 Abraham Geiger, *Judaism and its history* (New York: M. Thalmessinger, 1866); Claude G. Montefiore, *Some elements in the religious teaching of Jesus* (London: Macmillan, 1910).

11 George Foot-Moore, 'Christian writers on Judaism', *Harvard theological review* 14:5 (1921), 197–254; Robert Travers-Herford, *The Pharisees* (London: G. Allen & Unwin, 1924) and *Judaism in the New Testament period* (London: The Lindsey Press, 1928).

12 Joseph Klausner, *Jesus of Nazareth: his life, times, and teaching*, trans. Herbert Danby (New York: Macmillan, 1925; Hebrew original 1922); David Flusser, *Jesus*, trans. Ronald Walls (New York: Herder and Herder, 1969).

about a wider re-examination of Jesus, the apostle Paul, and first-century Jewish society from a specifically Jewish perspective. One consequence was the discouragement of the practice of maligning Judaism so as to make Jesus appear radically original.

The growing body of Jewish New Testament scholarship and the implications for understanding the relationship between Jews and Christians affected theologians, too. In *Faith and fratricide* (1974) and other writings, the American Catholic feminist Rosemary Radford Ruether developed the work of the British Anglican James Parkes and the French Jewish historian Jules Isaac in identifying the root cause of anti-semitism with Christianity.[13] Convinced that Jewish rejection of Jesus as Christ had inevitably led to the denigration of Judaism, Ruether came to question the legitimacy of high christology itself. As she put it, 'Anti-Judaism developed theologically in Christianity as the left-hand of Christology.'[14] For others, such revisionism was not adequate and a systematic overhaul of Christian theology, and the place of Judaism in it, was required. This culminated in the American Episcopalian Paul van Buren's three-volume *A theology of the Jewish–Christian reality* (1980–8), which attempted to unify Christian and Jewish revelation in terms of a single covenant and which saw the church's primary mission as a protector of Jewish *Torah* fidelity and statehood. Such landmarks in the intellectual landscape of inter-faith relations were, however, by no means representative of attitudes within the wider Christian community or even Christian scholarship in general.

In terms of Jewish–Christian relations the twentieth century has seen an attempt by increasing numbers of Christian individuals and institutions to recognise the legitimacy and vitality of post-biblical Judaism and to confront their traditional stereotypes and theologically informed prejudices. The unique relationship between the Jewish and Christian faith communities as a result of their shared origins, the resulting prejudices and difficulties in relating theologically to one another, and the communities' long memories of the often traumatic history of the interaction of their peoples, means that the relationship between Christianity and the Jewish other remains fragile.

---

13 James Parkes, *The conflict of the church and the synagogue: a study in the origins of antisemitism* (London: Soncino Press, 1934); Isaac, *The teaching of contempt*; Rosemary Radford Ruether, *Faith and fratricide: the theological roots of anti-semitism* (New York: Seabury Press, 1974).

14 Rosemary Radford Ruether, 'Anti-semitism and Christian theology', in Eva Fleischner (ed.), *Auschwitz: beginning of a new era: reflections on the Holocaust* (Jerusalem: KTAV, 1977), p. 79.

II
RELATIONS BETWEEN CHRISTIANS AND MUSLIMS

DAVID THOMAS

To European Christians at prayer on the outbreak of the First World War Islam was a matter of little concern, for Muslims lived in lands far away. By the turn of the millennium, however, indifference had given way to engagement with Muslims as neighbours in faith, and anxiety about the threat from Muslim extremists to livelihood and life. There has been no more dramatic change among Protestant and Catholic churches during the twentieth century than in their attitudes towards Islam, and the changes in these attitudes have been more fundamental than in any other period in the fourteen hundred years of shared Christian and Muslim history. They arise from an array of related factors, both those connected with the dramatic transformation experienced by the Islamic world, and also those that have issued from fresh Christian insights about non-Christians, and new moves towards them.

In 1914 almost the whole of the Islamic world was either under the direct rule of a European power or within its sphere of influence. The Ottoman empire, although in effect controlled from European capitals, constituted the one major sovereign Islamic entity, and Muslims everywhere looked to the sultan in Istanbul as the caliph, successor to the Prophet Muhammad as leader of the worldwide Muslim community and symbol of Muslim unity and aspirations. All this changed after the war when the empire was dismembered, and particularly in 1924 when the caliphate was abolished. Its former domains were split into separate states, and under Western influence these were compelled rapidly to come to terms with new political, economic, technological and cultural realities. Some Muslims enthusiastically embraced reform, though many were wary, sensing the potential threat to their traditional beliefs.

As the twentieth century progressed and European powers in turn relinquished their empires, other new states in Africa and Asia with substantial Muslim populations came into being and were faced with the same challenges of modernity as the former Ottoman possessions. Muslim communities in these states often experienced a dilemma between participating in the construction of a national life that was established on European values and norms, and at the same time striving to retain their traditional beliefs and practices. While Muslims in many new countries, for example in Africa, did not react immediately, in south Asia the only solution to this dilemma was seen as separation. Hence the founding of Pakistan, where Muslims could live according to the principles of their faith.

In the course of the latter decades of the century especially, self-confidence grew, boosted by the symbolic lead of the Ayatullah Khomeini in Iran, and Muslims all over the world became more conspicuous as people of strong religious sentiments who resisted Western influences. The reasons for this are highly complex, though prominent among them are the new oil wealth that enabled governments in parts of the Arab world to finance Islamic mission; widespread disillusionment with failed secular governments and a yearning for the certainty of religious values; and disenchantment with Western policies towards the Islamic world, particularly their myopic loyalty to Israel, leading to discontent with foreign ways.

In the middle of the century a number of prominent intellectuals voiced their rejection of extraneous influences and called for a return to religious ways. Among the most critical the Egyptian Sayyid Qutb (1906–66), whose two-year stay in the United States exacerbated his vehemence against the West, diagnosed Europe as suffering from a 'hideous schizophrenia that put to an end any working relationship between religion and practical life'.[15] While others were not so outspoken, many realised that the Islamic world was faced with an urgent challenge to rediscover itself, whether by returning to the teachings of scripture in their unalloyed form, or by reinterpreting them in the new circumstances in which Muslims lived.

Of course, in some parts of the world Christians and Muslims had existed beside one another for centuries. In the middle east, Egypt and Iran, Christian communities lived as religiously defined clients, *dhimmis*, of Muslim governments, while in south-eastern Europe, the Philippines and parts of west Africa, Muslim communities lived among larger Christian populations, and in Nigeria the two faiths were roughly equal. As might be expected, modes of co-existence had been worked out over time that enabled adherents of the two faiths to continue in tolerance and some security. But there was by no means peace and good will: the inter-necine fighting in Lebanon, Sudan, Bosnia-Herzegovina and Kosovo at various times in the century were all characterised, whether accurately or not, by Christian–Muslim hatred. The atrocities committed in the name of religion served as a regular reminder of

15 Sayyid Qutb, 'That hideous schizophrenia', in P. Griffiths (ed.), *Christianity through non-Christian eyes* (Maryknoll, NY: Orbis, 1990), p. 80.

the danger of religious differences and of the ambiguous potency of two religions that claimed to embody peace.

The differences between the two faiths and the urgent need for sober reappraisal of how they might approach one another with respect were brought home to Western Christians by the migration of Muslims to their countries. In the decades following the Second World War there was a steady influx of mainly manual workers from former colonies and allies, particularly into Germany from Turkey, into France from Algeria and Morocco, and into the United Kingdom from India and Pakistan.[16] Governments may originally have assumed that these workers would either leave after a short period or gradually merge into the host society. But not only did the majority stay, they settled into ways of life more characteristic of their old than their new surroundings. And thus communities of Muslims became integral parts of many cities and towns in western Europe, with their languages, foods, styles of dress and places of worship unmistakable indications of their presence.

Whether they were actively welcomed or merely tolerated at first, their continuing presence necessitated proper treatment by society and law. In the United Kingdom the Muslim outcry against Salman Rushdie's *The satanic verses* in 1988 and its barely veiled insults to the Prophet Muhammad shocked many in the wider community into realising the pronounced religious sensitivities of Muslims, and the stark difference between their insistence upon protection for revered sacred truth and the forbearance typical of many churchgoers. In France the exclusion from school in 1989 of two Muslim girls for wearing headscarves as signs of faith demonstrated the great difference between the laicised French state and Muslim citizens who regarded the public expression of faith as part of their lives. Both incidents raised fundamental issues about the right to preserve Islam in a non-Muslim context, freedom of expression, and the clash between religion and the state. How were the churches to respond?

A further event that impressed the Muslim presence on Christian minds was the overthrow of the shah of Iran in 1979 and the construction of an Islamic republic under the Ayatullah Khomeini. This experiment in statecraft focused the hopes of many Muslims, Sunnis as well as Shi'is, for a polity based on Islamic teachings. In many ways, Khomeini became a leader for Muslims worldwide and a symbol of a strong, self-sufficient, Islam.

16 J. S. Nielsen, *Muslims in western Europe*, 3rd edn (Edinburgh: Edinburgh University Press, 2004).

It is not surprising in light of renewed confidence among Muslims that in the latter years of the twentieth century extremist groups emerged prepared for fighting, killing and even martyrdom to usher in Islamic principles and ways of life and exterminate influences and threats from the West, or that the American commentator Samuel Huntington should predict increasing hostilities between the Islamic and Western blocs as part of an inevitable clash of civilisations.[17] Whether the extremist Muslims or Huntington were correct in their analysis or predictions is seriously open to question, though their perceptions of the divide between two cultures and faiths are indicative of the progressive problem of a resurgent Islam perceiving the West with its Christian foundation as an opponent, and in turn being seen in its fundamentalist intransigence as a real and present threat.

This is the background against which the attitudes of the churches changed through the twentieth century. In the 1920s it was possible for British Christians to write openly of Islam as a benighted and corrupt religion for which the only remedy was mass evangelisation. By the turn of the millennium, however, the rhetoric had changed (even though sentiments frequently had not) and Christian leaders were sometimes speaking of Muslims as partners in faith, and recalling the contribution of Islam to the foundations of modern European civilisation.

In the early part of the century Christians, and especially those whose churches operated missions in formal or informal conjunction with colonial powers, typically looked on Muslims as adherents of a repressive faith that stood in need of the gospel. For example, a report prepared for the Church of England Assembly in 1926 diagnosed the needs of Islam as follows:

> The educated classes, searching for light, need the mind of Christ to illuminate life with the high purpose of sacrificial service; the women of Islam, fettered by the laws of a barbaric age, need the emancipating power of the Gospel to lift them to their rightful place in both home and social life; the peasant and illiterate classes, frequently attached to some dervish order or other, need to know the fatherhood of God and the goal of their quest for the divine; and the Sufi mystic, seeking an experience of God, needs to be brought face to face with Christ as the Way, the Truth, and the Life.[18]

---

17 Samuel P. Huntington, 'The clash of civilizations?', *Foreign affairs* 72:3 (1993), 22–49.
18 *The world call to the church, the call from the Moslem world* (London: Press and Publications Board of the Church Assembly, 1926), p. 10.

The report makes clear repeatedly that the entire Islamic world is supine and ready to respond if the opportunity is only seized. Its sentiments anticipate the thoughts of the Dutch missionary Hendrik Kraemer as he was preparing for the 1938 International Missionary Council conference at Tambaram, southern India. Kraemer wrote: 'Islam in its constituent elements and apprehensions must be called a superficial religion ... Islam might be called a religion that has almost no questions and no answers.'[19] At the conference itself Kraemer's Barthian insistence upon the discontinuity between Christianity and other religions made a great impact. But he did not entirely carry the day, and the final conference statement left it an open question whether 'the non-Christian religions ... may be regarded as in some sense or to some degree manifesting God's revelation'.[20]

Coincidentally, the inclusivist stance (as it would now be termed) of the participants who recognised continuity between religions was echoed in the 1943 encyclical of Pope Pius XII, *Mystici corporis*, albeit in what has the appearance of a grudging concession: 'Even though by a certain unconscious desire and wish, they [all non-Catholics, including non-Christians] may be related to the Mystical Body of the Redeemer, they remain deprived of so many and so powerful gifts and helps from heaven.'[21] Here for the first time an official Catholic document held open the possibility that those outside the church, including those who were not Christians, might be saved. The thought it indirectly expresses momentously reverses the ancient dogma *extra ecclesiam nulla salus*, 'outside the church there is no salvation', and anticipates the groundbreaking teachings of the Second Vatican Council in the 1960s. It also contains in brief the insight articulated by the Jesuit theologian Karl Rahner (1904–84) that since God's grace is given to all through Christ, both those within the church and outside, all who respond to it can be called Christians, and those who respond unknowingly are 'anonymous Christians'.[22]

Rahner reached this insight on *a priori* theological grounds. In this he contrasts with another great Catholic thinker about relations between Christians and others, the French scholar Louis Massignon (1883–1962), who

19 Hendrik Kraemer, *The Christian message in a non-Christian world* (London: Edinburgh House Press, 1938), pp. 216–17.
20 *Tambaram-Madras series. International Missionary Council meeting at Tambaram, Madras, December 12th to 29th, 1938* (Oxford: Oxford University Press, 1939), vol. I, pp. 210–11.
21 Quoted in F. A. Sullivan, *Salvation outside the church? Tracing the history of the Catholic response* (London: Geoffrey Chapman, 1992), pp. 132f.
22 Karl Rahner, 'Christianity and the non-Christian religions', in *Theological investigations*, vol. v (London: Darton, Longman and Todd, 1966), pp. 115–34.

through years of immersion in Islamic mystical thought recognised Muslims as children of Abraham, guided by the Spirit.[23]

This is close to the teaching contained in the single most important document issued on Islam by any church in the twentieth century, or indeed before, in which the influence of these and other progressive scholars can be traced. This brief document was promulgated towards the end of the Second Vatican Council, on 28 October 1965, under the title 'Declaration on the relationship of the church to non-Christian religions', known from its opening words as *Nostra aetate*.

Its paragraph on Islam gives a detailed account of Muslim beliefs and practices, and underlines the fellowship with Christians these signify:

> The Church also has a high regard for the Muslims. They worship God, who is one, living and subsistent, merciful and almighty, the Creator of heaven and earth, who has spoken to men. They strive to submit themselves without reserve to the hidden decrees of God, just as Abraham submitted himself to God's plan, to whose faith Muslims eagerly link their own. Although not acknowledging him as God, they venerate Jesus as a prophet, his Virgin Mother they also honour and even at times devoutly invoke. Further, they await the day of judgement and the reward of God following the resurrection of the dead. For this reason they highly esteem an upright life and worship God, especially by way of prayer, alms-deeds and fasting.[24]

Traditional Catholics would find nothing objectionable here, but might be surprised by the statement that follows: 'This sacred Council now pleads with all to forget the past, and urges that a sincere effort be made to achieve mutual understanding.'[25]

Such idealism may be thought unrealistic. If so, it is matched by omission in the preceding description of any feature of Islam that might cause offence within the church, for example, direct references to the Prophet Muhammad and the Qur'an. A document that at first appears open and welcoming, in fact turns out have decharacterised true Islam.

But this was inevitable in light of the general statement about all non-Christian religions that prefaces the accounts of Islam and other faiths in the document. Here it is said that although the church 'rejects nothing that is true and holy in these religions', it nevertheless recognises a duty 'to proclaim

---

23 P. Rocalve, *Place et rôle de l'Islam et de l'Islamologie dans la vie et l'oeuvre de Louis Massignon* (Damascus: Publications de l'I.F.E.A.D., 1993).

24 Translated in Francesco Gioia (ed.), *Interreligious dialogue: the official teaching of the Catholic church (1963–1995)* (Boston: Pauline Books and Media, 1997), p. 38.

25 Ibid., p. 39.

without fail, Christ who is "the Way, the Truth and the Life" (Jn 14:6)',[26] thus highlighting the tension between the desire to accept the other as partner, and the imperative to proclaim Christian truth. This tension is not resolved by the council, and it became a major challenge for Christian thinkers in the decades that followed.

At the time of the council in 1964 Paul VI issued his encyclical *Ecclesiam suam* in which he mentioned Muslims warmly. His successor John Paul II likewise recalled the teachings of *Nostra aetate* in his first encyclical *Redemptor hominis* (1979), while in his later *Redemptoris missio* (1990) he stressed the presence of the Holy Spirit in individuals and societies throughout the world. However, he also made clear that the chief task of the church is mission, and that dialogue with Muslims and others is only one expression of this: 'Dialogue should be conducted and implemented with the conviction that *the Church is the ordinary means of salvation* and that *she alone* possesses the fullness of the means of salvation.'[27] Neither the pope's many visits to Islamic countries, his welcoming of Muslim leaders, nor even his dramatic invitation to world religions representatives to convene at Assisi on 27 October 1986 for a day of prayer for peace compromised this order of priorities – in fact, at the Assisi meeting each religious group performed its prayers separately.

The new importance which the Catholic church attached to relations with other faiths was signalled by the creation in 1964 of a secretariat for non-Christians within the curia; in 1988 this was renamed the Pontifical Council for Interreligious Dialogue. In accordance with its mandate, this council has produced documents on the tension hinted at in *Nostra aetate*, notably *Dialogue and witness* (1984) and *Dialogue and proclamation* (1991),[28] in which dialogue is explained as part of the wider evangelical task. In 2000 this relationship was made uncompromisingly clear in *Dominus Jesus*, a document from another Vatican dicastery, the Congregation for the Doctrine of the Faith: 'Inter-religious dialogue, therefore, as part of her evangelizing mission, is just one of the actions of the Church in her mission *ad gentes*.'[29]

In the Protestant churches there have also been clear gestures of openness towards Islam, though in a less distinctive manner. Formal relations were

---

26 Ibid., p. 38.   27 Ibid., p. 102.
28 Vatican Secretariat for non-Christians, 'The attitude of the church towards the followers of other religions: reflections and orientations on dialogue and mission', *Bulletin* 19:2 (1984), 126–41; Pontifical Council for Interreligious Dialogue, 'Dialogue and Proclamation: reflections and orientations on interreligious dialogue and the proclamation of the gospel of Jesus Christ', *Bulletin* 26:2 (1991), 201–50.
29 Congregation for the Doctrine of the Faith, *'Dominus Jesus' on the unicity and salvific universality of Jesus Christ and the church* (Vatican City, 2000).

developed by the World Council of Churches (WCC) which, after preparatory consultations at Broumana, Lebanon, in 1966, and Kandy, Sri Lanka, in 1967, about the advisability of meeting Muslims, organised a first meeting at Castigny, Switzerland, in 1969, and a multi-religious meeting at Ajaltoun, Lebanon, in 1970. In these gatherings the very different emphasis of the WCC from the Catholic church became apparent. Unable to speak with a single voice owing to the variety of churches from which it was constituted (the differences expressed at the Tambaram conference in 1938 had not disappeared), the WCC did not issue magisterial statements but emphasised the importance of faiths living side by side in respect and with practical co-operation.

In 1979, the WCC issued a key document on inter-religious relations, *Guidelines on dialogue with people of living faiths and ideologies*.[30] This is characterised by a recognition of the diversity of views about inter-religious matters among Christians, and consequently it advocates co-operation between faiths to build a 'community of communities' in which difference is tempered by respect.

As with the Catholic church, the member churches of the WCC recognised the tension between dialogue and mission, but were no more able to resolve it. The problem was graphically summed up in 1979 by Stanley Samartha: 'Dialogue emerged out of the womb of mission and it has never been easy for mission to cut the umbilical cord and to recognise the independence of the growing child without denying the relationship.'[31]

These developments among the Catholic and Protestant churches have taken place against the background outlined above of increasing self-assertiveness among Muslims in their homelands and adopted countries, escalating militancy among extremist Muslim groups, and widespread rejection of the West, leading often to distrust of the intentions behind Christian gestures of dialogue. Thus, while dialogue is acknowledged and pursued at the highest levels in the churches, the degree of its impact upon more than a few Muslims must be questioned. For many, the churches' gestures of outreach are seen in the same context as Western governments' actions in acting promptly to free oil-rich Kuwait in 1991 but doing too little too late to help Bosnian and Kosovo Muslims a few years later. Many reject dialogue as insincere, and a few resist it with armed force, while only some, mainly intellectuals living in the West, see the benefits of deepening mutual understanding and of furthering discussion towards greater honesty and respect.

---

30 Geneva: World Council of Churches Publications, 1979.
31 Stanley Samartha, 'Guidelines for dialogue', *Ecumenical review* 31 (1979), p. 130.

It must also be questioned whether the progress made by the official bodies in the churches has been noticed by many churchgoing Christians, or even their priests and ministers. In parts of the world where the two faiths have co-existed for centuries, official church statements have effected little wide-spread change in attitudes, although there has been an exponential increase in the number of specialist inter-faith meetings concerned with the differences between Christianity and Islam. The practical reality of Muslim neighbours or relations through conversion or marriage has brought home to some the necessity of knowing about and reflecting upon Islam, but for many this continued to be a marginal matter even in the years approaching 2000. All was to change with the atrocities of 11 September 2001, which concentrated in all minds the vigour of Islam (in whose name they had been committed), and raised for Christians greater challenges of comprehension and collaboration than their predecessors in 1914 could ever have imagined.

III
RELATIONS BETWEEN CHRISTIANS AND BUDDHISTS AND HINDUS

DAVID CHEETHAM

Buddhists

The history of relations between Christians and Buddhists in the twentieth century is varied and reflects many regional differences and specific historical circumstances. In this sense, an account of such a varied relationship cannot adopt a uniform approach or easily summarise the complexities of encounters and discussions that have taken place. On a theoretical level, an account might be given of some of the conceptual dialogue or comparative work that has been undertaken by individual scholars reflecting on dialogue and encounter with the other. Given the differences that surely exist between a theistic and a non-theistic religion, this has been a very creative discussion, but it is also work that has been undertaken more by Christian theologians than Buddhists.[32] Nevertheless, besides 'conceptual' or purely theological encounters, some understanding of Christian relations with Buddhists in

---

32 Notable exceptions include Thich Nhat Hanh, *Living Buddha, living Christ* (New York: Riverhead Books, 1995) and the Dalai Lama, *The good heart* (London: Rider, 1996).

the twentieth century must also be gleaned from considering the impact of nineteenth-century Christian missionary activities. This has significance not just as a key to comprehending particular historical encounters – for example, that in Sri Lanka – but also for understanding the sense of 'colonial guilt' that has often accompanied reflections in the second half of the twentieth century on 'the other'. Speaking in general, Christianity's reflection on its colonial past has initiated new postures towards other faiths and some radical gestures by some towards inclusion and dialogue.

Whereas in the West there are many Christian inter-faith groups who have been happy to 'cross over' into the Buddhist tradition to explore and incorporate some of the practices and meditation techniques, this is not necessarily repeated in other countries. For example, within India, Christian dialogue with other religions (although a more natural disposition within the south Asian consciousness) has often been tempered by a need to preserve identity. In the most recent times, the phenomenon of conversions from Scheduled (or Dalit) Castes has resulted in a certain competitiveness between Christians and Buddhists to win these groups. In Sri Lanka, the history and memory of tensions between Christians and Buddhists during the colonial era has continued to exercise an influence over contemporary efforts at understanding and has made the idea of 'common ground' a sometimes painful and difficult notion. Paradoxically, it was the actions of Christian missionaries that spurred on Buddhists to adopt far more sophisticated and aggressive 'missionary' methods ('Protestant Buddhism') in the defence of Buddhism against its opponents and in the propagation of Buddhism. The imitation of missionary methods proved to be crucial in establishing a Buddhist counter-propaganda machine. And so one of the results of this strife was the production of some of the strongest Buddhist polemics against Christianity (and the existence of God), which echoed some of the earliest debates that took place between Buddhists and the brahminical traditions of Hinduism.

Nevertheless, in places like Sri Lanka (and Cambodia), the Buddhist actions against Christian attempts to proselytise stem not from authentically Buddhist traditions about 'the other', but from a defensive mentality that has developed in the context of militant Christian missions. If dialogue between Christians and Buddhists in these parts of the world is to be positively advanced then it will first be necessary to rebuild trust and respect. This process has been given a significant boost by key figures such as Lynn de Silva (1919–82), a Sri Lankan Christian, who has sought to move the prevailing atmosphere away from diatribe and towards dialogue. The tangible outlet of this has been the founding of the journal *Dialogue* in the late 1960s. This journal has published articles on a wide range of significant themes, including the existence of God, the idea of the soul, working towards shared ethical practice, monastic life, globalisation and women in religion. Another figure (who took over from de Silva as editor of *Dialogue*), Aloysius Pieris (b. 1934), established the Tulana Research Institute in Sri Lanka in 1974 to promote Christian–Buddhist understanding.

From within the Roman Catholic tradition, one of the most prominent figures in Christian–Buddhist encounter was the monk and priest Thomas Merton (1915–68). Merton was attracted to Buddhism – particularly Zen – and explored the similarities (academically and in practice) between Christian mysticism and Buddhist thought. With Christian mysticism, in particular, he was drawn to the idea of the God who transcended all human comprehension and speech. Such approaches could help in finding points of contact with the Buddhist tradition. In similar vein, others have sought to highlight the notions of *kenosis* (divine self-emptying) in Christianity when seeking to make contact with the concept of *sunyata* (emptiness) in Buddhism.

In a West increasingly affected by the disorientation of a 'postmodern condition', and widespread interest in 'Eastern' techniques of meditation and spirituality, Buddhism has gained ground and a significant number of converts – at least when it comes to meditation practice. (Nevertheless, Western converts to Buddhism are still outnumbered by those 'ethnic' Buddhists in Western countries who trace their roots to Asia.) Moreover, in Christian theological reflection, there have been attempts to connect with Buddhism through postmodern theologies, so much so that such terms as 'Christian Buddhism' have gained a certain currency in postmodern theological thinking. Thus, the anti-realist British theologian Don Cupitt has called for a new Christianity which is 'Buddhist in form, Christian in content'.[33] Also, process theology (with its stress on 'becoming' rather than 'being') has found some affinity with the Buddhist worldview: for example, the North American process theologian John Cobb has been a prominent figure in Christian–Buddhist dialogue, particularly with Masao Abe of the Kyoto school. In the United States, the founding of a new journal (and conference series), *Buddhist–Christian studies*, by the university of Hawaii in 1980 (later under the auspices of the Society for Buddhist–Christian Studies) has provided another significant forum for discussion. Nevertheless, it has not always been easy to ascertain the common ground that would provide a

---

33 D. Cupitt, *Taking leave of God* (London: SCM, 1980), p. xiii.

platform for meaningful exchange and progress. There are differences such as: ideas of the self or non-self, the cycle of rebirth or the single life, salvation by 'grace' or effort, sin or ignorance, etc. However it is also possible that identifying such polarities is misleading. This is because the sheer diversity of beliefs and practices within the two religions means that they sometimes find themselves close together. An example of this might be the ideas of grace or saviour in Christianity in dialogue with comparable notions in the Amida traditions of Pure Land Buddhism. However, some remain sceptical that common ground is really possible and worry that it is potentially sought at the cost of losing the distinctiveness (and the support) of the different traditions. So a possible question might be, 'Does Christian–Buddhist exploration represent a genuine movement within the two religions towards each other, or is it only the concern of a few "enthusiasts"?' Only time will tell. In fact, it is possible that both traditions really see the other as providing illumination in some areas of their traditions whilst leaving other areas untouched (or 'unsurpassed'); that is, there is a sense of *complementarity*. Such complementarity has characterised the profound work of Aloysius Pieris with the joining of Buddhist *gnosis* and Christian *agape*. Nevertheless, it is possible that 'complementarity' can sometimes result in little challenge at the level of basic worldviews; that is, the traditions just talk past each other.

Looking to the future, Whelan Lai and Michael von Bruck warn: 'The isolation of specific elements has ... led to false assessments and lack of understanding in Buddhist–Christian dialogue.'[34] When it comes to the study of each religion we should remember that both are socially and historically embedded, which means that we cannot easily distil certain practices or philosophical worldviews for comparison and dialogue. Nevertheless, perhaps on a religious level, Christians and Buddhists are likely to continue to engage one another on matters relating to the nature of reality and the human condition and its solution. Neatly summing up the paradoxes of the encounter, Elizabeth Harris quotes Bishop Kenneth Fernando when he said that 'the strongest point about Christianity is that it has a Saviour. The strongest point about Buddhism is that it has no Saviour.'[35]

---

34 W. Lai and M. von Bruck (eds.), *Christianity and Buddhism: a multi-cultural history of their dialogue*, (Maryknoll, NY: Orbis, 2001), pp. 252–3.
35 Bishop Kenneth Fernando, cited in E. Harris, 'An interfaith future between Christianity and Buddhism: what cost? What benefit?', *World faiths encounter* 24 (November 1999), p. 17.

Hindus

Out of the nineteenth century, but resonating into the twentieth, are such figures as Swami Vivekananda (1863–1902). Vivekananda's eloquent speech at the first World Parliament of Religions in Chicago in 1893 had a profound impact on the future of Christian perceptions of Hinduism. Here was an effective spokesperson who turned the tables on 'fulfilment' ideas within Christian missiological reflection by (following Ramakrishna) suggesting all religions were equally valid. Moreover, he interpreted Jesus in the context of the *advaitic* tradition: that is, Jesus was just one manifestation of ultimate reality. Vivekananda's speech also drew a distinction between the materialist West and spiritual/mystical East, and although this is a hasty and erroneous idea it has nevertheless become a powerful paradigm that continues to influence popular prejudices. Another figure from the nineteenth century who powerfully articulated the sentiments that have emerged in some quarters of contemporary India is Dayananda Saraswati (1824–1883), the founder of the Arya Samaj, who bitterly criticised Christianity (together with other religions) for its exclusivist claims and for its policy in seeking conversions. There was in Saraswati's writings a desire to assert the supremacy of the 'pure' Vedic vision and revelation, which is superior to others; such sentiments are now the slogans of some contemporary Hindu fundamentalist groups in India.

Sarvapalli Radhakrishnan (1888–1975) is a majesterial figure whose vision concerning Hinduism's relationship with the other was influenced by Vivekananda and Ramakrishna. He also perceived *Vedanta* to be the ultimate expression of true religion which encompasses and includes the best within Christianity and other faiths. His tenure in the Spalding Chair for Eastern Religions and Ethics at Oxford University (1936–49) meant that Hindu–Christian dialogue gained a certain distinguished pedigree in the wider theology of religious debate. In addition, there is the massive influence of Mahatma Gandhi (1869–1948) who has had an enormous impact on the popular imagination. He admired Jesus (along with other great religious figures) as one who exemplified love and *ahimsa* (non-violence).

Critics of Christian–Hindu dialogue have pointed out the academic nature of much of it and its reflection of Western liberal Christian concerns. To what extent is the imperative towards dialogue a genuine issue in the Hindu mind? The echoes from the colonialist past have also been instrumental in causing suspicion about 'inter-religious dialogue' as a latent imperialist exercise that is merely an advanced version of earlier 'comparative' concerns. Or else, others have pointed out the need to recognise that within India itself the dialogue partners must include not just the high-caste brahminical representations of Hinduism, but also the unique predicaments and 'theological' expressions of the Scheduled Castes, or Dalits. It is in these lower castes that the conversions towards Christianity have been most evident, usually for socio-political reasons more than actual conversions to the gospel message.

Looking at the encounter between Hindus and Christians in India in the twentieth century, one can be struck by the diversity of opinions, from the uncompromising views of some conservative groups who would draw a sharp distinction between Christianity and the superstitions of an 'idolatrous' Hinduism, and those who have sought to absorb Hindu ideas and create a truly 'Indian' Christianity. In many cases this amounts to more than just inculturation. For example, one of the most distinctive features of Christian encounters with Hinduism has been the development of Christian ashrams. Famous innovators include Henri le Saux (1910–73) – later named Swami Abishiktananda – who founded the Saccidananda Asrama in south India, and the English Benedictine, Bede Griffiths (1906–93), who sought to reinterpret Christian metaphysics in line with Hindu philosophies, preferring monism over dualism. The Roman Catholic Brahmabandhav Upadhyaya (1861–1907), from a Bengali Brahmin background, argued that the Christian message 'must assume the Hindu garment which will make it acceptable to the people of India'.[36] He tried (unsuccessfully) to persuade the Vatican to accept his proposals. Moreover, P. Chenchiah (1886–1959) maintained that Christian converts in India should regard Hinduism as their 'spiritual mother'.[37] Nevertheless, not all express the same enthusiasm, and so other voices, like the Indian theologian Y. D. Tiwari, are concerned that the 'wide use of Hindu terms will weaken the Christian message'.[38]

India has produced some outstanding Christian theologians who are eager to engage with the Hindu culture and who have made distinctive contributions to the debate about Christianity and other religions. As well as those quoted above, they include such names as S. Samartha, P. Devanandan, A. J. Appasamy and M. Amaladoss. Looking to the future, Klaus Klostermaier makes a bold claim when he writes: 'Doctrinally Hinduism outside of India is very liberal; the openness for new ideas of modern Hindus in the west is so

---

36 Cited in J. Russell Chandan, 'The development of Christian theology in India', in R. S. Sugirtharajah and C. Hargreaves (eds.), *Readings in Indian Christian theology* (Delhi: ISPCK, 1993), p. 8.
37 Ibid.   38 Y. D. Tiwari, 'From Vedic dharma to the Christian faith', in ibid., p. 137.

great that dialogue is almost pointless.'[39] This reflects Klostermaier's view that the actual context of Hinduism in 'Bharat Mata', as he puts it, is crucial for understanding Hinduism and the socio-political complexities that affect the dialogue between different religious and social groups. However, the vast and multifarious nature of Hinduism in India should not prevent us from taking seriously the evolving diasporic expressions of Hindu belief and practice that will surely have an impact on future encounters. Furthermore, certain groups (inside and outside India) such as the Rashtriya Swayamsevak Sangh (RSS) or the Vishva Hindu Parishad (VHP) have influenced a 'semiticisation' of Hinduism (in order to make it more dogmatic, 'national', creedal and missionary) that will also have an important influence. In addition, perhaps, there is the increasing interest in the stereotypical 'mystic East' within some branches of 'new age' thinking in the West (largely through the popular culture of the 1960s) to consider. These new and evolving developments may indicate that the kind of encounter between Christians and Hindus will become more varied, complex and challenging in the twenty-first century.

IV
THEOLOGIES OF RELIGIONS

_____

DAVID CHEETHAM

Although it cannot be maintained that the 'theology of religions' as an important question for Christians is only a twentieth-century problem, it is nonetheless the case that the issues with which it is concerned have become increasingly prominent and acute. Various reasons might be offered for this: the increase in knowledge about other faiths, the dispersal of peoples and diasporic experience that has brought multi-culturalism into Western towns and cities. Moreover, there is the effect of globalisation and the communications revolution. In the West, perhaps also the collapse of confidence in the intellectual products of the European Enlightenment and in Western reason have been among significant factors that have led towards greater attention being given to insights from beyond purely Western canons and to greater openness to other traditions. Moreover, articulate voices have emerged from

---

39 K. Klostermaier, 'The future of Hindu–Christian Dialogue', in H. Coward (ed.), _Hindu–Christian dialogue: perspectives and encounters_ (Maryknoll: Orbis, 1989), p. 264.

areas that have a colonial past and these give new expressions to Christian theology and practice which are often critical of Western styles and methodologies. Many of these voices – especially Asian ones – have made important and informed contributions to the theology of religions.[40]

Some have seen it as the most important issue to have emerged in recent times: thus one missiologist remarked: 'This is the theological issue for mission in the 1990's and into the twenty-first century.'[41] Nevertheless, the twentieth century has brought forth a variety of different approaches to this issue; in fact, the *issue* itself is defined variously – reflecting sociological, political and ethical concerns as well as 'theological' ones. In this case, it is also more representative to speak of 'theologies of religions'. Moreover, it would be a superficial analysis indeed that merely sought to associate theologies of religions in the twentieth century to the collection of phenomena or trends mentioned above. Furthermore, to seek to construct an account which portrays the development of thinking in this field as a uniform progression away from less 'tolerant' traditional perspectives towards more inclusive or pluralistic ones would, at best, be misleading and at worst appear deliberately programmatic. Instead, it would be more correct to speak of the great deal of creativity and diversity – the sheer multiplicity of theologies of religion – that has characterised Christian reflection on 'the religious *other*' in the twentieth century. This has not always been original thinking; instead it might be said that in some cases the more standard 'exclusive' or 'inclusive' positions within the Christian tradition have undergone further elaboration and exploration and have benefited from greater erudition than in earlier times.

In the twentieth century, Christian theological reflection has been informed by a range of factors including academic theological work, the concerns of missionaries, emerging theologians from previously colonised areas such as India, students of comparative religion and inter-faith 'pioneers'. The vastly increased knowledge of the religious 'other' that began with missionary scholarship in the nineteenth century is clearly an important factor in the development of, first, comparative religion and, second, religious studies (and the 'inter-faith movement' as another offshoot). Such knowledge

---

40 See, for example, M. Amaladoss, *Making all things new: dialogue, pluralism and evangelisation in Asia* (Maryknoll, NY: Orbis, 1990); S. Samartha, *One Christ, many religions: towards a revised christology* (Maryknoll, NY: Orbis, 1991); S. Samartha, *Courage for Dialogue* (Maryknoll, NY: Orbis, 1981); R. Panikkar, *The unknown Christ of Hinduism* (Maryknoll, NY: Orbis, 1981).

41 G. H. Anderson, 'Theology of religions and missiology: a time of testing', in C. van Engen et al. (eds.), *The good news of the kingdom: mission theology for the third millennium* (Maryknoll, NY: Orbis, 1993), p. 201.

has also profoundly interrogated some older stereotypes (or myths) concerning other religions which were the imaginary 'dialogue' partners of the past. Nevertheless, the reasons for some of the more major theological contributions have resulted from influences that are not directly related to Christian reflections on other religions. If we look at one of the most influential theological figures of the twentieth century, Karl Barth (1886–1968), we see that the main reasons for his seemingly uncompromising view of religions as 'unbelief' stemmed not from an actual encounter with other faiths, or from a reflection on the place of the non-Christian within the Christian scheme, but from his vehement rejection of what he perceived as an impotent theological liberalism that resided in European universities at the end of the nineteenth century. Nevertheless, the separation of 'given' revelation from natural, or liberal, theology had a profound consequence for theologies of religions, and the Barthian view has been championed by conservatives who have wished to stress the radical discontinuity between Christianity and other faiths. The influence of Barth cannot be under-estimated and he is often placed into an 'exclusivist' camp (although it is possible that such a designation may actually represent a myopic reading of his work). There are background traces of his concerns to be found in many contemporary theologies, including the post-liberal theologies of the second half of the twentieth century and the 'radical orthodox' school to name but a few. Thus the post-liberal G. Lindbeck articulated an influential cultural-linguistic model that seeks to affirm the importance of the *intra-textual* (as opposed *extra*-textual) narrative of the Christian community, and is suspicious of ideas of 'common ground' or universal understanding. Also, influenced by the more 'radical orthodox' theological strategies, the Roman Catholic theologian Gavin D'Costa has stressed the tradition-specific character of religious discourse which means that our starting points are never 'above' the different religions, but from within them. In addition, this emphasis on the cultural location (or cultural integrity) of religious life has led to new theologies of religions which are keen to emphasise *difference*, rather than commonality, as being significant in the encounter and dialogue with other faiths. For example, the North American theologian S. Mark Heim has been innovative in stressing the multiple nature of the goals of different religions. That is, there are different 'salvations' which are not reducible to a single soteriological essence. This stress on difference, it is argued, makes the encounter and discussion between Christianity and other faiths more provocative, surprising and challenging.

More inclusive or universalist theologies of religions have their origin in the experience of missionaries, particularly in India, in the nineteenth and very early twentieth centuries. Nevertheless, earlier efforts at comparative work by some missionaries often betrayed what many perceived as colonialist influences and presumptions of superiority. This has led to questions of the motivation of Christians engaged in inter-faith dialogue. However, also from the middle of the nineteenth century came missionary voices that sought to be more inclusive of other religious traditions and interpret the Christian message as 'fulfilling' other religions. That is, they were seen as 'preparations' for the gospel. This notion of fulfilment found a sophisticated voice in J. N. Farquhar, author of *The crown of Hinduism* (1913). Farquhar's work has become a classic 'inclusivist' statement in the theology of religions and the impact of his thinking was felt at world missionary conferences held at Edinburgh (1910) and, even more, at Jerusalem (1928). In 1932–3 the influential Laymen's Foreign Missions Inquiry's multi-volumed *Re-thinking missions* (1932) was an avant-garde work which sought to reassess the traditional notion of mission as converting the heathen and asserted the value of the continued existence (rather than replacement or 'conversion from') of other faiths. This caused a significant controversy – being enthusiastically welcomed by liberals and heavily criticised by evangelicals – and formed the background of a pivotal world missionary conference held in Tambaram (1938). Here a Dutch scholar, Hendrik Kraemer, advanced a Barthian line in stressing the discontinuity between Christianity and other faiths. This was resisted by those who had sympathies with Farquhar and others, but the line taken by Kraemer was a definitive milestone for conservative thinking. This has remained the line taken by most conservatives in, for example, the Frankfurt Declaration of 1970.

From within the Roman Catholic tradition, Karl Rahner is another major theological figure to have dominated Catholic theological reflection on other religions in the twentieth century, not least because of his profound influence on the development of the thinking and statements on this issue in Vatican II (1962–5). Rahner's is a very profound contribution which began not as a deliberate reflection following a personal encounter with other faiths, but as a theological reflection within the Catholic tradition: a reflection on the love of God together with a complex and unique anthropology which saw God's grace as present in the very nature of humanity ('supernatural existential') and, as a further extension of this, that all of nature is 'graced'. The grace of Christ is present in other religions and therefore we may speak of the other as an 'anonymous Christian'. Moreover, other religions may be understood as 'ways of salvation'. The essence of what Rahner recommended found its way (though not in its entirety by any means) into the documents of Vatican II, which has radical implications for the theology of religions in the Catholic tradition. Thus *Lumen gentium* (1964) recommends dialogue and suggests that those in other faiths can achieve salvation through actions that are 'moved by grace' and the 'dictates of conscience'. *Nostra aetate* (1965), whilst affirming the uniqueness of Christ as 'the way, the truth and the life', nonetheless declares that one cannot reject what is 'true and holy' in other religions. Around this time, the Indian Catholic thinker Raimundo Panikkar published *The unknown Christ of Hinduism* (1964), which sought to discern the hidden Christ in the *advaitic* tradition of Hinduism. This important 'inclusive' work echoes something of Farquhar's thought fifty years earlier and has remained an influential work. Other prominent inclusive voices in the Catholic tradition include Jacques Dupuis who has sought to speak of the 'mutual complementarity' of religions.

During the early 1970s, the British philosopher and theologian John Hick proposed a 'Copernican revolution' in theology and recommended that all religions be seen as valid responses to the ultimate reality (the 'Real') behind them. His hypothesis has served as a major sophisticated statement of the pluralist position which has gained significant influence in the debate about other religions at the beginning of the twenty-first century.

In popular discussions it has become commonplace to use the threefold typology of exclusivism, inclusivism and pluralism when describing or 'categorising' some of the positions outlined above.[42] This is a paradigm that will continue to be useful and influential, but it has also been criticised for restricting the debate within its threefold boundaries or even for being overly programmatic in its tendency to suggest a progression from exclusivism towards pluralism. It is possible that some of the theologies of religions that emerge in the future will seek to address the issues without reference to this paradigm. This will undoubtedly create new discourses and thinking in the field which will enrich the debate still further.

It is clear that consideration of other religions and their competing claims to truth will continue to play a crucial role in the theological reflection of the twenty-first century. Moreover, current political tensions generated by divisions between peoples and acts of terrorism mean that critical theological and wider reflection on the relations between different cultures and religions will be increasingly perceived as an important task. Indeed, above other issues, it will be the theologian's response to 'the other' in light of contemporary

---

42 See A. Race, *Christians and religious pluralism* (London: SCM, 1983).

challenges that will be most keenly followed by those outside the Christian community in a world under the spectre of fundamentalism and terrorism. Some theologians have perceived an urgency to work towards more practical theologies. One instance of this is the 'global ethic' which was drafted by the Catholic theologian Hans Küng and launched at the 1993 World Parliament of Religions under the slogan: 'no peace among the nations without peace among the religions'. Moreover, others, such as P. Knitter, have called for theologies of religion which reflect the need for justice and peace. However, the nature of that reflection will be diverse, and the debate will continue to reflect the wide range of concerns, from the more particular and traditional to the more plural and universal, together with changing theological or intellectual trends and allegiances. Moreover, as the global inter-cultural experience gains even greater fluency in the future, it should be expected that non-Western Christian voices will increasingly inform and direct the future debates within this important theological concern.

28

Wealth and poverty

DUNCAN B. FORRESTER

The legacy of the nineteenth century

Social and economic changes in the nineteenth century ensured that Christian teaching on wealth and poverty when it was received in the early twentieth century had been profoundly affected by new challenges. The three most important nineteenth-century developments for our purposes were industrialisation, urbanisation and colonialism. Industrialisation transformed the nature of the economy, and was a major reason for the emergence of the new science of 'political economy'. Urbanisation brought into the cities of the industrialising nations a flood of people to work in the new factories. The rate of expansion was so rapid that the industrial cities developed vast and insanitary slums, and there was immense difficulty in providing even the most basic of services to the new industrial workforce and their families and dependants. Colonialism, particularly the growth of the British empire 'on which the sun never set', was an early form of what today is called 'globalisation'. The colonies provided plentiful supplies of raw materials for the new industries in the 'mother countries', and huge markets for finished products. Colonialism presented itself as in the interests of the populace of the colonies, and indeed the 'white colonies' absorbed some of the 'surplus population' from the mother countries. But by the late nineteenth century, in Asia and Africa it was fairly clear that there was a massive economic drain from the colonies to the imperial nations, on which their prosperity and wealth largely depended. This, of course, caused much poverty in the colonies, and in the industrial cities of the West the new mass poverty, or 'pauperism', showed itself as resistant to the forms of alleviation or remedy that had worked for much of the time in traditional societies with relatively simple modes of production and smallish social units. Mass poverty among the masses in the industrialised cities was closely related to a massive accumulation of capital. The traditional aristocracy whose wealth was usually based on land now had to face a new prosperous capitalist class of entrepreneurs whose wealth came from the new industrial growth and from the colonies.

These developments aroused both movements of protest and new forms of understanding society and the economy, particularly the classical political economy of Adam Smith and his allies and disciples. Evangelicals such as Thomas Chalmers saw a deep congruence between Christian theology and the new economics. The poor were, in Malthus' terms, the 'redundant population', and Chalmers taught that both the problem of poverty and its solution lay largely in the hands of the poor.

Various forms of socialism and, particularly in the second half of the nineteenth century, Marxism took a very critical position in relation to classical political economy and the new industrial capitalism. Christian social-ists regarded the masses of the urban poor as both the victims of capitalist development and as the core of new movements of protest and social change. The church, they felt, should identify itself with the industrial working class, and Christian theology should give some kind of endorsement to the socialist movement.

Other Christian responses to the new competitive capitalism arose mainly out of the liberal wing of the churches. The 'Social Gospel', in rather different forms, was influential in Germany and in the United States. For the leading German liberal theologian, Adolf von Harnack, 'the gospel and the poor' was *the* social question that had to be addressed. Yet Harnack and his like were reluctant to spell out in detail the political and economic implications of a Christian response to this pressing 'social question'. In America the powerful Social Gospel movement was identified with liberal theology and had as its major prophet Walter Rauschenbusch, whose classic work, *Christianity and the social crisis* (1907), inspired generations of young Christians with an eagerness for social and political involvement particularly in tackling poverty and its effects on the individual and society.

From 1891 when Pope Leo XIII promulgated his encyclical *Rerum novarum* there has developed a coherent body of official Roman Catholic social teaching which has all along been deeply concerned with issues of wealth and poverty, and with the rights of workers. To begin with, this teaching saw itself as offering a 'third way' between capitalism and individualism, on the one hand, and socialism and collectivist responses to questions of wealth and poverty, on the other. At the beginning there was much suspicion of modern-ity in all its manifestations, and the third way that was offered was highly traditionalist. But gradually Roman Catholic social teaching became embo-died in radical popular movements for social change and in conservative

Christian Democratic political parties. It claimed to be even-handed in its critiques of capitalism and socialism, and consistent in its advocacy of a Catholic 'third way'.

The red pastor of Safenwil

As the confidence of the Western world disintegrated in the carnage of the First World War, in the small Swiss parish of Safenwil in the Aargau there was a young minister who was not afraid to take sides, and who saw it as his duty as a pastor and a theologian to align himself with the cause of the poor and the weak. His preaching and his political stances caused offence to the more conservative and prosperous members of his congregation. But the workers and the poor in the parish regarded him with real affection as being one who was on their side. His name was Karl Barth, and he has often been spoken of as the greatest Protestant theologian of the twentieth century.

Barth from the beginning was determined to ground his political, economic and social stances on rigorously worked-out theology, and indeed his consistently radical position on economic issues was rooted in his radical post-liberal theology. He believed that the war had revealed the frailty of the theological liberalism of such as Harnack, and he sought a more radical theology that resulted from a re-engagement with what he called 'the strange new world in the Bible'. His guides were the leaders of the movement called 'religious socialism', particularly Christoph Blumhardt, Hermann Kutter and Leonardt Ragaz. His encounter at Safenwil with the realities of poverty made a profound and enduring impression on Barth and on his theology. He wrote in 1927: 'In the class conflict which I saw concretely before me in my congregation I was touched for the first time by the real problems of real life.' As a result he studied factory acts and trade unionism, and reflected on the class struggles in the locality, involving most of the members of his congregation. 'A real Christian must become a socialist,' he declared in 1915, and 'a real socialist must be a Christian'. It has also been suggested, by F. W. Marquardt and others, that socialism was throughout his career at the very heart of Barth's theology. Certainly he could still nail his socialist colours to the mast in 1946, when he was an immensely distinguished professor of dogmatics, declaring:

> The Church is witness of the fact that the Son of man came to seek and to save the lost. And this implies that – casting all false impartiality aside – the Church must concentrate first on the lower and lowest levels of human society. The poor, the socially and economically weak and threatened, will

always be the object of its primary and particular concern, and it will always insist on the State's special responsibility for these weaker members of society . . . The Church must stand for social justice in the political sphere. And in choosing between the various socialistic possibilities . . . it will always choose the movement from which it can expect the greatest measure of social justice . . .[1]

Barth's influence on theology and on the churches was profound. But as so often happens with really great thinkers, his disciples divided into two groups: the 'left Barthians' who saw Barth's teaching as pointing unwaveringly towards poverty as a central issue for theological ethics, and socialism in one or the other of its varieties as showing the way to deal with poverty, and the 'right Barthians' who used some parts of Barth's theology to support conservative positions on economic, ecclesiastical and social issues. But Barth ensured that what was later to be spoken of as the 'preferential option for the poor' was to be steadily near the top of the Protestant churches' agenda during the twentieth century.

Poverty and philosophical idealism

From the late nineteenth century for a number of decades, a form of philosophical idealism influenced by Hegel, sympathetic to liberal theology, and committed to the need for radical social reform was very influential in British academic life, particularly at Balliol college, Oxford, and in the Scottish universities. One of the early leaders of this movement, Benjamin Jowett, the master of Balliol in the late nineteenth century, and one of his successors, Edward Caird, used to say to the brightest and best of their students, 'Go and find your friends among the poor.'[2] As a consequence many of them went to the east end of London, and the slums of Manchester and Glasgow, and they worked in settlements and slum parishes, they established youth clubs, they worked with unemployed people, they helped provide medical care for malnourished children with rickets, they taught in adult education classes. They got to know poor people. But when they tried to make friends, they found great problems. An ugly ditch of inequality seemed to be set between their world and the world of the poor. They were excluded from each other's

1 Karl Barth, 'The Christian community and the civil community', in *Against the stream: shorter post-war writings, 1946–52* (London: SCM, 1954), p. 38.
2 Norman Dennis and A. H. Halsey, *English ethical socialism: Thomas More to R. H. Tawney* (Oxford: Clarendon Press, 1988), p. 153.

lives. Individual idealistic efforts by privileged and able young academics, however strenuous, were not enough to span the chasm.

The idealistic young men realised that there were great structural obstacles to friendship. By going to the slums and meeting poor people they saw that they must put the poor at the heart of their concern, that they must speak for the voiceless, that they must work to make Britain a place where friendship was possible, the forces that corrode, corrupt or impede friendship removed. They went through a kind of intellectual and emotional conversion which was to have profound repercussions. The young men who responded included Richard Tawney, William Beveridge and William Temple.

Tawney throughout the 1920s and 1930s denounced the 'mammon-worship' that condemned multitudes to poverty and degradation and despair. He called for a fraternal society, a community of friends, in which the equal worth of every human being before God is fully recognised. Tawney taught economic history for most of his working life at the London School of Economics. His scholarly writings were not particularly voluminous, but some of them, most notably *The acquisitive society* (1921) and *Equality* (1931), were immensely influential and intelligent manifestos. He argued that from the birth of modern industrial capitalism the church and theology had withdrawn into the private and domestic realms and away from all serious and thoughtful engagement with public issues. The vacuum thus created was, he said, occupied by another creed, 'a persuasive, self-confident and militant gospel proclaiming the absolute value of economic success'. This new, and false, gospel was seen by Tawney as destructive of fellowship and of concern for the poor, and as a consequence radically opposed to Christianity. 'Compromise is as impossible,' he wrote, 'between the Church of Christ and the idolatry of wealth, which is the practical religion of capitalist societies, as it was between the Church and the State idolatry of the Roman Empire.'[3] Christianity, taken seriously, involved for him an engagement with the struggle against poverty, for Christianity is not only concerned with the destiny of the individual, but with the establishment of fraternity, justice and compassion in society. In the conflict between Christianity and the idolatry of capitalism, Tawney issued calls for 'intellectual conversion' – a turning from the values of capitalism towards God's reign and towards the poor, and the values of justice and equality, which were rooted in the Christian faith. His continuing influence in promoting Christian socialism and putting the issue of poverty at the heart of his concern has been prodigious.

3 Richard Tawney, *Religion and the rise of capitalism* (London: John Murray, 1926), p. 286.

William Beveridge, Tawney's brother-in-law, but less specifically committed religiously, after acting as sub-warden of the Toynbee Hall settlement in east London, in the 1940s sounded the call to do battle with the five 'giants' – squalor, idleness, want, disease and ignorance – which stood in the way of a more Christian and a more caring Britain, in which friendship and mutual support would be possible because the gulf between rich and poor would be bridged. When a sequence of reports from Beveridge outlining a welfare state were published, the archbishop of Canterbury said, 'This is the first time that anyone has set out to embody the whole spirit of the Christian ethic in an Act of Parliament!'

William Temple, as archbishop of York and then of Canterbury, recruited Christian intellectuals to share in the task of reshaping the social order, and mobilised church support for a more just, equal and fraternal Britain. His little book *Christianity and social order* (1942) was immensely influential, and can be read as a kind of manifesto calling for the eradication of poverty. It has aptly been described as one of the foundation piers of the welfare state. Temple, as a young man, was deeply influenced by philosophical idealism; later he responded to the new 'theology of crisis' coming from Barth and others. He had a huge influence on planning for 'post-war reconstruction', and he managed to combine to a quite extraordinary extent the roles, often believed to be contradictory, of prophet and of church leader. *Christianity and social order* concludes with practical suggestions for government, which together express Temple's social vision and his special concern with poverty. They also outline with considerable clarity the type of welfare state that was implemented in Britain in the late 1940s, with strong support from the churches and Christian opinion. 'Every child should find itself a member of a family housed with decency and dignity,' Temple wrote; there should be education for all, together with fair and decent wages, and worker participation in the conduct of industry. Every citizen should be guaranteed leisure and holidays with pay, and 'liberty in the forms of freedom of worship, of speech, of assembly, and of association for special purposes'. Finally, anticipating criticism, he asked: 'Utopian? Only in the sense that we cannot have it all tomorrow. But we can set ourselves to advance towards the six-fold objective. It can all be summed up in a phrase: *the aim of a Christian social order is the fullest possible development of individual personality in the widest and deepest fellowship.*'[4]

4 William Temple, *Christianity and social order* (Harmondsworth: Penguin, 1942), pp. 73–4.

Temple, Tawney, Beveridge, and many others as well, all found out that personal change and personal commitment were important, but they were not enough. The structures and processes that caused poverty and impeded friendship had to be unmasked, confronted, reformed or replaced. Structures that enabled and expressed friendship had to be established. For these, and many others, poverty was the key issue that had to be tackled in any decent society. And for most of them this concern was rooted in and arose from their Christian faith.

Tawney and Temple, and the influential band of academics and professionals who regarded themselves as in some sense or other Christian socialists, and most of whom had been deeply influenced by the kind of Idealist philosophy that was represented by thinkers like T. H. Green, Bernard Bosanquet and others, collectively had a major impact on policy and political priorities in Britain, particularly in the 1940s. But it has also to be said that until the 1950s there was rather little serious intellectual engagement either with 'scientific socialism' in its Marxist garb, or with the ideologies of capitalism, represented from the 1940s in the thought of such as Friedrich von Hayek, whose influential *The road to serfdom* (1944) argued that all forms of socialism necessarily end up as totalitarian forms of oppression. But those we have been considering in this section had one great achievement to their credit: the crystallisation of a consensus on which the British welfare state could be built in the 1940s and 1950s.

Christian neo-liberalism

In most of the countries of the Western world there was for a couple of decades after the Second World War a broad left-of-centre consensus that the welfare state was a good thing, and that industry and the economy should be made socially accountable, perhaps through public ownership of 'the commanding heights' of the economy, and through centralised economic planning. Redistribution through the taxation and welfare systems was commonly advocated as the most appropriate way for avoiding high levels of inequality and dealing with the problem of poverty. Right-wing critics of this consensus bided their time, sharpening their intellectual tools as they awaited the expected collapse of the social democratic welfare consensus from its own inner contradictions. Thinkers such as Hayek, Karl Popper, whose famous *The open society and its enemies* was first published in 1945, and the economist Milton Friedman worked to develop a critique of the welfare consensus and proposals for what should follow its collapse. In their wilderness years around informal networks such as the Mont Pelerin Society they worked quietly on developing a consistent and well-thought-out neo-liberal position, espousing the free market and resisting the expansion of state interference. They were against egalitarian policies of redistribution, and welfare policies which they saw as encouraging dependency and eroding individual responsibility. Social justice was declared to be a dangerous and misleading 'myth' by Hayek. They moved centre stage in Britain with the emergence as prime minister of Margaret Thatcher, in the United States with the development of Reaganism, and in a number of other countries, especially around the time of the spectacular collapse of the communist dictatorships of eastern Europe in 1989.

One of Margaret Thatcher's most prominent advisers, Keith Joseph, declared baldly at a time when social scientists and politicians were wrestling with the understanding of poverty, and how policy could most appropriately respond, 'A family is poor if it cannot afford to eat.'[5] Inequality was no longer considered a social problem by the neo-conservatives; indeed, in a free market it might have huge economic advantages, which would 'trickle down' to benefit the poor as well as the wealthy. Welfare provision was to be reorganised in accordance with theories that were strikingly similar to those popular in the nineteenth century. New right social theorists in the United States, such as Charles Murray and Lawrence Meade, attacked the welfare state and policies of redistribution as fundamentally ill conceived and economically disastrous.

Particularly in Britain and America there were strenuous efforts to relate new right policies to Christian faith. Margaret Thatcher, for instance in the 'Sermon on the Mound' which she delivered in 1988 to the General Assembly of the Church of Scotland, claimed to root both the general orientation and the particular policies of her government on the central affirmations of the Christian faith. She affirmed consistently that she acted on principle and on conviction rather than pragmatism or electoral advantage. She described her government as not being based on expediency. 'It was successful', she argued, 'because it was based on clear, firmly-held principles which were themselves based on a right understanding of politics, economics and above all human nature.'[6] And these principles she believed were at their root Christian.

Many of the most significant Christian thinkers who supported the new right did so with significant reservations. The economist Brian Griffiths, for

---

5 Keith Joseph and Jonathan Sumption, *Equality* (London: John Murray, 1979), pp. 27–8.
6 *The Scotsman*, 23 November 1996.

instance, who was for a time Margaret Thatcher's chief economic adviser, had public reservations about the extreme individualism that was characteristic of the Thatcherite project, and believed that the market could only function acceptably if it was in a clear moral framework that put certain limits on the marketplace, particularly to protect the poor and the vulnerable. A special concern – or what others would call a 'preferential option' – for the poor is not for Christians a matter of choice: both government and the market, Griffiths argued, must have a special care for the poor if they are to be acceptable to Christians. Rather than regarding himself as an advocate of the free market economy, Griffiths saw himself as committed to exploring Christian alternatives to capitalism and socialism. A similar position was taken up by the conservative politician and businessman who was an evangelical Christian, Sir Fred Catherwood.

In the United States the new right found theological support from evangelical Christians and from prominent conservative Roman Catholics such as Richard Neuhaus and Michael Novak. In his vindication of liberal democracy and the market economy, Novak concludes his argument with a 'theology of democratic capitalism', in which he argues that neither a democratic polity nor a market economy makes sense apart from 'certain specific views of human life and human hope'.[7] Like Catherwood and Griffiths, both evangelical Protestants, Novak and Neuhaus as Roman Catholics advocate a Christian polity and economy and are deeply suspicious of the socialist and Christian socialist projects. Novak endorses what he sees as Roman Catholic social teaching's critique of socialism, and its advocacy of a 'third way'.

Roman Catholic social teaching and practice

The tradition of Roman Catholic social teaching, which had begun to revive in the late nineteenth century, flourished creatively under the influence of seminal thinkers such as Jacques Maritain in France and John Courtney Murray in the United States. It provided the ideological underpinning for the right-of-centre Christian Democratic parties influential in many countries in Europe. Maritain and Murray and many others drew traditional Roman Catholic teaching into the modern debates about social and economic issues such as poverty and wealth, and in the process adapted the teaching and its emphases to make it capable of holding its own in the general liberal

---

7 Michael Novak, *The spirit of democratic capitalism* (New York: Simon and Schuster, 1982), pp. 333–60.

democratic forum of debate about social issues. Poverty was no longer seen as simply the occasion for charity, or for the voluntary embracing of 'holy poverty' as a way to holiness. It now became a problem or a malady to be tackled with all the resources that social theory and practical Christian commitment could afford. Through popular movements such as the JOC (*Jeunesse Ouvrière Chrétienne*) young Catholics were encouraged and trained to work with and for the poor, and to question the existing social order on a Christian basis. Catholic Action, defined by Maritain as 'works whose object is to make the Christian life and spirit penetrate into the profane and secular, into social life and into particular social activities',[8] became a major influence on ways of responding to poverty .

Although Marxism in general had little impact on Catholic social teaching until the 1960s, there was one aspect of Marxist teaching which seemed far earlier to be strikingly relevant – the existence of what Marxists called the 'proletariat'. Many Catholics were deeply concerned that in most of the countries of western Europe there was an industrial proletariat of the poor which was deeply alienated from the church and from the Christian faith. Some Catholics were impressed with the Marxists' claim that the urbanised industrial poor were a *class* in a situation which was inevitably one of class conflict. And without embracing fully the Marxist understanding of the proletariat as a kind of chosen people who were the harbingers of the future, it was argued that there was a Christian responsibility to take sides, to stand with the poor, to identify with the proletariat, even in its struggle against the bourgeoisie.

A missionary and radical response to poverty which created much excitement in the 1940s to 1960s was the development, particularly in France, of the worker-priest movement.[9] Radical priests, with or without the encouragement of their bishops, sought solidarity with the poor. They found labouring jobs in industry, and said mass in their lodgings or occasionally in the factories, late at night or early in the morning, gathering around them small groups of industrial workers, and involving themselves fully in the life of the working poor. This meant taking a full part in radical politics of a sort that presupposed class struggle. The Vatican became deeply concerned and attempted, without total success, to suppress the movement. It was

---

8 Jacques Maritain, *Scholasticism and politics*, 3rd edn (London: Bles, 1954), p. 158.
9 John Petrie (trans.), *The worker priests: a collective documentation* (London: Routledge and Kegan Paul, 1954); Oscar L. Arnal, *Priests in working-class blue: the history of the worker-priests (1943–1954)* (New York: Paulist Press, 1986).

clearly alarmed at the phenomenon of priests identifying with the proletariat, and taking sides in class conflicts.

The Vatican also declared that 'work in a factory is incompatible with the sacerdotal life and obligations', for 'the working priest is not only plunged in a materialist atmosphere deleterious to spiritual life and often even dangerous for his chastity, but is also led in spite of himself to think like his worker comrades on trade unions and social matters, to take part in their struggles, which gravely involve him so that he is led to participate in the class struggle which is inadmissible for a priest'.[10] It was indeed odd that the authorities did not realise that their criticisms of the worker priests also suggested a radical critique of modern industrial society whose 'materialist atmosphere' presumably endangered also the spiritual life of Christian working people. But already alliances, dialogue and new understandings had arisen between significant radical Catholics and communists, particularly in France, where the worker-priest movement was strongest.

Liberation Theology

The worker-priest movement was one of the influences behind the rise of Liberation Theology, initially in Latin America, from the early 1960s. Liberation Theology from the beginning saw the poor as involved in a social structure that was profoundly exploitative and unjust. As José Miguez Bonino put it:

> The poor, the oppressed, the humiliated *are a class* and *live in countries* . . . Are we really for the poor and the oppressed if we fail to see them as a class, as members of oppressed societies? If we fail to say *how*, are we 'for them' in their concrete historical situation? Can we claim a solidarity which has nothing to say about the actual historical forms in which their struggle to overcome oppression is carried forward? . . . Is it possible to claim a solidarity with the poor and hover above right and left as if the choice did not have anything to do with the matter?[11]

The primary issue for theology is not, according to the liberation theologians, an abstract concept, even 'poverty', 'inequality', or 'justice'. It is rather poor *people*, and the question why they are poor, and what can be done about it. But who are the poor? Marxist analysis encouraged the liberation theologians

---

10 Cardinal Pizzardo, quoted in the *Guardian*, 15 September 1959.
11 José Miguez Bonino, *Revolutionary theology comes of age* (London: SPCK, 1975), p. 148.

to emphasise the necessity of understanding the poor as part of a class system of social stratification, which is itself inevitably locked into class conflict.

Bonino and the other liberation theologians challenged the Western political theologies as represented by Jürgen Moltmann, Johann Baptist Metz and others with being too critically detached from the actual struggles of the poor. Liberation Theology, they argued, is not the reduction of the gospel to a political programme, but the attempt to illuminate what is going on with the help of the best social and economic theory available – at the time generally considered by the liberation theologians to be Marxism. Discernment of the truth and the call of God is, according to the liberation theologians, only possible for those who are themselves deeply engaged. Understanding comes from practice and commitment; it is not directly derived from theory. The liberation theologians challenged their European and North American theological colleagues to spell out in practice what they meant by identification with the poor and oppressed. As the most influential of all the liberation theologians, Gustavo Gutiérrez, put it:

> All the political theologies, the theologies of hope, of revolution and of liberation, are not worth one act of genuine solidarity with exploited social classes. They are not worth one act of faith, love and hope committed – in one way or another – to active participation to liberate man from everything that dehumanizes him and prevents him from living according to the will of the Father.[12]

The agenda of theology 'is no longer how we are to speak of God in a world come of age; it is rather how to proclaim him Father in a world that is not human, and what the implications might be of telling non-humans that they are children of God'.[13] It puts the poor and the problem of poverty at the heart of its faith and its concern. Liberation Theology also insisted that theology must operate in dialogue with the best social analysis available if it was to be able to discern the signs of the times. And this, for all the liberation theologians as for the worker priests, meant Marxism. For them, Marxism provided a compelling analysis of exploitation and oppression, of social division and injustice. Most other available options, they believed, are bland about social conflict, or can hardly see it because they are so obsessed with equilibrium, harmony and social cohesion. Marxism was seen as providing both illumination and guidance.

---

12 Gustavo Gutiérrez, *A theology of liberation* (London: SCM, 1974), p. 308.
13 Gustavo Gutiérrez, 'Liberation praxis and Christian faith', in Rosino Gibellini (ed.), *Frontiers of theology in Latin America* (London: SCM, 1975), p. x.

The conferences of the Latin American Catholic bishops at Medellín (1968) and then at Puebla (1979) strongly affirmed the preferential option for the poor, rooted in God's love which is both universal and preferential, as expressed particularly in the Exodus and the incarnation. This option was both an expression of Christian faith and a foundation for a new kind of theology.

Boff and Pixley agree that the option for the poor 'is one form – and today the decisive one – of Christian love'.[14] They affirm with the Vatican that God's love is universal as well as preferential; its universality demands that it be preferential and adapted to need.[15] But along with the other liberation theologians they are reluctant to regard the preferential option as essentially a charitable disposition towards the poor, and something that the church has consistently expressed down the centuries. The church, they believe, has often deserted the poor, or patronised them, or effectively denied them a place of honour in the church. The time has come, they believe, to take conflicts of interest and class conflicts seriously. The church and Christians must work out where they stand: are they alongside the poor, in solidarity with them in their sufferings and in their struggle, or are they by default against the poor?

The Vatican under the Polish Pope John Paul II, who was deeply suspicious of anything to do with Marxism, was quick to attempt to tone down and spiritualise the Latin American understanding of the preferential option for the poor. In an address to the cardinals in 1984, John Paul II traced the preferential option back to the Vatican II document *Lumen gentium*, which states that the church 'recognizes in the poor and the suffering the likeness of her poor and suffering Founder. She does all she can do to relieve their need and in them she strives to serve Christ.'[16] According to the *Instruction on Christian freedom and liberation* published in 1986, nothing new or different has occurred; the church has always cared for the poor:

> Those who are oppressed by poverty are the object of a love or preference on the part of the Church, which since her origin and in spite of failings of many of her members has not ceased to work for their relief, defence and liberation. She has done this through numberless works of charity which remain always and everywhere indispensable ... The Church shows her solidarity

---

14 Clodovis Boff and G. V. Pixley, *The Bible, the church and the poor* (Maryknoll, NY: Orbis, 1990), p. 219.
15 On this see Stephen J. Pope, 'Proper and improper partiality and the preferential option for the poor', *Theological studies* 54 (1993), 242–71.
16 Cited in ibid.

with those who do not count in society by which they are rejected spiritually and sometimes physically . . . The special option for the poor, far from being a sin of particularism or sectarianism, manifests the universality of the Church's being and mission. The option excludes no one.[17]

The Vatican was deeply concerned because it believed that the liberation theologians accepted and endorsed uncritically a Marxist understanding of class struggle which saw the only way forward as direct action, ultimately often involving violence on the part of the poor and their allies. The implications of such an understanding were felt to be alarming. The preferential option, the Vatican thought, had become a political alliance to struggle for the overthrow of the existing social and economic order – and perhaps the hierarchical ordering of the church as well. This, they suggested, was a radical politicisation of the gospel, and rested on a misunderstanding of the nature of the church and its calling. The weakening of Marxist movements worldwide in the aftermath of the collapse of the old Soviet Union and its satellites, together with economic and political changes in many countries of Latin America, have made expectations of radical social change as a consequence of class struggle less plausible today. But if the idea of the preferential option for the poor as meaning primarily identification with the poor in a class struggle to usher in a new order is no longer compelling, a more theologically rooted and sober account of the preferential option remains influential.

It was precisely the endorsement of Marxism, an explicitly atheistic teaching, with its positive attitude to class struggle that turned the Vatican against Liberation Theology, as it had earlier denounced the worker priests. In 1984 the Sacred Congregation for the Doctrine of the Faith issued a document, *Instruction on certain aspects of Liberation Theology*, followed up in 1986 with another document, *Instruction on Christian freedom and liberation*. In these documents there was mixed a traditional concern for charity towards the poor and a firm injunction against taking sides economically and politically, or revising theology in the light of a dialogue with Marxism. A 'preferential option for the poor' was affirmed in general terms, but these documents can hardly be read as other than a reprimand to the liberation theologians, particularly for their use of Marxist analysis, for their recognition of the class struggle, and for what was regarded as their politicisation of the gospel. They were followed up by a series of sanctions against prominent liberation

---

17 Congregation for the Doctrine of the Faith, *Instruction on Christian freedom and liberation* (Vatican City, 1986), par. 68.

theologians and prelates who supported them, and by schoolmasterly visits to Latin America by the pope. But it was not so much the Vatican's intervention as the collapse of the communist regimes in Europe around 1989, and the general disenchantment with Marxism that followed, which contributed in a rapidly changing context to the decline of Liberation Theology in Latin America. Here and there it continues to flourish, as do its offspring in a variety of context-specific forms of Liberation Theology in Africa, Asia and elsewhere.

The churches and the preferential option for the poor

The preferential option for the poor took a distinctive shape in the United States in the 1980s. Already the Catholic church in the States had accepted the non-authoritarian dynamics of a liberal democratic society, but it was a considerable surprise when the bishops on a variety of issues, but particularly peace and the economy, issued documents that made no claim to be definitive statements from above intended to foreclose the discussion. Instead they issued for general discussion several drafts, and invited responses from all sorts of people, before a document reached its final shape. And the final document was more an agenda for responsible discussion and decision-making than an authoritative pronouncement intended to bind the consciences of the faithful.

The position of the poor had a central place in the pastoral letter *Economic justice for all*: 'Decisions must be judged in light of what they do for the poor, what they do to the poor, and what they enable the poor to do *for themselves*. The fundamental moral criterion for all economic decisions, policies and institutions is this: They must be at the service of *all people, especially the poor*,' the bishops wrote.[18] Individuals and the nation, not just Christians and particularly Catholics, were called upon to make a fundamental option for the poor, assessing public policy 'from the viewpoint of the poor and powerless'. 'The deprivation and powerlessness of the poor wounds the whole community . . . These wounds will be healed only by greater solidarity with the poor and among the poor themselves.'[19] More than charity, important as that is, is required: 'Alleviating poverty will require fundamental

---

18 US Catholic Bishops, *Economic justice for all: Catholic social teaching and the US economy* (Washington: National Conference of Catholic Bishops, 1986), par. 24.
19 Ibid., par. 88.

changes in social and economic structures that perpetuate glaring inequalities and cut off millions of citizens from full participation in the economic and social life of the nation.'[20]

Economic justice for all came just at a time when there was a huge resurgence of neo-conservatism in America and many of the countries of western Europe. It was roundly denounced by some as being based on old-fashioned socialist ideas and welfarism rather than rigorous theology. But, like a number of other church statements on poverty of around the same time, it arose from two factors in particular: first, that the church was present in areas of deep and persistent poverty in the States, and, second, that the bishops could not but attend to the increasingly pressing issues of global poverty and the anger and dismay that underlay the development of Liberation Theology in Latin America and elsewhere.

Other churches took not dissimilar initiatives, demonstrating that although they might hardly present themselves as churches *of* the poor, they could be churches *for* the poor. The Church of England's remarkable report *Faith in the city* (1985) was the result of bishops and other church leaders attending to the cries of fear, rage and despair arising from many of the areas of urban deprivation. Poverty, the report affirmed, 'is not only about shortage of money. It is about rights and relationships, about how people are treated and how they regard themselves; about powerlessness, exclusion and loss of dignity. Yet the lack of an adequate income is at its heart.'[21] The evidence of poor people was taken very seriously in the work of the commission, and members of the commission spent considerable time in deprived areas collecting evidence and testimony. The final report was the product of a church which took its responsibility for and to the poor seriously, but which could hardly be called a church of the poor.

Prosperity religion

From the 1970s there was an extraordinary, unexpected and rapid expansion of Pentecostal Christianity, first in Latin America and then in many parts of the southern hemisphere, in Korea, and in the United States.[22] Many of these

---

20 Ibid., par. 187.
21 Archbishop of Canterbury's Commission on Urban Priority Areas, *Faith in the city: a call for action by church and nation* (London: Church Information Office, 1985), p. 195.
22 The best account of this is David Martin, *Tongues of fire: the explosion of Protestantism in Latin America* (Oxford: Blackwell, 1990). See also Steve Brouwer, Paul Gifford and Susan Rose, *Exporting the American gospel* (New York: Routledge, 1996).

churches appeared to offer the poor an attractive and clear way of social and economic improvement by adopting a disciplined and ascetic lifestyle. An increasing number of these churches bought into the new style of 'prosperity religion' espoused by some right-wing church leaders in the United States, most notably Oral Roberts, who spoke freely of the returns guaranteed on our investment made with God. These leaders emphasised texts from the Bible, most notably from Deuteronomy, and in particular 3 John 2: 'Beloved, I wish above all things that thou mayest prosper and be in health, even as thy soul prospereth.'[23] Accordingly, there was a Christian imperative to get rich by honest means. One of the early leaders of the prosperity religion movement, Russell H. Conwell, himself a Baptist, declared: 'I say that you ought to get rich, and it is your duty to get rich. To make money honestly is to preach the gospel.'

But the mainstream churches can be, and sometimes are, a very unusual kind of community of moral discourse and action, precisely because it includes both some of the rich and powerful and some of the poor. When they begin to communicate honestly and directly within the church important new insights and understandings may emerge out of the sharing of challenges and insights. And some of the conclusions may be of importance to the broader society.

Ecumenism and globalisation

The ecumenical movement – which William Temple spoke of as 'the great new fact of our era' – gradually after the World Missionary Conference of 1910 in Edinburgh drew almost all the major churches not so much into unity as into dialogue and commitment to one another. The churches slowly came to feel that in a sense they were accountable to one another, and able to challenge and enlighten one another. For our present purposes this was particularly significant because many of the younger churches of Africa and Asia were almost entirely composed of the poorer and weaker sections of society.

This was particularly true in India, where as a result of the 'mass movements' of the late nineteenth and early twentieth centuries the vast majority of Christians came from low-status caste groups labelled collectively 'untouchables', 'depressed classes' 'Scheduled Castes', by Gandhi 'Harijans', or 'Children of God', or today 'Dalits'. The caste system is a rigid and resilient

23 3 John 2 (AV).

hierarchical ordering of society in terms of purity and pollution. But in practice it corresponds very closely to a hierarchy of wealth and power. Certainly those at the foot of the hierarchy – those who used to be called 'untouchables' or even 'unseeables' – are normally the poorest of the poor. Since the caste system is legitimated by brahminical Hinduism, the Dalits' struggle to improve their collective lot and affirm their dignity has often taken the shape of a rebellion against Hinduism. The leader of the 'untouchables' at the time of independence was Dr Ambedkar who, in October 1956 in a dramatic act of defiance against Hinduism, and disillusion with Gandhian techniques for improving the position of the poorest and weakest in Indian society, led a massive public conversion of nearly half a million 'untouchables' to Buddhism. By 1960 there were some three million ex-'untouchable' converts to Buddhism, and by 2000 there were some eight million of these neo-Buddhists in India. Conversions of ex-'untouchables' to Christianity have continued after the great 'mass movements' of the nineteenth and early twentieth centuries, and there have been smaller conversion movements to Islam in a number of places. Hinduism was widely felt among the ex-'untouchables' to be systematically degrading to them in insisting on their resignation to their poverty and degradation. Conversion to a faith other than Hinduism was felt to be an affirmation of their dignity, and also a way of improving their material lot. And in many cases both hopes were realised.

Christianity and development

Within the ecumenical forum, the global issue of poverty began to be addressed, and the distinctive and challenging contribution of poor churches was recognised, while the more prosperous churches sought ways of sharing resources. Immediately after the Second World War many churches became deeply involved in relief, aid and development work, particularly in those countries that had been most deeply devastated by the war and were struggling to recover. This rapidly became institutionalised in a variety of aid and development agencies, some like Christian Aid in Britain being ecumenical, others being based in particular churches. The largest, and in many ways the most significant, of these was Caritas Internationalis, which co-ordinated Roman Catholic development work worldwide, and gave a strategic and theological lead. Increasingly these agencies came to stress partnership rather than a relationship of donor and recipient, which can easily create a false dependency. Both nationally and ecumenically poor and prosperous churches recognised that they were accountable to one another and committed to sharing.

The first major challenge to the notion of development came from the early liberation theologians, particularly Gustavo Gutiérrez. He and others argued that development work involved change within existing institutional structures, and thus did not 'attack the roots of the evil'. What they called developmentalism had shown itself to be merely 'a timid reformism really ineffective on the long run and counterproductive to achieving a real transformation'. What is needed is 'a radical break from the status quo, that is, a profound transformation of the private property system, access to power of the exploited class, and a socialist revolution that would break this dependence and would allow the change to a new society, a socialist society – or at least allow that such a society might be possible'.[24]

From the 1990s the major Christian development agencies endeavoured to take very seriously the critique of the liberation theologians. The stress now became on the preferential option for the poor, on partnership in the sharing of resources, and on direct challenges to governments, transnational corporations and agencies. In addition to crisis aid and co-operation in a wide range of development agencies, there were several well-focused campaigns, concentrating on issues such as third world indebtedness and injustice in trading relationships.

The globalisation that was a dominant feature of world economic relations, particularly after the end of the Cold War, raised very pressing issues of the Christian conscience. At its simplest, globalisation means the worldwide dominance of the free market, which is often understood as working to the huge advantage of the wealthy industrialised countries, and as having devastating consequences on the poorer countries. The central bodies in the globalisation process, particularly the World Bank, the International Monetary Fund and the World Trade Organisation, are expected to monitor what is happening and ensure that things run smoothly. They are regarded with much suspicion by many, especially when monitoring structural adjustment programmes for countries going through a major economic crisis, often caused by massive debt. The problem of third world debt is particularly intractable. Yet the notable millennium campaign on the issue of debt, Jubilee 2000, certainly had considerable impact on politicians, non-governmental organisations, and the public.

---

24 Gutiérrez, *Theology of liberation*, pp. 26–7.

At the end of the century, both globally and within most nations, the problem of poverty was worse than it had been a hundred years before. The gap between the wealthy industrialised societies and the poorest nations had widened steadily, and even in prosperous nations like the United States a substantial proportion of the population was living in poverty. But the churches' response to poverty had changed substantially in response to new circumstances and new challenges. Issues of poverty and wealth were bound to remain high on the churches' agenda.

29

Male and female

I

MARRIAGE AND THE FAMILY

ADRIAN THATCHER

The secular understanding of sexuality and intimate human relationships changed markedly in the twentieth century, and this impacted heavily on the institutions of marriage and family. The churches' engagement with these changes was diffuse, divisive and slow. They responded differently to the arrival of reliable contraception and legal abortion, and to the demands both for easy extrication from failed marriages, and for remarriage or 'further marriage'. The expectation that couples should refrain from sexual intercourse until marriage has been generally abandoned by couples themselves, and is under severe strain even among conservative Christians. Since the average age of first marriage (in England and Wales in 2000) was thirty-one for men and twenty-eight for women[1] it is not difficult to see why. At the end of the twentieth century, over 40 per cent of marriages in those countries were predicted to end in divorce, and 39 per cent of children were born outside of marriage.[2] The figures are similar in Canada and the USA. In some countries married people were already becoming a minority of the adult population.

Contraception

An enlightening window into the mind of Anglicanism over the century regarding marriage and family is the stream of resolutions emanating from

---

1 Statistics provided by One Plus One, on-line at oneplusone.org.uk (accessed 31.10.03).
2 Lord Chancellor's Advisory Group on Marriage and Relationship Support, *Moving forward together* (London: COI Communications, 2002), p. 18.

successive Lambeth Conferences (of bishops of churches throughout the Anglican communion). It is probably fair to say that most Protestant churches were in sympathy with the resolutions on marriage and family. In 1920 the Lambeth Conference issued 'an emphatic warning against the use of unnatural means for the avoidance of conception . . . and against the evils with which the extension of such use threatens the race'.[3] The teaching that 'encourages married people in the deliberate cultivation of sexual union as an end in itself' was opposed. Marriage was said to be subject to two 'governing considerations'. One was 'the continuation of the race through the gift and heritage of children; the other is the paramount importance in married life of deliberate and thoughtful self-control'. Resolution 69 condemned as 'an invitation to vice' 'the distribution or use, before exposure to infection, of so-called prophylactics', and resolution 70 combined 'the open or secret sale of contraceptives' with 'the continued existence of brothels' as 'incentives to vice'.[4]

There is no hint of the changes on contraception and sexual union that were to come ten years later. The 1930 conference acknowledged 'that intercourse between husband and wife as the consummation of marriage has a value of its own within that sacrament, and that thereby married love is enhanced and its character strengthened'.[5] This reads like a clear reversal of the earlier teaching that sexual intercourse should not be an end in itself. The two 'governing considerations' of Christian marriage remain, but this time the 'deliberate and thoughtful self-control' required of married couples may be aided, for '[w]here there is clearly felt moral obligation to limit or avoid parenthood, the method must be decided on Christian principles'.[6] The 'primary and obvious method' is said to be 'complete abstinence from intercourse', but 'in those cases where there is such a clearly felt moral obligation to limit or avoid parenthood, and where there is a morally sound reason for avoiding complete abstinence, the Conference agrees that other methods may be used, provided that this is done in the light of the same Christian principles'. The conference was able to affirm that the primary purpose of marriage is procreation, while allowing that some married couples may choose not to procreate.

The 1958 Lambeth Conference was more confident in the 1930 decisions, handing over to parents 'the responsibility for deciding upon the number and

3 Lambeth Conference 1920, resolution 68. All resolutions from all Lambeth Conferences are conveniently available on-line at http://www.anglicancommunion.org/acns/archive/(accessed 28.07.03). All subsequent references to Lambeth Conference resolutions are from this source.
4 Ibid.   5 Lambeth Conference 1930, resolution 13.
6 Lambeth Conference 1930, resolution 15.

frequency of children' which 'has been laid by God upon the consciences of parents everywhere'.[7] This 'planning', carried out 'in such ways as are mutually acceptable to husband and wife in Christian conscience, is a right and important factor in Christian family life and should be the result of positive choice before God'. This position is also taken by the Orthodox churches, at least later in the century.[8] The resolution was invoked ten years later, by which time oral contraceptives had become widely available and the conference found itself 'unable to agree with the Pope's conclusion that all methods of conception control other than abstinence from sexual intercourse or its confinement to periods of infecundity are contrary to the "order established by God"'.[9]

The pope was Paul VI, and his conclusion was stated in his encyclical letter *Humanae vitae* published earlier that year. In 1930 his predecessor Pius XI, with the Anglicans firmly in his sights, contemptuously dismissed 'some' who, 'openly departing from the uninterrupted Christian tradition', had 'judged it possible solemnly to declare another doctrine regarding this question'.[10] He ruled that 'any use whatsoever of matrimony exercised in such a way that the act is deliberately frustrated in its natural power to generate life is an offense against the law of God and of nature, and those who indulge in such are branded with the guilt of a grave sin'.

The Second Vatican Council document *Gaudium et spes* praised married love. It is 'eminently human' and 'can enrich the expressions of body and mind with a unique dignity, ennobling these expressions as special ingredients and signs of the friendship distinctive of marriage'.[11] *Humanae vitae* (1968) praised married love in yet more glowing terms while simultaneously adding a further argument against contraception on the back of it – since conjugal love 'is a very special form of personal friendship whereby the spouses generously share everything with each other',[12] contraception comes to be depicted as a withholding of each partner from the other, a failure to share

---

7 Lambeth Conference 1958, resolution 115.
8 William Basil Zion, *Eros and transformation: sexuality and marriage – an Eastern Orthodox perspective* (Lanham, MD and London: University Press of America, 1992), ch. 7, 'Orthodoxy and contraception', pp. 239–62.
9 Lambeth Conference 1968, resolution 22.
10 Pope Pius XI, *Casti connubii* [*Chaste marriage*] (1930), par. 56. Available on-line at http://www.vatican.va/holy_father/pius_xi/encyclicals/documents (accessed 29.07.03).
11 *Gaudium et spes* [Pastoral Constitution on the Church in the Modern World] (1965), par. 49. Available on-line at http://www.vatican.va/archive/hist_councils/ii_vatican_council/documents (accessed 29.07.03).
12 Pope Paul VI, *Humanae vitae* (1968), section 9. Available on-line at http://www.vatican.va/holy_father/paul_vi/encyclicals/documents (accessed 29.07.03).

the God-given power of fecundity.[13] Whereas Anglicans had posited 'govern-ing considerations' concerning married intercourse the pope posited an 'inseparable connection, established by God, which man on his own initiative may not break, between the unitive significance and the procreative signifi-cance which are both inherent to the marriage act'.[14] Pope John Paul II was to emphasise further this 'unbreakable connection'.[15] If Paul VI had specified that *marriage itself*, instead of every act of love-making within marriage, contained potentially unitive and procreative significance, the Anglican and Roman positions would have been much closer.[16]

Marriage

The century saw changes to the churches' understanding of marriage in at least three areas – the importance of human love, the positive value of sex-ual experience, and the place within marriage of children. The theological legitimation of divorce and further marriage is a further, dubious, twentieth-century achievement. One way of tracing the first three of these changes is to compare the 1662 *Book of common prayer* Form of Solemnization of Matrimony, in common use for much of the century, with the Anglican *Common worship* Marriage Service released in 2000. The earlier book stated in its preface that marriage was not to be 'enterprised' 'to satisfy men's carnal lusts and appetites, like brute beasts that have no understanding', and then set out the threefold purpose of marriage. The first purpose was 'the procre-ation of children, to be brought up in the fear and nurture of the Lord . . .'.[17] (We have seen the Lambeth Conference reasserting this conviction.) The second (directly following St Paul) was 'a remedy against sin, and to avoid fornication'; the third was for 'mutual society, help and comfort'.

The 1928 revised (and never finally authorised) prayer book removed both the references to lusts and beasts and to the purposes of marriage, being minimalist in its descriptions. But controversy is only postponed by silence.

13 Ibid., section 13. On this point, and for a detailed analysis of Roman Catholic teaching on contraception, see Adrian Thatcher, *Marriage after modernity* (New York: New York University Press; Sheffield: Sheffield Academic Press, 1999), pp. 171–208.

14 *Humanae vitae*, section 12.

15 Pope John Paul II, *Familiaris consortio* (1981), section 32. Available on-line at http://www.vatican.va/holy_father/john_paul_ii/apost_exhortations/documents/. Pope John Paul II, *Letter to families*, section 10. Available on-line at http://www.vatican.va/holy_father/john_paul_ii/letters/documents/. (Both accessed 29.07.03.)

16 See Margaret Monahan Hogan, *Finality and marriage*, Marquette studies in philosophy (Marquette: Marquette University Press, 1993), pp. 102–5.

17 On-line at www.eskimo.com/~lhowell/bcp1662/ (accessed 29.07.03). There are several on-line versions of *The book of common prayer*.

There is no mention of divine or human love in the prefaces of either service, whereas love occurs frequently in the welcome and the preface of *Common worship*, and the atmosphere of the new service is saturated with it. A reason for 'the gift of marriage' is 'that as man and woman grow together in love and trust, they shall be united with one another in heart, body and mind, as Christ is united with his bride, the Church'.[18] There is in this declaration a skilful use of Ephesians 5:25 which avoids the gender imbalance of that and surrounding verses.

Whereas there is a negative view of sex in the earlier service, in the new one 'The gift of marriage brings husband and wife together in the delight and tenderness of sexual union and joyful commitment to the end of their lives.' But, whereas procreation comes first in the older service, one might validly infer from the new service that there is no obligation to have children at all. Marriage 'is given as the foundation of family life in which children are [born and] (*sic*) nurtured . . .' In other words there is a necessary connection between having children and being married, but no such connection between being married and having children. In these three ways the liturgy expresses long-term changes going on far outside itself. This third change is ambiguous. By 2000 the practice of contraception, even within marriage, had extended far beyond the guidelines of the 1968 Lambeth Conference in its riposte to *Humanae vitae*. That conference assumed that fertile couples would normally be parents (the title of resolution 22 was 'Responsible parenthood'). No such assumption was being made in 2000.

Wives and husbands

Polygamy remained a problem for the churches throughout the century in many of the churches of west Africa and elsewhere. Pius XI held that Jesus Christ had already condemned the practice because his teaching on marriage demanded 'in the first place the complete unity of matrimony which the Creator Himself laid down in the beginning when He wished it to be not otherwise than between one man and one woman'.[19] The Lambeth Conference of 1958 was typically more subtle, declaring 'that monogamy is the divine will', while acknowledging 'that the introduction of monogamy into societies that practise polygamy involves a social and economic revolution and raises problems which the Christian Church has as yet not solved'.[20]

---

18 On-line at www.cofe.anglican.org/commonworship/marriage/(accessed 29.07.03).
19 Pius XI, *Casti connubii*, pars. 20–1.
20 Lambeth Conference 1958, resolution 120 (a) and (b). And see Lambeth Conference 1968, resolution 23.

But the bishops also appealed to the emerging feminist agenda in order to deal with the problem. The conference declared 'that the problem of polygamy is bound up with the limitations of opportunities for women in society' and urged the church to 'make every effort to advance the status of women in every possible way, especially in the sphere of education'.[21] Adrian Hastings, in his influential 1973 work *Christian marriage in Africa*, used this argument against it. He held its wrongness lay, not in being disguised adultery, but in the psychological damage it caused to wives, and in the lack of 'recognition of the dignity and equal status of women' which was contrary to the gospel.[22]

The churches were also divided throughout the century regarding the subordination of wives to husbands. This of course is entangled with the internal problem of how to read the Bible (a hermeneutic problem) and the external problem of responding to the changing status of women in relation to men more generally (an ethical and a credibility problem). In *Casti connubii* Pius XI could have been speaking for most Christians when, between the great wars, he reaffirmed 'the primacy of the husband with regard to the wife and children, the ready subjection of the wife and her willing obedience'.[23] Such obedience was, of course, universally required of all brides. At least Pius XI added that subjection to a husband 'does not deny or take away the liberty which fully belongs to the woman both in view of her dignity as a human person, and in view of her most noble office as wife and mother and companion; nor does it bid her obey her husband's every request if not in harmony with right reason or with the dignity due to wife'.[24] And he went well beyond St Paul in asserting that 'if the man is the head, the woman is the heart, and as he occupies the chief place in ruling, so she may and ought to claim for herself the chief place in love'.

These qualifications appear progressive when compared with the Southern Baptist Convention's 'stance on marriage and family' of 1998 which many will think insulting to women and detrimental to Christian marriage generally. While affirming the 'equal worth' of husband and wife since they both are 'created in God's image', the 'stance' recapitulates the subordinationism of Ephesians 5:21–33 by affirming that a husband 'has the God-given responsibility to provide for, to protect, and to lead his family. A wife is to submit herself graciously to the servant leadership of her husband even as the church

---

21 Lambeth Conference 1958, resolution 120 (d).
22 Adrian Hastings, *Christian marriage in Africa* (London: SPCK, 1973), pp. 75–6.
23 *Casti connubii*, par. 26.   24 Ibid., par. 27.

willingly submits to the headship of Christ.'[25] She is 'to respect her husband and to serve as his helper in managing the household and nurturing the next generation'.

Subsequent historians are likely to look back on this 'stance' as a direct (and dangerous) consequence of biblical literalism that has regard for neither the 'horizon' of the text nor the 'horizon' of the reader. The Southern Baptists have probably interpreted accurately the 'authorial intent' of the passage (assuming – generously – that one can still speak in this way!). The husband loves; the wife submits and respects. The asymmetrical relationship between God and God's people, and between Christ and the church, is applied uncritically to the married relationship (so that the husband stands for God and for Christ). Leaving aside the record of husbands as household managers (and that 'servant leadership' is an oxymoron that should fool no one), perhaps the saddest feature of the 'stance' is its lack of awareness of the link between the theology of male power it authorises and the perpetuation and legitimation of domestic violence. *Casti connubii*, with its appeal to the wife's dignity and to 'harmony with right reason', and the careful application of the analogy in Ephesians 5 to the *mutual* love of husbands and wives in *Common worship*, are preferable to the theological chauvinism of the Southern Baptists.

Family life

Churches have also differed in the justifications for their emphases on family life. All of them consistently affirm that marriage, whether understood as a sacrament, an ordinance, an estate, or a 'gift of God in creation', is the basis of family life. A problem for a purely biblically based theology of the family lies in the mixed messages that the New Testament conveys about the desirability of marrying *at all*, in the apparent priority of the spiritual family of the church or the reign of God over the biological unit,[26] and in the questionable morality of the household codes.[27] The Lambeth Conference of 1958, intriguingly, recorded 'its profound conviction that the idea of the human family is rooted in the Godhead and that consequently all problems of sex relations, the

---

25 On-line at http://www.sbc.net/bfm/default.asp (accessed 30.07.03).
26 For a positive interpretation of these matters, see Stephen G. Post, *More lasting unions: Christianity, the family, and society* (Grand Rapids and Cambridge, UK: Eerdmans, 2000).
27 Col. 3:18—4:1; Eph. 5:22—6:9; 1 Pet. 2:18—3:7. See also 1 Tim. 2:8–15, 6:1–2; Titus 2:1–10. On household codes see James D. G. Dunn, 'The household rules in the New Testament', in Stephen C. Barton (ed.), *The family in theological perspective* (Edinburgh; T&T Clark, 2000), pp. 43–64.

procreation of children, and the organisation of family life must be related, consciously and directly, to the creative, redemptive, and sanctifying power of God'.[28] Unfortunately nothing was said about *how* these problems were to be related to the Godhead. Is there a proleptic hint here, reminiscent of the trinitarian theology of the last quarter of the century, that familial relations may share in the relations of the Persons of the one God? The conference also issued a 'summary of the marks of a Christian family', which included worship on Sundays and common prayer and Bible reading. But it is to the Roman Catholic church, and in particular to Pope John Paul II's apostolic exhortation *Familiaris consortio* – 'On the role of the Christian family in the modern world' – that one must turn for an explicit 'theology of the family'.

This work is much more explicit about how the human family is rooted in the Godhead. 'God is love', the pope says, citing 1 John 4:8, 'and in Himself He lives a mystery of personal loving communion. Creating the human race in His own image and continually keeping it in being, God inscribed in the humanity of man and woman the vocation, and thus the capacity and responsibility, of love and communion.'[29] In the *Letter to families* of 1994, the trinitarian suggestiveness becomes a carefully formulated analogy: 'The family is in fact a community of persons whose proper way of existing and living together is communion: *communio personarum*. Here too, while always acknowledging the absolute transcendence of the Creator with regard to his creatures, we can see the family's ultimate relationship to the divine "We". *Only persons are capable of living "in communion"*.'[30] By virtue of their indissoluble love, 'spouses are therefore the permanent reminder to the Church of what happened on the Cross'.[31] The relationship between the family and the life of the church is expounded by means of the doctrine of the 'domestic church'. There are 'many profound bonds linking the Church and the Christian family and establishing the family as a "Church in miniature" (*Ecclesia domestica*), in such a way that in its own way the family is a living image and historical representation of the mystery of the Church'.[32] Indeed, so close is the inter-relationship between the universal church and the domestic church that 'the future of evangelization depends in great part on the Church of the home'.[33]

28 Lambeth Conference 1958, resolution 112: repeated verbatim at the 1968 conference (resolution 22).
29 *Familiaris consortio*, section 11.   30 *Letter to families*, section 7.
31 Ibid., section 13.   32 *Familiaris consortio*, section 49.   33 Ibid., section 52.

Divorce

Since the 1960s, the divorce rate has more than doubled in the United Kingdom, the United States, France, Australia and elsewhere. It is predicted that 40 per cent of all marriages performed in 2000 onwards will end in divorce. One influential writer posits, as a partial explanation for broken marriages, 'the widespread diffusion of a historically new and distinctive set of ideas about divorce in the last third of the twentieth century'.[34] These included the transition 'from an ethic of obligation to others and toward an obligation to self', and the spread of market values to personal and family life. The positive advantage of easy extrication from violent or otherwise intolerable marriages should not be under-estimated. There is impressive unanimity among the churches that marriage is an unconditional, lifelong, commitment. Protestants and Roman Catholics now use the biblical term 'covenant' in relation to it. But there has been an undoubted accommodation of the divorce culture by the churches. All of them affirm the saying of Jesus, 'What therefore God has joined together, let not man put asunder,'[35] but their interpretations of it vary widely. For the Roman Catholic and Orthodox churches, marriage is a sacrament. In Roman Catholic theology, part of what makes a marriage a sacrament *is* its indissolubility. Divorce of a validly married couple is therefore impossible. However, if the consent given in a marriage service can be judged to have been defective, then God has not joined them together, and the marriage can be annulled. In the early 1960s, about 300 declarations of nullity came from the United States each year; by 1996 that figure had grown to over 60,000. Grounds for annulment include ignorance, lack of the use of reason, and lack of due discretion.[36] Orthodox churches, on the other hand, recognise both the sacrament of marriage *and* the possibility of marriage dissolution. That is because God gives the church the power to 'bind' and 'loose' (Matt. 16:19). In 'putting asunder', then, God, not 'man', puts asunder what God has joined. Similar rises in numbers of divorces are reported among the Orthodox.

The position in Protestant and Anglican churches is more difficult. Protestants are unanimous that marriage is not a sacrament. John Witte has described

---

34 Barbara Dafoe Whitehead, *The divorce culture* (New York: Vintage, 1998), p. 4.
35 Mark 10:9 (Revised Standard Version); and see Matt. 19:6.
36 For a fuller list of reasons and an explanation of them see Paul Robbins, 'Marriage nullity in the Catholic church: not every wedding produces a marriage', in Adrian Thatcher (ed.), *Celebrating Christian marriage* (Edinburgh and New York: T&T Clark, 2001), pp. 311–24.

how in the twentieth century a 'contractual view of marriage has come to dominate American law, lore, and life', and: 'The roles of the church, state, and broader community in marriage formation, maintenance, and dissolution have been gradually truncated in deference to the constitutional principles of sexual autonomy and separation of church and state.'[37] The relationship between this undoubted trend and the Protestant culture that hosted it is contentious. Theologically, Protestants have been closest to the rise of biblical and historical criticism, and mainline churches have been influenced by this, allowing them to conclude that, contrary to earlier teaching, Jesus was not, for example, founding a new law of marriage. The 'exception clauses' in Matthew's gospel [38] permitting the divorce of wives in cases of 'unchastity' (*porneia*) were thought to allow greater latitude of interpretation. Liberal Protestants would regard the injunction of Jesus as the expression of an ideal to which there may regrettably be exceptions. What though of Christians who believe the words of scripture are, literally (even if not infallibly), the word or words of Godself? They might, with other Christians, contrast the ideal of permanent marriage with other Christian values, in particular the admission of and repentance from sin and the need for forgiveness; or, with Christians in earlier centuries, allow for separation but no remarriage.

Styles of response

During the last two decades of the century there was a clearer understanding of the economic costs of divorce, the growing poverty of divorced women, and the impact of broken families and father absence on children, causing the ethical socialist A. H. Halsey to observe in 1993 (in Britain) that 'the children of parents who do not follow the traditional norm (i.e. taking on personal, active and long-term responsibility for the social upbringing of the children they generate) are thereby disadvantaged in many major aspects of their chances of living a successful life'. He had evidence, amply confirmed since, that 'such children tend to die earlier, to have more illness, to do less well at school, to exist at a lower level of nutrition, comfort and conviviality, to suffer more unemployment, to be more prone to deviance and crime, and finally to repeat the cycle of unstable parenting from which they themselves have suffered'.[39] The impact of divorce, particularly on children, seemed to

---

37 John Witte, Jr, *From sacrament to contract: marriage, religion, and law in the Western tradition* (Louisville: Westminster John Knox Press, 1997), p. 195.
38 Matt. 5:32; 19:9.
39 A. H. Halsey, 'Foreword', in Norman Dennis and George Erdos (eds.), *Families without fatherhood* (London: Institute of Economic Affairs Health and Welfare Unit, 1993), p. xii.

justify the almost apocalyptic warnings of the churches, earlier in the century, about the consequences of the weakening of the institution of marriage. In this respect at least, their testimony was prophetic.

The flagship book in a major project in the United States on 'The Family, Religion and Culture' in 1997 posited 'three styles of religious response'[40] to the 'family crisis' over divorce. Both the crisis and the styles of response can be found far beyond the United States. These are liberal or 'mainline' Protestant, conservative Protestant, and Roman Catholic. The liberal Protestant response was barely a response at all since marriage in that tradition was already beginning to be replaced with a language that spoke instead of loving and just relationships. The table of contents of the 1991 Presbyterian church report[41] did not even mention marriage, and a mere three and a half pages (out of nearly 200) were devoted to it. The Catholic response 'never fully came to terms with its inadequate views on gender' (and many will add contraception and the absolute prohibition of abortion and divorce to the list). The conservative response is diffuse, with fundamentalists and the 'religious right' seeking an opportunity to push back hard-won reforms regarding the rights of wives, women (and lesbian and gay people) in the name of biblical, traditional or family values, while other conservatives argue for appropriate development of deeply rooted theological and social traditions.

But these styles of response, as we have seen, have been identifiable throughout the century. The liberal style is most in tune with culture but most likely to accommodate itself to it. The conservative Protestant style appeals directly to the Bible, whose message is thought to remain the same amidst the vagaries of sexual chaos, while the Roman style blends appeals to scripture, tradition and its own (diminishing) teaching authority. These styles determined the mid-century arguments over contraception. The Roman style retains a strong emphasis on the tradition of natural law, alongside tradition and scripture. The liberal Lambeth Conference of 1930 blends scripture (the emphasis on the life of discipline) and tradition (e.g., that the primary purpose of marriage is children) with concern for the pastoral

---

40 Don S. Browning, Bonnie J. Miller-McLemore, Pamela D. Couture, K. Brynolf Lyon and Robert M. Franklin, *From culture wars to common ground: religion and the American family debate* (Louisville: Westminster John Knox Press, 1997), p. 43. Among the many achievements of the project were nineteen scholarly books in the area of family and marriage.

41 General Assembly Special Committee on Human Sexuality, Presbyterian Church (USA), *Keeping body and soul together: sexuality, spirituality and social justice* (Tampa, FL: Jan, 1991).

consequences of the continuity of the ban on contraceptive use. Among conservative Protestants little has been said about contraception within marriage. And that is because scripture has little to say about it.

One of the ambiguous changes to the theology of marriage in the twentieth century has been the weakening, outside Roman Catholicism, of its procreative purpose. Again the three styles are at work. Since the Bible does not say that the purpose of marriage is that of having children, but tradition does, it is not surprising that Protestants, liberal and conservative, are untroubled by the intention of some fertile couples to remain childless,[42] while in Catholicism all sexual intercourse has to be officially open to conception. A positive theology of, and for, children is still awaited. Couples marry later than in any previous age. Most wives do paid work outside the home, and some couples see the arrival of children as frustrating their promising careers. There may be other more selfish reasons to do with money and avoiding sleepless nights. The Protestant churches seem scarcely to have noticed this subtle change. Many Christians, liberal and conservative, accommodate to the culture in this respect by coalescing with the view, mistakenly, that marriage is a purely private relationship where the involvement of families and community is reduced.

There is no developed doctrine of the Trinity in scripture, so there is not going to be any appeal to it in grounding a theological account of human families among Christians who do not value tradition. Equally, for those Christians who think the teaching of scripture is a historical constant, and that scripture teaches couples should not have sex until they are married, there can be no concession to the rising age of first marriages, even though those same Christians believe celibacy to be a rare gift. A painful wedge is therefore driven between the sexuality and the spirituality of a whole generation. Liberal Protestants are at least realists here. There is a way of easing the problem for all three strands: the recovery of the tradition of betrothal has the merits of being biblical and historical, and it posits a phased entry into marriage. The new century may also see older traditions regarding the entry into marriage through the separate events of spousals and nuptials as the solution to the very widespread practice of living together pre-nuptially.[43]

42 See part 5, 'Children and marriage', of Thatcher (ed.), *Celebrating Christian marriage*, pp. 219–50.
43 Adrian Thatcher, *Living together and Christian ethics* (Cambridge: Cambridge University Press, 2002).

'Critical familism'

The Family, Religion and Culture project argued for a 'critical familism' which entailed 'a full equality between husband and wife', an analysis 'of the *power relations* between husband, wife, children, and surrounding economic and governmental institutions', and the deep, co-operative, involvement of civil society in promoting the 'common good'.[44] The project promoted 'equal-regard marriages and families' and by means of its many books it described 'the religiocultural vision and social supports needed to inspire and maintain them'.[45] The broad vision was by no means confined to Christianity.[46] But the churches and the Christians within them who represent the three strands remain divided and seem not to be listening to each other. It will take much greater courage and insight, prayer and imagination, faithfulness and responsiveness, for churches to commend their teaching in the new century in a way that promotes marriage and the common good, brings sexuality and spirituality together, and nurtures both.

II
HOMOSEXUALITY

DAVID HILLIARD

In Western societies at the beginning of the twentieth century the present-day concept of homosexuality as a condition or orientation that is different from heterosexuality, and 'the homosexual' as a distinct and identifiable minority, was beginning to solidify.[47] A shadowy homosexual underworld with its own codes, slang and meeting places already existed in the larger cities of Europe and North America, but the great majority of homosexually inclined people, fearful of social stigma, concealed their 'secret' and remained invisible. The Christian church everywhere agreed that all sexual activity

---

44 Browning et al., *From culture wars*, p. 2.   45 Ibid., p. 3.
46 Don S. Browning, *Marriage and modernization: how globalization threatens marriage and what to do about it* (Grand Rapids and Cambridge, UK: Eerdmans, 2003).
47 Historical surveys of homosexuality in the twentieth century include Nicholas C. Edsall, *Toward Stonewall: homosexuality and society in the modern Western world* (Charlottesville: University of Virginia Press, 2003); Jeffrey Weeks, *Coming out: homosexual politics in Britain from the nineteenth century to the present*, revd edn (London: Quartet, 1990).

between people of the same sex was intrinsically wrong and unnatural, because it violated the God-ordained pattern for human sexuality ('male and female he created them') and was specifically condemned in both the Old and the New Testaments.[48] However, there was a general reticence within the church, as in the wider society, about any open discussion of homosexuality, so that the subject was mentioned only rarely, and obliquely, in public discourse. Because female sexuality was seen only in relation to male behaviour, lesbianism was ignored. At the same time, there were hints of a less negative approach, which did not regard a homosexual orientation as a sign of inherent moral weakness and upheld the ideal of chaste friendship between people of the same sex.

The ambiguous relationship of homosexuals with the Christian church at the beginning of the twentieth century can be illustrated by the circle around Oscar Wilde. In November 1900 Wilde died in Paris and on his deathbed was received into the Roman Catholic church. Several of his closest friends likewise found a religious home in Roman Catholicism. So too did a cluster of lesbian writers, including Radclyffe Hall, author of the novel *The well of loneliness* (1928).[49] This attraction to Catholicism in its Roman or Anglican forms was quite common in this period among English and American homosexuals and lesbians with literary, artistic and religious interests. In many cases it was a demonstration of rebellion against Protestant and heterosexual respectability. Some were drawn to the Catholic religion by the apparent security or superiority of ancient traditions and rituals and the opportunity for absolution from sinful acts through the practice of auricular confession. Catholicism also provided these converts with an aesthetic style, devotional language, rituals and imagery through which they could express, in a coded way, a sense of difference and articulate homoerotic desire.

During the first half of the twentieth century there was a significant overlap between urban homosexual sub-cultures and the Anglo-Catholic wing of the Church of England. As a sexual minority, homosexuals sensed an affinity with Anglo-Catholicism as a minority party in the national church with its emphasis on beauty in worship and 'correct' ceremonial, its distinctive genre of 'camp' humour, and the reputation of some of its clergy for

---

48 For example, Rom. 1:26–7; 1 Cor. 6:9–10.
49 Joanne Glasgow, 'What's a nice lesbian like you doing in the church of Torquemada? Radclyffe Hall and other Catholic converts', in Karla Jay and Joanne Glasgow (eds.), *Lesbian texts and contexts: radical revisions* (New York: New York University Press, 1990), pp. 241–54.

being pastorally sensitive. Anglo-Catholic churches and societies, in England and also in the United States and other countries, were often discreet meeting places for homosexuals at a time when they had few alternatives.

There is much evidence from the first half of the twentieth century that a substantial number of men with homosexual inclinations devoted their lives to religious institutions. Within the Roman Catholic church, devout young men who were not sexually attracted to women and sought to be free of the social pressure to marry were often drawn, for reasons of which they were only dimly aware, to the priesthood or the religious life. This offered a respected and religiously sanctioned alternative to marriage. Seminaries and religious houses, as all-male communities, were structured so as to prevent or conceal any expression of homosexuality; to preserve the harmony of the community 'particular friendships' were forbidden. In both Western Catholicism and Eastern Orthodoxy, however, some monastic communities were willing to accommodate affectionate relationships between their members.[50] For similar reasons, young men and women with homosexual feelings were sometimes drawn to overseas missionary work, which offered the prospect of adventure in foreign lands and freedom from conventional domesticity. In Western urban societies there was always a significant, if secretive, homosexual presence among church organists and leaders of choirs. In the Protestant churches, unmarried clergymen often found emotionally fulfilling work in education as teachers in theological colleges, as chaplains to boys' schools or youth organisations, or in ministry to university students.

Between the 1920s and the 1950s there were three shifts in Western Christian thinking that had implications for attitudes to homosexuality. The first was a new theology of marriage, based on a revisiting of biblical texts on human love and marriage, which emphasised mutual commitment and emotional intimacy as equal in importance to the procreation of children. The idea that sexual intercourse had a positive value as an expression of love between partners was later extended (as traditionalists had feared) to justify sexual activity within same-sex relationships. The second was the incorporation of the insights of psychology into the training of clergy for ministries of pastoral care and counselling. The new literature of pastoral theology reflected the dominant 'medical model' of homosexuality: the idea that 'the homosexual' had a psychological illness that required professional 'help' and treatment rather than punishment. The third trend, beginning in

---

50 For personal accounts, see Geoffrey Moorhouse, *Against all reason* (London: Weidenfeld and Nicolson, 1969), ch. 7.

English-speaking countries, was a questioning of the traditional association between law and morality, crime and sin. Within the major Protestant and Anglican churches there was growing support for the view that the existing (erratically enforced) legal prohibitions against male homosexual acts should be removed, without implying approval of such behaviour. Meanwhile, the context within which Christians discussed homosexuality was altered by the apparent findings of sex research. Surveys of sexual behaviour, such as that by Alfred Kinsey and his associates in the United States (1948, 1953), seemed to show that the incidence of homosexuality was higher than had been thought and challenged received notions of what was sexually normal and 'natural'.

Throughout this period the traditional condemnation of homosexuality by the Christian church was taken for granted, though a few theologians wondered whether its foundational arguments were entirely watertight. In England a pivotal figure was D. S. Bailey, who authored a 1954 report on homosexuality for the Church of England Moral Welfare Council and *Homosexuality and the western Christian tradition* (1955), which questioned the traditional homosexual interpretation of the 'sin of Sodom' (Gen. 19:4–11). In France a physician and theologian, Marc Oraison, published *Vie chrétienne et problèmes de la sexualité* (1952), which suggested that in sexual matters, including homosexuality, the conditions for grave subjective sin were rarely met. Oraison's writings ran into trouble with the Vatican. The decade of the 1960s saw the birth of radical theology and the popularisation of situation ethics ('the rule of love') as the 'new morality'. Two influential works of this period argued that Christians should accept loving relationships between people of the same sex: *Towards a Quaker view of sex* (1963), and *Time for consent* (1967) by a liberal Anglican theologian, Norman Pittenger. Meanwhile, on the west coast of the United States in San Francisco, a city whose reputation for tolerance after the Second World War attracted a sizeable homosexual population, in 1964 a group of activists and sympathetic ministers set up the Council on Religion and the Homosexual, to encourage dialogue and study. In Los Angeles in 1968 Troy Perry, formerly a Pentecostal pastor, founded the Metropolitan Community church as an 'inclusive' church to meet the need of homosexuals. It later grew into an international 'fellowship'. Faint cracks were appearing in the Christian consensus on homosexuality.

The cultural landscape changed dramatically in the late 1960s and early 1970s. In Western societies this was a period of social ferment and radical movements which challenged established authorities and demanded to be heard. The modern gay movement had its symbolic beginning in Greenwich Village, New York, in 1969. From there 'gay liberation' spread rapidly to the cities of North America, western Europe and Australasia, overtaking the existing (reformist) homosexual rights organisations.[51] For the first time on a large scale homosexuals and lesbians began to speak and write about themselves and claimed the same rights in society as other minority groups. The word 'homosexual' (a mid-nineteenth-century medical label) was displaced by 'gay' (a word with obscure origins) as signifying a positive sexual identity. From the 1990s this was in turn challenged by the more fluid term 'queer', which signified a critique of existing sexual categories and identities. The new wave of gay radicalism permanently changed the shape of homosexual life in Western societies. During the 1970s, initially in the major cities of North America, western Europe and Australia, there emerged a visible 'gay community', with its own magazines and newspapers, counselling services, sporting clubs and communal celebrations. By the end of the twentieth century gay and lesbian cultures, linked internationally by the internet, were taking shape in parts of Asia, Africa and South America.

The great majority of Christians did not approve of the growing visibility of homosexuality and the self-assertive rhetoric of gay liberation ('gay is good'). From the 1970s public opinion in Western societies liberalised on most areas of sexual behaviour and this shift was gradually reflected to some extent within the major churches. It also provoked resistance. Conservative Christians of all denominations deplored what they saw as the promotion of a sinful and destructive 'homosexual lifestyle' which undermined both the institution of marriage and the moral foundations of Christian society. They fought, sometimes with a high level of grassroots support, against what they saw as the 'homosexual lobby' with its sinister 'gay agenda'.

As society's attitudes changed, the Christian churches began to look again at homosexuality. In the Anglican and Protestant churches the usual method was to set up a working party or task group on the subject. By the end of the twentieth century few denominations had not addressed the subject, and for some it was a recurring and contentious issue. This process was accompanied by an endless flow of statements, resolutions, theological works and popular pamphlets on homosexuality. Debate within the churches clustered around six issues in particular:

- the authority and meaning of those biblical texts that referred to homosexual activity and how they should be interpreted and applied in the contemporary world

51 Weeks, *Coming out*, chs. 16–17.

- the question of whether it was possible or desirable to seek to change a person's homosexual orientation or whether this should be seen as a 'gift from God'
- the extent to which churches should support legal equality for homosexual minorities in society
- the admission of known gay and lesbian people into church membership and positions of leadership within the local congregation
- whether the church should support, and bless, 'stable' same-sex unions
- the ordination of publicly affirmed lesbians and gay men

As with many other moral issues, the divide between 'liberal' and 'conservative' sliced across denominational boundaries. The strongest opponents of liberal views were evangelicals (though some evangelicals dissented[52]), who saw themselves as upholding the 'clear and consistent' teaching of scripture, reinforced by the Christian moral tradition, in which homosexual behaviour was expressly forbidden and condemned. Gay Christians should therefore live a celibate life. Revisionists argued, on the other hand, that the negative references to homosexuality in scripture had been shaped by the social and cultural values of the ancient world and that the biblical writers had no knowledge of homosexual orientation, sexual identity or adult homosexual relationships: *'Biblical judgments against homosexuality are not relevant in today's debate.* They should no longer be used in denominational discussions about homosexuality ... *not because the Bible is not authoritative,* but simply because it does not address the issues involved.'[53] The church needed, they said, to develop a new theology of sexuality, based on human experience, modern scientific knowledge and a reinterpretation of Christian texts, which accepted same-sex relationships as natural and good.

The great majority of church reports, statements and discussion papers on homosexuality oscillated between non-punitive disapproval and a cautious acceptance, hedged with qualifications.[54] In their exegesis and evaluation of the relevant biblical passages, and their interpretation of social scientific evidence, they revealed sharp differences of opinion among scholars. Usually they supported the decriminalisation of homosexual acts and the

---

52 For example, Michael Vasey, *Strangers and friends: a new exploration of homosexuality and the Bible* (London: Hodder and Stoughton, 1995).
53 Robin Scroggs, *The New Testament and homosexuality: contextual background for contemporary debate* (Philadelphia: Fortress Press, 1983), p. 127.
54 For example, Anglican Church of Australia, *Faithfulness in fellowship: reflections on homosexuality and the church. Papers from the doctrine panel of the Anglican Church of Australia* (Melbourne: John Garratt Publishing, 2001).

elimination of 'unjust' discrimination in the secular sphere. Generally they agreed that homosexuals should be received into church membership. Some, such as a 1979 report by a Church of England committee, were prepared to allow that Christians 'may justifiably choose to enter into a homosexual relationship' comparable to marriage.[55] At the beginning of the twenty-first century the most liberal voices were from Germany, Scandinavia and the Netherlands where (though the issue remained controversial) several Protestant synods had voted to allow clergy to conduct blessing ceremonies for same-sex unions.[56] In North America and the United Kingdom very few denominations were prepared explicitly to approve the ordination of openly gay or lesbian candidates for the ministry who did not promise life-long sexual abstinence. However, clergy who were discreet about their sexuality and their partnerships were often tolerated.

Gay and lesbian members of the main Christian denominations found themselves under fire from two directions. Many in the wider gay community wondered how anyone could remain within institutions that were a source of oppression and sexual guilt, while many within the churches saw the acceptance of homosexual behaviour as disobedience to the revealed will of God. Gay and lesbian Christians frequently 'shopped' and switched to denominations or congregations they found more welcoming. In the United States during the 1970s activists who were members of the major denominations formed groups for mutual support which evolved into national organisations. The Unitarian Universalist Gay Caucus, founded in 1971, was followed by Dignity (Roman Catholics), Lutherans Concerned, Presbyterians for Lesbian & Gay Concerns, Integrity (Episcopalians), Affirmation (United Methodists), Kinship (Seventh-day Adventists), Axios (Eastern Christians) and many others.[57] They published newsletters and pamphlets, held conferences, and sought to have a voice at national meetings that shaped denominational policies. There was a different pattern in the United Kingdom and Europe, where the principal campaigning organisations were ecumenical in their membership. Among them were the Lesbian and Gay Christian movement (United Kingdom), Communauté du Christ Libérateur

---

55 Church of England, General Synod Board for Social Responsibility, *Homosexual relationships: a contribution to discussion* (London: CIO Publishing, 1979), p. 52.
56 For the Netherlands, see Donald Mader, 'Exclusion, toleration, acceptance, integration: the experience of Dutch Reformed churches with homosexuality and homosexuals in the church', *Journal of homosexuality* 25:4 (1993), 101–19.
57 Each of these organisations has a website.

(Belgium), David et Jonathan (France) and Homosexuelle und Kirche (Germany).

The Roman Catholic church responded to the gay movement, and the emergence of men and women who proclaimed themselves as both gay and Catholic, by official pronouncements from the Vatican and a carefully worded section (pars. 2357–9) in the *Catechism of the Catholic church* (1994). An important document was prepared by the Congregation for the Doctrine of the Faith: *Letter to the bishops of the Catholic church on the pastoral care of homosexual persons* (1986). The *Letter*, using the language of the Catholic natural law tradition, described the homosexual inclination as 'an objective disorder'. Although homosexual persons are 'often generous and giving of themselves', homosexual activity was never a morally acceptable option and therefore had no claim to protection by civil rights legislation.[58] Statements on homosexuality by some bishops and regional bishops' conferences emphasised more the need for pastoral care and, by omission rather than direct assertion, toned down the strict application of the church's absolute moral rules. A few theologians directly challenged the church's official teaching. During the 1990s the public position of the Roman Catholic church, especially in the United States, was weakened by the exposure of sexual misconduct when a substantial number (though a small minority) of priests and religious brothers were found guilty of sexual abuse of children or having sexual relationships with teenage boys. The 'gay priest' and the 'paedophile priest' became subjects of academic studies, magazine articles and polemical works.[59] Nervous conservatives, seemingly blind to the existence of homosexuals among themselves, began calling for gay men to be excluded from seminaries and the priesthood.

The tensions in Christian attitudes to homosexuality were sharpened with the appearance of AIDS (Acquired Immunity Deficiency Syndrome), which was first identified in the United States in 1981 and spread rapidly to Europe and elsewhere. In Western countries the great majority of those infected were homosexual males, so that AIDS was labelled as a 'gay disease'. The Christian churches brought an ethical and theological dimension into the public discussion of AIDS. Many Christian leaders advocated compassion for people with AIDS while also calling for a change in sexual behaviour. Some

58 Catholic church, Congregation for the Doctrine of the Faith, *Letter to the bishops of the Catholic church on the pastoral care of homosexual persons* (London: Catholic Truth Society, 1986), pars. 3, 7, 10.

59 Philip Jenkins, *Pedophiles and priests: anatomy of a contemporary crisis* (New York: Oxford University Press, 1996); Mark D. Jordan, *The silence of Sodom: homosexuality in modern Catholicism* (Chicago: University of Chicago Press, 2000), chs. 6–7.

Christians were active in providing practical and pastoral support within urban gay communities. Fundamentalists claimed that AIDS was a judgement of God on unrepentant sexual immorality.

In the aftermath of the gay movement, some Christians began to argue that a shared sexual identity and experience of living as lesbian and gay people provided a basis for a reconstruction of Christian theology. This was gay (or queer) theology; it drew upon the ideas of Black, Liberation and feminist theologies.[60] Writers of gay theology, such as Gary Comstock, rejected many of the categories of traditional Christian theology because of their 'hetero-sexist' assumptions. Appealing to a God of justice, they saw liberation from sexual oppression and unjust structures as an essential element of salvation. Lesbian feminist theologians explored the idea of the human body as the site of divine revelation and the spiritual meaning of sexual pleasure. The majority of gay and lesbian Christians were untouched by the speculations of gay theology, or by those who advocated a distinctively queer spirituality, but implicitly, by their presence in congregations, they raised questions about human sexuality and the nature of the church.

Until the 1990s the public debate on homosexuality was confined to the churches of western Europe, North America and Australasia. The Eastern Orthodox churches did not see their traditional teaching on homosexuality as open to question, nor was homosexuality a major issue for the churches in Africa. This changed at the Lambeth Conference of bishops of the Anglican communion in 1998, when the bishops of flourishing churches in east and west Africa, conservative in their theology, did much to ensure the adoption by the conference of a resolution on human sexuality that made few concessions to liberal opinion.[61]

Anglican opinion was further polarised in 2003 when a succession of separate events became international news stories. These included the approval by the diocese of New Westminster (Vancouver) in Canada of a public rite of blessing for same-sex couples; and the election as bishop by the diocese of New Hampshire in the United States of a gay priest living openly with his male partner. The leaders of conservative national churches, mainly

---

60 For a review of recent publications, see Laurel C. Schneider, 'Homosexuality, queer theory, and Christian theology', *Religious studies review* 26 (2000), 3–12.
61 Kevin Ward, 'Same-sex relations in Africa and the debate on homosexuality in east African Anglicanism', *Anglican theological review* 83 (2002), 81–111. For a South African viewpoint, see Paul Germond and Steve de Gruchy (eds.), *Aliens in the household of God: homosexuality and Christian faith in South Africa* (Cape Town: David Philip, 1997).

in the non-Western world and led by the primate of Nigeria, were outraged at what they saw as the condoning of sin and the rejection of traditional Anglican teaching on human sexuality. The resulting international debate over the acceptance of homosexual practice was widely portrayed as a theological and geographical division between global North and South, but the reality was less tidy. Many observers predicted that the issue would push the Anglican communion to a split or an internal realignment.

At the beginning of the twenty-first century there is no unified Christian voice on homosexuality but several divergent currents. For conservative Christians in all denominations the traditional condemnation of homosexual behaviour has become a litmus test of fidelity to scripture and doctrinal orthodoxy. Others, while seeing homosexual relationships as a falling short of God's ideal, are less combative and more disposed to find ways of meeting pastoral needs. Liberal Christians argue the case for a reinterpretation of biblical texts that would allow committed same-sex relationships. Radicals advocate a new theology of human sexuality and the full inclusion of gay and lesbian people (and other sexual minorities) in church life. Each position claims to be gaining ground somewhere; none of them shows any sign of dissolving. All that can be said with certainty is that homosexuality will continue to divide the Christian churches for some time.

III
PATRIARCHY AND WOMEN'S EMANCIPATION

PIRJO MARKKOLA

A history that ignores women and minorities is a poor reflection of our Christian heritage.　　　　(*Christianity today*, 20 July 1992, p. 20)

The Christian conception of the world is explicitly based on gender differ-ence. Through centuries the social understanding of gender difference has defined the lives of women and men, and the conceptions of appropriate gender relations have been based on those definitions. In every society there are some commonly shared notions of proper femininity and masculinity. These notions are constructed and negotiated in the social context of every-day life. Furthermore, socially acceptable ways of being female or male depend on other categories such as class and ethnicity.

Hierarchical gender relations placed women and men in different positions in the social processes by which societies were constructed in the twentieth century. The churches have undoubtedly contributed to the upholding of patriarchal social structures. In the early twentieth century, many leaders of the Christian churches opposed feminism and the women's rights movement, and that gave a justification for considering religion – and religious circles – as hostile to women's emancipation. Since then, the relationship between the patriarchal conception of the world and women's emancipation has been one of the ongoing debates within the Christian churches as well as between churches and other social institutions. Nevertheless, the churches can hardly be accused of being the sole representatives of patriarchal values. Furthermore, the churches have proved to be more or less open to the redefinitions of their views on gender relations.

For the Christian churches, the relationship between patriarchy and women's emancipation can be divided into two major themes and several sub-themes. Very often the issue of patriarchy and women's emancipation has been seen as an ordination controversy, i.e., whether women can acquire full clergy rights or not. This is an important aspect, of course, and cannot be ignored here. However, there are also other crucial questions regarding gender relations in the churches. How have the Christian churches positioned themselves towards women's emancipation and the demand for gender equality? In this section, we will first discuss patriarchy and women's emancipation on a general level. Secondly, we will briefly examine the question of women's ordination in various Christian churches in the twentieth century.

The international women's rights movement of the late nineteenth and early twentieth centuries stated that women's inferior status in church and society demanded changes. In many countries, women's economic and political emancipation soon challenged the Christian churches, Catholic as well as Protestant, and the churches responded to those challenges. Feminists opposed the patriarchal structures; however, they were divided in their views on the role of Christianity in the oppression of women. Some feminists considered the churches as the ultimate bastions of patriarchy while others interpreted Christianity as the basis for women's emancipation.[62]

---

62 See, e.g., Karen Offen, *European feminisms 1700–1950: a political history* (Stanford: Stanford University Press, 2000), pp. 196–200, 254; Johanna Stuckey, *Feminist spirituality: an introduction to feminist theology in Judaism, Christianity, Islam and feminist goddess worship* (Toronto: Center for Feminist Research, York University, 1998), pp. 17–19; Inger Hammar, 'From Frederika Bremer to Ellen Key: calling, gender and the emancipation debate in Sweden, c. 1830–1900', in Pirjo Markkola (ed.), *Gender and vocation:*

Within the Christian churches, a division between conservative or hierarchical views and liberal or egalitarian views became decisive in gender issues. The conservatives – both male and female – favoured traditional gender roles based on a fundamentalist interpretation of the Bible. They argued that the order of creation established different and hierarchical gender roles. Women and men were equal as persons, but they had different roles. In their worldview, women were created to serve men; in society women were primarily to be mothers and homemakers. For the conservatives, women's economic and political emancipation entailed a serious threat against a God-given social order. At the same time the liberals argued that God had created women equal with men; therefore, they should be granted equal social and political rights. For the liberal egalitarians, both men and women were created in the image of God (*imago Dei*). Additionally, they based their arguments on the conception of spiritual equality: at Pentecost, the Holy Spirit descended upon men and women equally. Furthermore, they relied on Paul's words emphasising that all are one in Christ.[63]

The twentieth-century changes in economic structures and political systems brought about new challenges transforming the conservative and the liberal views. By the 1920s, at the latest, it was possible to speak about Catholic feminism, for example in England and in continental Europe. Many Catholic women demanded better education for women, suffrage, single women's employment and reform of married women's legal rights. Political feminism, openly opposed by the first popes of the twentieth century, was successful in achieving political rights for women in several European countries. In 1919, Benedict XV relinquished his predecessors' opposition to female political involvement. His successors encouraged Catholic laywomen to play a more active role in the life of the church.[64] Politics, particularly women's right to vote, so clearly condemned at the beginning of the twentieth century, had by now become an encouraged activity for Catholic women.

Nevertheless, the Holy See was slow to revise the patriarchal conception of women's role in the family. The patriarchal values and women's

women, religion and social change in the Nordic countries, 1830–1940 (Helsinki: Finnish Literature Society, 2000), pp. 55–7; Pirjo Markkola, 'The calling of women: gender, religion and social reform in Finland, 1860–1920', in ibid., pp. 132–40.

63 Rosemary R. Ruether, 'Christianity', in Arvind Sharma (ed.), *Women in world religions* (Albany: State University of New York Press, 1987), pp. 207–9.

64 Offen, *European feminisms*, pp. 198–200, 290, 335–6; Richard L. Camp, 'From passive subordination to complementary partnership: the papal conception of a woman's place in church and society since 1878', *Catholic historical review* 76 (1990), 506–25.

emancipation were closely intertwined with the notions of family and marriage. Gender-specific family roles were promoted by the Catholic church in the 1920s and 1930s, but the Vatican's teaching on patriarchal order in the family was changing. The ideal of a wife's subordination to her husband gradually gave way to a more egalitarian conceptualisation of marriage. Marital equality was accentuated in the post-war era. Yet, essentialist views of gender differences and women's God-given, unique qualities were pronounced and motherhood as women's vocation was emphasised. Women's equal but complementary status continued to be a formal Catholic understanding in the 1960s and 1970s.[65] The Catholic church attempted to adjust the patriarchal ideology to demands for women's economic and political emancipation in the twentieth century. At the same time, it aimed at upholding the traditional ideas on women's unique, irreplaceable, role in family, church and society.

In the latter part of the twentieth century, the influence of the modern feminist movement encouraged many churchwomen to question the patriarchal gender order prevalent in their churches. Women's active involvement and traditional role in everyday parish activities were highly valued by their churches, but women's participation in the decision-making represented a more problematic issue. In Australia, for example, the Anglican church faced growing demands from the feminist movement. Gradually, women gained access to parish councils and vestry meetings. In North America, many Protestant denominations made women eligible to the ruling boards or councils, but only a few women attained significant leadership positions.[66] The fact that women's participation comprised a problem indicates the hierarchical and complex nature of gender relations in the Christian churches.

In Catholic history, the Second Vatican Council of the 1960s has sometimes been regarded as a starting point in which gender relations and the position of women were redefined. The council did not introduce this controversy to the Catholic agenda, but it promoted new directions in the church, especially in Latin American and other predominantly Catholic countries. Women were encouraged to participate in community life; Pope John XXIII even explicitly vindicated a more visible public role of women. Additionally, the growth of

---

65 Camp, 'From passive subordination'; Offen, *European feminisms*, pp. 335–6.
66 Brian H. Fletcher, 'Anglicanism and national identity', *Journal of religious history* 25 (2001), p. 34; Rosemary Radford Ruether and Rosemary Skinner Keller, *Women and religion in America*, vol. III: *1900–1968* (San Francisco: Harper & Row, 1986), pp. 266–7, 276–7.

Liberation Theology and feminist theology questioned many patriarchal structures supported and promoted by the Catholic church. The second general conference of Latin American bishops in 1968 introduced the conception of the 'church of the poor', playing a significant role in the redefinition of women's social role as well. Public patriarchal relations seemed to be an acceptable target of criticism for the progressive clergy, but women's emancipation in private matters constituted a silenced issue. The final document of the third general conference of Latin American bishops in 1979 speaks of the oppression and exploitation of women in public life, states women's double oppression and marginalisation, and confirms women's spiritual equality; however, women's body rights and reproductive rights were not on the agenda. The feminist understandings of family and sexuality as the locus of women's oppression appeared to be secondary to the male liberation theologians' tendency to locate women's oppression in capitalist power relations.[67] The feminist concerns of reproductive rights were equally disturbing for the conservative as well as the radical clergy.

In general, the most difficult gender issues seem to be related to female sexuality and women's bodies. This has been particularly obvious in the ecumenical movement and the World Council of Churches. The study programme on the 'Community of Women and Men in the Church' suggested in 1981 that 'religious teachings and practices concerning the inferiority of women were linked to attitudes towards female sexuality and especially to female bodily functions such as menstruation'. After 1981 the WCC sponsored another programme on 'Female Sexuality and Bodily Functions in Different Religious Traditions'. The study was limited in its size and scope; however, it showed that female sexuality was a crucial historical and theological question.[68] Notions of sexuality have also flavoured the ways in which the ordination of women has been a controversial issue in Christendom.

Priesthood was traditionally a male vocation in the Christian churches. In the nineteenth century, however, new views about ministry were being pronounced and women's vocation was debated particularly in the Protestant churches. For the Roman Catholic and the Orthodox churches, and also for the Anglican church, this issue became actualised later. Even

---

67 Sonia E. Alvarez, 'Women's participation in the Brazilian "People's church": a critical appraisal', *Feminist studies* 16 (1990), 381–408; Elina Vuola, *Limits of liberation: praxis as method in Latin American Liberation Theology and feminist theology* (Helsinki: The Finnish Academy of Science and Letters, 1997), pp. 181–97.

68 Janet Crawford, 'The community of women and men in the church: where are we now?', *Ecumenical review* 40 (1988), pp. 46–7.

today, the ordination issue divides the Orthodox churches and the Catholic church, which do not ordain women, from many churches of the Anglican and Protestant traditions, which ordain women as ministers and, in some cases, as bishops.[69]

Nonetheless, the willingness of the Protestant churches to recruit female clergy should not be exaggerated. In 1890, around 7 per cent of the US denominations granted full clergy rights to women; in 1920, the figure was approximately 30 per cent. The American Association of Women Ministers was founded in 1919 to secure equal opportunities for women in the churches. In the mainline denominations, the churches were controlled by men. In 1940, virtually all pastors were men. The only mainline Protestant group with a significant number of female pastors was the Friends (Quakers). Both fundamentalists and mainline US Protestants were not eager to welcome women as pastors, nor did they trust women with other forms of leadership in their churches; in 1940, over 90 per cent of local trustees were men. Furthermore, attempts to promote ecumenical work created a hindrance for women's ordination.[70] Many ecumenical activists considered denominational disagreement on women's ordination as a major obstacle to co-operation between the Christian churches.

The United Church of Canada ordained the first woman in 1936, after an eighteen-year struggle.[71] South of the border, Presbyterians and Methodists opened the ministry for women in the 1950s, and the Lutherans accepted women's ordination in 1970; however, even today, the Lutheran church – Missouri synod reserves the pastorate for men only. In this respect, fellow Europeans were early on; the first women were ordained in the Netherlands and Germany in the 1920s. The Lutherans in Denmark changed the ordination rules in 1948; Sweden followed ten years later. In 1999, over 70 per cent of the Lutheran churches in the world ordained women. Furthermore, a handful of female Lutheran bishops were consecrated in the 1990s, e.g., in Denmark, Germany, Nicaragua, Norway and Sweden.[72]

69 Mark Chaves, 'Ordaining women: the diffusion of an organizational innovation', *American journal of sociology* 101 (1996), p. 862; Sara Butler, 'The ordination of women: a new obstacle to the recognition of Anglican orders', *Anglican theological review* 78 (1996), 96–113.

70 Chaves, 'Ordaining women', pp. 842–4; Michael S. Hamilton, 'Women, public ministry, and American fundamentalism, 1920–1950', *Religion and American culture. A journal of interpretation* 3 (1993), pp. 180–1.

71 Valerie J. Korinek, 'No women need apply: the ordination of women in the United church, 1918–65', *Canadian historical review* 74 (1993), p. 473.

72 Chaves, 'Ordaining women', p. 868; Ruether and Keller, *Women and religion in America*, pp. 339–83.

The Anglican church debated the ordination of women for almost fifty years until 1968, when the member churches were given the freedom to decide the issue themselves. In North America, both the General Convention of the Episcopal church and the Anglican Church of Canada approved women's ordination in 1976. The debate continued elsewhere; in 1992, the Church of England and the Anglican Church of Australia decided to allow the ordination of women as priests.[73]

In fact, women's entry into the clergy became mostly a post-1970 phenomenon. Even the churches that opened ministry for women early witnessed an increase in the numbers of ordained women only in the 1970s and 1980s. For example, in the United States no more than 1 per cent of the ministers in the United Methodist church were female in 1977, but in 1997 the percentage was eleven. Within some churches there were also new organisations created to promote women's careers. Even the latecomers could show quick development. The Lutheran Church of Finland first ordained women in 1988; yet in 1999 approximately 25 per cent of parish clergy, 54 per cent of the hospital counsellors and 63 per cent of family counsellors were women.[74] These figures also reveal a tendency familiar in many churches: female clergy are inclined to concentrate on counselling and assisting positions. Ordination does not necessarily entail gender equality.

In the Catholic church, women's rights were discussed by the members of the Second Vatican Council in 1965. In the 1970s, the issue of women's ordination was on stage several times; first, in 1971 the bishops discussed but rejected a resolution favouring the ordination of women. In 1973, when a 'Study Commission on the Role of Women in Church and Society' was established, ordination was excluded from the agenda. In 1977, the Holy See proclaimed that 'Christ established a bond between maleness and the priesthood which could not be altered'.[75] Catholic feminists did not give up their demand for women's ordination, but Pope John Paul II was unwavering. In the apostolic letter of 1994 he once again prohibited women's

---

73 Rima L. Schultz, 'Woman's work and woman's calling in the episcopal church: Chicago, 1880–1989', in Catherine M. Prelinger (ed.), *Episcopal women: gender, spirituality, and commitment in an American mainline denomination* (New York and Oxford: Oxford University Press, 1992), p. 56; Butler, 'Ordination of women', p. 96; Fletcher, 'Anglicanism and national identity', p. 341.

74 Chaves, 'Ordaining women', pp. 840–1, 868; Kari Salonen, Kimmo Kääriäinen and Kati Niemelä, *The church at the turn of the millennium: the Evangelical Lutheran Church of Finland from 1996 to 1999*, publication no. 51, The Research Institute of the Evangelical Lutheran Church of Finland, http://evl.fi/kkh/ktk/english/p51.htm.

75 Camp, 'From passive subordination'.

ordination, arguing that the Lord chose the twelve men whom he made the foundation of his church.[76] The same argument has often been used by the opponents of women's ordination in the other Christian churches, too.

The women's diaconate introduced in the nineteenth century formed a female vocation, offering single women an opportunity to serve the Protestant churches. There were differing practices within different denominations, but a rather general model was that deaconesses were recruited to perform charitable work in the parishes. Still, in the twentieth century, some churches – e.g., the United Church of Canada – attempted to channel women's work into the deaconess orders and thus bar women's entry to the ordained ministry. As deaconesses women could teach, preach and in some cases baptise, but they would not administer the other sacraments. Furthermore, e.g., in the Anglican church, male deacons were considered clergy; however, as late as in 1968 the Anglican clergy was not able to make up its mind whether deaconesses were 'within the diaconate'.[77] Women's work in the church and men's work in the church were not symmetrical.

IV

THE CHURCH AS WOMEN'S SPACE

———

PIRJO MARKKOLA

Women have outnumbered men in the Christian churches, but authority and power have stayed in the hands of men throughout centuries. It was only in the second half of the twentieth century that the situation began to change on a larger scale. Women gradually got involved in the decision-making bodies of the churches and the number of female clergy increased. Likewise, the definitions of femininity and masculinity have little by little changed.[78]

---

76 Butler, 'Ordination of women'.
77 Korinek, 'No women need apply', pp. 483–5; Mary A. MacFarlane, 'Faithful and courageous handmaidens: deaconesses in the United Church of Canada, 1925–1945', Elizabeth Gillan Muir and Marilyn Färdig Whiteley (eds.), *Changing roles of women within the Christian churches in Canada* (Toronto: University of Toronto Press, 1995), pp. 239–55; Catherine M. Prelinger, 'The female diaconate in the Anglican church: what kind of ministry for women?', in Gail Malmgreen (ed.), *Religion in the lives of English women, 1760–1930* (Bloomington and Indianapolis: Indiana University Press, 1986), pp. 186–7.
78 Schultz, 'Woman's work', in Prelinger, *Episcopal women*, p. 19; Crawford, 'The community', p. 42; Callum G. Brown, *The death of Christian Britain: understanding secularisation 1800–2000* (London and New York: Routledge, 2001), pp. 58–9, 156–61.

Contesting interpretations suggest that Christianity was used to legitimise different definitions of gender relations. In this section we will discuss the ways in which women have found their space in the churches and the ways in which those ways have changed in the twentieth century. The issue will be discussed both in a local setting and on an international and ecumenical level.

The churches and revivalist movements have offered women many meaningful positions. In nineteenth- and early twentieth-century Europe and North America, Protestant women actively contributed to social work, which was based on revivalist religious values. They founded deaconess institutions, orphanages and homes for 'fallen women'. They engaged in philanthropic work among the urban poor and supported the work of deaconesses and missionaries. Moreover, women were active in various home mission and moral reform organisations.[79] In these efforts they were simultaneously encouraged and discouraged. Women who were expanding their social activities were questioning and challenging the social consequences of gender difference, but usually based their arguments on differences between men and women rather than on denying them.

Religious reform movements empowered women, but at the same time they defined gendered fields of activity. The Christian framework fostered several conceptions of women's vocation. Some women found their vocation in the formalised context of the Catholic orders or the Protestant deaconess movement; others devoted themselves to social work among women and children, whereas some other women – both Protestant and Catholic – began to argue for women's rights and actively paved their way to politics. All these women extended their social work beyond the family, but they interpreted their religious vocation in differing ways. The concept of 'woman's calling' continued to be central in women's organisations and new female occupations in the twentieth century, albeit the old-fashioned concept was often replaced with more modern concepts of vocation, ministry or career.[80] According to the Christian ideology, women's calling was to serve the social collective as mothers and daughters, i.e., in the households. At a time when

---

79 See, e.g., Ruether and Keller, *Women and religion in America*; Susan Hill Lindley, *You have stept out of your place: a history of women and religion in America* (Louisville: Westminster John Knox Press, 1996); Elizabeth Smyth, 'Christian perfection and service to neighbours', in Muir and Whiteley, *Changing roles of women*, pp. 40–1; Malmgreen, *Religion in the lives*; Markkola, *Gender and vocation*.

80 Schultz, 'Woman's work', in Prelinger, *Episcopal women*, pp. 52–3; and Randi R. Warne, 'Nellie McClung's social gospel', in Muir and Whiteley, *Changing roles of women*, pp. 40–1, 344–9, respectively.

economic changes were undermining the household unit, the definitions of women's proper calling were re-evaluated.

In the 1920s and 1930s, the progressive tone of the reform movements gave way to a more traditional notion of gender relations in many churches. Particularly in the United States, several church women assumed a new conception of ideal womanhood, that of a wife-companion. Women's work became more integrated into the general work of the church; simultaneously, many women's groups lost their independence. Instead of being social innovators, they turned into fundraisers.[81] Integration and separation was a constant dilemma in women's mobilisation both in religious and secular settings.

The Catholic church provided female space for women religious. In Ireland, the Catholic church attracted numerous women in the twentieth century. At the beginning of the century, the number of women religious was just over 8,000, and the number of religious orders was thirty-five. In 1989 the total number of female religious was 11,415; about 400 of them were cloistered contemplatives.[82] In North America, Catholic sisterhoods in the early twentieth century offered a serious alternative for many immigrant women; in the immigrant communities they also served as educational institutions for working-class girls, facilitating upward social mobility. It has been argued that women religious belonged to the best-educated sections of the parishes they served.[83]

Laywomen also found their space in the Catholic church. Throughout the century they were dynamic parish members, for example in the United States, Italy, Spain and many other countries. In Latin America, Catholic women became active participants in the new church community organisations founded after the Second Vatican Council in the 1960s. Research on women's participation in the People's church in Brazil, however, reveals that women are offered rather traditional activities, i.e., mothers' clubs and housewives' associations, reinforcing traditional gender roles. Women's participation also involves cleaning up after the meetings and other typical female work.[84] Many women consider this important and satisfying, but

81 Schultz, 'Woman's work', in Prelinger (ed.), Episcopal women, pp. 24–5.
82 Margaret MacCurtain, 'Late in the field: Catholic Sisters in twentieth-century Ireland and the new religious history', Journal of women's history 7 (1995), p. 54.
83 Leslie Woodcock Tentler, 'On the margins: the state of American Catholic history', American quarterly 45 (1993), pp. 107–8.
84 Alvarez, 'Women's participation'.

the radical message of equality and the reality of women's experience do not meet.

African churches have likewise relied on women's contributions – both material and spiritual. Women's organisations in many parts of Africa have been powerful and relatively independent. The prophetic churches, in particular, give space for revivalist meetings or prayer and faith healings organised by women's organisations. Additionally, women often raise funds for the churches and for charity, sometimes even paying the clergyman's salary.[85] African cultures give a considerable importance to motherhood; nevertheless, the Catholic sisterhoods have managed to attract many women. In addition to the European sisterhoods, there were several African women's orders founded in the 1920s and 1930s. In 1979, the number of women religious in Africa was almost 33,700; about 12,000 of them were Africans. However, for a woman to enter the religious life represented a radical choice; in a society highly valuing maternity, choosing childlessness could become a source of enduring pain.[86]

Church as women's space has many aspects. Many women appreciated the traditional roles churches offered them, whereas other women expected their churches to promote gender equality and to support women. Research on Norwegian missionary movements in the twentieth century represents a good example of diverse meanings women gave to their activities in the church. In the various missionary organisations women found meaningful positions as humble participants, in formal leadership positions and in informal spiritual leadership. The majority of women assumed a traditional role reserved for them. Formal leadership positions were sometimes acquired by female missionaries in the field, who saw a controversy between responsible work carried out by them and the subordinated position they were offered by the organisation, and became openly rebellious, challenging established power relations. Informal spiritual leadership was occasionally practised in local communities, in which women could gain influence and authority, but still stayed within the proper female sphere.[87]

Missionary work, expanding in the nineteenth century, changed its character in the twentieth century. For women missionaries, there were two differing tendencies after the First World War. For the North American

85 Elizabeth Isichei, *A history of Christianity in Africa: from antiquity to the present* (Lawrenceville, NJ: Africa World Press Inc., 1995), pp. 277, 291, 303, 350.
86 Ibid., pp. 191, 241, 333.
87 Bjørg Seland, '"Called by the Lord" – women's place in the Norwegian missionary movement', in Markkola, *Gender and vocation*, pp. 91–106.

female missionaries, a new era spelled a loss of independence. Their missionary work became more tightly integrated into the church organisations led by men and the earlier women's missionary associations almost disappeared. For many European female missionaries, on the contrary, the twentieth century brought about a different experience. Women's status as missionaries became better established in the missionary organisations. Yet the development was extremely slow. In the 1960s and 1970s female missionaries still had to struggle to make their voices heard in their organisations. There is also evidence from the 1990s that changing missiological conceptions affect the role of female missionaries. Missionary strategies aiming at the emergence of new churches have in some organisations emphasised the role of male missionaries and undermined the position of women missionaries.[88] In other words, while the powers of male missionaries remain largely intact, the delegation of major responsibility for education, charity and social work to the new churches in Africa and Asia has meant the transfer of women's work from the hands of the missionaries to the hands of the local women.

The church as women's space remains a multi-faceted issue. Women have different expectations and diverse needs worldwide. Even within one community there are different needs of women. Spiritual and religious expectations also vary. However, problems like poverty, hunger and violence are gendered issues that the churches address both locally and internationally. Many problems women face are relatively similar; yet there are cultural and regional differences. In many cultures, the Christian churches have empowered women to reflect on their oppression in the society at large. Asian women, for example, founded a theological journal, *In God's image*, in 1982 to address women's concerns. They named their oppression 'as a sinful situation tied for centuries to the chains of patriarchy'.[89] Within a Christian context, women have discussed discrimination and violence against women; simultaneously, they have critiqued patriarchal church traditions and practices.

The issue of the church as women's space has been discussed in the international and ecumenical settings, too. The discrepancy between principles and practices was articulated in the first World Council of Churches

88 Dana L. Robert, 'From missions to mission to beyond missions: the historiography of American Protestant foreign mission since World War II', *International bulletin of missionary research* 18 (1994), 146–61; Mary Taylor Huber and Nancy C. Lutkehaus (eds.), *Gendered missions: Women and men in missionary discourse and practice* (Ann Arbor: University of Michigan Press, 1999).
89 Yong Ting Jin, 'On being church. Asian women's voices and visions', *Ecumenical review* 53 (2001), pp. 109–11.

assembly in Amsterdam in 1948: 'The Church as the Body of Christ consists of men and women, created as responsible persons to glorify God and to do His Will.' However, 'this truth accepted in theory, is too often ignored in practice'.[90] The first worldwide study on women's work and place in the churches was published after the First Assembly. It concluded that women were seeking the right to serve, but the institutional churches largely ignored the need for their services; additionally, women were not encouraged to develop their talents. In 1974, during the time when international feminism was highlighting women's demands for equality, the WCC sub-unit on Women in Church and Society organised a consultation on discrimination against women. The participants in the consultation argued that 'the sin of sexism was present in the church as well as in society'; therefore, they recommended a special study programme on gender relations.[91]

In 1975, the United Nations declared a women's decade, and the Christian churches responded. In the same year, the fifth World Council of Churches assembly was held in Nairobi. In the history of the WCC the Nairobi meeting itself represented a noteworthy milestone. For the first time women were visibly present in the assembly, representing 22 per cent of the delegates (cf. 6 per cent in Amsterdam). Women also made their voice heard in the meetings, reports and recommendations. The assembly accepted a study programme on the 'Community of Women and Men in the Church'. The worldwide programme was initiated in 1978 and continued until the end of 1981. However, the study was not aimed at fighting sexism in the churches nor promoting women's issues as such. It was a programme about community, arguing that the church's unity must include both women and men in mutual partnership. Nevertheless, the study had influence on women's participation, for example in the sixth WCC assembly in Vancouver in 1983.[92]

The year 1985 spelled an end of the UN decade for women. Soon afterwards, the World Council of Churches declared the 'ecumenical decade of churches in solidarity with women' (1988–98), inviting the churches to promote women's full participation in the church and community life.[93] The decade itself is a sign of the need to keep gender issues on the agenda of the Christian churches. Gender relations and women's space in the churches are unsolved dilemmas worldwide. The relationship between

90 Crawford, 'The community', p. 37.   91 Ibid., p. 38.   92 Ibid., pp. 38–9.
93 Ibid., p. 43; Janet Crawford, 'Women and ecclesiology. Two ecumenical streams?' *Ecumenical review* 53 (2001), p. 4.

Christian faith and emancipation is far from solved for women, too. For many women, Christendom stands as the symbol of the patriarchal power at work. For many other women, Christianity represents the cornerstone of women's emancipation. The church as women's space gives room for varied conceptions of gender relations.

30

Christianity and the sciences

PETER J. BOWLER

There is a widespread assumption that the late nineteenth century was a period in which the conflict between science and religion moved into the open, with materialistic scientists openly bidding to replace Christianity as a source of cultural authority. The twentieth century then appears as an era in which the churches attempted to fight back, denying science's claim to have explained away the mysteries of the cosmos and the human spirit. Even if religion as a whole was in decline (at least in Europe), the specific challenges offered by the materialist view of nature were identified more clearly and alternative visions offered that would blunt science's ability to undermine faith.

In fact the story of the relationship between Christianity and the sciences in the twentieth century is a good deal more complex than this simple image of conflict would imply. Historians of the nineteenth century itself have noted how the image of a necessary confrontation between science and religion was deliberately manufactured by the advocates of materialism or (as T. H. Huxley would have preferred to call it) scientific naturalism. As James R. Moore has noted,[1] this image derives from late nineteenth-century writers such as J. W. Draper and A. D. White, both of whom endorsed the argument that science was wresting authority from religion. Paradoxically, the image of late nineteenth-century culture as dominated by science-inspired materialism was consolidated by the later opponents of that movement, who presented themselves as challenging an entrenched dogma.

In fact, neither the scientific profession nor late nineteenth-century culture as a whole had been dominated by the materialism promoted by Huxley and Draper. Eminent scientists from the biologist Louis Pasteur to the physicist

---

1 J. R. Moore, *The post-Darwinian controversies: a study of the Protestant struggle to come to terms with Darwin in Great Britain and America, 1870–1900* (New York: Cambridge University Press, 1979).

Lord Kelvin had retained their Christian faith and worked to ensure that it was compatible with their scientific worldview. Darwin's theory of natural selection had been challenged by various non-Darwinian theories of evolution which retained a sense of order and purpose in nature. Early twentieth-century critics of Darwinism such as Henri Bergson and George Bernard Shaw were not initiating a counter-attack, but merely updating a tradition that had held its ground in the preceding decades.

What changed around 1900 was the self-confidence of the forces opposed to materialism. There was a new sense that science had recognised the limitations of the naturalistic programme and was now throwing its weight behind the drive to see life and mind as purposeful agents within a meaningful cosmos. For thinkers such as Bergson and Shaw this had little to do with the revival of traditional religious values. But liberal Christians, at least in the English-speaking world, now saw an opportunity to seize the initiative by capitalising on the latest developments in science to create a new natural theology in which evolution was shaped by the purposeful activities of living things in such a way that it eventually achieved the divine goal of creating the human species. The idea of progress was retained as the hallmark of evolution and the framework within which human actions would achieve God's will in the world.

There were two problems with this programme. The first was that it had very mixed fortunes in terms of its scientific credentials. The physicists, at least, did overthrow the old form of materialism by showing that the world was not deterministic, and might even need the mind of an observer to manifest itself at all. But in biology, the creative evolutionism of Bergson and Shaw was being exposed for what it was – a vestige of the old Lamarckism, increasingly out of touch with the new science of genetics that was now providing a secure foundation for the theory of natural selection. The second problem was that the new natural theology could be promoted by outright opponents of Christianity such as Shaw, suggesting to many traditional Christians that the liberals had sold the pass to the enemy in their anxiety to make a compromise with new ideas such as evolutionism.

In this context, it is hardly surprising that the middle decades of the century should witness a resurgence of outright opposition to many aspects of science by more conservative theological forces. But this opposition took several different forms. In America, the evangelical movement known as fundamentalism became increasingly identified with opposition to Darwinism, but tried to take on science within its own territory. Efforts were made to argue that scientific geology could be reinterpreted to provide evidence of a recent creation and worldwide deluge. The movement known as creationism thus still welcomed the study of nature, but argued for a 'creation science' which supported rather than undermined traditional Christian beliefs. In Europe, however, there was a deeper challenge to the authority of science from the Neo-Orthodoxy of theologians such as Karl Barth. For them, to defend the faith it was necessary to focus on human sinfulness and the need for salvation. Anything that distracted from this was unwelcome, including even a natural theology which sought to demonstrate God's designing hand in nature.

The late twentieth century has seen these debates move into new phases as the focus of both scientific and theological attention shifts. In America, interest in 'young earth' creationism has waned, although opposition to Darwinism remains intense. Liberal Christians in both America and Europe have, however, survived the onslaught of Neo-Orthodoxy and have continued to seek a natural theology that uses as much established scientific knowledge as possible. Evolutionism is accepted, and efforts have been made to argue that even a Darwinian interpretation may not be incompatible with Christian values. More positively, the latest developments in physics and cosmology have been used to argue that the universe described by science gives evidence that it has indeed been designed in a way that makes possible the emergence of thinking, moral, beings such as ourselves. The diversity of Christian responses to science is thus maintained.

The new natural theology and modernism

The opponents of religion had used scientific materialism and the Darwinian theory of evolution to challenge many aspects of traditional Christian belief. But even advocates of the naturalistic position such as Herbert Spencer were committed to the idea of progress, and to the assumption that human moral values were a pre-determined outcome of the ascent of life. This made it relatively easy for liberal Protestants to argue that evolution could be incorporated into traditional natural theology because the ultimate outcome of the process indicated its underlying divine purpose. The Darwinian theory of natural selection was more difficult to take on board, since it not only proclaimed struggle to be the driving force of nature, but also treated every adaptive character as the product of trial and error. But the widespread assumption that selection was supplemented by the Lamarckian process of the inheritance of acquired characters allowed this problem to be evaded: if evolution adapted structures to new habits deliberately chosen by the animals themselves, a form of teleology was preserved. In America, the Quaker paleontologist Edward Drinker Cope explicitly hailed the 'growth force' of life as the divine creative power transferred into nature itself. Provided one adopted a vitalist, rather than a mechanist, view of life, evolution was not a threat to teleology.[2]

Historians of science have tended to focus on the expansion of mechanist thought within twentieth-century biology. Yet the early decades of the century saw an explosion of interest in Henri Bergson's explicitly vitalist philosophy of 'creative evolution', and even within science there was continued support for a less mechanist approach to the study of living things. Although widely hailed as a new and non-materialist approach to evolution, this movement merely preserved the views of the previous generation of Lamarckians, but with a somewhat greater emphasis on the open-endedness and unpredictability of the direction of progress. For many Christians, however, it was possible to ignore the implication that humanity was not the intended goal of creation. Intelligent and moral beings such as ourselves would emerge sooner or later, so the ultimate purpose of the whole process was preserved. A whole generation of anti-mechanist biologists and liberal theologians hailed Bergson's philosophy as the foundation of a new approach to science and a new natural theology. In the course of the 1920s this position was supplemented by the psychologist C. Lloyd Morgan's philosophy of emergent evolution (in which new properties such as life, mind and spirit 'emerged' at certain levels of increased complexity) and the philosopher-statesman Jan Christiaan Smuts' emphasis on 'holism' as the key to understanding how living things could exhibit qualities unpredictable from a mechanist analysis of their separate parts. Although the new science of genetics was undermining Lamarckism and creating a new foundation for the theory of natural selection, it was possible for theologians to imagine, at least until around 1930, that the direction in which science itself was moving favoured the non-mechanist philosophy that was an essential component of the new natural theology.[3]

---

2 P. J. Bowler, *The eclipse of Darwinism: anti-Darwinian evolution theories in the decades around 1900* (Baltimore: Johns Hopkins University Press, 1983); P. J. Bowler, *The non-Darwinian revolution: reinterpreting a historical myth* (Baltimore: Johns Hopkins University Press, 1988). See also Moore, *Post-Darwinian controversies* and J. Durant (ed.), *Darwinism and divinity: essays on evolution and religious belief* (Oxford: Blackwell, 1985).

3 On developments in early twentieth-century Britain see P. J. Bowler, *Reconciling science and religion: the debate in early twentieth-century Britain* (Chicago: University of Chicago Press, 2001) and more generally A. Hastings, *A history of English Christianity, 1920–1985* (London: Collins, 1986).

In physics too, science seemed to be on the side of compromise. The pioneer of radio Sir Oliver Lodge hailed the ether through which electromagnetic waves are transmitted as the unifying foundation of nature and the material basis for the soul to survive the death of the gross physical body. Lodge contributed to the popular interest in spiritualism following the war.[4] Although Einstein's theory of relativity undermined Lodge's support for the ether, developments in atomic physics seemed to challenge old-fashioned materialism in a new and more fundamental way. Few theologians understood the details of Heisenberg's uncertainty principle or Schroedinger's wave mechanics, but popular accounts seemed to imply that nature could no longer be seen as a collection of billiard-ball atoms driven by purely mechanical forces. As writers such as the physicist-cosmologists Arthur Eddington and James Jeans proclaimed, science now required the observer to be included in the equation defining any observation of the physical world. Eddington, a Quaker, proclaimed in his *Nature of the physical world* of 1928 that the new physics enabled the scientist to become a religious thinker again, since the concept of a universal consciousness equivalent to God was no longer incompatible with scientific theory.

The new natural theology was based on the idea of progress, and historians have often assumed that this idea lost much of its influence in the early twentieth century, especially following the trauma of World War I. This may be a valid interpetation of the situation in continental Europe, but it does not apply to the English-speaking world, at least for the 1920s. In Germany, a teleological vision of nature was articulated by Rudolph Otto, professor of theology at Göttingen, but Protestant thought turned increasingly toward a harsher view of the human sitation (discussed below). In Britain and America, though, liberal Christians welcomed the opportunity for a reconciliation with science provided by the new natural theology. Progress was the central theme of evolution, and the emergence of the human spirit could be seen as a key step toward achieving the divine purpose. This interpretation became a key feature of the modernist movement within the Anglican church, which was active through conferences and publications through the 1920s.[5] Charles Raven promoted the new natural theology in books such as his *Creator Spirit* of 1927. But Raven was committed to an explicitly non-mechanist and

4 J. Oppenheim, *The other world: spiritualism and psychic research in England, 1850–1914* (Cambridge: Cambridge University Press, 1985).
5 K. W. Clements, *Lovers of discord: twentieth century theological controversies in England* (London: SPCK, 1988); A. M. G. Stephenson, *The rise and decline of English modernism* (London: SPCK, 1984).

Lamarckian view of biology, and remained so throughout the rest of his life.[6] Other modernists, including E. W. Barnes, bishop of Birmingham, realised that Darwinism was now making a comeback in biology and saw that the movement was vulnerable if it continued to link itself to an outdated scientific position.

Most Nonconformist churches did not experience movements equivalent to modernism, and indeed many ministers and theologians thought that the modernists had abandoned the core Christian teachings on sin and the need for salvation. The Congregationalists had experienced a brief flurry of interest in the 'new theology' of R. J. Campbell in 1907, and a few Congregationalists continued to promote a liberal position into the 1920s. In Scotland, Presbyterians such as James Y. Simpson endorsed the new natural theology. But in general the trend among nonconformists was to resist the kind of liberalisation promoted by the Anglican modernists. By the mid-1930s the weaknesses of the new natural theology were being exposed. It was not so much the challenge from science that undermined modernism: Darwinism may have been revived in biology, but in physics the new idealism of Eddington and Jeans still gave hope to the opponents of materialism. But as critics from both the Catholic and evangelical wings of the Anglican church had warned, modernism denatured Christianity by ignoring human sinfulness in order to take on board ideas such as progressive evolution. What was left was an emotionally unsatisfying vision of the human situation which appeared increasingly out of touch with the political and economic realities of the 1930s. The modernists' faith in progress seemed an unrealistic response to the Depression and the rise of fascism in Europe.

Human nature and the new psychology

The modernist position treated human moral and spiritual qualities as the intended product of a divinely ordained evolutionary process. There was still a problem with the concept of original sin, but by the early twentieth century liberals such as the Anglican F. R. Tennant were arguing that the fall could be interpreted as the awakening of the moral conscience in the earliest forms of humanity as they emerged from their brute ancestry. E. W. Barnes gained notoriety for his 'gorilla sermons' (reprinted in his *Should such a faith offend?* of

---

6 F. W. Dillistone, *Charles Raven: naturalist, historian, theologian* (London: Hodder and Stoughton, 1975).

1927) in which he drove home the need for the concept of the fall to be reinterpreted if Christianity was to take on board the idea of evolution.[7] The idea that the sinful part of human nature was a remnant of its animal ancestry allowed the modernists to be complacent at first over the threat posed by the new psychology of Sigmund Freud. In the 1920s there were efforts to dismiss Freud's view of the unconscious as merely a refinement of earlier evolutionary ideas. It was the opponents of modernism who saw the threat posed by analytical psychology's vision of the subconscious mind driven by purely animal urges over which the conscious mind had little control. The threat was even more apparent when Freud began to argue that religion itself was a by-product of the tensions created between the conscious and unconscious parts of the mind. By the 1930s most religious thinkers, liberal or conservative, were arguing against the influence of Freud's view of human nature.[8] They were anxious to preserve a role for the higher spiritual qualities which had the potential, at least, to reach beyond the animal past. In effect, Freud threatened liberal theology by undermining the assumption that evolution was a progressive force designed to create spiritual beings.

Freud was not the only threat from the new psychology, and in some respects the behaviourist movement promoted by James Watson in America offered a more obvious challenge. If this approach were applied to the human as well as the animal mind, we would be reduced to mere automata, wide open to manipulation by behavioural conditioning, as in Aldous Huxley's *Brave new world*. Even the British modernists treated this as a *reductio ad absurdam* of the materialist position, although they were fortunate that the movement gained less support within academic psychology on the European side of the Atlantic.

Opposition to the new natural theology: Roman Catholicism

The Roman Catholic church had stamped out its own modernist movement at the turn of the century, and at that point had seemed to turn its back very firmly against the theory of evolution. Efforts to argue that evolution could be seen as the unfolding of a divine plan were resisted, most obviously

---

7 J. Barnes, *Ahead of his age: Bishop Barnes of Birmingham* (London: Collins, 1979).
8 J. H. Roberts, 'Psychoanalysis and American Christianity, 1900–1945', in D. C. Lindberg and R. L. Numbers (eds.), *When science and Christianity meet* (Chicago: University of Chicago Press, 2003), pp. 225–44.

because any connection between humans and animals was thought to undermine the unique spiritual status of the human soul. In 1909, however, the Pontifical Biblical Commission formally removed the ban on discussion of bodily evolution by proclaiming that the text of the creation story in Genesis need not be taken literally. From this point on, liberal thinkers within the church began to develop the argument that a non-Darwinian and teleological version of evolutionism was acceptable, provided it was made clear that only the human body had been formed in this way, the soul being a divine creation. Catholics were thus able to go some way with the supporters of the new natural theology. They could accept the arguments of vitalist biologists and anti-materialist physicists, and (within very strict limits) explore the idea of progressive evolution. But all forms of mental and moral development, including the theory of emergent evolution, were off-limits. When the Jesuit palaeontologist Teilhard de Chardin developed a form of theistic evolutionism, he was forbidden to publish, and his views only had an impact posthumously in the 1950s.

A key figure in the movement to make boldly evolution acceptable was the Belgian scholar Canon Henri de Dorlodot. He sidestepped the question of the mechanism of evolution by insisting that this was outside the realm of theology. In his *Darwinism and Catholic thought* (trans. 1925) he noted that even Darwin had conceded a divine origin for life itself, but argued that there was nothing in scripture to rule out spontaneous generation or bodily evolution. Many of the church fathers seem to have accepted spontaneous generation. Dorlodot's position was explored further in Ernest Messenger's *Evolution and theology* of 1931, which strongly implied that the actual process of evolution was divinely pre-ordained, but made it clear that, even so, only the human body could have been formed in this way. The soul was a direct product of supernatural activity. In effect, Dorlodot and Messenger paved the way for what became the orthodox position of the church in the later twentieth century. In the 1930s, though, there were still many Catholics who took a much more conservative position. The popular writer Hilaire Belloc emerged as one of the more effective opponents of the materialist view of evolution expressed by figures such as H. G. Wells, and it is clear that Belloc rejected any form of evolution that included ape-human intermediates. He gained some credibility for the Catholic position by arguing that the church had been the only institution that had held the line against materialism.[9]

9 Bowler, *Reconciling science and religion*, chs. 9 and 11.

Opposition to the new natural theology: Neo-Orthodoxy

The theological liberalism that had allowed the new natural theology to flourish in the English-speaking world also came under attack from the harsher vision of the human situation being developed in Germany by Karl Barth. This was a challenge not to the scientific credibility of the thesis, but to the whole project in which the study of nature was allowed to supplement scripture in defining the human situation.[10] German theologians in the 1930s were only too well aware of the challenges emerging in the real world to any expectation that nature and history were somehow on the side of human perfectibility. Barth stressed the sinfulness of humanity and the absolute need for redemption from a source outside this world. From such a perspective, natural theology became not only wrong (because there was no reason to suppose that nature was benevolent and purposeful) but irrelevant and dangerous (because to become involved with it was to lose sight of the true nature of humanity). In America the sternly realistic social ethics of Reinhold Niebuhr also provided a new foundation for Protestant thought along lines which dismissed the liberals' optimistic faith in progress as both naive and unChristian.

The impact of these new theological perspectives on the new natural theology was rapid and devastating. Even within its heartland, the Anglican church, modernism withered as a new generation finally abandoned the hope that nature provided some guarantee for the human future and turned back to a recognition of human sinfulness. Charles Raven saw his influence crumble at Cambridge as young Christians turned in droves to the Neo-Orthodox approach brought in by Edwyn Hoskins' translation of Barth. The period surrounding World War II would experience a temporary revival of popular interest in Christianity across Europe, but this coincided with a rejection of the liberal view that had allowed the new natural theology to flourish.

Opposition to the new natural theology: American fundamentalism

In America, Niebuhr's position may have appealed to the theologically sophisticated, but there was also grassroots opposition to the Darwinian

---

10 On Barth and natural theology see S. A. Matczak, *Karl Barth on God: the knowledge of the divine existence* (New York: St Paul's Publications, 1962), pp. 253–69.

theory from the movement known as fundamentalism. Creationism has attracted much attention from historians – so much that it has tended to distort our perception of the wider interaction between Christianity and science in the twentieth century. But the popular image of its activities has been significantly distorted, and this at least has been corrected by the latest studies. Creationism arose within social groups that were both theologically and politically conservative. Fundamentalists resented the liberalisation of their faith which, they felt, had undermined traditional moral values by treating the human race as merely improved animals. Like other conservative opponents of evolutionism, they wanted to preserve the unique status of the human spirit. But they were also concerned to preserve the veracity of the word of God, and were thus pre-disposed to reject evolution because of its incompatibility with the details of the Genesis creation story. In its later versions, creationism also differed from other conservative responses by choosing to engage science on its own territory. Where Neo-Orthodoxy turned its back on natural theology, creationism sought to revive the scientific plausibility of the argument from design and to devise what could be presented as a scientifically respectable view of earth history more in line with Genesis. It is thus no accident that many creationists have been trained in the practical sciences or in medicine – they have no interest in rejecting the technological benefits that arise from understanding how nature works on a day-to-day basis.[11]

The first outburst of American creationism peaked in the 1920s, although historians have now challenged many of the myths surrounding this episode, including the assumption that it marked the highpoint of creationist influence. Not all fundamentalists were opponents of evolutionism, and few states actually banned the teaching of evolution, although the creationists were remarkably successful in keeping it out of the schools for the next several decades.[12]

The 1920s saw the early origins of what later became known as young-earth creationism, based on the claim that all sedimentary rocks were laid down in Noah's flood. This idea came into its own in the 1950s as the creationists woke up to the fact that a resurgent Darwinism was demanding access to the educational system. A number of American states now passed legislation requiring that equal time be given in the public schools to the

11 R. L. Numbers, *The creationists* (New York: Knopf, 1992).
12 E. J. Larson, *Summer for the gods: the Scopes trial and America's continuing debate over science and religion* (New York: Basic Books, 1998); R. L. Numbers, *Darwinism comes to America* (Cambridge, MA: Harvard University Press, 1998).

teachings of 'creation science.' The American Civil Liberties Union contested these laws on the grounds that they violated the constitutional prohibition on the teaching of religion in the schools, the basis of their argument being that flood geology was obviously inspired by the desire to preserve the veracity of Genesis. In the 1980s the creationist movement changed its tactics and began to concentrate on the traditional concept of design as a scientifically valid argument against Darwinian natural selection. Michael Behe and others developed the concept of intelligent design, according to which some organic structures and processes can be shown to be so irreducibly complex that they cannot have been built up by gradual steps from simpler origins, least of all by trial and error.[13] Creation by an intelligent God is the only alternative explanation.

Reviving the synthesis

The conservatism of the creationist movement in the United States contrasts with the more imaginative efforts that have been made by liberal Christian thinkers to explore a reconciliation with science. The 1930s and 1940s saw a sharp decline in the fortunes of theological modernism in the English-speaking world under the influence of Protestant Neo-Orthodoxy. Roman Catholicism also gained renewed impetus through its resistance to the materialism and liberalism that had so spectacularly failed to anticipate the social and moral disasters of the Depression and the rise of fascism. But in the 1950s the effort to reforge a synthesis between liberal theology and science began again, in effect reviving the new natural theology that had burgeoned in the early twentieth century. Evolutionism was still central to this view of the cosmos, all the more so now that cosmologists too saw the physical universe as a system evolving from the 'big bang'. Darwinian natural selection remained a problem: this had become the biologists' preferred explanation of evolution, and Christians struggled to come to terms with this situation. But as in the period around 1930, the physical sciences seemed to offer better hope for the creation of a less materialistic view of the world. Development in sub-atomic physics confirmed the less deterministic view of nature pioneered by quantum mechanics, although the precise way in which these insights could be used to defend free will proved elusive. More significantly, physicists joined forces with the cosmologists to show that

---

13 M. Behe, *Nature's black box: the biochemical challenge to evolution* (New York: Simon and Schuster, 1996).

many of the underlying physical processes which govern the evolution of the universe seem to be pre-designed to allow the emergence of stars, planets and ultimately life itself. The notion of design has been reformulated to allow for the fact of progressive evolution.

An early sign of the new enthusiasm for teleological evolutionism was the positive reception accorded to Teilhard de Chardin's *Phenomenon of man* when it was finally published in the 1950s (trans. 1959). Teilhard ignored Darwinism to present evolution as a divinely planned unfolding of nature toward the human spirit and beyond. This was a philosophy derived from the non-Darwinian thinking popular in the early decades of the century. It was welcomed by theological liberals such as Charles Raven, and roundly condemned by the new generation of scientific biologists. From this time onwards, liberal theologians outside the Roman Catholic church have accepted the need to come to terms with the idea that the human spirit must have evolved along with the body. The Darwinian selection theory has, however, continued as a stumbling block, and there has been a tendency (disappointing from the scientists' point of view) to ignore the theory in favour of poorly articulated teleological alternatives. In the closing years of the twentieth century, however, some theologians have begun to seek avenues by which their faith can be reconciled even with Darwinism. They point out that suffering may be a necessary consequence of the Creator's decision to allow evolution to proceed freely, thereby ensuring that its end-products still have free will. They also note that Christianity is the only religion in which suffering is an integral part of the message of salvation.[14]

More generally, the writings of theologians with scientific training, including Arthur Peacocke and John Polkinghorne, have explored the implications of new discoveries in physics and cosmology for a revival of the design argument.[15] They point out that many of the universal constants that determine how the laws of nature operate seem to have been fine-tuned to ensure that the evolution of the universe takes place in such a way that meaningful structures can appear. With only the slightest difference from the known figure for any one of a number of constants, there would be no stars or planets, or stars would burn out too quickly for life to evolve. There seems a

---

14 E.g., Kenneth R. Miller, *Finding Darwin's God: a scientist's search for common ground between God and evolution* (New York: Perennial, 2000).
15 A. R. Peacocke, *Creation and the world of science* (Oxford: Oxford University Press, 1980); J. C. Polkinghorne, *Belief in God in an age of science* (New Haven: Yale University Press, 1998). See also I. G. Barbour, *Religion and science: historical and contemporary issues* (London: SCM, 1998).

strong implication that these constants were determined at the initial 'big bang' from which the universe began by a Creator who wished to see certain outcomes to the evolution of the cosmos, including the appearance of living things capable of moral and spiritual activity. This form of reconciliation between science and religion is being actively promoted in many quarters as an alternative to the creationists' attempt to replace many of the key ideas of modern science. In spirit, if not in detail, it is very much a resurgence of ideas and values of the new natural theology popular among theological liberals nearly a century earlier.

31

Literature and the arts

I

LITERATURE AND FILM

DAVID JASPER

Literature

The outbreak of the Great War in 1914 marked the effective end of the nineteenth century, and with it the age of the great religious novel in Europe and its reflection on the shifting experience of Christianity after the Enlightenment and in the age of industrialisation, not least as the churches expanded globally with the growth of the colonial powers. The terrible years of the war destabilised and eroded theology and belief, and if the young English poet Wilfred Owen had already lapsed from his Christian faith even by 1913, his experiences at the front provoked a rage against the faith and a despair, later to be finely caught in Benjamin Britten's setting of his poetry to music in the *War requiem* (1961), that was to herald the new century. At the same time the anxious literature of avant-garde modernism, with its attack on realism and mimesis, emerged in sceptical protest against the 'totalizing religious and political frameworks of the nineteenth century'.[1] Stephen, in James Joyce's *Stephen hero* (1904–6) is told by a priest that his essay on 'Art and life' 'represents the sum of modern unrest and modern freethinking'. Twenty years later, E. M. Forster in *A passage to India* (1924) allows only a minor role for the European missionaries in Chandrapore, India, and their 'poor, chattering Christianity'.

Throughout the twentieth century, however, Christianity, even as it began to fade in the churches, continued to haunt fiction, while the novel challenged

1 Christopher Butler, *Early modernism: literature, music and painting in Europe 1900–1916* (Oxford: Clarendon Press, 1994), pp. 1–2.

582

Christian orthodoxy with the freedoms of literature and was adapted with increasing sophistication for cinema. Perhaps the most notorious example of this in the mid years of the century is Nikos Kanzantzakis' Ὁ τελευταῖος πειρασμος (1955), which was immediately blacklisted by the Vatican. Translated in 1960 as *The last temptation of Christ*, the novel was the subject of Martin Scorsese's challenging and deeply theological, though flawed, film of 1988. Yet still the 'Catholic novel' flourished throughout the twentieth century in the work of such writers as Evelyn Waugh, Graham Greene and most recently David Lodge in Britain, François Mauriac and Julien Green in France and Flannery O'Connor in the USA, to name but a few. Waugh described the theme of his *Brideshead revisited* (1945) as 'the operation of divine grace on a group of diverse but closely connected characters', while the work of grace is central to the gothic fictions of O'Connor, who wrote in her note to the second edition of *Wise blood* (1962) – which was also made into a fine film by John Huston –:

> That belief in Christ is to some a matter of life and death has been a stumbling block for readers who would prefer to think it a matter of no great consequence. For them Hazel Motes' [the main character of the novel] integrity lies in his trying with such vigor to get rid of the ragged figure who moves from tree to tree in the back of his mind. For the author Hazel's integrity lies in his not being able to.[2]

At the other end of the fictional spectrum, the elaborate science fiction fantasies and children's 'Narnia' books of C. S. Lewis have continued to attract a huge readership, drawn by his deeply held but ultimately rather simplistic Christian faith. Lewis and his fellow 'Inklings', among whom J. R. R. Tolkien has recently enjoyed an enormous revival through the commercial success of the filming of his epic fantasy *The lord of the rings* (1954–5), draw on their work in early and middle English literature and the genre of fantasy literature in Victorian fiction, notably that of George Macdonald. At the same time, the New Testament has continued to be a direct influence on fiction in such diverse fictional works as Jorge Luis Borges' 'The gospel of Mark' (in the late collection of stories entitled *Dr. Brodie's report* (1971)), Robert Graves' *King Jesus* (1946) and Kazantzakis' *Christ recrucified* (1954). Literature, like twentieth-century art, has frequently interwoven the passion story with the wars and tragedies our time, as in the American William Faulkner's Pulitzer Prize-winning *A fable* (1954), which is an extended parable

2 Flannery O'Connor, Author's Note to the Second Edition of *Wise blood* (London: Faber and Faber, 1968).

of the passion set within the First World War. In an early critical study of this theme in fiction, *The novelist and the passion story* (1960), the theologian F. W. Dillistone defends the power of 'story', writing: 'The events happened more than 1900 years ago, but through the story they become entirely contemporary. The movement of the story corresponds, we know, to the movement of human life everywhere, and it is always possible that the goal towards which the story leads may find its counterpart with the circumstances of a wholly different age.'[3] The American John Irving's *A prayer for Owen Meany* (1989) is one of the more imaginative retellings of the gospel story, its comic oddities only made clear in the final moment of Owen's 'passion', the event for which his whole strange life has been a preparation.

The cross and passion have powerfully funded the literature of liberation, either in such work as the novels of James Baldwin in the United States, or in post-colonial fiction. Baldwin's short story 'Going to meet the man' (1948) is a disturbing and violent account of the lynching and hanging of an African American man in the American deep south seen through the eyes of a young white boy. The Kenyan novelist Ngũgĩ Wa Thiong'o wrote his novel *Devil on the cross* (1980) – which he himself translated from the Gĩkũyũ – while detained in prison without trial. Its apocalyptic opening begins with the words, 'Certain people in Ilmorog, our Ilmorog, told me that this story was too disgraceful, too shameful, that it should be concealed in the depths of everlasting darkness.' In his novel *Incognito* (1962), first published in French, the Rumanian dissident writer Petru Dumitriu portrays the impossible possibility of Christian faith under the communist regimes of the eastern bloc. Other writers who have employed the power of literature to sustain spiritual values under Soviet repression are Alexander Solzhenitsyn and the Christian poet Irina Ratushinskaya.

The growth of the ecumenical liturgical movement, beginning in France in the nineteenth century, has encouraged a revival, mostly in English and often in verse, of religious drama and the modern production of the medieval miracle cycles in York and elsewhere. The best known of such plays is T. S. Eliot's *Murder in the cathedral* (1935), concerned with the murder of Archbishop Thomas Becket in 1170, and written to be performed in Canterbury cathedral. It was followed in the next year by Charles Williams' *Thomas Cranmer of Canterbury*, also first performed in the chapter house of Canterbury cathedral, on 20 June 1936. Alongside such deliberate portrayals of Christian history 'on site' in medieval settings, the rapid growth of radio

---

3 F. W. Dillistone, *The novelist and the passion story* (London: Collins, 1960), pp. 11–12.

broadcasting soon began to attract major literary figures. In February 1940, J. W. Welch, director of religious broadcasting for the BBC, asked Dorothy Sayers to write a series of plays on the life of our Lord for the Sunday Children's Hour. The result was the twelve plays of *The man born to be king* (1943), which after the initial press conference attracted hostility from Christian quarters, Welch writing that 'on the appearance of . . . . sensational and inaccurate reports, without having heard or read one line of any of the plays . . . . people condemned the plays as "irreverent", "blasphemous", "vulgar" and so on. These correspondents condemned plays they had never seen or heard, and the language applied to Our Lord by his contemporaries was, almost word for word, now applied to Miss Sayers.'[4] This is just one example of the uneasy relationship between the gospel story and modern mass media that is repeated time and again in the history of radio and television as well as the cinema. For example, the beginnings of the commercial film industry in Australia were largely funded by the Salvation Army, which saw the cinema as a potential pulpit for their preaching of the gospel. This, however, turned out not to be the case, as films began to cater for the demands of a paying audience who wanted to be entertained and excited rather than preached at and converted.

Among the most recent plays based on the gospels is the trilogy of the Glasgow poet Edwin Morgan, *A. D.* (2000), which also met with opposition from local church groups on its first performance to celebrate the millennium in Glasgow. Morgan is not a Christian and declared that his 'ambition [was] to tell a good story'. Jesus is here portrayed as 'a human figure in an inhuman time', his character a radical departure from the gospel narratives as he fathers a child by an unmarried woman and is the object of the openly gay affection of 'the disciple whom Jesus loved'. Edwin Morgan, like T. S. Eliot, is primarily a poet, and the twentieth century saw an outpouring of poetry inspired by the Bible and of 'Christian verse', while at the same time there was an increasing uncertainty as to what this exactly meant. Peter Levi writes in his introduction to *The Penguin book of English Christian verse* (1984): 'By the vaguest definition, Christian poetry might be any verse written by a Christian, or in a Christian framework or language, in Christian centuries, in a Christian society.'[5] Some half a century earlier, Lord David Cecil, in his introduction to the first *Oxford book of Christian verse* (1940), had been clear that there is a specific division of poetry called 'Christian', which excludes

4 J. W. Welch, Foreword to Dorothy L. Sayers, *The man born to be king: a play-cycle on the life of our Lord and Saviour Jesus Christ* (London: Victor Gollancz, 1943), pp. 9–10.
5 Peter Levi (ed.), *The Penguin book of English Christian verse* (Harmondsworth: Penguin, 1984), p. 19.

great areas of human behaviour (sexual, political, military) and leaves little room for doubt or exploration. Furthermore, he believed that there was a revival in such poetry after the First World War, remarking that 'since 1918 Christianity has raised her head again',[6] specifically in the writings of T. S. Eliot. Certainly many of the major British poets of the twentieth century were Christian, and their faith directly inspired much of their writings – among them W. H. Auden, R. S. Thomas, Geoffrey Hill, Jack Clemo and David Jones.

In France in the earlier years of the century, Catholic poetry emerged powerfully in the work of the deeply theological convert Charles Péguy, whose great monologue *The portal of the mystery of hope* (1910) has recently been republished in English.[7] In post-colonial literature, Christian poetry has frequently been absorbed into a syncretistic context as in the work of the Nigerian poet Christopher Okigbo, a writer who finds no conflict between his professed faith and the religious traditions of his own Igbo peoples of eastern Nigeria. Indeed, in 1958 Okigbo remarked, 'When I started taking poetry very seriously, it was as though I had felt a sudden call to begin performing my full functions as the chief priest of Idoto.'[8] Idoto is the local river-goddess.

In the poetry of the Holocaust and later the communist bloc, the powerful images of the passion narratives were frequently used to describe the sufferings of innocent victims. The Polish poet Czeslaw Milosz translated his own poem 'A poor Christian looks at the ghetto' into English verse:

> What will I tell him, I, a Jew of the New Testament,
> Waiting two thousand years for the second coming of Jesus?
> My broken body will deliver me to his sight
> And he will count me among the helpers of death:
> The uncircumcised.[9]

Film

The commercial cinema has had, from its beginnings, an uneasy but energetic relationship with the gospel story and with the history of the

---

6 Lord David Cecil, *The Oxford book of Christian verse* (Oxford: Oxford University Press, 1940), p. xxxiii.

7 Charles Péguy, *The portal of the mystery of hope*, trans. David Louis Schindler, Jr (Edinburgh: T&T Clark, 1996).

8 In Marjory Whitelaw, 'Interview with Christopher Okigbo, 1965', *Journal of Commonwealth literature* 9 (1970), p. 36.

9 In George Steiner (ed.), *The Penguin book of modern verse translation* (Harmondsworth: Penguin, 1966), p. 233.

Christian church. Although there have been huge 'Christian' box office successes such as the 1977 film *Jesus of Nazareth*, directed by Franco Zeffirelli (yet even this, before its release, attracted the opprobrium of fundamentalist groups who had never even seen it), on the whole the gospel has not fared well in the context of the Hollywood epic. Of George Stevens' reverent *The greatest story ever told* (1965), it was said by a critic in the New Yorker: 'If the subject matter weren't sacred, we would be responding to the picture in the most charitable way by laughing at it from start to finish.'[10] More notorious was the furore surrounding the release of Martin Scorsese' film of Kazantzakis' already controversial novel *The last temptation of Christ* (1988). A fine, though flawed, and deeply serious film that explores the struggle between Jesus' divinity and his humanity, *The last temptation* illustrates the extreme difficulty of exploring theological issues in the context of the commercial cinema.

For Hollywood sets out primarily to entertain, the cinema being a means to escape from reality for an hour or two through a medium that is supremely an art of illusion. Miracles then become easy, solved by the sleight of hand of the director and the camera operator. The results have not always been bad, though the temptation to adapt the Christian story for grand epic purposes was strong from the start, and even the early silent film *From the manger to the cross* (1913) – with its magnificently aristocratic Jesus played by Robert Henderson-Bland – realised film's potential to show us the 'real thing' by filming on location in Egypt, the holy family resting on its flight from Herod in the very shadow of the Sphinx itself. But it was the director Cecil B. de Mille in *The King of kings* (1927) who realised the full epic potential of the life of Christ for the mass audience, shamelessly attracting the viewers' attention at the very beginning with a scantily clad Mary Magdalene, and maintaining the romantic interest in an unlikely love triangle between Mary, Judas Iscariot and Jesus. This epic tradition reached its full flowering in the two 'lives of Jesus' of the 1960s, Nicholas Ray's *King of kings* (1961) and Stevens' *The greatest story ever told*. At the same time, the character of Jesus granted an appearance of gravity to a number of epics with a walk-on role, most notably in the hugely successful *Ben-Hur* (1959), which was based on Lew Wallace's best-selling novel of 1880. Both book and film represent an odd and unacknowledged extension of the critical search for the Jesus of history, as writer and

10 Quoted in Bruce Babington and Peter William Evans, *Biblical epics: sacred narrative in the Hollywood cinema* (Manchester: Manchester University Press, 1993), p. 1.

director expended great energy in seeking to ensure that their portrayals of history were 'accurate' in every detail.[11]

Apart from Hollywood, less mainstream cinema has tried its hand at making films of the gospel story, perhaps the most successful example being Pier Paulo Pasolini's *Il vangelo secondo Matteo* (*The gospel according to St Matthew*) (1966), a low-budget production with unknown actors that achieves consistency partly because it simply adapts the text of Matthew as screenplay. Another Italian film, made two years later, Valerio Zurlini's *Seduto alla sua destra* (1968) is a strange allegory using the gospel narrative to illustrate the last days of African revolutionary Patrice Lumumba. Screened in America as *Black Jesus*, it was reported in the *Saturday review* that 'the film makes no attempt to propagandize one way or the other; rather, it presents a bloody equation of our time with an event (perhaps myth) of two thousand years ago'.[12] Very different, and infinitely more bloody, is Mel Gibson's *The passion of the Christ* (2003) of which the director Gibson, a devout conservative Roman Catholic, is reported to have said (in the *Guardian* for 4 August 2003), that the 'Holy Ghost was working through me on this film, and I was just directing traffic'. The film portrays the final twelve hours of the life of Jesus, is largely without star actors, and is 'historically accurate' inasmuch as the dialogue is in Aramaic and Latin. Before it was even shown, the film attracted criticism from a number of religious quarters – Christian evangelical, Catholic and Jewish.

Much attention has been given to the film's extreme, even gratuitous, violence, particularly during the scourging of Jesus by the Roman soldiers. However, the restrained narratives of the canonical gospels stand in contrast to other contemporary accounts of torture, for example in 4 Maccabees 6,[13] and in this latter graphic tradition Gibson's film stands as a deeply uncomfortable, almost liturgical, film that draws upon a particular kind of Roman Catholic spirituality, portraying the last hours of Jesus' life as a self-conscious battle with Satan. Joyless and relentless, at once deeply pious and disturbingly voyeuristic, *The passion* attracted huge audiences and diverse responses. It is certainly a major contribution to the genre of film lives of Christ.

11 For a recent survey of the history of the 'quest for the historical Jesus', see Gregory W. Dawes (ed.), *The historical Jesus quest* (Louisville: Westminster John Knox Press, 2000).

12 *Saturday review*, 11 September 1971. Quoted in Roy Kinnard and Tim Davis, *Divine images: a history of Jesus on the screen* (New York: Citadel Press, 1992), p. 167.

13 See Stephen D. Moore, *God's gym: divine male bodies of the Bible* (New York and London: Routledge, 1996), pp. 6–7; Martin Hengel, *Crucifixion in the ancient world and the folly of the message of the cross*, trans. John Bowden (Philadelphia: Fortress Press, 1977).

Jesus has also been subjected to clown makeup in the puerile musical *Godspell* (1973), rock music superstardom in Norman Jewison's *Jesus Christ, superstar* (1973) – also a highly successful stage production – and the satirical attention of the British Monty Python in their *Life of Brian* (1979), which not unexpectedly attracted huge criticism from Christian groups and churches (especially for its all-singing, all-dancing crucifixion scene), and an even larger cult following. In fact, *The life of Brian* is an often biting satire on the church and the absurdities and extremes of Christian belief and practice, as when the crowd insist with one voice and in unison that 'we do all think for ourselves'. Brian, the reluctant Messiah (Graham Chapman), is continually being mistaken for the real Jesus (Ken Colley), from the moment when the three kings go to the wrong stable, to be confronted with Brian's ghastly mother, the Virgin Mandy (Terry Jones). In many respects the film draws on the comic traditions of the medieval miracle plays which also parallel the gospel narratives with comic variations on them, as in the great *Second shepherds play* of the Wakefield pageants. The tradition of the miracle cycles is also employed to great, and unexpectedly successful, effect in the French Canadian film *Jesus of Montreal* (1989), which uses the idea of the actor playing the role of Jesus in a play gradually assuming the character himself and thus 'expressing the genuine need for spiritual fulfillment in a corrupt modern society, and the potential achievement of that spiritual fulfillment through pure artistic expression'.[14]

Like the gospels, the history of the Christian church has not fared particularly well in the cinema, too often subjected to the stilted, over-pious, form of the grand epic, as in Harry Koster's 1953 adaptation of Lloyd C. Douglas' novel *The robe*, which is the story of the Roman tribune Marcellus (Richard Burton) and his slave Demetrius (Victor Mature). Marcellus witnesses the crucifixion, is converted and eventually dies the death of a martyr. Always seeking suitable subjects to satisfy the commercial demands of sex and violence in exotic settings, the cinema has frequently visited the world of the medieval church and the cruelty of the Inquisition, as in the 1986 adaptation of Umberto Eco's novel *The name of the rose*, with Sean Connery as a sort of Franciscan Sherlock Holmes investigating a series of mysterious deaths in a remote monastery. Occasionally the cinema has managed to combine fine film-making with serious portrayals of dilemmas of faith, as in Fred Zinneman's *A man for all seasons* (1966) in which Paul Schofield portrays Sir Thomas More

---

14 Kinnard and Davis, *Divine images*, p. 213.

refusing to bend his beliefs and faith in the Church of Rome to the whims of Henry VIII (Robert Shaw), and finally suffering execution as a result. Roland Joffé's *The mission* (1986) explores the brutal oppression of Portuguese and Spanish imperialism in eighteenth-century South America, and the role played by the church in its atrocities as the emissary of the pope, Altamirano (Ray McAnally) decides, for the sake of church interests, to close the Jesuit missions to the native tribes in order to allow for the expansion of the slave trade. The serious questions that are raised in this film about the 'civilising' of 'primitive peoples' by European missions are set against the visual backdrop of the tropical forest, representing the biblical Eden story and its motif of lost innocence.[15] The capacity of the cinema to employ a biblical background to films that leave the audience barely conscious of the references that are driving the narrative has been most successfully (and arguably most subtly) exploited by Clint Eastwood in his magnificent trilogy of Westerns, *High plains drifter* (1972), *Pale rider* (1985) and *Unforgiven* (1992). In each case there is an adaptation of apocalyptic themes, most overtly seen in the title of the second film and its use of Revelation 6:8, 'And I saw, and behold, a pale horse, and its rider's name was Death, and Hades followed him.' Nowhere is this verse better illustrated than in the last fifteen minutes of *Unforgiven*, leaving the viewer disturbed and unsettled by the necessary but vicious revenge upon the people of Big Whiskey and a fade-out on a dark and stormy night.

The necessarily highly selective literature and films that have been referred to in this chapter represent a further episode in the ancient, problematic, relation between the Christian church, with its Bible and its faith, and the arts. Since the early church took over the Jewish prohibition of idolatry,[16] the troubled love affair between Christianity and the arts has been both a provocation and a revilement of works of creativity and genius. As novelists, poets and playwrights have found inspiration in the Bible and Christianity, there remained in the twentieth century the suspicion that the 'truth' of the gospel and Christian belief was being somehow undermined by artistic fabrication, even while the arts might gloriously reveal the faith in new and contemporary ways or give serious expression to its dilemmas and problems. At the same time, the enduring sense of the novel, the poem and the play

---

15 See further Vaughan Roberts, 'Between Eden and Armageddon: institutions, individuals, and identification in *The mission*, *The name of the rose*, and *Priest'*, in Clive Marsh and Gaye Ortiz (eds.), *Explorations in theology and film* (Oxford: Blackwell, 1997), pp. 180–92.

16 See George Pattison, *Art, modernity and faith: towards a theology of art* (London: Macmillan, 1991), ch. 2.

as handmaids of religion has ensured the continuing popularity of writings that present the fundamentals of Christian belief in attractive and accessible form. The theme of 'story' was central to the 1981 report of the Doctrine Commission of the Church of England, *Believing in the church*, where, in a tone of some surprise, we find the words:

> Recent theology . . . has thrown up a new term which we might want to use: 'story'. Story, like myth, is a word with many possible meanings. On the one hand, it is hallowed in Christian usage: 'Tell me the old, old story'; on the other, it can be used in a debunking way, as when people say that Christianity is 'only a story' or 'only a collection of old stories'. In this chapter we shall try to show that it can be used in a positive way . . .[17]

Theologians may speak thus. For novelists, poets and playwrights such positivity is always dangerous, especially when theological issues lie at the heart of their creative impulse. Thus Nikos Kazantzakis begins the prologue to his much vilified *Last temptation* with the pained but deeply biblical words:

> The dual substance of Christ – the yearning, so human, so superhuman, of man to attain to God, or more exactly, to return to God and identify himself with him – has always been a deep inscrutable mystery to me. This nostalgia for God, at once so mysterious and so real, has opened in me large wounds and also large flowing springs.[18]

For the film-maker as the most recent newcomer to the company of artists, the problem is even more complex. Not only are there the ancient fears of what the eye sees (in the long tradition of Christian iconoclasm), but the environment of the commercial cinema with its absolute dependence on box office success, except in the case of a very few and little seen art-house films or the relatively small-scale (though often important) film industries of former eastern European or third world countries, and its widely held but rather naive addiction to notions of mimetic truth, has condemned it to a simplified vision that is too easily open to misunderstanding by others whose Christian vision is often itself too simple and rigid. In the lives of Christ, the struggle by film-makers to preserve Jesus' divine nature too easily detaches him from the rest of humanity, while the too human Jesus fails for the opposite reason. In short, the cinema has not found christology easy. Thus it was said of Nicholas

---

17 John Barton and John Halliburton, 'Story and liturgy', in *Believing in the church: the corporate nature of faith*, a report by the Doctrine Commission of the Church of England (London: SPCK, 1981), p. 79.
18 Nikos Kazantzakis, *The last temptation*, trans. P. A. Bien (London: Faber and Faber, 1975), p. 7.

Ray when he was searching for an actor to play Jesus in *King of kings*, that he eventually found one who was neither human nor divine: he found the heartthrob Jeffrey Hunter, an anodyne successor to Ray's real hero, the truly tragic James Dean.

II
MUSIC AND CHRISTIANITY IN THE
TWENTIETH CENTURY

ANDREW WILSON-DICKSON

This section compares the unchanging traditions of the Eastern churches with the influence of popular and classical music on Western worship. It also observes the migration of music across denominations and a broadening of the musical types accepted in the worship of Western Christianity.

Whoever first suggested music to be a universal language might well have been living in nineteenth-century Europe, in an age when Western culture was still certain of its uniqueness and superiority. At that time, objective examination of other more ancient musical traditions was too much to ask, even of great musical minds. Thus the great iconoclast and revolutionary, Berlioz, summarised the European perception of a Chinese musician: 'He has a music which we find abominable, atrocious; he sings like yawning dogs, like cats vomiting after having swallowed a fishbone; the instruments accompanying the singing seem to us true instruments of torture.'[19] In Britain and the United States, such cultural isolationism was complemented by unimaginative composition and encouraged by conservative audiences. The music reviews of Corno di Bassetto (George Bernard Shaw) at the end of the century are unusually perceptive of the situation.

Conservatism and elitism were further entrenched in the parochial world of Christian worship. Abroad, missionaries bringing the gospel to the unsaved millions continued to package it with capitalist ideology and a European hymnbook. At home, the educated musicians of British cathedrals assumed their anthems and chanting to be the ideal for local parishes and spared no scorn for the popular music of the nonconformists.

---

19 H. Berlioz, *À travers chants* (Paris: Michel Levy Frères, 1852), 'Moeurs musicales de la Chine', pp. 252–8, trans. Nguyen Kim-Oanh and Fredric Lieberman (http://arts.ucsc.edu/faculty/lieberman/Chinese.html).

One feature of the twentieth century is a stumbling journey away from this feudal scene and towards a tentatively emerging acceptance – even a celebration – of the diversity of musical style in worship. Another, not dealt with here, is a profound change of attitude to the nature of foreign mission and the recognition that indigenous languages and musical styles are a right for all Christian worshippers.

Popular music and Western Christianity

Where the influence of modern secular music is strictly curbed in the Eastern churches, the Western remain as divided on the matter as at the Reformation. From at least as far back as the mid-nineteenth century the majority have embraced local secular styles. Ira D. Sankey was typical in his adoption of the idiom of the drawing-room ballad ('The ninety and nine', 1874, 'Hiding in Thee', 1877) to the accompaniment of the harmonium. Though the large-scale gatherings of such North American Protestant evangelists were for proselytising, not for worship, the musical influence on congregations is still remarkably strong and spread as far afield as the Pacific islands and South Korea. Indeed, areas of Christian expansion (for example South America and many parts of Africa) have embraced local secular music in a similar manner to the following description which relates to the Protestant English-speaking world.

The musical style of Evangelical free churches has evolved in the twentieth century roughly in parallel with changes in secular musical fashion. For white worshippers in the USA and UK, the style of music-hall dominated the worship song in the early part of the century (Charles Alexander, Homer Rodeheaver), followed by music of the dance-floor ((Norman Clayton, George Beverley Shea assisting Billy Graham) and, more recently, folk, rock and musical theatre.

Black free churches moved in a similar direction but also drew on the unique repertoire and traditions of the shout and the spiritual. In the twentieth century, however, black song-leaders and ensembles have had a strong hand in creating the most popular secular genres of the century (for example, blues, jazz and soul) rather than being driven by them. The songs of Charles A. Tindley and Thomas A. Dorsey (*Gospel pearls*, 1921) have been highly influential, with an expanding tradition of solo singing (Mahalia Jackson, James Cleveland, Shirley Caesar) and vocal ensembles (Golden Gate Quartet, Mighty Clouds of Joy, Take 6). Through the century there has been a steady move from harmonic and metrical simplicity to a sophistication of chord-types in complex polyrhythms borrowed from Brazilian and African cultures.

Alongside this evolution has come a change in the use of instruments to accompany worship. At the beginning of the century the piano became the dominant indoor instrument (it was Alexander's preferred resource) but later the use of the guitar and instrumental bands became widespread. By the 1960s these featured electric instruments – the Hammond organ (still a ubiquitous sound in black churches) followed by the synthesiser, the electric guitar, bass guitar, drum-kit and ethnic percussion. At the beginning of the twenty-first century most lively Evangelical churches will accompany their worship with such forces.

The insistent emphasis on the 'new' (the openings to Psalms 96 and 98 are consistently cited in evangelical circles) has produced a large-scale industry for the creation and dissemination of new songs. These are launched at residential gatherings (such as Spring Harvest and Greenbelt in the UK, Hillsong in Australia or the International Worship Institute Conference in Dallas) and then adopted locally until supplanted by others. The songs in their initial presentation are usually written and sung by the same person (Graham Kendrick was the dominant British figure of the 1980s and 1990s), the text usually in the first person and the vocal style ornamental. Such songs, sung congregationally, become simplified, the syncopations and improvised embellishments tending to disappear. While oral transmission of this music is widespread, contemporary electronic means are used to disseminate it in print and recording. Radio remains an important medium for black gospel music, but it is the internet that has revolutionised access to the repertoire.

Stylistically, Western Christian song has reflected almost every popular musical genre of the previous hundred years, recently including music of the club culture. In all these cases the theological *raison d'être* is the possibility of redeeming the music of the fallen world. This cannot be better summarised than in Luther's wish 'that the evil, vexatious melodies, the useless and shameful songs to be sung in the streets, fields, houses and elsewhere, may lose their bad effects if they can have good, useful Christian texts . . .'[20]

Western music and tradition

The liturgies and music of the Eastern churches (Greek, Coptic and Ethiopian in particular) continue to be inextricable, and given validity through links to the past. The twentieth century has seen little change here; music may be newly composed or elaborated, but, like its icons, the style and manner is

---

20 M. Luther, *An order of mass and communion for the church at Wittenberg* (1525), trans. U. S. Leupold, in *Luther's works* (Philadelphia: Fortress Press, 1965), vol. LIII, p. 36.

hallowed by tradition and change is hard to perceive. The rapidly evolving style of secular music, brought on by the increased mobility of populations and the invasive influence of television, has thus had almost no effect on the liturgical traditions of these churches, even though some non-liturgical contexts (youth meetings, for example) may admit the use of local modern instruments and song styles.

In the West, the tainting of the liturgy by popular music remains anathema to a minority, such as strict Calvinists, who still adhere to the principles that only biblical texts may be uttered in worship, in 'the vulgar tongue', and that instrumental accompaniment is unacceptable. The melodies sung by some Free churches in the Isle of Lewis, for example, or in some reformed Presbyterian churches in the southern states of North America, are the same melodies published in Calvin's *Genevan psalter* of 1562, or their close relatives, and are sung in a unique style almost unchanged since the seventeenth century. For such communities, external influences are a constant threat to which a proportion succumb.

Parts of the Anglican church are also isolationist, through the high value placed on tradition. As a result, Anglo-Catholics have continued to inhabit the repertoire of cathedral music, and choirs surrounded by the symbolism of the Oxford movement are still supported, at considerable cost. However, the human resources are diminishing, and in the last twenty years of the century girl singers have been introduced, to the consternation of traditionalists.

The Royal School of Church Music has continued to be the chief engine in Britain and its former colonies for the co-ordination of parish church choirs. In the last thirty years of the century, this organisation (and others such the Music In Worship Foundation) has broadened its brief to encourage the use of orchestral instruments in worship and to develop congregational singing.

Classical music and its influence

The social upheaval and cultural uncertainty following the First World War found a strong reaction amongst European composers. In the concert hall, a number dealt with Christian texts, but subjected eternal truths to unusual scrutiny, no longer viewed in the context of arrogance and empire but often by the dimmer light of an evil world. Thus in Britain, Gustav Holst set a controversial gnostic text in his *Hymn of Jesus* (1916), Vaughan Williams moved his music into a new arena of tension with *Job* (1930) and *Dona nobis pacem* (1936), and two pacifist composers, Michael Tippett and Benjamin Britten, engaged with Christian themes from their personal perspectives. Their most enduring examples are Tippett's *A child of our time* (1941) and

Britten's *War requiem* (requiem texts interlaced with the war poems of Wilfred Owen, 1962). Composers on mainland Europe contributed to similar themes: Bohuslav Martinu's *Field mass* (1939), Frank Martin's *In terra pax* (1944) and Messiaen's *Quatuor pour la fin du temps* (written and first performed in a German POW camp, 1941).

The latter half of the century saw a change of perspective. The obscurantism of the European musical 'avant-garde' of the 1950s and 1960s created a serious barrier to appreciation by most audiences. This aggressive post-1945 revolution (in the hands of Stockhausen, Boulez and Xenakis, for example) had exhausted itself by the 1970s and its place was taken by a renewed exploration of harmoniousness and predictability. More than that, composers began to explore this in a context of spirituality, suggested by structures with slow rates of change and by the setting of liturgical texts. Composers who have moved precipitately from one state to the other include Henryk Górecki in his hugely successful Third Symphony ('Symphony of sorrowful songs', 1976), followed by Beatus Vir (1979) and Miserere (1981), together with two composers of an Orthodox Christian background, the Estonian Arvo Pärt (*St John passion*, 1982–8) and John Tavener (*The protecting veil*, 1987, *Akathist of thanksgiving*, 1988). Tavener received extraordinary acclaim for 'Song for Athene' (1993), sung at the close of the funeral of Lady Diana, Princess of Wales.

Where the worship music of the free and Evangelical churches in Britain has remained largely untouched by developments in classical music, those which have had traditionally close contact (Roman Catholic and Anglican) have been beneficially affected by the developments described above, in spite of diminishing resources for, and interest in, the commissioning of new work.

The Anglican church

In the Anglican church, the lacklustre world of the previous century continued to dominate cathedral worship until the 1920s, though with the greater technical proficiency exemplified by Charles Villiers Stanford. The modality of folk-melody and of music from the pre-diatonic era was explored by Vaughan Williams (*Mass*, 1921) and by Herbert Howells (canticle settings from the 1930s). The acerbic language of Kenneth Leighton and William Mathias followed, and the few works specifically for the liturgy by Benjamin Britten (Missa Brevis, 1959) and Michael Tippett (Evening Canticles, 1961) heralded an era of greater aural challenge for congregations. This has been taken up by more recent figures such as Jonathan Harvey (b. 1939). Significantly, none of these composers have been employees of the church.

Musical conservatism in Anglican hymnody, exemplified by *Hymns ancient and modern*, was threatened by the work of the poet laureate Robert Bridges and by the appearance of the *English hymnal* in 1906, edited by Percy Dearmer (text) and Ralph Vaughan Williams (music). The latter reintroduced excellent music from far back in British history – from art-music (Thomas Tallis, Orlando Gibbons) to folk-song, as well as his own compositions. The association of folk-song melodies with hymn-texts has permanently changed the hymn repertoire for many churches. *Songs of praise* (1925/1931) from the same editors (with Martin Shaw) continued in this direction. An indication of more uncomfortable forces of change came in the 1950s with the Twentieth Century Church Light Music Group's *Thirty 20th-century hymn tunes* (1960), strongly influenced by ballroom-dance music. Low Anglican churches have since increasingly adopted worship songs in contemporary idioms (led by an instrumental group) as a foil to older musical forms. Traditional hymnody has been renewed by a number of fine authors (Brian Wren, Alan Gaunt, Fred Kaan, Christopher Idle), though without a corresponding enlivening of music.

Mainland Europe

The Roman Catholic church's time-honoured position as a patron of the arts should have given the church a positive and creative reason to be in touch with the latest thinking in art-music. But by the later nineteenth century its musicians were seduced by the easy sentiments of light opera (exemplified by Gounod's liturgical works). By the beginning of the twentieth century, European art-composers found such emotional gestures sterile, and pursued paths which the Roman church could not, or would not, follow. The disintegration of tonality in the concert hall and the many alternatives proposed in its wake were ill suited to the liturgy, aesthetically and technically. There have been exceptions of course: the outstanding figure in the French composer-organist tradition, Olivier Messiaen (1908–92), organist of the Trinité in Paris for more than sixty years, or the contributions to liturgical music by Jean Langlais (1907–90). However, not only were the turbulent and radical changes of the secular world informing the music of these composers, but so was the church's chant, traditional yet under-valued. In his *motu proprio* of 1903, Pope Pius X strongly encouraged a deeper awareness of the church's legacy of its chant. As a result, this monodic repertoire, like an ancient oil-painting restored by scholars to its former hue, became a strong inspiration to musicians, including the two mentioned above. The hope that the chant would become universally sung was never fully realised, but its influence on composers has been remarkable; by pre-dating tonality, the chant became a renewing force for twentieth-century harmony.

In Germany, the Lutheran chorale provided a similar impetus for composers for the liturgy. Until the Nazism of Hitler overwhelmed them, a number of composers (notably Hugo Distler) worked creatively towards a musical renewal, republishing the most ancient versions of chorales and composing new music around them, following the methods of seventeenth- and eighteenth-century composers. Since that time, churches have continued to benefit from the generous musical resources that are a legacy of Luther's reforms, with some enriching results. However, the withdrawal of such funding is making the maintaining of high standards a struggle.

In the parish churches of France, Italy and Spain, however, musical resources have always been thin. Clerics became increasingly concerned by the remoteness of the liturgy to the congregations it was supposed to serve. Some exercised increasing pressure to permit worship in the vernacular, as a move towards a renewed sense of community and away from a pietist individualism. This was formalised by the Second Vatican Council in 1963 and, although not banned, Latin vanished from the liturgy almost overnight and with it the musical traditions of millennia. In every area, churches were forced to propose and adopt local solutions around the few musicians with the dedication and imagination to respond to change. The father of these in France is Joseph Gelineau (b. 1920), who has worked tirelessly since the 1950s, from the publication of his still-famous vernacular psalm-settings to his more recent work with the Taizé community. Since the 1970s, André Gouzes has been developing and publishing an extensive body of parish choral music, *La Liturgie Chorale du Peuple de Dieu*, springing from the worshipping community at L'Abbaye de Sylvanès, his *'atelier de musique liturgique'*. Gouzes travels widely with his choirs in France to encourage and train at local level.

Ecumenical trends

In Britain, there is an increasing overlap in musical resources, to the point where the value and expense of printing denominationally specific hymn-books is being questioned. First, their selection of traditional hymns reveals increasingly common ground. Second, the music that lies beyond hymns (psalms and many other types of liturgical song) is of increasing general interest and is contained in compilations with no denominational affiliation (*Mission praise* (1983 on), *Songs of fellowship* (1991 on)). Psalm-singing is no longer denominationally so well defined. Thus Anglican chant outside cathedrals is in diminishing use, with new metrical settings and occasional responsorial versions (traditionally the province of the free and the Roman Catholic churches respectively) making an appearance. Hymns and tunes of Protestant origin are increasingly popular in British Roman Catholic churches. Most hymnbooks include a selection of the music of the ecumenical Taizé community, which from the 1970s has provided Protestant churches with a meditative rather than passionately expressive repertoire of song (something that the Roman Catholic community has had for centuries).

A recent dimension to British church singing is the music of the world church. The first circulation of this was in the 1980 edition of *Cantate Domino*, edited by Erik Routley, though little known outside its commissioning organisation, the World Council of Churches. Since then, John L. Bell of the Iona community has compiled a number of songs in many languages which have reached a far wider worshipping public (*Many and great*, 1990, *Sent by the Lord*, 1991). Although losing in transplantation, they are an antidote to denominational isolation and represent a continuing trend.

In summary, where the Eastern churches have guarded their traditions jealously, the twentieth century has witnessed a burgeoning of music for Western church worship even greater than the previous century and increasingly varied in style and excellence. There are clear signs that this material is migrating freely across denominational boundaries, challenging the traditional constitutional barriers to the fellowship of all saints. In this sense, music does have the potential to be universal.

III
CHRISTIANITY AND ART

JUTTA VINZENT

The most distinct feature of Christianity and art in the twentieth century is the secularisation of culture and thus a change in patronage: while modern art claims autonomy, churches play a diminishing role in commissioning art. Accordingly, the story of Christianity and art in the twentieth century can be told in two major narratives: one narrative encompasses the art commissioned by churches, in short church art, the other the story of Christian iconography and themes in modern and contemporary art. Works of the former category are usually kept in churches, those of the latter in museums and galleries, although as Inken Mädler observed in 1997, 'eine Art

Musealisierung kirchlicher Räume ist derzeit ebenso zu konstatieren wie die zunehmende *Sakralisierung . . . musealer Räume*:[21] churches are used as museums in a literal sense (churches become museums) and a transferred sense (visitors to churches treat the building and its content as a museum), and art museums are approached with a secular reverence, as Carol Duncan proclaims in *Civilising rituals*.[22] Apart from the patronage and the holdings of the works, the split also goes through the disciplines: theologians and art historians seem to concentrate on different artists, topics and works. John Dillenberger classifies theologians and their methods in relation to the arts into three types: the first is that in which no relation is seen between the arts and theological work (for example, Rudolf Bultmann and Karl Barth), the second is one in which a positive relation is articulated (for example, Langdon Gilkey and Paul Tillich), and the third is one in which the arts provide paradigms influencing the nature of the theological method (for example, Hans Urs von Balthasar and Karl Rahner).[23] For art historians specialising in the twentieth century, Christianity plays a subordinate role.

The division between church and modern art is due to the exclusion of modern art by churches (for example, the Roman Catholic church denounced modern art in an 'instruction' for the ordinary of 1952),[24] but also to the striving for autonomy of the art object in the twentieth century: art objects should stand for themselves and thus should be dealing with art (preferably abstract), be promoted by art dealers and be exhibited in art galleries.

One possible way of looking at the relationship between Christianity and art in the twentieth century would be to focus on the perception of the spectator rather than on the art objects. The prominent Roman Catholic theologian Karl Rahner, for example, suggests that art works should be viewed religiously.[25] His so-called *religiöses Sehen* (religious seeing) applies to any art regardless of its iconography. *Seeing*, however, is not a universal

---

21 Inken Mädler, *Kirche und bildende Kunst der Moderne. Ein an F. D. E. Schleiermacher orientierter Beitrag zur theologischen Urteilsbildung*, Beiträge zur historischen Theologie 100 (Tübingen: Mohr Siebeck, 1997), p. 33.

22 Carol Duncan, *Civilising rituals* (London and New York: Routledge, 1995), esp. pp. 7–20.

23 John Dillenberger, *A theology of artistic sensibilities: the visual arts and the church* (London: SCM, 1986), pp. 217–27.

24 Alaphridus Ottaviani (Adsessor), 'Instructio. Ad locorum ordinarios: "De arte sacra"' (Acta SS. Congregationum. Suprema Sacra Congregatio S. Officii, part 1), *Acta Apostolicae Sedis* 44 (1952), 542–5.

25 Karl Rahner, 'Zur Theologie des Bildes', in Rainer Beck, Rainer Volp and Gisela Schmirber (eds.), *Die Kunst und die Kirchen: der Streit um die Bilder heute* (Munich: Bruckmann, 1984), p. 218.

experience, but differs individually and culturally. Thus the following division between church art and modern art is based on patronage and iconography.

Church art

Church art encompasses churches and their decoration and smaller objects and vestments. Objects are usually based on Christian iconography and thus are often figurative, but can also be abstract as in the interior design of Heinz Mack (b. 1931) for the Roman Catholic church of St Theresia, Kaiserslautern, Germany (1992–4). Finished works of church art naturally represent the way in which the church (the actual communities of a parish or diocese) wants to have Christianity represented. Other projects will not be realised, as demonstrated by the long-lasting debate around the stained glass windows designed by Johannes Schreiter (b. 1930) for the Protestant Holy Spirit church in Heidelberg, Germany (finally installed in 2002). Drawing back to the usage of the church as a library (housing the Bibliotheca Palatina) between 1421 and 1623, in which knowledge of former times was gathered and studied, the ten windows deal with typical twentieth-century spiritual, scientific, economic and political topics, probably most obvious in the window with the theme 'stock market' and that of 'biology', the latter showing a DNA-spiral molecular pattern. All of the windows present signed copies of the documents portrayed. In this manner Schreiter points out the finite character of technical progress and human achievement.

Apart from the subject and style of the art works, the question as to whether the executing artist is a believer sometimes plays a role. The Catholic philosopher Jacques Maritain (1882–1973), for example, although interested in the revitalisation of art in the church, believed that art for the church must be done by believers.[26]

The need of the church to have artists who produce its religious objects, architecture and interior design has led to the publication of journals such as the German *Kunst und Kirche*, an ecumenical journal of the Protestant and Catholic churches, the French *Art chrétien* and the American *Liturgical arts*.

Usually artists producing church art are unknown to the canon of modern art. A considerable number of churches, however, have interior designs by well-known modern artists. The Dominican Father Marie-Alain Couturier (1897–1954) was the first in France to commission modern artists (most of

26 Dillenberger, *Theology of artistic sensibilities*, p. 193.

them working in France) for Notre Dame de Toute Grâce in Assy (near Chamonix), France, from 1939. Works executed there include *The virgin of the litany* (a mosaic on the façade) by Fernand Léger (1881–1954), stained glass from designs by the Catholic Georges Rouault (1871–1958), *Saint Dominic* by Henri Matisse (1869–1954), *St Francis of Sales* by Pierre Bonnard (1867–1947), and further works by the sculptor Germaine Richier (1902–59), the Cubist Georges Braques (1882–1963), Marc Chagall (1887–1985) and Jacques Lipchitz (1891–1973). The finished project was not only appreciated, but also attacked by reactionary conservatives both in France and in Rome for the lack of a religious object, the strangeness of the forms, the manifestation of modern freedom and subjectivity, and the lack of faith or ecclesial membership of the artists.[27] The project may have influenced the change from a balanced tone on art in Pius XII's encyclical *Mediator Dei* (1947) to an 'instruction' on sacred art issued by the Vatican in 1952, as mentioned above.

In Britain, the Anglican cathedral of St Michael in Coventry, erected by Basil Spence (1907–76) next to the ruins of the old cathedral between 1954 and 1962, commissioned modern artists working in England at the time: the visitor is greeted by a nineteen-foot-high sculpture of *St Michael and the devil* by Jacob Epstein (1880–1959) on the outside wall; apart from the baptistery window designed by John Piper (1903–92) and a crucifixion by Geoffrey Clarke (b. 1924), the interior of the cathedral is dominated by a *Christ in Glory*, a seventy-five-foot tapestry woven after designs by Graham Sutherland (1903–80). The new church together with the still monumental ruins of the fourteenth-century old cathedral, hit by German bombing on the night of 14 November 1940, has become a symbol for reconciliation after the war.

In the USA, the Rothko chapel in Houston, Texas, opened in 1971, was made possible by the world-famous art collectors John (b.1904) and Dominique de Ménil (1908–98), the latter being heiress to the Schlumberger Ltd oil service company fortune. The non-denominational church houses fourteen dark maroon/black canvases by the American abstract expressionist Mark Rothko (1903–70). These abstract colour field paintings create a modern meditative environment open to any religion.

Apart from the interior designs, churches have been planned by modern architects: a prominent example is Notre Dame du Haut in Ronchamp, France, designed by Le Corbusier (1887–1965) and built between 1950 and 1954 as a

---

27 Thomas F. O'Meara, 'Modern art and the sacred: the prophetic ministry of Alain Couturier, O. P.', *Spirituality today* 38 (1986), 31–40.

pilgrim chapel. The roof in particular is characteristic of the modern artist's style. The Crystal cathedral (Anaheim, California, USA) was designed by Philip Johnson (b. 1906), known for his unabashedly neo-Georgian plan for the AT&T headquarters in New York city (1978–84); since 1992, the Sony building has brought postmodern architectural debate into the public forum. Johnson's church was built in 1980 with over 10,000 panels of glass, so that the walls of the church mirror the environment, creating the impression of a vanishing church that is neither distinguished nor consonant as a Christian building.

Behind these projects is the belief that church art should not necessarily be produced by believers (which, for Couturier, had resulted in poor art in the past). The commissions usually result from a personal friendship between the modern artist and those from the churches in charge of the projects. They do not necessarily represent the understanding of the official churches; most often these projects are based on individual initiative.

Christian themes in modern and contemporary art

Christian themes play an important part in 'autonomous' painting, graphic art and sculpture in the twentieth century. At different times, they fulfilled different purposes, of which the following represents a selection: Christ as an identification figure for the artist, the political use of Christian iconography, and Christian themes and globalisation. Apart from these explicit usages of Christian themes, some art of the twentieth century and Christianity have also implicit parallels, particularly the search for the spiritual; this goes not only for works of art, but also for writings by artists, such as the book *Concerning the spiritual in art* (originally published as *Über das Geistige in der Kunst* in 1911) by the expressionist Wassily Kandinsky (1866–1944) and the essay 'The sublime is now' by the abstract expressionist Barnett Newman (1905–70). In this 1948 writing, Newman explained his concept of the modern sublime by drawing explicit parallels to Christianity that reflect its secularisation: 'Instead of making *cathedrals* out of Christ, man, or "life", we are making [them] out of ourselves, out of our own feelings.'[28]

THE ARTIST'S IDENTIFICATION WITH CHRIST

The identification with Christ was a result of the nineteenth century which, along with the development of the autonomy of the art work, defined the role of the artist as autonomous; artists invented a self-image as the outsider

---

28 Barnett Newman, *Selected writings and interviews* (New York: Alfred A. Knopf, 1990), p. 173. Italics and brackets correspond with the original.

of society, being misunderstood and suffering as Christ did, who later would resurrect and be revered (an underlying thought may also have been the idea of God as Creator parallel to the artist as creator). Following the Pont-Aven group (Paul Gauguin, Vincent van Gogh and Emile Bernard) and the French and German symbolists (among others Odilon Redon and Max Klinger), it was particularly the expressionists who identified themselves with Christ.

Since the spiritual was such a high influence many expressionists used religious themes 'as vehicles to consider the essence of the nature of the world and of themselves'.[29] However, they did not make the setting contemporary as did James Ensor in the nineteenth century (e.g., *Christ's entry into Brussels in 1889* of 1888, oil on canvas, J. Paul Getty Museum, Los Angeles), but painted the religious subjects in their typical expressionist style, using bright colours and flat patterning.

While Ernst Barlach (e.g., *Monks reading*, 1932, cast stucco, Ernst Barlach Stiftung, Güstrow) and Wassily Kandinsky (e.g., *All saints I*, 1911, oil on card, Städtische Galerie im Lenbachhaus, Munich) focused on themes of Christian belief and life, it was Emil Nolde (1867–1956) who referred specifically to the New Testament.

From 1909, Nolde began a series of religious paintings that were called his greatest contribution to the art of the twentieth century. The most celebrated one is *Last Supper* (1909, oil on canvas, Statens Museum für Kunst, the Royal Museum of Fine Arts, Copenhagen), which was also the first in this succession. Nolde represents the traditional subject in his usual style of the time, modelling with colour to the extreme of an emotional outburst. The combination of a modernist style with a traditional subject, typical for expressionism, caused, as Shearer West writes, 'strong reaction among his contemporaries, who felt that he was both desecrating religion through his blazing impasted style and caricatural representations of holy figures'.[30] Indeed, Nolde's *Pentecost* painting (1909, Nationalgalerie, Berlin) was rejected not only by the jury of the Berlin Secession, but also by the church and the public.

Although the artist did not represent himself as Christ in these works, Nolde 'empathised with the isolation of the freethinker, the "chosen one", both blessed and tormented with special gifts. A similar self-identification

---

29 Peter Vergo and Felicity Lunn, *Emil Nolde* (London: Whitechapel Art Gallery, 1996), p. 112.

30 Shearer West, *The visual arts in Germany, 1890–1937: utopia and despair* (Manchester: Manchester University Press, 2000), p. 69.

occurs in later religious works such as *The Last Supper* and *Pentecost*, in which the figure of Christ dominates the composition.'[31] The interpretation of the artist's implicit identification with Christ is also supported by Nolde's autobiography which emphasises the artist's deep religious feelings from early years.[32]

POLITICAL USE OF CHRISTIAN ICONOGRAPHY IN THE MIDDLE OF THE CENTURY

The most popular Christian theme used politically is the crucifixion. During World War I, Max Beckmann (1884–1950) explored it extensively (e.g., *Descent from the cross*, 1917, oil on canvas, the Museum of Modern Art, New York).

During and after World War II, the crucifixion of Christ was also used not only for suffering in general, but for the Nazi persecution of the Jews. As such, the genuine Christian symbol becomes a symbol for the suffering Jew. This can be seen in the numerous crucifixion paintings by Marc Chagall (1887–1985), who was himself persecuted by the National Socialists (he fled from Marseille to the USA in May 1941). Since 1937 the crucifixion features in his paintings and works on paper as such a symbol. As in many works to follow, in *White crucifixion* (1938, oil on canvas, the Art Institute of Chicago), the first finished painting of the series, Chagall represents Christ as a Jew (dressed with a talith, the traditional Jewish prayer shawl, and the menorah, the seven-armed candelabrum, at his feet) amongst symbols of emigration (émigrés fleeing on foot and by boat), the pogroms (a burning synagogue and a torah roll, a plundered village) and resistance (a group of fighting, unarmed people). In other works, the crucifixion is set in an eastern European village, while the crucified is depicted as a contemporary Jew (e.g., *The crucified*, 1944, gouache on paper, Israel Museum, Jerusalem). Chagall includes a self-portrait in these scenes of crucifixion, as painter (e.g., *The soul of the city*, 1945, oil on canvas, Musée National d'Art Moderne, Centre Georges Pompidou, Paris), witness and mourner (e.g., *The crucified*, 1944), but never as the crucified himself. Although Chagall produced works for churches (e.g., stained glass windows for the choir of Fraumünster, Zurich, 1970), a large collection of his works with religious themes (also from the Old Testament) are kept neither in a church nor in a synagogue, but in the Chagall Museum of the Bible in Nice, France.

---

31 Vergo and Lunn, *Emil Nolde*, p. 112.
32 Emil Nolde, *Das eigene Leben* (Berlin: Rembrandt-Verlag, 1931), esp. pp. 49f.

In the second half of the twentieth century, the crucifixion has not lost its attraction to artists: while Francis Bacon (1909–92) painted an unconventional triptych in 1965, highlighting the fleshly pain (*Three studies for a crucifixion*, 1962, oil with sand on canvas, Solomon R. Guggenheim Museum, New York), Arnulf Rainer (b. 1929) created a few more traditional crucifixions from the mid-1950s (e.g., *Weinkruzifix*, 1957/1978, Tate Modern, London); so did Craigie Aitchison (b. 1926) who used the Christian symbol in numerous images from 1958, existentially expressing his own loneliness (e.g., *Crucifixion*, 1984, Museum and Art Gallery, Birmingham).

Apart from the crucifixion, further Christian themes used politically in the twentieth century include the flight to Egypt (e.g., Max Beckmann, *Departure triptych*, 1932/3, oil on canvas, the Museum of Modern Art, New York) as a symbol for emigration and the prodigal son (e.g., Hans Feibusch, *Prodigal son*, 1943, oil on canvas, private collection) to express the hope of returning home.

CHRISTIAN THEMES AND GLOBAL UNDERSTANDING

The use of Christian iconography continues until today. However, in a more globalised world, the field has developed from studies on Christian themes to those on religious themes, including not only the Abrahamic religions, but also all world religions: monographs such as *Religion, art and visual culture* deal with Christianity alongside Judaism, Islam, Hinduism and Buddhism and new journals emphasise religion instead of Christianity, such as the Boston university journal *Religion and the arts*, founded in 1996.

Despite the broadening of the subject, at the end of the twentieth century Christian iconography still had the power to create controversy, as demonstrated by the dispute around Chris Ofili's *Holy Virgin Mary* (1996, mixed material with elephant dung on canvas, the Saatchi Gallery, London). Shown in the exhibition *Sensation* at the Brooklyn Museum of Art, New York in 1999, the painting evoked such a public outcry that the New York city mayor at the time, Rudy Giuliani, threatened to cut off financial support for the museum.[33] What caused the controversy was the way in which Ofili (b. 1968) represented the ever-popular subject: apart from ethno-cultural aspects (his Madonna has black skin) and the pornographic context (she wears a stylised blue shawl against a field of yellow on which he pasted magazine cut-outs of female genitalia), what really upset the American public was the representation of

---

33 S. Brent Plate (ed.), *Religion, art and visual culture: a cross-cultural reader* (New York and Basingstoke: Palgrave, 2002), p. 1.

the Virgin Mary with one visible breast made of elephant dung.[34] Dung is a material which the British-Nigerian artist had already used in works exhibited at the Turner Prize show in 1998, which he won, for example in *Afrodizzia* (1996, mixed material with elephant dung on canvas, the Saatchi Gallery, London). More than the work itself, the debate around the *Holy Virgin Mary's* exhibition in New York (and the physical attack by a 72-year-old Christian, Dennis Heiner, who threw white paint across the work when exhibited in New York) demonstrates cultural differences in a globalised world: while the dung in African cultures has a spiritually symbolic meaning representing fertility, Western cultures view it as dirt. Thus the American public interpreted the painting as a symbol of sensation and provocation, while the artist, a practising Catholic, used the language of his inheritance for a Christian theme, thus conjoining symbols of different cultures.

IV
CHURCH ARCHITECTURE

NIGEL YATES

The design of church buildings in the twentieth century has been fraught with difficulty. On the one hand architects have been keen to adopt some of the radical ideas seen in the design of secular public buildings in that of ecclesiastical ones. On the other hand the deep conservatism of both clergy and laity have tended to resist these attempts, and the fact that major liturgical reform did not really get under way until the 1960s also delayed any need to reorder churches to meet new liturgical requirements. Although there were moves towards liturgical reform in parts of Roman Catholic Europe, notably Belgium, France and Germany, and a consequent desire to design a new type of church building, immediately after the First World War, they had little impact on most other parts of the Christian world, and it was not until the Second Vatican Council authorised a complete and radical overhaul of the liturgy of the Roman Catholic church that a major shift in liturgical attitudes and the design of church buildings began to make its impact on most Christian churches. The growth of the ecumenical movement had, even in the period before the First World War, meant that liturgical innovation in one

----

34 Ibid.

church had an impact in others, but in the first half of the century that impact was still the working through of the ideas that had transformed Anglican worship and church buildings as a result of ecclesiology and ritualism in the second half of the nineteenth century, and the influence that had had on the other Protestant churches of the English-speaking world. Throughout the twentieth century there were Christian churches, notably the Eastern Orthodox churches and some of the more extreme Protestant churches, in which the consensus about liturgical reform and the consequent design of church buildings had no impact whatsoever. However, within the Roman Catholic, Anglican, Lutheran and many of the Reformed churches, the ideas that had begun to emerge, tentatively between the 1920s and the 1950s and more confidently from the 1960s, were to be expressed in the design of new churches and in the reordering of existing ones.

The slowness with which this programme was adopted proved frustrating for some architects and theologians. In England a number of them formed themselves into a body called the New Churches Research Group in 1957 and five years later ten of their number expressed these frustrations in a very significant volume of essays. In an introductory contribution the editor deplored the fact that

> if anything that can properly be described as modern church architecture exists at all today it does so only in embryonic form. There are plenty of new churches: they have been going up in their hundreds during the last few years all over the world, from Finland to Australia. How many of these churches can really be called *modern* buildings is another matter altogether. The great majority are essentially backward-looking; they merely take the formal concepts of the past and deck them out in a new brightly coloured wrapper.[35]

There is little doubt that the sort of church Hammond had in mind was one like St Michael's, New Marston, built in 1955, where art and construction are modern but the liturgical arrangement wholly traditional (fig. 31.1). Whilst some of Hammond's allegations, and those of his co-essayists, could not be denied, they were able to draw attention to a significant number of buildings in Europe, and even a few in the British Isles and the United States, in which an attempt had been made to design churches in which the liturgical action was placed centrally within the building rather than at one end of a rectangular, and preferably aisled, structure, as had been the ideal of the nineteenth-century neo-gothicists. There was a movement in both the Roman Catholic

---

35 Peter Hammond (ed.), *Towards a church architecture* (London: The Architectural Press, 1962), p. 15.

Figure 31.1 St Michael and All Angels, New Marston, Oxford, 1955

and Anglican churches in the years immediately prior to and after the Second World War in which liturgical writers endeavoured to emphasise that making the liturgical action less remote, and involving the laity as actors rather than spectators, was to recover the true purpose of Christian worship as understood by the early Christian church and, to a more limited extent, the reformers of the sixteenth century.

Some Roman Catholic commentators, in the days before the Second Vatican Council, dismissed such agendas as 'reckless' and 'iconoclastic',[36] and buildings with central altars, and with the congregation placed around them on two or more sides, as seen in the churches of Rudolf Schwarz and Emil Steffan in Germany, or Reiner Senn in France, remained rare.[37] In Ireland the church of Christ the King, Turner's Cross, Cork, designed in 1927 by Barry Byrne, a Chicago-based architect and former pupil of Frank Lloyd Wright, still had its altar at the east end and was flanked by two side altars, though the seating was angled to face them in four blocks. Christ the King was 'at least thirty years ahead of its time' in its architectural

36 P. F. Anson, *Fashions in church furnishings 1840–1940*, 2nd edn (London: Studio Vista, 1965), pp. 356–67.
37 Hammond, *Towards a church architecture*, pp. 129–48, 161–71; for Schwartz's work, and that of those influenced by him in Germany and Switzerland, see also Peter Hammond, *Liturgy and architecture* (London: Barrie and Rockliffe, 1960), pp. 55–65.

composition. Far more typical of Irish Roman Catholic taste were the neo-classical cathedrals of 1930–6 at Mullingar and even later (1949–65) at Galway.[38] A similar commitment to traditional building styles among Roman Catholics could be detected in many other parts of the world. English exceptions to this rule were the churches of the First Martyrs in Bradford (1935), a circular building in which the pulpit was placed behind a central altar, and St Peter's at Gorleston-on-Sea (1939), a cruciform building in which the congregation was placed on four sides of a central altar.[39]

For Anglicans a major catalyst for liturgical reform and new styles of church architecture was the Parish and People movement, launched in 1950, and the replacement in the two decades that followed of either mattins or a non-communicating sung eucharist as the principal Sunday service by a parish communion, frequently though not invariably followed by a parish breakfast. Early experiments with this new type of service, which encouraged greater participation by the laity, had been made from the late 1920s and had been advocated in a seminal work by a member of the Society of the Sacred Mission.[40] However, even when they were happy to adopt the idea of the parish communion, most Anglicans were unwilling to get too far away from the ecclesiological ordering of churches in which the altar was at the east end and the choir was placed between the altar and the congregation. This was still shown in the plans of the John Keble Church at Mill Hill (1936) and St Michael's at Wythenshawe (1937), though at the latter the seating was arranged so that most of the congregation had a clear view of the sanctuary.[41] One of the first Anglican churches to break away from this idea and to make the altar central in the building, with the choir stalls incorporated in the seating which surrounds the altar on three sides, was St Paul's, Bow Common, designed by Robert Maguire and Keith Murray, and opened in 1960.[42]

The other Protestant churches were not greatly influenced by either the liturgical ideas of progressive Anglican and Roman Catholic writers or modern church design. Though some early twentieth-century Lutheran churches, such as Högalid church in Stockholm (1918–23) and Grundtvig's church in Copenhagen (1921–6) had striking modern exteriors, their internal

---

38 Richard Hurley, *Irish church architecture in the era of Vatican II* (Dublin: Dominican Publications, 2001), pp. 23–5, 112–14.
39 Hammond, *Liturgy and architecture*, pp. 69–70.
40 A. G. Hebert, *Liturgy and society: the function of the church in the modern world* (London: Faber and Faber, 1935), esp. ch. 9.
41 Hammond, *Liturgy and architecture*, pp. 71–4.
42 Hammond, *Towards a church architecture*, pp. 154–8. Both architects contributed essays to this volume.

arrangements and furnishings were extremely traditional. In some of the more recent Finnish Lutheran churches, such as that at Orivesi (1961), the furnishings as well as the fabric were contemporary, but the altar, font and pulpit were still placed in a separate, railed, apsidal sanctuary, though the seating was angled so that the whole congregation had a clear view of the sanctuary. The church at Stengård in Denmark had a freestanding brick altar with steps behind to reach the pulpit, and the font in front of the pulpit. Seats faced the sanctuary from two different directions if the adjacent hall was opened to provide for a large congregation. The reluctance of Calvinists and other Protestants of the reformed tradition to adopt modern ideas of church architecture and liturgical arrangement was largely because it was preaching rather than the eucharist which was the core of their worship and their needs had been adequately met by focusing the congregation on the pulpit. Nevertheless there were a few interesting experiments influenced by the Anglican or Roman Catholic liturgical movements. The Dutch Reformed churches at Aardenhout and Nagele had sanctuaries that gave a separate and balanced emphasis to both the pulpit and the communion table, and at Aardenhout the congregation faced the pulpit from two different directions. The Swiss Reformed churches at Reinach, a suburb of Basel, and Effretikon, near Zurich, were L-shaped buildings with their pulpits and communion tables placed in the angle of the building with seats facing them from two different directions.[43] St Columba's Church of Scotland church at Glenrothes (1960) had seating for the congregation placed on three sides of a central platform with seating for the elders and choir on the fourth side, behind the pulpit. The pulpit was placed at the back of the platform, towards one corner, with a freestanding communion table at the front, and the font between the pulpit and the altar. The church of the Taizé community, built in 1962, had a central altar and no fixed pulpit, being designed to be the setting for a rich liturgy with strong Roman Catholic and Eastern Orthodox influences.[44]

An interesting feature of Anglican and Lutheran architecture since the 1920s has been the attempt to give traditional designs and liturgical arrangements a modern interpretation. A good example was All Saints at Bawdeswell in Norfolk (1955), which is a modern interpretation of an eighteenth-century

---

43 E. S. Heathcote, *Church builders* (Chichester: Academy Editions, 1997), pp. 20–1, 84; G. E. Kidder-Smith, *The new churches of Europe* (London: The Architectural Press, 1964), pp. 23–5, 68–71, 220–5, 274–81; photograph of Högalid church interior in Hebert, *Liturgy and society*, plate XIII.
44 Robert Maguire and Keith Murray, *Modern churches of the world* (London: Studio Vista, 1965), pp. 123–5, 154–7.

Anglican building complete with three-decker pulpit, Laudian altar and the choir in a west gallery.[45] The Evangelical church at Essen, Germany, designed by Otto Bertning in 1929–30, was a modern interpretation of traditional Lutheran architecture of the seventeenth and eighteenth centuries complete with galleries; the pulpit, altar and font are placed one in front of the other, with the organ and choir behind them.[46] The church at Gravberget in Norway was an interesting reinterpretation of the traditional stave church. It was a square building rising to form a spire, but arranged diagonally inside so that the altar was placed in one angle of the building and seating faced it from two sides. Each of the four sides of the interior had a gallery, divided into four separate boxes along the two walls that met behind the altar; along the other two walls a slightly longer gallery was divided into five separate boxes. The pulpit was placed behind the altar in the traditional German position, which had occasionally been used in Scandinavia in the eighteenth and early nineteenth centuries.[47]

In the 1960s church architecture, according to Peter Hammond and Frederic Debuyst, was still desperately conservative. The latter described much of the church architecture of this period as 'essentially backward-looking, unauthentic . . . a compromise between the old medieval, symbolic and monumental concept of church building, and the new vision of things . . . The great mass of the faithful, Catholics as well as Protestants, are not yet disturbed by this fact. They are probably not even aware of it.'[48] All this was about to change. The major catalyst was the liturgical reforms of the Second Vatican Council which formalised, and indeed went some way beyond, the liturgical experiments that had taken place in some parts of Europe since the 1930s. The emphasis was strongly on congregational participation. These changes were paralleled by very similar developments in the Anglican church, strongly influenced by the Parish and People movement. By the 1970s Roman Catholic and Anglican initiatives were also beginning to have an impact on other Christian denominations. However, as in the inter-war period, it was the Roman Catholics who still made the running in matters of church design. It is interesting to compare the much more liturgically radical designs of the new Roman Catholic cathedrals in Liverpool (1967) and Clifton, Bristol (1973) with their more conservative Anglican counterparts at

45 Hammond, *Liturgy and architecture*, pp. 106–7.
46 Maguire and Murray, *Modern churches*, pp. 26–9.
47 Kidder-Smith, *New churches of Europe*, pp. 229–33.
48 Frederic Debuyst, *Modern architecture and Christian celebration* (London: Lutterworth Press, 1968), p. 9.

Coventry (1962) and Guildford (1966). In terms of its individual furnishings, Coventry was a spectacularly modern building, but it was still arranged with the main altar at one end of a long rectangle, and with the choir stalls placed between the altar and the congregation. Liverpool and Clifton were, by contrast, both circular buildings. At Liverpool the congregation was seated around the main altar with the choir forming one segment of this seating.[49] Another good example of a Roman Catholic church designed for congregational participation in worship was that of Leyland (Lancs), another circular building opened in 1964, and incorporating freestanding stations of the cross by Arthur Dooley and abstract stained glass by Patrick Reyntiens.[50]

One of the key elements in the new architectural thinking that stemmed from the liturgical revolution of the 1960s was flexibility and the desire to reduce furnishings to the absolute minimum necessary for the much more informal styles of worship favoured by liturgical reformers. A group of such churches was built in Belgium by the architect Marc Dessauvage: Willebroek (1963), Ezemaal (1964), Aarschot (1965) and Westmalle (1967). They were provided with square altars behind which the celebrant could face the people and freestanding tabernacles for the reservation of the sacrament. It was considered essential that all church furniture, apart from the altar and the tabernacle, should be 'mobile, so that their position can be changed according to the different kind of celebration', and that there should be 'space free of all furnishing, where one can move with ease . . . for the solemn celebrations'.[51] There was also a desire that churches should reflect the environment within which they were built. This was achieved in Ireland by the Donegal architect Liam McCormick, who 'possessed a natural instinct for landscape, his buildings grew out of their surroundings . . . calling forth a response in a wealth of mostly natural forms and materials of timber, stone and slate'.[52] His church of St Aengus at Burt (1967) was a circular design inspired by the nearby stone fort, the Grianán of Aileach. Another church, St Michael's at Creeslough (1971), was strongly influenced by Le Corbusier's Notre Dame de Ronchamp. A third, St Columcille's at Glenties (1974), had seating at different levels.

Some of the most exciting Roman Catholic architecture was not in Europe or America but in the rapidly expanding Christian communities in Africa.

49 W. E. A. Lockett (ed.), *The modern architectural setting of the liturgy* (Liverpool: Liverpool University Press, 1964), plates 12 and 13.
50 Bryan Little, *Catholic churches since 1623* (London: Robert Hale, 1966), pp. 219–21, plates 40(a) and (b).
51 Debuyst, *Modern architecture*, pp. 55–8, 64, 66.
52 Hurley, *Irish church architecture*, pp. 48–50, 60–1, 81–3.

Here architects were not hidebound by the nostalgia for traditional church buildings, but could design buildings which were essentially practical, and which from time to time would incorporate features designed to relate these new buildings to their indigenous context. The cathedral at Mityana in Uganda, designed by Justus Dahinden in 1972, has a short tower in which African drums can be played to call the people to the services, and comprises 'three spherical segments ... which represents an ancient Bantu building symbol ... The structure is conceived as the focus of an urban complex which includes a school, social centre, Carmelite Convent, presbytery, parish hall and health centre.'[53]

It was not just in Africa that such multi-purpose complexes were being built. Increasingly, throughout the world, from the 1970s new churches were being constructed as parts of groups of buildings that had both religious and secular functions, rather than as freestanding structures. The opportunity was sometimes taken to build new churches or chapels for existing complexes of buildings. A good example is the Falklands Island Memorial chapel at Pangbourne college, near Reading, opened in March 2000. 'Built to commemorate the lives and sacrifice of all those who died in the South Atlantic in 1982' it is, according to its publicity brochure, 'reminiscent of the shape of a ship – almond or "mandorla" shaped – denoting hands "cupped" in prayer' (fig. 31.2).

Whilst the liturgical revolution of the 1960s encouraged much good church-building it also threatened existing buildings in which over-zealous clergy and laity were determined that the architecture and furnishings of previous generations should not be allowed to get in the way of essential reordering. In Ireland the Roman Catholic cathedral at Killarney had all its original furnishings, designed by the distinguished Victorian architect A. W. N. Pugin, removed in 1970. A similarly disastrous reordering at Pugin's other Irish cathedral, Enniscorthy, was partially reversed in 1994, when his canopied pulpit and episcopal throne were reinstated and much of the original decoration restored or replicated.[54] Such action conflicted with a growing emphasis on the conservation of historic buildings, encouraged by local planning authorities, and bodies were set up by the churches, such as the Council for the Care of Churches by the Church of England, or the Committee on Artistic Matters by the Church of Scotland, to prevent such buildings being damaged by ill-considered reordering. In the United States

53 Heathcote, *Church builders*, pp. 91–3; for a comparable Anglican cathedral at Mbala, Uganda, see Lockett, *Architectural setting*, plates 23 and 24.
54 Hurley, *Irish church architecture*, pp. 115–16, 120–2.

Figure 31.2 The Falkland Islands Memorial chapel at Pangbourne college, Reading, 2000. Photograph by David Robinson

the impact of the conservation lobby has been such that many surviving churches of the colonial period, in which the furnishings had been altered during the nineteenth century, have been restored to their original, seventeenth- or eighteenth-century, appearance.

The damage caused to church buildings in Britain and Europe during the Second World War offered major opportunities for intelligent reconstruction in the post-war period. Whereas, on the whole, British churches were rebuilt so as to reinstate what had been lost, in mainland Europe architects were prepared to be more radical, as indeed they were in the adaptation of existing buildings to modern liturgical requirements. Good examples of such adaptations were the churches of St Roch, Duisdorf, where a new nave and chancel were placed at right angles to the existing nave and apsidal chancel, the latter being used as a new baptistery, and St Maurice, Cologne, where the former church was used as an open courtyard in front of a new fan-shaped building.[55] The Protestant church at Trier, which had occupied the fourth-century throne room of the former Roman imperial palace since 1856, was severely damaged during the war. Afterwards advantage was taken to replace the heavy nineteenth-century furnishings with a much lighter and more spacious interior. The impact of this successful modern interior in one of the city's most ancient buildings was not lost on the Roman Catholics of Trier, who took advantage of the liturgical reforms required by the Second Vatican Council to reorder some of their own buildings in a similarly successful manner, as seen in the new circular sanctuary under the crossing of the thirteenth century Liebfrauenkirche. A rare British example of an attempt to achieve something innovative as a result of damage to the existing building was at Llandaff cathedral, where the work of post-war reconstruction was undertaken under the direction of George Pace between 1949 and 1957: the medieval fabric was restored but the building was given a new chapel off the north aisle and the choir separated from the nave by a new organ loft on concrete arches, the front of which was used to display Sir Jacob Epstein's *Christ in majesty* (fig. 31.3).

The reluctance in Britain, the United States and much of the English-speaking world to be creative in adapting existing buildings to modern liturgical requirements has resulted in many churches being awkwardly reordered within their existing fabrics. This was shown in the plans for several reorderings within the Anglican diocese of Lichfield, though a proposal for the church in the Birmingham suburb of Sheldon, where the population had increased from 400 in 1930 to 35,000 in 1960, was more interesting. The north aisle was to be turned into the chancel, a new nave built on to the south wall of the existing nave, and the existing chancel turned into a side chapel.[56] It is, however, the case that whilst church architecture in the middle years of the twentieth century suffered from the stranglehold of

---

55 Hammond, *Liturgy and architecture*, pp. 143–4.
56 Gilbert Cope (ed.), *Making the building serve the liturgy* (London: A. R. Mowbray, 1962), pp. 62–71.

Figure 31.3 The nave of Llandaff cathedral, Cardiff, showing the new organ case and sculpture of *Christ in majesty*, 1957

outdated liturgical thinking, that of the last forty years has too often responded to the demands of liturgical reformers by solutions which have been both ineffective in liturgical terms and damaging to the quality of important buildings inherited from previous ages.

32

Role models

HUGH McLEOD

Every century of Christian history has had its saints, regarded as holy men and women by their fellow believers, and held up as models by religious authority. But ideas of holiness are continually evolving: the saints of one generation may seem quite unsaintly to another generation. And if saints are exceptional individuals, more numerous are those who have been seen or have been presented as models of what it means to be a Christian within a particular profession. Here too perceptions may change radically as the status of particular professions in Christian thinking changes.

While many important books have been written on the Christian saints of earlier centuries,[1] very little attempt has so far been made to explore twentieth-century concepts of sanctity, and the role models presented to or adopted by Christians in that century.[2] In view of the paucity of relevant secondary sources, this chapter is a preliminary exploration of the theme, and it is limited to notions of sanctity and role models recognised in the Western world.

Saints

Addressing pilgrims who had come to Rome for the beatification of Mother Teresa of Calcutta on 20 October 2003, Pope John Paul II declared that she had been 'one of the greatest missionaries of the twentieth century':

> The Lord made this simple woman who came from one of Europe's poorest regions a chosen instrument (cf. Acts 9:15) to proclaim the gospel to the entire world, not by preaching but by daily acts of love towards the poorest

---

1 See, for instance, Stephen Wilson (ed.), *Saints and their cults* (Cambridge: Cambridge University Press, 1983).

2 A major exception is Kenneth Woodward, *Making saints: inside the Vatican: who become saints, who do not, and why* (London: Chatto & Windus, 1991). This is, however, focused on one aspect of the subject, namely formal saint-making processes in the Roman Catholic church.

of the poor. A missionary with the most universal language: the language of love that knows no bounds or exclusion and has no preferences other than for the most forsaken.

He went on to note that she had found her strength in prayer and in 'the silent contemplation of Jesus Christ, his Holy Face, his Sacred Heart'. He also described her as 'a missionary of life':

> She always spoke out in defence of human life, even when her message was unwelcome ... Her very smile was a 'Yes' to life, a joyful 'yes', born of profound faith and love, a 'yes' purified in the crucible of suffering. She renewed that 'yes' each morning in union with Mary, at the foot of Christ's Cross. The 'thirst' of the crucified Jesus became Mother Teresa's own thirst and the inspiration of her path of holiness.

The pope concluded by claiming that Mother Teresa was 'truly a mother': 'A mother to the poor and a mother to children. A mother to so many girls and young people who had her as their spiritual guide and shared in her mission.'[3]

According to Michael Walsh, John Paul 'talked constantly of saints, and of their role in the founding and preservation of Western civilization. They are in his eyes, and the minds of many, models of Christian living whom, through its official procedures of beatification and canonization, the Church sets before the faithful for emulation.'[4] Mother Teresa achieved beatification only six years after her death. One may assume that the pope regarded her as a supreme female role model: a nun, but also a mother; an ascetic, yet one fully involved in the life of a great city; a warm and loving personality, and also a champion of traditional Catholic teachings – not least on the subjects of contraception and abortion, to which John Paul referred obliquely in his address. She had been born Agnes Bojaxhiu of Albanian parents in Skopje in 1910. (In spite of the pope's reference to her as 'a simple woman', her parents were comfortably off and gave her a good education.) She had spent most of her life in India, initially as a teacher in a school run by the Loreto nuns. In 1950 she founded the Missionaries of Charity, an order dedicated to work among the most isolated and deprived of Calcutta's poor – first by providing schooling for slum children, and later by caring for dying beggars, for lepers and for orphans. After overcoming opposition from Hindus who saw her work as a form of proselytism, she won recognition first from local

---

3 www.motherteresacause.info/20October2003.htm, accessed 31 July 2004.
4 Michael Walsh, *John Paul II* (London: Harper Collins, 1994), pp. 120–1.

newspapers, then from the Indian government, then from Pope Paul VI, and finally from the Western media, which made her an international celebrity.

While many of those selected by the Vatican as role models achieve only limited recognition from the mass of Catholics, this cannot be said of Mother Teresa, who was widely regarded as a living saint in her lifetime, and continues to be loved and revered since her death. In July 2004 there were about 240,000 references to her on the internet. (This scarcely compares with the 3.9 million references to Jesus Christ, the 2.2 million to George W. Bush, or the 1.8 million to the Beatles. But she is about on a par with Karl Marx and Adolf Hitler, and a long way ahead of St Teresa of Lisieux, after whom she took her name.) An American Catholic website which includes a section of 'readers' stories of Mother Teresa's inspiration' includes accounts of miracles, varying from healings to success in examinations, but the main emphasis is on her humility, self-sacrifice and compassion. As one reader wrote, 'Mother Teresa loved all people with compassion and care, just as they are. Saint and sinner alike.'[5]

Mother Teresa may be remembered in history as the first Catholic saint who owed her worldwide reputation to television – in particular, Malcolm Muggeridge's BBC documentary of 1969, *Something beautiful for God.* However, her style of sanctity was little different from that of many saints of the nineteenth, or even the eighteenth, century. A telling comment is that of the singer Bob Geldof, who had tried to kiss her, and only realised later that she only let lepers kiss her.[6] It is a sign of the changing treatment of religion on British television that it was also a British documentary, Christopher Hitchens' *Hell's angel* (1994), that did most to publicise the views of Mother Teresa's critics. The indictment focused on three main points: that any good she did was more than outweighed by the damaging consequences of her opposition to contraception and abortion; that standards of medical care in her institutions were often poor; and that, in cultivating powerful patrons, she gave respectability to brutal dictators and corrupt businessmen. The first of these points has little merit: Mother Teresa was a conservative Catholic who remained faithful all her life to the beliefs in which she was brought up in the 1920s, and who assumed that a faithful Catholic must accept all of the church's teachings, rather than picking and choosing. One may object to the conservative Catholic position, but it is naive to suppose that a conservative Catholic can or should think otherwise. The other criticisms have more

5 www.americancatholic.org/Features?Teresa/viewstory.asp, accessed 31 July 2004.
6 Paul Williams, *Mother Teresa* (Indianapolis: Alpha, 2002), p. 191.

validity. Yet the practices condemned by Hitchens may be seen as a product of her order's history, as well as reflecting the very traditional character of her Catholicism. The Missionaries of Charity grew from nothing to become a worldwide organisation by a single-minded pursuit of patrons wherever they could be found, and without asking political questions. In this they followed long-established traditions in Catholic charitable work, which have only come to be widely criticised since the 1960s.

While Pope John Paul II was a friend of Mother Teresa, he was also a devotee of the most widely popular male 'living saint' of the twentieth century. Padre Pio, canonised in 2002, also followed a traditional model. In fact, by comparison with him, Mother Teresa's powers seem rather tame. Born in a poor south Italian family in 1887, he became a Capuchin friar, and in 1918 received stigmata. Revered primarily as a miracle-worker, reputed to be able to bilocate and levitate, he also had a great reputation as a confessor. He was said to be able to see into the future, to have been given a vision of heaven, and to have miraculously prevented the bombing of his monastery by the Americans during World War II. Pictures of the saint have also been credited with miraculous properties. In the 1990s it was claimed that a million pilgrims a year visited the monastery where he lived and died.[7]

The Catholic church has formal procedures for beatification and canonisation – simplified by John Paul II, a great traveller who, on visiting a new country, liked to announce the beatification of one of its sons or daughters. The number of beatifications in the first eleven years of his papacy exceeded the combined total of his seven twentieth-century predecessors.[8] Of course, political considerations play a major part in determining which candidates do achieve the goal. For instance, beatifications and canonisations reflect the Vatican's recognition of a particular nation or ethnic group, and they are often used to make a historical point with contemporary relevance. A striking example, discussed at length by Woodward, was the attempt by 'progressive' bishops during the latter stages of Vatican II to secure the canonisation by acclamation of Pope John XXIII, and the counter-claims by 'conservatives' that Pius XII had a better case. Paul VI decided that both cases should be investigated, but that the normal procedures should be followed.[9] Most of those who gain the official status of saints have been priests or nuns. Lay saints are infrequent except in the case of martyrs, and

---

7 http://members.aol.com/goodyburk/padrepio.html, accessed 31 July 2004; Woodward, *Making saints*, pp. 184–90.
8 Woodward, *Making saints*, pp. 116–20.   9 Ibid., pp. 280–301.

married saints, as Woodward shows in a discussion of 'Sanctity and sexuality', are particularly rare.[10]

There are of course many people who have been presented as role models to their fellow laity without being recognised as saints, and I shall return later to some examples. Protestant churches do not have any procedure for recognising saints, and saints play a much smaller part in Protestant than in Catholic or Orthodox life. However, Protestants certainly have their heroes of the faith, who provide outstanding examples of what it means to be a Christian at a particular time or in a particular place.

Protestant ideals have evolved more quickly than Catholic, but for a relatively long period – from the later nineteenth century up to about 1960 – the most widely recognised Protestant ideal of the Christian was the missionary. Protestant Sunday schools entertained their pupils with tales of missionary heroism and rewarded those who attended most regularly or showed the most knowledge by giving them biographies of famous missionaries. Missionaries were even celebrated in films, such as *The inn of the sixth happiness* (1958) – until a more critical view of Christian missions began to become conventional in the 1960s.

This film was based on the life of Gladys Aylward (1902–70), a working-class Londoner, rejected by the China Inland mission because of her lack of education, who nonetheless made her own way to China, arriving in 1932 during the war with Japan. She joined an elderly missionary who ran an inn in a remote mountain area. The inn was used as a base for evangelism, and also for housing orphans. Her exploits there became, in the words of the British *Sunday school chronicle*, 'one of the most amazing stories of Christian devotion and heroism of our own time'. Her finest hour came when she led a hundred orphans 'across mountains and over rivers' to safety in a province not occupied by the Japanese. Equally important to her reputation as a Christian heroine was her campaign against the binding of young girls' feet.[11]

Aylward was still alive when Ingrid Bergman portrayed her in the cinema and she could as much be called a 'living saint' as Mother Teresa or Padre Pio. Indeed she could be termed a model Protestant saint of her time. The overriding emphasis in the Aylward legend is on the lone individual, called by God for special work, and pursuing her vocation in the face of overwhelming odds, including the opposition of powerful religious authorities. In this, her

---

10 Ibid., pp. 336–52.
11 *Sunday school chronicle*, 7 May 1953; www.gospelcom.net/chi/glimpsef/GLIMPSES/glmps006/shtml, accessed 2 August 2004.

story has much in common with Mother Teresa's. More distinctively Protestant is the strong element of adventure: Protestant saints were expected to be men and women of action, and in Aylward's case this included being shot at by the Japanese. Then there is her work in opposition to foot-binding. Although Protestant missionaries in the early twentieth century were divided between those who gave priority to the Social Gospel and those who gave priority to individual conversion, even the latter believed that social reform was part of the Christian message, and that Christianity would bring about a more humane society and one which would give women a better deal.

The 1960s brought changes in attitudes towards missionaries, including calls for a moratorium on missions. With the end of most of the European empires, Christian opinion was increasingly critical of the associations between missions and colonialism. Non- or anti-Christian opinion also became more vocal, and often condemned missions as a form of cultural aggression. Liberal Christians were highly receptive to these arguments, while conservative evangelicals largely rejected them – with the result that Protestant missions came increasingly to be dominated by the latter. They accepted many of the criticisms of colonialism, and recognised the right of African and Asian Christians to run their own churches, and to adapt forms of worship to local cultural forms. But they could not accept anything that detracted from the urgency of the Great Commission. The old division between liberals committed to social improvement and evangelicals preoc-cupied with conversion thus deepened in the 1960s and after. And this was inevitably reflected in different choices of role models.

The most widely admired Protestant hero of the second half of the century was probably Martin Luther King Jr (1929–68). For most liberals and many evangelicals the Civil Rights movement was the supreme example of a twentieth-century Christian crusade, fought with the Christian weapons of non-violent resistance. King's inspiring oratory, drawing repeatedly on scrip-tural language and motifs, was seen as an outstanding example of the application of the Bible to contemporary politics. He was the American Moses who, as he declared in his last speech, on the eve of his assassination, had been to the mountain-top, but would not get to the promised land. His still mysterious death established him as a martyr. King's liberal theology was very different from that of Gladys Aylward, but like her he believed that he had a divine calling. After he had received a death threat during the Montgomery bus boycott in 1956, God had spoken to him, saying: 'Martin Luther, stand up for righteousness. Stand up for justice. Stand up for truth.

And lo, I will be with you, even unto the end of the world.'[12] An intriguing aspect of the King legend is that attempts to discredit him on the grounds of his sexual behaviour have had little impact. Protestants attach high importance to the family. They see no merit in celibacy, but they do expect marital fidelity. The fanatically anti-communist director of the FBI, J. Edgar Hoover, believed that King was a communist, or at least under communist influence. The FBI therefore bugged hotel rooms used by King during his campaigns, in the hope of finding evidence that would discredit him. The bugging did not prove King was a communist, but did establish that he had committed adultery. However, the attempts to use this evidence against him failed at the time, and have done very little to dent his heroic reputation since his untimely death in 1968.

Martyrs are to a considerable degree exempt from the suspicions and accusations that follow most prominent individuals. It is therefore not surprising that the other leading twentieth-century contender for Protestant sainthood is Dietrich Bonhoeffer, who was killed by the Nazis in 1945, but whose reputation took off after the publication of *Widerstand und Ergebung*, translated into English in 1953 as *Letters and papers from prison*. King and Bonhoeffer were representative of a growing tendency to celebrate as supreme Christian heroes those who gave their lives in fighting against tyrannical governments or oppressive social systems. They could be seen as martyrs not only in the cause of the faith, but of humanity in general.[13]

For those Protestants who regard King and Bonhoeffer as too political or as insufficiently conservative in their theology, the most widely favoured hero would probably be the American evangelist Billy Graham (b. 1918) – though even he is too liberal for some American fundamentalists. Graham became America's most famous revivalist as a result of the Los Angeles crusade in 1949; after a false start with Harry Truman, he established a rapport with Eisenhower, and for many years thereafter friendly relations with Graham were deemed an essential part of being an American president or presidential candidate; his crusades in London and Glasgow in 1954 and 1955 made him an international star; by the 1960s and 1970s he was able to attract huge audiences in Germany and South Korea; and in the 1980s he was even preaching in Moscow. Apart from his skills as a preacher and his successful avoidance of the scandals that have bedevilled so many mass evangelists, three other

---

12 Stephen B. Oates, *Let the trumpet sound: the life of Martin Luther King, Jr* (London: Search Press, 1982), pp. 88–9.
13 See Andrew Chandler (ed.), *The terrible alternative: Christian martyrdom in the twentieth century* (London: Cassell, 1998).

aspects of his unique popularity are noteworthy. First, his persona was an important part of his appeal: he was seen as a warm, relaxed and friendly person, with whom you might enjoy a round of golf. (Graham is in fact a fervent golfer, and indeed experienced his call to be a preacher while on the eighteenth green of a Florida golf course.) Second, he has been a skilled theological tight-rope walker: his theology has remained sufficiently conservative to retain the respect of most of his fellow evangelicals, yet at the same time his style of presenting the message has mellowed over the years, and contains enough generally acceptable clichés to make him attractive to presidents and to the American public generally. Third, he has proved very adaptable, accepting that the over-riding need to present the message of salvation must be combined with a willingness to listen to new ideas and to try out new methods. His roots are in Bible Belt fundamentalism, and much of what he said in his early years was little different from what is being said by the 'televangelists' of recent times. A first major turning point was the New York crusade of 1957, when he declared his willingness to work with any church that would work with him, including some reckoned by his friends to be irredeemably liberal, and when he invited Martin Luther King to speak at one of his rallies. (He had already in 1954 insisting on addressing only desegregated audiences.) In the 1980s he started talking about ecological issues, cancelling third world debt, disarmament, and the dangers of retaining capital punishment when the poor seldom get adequate lawyers.[14] *Time* magazine included Graham among 100 'heroes and icons' of the twentieth century, mainly because of his role as a symbol of America as Americans liked to imagine it, and his power to confer legitimacy on presidents and wars.[15]

Statesmen, warriors, peace-makers, businessmen . . .

If saints and martyrs were in the twentieth century, as in any other, the supreme Christian heroes, many other role models were available, including such well-established types as the Christian statesman, warrior, peace-maker, businessman or philanthropist, as well as more characteristically twentieth-century figures, such as the Christian athlete or entertainer. More controversially, there were, as in the nineteenth century, nationalist heroes, such as

---

14 William Martin, *The Billy Graham story: a prophet with honour* (London: Hutchinson, 1992), pp. 167–72, 225–38, 588–91.
15 www.time.com/time/time100/heroes/graham01.html, accessed 2 August 2004.

Archbishop Stepinac in Croatia, who symbolised the cause of their own people while being reviled by hostile neighbours.

Those who laid claim to the title of Christian statesmen, or who have been so regarded by their followers, have espoused widely different politics and they have included some whose claims to this title would have been rejected by almost everyone else. Here one should distinguish between the many statesmen who have been devout Christians, but have not exploited their religion for electoral purposes, and those who have made their religion an essential part of their public persona, in an attempt to appeal to the church-going electorate. In the 1920s and 1930s, a pious image was cultivated by statesmen as diverse as Stanley Baldwin, Chiang Kai-Shek and Adolf Hitler. In the 1940s, 1950s and 1960s, many of Europe's most powerful politicians, among them Konrad Adenauer, Alcide De Gasperi, Robert Schuman and Charles de Gaulle, were well known to be practising Catholics – as were the Spanish and Portuguese dictators, Franco and Salazar. In the 1980s, a crucial aspect of Ronald Reagan's electoral successes was his strong appeal to conservative Protestants.

Hitler's use of religious language and occasional participation in church services, especially during the period 1932–4, has generally been seen as a form of cynical opportunism, guided by his need to gain the support of the churches during the period when he was not yet in power or not yet fully in control. This still seems to me the best explanation of his motives, though Steigmann-Gall argues in a recent book that his religiosity was sincere.[16] What is clear, however, was that he persuaded many Protestants, and to a lesser extent Catholics. Wishful thinking certainly played a role here. As in most political movements there were many people who longed to believe that their leader was sincere and that he believed the same things that they did. In 1933, Martin Niemöller, the later Confessing Church leader and concentration camp prisoner, proclaimed: 'Today Christians, not international atheists, are at the head of Germany.' In a service to mark Hitler's birthday on 20 April 1933 a Berlin pastor referred to Hitler as '[t]he leader sent to us from God in a time of deepest need for body and soul' and claimed that he was not only an 'orator' but a 'preacher' and a 'rouser of consciences'. And a disillusioned former follower skilfully delineated the methods by which Hitler won the trust of many Christians:

16 Richard Steigmann-Gall, *The Holy Reich: Nazi conceptions of Christianity, 1919–1945* (Cambridge: Cambridge University Press, 2003).

He made free use of the Christian vocabulary, talked about the blessing of the Almighty and the Christian confessions which would become pillars of the new State, he rang bells and pulled out all the organ-stops. He assumed the earnestness of a man who is utterly weighed down by historic responsibility. He handed out pious stories to the press, especially the Church papers. It was reported, for example, that he showed his tattered Bible to some deaconesses and declared that he drew the strength for his great work from the Word of God. He was able to introduce a pietistic timbre into his voice which caused many religious people to welcome him as a man sent from God.[17]

In the very different political world of inter-war Britain, Stanley Baldwin, leader of the Conservative Party and prime minister 1923–4, 1924–9 and 1935–7, made a deliberate and fairly successful attempt to win the support of the churches. Although an Anglican, Baldwin also had family connections with Methodism, and he emphasised these Nonconformist roots in order to win over formerly Liberal voters who were looking for a new political home. The 1924 election, when Baldwin won a large majority, was said to have been the first in which substantial numbers of Nonconformists voted Conservative. Baldwin's version of the Christian statesman was partly founded on an image of honesty, reliability and straightforwardness (symbolised by his pipe) – he was, according to a party slogan, 'The man you can trust'. In the 1920s his Christian politics focused on reconciliation between classes and rejection of what he presented as the confrontational politics of the Labour Party (and of more aggressively anti-union Conservative colleagues). In the 1930s his main theme was the defence of democracy, individual freedom and Christian civilisation against communist and fascist totalitarianism.[18]

The 'Christian statesmen' of the 1920s and 1930s were mainly on the right. Except in the English-speaking world, socialist, and even liberal, politics still tended towards anti-clericalism or even secularism, though Sweden had its 'Christian social democrats' and Germany and Switzerland their 'religious socialists'. However, in Britain the most revered figure of the Labour movement, Keir Hardie, who had died in 1915, was a Christian socialist, and this tradition was continued by major figures of the inter-war years, such as

---

17 James Bentley, *Martin Niemöller* (London: Hodder & Stoughton, 1984), pp. 42–3; Manfred Gailus, *Protestantismus und Nationalsozialismus: Studien zur nationalsozialistischen Durchdringung des protestantischen Sozialmilieus in Berlin* (Cologne: Böhlau, 2001), pp. 109–10.

18 Philip Williamson, *Stanley Baldwin: Conservative leadership and national values* (Cambridge: Cambridge University Press, 1999), pp. 37, 277–93, 354–5.

Arthur Henderson, foreign secretary 1929–31, and George Lansbury, leader of the Labour Party 1931–5. Lansbury, whom Clement Attlee once compared to Gandhi, and who was described by the historian A. J. P. Taylor as 'the most lovable figure in modern politics', had the status of a Christian socialist saint in the eyes both of his many admirers and of his detractors. The latter felt that he was too saintly to be an effective politician. This was the burden of the trade union leader Ernest Bevin's notorious attack on Lansbury's pacifism at the party conference in 1935 that precipitated the latter's resignation. Bevin was credited with the comment that 'Lansbury's been dressed in saint's clothes for years waiting for martyrdom. All I did was set fire to the faggots.' While saints in politics are unlikely to be universally admired, Lansbury owed his great popularity to the fact that he was seen as a politician of rare honesty and integrity. He lived in the east end of London in the midst of his constituents, and as mayor of the impoverished borough of Poplar in the 1920s he and other councillors had gone to jail for refusing to make legally required payments which he believed the people of Poplar could not afford. As one of his biographers comments: 'He did not seek personal wealth or social status. Above all, he practised in his public and his private life the Christian principles which inspired his socialism, pacifism, internationalism and support for women's rights. An unbridled passion for social justice and unshakable belief in democracy sustained Lansbury's lifetime of public service in local government and on the national stage.'[19]

'Christian statesmen' will inevitably make some decisions that disappoint or even shock their admirers. The most admired political figures have therefore often been campaigners, who never achieved, or never sought, political power. The prototype of modern campaigns was the movement to abolish the slave trade, with its origins in the later eighteenth century. The nineteenth century brought many more such humanitarian crusades, often led by Christians and drawing heavily on biblical arguments. In the twentieth century biblical arguments have less frequently been to the fore, but Christians have continued to be prominent in campaigns of many kinds: movements for peace, for racial justice, on behalf of refugees and political prisoners, to alleviate hunger, and so on. The life of a professional campaigner is one of pronounced highs and lows and of potential tension not only with the state but with the church. Many campaigners inspired by their Christian faith experienced disappointment at lack of support from the

19 John Shepherd, *George Lansbury: at the heart of Old Labour* (Oxford: Oxford University Press, 2002), pp. 2–3, 327, 362.

church hierarchy. Martin Luther King Jr, since his death the most revered of twentieth-century Christian campaigners, had his share of such frustrations. For instance, his famous 'Letter from a Birmingham Jail' was provoked by criticism from many of the white clergy in that city. King's principal power-base always lay in the black churches, and he also enjoyed very important support from white churches in the north. However, there were also Christian campaigners whose relationship with their churches came under intolerable strain. A notable example was Danilo Dolci. His work, starting in the 1950s, to ameliorate conditions of life and challenge the authority of the mafia in the impoverished villages of western Sicily was prompted by his Christian faith, but eventually led him to break from the Catholic church, when support for his work was not forthcoming.

The warrior and the peace-maker both have their place in Christian history. The twentieth century with its almost uninterrupted history of bloody conflict has had its share of both – the Christian warriors inevitably receiving most acclaim in their lifetime, while the peace-makers have been more warmly remembered after their deaths. Field-Marshal Sir Douglas Haig, the chief commander of the British forces in World War I, is a case in point. A Scottish Presbyterian by upbringing, but no sectarian, he firmly believed that he was God's agent in the battle against the evil of Prussian militarism. He regularly sought the guidance both of God and of his chaplain, who was his closest confidant, and he attached enormous importance to the role of the chaplains in the British army. Since his death in 1928 Haig's leadership, including his reliance on divine guidance, has been subject to severe criticism, but during the war and in its immediate aftermath he was a national hero, and in the eyes of many a model Christian.[20]

Christians have also been prominent as peace-makers of many kinds. Those who have achieved iconic status include those who have used non-violent methods of resistance to oppressive governments or social systems, such as Martin Luther King Jr or Desmond Tutu, both winners of the Nobel peace prize; those who have tried to mitigate the cruelties of war and to bring reconciliation afterwards, such as George Bell, Anglican bishop of Chichester, who condemned saturation bombing of German cities during World War II, formed links with German resisters during the war, and maintained close relationships with the German churches after the war; war resisters such as the Austrian Catholic peasant, Franz Jägerstätter, executed by the Nazis for

---

20 Michael Snape, *God and the British soldier* (London: Routledge, 2005) includes a valuable analysis of the role of religion in British military leadership in the two world wars.

refusing to fight, or the Berrigan brothers, imprisoned during the Vietnam war; those who have acted as mediators, such as Jimmy Carter, winner of the Nobel peace prize in 2002, and the only United States president of recent times the sincerity of whose religion nobody questions. As Hendrik Hertzberg commented in an internet essay: 'Carter was Christian before Christian was cool.'

Since being voted out of office in 1980, Carter has devoted himself to a variety of humanitarian and peace causes. Hertzberg went on to state that Carter's style of leadership 'was and is more religious than political in nature', and to declare: 'Jimmy Carter is a saint.' His following explanation provided a good statement of Carter's claims to be regarded as a distinctively Protestant, later twentieth-century, saint. The essence of the case was that Carter is a man of action, who 'hasn't just talked' about peace or democracy or the relief of poverty, but has taken risks, and has shown 'persistence' and 'stubbornness' to make these a reality. It is also characteristic of this Protestant style of sainthood that in his plea for canonisation Hertzberg makes no claim that his candidate is perfect. He admits that Carter suffers from 'self-righteousness', and a willingness to talk at excessive length and sometimes on inappropriate topics.[21]

The Christian businessman was a characteristic figure of the nineteenth century. He was less familiar in the twentieth century, both because of changes in business and changes in Christianity. Men like Sir Titus Salt, 'the great philanthropist', founder of the model village of Saltaire near Bradford, typically headed a family-owned firm, in which they had a great deal of freedom to mix the pursuit of profit with the realisation of their religious or political visions. Many of them were self-made men. They were often upheld as model Christians, both because of the energy, enterprise and self-discipline shown in the making of their fortunes, and because of the good uses to which their riches had been put. With the growing dominance of large limited-liability companies, run by professional managers, the scope for such benevolent initiatives was limited. Celebration of successful businessmen had been a Protestant speciality. For instance, Salt was the subject of an enthusiastic biography, written by a Wesleyan minister, who quite explicitly presented him as a role model for young men. On the other hand the growing influence of the Social Gospel from the late nineteenth century onwards had made Protestant preachers much more suspicious of apparently generous business magnates, and more inclined to see them through the eyes of their

21 www.pbs.org/newshour/character/essays/carter.html, accessed 2 Aug 2004.

workforce. Reinhold Niebuhr who, before going to his chair at Union theological seminary in New York, had been a pastor in Detroit in the 1920s, was scathing about the benevolent pretensions of Henry Ford, his main complaint being that, whatever good Ford may have done, he was a dictator. The same criticism could certainly have been made of many of the heroes of nineteenth-century industry.

David Jeremy's investigation of the links between business and religion in twentieth-century Britain suggests that the proportion of leading business-men who are known to have had some degree of religious involvement fell from 50 per cent in 1907 to 36 per cent in 1955, and that the presence of businessmen in positions of lay leadership in the churches also fell during this period. Throughout the period there were businessmen who were promi-nent and strongly committed Christians, but very few were regarded as role models in the way that so many of their predecessors in the previous century had been. Jeremy's study of the laymen and -women who held the vice-presidency of the Methodist Conference between 1932 and 2000 showed a heavy preponderance of businessmen up to 1950, after which the professions predominated. An interesting finding is that the businessmen who achieved this distinction were often relatively obscure men with a reputation as local preachers, chosen in preference to well-known magnates, such as the mem-bers of the very wealthy Rank dynasty.[22]

On the other hand, the enormous growth of the entertainment industry, as reflected in films, television and professional sport, has brought new kinds of Christian role model. The Christian athlete originated in the 'muscular Christianity' of Britain and the United States in the later nineteenth century. He was an amateur, often a student. He stood for such values as 'fair play' and 'team spirit', and while he would show every degree of 'pluck' and 'grit' in pursuit of victory, he was also a 'good loser'. Sport was a part of the full life, and indeed an important part, since God had given us bodies, as well as minds and souls; but sport was only a part of life and should not take precedence over other things that were *more* important.[23] By the early twentieth century most of these ideals were under threat. They seemed of little relevance to the

22 David Jeremy, *Capitalists and Christians: Business Leaders and the Churches in Britain, 1900–1960* (Oxford: Oxford University Press, 1990), p. 113; David Jeremy, 'Twentieth-century Protestant Nonconformists in the world of business', in Alan P. F. Sell and Anthony R. Cross (eds.), *Protestant Nonconformity in the twentieth century* (Carlisle: Paternoster, 2003), pp. 264–312.
23 Clifford Putney, *Muscular Christianity: manhood and sports in Protestant America, 1880–1920* (Cambridge, MA: Harvard University Press, 2001), pp. 60–1, 69–71.

professionals who had a dominant influence on the most popular sports. Moreover, competition played a growing role at all levels of sport, and it was increasingly important as a source of prestige for communities and nations, as well as for the individual athlete. One of the first Christian sporting heroes had been C. T. Studd, the England cricketer of the 1880s, who abandoned this career at an early stage to become a missionary in China. In later life he regretted that he had devoted so much time to something so unimportant as cricket.

An indication of how far perceptions of sport and its significance changed during the twentieth century can be seen in comparison between Studd and the British triple-jumper, Jonathan Edwards. Edwards broke the world record in 1995 and was Olympic champion in 2000. His conservative evangelical theology is not too far removed from that of Studd, and like Studd he feels called to be an evangelist. But his way of responding to this call has been very different. According to his biographer, 'He has always interpreted his athletics prowess as a gift from God . . . Unlike most athletes the accumulation of wealth and fame were never Edwards' primary motives for being a sportsman . . . he felt he was answering a call to be an evangelist, a witness to God in running spikes.' Following the logic of this vocation led him to one of the most controversial decisions of his career. Having for long refused to compete on Sundays, in 1992 he lifted the ban, recognising that so many major events were held on that day that he was thereby excluding himself from reaching the top. He inevitably faced charges of apostasy from fellow evangelicals, and of hypocrisy from religious sceptics. But he justified his decision by saying that it was based not only on a new understanding of scripture, but on the fact that God had sent him a message through a dream that one of his fellow church members had had. Edwards believed that God took a close interest in his athletics career, and spoke to him both through his successes and through his failures. When he recovered with unexpected rapidity from an injury, he saw it literally as a miracle.[24]

While Edwards has been presented as a role model for young Christians, other individual athletes or teams have been seen literally as Christian champions, competing as a representative of their religion. Scotland's two leading football teams, Glasgow Rangers and Glasgow Celtic, have for most of their history had respectively a Protestant and a Catholic identity, and football has been the main focus for sectarian antagonism in the country.

---

24 Malcolm Folley, *A time to jump* (London: Harper Collins, 2000), pp. 2–3, 7–8, 244–5; *Guardian*, 23 August 2003.

Catholics were for long excluded from playing for Rangers. Celtic occasionally employed Protestant players, but its link with the Catholic church was
particularly close. The club was founded by a Marist brother. Celtic Park has
been used for open air masses. In the 1930s players and management made
pilgrimages to Lourdes, and in the early years the pope was informed by
telegram of major victories.[25]

The most notable individual sporting champion of Catholicism was Gino
Bartali, 'the pious', an outstanding Italian cyclist of the 1930s and 1940s, whose
victories attained added piquancy from the fact that his main rival, Fausto
Coppi, was a communist sympathiser. At the height of the Catholic–
communist conflict Bartali was praised by Pius XII as an example of staunch
Catholicism. His victory in the Tour de France in 1948 followed a phone-call
from Alcide De Gasperi at a crucial point in the Tour, in which the Italian
premier is said to have reminded the Catholic cyclist of the political and
religious significance of the race. Bartali was presented by the Catholic press
as a model family man, and the contrast appeared especially stark when
Coppi was involved in a much-publicised extra-marital affair.[26]

If many aspects of modern sport have made the search for Christian role
models difficult, it has been even more difficult to find such models in the
worlds of cinema, television and popular music – though the search has been
even more urgent in view of their immense influence on twentieth-century
life, first in the United States, but increasingly throughout the world. Some,
perhaps many, singers and actors have been in their own way strongly
religious, but have had little potential as role models. Elvis Presley is a case
in point. Up to the 1950s stars of the entertainment world were generally
expected to maintain a respectful attitude towards the religion of their
country, whatever their private beliefs or practices, but few could be drawn
upon as models of piety. In the 1960s a new style of more openly rebellious
entertainer emerged, exemplified by John Lennon's claim that the Beatles
were 'more popular than Jesus Christ', and his plea for atheism and anarchy
in the song *Imagine*. By contrast, those entertainers whose Christian credentials were clearest, such as Cliff Richard or Pat Boone, presented a public
image of likeability and clean-cut honesty, but also of blandness. The
Christian entertainer was perhaps able to flourish more easily in the 1940s
and 1950s. The best example might be Bing Crosby, who was a singer of

---

25 See Bill Murray, *The old firm* (Edinburgh: John Donald, 1984).
26 Stefano Pivato, 'The bicycle as a political symbol: Italy, 1885–1955', *International journal
    of the history of sport* 7 (1990), pp. 181–4; Geoffrey Wheatcroft, *Le Tour: a history of the
    Tour de France* (London: Simon and Schusster, 2003), p. 146.

worldwide renown, a popular film actor, and a loyal Catholic. His portrayal of the relaxed and charming New York slum priest Fr Chuck O'Malley in the 1944 musical *Going my way* earned him not only an Oscar but a private audience with Pope Pius XII.

Conclusion

Finally, a significant absence should be noted – the relative paucity of writers and other intellectuals among twentieth-century Christian role models. This is not because of a lack of interest on the part of the church authorities. Pius XII, in particular, believed that as pope he must be abreast of the latest developments in science, technology and the arts. He frequently addressed congresses, and presided at receptions for intellectuals of many kinds. Nor can it be said that there have been few Christian intellectuals, or even that Christians have been less numerous in the intelligentsia than in other social groups. It is likely that at most times both committed believers and committed unbelievers have been over-represented among intellectuals. In 1993–4, a leading French historian of the early modern period, Jean Delumeau, was able to gather together a formidable team of historians who were also Christians to write about the relationship between their religious beliefs and their practice of history.[27] No doubt the same could have been done in many other fields of scholarship. This paucity of recognised role models is partly because writers and artists who value their independence and integrity are reluctant to be commandeered to assist with someone else's agenda: Graham Greene, the greatest English novelist of the 1930s and 1940s, objected to being called 'a Catholic novelist', saying that he was 'a novelist who happens to be a Catholic'.

It remains true that at most points in the twentieth century the figures who have had the highest profile in the world of ideas and artistic creation have been non-Christian or even anti-Christian. There have been variations over time. For instance, Adrian Hastings, in his history of Christianity in twentieth-century England, sees the period from about 1935 to 1960 as the period richest in Christian cultural heroes – in sharp contrast both to the early and to the later decades of the century. He notes the popularity in these middle years of poets and novelists such as Eliot, Greene and Waugh, of historians such as Toynbee and Butterfield, and especially of the Christian apologetics of

---

27 Jean Delumeau (ed.), *L'historien et la foi* (Paris: Fayard, 1996).

C. S. Lewis, who played an important part in the vastly increased amount of religious broadcasting during World War II. He also notes the unique reputation, as intellectual and social reformer, as well as ecumenical leader, of William Temple who, while archbishop of York and then Canterbury, exercised a wide-ranging influence of a kind paralleled by none of his successors and very few of his predecessors.[28] To this list might be added Sir Arthur Eddington, professor of astronomy at Cambridge, who, as a distinguished research scientist who was also a skilled populariser, had a role in the Britain of the 1920s and 1930s somewhat akin to that of Richard Dawkins in the 1980s and 1990s – with the difference that Eddington was a Quaker, dedicated to showing the positive relationship between science and religion. Cholvy and Hilaire suggest a similar chronology for France. Hilaire calls the 1930s 'a golden age of Christian thought and literature', distinguished by such widely known and admired figures as the philosopher Maritain, the poet Claudel, and the novelists Mauriac and Bernanos.[29]

An important, but as yet hardly explored, aspect of the crisis of Christianity in the West since the 1960s has been the dwindling number of such Christian cultural heroes. In the period after 1960 the popular influence of Christian writers, artists and intellectuals was greatest in countries like Poland and the Soviet Union, where Christianity was associated with dissidence.

28 Adrian Hastings, *A history of English Christianity 1920–2000* (London: SCM, 2001), pp. 288–301, 491–504; John Kent, *William Temple: church, state and society in Britain 1880–1950* (Cambridge: Cambridge University Press, 1992).
29 Gérard Cholvy and Yves-Marie Hilaire, *Histoire religieuse de la France contemporaine 1930–1988* (Toulouse: Privat, 1988), pp. 24–9.

Being a Christian at the end
of the twentieth century

HUGH McLEOD

When being a Christian was dangerous

There are many parts of the world where it was dangerous to be a Christian in the twentieth century. The Bolshevik revolution of 1917 in Russia marks the beginning of a period in which numerous governments conducted sustained attacks against religion in general, against Christianity, or against particular forms of Christianity. According to Chandler and Harvey, more Christians suffered martyrdom in the twentieth century than in any other.[1] These attacks took their most extreme forms during such periods as Stalin's Terror in the 1930s or the Cultural revolution of 1966–76 in China, when religion was one of many forms of 'counter-revolutionary' activity to face systematic attack, or in Hoxha's Albania, which in 1967 declared itself the world's first 'atheist state'. Most communist-ruled states have persecuted Christianity systematically, but with fewer extremes of violence. More typical than the killings or imprisonment suffered by the few have been the more mundane forms of exclusion suffered by the majority of Christians living under a hostile state: discrimination in education or the job market, the lack of churches or clergy, ridicule by those in authority, and the systematic use of schools and media to discredit their beliefs.

Revolutionary attacks on religion in general or Christianity in particular were informed by nineteenth-century critiques of religion as unscientific and as 'opium' provided by the masters to keep the workers contented. But they were motivated mainly by the belief that the churches were essential parts of an old order which had to be swept away if a new ideal society of justice, equality and enlightenment was to be brought into being. All too often,

---

1 Andrew Chandler and Anthony Harvey, 'Introduction', in Andrew Chandler (ed.), *The terrible alternative: Christian martyrdom in the twentieth century* (London: Cassell, 1998), p. 11.

however, the revolutionary government evolved into a totalitarian state. As that happened, churches, however willing to work with the new regime, were seen as potentially dangerous because they were at least partly independent of state control and could become a focus for dissent. In Asia, Africa and, indeed, Mexico, attacks on Christianity, even if ostensibly grounded in Marxism, were also likely to have a strong nationalist edge. The argument that Christianity was an alien import, imposed by Western imperialism, seemed plausible enough in, for instance, China, where there were still many first-generation Christians. But it was also used in Mexico, although Mexican Catholicism had a continuous centuries-long history: Diego Rivera and the other artists of the revolution still harked back to an idealised pre-Columban era and emphasised Catholicism's colonial origins.

More selective attacks on particular Christian denominations or on Christians adhering to a particular kind of theology or politics have had very varied causes. Most often the cause for concern has been the association between a particular form of Christianity and national or ethnic identity. Thus, for instance, Stalin banned the Greek Catholic, or Uniate, church because of its links with Ukrainian nationalism; several thousand Catholic priests were killed by the Nazi occupiers of Poland. (John Paul II's views on the priesthood, and much else, were shaped by the fact that his ordination in 1946 followed a secret training in Poland during World War II.) In the first half of the twentieth century Christian clergy were frequently targeted by left-wing governments or by revolutionary movements because of their actual or presumed right-wing sympathies. This happened most notoriously during the Spanish civil war between 1936 and 1939, when several thousand Catholic priests and nuns were killed by Republicans (while smaller numbers of Basque priests were being killed by the Nationalists). It also happened on a lesser scale in the Asturias uprising of 1934, and in the Finnish civil war of 1918 when the victims were Lutheran pastors. In the period from the 1960s to the 1980s clergy, nuns and lay activists were often targeted by right-wing military regimes in Latin America and Asia because of their actual or presumed left-wing sympathies. Here the most notorious example was El Salvador, where the victims of the death-squads included the Catholic archbishop, Oscar Romero, and six Jesuits killed in one night, as well as many humbler victims, such as the Jesuits' housekeeper and her daughter.

In some ways, the 1990s were a quieter period after the dramas, the tragedies and the martyrdoms of the 1970s and 1980s. Brazil had returned to civilian rule in 1985; the years 1989–91 brought the disintegration of the Soviet bloc and then of the Soviet Union itself; apartheid in South Africa ended in

1994; in many parts of Africa and Latin America, and in some parts of Asia, this period brought an end to long-running military dictatorships or civil wars, and the holding of elections. This often brought great extensions of religious as well as political freedom.

Being a Christian was still dangerous in some parts of the world, but the nature of the danger was changing. In Yugoslavia, as in Ireland, the danger might arise from being a member of the wrong branch of Christianity. In many parts of central and eastern Europe ethnic and national identities have been for centuries closely bound up with adherence to specific forms of Christianity. In the later 1980s and early 1990s the Soviet Union and the other multi-national states of eastern Europe were coming under increasing pressure from nationalist movements in which distinctive religious identities generally played a part – even if they were manipulated by communist politicians who had devoted much of their lives to trying to suppress religion. In the majority of cases the nationalist movements obtained their objectives without resorting to force or facing violent suppression. But the break-up of Yugoslavia was accompanied by violence on a terrible scale in which the division between Orthodox, Catholic and Muslim played an essential part.[2] The leaders of the Catholic church in Croatia, the Serbian Orthodox church in Serbia, and the Muslim community in Bosnia-Herzegovina all championed their own people, bolstered national morale by frequent reference to struggles and sufferings in the past, and forged close links with nationalist politicians. The frequency with which the various armies desecrated the holy places of their enemies emphasised the importance of religious sites and symbols in the struggle.

The 1990s also brought growing tension and sometimes violence between Christians and Muslims, and between Christians and Hindus. In some Islamic states becoming a Christian could be a life-threatening choice. In Khomeini's Iran apostasy from Islam was a capital offence, and in Pakistan some Christians have been sentenced to death for blasphemy. More often the threat comes from local militants or from relatives who see apostasy from Islam as a threat to family honour. Meanwhile, in predominantly Christian countries, Muslims have faced denigration from racist political parties and from sections of the press, and sometimes violent attacks – though these have been less often in the name of Christianity than of 'civilisation' or 'Western values'.

---

2 Vjekoslav Perica, *Balkan idols: religion and nationalism in Yugoslav states* (Oxford: Oxford University Press, 2002).

Tensions between Christians and Muslims have been most acute in countries such as Nigeria, where numbers are fairly equal at the national level, and where religion has become bound up with inter-regional conflicts. In this highly competitive situation, fear plays a big role. Christians fear that Muslims intend to achieve political dominance and impose shari'a law, as has happened in some northern states. Muslims fear the economic and cultural power of Christians, with backing from the United States and Europe, which threatens to undermine their values and way of life. Thus an event as apparently trivial as the holding of the 'Miss World' contest in Abuja in 2002 could lead to church-burnings, attacks on Christians, and two hundred deaths. Muslims who regarded the event as immoral, and particularly resented the fact that it was being held during Ramadan, then read about remarks in a Lagos newspaper which they deemed insulting to the Prophet. As so often in recent years, it only required a tiny spark to ignite the fire of communal violence.

The decline of old and the rise of new Christendoms

By the end of the twentieth century, the attempts to suppress Christianity by force, which had played such a large part in the history of the twentieth century, had largely been abandoned. On the other hand, 'Christendoms' of the kind that were familiar at the beginning of the century had become a rarity. In the former Catholic strongholds of Ireland, Poland and southern Europe the Catholic church remained a very important institution, but it could no longer dominate the lives of communities in the ways that it had done a generation or two earlier. It faced competition from secularism, from 'alternative spiritualities' of all kinds, and in particular from the propagation through the press, television and advertising of alternative values, such as individual self-fulfilment, sexual freedom, and consumerism. Most people still called themselves Catholics and maintained some links with their church, but the spirit of the age was opposed to any kind of exclusivism.

In Limerzel, which may be taken as representative of Europe's Catholic heartlands, the Catholic culture, still dominant at the middle of the twentieth century, began to decline in the 1960s. Yves Lambert describes the 1960s, 1970s and 1980s as 'a period of sometimes dramatic conflicts between parents who are attached to Catholic practice and young people (and then adolescents) who are increasingly reticent'. Vatican II had of course brought changes in the liturgy, which most people accepted, though these were resented by some of the older people. The clergy realised that they could no longer command, but now had to woo the people. As a result, styles of preaching changed. A farmer's wife commented in 1976: 'Now they don't talk much about sins: in earlier times they insisted, *oh la la*! But people won't respond to that any more, they won't listen to them any more! Now it's charity, good relations between families, between neighbours.' And a shopkeeper said: 'They [the priests] have been forced to adapt themselves too. In earlier times we were there behind our counter, but now people want to serve themselves. Well, in church it's similar: there's no longer a holy table, you can touch the host!' Limerzel still had its own priest, but many neighbouring parishes did not. By necessity, a new kind of Catholicism was emerging in which a large part of the roles once monopolised by the clergy had been taken over by laypeople.[3]

Pluralism was indeed a fact of contemporary life. In most parts of the world Christianity was increasingly a matter of personal choice rather than inherited identity. In Africa and Latin America, the big growth was in 'born again' forms of religion. 'Christendoms' of a new kind were emerging in many parts of sub-Saharan Africa, where Christianity was growing spectacularly, but was taking a huge variety of local forms.[4] In the intensely religious culture of Accra or Kampala, belief in God, in miracles and in the spirit-world were widely taken for granted, and the competition was between rival forms of supernatural belief.

In the 1960s the leaders of newly independent African states frequently attempted an even-handed approach, in which they sought support from all the main religious groups in their country. By the 1990s, their successors were often identifying more explicitly with particular religions and denominations. The leaders in this trend were Muslims in Sudan and Nigeria. But in 1991 President Frederick Chiluba declared Zambia to be a 'Christian state'. In a speech replete with biblical references, he declared: 'The Bible, which is the Word of God, abounds with proof that a nation is blessed, whenever it enters into a covenant with God and obeys the word of God.' At a time when the ideal of 'Christendom' had, on principle, or from sheer realism, been abandoned by most Europeans, it was being eagerly embraced in Africa. Chiluba's links were with the 'born-again' churches, and his declaration aroused suspicion not only from the small Muslim minority, but also from many Roman Catholics. However, in the previous year, presidents, prime ministers

---

3 Yves Lambert, *Dieu change en Bretagne* (Paris: Editions du Cerf, 1985), pp. 243–55.
4 Philip Jenkins, *The next Christendom: the coming of global Christianity* (New York: Oxford University Press, 2002).

or other leading political figures of eight African countries had participated in a prayer breakfast in a Lusaka hotel at the invitation of Chiluba's predecessor, Kenneth Kaunda. According to Paul Gifford, 'This breakfast is significant in portraying the way that Christianity is seen in some parts of southern Africa – as something totally good, which enhances the standing of all associated with it.'[5]

The political benefits that association with Christianity offered arose partly from the degree to which Christianity had penetrated popular culture. In the case of Ghana, Gifford noted that in the 1990s about half of the cars, buses and taxis carried Christian slogans, that businesses frequently bore such names as 'King of Kings Electrical' or 'The Lord is my Light Car Wash', and that about a third of those advertising in the lonely hearts columns of the tabloid press specifically asked for a Christian partner. Equally significant was the way in which Accra's booming Pentecostal churches fulfilled a variety of other social functions. At the most up-market of these, where young members of the congregation are 'beautifully dressed, groomed and made-up', the church sees it as one of its tasks to help members find suitable partners and then prepare them for marriage. These churches are also notable for modern styles of music, appealing directly to the young. Gospel music, mixing Western with traditional Ghanaian elements, is performed not only in church, but on the radio, while tapes are sold in markets and reviewed in the press. Churches are also significant employers. And in a touch reminiscent of Britain or the United States in the nineteenth century, Gifford notes that in any kind of long-distance public transport it is normal to find someone standing at the front preaching and then holding a collection for an evangelistic enterprise or charity. The popularity of the 'born again' churches, he argues, is partly explained by the way in which they mix the old with the ultra-modern. They are modern in their ready use of the latest technology, and in their links with the United States. 'Over much of Africa, the young listen to Michael Jackson tapes, watch Rambo videos, smoke Marlboro, drink Coca Cola, and wear Levis, NY Giants baseball caps and Nike trainers (or imitations thereof) . . .' Evangelical Christianity can readily be seen as part of the same package. On the other hand, the frankly 'pre-modern' theology of these churches, and especially their stress on deliverance from demons, is more in tune with popular ways of thinking than the more 'rational' style of the 'mainline' churches.[6]

5 Paul Gifford, *African Christianity: its public role* (London: Hurst, 1998), pp. 195–205.
6 Ibid., pp. 61–2, 76–109.

After communism

In Europe and North America in the latter years of the twentieth century, Christians had seen one old enemy decisively defeated, as the Soviet empire collapsed. For many people anti-communism had for long been a major part of their Christian identity. This was most obviously true in countries where Christians had faced long years of communist persecution. But it was equally true in the United States, where it had been the main plank of foreign policy for several decades and where more than 100,000 people had given their lives in that cause. In 1989 and the years immediately following there was a temptation to indulge in Christian triumphalism. Evangelical Protestants saw eastern Europe as a vast and very promising mission field – though they soon found that the results fell far short of their hopes. Traditionalist Catholics everywhere, but especially in Poland, saw John Paul II as the hero of the hour. The defeat of communism appeared to offer a golden opportunity to reassert Poland's true identity as a Catholic nation. This was certainly the view of Poland's first post-communist president, Lech Wałęsa, who infuriated non-Catholics by wearing a picture of the Black Madonna pinned to his jacket. Catholic religious education was reintroduced in state schools, strict limits were imposed on legal abortion, and the church demanded stricter controls on pornography, blasphemy and the activities of Protestant sects. Before long the Catholic church faced complaints that it was 'too powerful', and the 1990s saw increasing criticism of the Catholic hierarchy and a decline in churchgoing.[7]

On the other hand there were parts of central and eastern Europe where churchgoing Christians entered the new era of political and religious freedom as a small minority. This was the situation in Estonia, the Czech Republic and the former East Germany, where the communist anti-religious policies had been able to build on the solid foundations of strong pre-existing traditions of anti-clericalism and religious scepticism. In the two former countries, nineteenth-century nationalism had frequently developed an anti-clerical edge in opposition respectively to the dominance of a German-speaking elite in the Lutheran church and to the links between the Habsburgs and the Catholic church. In East Germany the communists were able to build on traditions both of working-class secularism and of bourgeois atheism. In 2003

---

7 Zdzislaw Mach, 'The Roman Catholic church in Poland and the dynamics of social identity in Polish society', in Tom Inglis, Zdzislaw Mach and Rafal Mazanek (eds.), *Religion and politics: east–west contrasts from contemporary Europe* (Dublin: University College Press, 2000), pp. 113–28.

it was claimed that the territory of the former East Germany (now of course contained within a reunited, though western-dominated, nation), was 'still the most areligious part of the world'.[8] In Germany's 'new states' 70 per cent of the population claimed to be 'without religion'. Here, it seems, the communists had been unusually successful in propagating what they termed 'the scientific worldview', which included atheism, belief in science as the only reliable source of knowledge, and a rejection of anything that could be termed 'mystical' or 'magical'. Other factors may have contributed to this extreme situation. It seems probable, in view of the many forms of discrimination that they faced, that Christians were over-represented among those who migrated to the west before the erection of the Berlin Wall in 1961. At the present day, being of no religion (like voting for the PDS, the revamped Communist Party) may be a way of maintaining a defiant separate identity in a state where many 'Ossis' feel like second-class citizens.

The West: Christians under attack?

In most western European countries and in North America, on the other hand, the great majority of the population were at least nominally Christian. Committed and active church members were in no sense a deprived or excluded group. They were often drawn disproportionately from the professional and managerial classes and they were well represented in positions of power and authority. Yet they too often felt alienated from much contemporary culture. A typical complaint was that of the Catholic historian Adrian Hastings, who referred to the 'inexpressibly secular and shallow nature' of much contemporary culture, 'fed unrelentingly on soap opera, sitcom, the novels of Jeffrey Archer and such trivia' and 'severed for the most part from the Christian past by sheer ignorance'.[9] Christians in the late twentieth century seldom faced the political hostility that had been common in cities like Berlin a few decades earlier. If there was a focus for their anxieties, it was most likely to be the media. Thus the British sociologist Grace Davie suggests that 'disproportionate numbers of those who have little or no interest in religion (in both a personal and a professional sense) are present in the circles which dominate the media. Such dominance may be one (possibly the principal) reason for the persistence of dismissive attitudes to religion in

8 Thomas Schmidt and Monika Wohlrab-Sahr, 'Still the most areligious part of the world: developments in the religious field in eastern Germany since 1990', *International journal of practical theology* 7 (2003), 86–100.
9 Adrian Hastings, *A history of English Christianity 1920–2000* (London: SCM, 2001), p. lix.

modern Europe.'¹⁰ Nor are complaints about the quality of media coverage of religion exclusive to Europe: the American historian Jeff Cox complains that the *New York times* 'has only three stories about religion': 'It appears in their columns either as marginal, and therefore unimportant or picturesque, or as a phenomenon which everyone thought was dead but remains surprisingly alive, or as reactive, anti-modern and "fundamentalist", and therefore a threat to all the values we hold dear.'¹¹

The press has been a key player in Western societies since the early nineteenth century, and was already playing a big part in the battles between clericals and anti-clericals in the latter part of that century. It is beyond the scope of this chapter to determine whether media hostility to the churches was greater in the 1990s than the 1890s, or, if so, when this came about and why. The important point, however, is that many contemporary Christians *believe* that the media are dominated by people who are anti-religious, or at least areligious. These anxieties focus principally on television, though to a lesser extent on other media too. Two more general and one specific point can also be made. First, it is a more or less general complaint, not only of Christians or others interested in religion, but also of those interested in, for instance, the arts, science or politics, that commercial pressures have led television to be increasingly dominated by programmes that are seen as having a mass appeal, and that only a very limited range of topics, most notably sex, sport and crime, are seen as having this appeal. Second, it is argued that the nature of television as a medium tends to encourage a particular style – 'short, quick, simple, new, informative, challenging, entertaining',¹² to which the churches in Europe have not adapted very well – though maybe conservative Protestants in the United States have been more successful. Third, in some countries or regions where the church has been very powerful, the media have played a key role in undermining its authority. This happened in Boston, most Catholic of great American cities, where the *Boston globe* took the leading part in exposing paedophile priests and cover-ups by the archdiocese. An even more striking case is Ireland where the sociologist Tom Inglis argues that since the 1970s increasingly outspoken and

---

10 Grace Davie, *Religion in modern Europe: a memory mutates* (Oxford: Oxford University Press, 2000), p. 104.

11 Jeffrey Cox, 'Master narratives of long-term religious change', in Hugh McLeod and Werner Ustorf (eds.), *The decline of Christendom in western Europe 1750–2000* (Cambridge: Cambridge University Press, 2003), p. 202.

12 Tom Inglis, 'Irish civil society: from church to media domination', in Inglis, Mach and Mazanek, *Religion and politics*, p. 65.

self-confident media have gradually displaced the clergy as the 'moral police-men' and chief shapers of public opinion.[13]

One way of responding to secularism and pluralism was that adopted by the 'religious right', which emerged in the United States in the later 1970s.[14] The best-known of the groups that emerged around this time was the 'Moral Majority' led by the Independent Baptist preacher and televangelist Jerry Falwell. The title chosen by Falwell for his movement well expresses its split personality. On the one hand, Falwell claimed to be speaking for the majority of Americans who, in his view, were religious, committed to traditional moral values, and more generally conservative. On the other hand he feared that a new pseudo-religion of 'secular humanism' had conquered the commanding heights in American society and exercised an all-powerful influence through the media and the education system. America was a chosen nation, but one that had lost its way. The decisive catalyst was the Supreme Court decision of 1973 legalising abortion. But 'secular humanist' influence was seen in many other places, including the teaching of evolution in schools, the earlier Supreme Court decisions banning school prayers, and such symptoms of 'the decline of the family' as the increasing entry of mothers into the labour market, rising divorce rates and the growing tolerance of homosexuality. Yet, in spite of their combative style and frequent warnings that their nation has lost its way, the 'religious right' was in many respects in the mainstream of American opinion. For instance, they fully shared the widespread enthusiasm for free enterprise, the death penalty and uncompromising defence of American interests overseas.

The 'religious right' were as much disliked by the majority of their fellow Christians as by secularists. Yet some Christians may have secretly envied the conservatives' uninhibited style. This arose partly from the nature of their theology, but partly also from the fact that in the last quarter of the twentieth century conservative Protestants were often holding their own or even expanding, at a time when both Catholics and liberal Protestants were suffering serious losses. The latter were painfully aware of the problems that their churches faced. The many revelations concerning paedophile priests had particularly damaging effects on the Catholic self-image, as well

13 Ibid., p. 67.
14 The most accessible of the numerous books is Walter H. Capps, *The new religious right: piety, patriotism and politics* (Columbia: Columbia University Press, 1994). A stimulating interpretation (though the title has proved premature) is Steve Bruce, *The rise and fall of the new Christian right: conservative Protestant politics in America 1978–1988* (Oxford: Oxford University Press, 1988).

as on relations between clergy and laity. But most of the churches faced the problems of an ageing membership, declining resources, and a feeling of not being heard. One response to this situation was a strong strain of self-criticism and determination to learn from mistakes made in the past. An example had been set back in 1945 by German Protestants in their Stuttgart Declaration, in which they confessed that they had done too little to oppose the crimes of the Nazis. At the Rustenburg conference in 1990 a similar confession was made by South African theologians who had supported or failed to oppose apartheid. In the 1990s, John Paul II apologised for various wrongs committed by his church – sometimes in the distant past – and the Anglican church in Australia apologised for wrongs done to the aboriginals. The positive agenda springing from this determination to learn from mistakes made in the past can be summed up as what the World Council of Churches at its Vancouver assembly in 1983 called 'justice, peace and the integrity of creation'. Just as the 'religious right', while condemning much of contemporary culture, made common cause with secular conservatives on certain issues, 'mainstream' churches made common cause with secular progressives on, for instance, cancelling third world debt, anti-racism, or opposition to the death penalty. The most significant contribution of Christians to such causes has probably been at the level of action by individuals responding to the need of other individuals, in ways ranging from soup kitchens and work for aid agencies to the befriending of death row prisoners. Research in the 1990s in the United States and United Kingdom suggested that churchgoers were considerably more likely than the population as a whole to give to charities and to be active in voluntary organisations.[15]

The re-emergence of Christians in China?

The biggest question-mark at the end of the twentieth century hung over the present position and future prospects of Christianity in China. Nowhere had the fortunes of twentieth-century Christianity fluctuated so much. It was clear that Christianity was again growing in the world's most populous nation, but estimates of the extent of this growth varied wildly. The habitually optimistic Donald Barrett suggested 90 million Chinese Christians; the more circumspect Philip Jenkins proposed 50 million; and the very circumspect Bob Whyte, conscious of the numbers of false dawns in Chinese

---

15 Robin Gill, *Moral communities* (Exeter: Exeter University Press, 1992); Robert D. Putnam, *Bowling alone* (New York: Simon & Schuster, 2000), p. 67.

Christian history, was in the later 1980s reluctant to go much above 6 million.[16] In a country where Christians have only recently emerged from a period of severe persecution there are clearly many who might regard themselves as Christians but who are cautious about making any public commitment. To add to the problems of counting Christians, there are many people who read the Bible and Christian books, but stop short of declaring themselves converts. In few countries is the legal status of Christianity so unclear. Members of the officially tolerated Protestant and Catholic churches can expect rapid reprisals if they are seen as doing anything beyond what is officially allowed – and certainly any hint of political dissent would be severely punished. On the other hand it is well known that large numbers of religious meetings, sometimes involving considerable numbers of people, take place outside the officially recognised institutions. On the one hand the laws prohibit religious discrimination; yet on the other hand, it is widely believed that professing believers will face difficulties in their places of work or study and may be unable to progress in their professions. Historically, as elsewhere in Asia, Christianity has won converts from ethnic minorities and other marginalised groups. Some of the biggest growth of Christianity in recent years has been in areas of rural poverty, where faith-healings and exorcisms have attracted a lot of interest.[17] On the other hand, Christianity's present appeal is often to intellectuals or to other well-educated people, disillusioned with Marxism since the Cultural revolution. For them, Christianity appears as a 'modern' religion, which has come to terms with the post-Enlightenment world, and potentially offers the moral underpinnings which their society no longer possesses.[18]

---

16 David B. Barrett, George T. Kurian and Todd M. Johnson (eds.), *World Christian encyclopaedia*, 2 vols. (Oxford: Oxford University Press, 2001), p. 191; Jenkins, *The next Christendom*, p. 70; Bob Whyte, *Unfinished encounter: China and Christianity* (London: Fount, 1988), p. 410.

17 Whyte, *Unfinished encounter*, pp. 411–15.

18 Edmond Tang, 'The second Enlightenment: the spiritual quest of Chinese intellectuals', in T. Murayama and W. Ustorf (eds.), *Identity and marginality: Christianity in north east Asia* (Frankfurt am Main: Peter Lang, 2000), pp. 55–70.

Bibliography

Chapter 1

Barrett, David B., George T. Kurian and Todd M. Johnson, *World Christian encyclopaedia*, 2 vols. (Oxford: Oxford University Press, 2001)

Bebbington, David W., *Evangelicalism in modern Britain: a history from the 1730s to the 1980s* (London: Unwin Hyman, 1989)

Brasher, Brenda, *Give me that online religion* (San Francisco: Jossey Bass, 2001)

Conway, John S., *The Nazi persecution of the churches* (London: Weidenfeld & Nicolson, 1968)

Davie, Grace, *Religion in modern Europe: a memory mutates* (Oxford: Oxford University Press, 2000)

Davie, Grace, Paul Heelas and Linda Woodhead (eds.), *Predicting religion: Christian, secular and alternative futures* (Aldershot: Ashgate, 2003)

Ford, David F. (ed.), *The modern theologians: an introduction to Christian theology in the twentieth century*, 2nd edn (Oxford: Blackwell, 1997)

Hobsbawm, Eric J., *Age of extremes: the short twentieth century, 1914–1991* (London: Michael Joseph, 1994)

Marsden, George M., *Fundamentalism and American culture: the shaping of twentieth century Evangelicalism 1870–1925* (New York: Oxford University Press, 1980)

Martin, David, *Does Christianity cause war?* (Oxford: Oxford University Press, 1997)

Nash, David, 'Religious sensibilities in the age of the internet: freethought culture and the historical context of communication media', in Stewart M. Hoover and Lynn Schofield Clark (eds.), *Practicing religion in the age of the media: explorations in media, religion and culture* (New York: Columbia University Press, 2002), pp. 276–90

Porterfield, Amanda, *The transformation of American religion: the story of a late-twentieth-century awakening* (New York: Oxford University Press, 2001)

Steigmann-Gall, Richard, *The Holy Reich: Nazi conceptions of Christianity 1919–45* (Cambridge: Cambridge University Press, 2003)

Townshend, Charles, *Terrorism: a very short introduction* (Oxford: Oxford University Press, 2002)

Chapter 2

Bew, Paul, Peter Gibbon and Henry Patterson, *Northern Ireland, 1921–1996* (London: Serif, 1996)

Bibby, Reginald W., *Fragmented gods: the poverty and potential of religion in Canada* (Toronto: Stoddart, 1990)

Bibliography

Cox, Jeffrey, *English churches in a secular society: Lambeth 1870–1930* (Oxford: Oxford University Press, 1982)

Imperial faultlines: Christianity and colonial power in India, 1818–1940 (Stanford, CA: Stanford University Press, 2002)

Diamond, Norma, 'Christianity and the Hua Miao: writing and power', in Daniel H. Bays (ed.), *Christianity in China from the eighteenth century to the present* (Stanford, CA: Stanford University Press, 1996), pp. 138–57

Fields, Karen E., 'Christian missionaries as anticolonial militants', *Theory and society* 11 (1982), 95–108

Glazer, Nathan, and Daniel P. Moynihan, *Beyond the melting pot*, 2nd edn (Cambridge, MA: Harvard University Press, 1970)

Gugelot, Frédéric, *La conversion des intellectuels au catholicisme en France (1885–1935)* (Paris: CNRS, 1998)

Hölscher, Lucian (ed.), *Datenatlas zur religiösen Geographie im protestantischen Deutschland*, 4 vols. (Berlin: Walter De Gruyter, 2001)

Lambert, Yves, *Dieu change en Bretagne* (Paris: Editions du Cerf, 1985)

McLeod, Hugh, 'White collar values and the role of religion', in Geoffrey Crossick (ed.), *The lower middle class in Britain 1870–1914* (London: Croom Helm, 1977), pp. 61–88

'New perspectives on Victorian working class religion: the oral evidence', *Oral history* 14 (1986), 31–49

Piety and poverty: working class religion in Berlin, London and New York, 1870–1914 (New York: Holmes & Meier, 1996)

Religion and the people of western Europe, 1789–1989 (Oxford: Oxford University Press, 1997)

McRoberts, Kenneth, *Quebec: social change and political crisis*, 3rd edn (Toronto: McClelland & Stewart, 1988)

Thompson, Paul, with Tony Wailey and Trevor Lummis, *Living the fishing* (London: Routledge, 1983)

Williams, S. C., *Religious belief and popular culture: Southwark c.1880–1939* (Oxford: Oxford University Press, 1999)

Chapter 3

Bernstein, C., and M. Politi, *Holiness: John Paul II and the hidden history of our time* (London: Doubleday, 1996)

Carlen, C., IHM (ed.), *The papal encyclicals, 1846–1978*, 5 vols. (Ann Arbor: Pierian Press, 1990–7)

Chadwick, O., *Britain and the Vatican during the Second World War* (Cambridge: Cambridge University Press, 1986)

Coppa, Frank J., *The modern papacy since 1789* (London and New York: Longman, 1998)

Cornwell, J., *Like a thief in the night: the death of Pope John Paul I* (London: Viking, 1989)

Hitler's pope: the secret history of Pius XII (London: Viking, 1999)

Dwyer, J. A. (ed.), *The new dictionary of Catholic social thought* (Collegeville, MN: Liturgical Press, 1994)

Falconi, C., *The popes of the twentieth century* (London: Weidenfeld & Nicolson, 1967)

Hansom, Eric. O., *The Catholic church in world politics* (Princeton: University of Princeton Press, 1987)

Hastings, A. (ed.), *Modern Catholicism: Vatican II and after* (London: SPCK, 1992)

Hebblethwaite, P., *John XXIII: pope of the council* (London: Geoffrey Chapman, 1984)

    Paul VI: the first modern pope (London: HarperCollins, 1993)

Kent, P. C., *The pope and the duce* (London and Basingstoke: Macmillan, 1983)

    The lonely Cold War of Pius XII (Toronto: McGill-Queen's University Press, 2002)

Kent, P. C., and J. F. Pollard (eds.), *Papal diplomacy in the modern age* (Westport, CN: Praeger, 1994)

Kirby, D. (ed.), *Religion and the Cold War* (Basingstoke: Palgrave, 2003)

Leung, B., *Sino–Vatican relations: problems in conflicting authority, 1976–1986* (Cambridge: Cambridge University Press, 1992)

Levillain, P. (ed.), *The papacy: an encyclopedia*, 3 vols. (London: Routledge, 2002)

Lewy, G., *The Catholic church and Nazi Germany* (London: Weidenfeld & Nicolson, 1964)

Luxmoore, J., 'The cardinal and the communists', *The Tablet*, 2 September 2000

Luxmoore, J., and J. Babiuch, *The Vatican and the red flag: the struggle for the soul of eastern Europe* (London: Geoffrey Chapman, 1999)

Molony, J. N., *The emergence of political Catholicism in Italy: Partito Popolare: 1919–1926* (London: Croom Helm, 1977)

O'Grady, D., 'Casaroli's long march', *The Tablet*, 9 September 2000

Passalecq, G., and B. Suchecky, *The hidden encyclical of Pius XI* (New York and London: Harcourt Brace, 1997)

Pawley, B., and M. Pawley, *Rome and Canterbury through four centuries* (London and Oxford: Mowbray, 1981)

Pollard, J. F., *The Vatican and the fascist regime in Italy, 1929–1932: a study in conflict* (Cambridge: Cambridge University Press, 1985)

    The unknown pope: Benedict XV (1914–1922) and the pursuit of peace (London: Cassell, 1999)

    'The papacy in two world wars: Benedict XV and Pius XII compared', in G. Sorensen and R. Mallett (eds.), *International fascism, 1919–1945* (London: Frank Cass, 2002)

    Money and the rise of the modern papacy: financing the Vatican, 1850–1950 (Cambridge: Cambridge University Press, 2004)

Raw, C., *The money-changers: how the Vatican bank enabled Roberto Calvi to steal $4250 million for the heads of the P2 masonic lodge* (London: HarperCollins, 1992)

Rhodes, A., *The Vatican in the age of the dictators* (London: Hodder & Stoughton, 1973)

Sanchez, J., *Pius XII and the Holocaust: understanding the debate* (Washington: Catholic University of America Press, 2002)

Spinosa, A., *Pio XII: l'ultimo papa* (Milan: Mursia, 1992)

Stehle, S., *The eastern politics of the Vatican, 1917–1979* (Athens, OH: Ohio University Press, 1981), chs. IX and X

Stehlin, S., *Weimar and the Vatican, 1919–1933: German–Vatican diplomatic relations in the interwar years* (Princeton: Princeton University Press, 1983)

Walsh, M. J., *John Paul II* (London: Geoffrey Chapman, 1994)

Willey, D., *God's politician: John Paul at the Vatican* (London: Faber & Faber, 1992)

Yallop, D., *In God's name: an investigation into the murder of Pope John Paul I* (London: Corgi, 1984)

Chapter 4

Bell, G. K. A., *Documents on Christian unity*, 4 vols. (London: Oxford University Press, 1924, 1930, 1948, 1958)

Boegner, M., *The long road to unity* (London: Collins, 1970)

Bria, I., and D. Heller, *Ecumenical pilgrims* (Geneva: WCC Publications, 1995)

Clements, K., *Faith on the frontier: a life of J. H. Oldham* (Edinburgh: T&T Clark, 1999)

Ehrenstrom, N., and W. G. Muelder (eds.), *Institutionalism and church unity* (London: SCM, 1963)

Fey, H. (ed.), *The ecumenical advance: a history of the Ecumenical movement, volume 2, 1948–1968* (London: SPCK, 1970)

Gairdner, W. H. T., *Edinburgh 1910* (Edinburgh, 1910)

Gunneman, H., *The shaping of the United Church of Christ* (New York: United Church Press, 1977)

Hopkins, C. H. *John R. Mott 1865–1955, a biography* (Grand Rapids: Eerdmans, 1979)

Hudson, D., *The Ecumenical movement in world affairs* (London: Weidenfeld & Nicolson, 1969)

Iremonger, F. A. *William Temple* (London: Oxford University Press, 1948)

Jackson, E., *Red tape and the gospel* (Birmingham: Phlogiston, 1980)

Jasper, R. C. D., *Arthur Cayley Headlam: life and letters of a bishop* (London: Faith Press, 1960)
George Bell, bishop of Chichester (London: Oxford University Press, 1967)

Lossky, N., et al., *Dictionary of the ecumenical movement*, 2nd edn (Geneva: WCC Publications, 2004)

Meyer, H., and W. G. Rusch (eds.), *Growth in agreement II* (Geneva: WCC Publications, 2000)

Meyer, H., and L. Vischer (eds.), *Growth in agreement* (Geneva: World Council of Churches, 1984)

Reports of Faith and Order conferences: Lausanne 1927, Edinburgh 1937, Lund 1952, Montreal 1964, Santiago da Compostela 1993

Reports of Life and Work conferences: Stockholm 1925, Oxford 1937

Reports of World Council of Churches assemblies: Amsterdam 1948, Evanston 1954, New Delhi 1961, Uppsala 1968, Nairobi 1975, Vancouver 1983, Canberra 1991, Harare 1998

Reports of World Missionary conferences: Edinburgh 1910, Jerusalem 1928, Tambaram 1938

Rouse, R., and S. C. Neill, *A history of the Ecumenical movement, 1517–1948* (London: SPCK, 1954)

Ruedi-Weber, H., *Asia and the Ecumenical movement* (London: SCM, 1966)

Schmidt, S., *Augustin Bea, the cardinal of unity* (New Rochelle, NY: New City Press, 1992)

Sundkler, B., *Church of South India: the movement towards union, 1900–1947* (London: Lutterworth, 1954)
Nathan Söderblom: his life and work (London: Lutterworth, 1968)

Wilson, B. R., *Religion in secular society* (London: Watts, 1966)

World Missionary Conference 1910: Report of Commission VIII, co-operation and the promotion of unity (Edinburgh: Oliphant, Anderson and Ferrier, 1910)

Chapter 5

Barrett, David, et al., *World Christian encyclopedia*, 2nd edn, 2 vols. (Oxford: Oxford University Press, 2002) de Benoist, Joseph-Roger, *Eglise et pouvoir colonial au Soudan français* (Paris: Karthala, 1987)

Clements, Keith, *Faith on the frontier: a life of J. H. Oldham* (Edinburgh: T&T Clark, 1999)

Cooper, Frederick, *Decolonization and African society* (Cambridge: Cambridge University Press, 1996)

Farah, Rariq, *In troubled waters: a history of the Anglican church in Jerusalem 1841–1998* (Dorset: Christians Aware, 2002)

Hastings, Adrian, *The church in Africa 1450–1950* (Oxford: Clarendon Press, 1994)

'The clash of nationalism and universalism within twentieth-century missionary Christianity', unpublished paper, 2001

Hogan, Edmund H., *The Irish missionary movement: a historical survey 1830–1980* (Dublin: Gill & Macmillan, 1990)

Holtrop, Pieter N., and Hugh McLeod, *Missions and missionaries* (Woodbridge, Suffolk: Boydell Press, 2000)

Jedin, H., *The history of the church, volume X: the church in the modern age* (London: Burnes & Oates, 1981)

Jenkins, Philip, *The next Christendom: the coming of global Christianity* (Oxford: Oxford University Press, 2002)

Kraemer, Hendrik, *The Christian message in the non-Christian world* (London: Edinburgh House Press, 1938)

Martin, David, *Pentecostalism: the world their parish* (Oxford: Blackwell, 2002)

Nguyen, Huy Lai, 'Vietnam', in Adrian Hastings (ed.), *The church and the nations* (London: Sheed & Ward, 1959), pp. 171–92

Oliver, Roland, *The missionary factor in east Africa* (London: Longmans, 1952)

Orr, Rodney, 'African American missionaries to east Africa, 1900–1926: a study in the ethnic reconnection of the gospel', PhD dissertation, University of Edinburgh, 1999

Picciola, André, *Missionaires en Afrique: l'Afrique occidentale de 1840 a 1940* (Paris: Denoel, 1987)

Quinn, Frederick, *The French overseas empire* (Westport, CN: Praeger, 2000)

Said, Edward, *Out of place: a memoir* (New York: Alfred Knopf, 1999)

Shehata, Samy, 'An evaluation of the mission of the Episcopal church in Egypt 1918–1925', MA dissertation, Birmingham university, 2001

Shelley, Michael T., 'The life and thought of W. H. T. Gairdner 1873–1928: a critical evaluation of a scholar-missionary', PhD dissertation, Birmingham university, 1988

Stacpoole, Alberic (ed.), *Vatican II by those who were there* (London: Chapman, 1986)

Stanley, Brian, *The Bible and the flag: Protestant missions and British imperialism in the nineteenth and twentieth centuries* (Leicester: Apollos, 1990)

Sundquist, Scott W., *A dictionary of Asian Christianity* (Grand Rapids: Eerdmans, 2001)

Tuck, Patrick J. N., *French Catholic missionaries and the politics of imperialism in Vietnam, 1857–1914* (Liverpool: Liverpool University Press, 1987)

Yates, Timothy, *Christian mission in the twentieth century* (Cambridge: Cambridge University Press, 1994)

Chapter 6

Anderson, Allan, *An introduction to Pentecostalism: global charismatic Christianity* (Cambridge: Cambridge University Press, 2004)

Bibliography

Anderson, Allan, and Edmond Tang (eds.), *Asian and Pentecostal: the charismatic face of Asian Christianity* (Oxford: Regnum, 2005)

Anderson, Robert M., *Vision of the disinherited: the making of American Pentecostalism* (Oxford: Oxford University Press, 1979)

Barrett, D. B., and T. M. Johnson, 'Annual statistical table on global mission: 2003', *International bulletin of missionary research* 27:1 (2003), 24–5

Bartleman, Frank, *Azusa Street* (S. Plainfield, NJ: Bridge Publishing, 1980)

Berg, Mike, and Paul Pretiz, *Spontaneous combustion: grass-roots Christianity Latin American style* (Pasadena, CA: William Carey Library, 1996)

Burgess, S. M., and E. M. van der Maas (eds.), *New international dictionary of Pentecostal and Charismatic movements* (Grand Rapids: Zondervan, 2002)

Cox, Harvey, *Fire from heaven: the rise of Pentecostal spirituality and the reshaping of religion in the twenty-first century* (London: Cassell, 1996)

Dayton, Donald W., *Theological roots of Pentecostalism* (Metuchen, NJ and London: Scarecrow Press, 1987)

Faupel, D. William, *The everlasting gospel: the significance of eschatology in the development of Pentecostal thought* (Sheffield: Sheffield Academic Press, 1996)

Gifford, Paul, *African Christianity: its public role* (London: Hurst, 1998)

Hedlund, Roger E. (ed.), *Christianity is Indian: the emergence of an indigenous community* (Delhi: ISPCK, 2000)

Hollenweger, Walter J., *The Pentecostals* (London: SCM, 1972)

Hoover, Willis C., *History of the Pentecostal revival in Chile* (Santiago: Imprenta Eben-Ezer, 2000)

Johnstone, P., and J. Mandryk, *Operation world: 21st century edition* (Carlisle: Paternoster, 2001)

Kay, William K., *Pentecostals in Britain* (Carlisle: Paternoster, 2000)

Martin, David, *Tongues of fire: the explosion of Protestantism in Latin America* (Oxford: Blackwell, 1990)

McGee, Gary B., '"Latter rain" falling in the east: early-twentieth-century Pentecostalism in India and the debate over speaking in tongues', *Church history* 68:3 (1999), 648–65

Synan, Vinson, *The Holiness-Pentecostal tradition: Charismatic movements in the twentieth century* (Grand Rapids and Cambridge: Eerdmans, 1997)

Chapter 7

Anderson, Allan, *Zion and Pentecost: the spirituality and experience of Pentecostal and Zionist/Apostolic churches in South Africa* (Pretoria: University of South Africa Press, 2000)
  African reformation: African initiated Christianity in the 20th century (Trenton, NJ and Asmara, Eritrea: Africa World Press, 2001)

Anderson, Allan, and Edmond Tang (eds.), *Asian and Pentecostal: the charismatic face of Asian Christianity* (Oxford: Regnum, 2005)

Barrie-Anthony, Steven, 'India, religion in contemporary', in J. Gordon Melton and Martin Baumann (eds.), *Religions of the world: a comprehensive encyclopedia of beliefs and practices*, 4 vols. (Santa Barbara, CA: ABC-Clio, 2002) vol. II, pp. 627–35

Bays, Daniel, 'Christian revival in China, 1900–1937', in Edith L. Blumhofer and Randall Balmer (eds.), *Modern Christian revivals* (Chicago: University of Illinois Press, 1993)

Daneel, Marthinus, *Old and new in southern Shona Independent churches*, vol. 1 (The Hague: Mouton, 1971)

Quest for belonging (Gweru, Zimbabwe: Mambo Press, 1987)

Deng Zhaoming, *The torch of the testimony in China* (Hong Kong: Christian Study Centre on Chinese Religion & Culture, 1998)

Gao Shining, 'Twenty-first century Chinese Christianity and the Chinese social process', *China study journal* 15:2/3 (December 2000), 14–18

Grenfell, James, 'Simâo Toco: an Angolan prophet', *Journal of religion in Africa* 28:2 (1998), 210–26

Harper, Ann C., 'The Iglesia Ni Cristo and evangelical Christianity', *Journal of Asian mission* 3:1 (2001), 101–19

Harper, George W., 'Philippine tongues of fire? Latin American Pentecostalism and the future of Filipino Christianity', *Journal of Asian mission* 2:2 (2000), 225–59

Hastings, Adrian, *A history of African Christianity 1950–1975* (Cambridge: Cambridge University Press, 1979)

The church in Africa 1450–1950 (Oxford: Clarendon Press, 1994)

Hedlund, Roger E., *Quest for identity: India's churches of indigenous origin* (Delhi: ISPCK, 2000)

Hedlund, Roger E. (ed.), *Christianity is Indian: the emergence of an indigenous community* (Delhi: ISPCK, 2000)

Hoehler-Fatton, Cynthia, *Women of fire and spirit: history, faith and gender in Roho religion in western Kenya* (Oxford: Oxford University Press, 1996)

Isichei, Elizabeth, *A history of Christianity in Africa* (London: SCM, 1995)

Johnstone, P., and J. Mandryk, *Operation world: 21st century edition* (Carlisle: Paternoster, 2001)

Lambert, Tony, *Resurrection of the Chinese church*, 2nd edn (Chicago: OMF, 1994)

Leung Ka-lung, *The rural churches of mainland China since 1978* (Hong Kong: Alliance Bible Seminary, 1999)

Maggay, Melba P., 'Towards sensitive engagement with Filipino indigenous consciousness', *International review of mission* 87:346 (1998), 361–73

Martin, Marie-Louise, *Kimbangu: an African prophet and his church* (Oxford: Blackwell, 1975)

Peel, J. D. Y., *Aladura: a religious movement among the Yoruba* (Oxford: Oxford University Press, 1968)

Salazar, Robert C. (ed.), *New religious movements in Asia and the Pacific Islands: implications for church and society* (Manila: De La Salle University Press, 1994)

Somaratna, G. P. V., *Origins of the Pentecostal mission in Sri Lanka* (Nugegoda: Margaya Fellowship, 1996)

Sundkler, B. G. M., *Zulu Zion and some Swazi Zionists* (London: Oxford University Press, 1976)

Turner, Harold W., *History of an African Independent church (1) The Church of the Lord (Aladura)* (Oxford: Clarendon Press, 1967)

Religious innovation in Africa (Boston, MA: G.K. Hall, 1979)

Waehrisch-Oblau, Claudia, 'Healing prayers and healing testimonies in mainland Chinese churches', *China study journal* 14:2 (August 1999), 5–21

Chapter 8

Abrams, R. H., *Preachers present arms: the role of the American churches and clergy in World Wars I and II, with some observations on the war in Vietnam* (Scottdale, PA: Herald Press, 1969)

Bailey, C. E., 'The British Protestant theologians in the First World War: Germanophobia unleashed', *Harvard theological review* 77 (1984), 195–221

Becker, A., *War and faith: the religious imagination in France, 1914–1930* (Oxford: Berg, 1998)

Becker, A., and S. Audoin-Rouzeau, *1914–1918: understanding the Great War* (London: Profile Books, 2002)

Brown, S. J., '"A solemn purification by fire": responses to the Great War in the Scottish Presbyterian churches', *Journal of ecclesiastical history* 45 (1994), 82–104

Chickering, R., *Imperial Germany and the Great War, 1914–1918* (Cambridge: Cambridge University Press, 1998)

Cornwall, M., *The undermining of Austria-Hungary: the battle for hearts and minds* (Basingstoke: Macmillan, 2000)

Crerar, D., *Padres in no man's land: Canadian chaplains and the Great War* (Montreal: McGill-Queen's University Press, 1995)

Dansette, A., *Religious history of modern France volume II: under the Third Republic* (Edinburgh: Nelson, 1961)

Hoover, A. J., *The gospel of nationalism: German patriotic preaching from Napoleon to Versailles* (Stuttgart: Franz Steiner, 1986)

  God, Germany, and Britain in the Great War: a study in clerical nationalism (New York: Praeger, 1989)

Hope, N., *German and Scandinavian Protestantism 1700–1918* (Oxford: Clarendon Press, 1995)

Krumeich, G., and H. Lehmann (eds.), *'Gott mit uns': Nation, Religion und Gewalt im 19. und frühen 20. Jahrhundert* (Göttingen: Vandenhoeck und Ruprecht, 2000)

McKernan, M., *Australian churches at war: attitudes and activities of the major churches 1914–1918* (Sydney and Canberra: Catholic Theological Faculty and Australian War Memorial, 1980)

McMillan, J. F., 'French Catholics: *rumeurs infâmes* and the *union sacrée*, 1914–1918', in F. Coetzee and M. Shevin-Coetzee (eds.), *Authority, identity and the social history of the Great War* (Providence and Oxford: Berghahn Books, 1995)

Missalla, H., *'Gott mit uns' – die deutsche katholische Kriegspredigt 1914–1918* (Munich: Kösel, 1968)

Moses, J. A., 'The British and German churches and the perception of war, 1908–1914', *War and society* 5 (1987), 23–44

  'State, war, revolution and the German Evangelical church, 1914–18', *Journal of religious history* 17 (1992), 47–59

Nagler, J., 'Pandora's box: propaganda and war hysteria in the United States during World War I', in R. Chickering and S. Förster (eds.), *Great War, total war: combat and mobilization on the western front, 1914–1918* (Cambridge: Cambridge University Press, 2000)

Perry, N., and L. Echeverría, *Under the heel of Mary* (London: Routledge, 1988)

Piper, J. F., *The American churches in World War I* (Athens, OH: Ohio University Press, 1985)

Pollard, J. F., *The unknown pope: Benedict XV (1914–1922) and the pursuit of peace* (London: Geoffrey Chapman, 1999)

Pressel, W., *Die Kriegspredigt 1914–1918 in der evangelischen Kirche Deutschlands* (Göttingen: Vandenhoeck und Ruprecht, 1967)

Schweitzer, R., *The cross and the trenches: religious faith and doubt among British and American Great War soldiers* (Westport, CT: Prager, 2003)

Sherman, D. J., 'Bodies and names: the emergence of commemoration in interwar France', *American historical review* 103 (1998), 443–66

Snape, M., *God and the British soldier* (London: Routledge, 2005)

Strachan, H., *The First World War volume I: to arms* (Oxford: Oxford University Press, 2001)

The First World War: a new illustrated history (London: Simon and Schuster, 2003)

Wilkinson, A., *The Church of England and the First World War* (London: SPCK, 1978)

Dissent or conform? War, peace and the English churches, 1900–1945 (London: SCM, 1986)

Živojinović, D. R., 'Pope Benedict XV's peace efforts (1914–1917)', in R. Bosworth and G. Cresciani (eds.), *Altro polo: a volume of Italian studies* (Sydney: University of Sydney Press, 1979)

Chapter 9

Agostino, M., *Le Pape Pie XI et l'opinion publique (1922–1939)* (Rome: Ecole Française de Rome, 1991)

Altermatt, U., *Der Weg der Schweizer Katholiken ins Ghetto*, 2nd edn (Zurich: Benziger, 1991)

Bakvis, H., *Catholic power in the Netherlands* (Kingston and Montreal: McGill-Queen's University Press, 1981)

Baranowski, S., *The Confessing Church, conservative elites and the Nazi state* (Lewiston: Edwin Mellen, 1986)

Buchanan, T., and M. Conway (eds.), *Political Catholicism in Europe 1918–1965* (Oxford: Oxford University Press, 1996)

Carsten, F. L., *Fascist movements in Austria: from Schönerer to Hitler* (London and Beverly Hills: Sage, 1977)

Conway, M., 'Building the Christian city: Catholics and politics in inter-war Francophone Belgium', *Past and present* 128 (1990), 117–51

Catholic politics in Europe (London and New York: Routledge, 1997)

Delbreil, J.-C., *Centrisme et démocratie chrétienne en France: le Parti Démocrate Populaire des origines au MRP (1919–1944)* (Paris: Sorbonne, 1990)

Durand, J.-D., *L'Europe de la démocratie chrétienne* (Brussels: Complexe, 1995)

Fouilloux, E., 'Le catholicisme', in J.-M. Mayeur (ed.), *Histoire du Christianisme*, vol. XII (Paris: Desclée-Fayard, 1990), pp. 116–239

Garvik, O. (ed.), *Kristelig Folkeparti. Mellom tro og makt* (Oslo: Cappelen, 1983)

Gellott, L., 'Defending Catholic interests in the Christian state: the role of Catholic Action in Austria 1933–1938', *The Catholic historical review* 74 (1988), 571–89

Gerard, E., *De Katholieke Partij in crisis: partijpolitiek leven in België (1918–1940)* (Leuven: Kritak, 1985)

Helmreich, E. C., *The German churches under Hitler: background, struggle and epilogue* (Detroit: Wayne State University Press, 1979)

Jelinek, Y., *The parish republic: Hlinka's Slovak People's Party 1939–1945* (New York and London: East European Quarterly, 1976)

Bibliography

Kaiser, W., and H. Wohnout (eds.), *Political Catholicism in Europe 1918–45*, vol. 1 (London and New York: Routledge, 2004)

Kalyvas, S., *The rise of Christian Democracy in Europe* (Ithaca and London: Cornell University Press, 1996)

Keogh, D., *The Vatican, the bishops and Irish politics 1919–39* (Cambridge: Cambridge University Press, 1986)

Kossmann, E. H., *The Low Countries 1780–1940* (Oxford: Oxford University Press, 1978)

Kselman, T., and J. Buttigieg (eds.), *European Christian democracy: historical legacies and comparative perspectives* (Notre Dame: Notre Dame University Press, 2003)

Lannon, F., *Privilege, persecution and prophecy: the Catholic church in Spain, 1875–1975* (Oxford: Oxford University Press, 1987)

Lundkvist, S., 'Popular movements and reforms', in S. Koblik (ed.), *Sweden's development from poverty to affluence 1750–1970* (Minneapolis: University of Minnesota Press, 1975), pp. 180–93

McMillan, J., 'Catholicism and nationalism in France: the case of the *Fédération Nationale Catholique*, 1924–1939', in F. Tallett and N. Atkin (eds.), *Catholicism in Britain and France since 1789* (London and Rio Grande: Hambledon, 1996), pp. 151–63

Moeller, R. G., *German peasants and agrarian politics, 1914–1924: the Rhineland and Westphalia* (Chapel Hill and London: University of North Carolina Press, 1986)

Moro, R., *La formazione della classe dirigente cattolica* (Bologna: Il Mulino, 1979)

Morsey, R., *Der Untergang des politischen Katholizismus: die Zentrumspartei zwischen christlichem Selbstverständnis und 'nationaler Erhebung' 1932–1933* (Stuttgart and Zurich: Belser, 1977)

Patch, W., *The Christian trade unions in the Weimar Republic 1918–1933: the failure of 'corporate pluralism'* (New Haven and London: Yale University Press, 1985)

Pollard, J., *The Vatican and Italian fascism 1929–1932* (Cambridge: Cambridge University Press, 1985)

Przeciszewski, M., 'L'association catholique de la jeunesse académique, "Odrodzenie" (La Renaissance): aperçu historique', *Revue du nord* 70 (1988), 333–47

Righart, H., *De katholieke zuil in Europa* (Meppel: Boom, 1986)

Schwarz-Lausten, M., *A church history of Denmark* (Aldershot and Burlington: Ashgate, 2002)

Spinka, M., 'The religious situation in Czechoslovakia', in R. Kerner (ed.), *Czechoslovakia: twenty years of independence* (Berkeley and Los Angeles: University of California Press, 1940), pp. 284–301

Stehlin, S., 'The emergence of a new Vatican diplomacy during the Great War and its aftermath, 1914–1929', in P. Kent and J. Pollard (eds.), *Papal diplomacy in the modern age* (Westport, CT and London: Praeger, 1994), pp. 75–85

Steigmann-Gall, R., *The Holy Reich: Nazi conceptions of Christianity 1919–1945* (Cambridge: Cambridge University Press, 2003)

Vardys, V. S., *The Catholic church, dissent and nationality in Soviet Lithuania* (Boulder: East European Quarterly, 1978)

Vincent, M., *Catholicism in the Second Spanish Republic: religion and politics in Salamanca 1930–1936* (Oxford: Oxford University Press, 1996)

Wintle, M., *Pillars of piety: religion in the Netherlands in the nineteenth century* (Hull: Hull University Press, 1987)

Wright, J. R. C., *'Above parties': the political attitudes of the German Protestant church leadership 1918–1933* (Oxford: Oxford University Press, 1974)

Wolff, R. J., and J. K. Hoensch (eds.), *Catholics, the state and the European radical right 1919–1945* (Boulder: Social Science Monographs, 1987)

Chapter 10

Abel, Christopher, *Política, iglesia y partidos en Colombia* (Bogotá: FAES/Universidad Nacional de Colombia, 1987)

Badanelli, Pedro, *Perón, la iglesia y un cura* (Buenos Aires: Editorial Tartessos, 1960)

Bailey, David C., *Viva Cristo Rey: the Cristero rebellion and the church-state conflict in Mexico* (Bloomington: Indiana University Press, 1974)

Bruneau, Thomas, *The political transformation of the Brazilian Catholic church* (Cambridge: Cambridge University Press, 1974)

The church in Brazil: the politics of religion (Austin: University of Texas Press, 1982)

Câmara, Dom Helder, *The conversions of a bishop*, an interview with José de Broucker (London: Collins, 1977)

Falcoff, Mark, and Fredrick B. Pike (eds.), *The Spanish Civil war, 1936–39: American hemispheric perspectives* (Lincoln, NE: University of Nebraska Press, 1982)

Gabaglia, L. P. R., *O Cardeal Leme 1882–1942* (Rio de Janeiro: Livraria José Olympio, 1962)

Garrard-Burnett, Virginia, *Protestantism in Guatemala: living in the new Jerusalem* (Austin: University of Texas Press, 1998)

Griffiths, Leslie, 'Religion and the search for identity: campaigning against Voodoo and illiteracy in Haiti, 1939–43', in Holger Bernt Hansen and Michael Twaddle (eds.), *Christian missionaries and the state in the third world* (Oxford: James Currey, 2002), pp. 255–65

Ivereigh, Austen, *Catholicism and politics in Argentina 1810–1960* (Basingstoke: Macmillan, 1995)

Ivereigh, Austen (ed.), *Politics of religion in an age of revival: studies in nineteenth century Europe and Latin America* (London: Institute of Latin American Studies, 2000)

Londoño-Vega, Patricia, *Religion, culture and society in Colombia: Medellín and Antioquia 1870–1930* (Oxford: Oxford University Press, 2002)

Lundius, Jan, and Mats Lundahl, *Peasants and religion: a socioeconomic study of Dios Olivorio and the Padre Sola movement in the Dominican Republic* (London: Routledge, 2000)

Lynch, John, 'The Catholic church in Latin America, 1830–1930', in Leslie Bethell (ed.), *The Cambridge history of Latin America Vol. IV c.1870–c.1930* (Cambridge: Cambridge University Press, 1986), pp. 527–96

Mecham, J. Lloyd, *Church and state in Latin America: a history of politico-ecclesiastical relations*, revd edn (Durham, NC: University of North Carolina Press, 1968)

Meyer, Jean A., *The Cristero rebellion: the Mexican people between church and state 1926–1929*, trans. Richard Southern (Cambridge: Cambridge University Press, 1976)

Pike, Fredrick B., *Hispanismo: Spanish liberals and conservatives and their relations with Spanish America, 1898–1936* (Notre Dame: Louisiana State University Press, 1971)

Smith, Brian, *The church and politics in Chile* (Princeton: Princeton University Press, 1982)

Watters, Mary, *A history of the church in Venezuela 1810–1930* (Durham, NC: University of North Carolina Press, 1933)

Yaremko, Jason, *U.S. Protestant missions in eastern Cuba, 1898–1935: salvation and conflict in the cradle of independence* (Ann Arbor: UMI, 1998)

Chapter 11

Anderson, Allan, *African reformation: African initiated Christianity in the 20th century* (Trenton, NJ: Africa World Press, 2001)

Baeta, C. G. (ed.), *Christianity in tropical Africa* (London: Oxford University Press, 1968)

Beetham, T. A., *Christianity and the new Africa* (London: Pall Mall, 1967)

Berger, E., *Labour, race and colonial rule, 1924–1960* (Oxford: Clarendon Press, 1974)

Birmingham, D., *The decolonization of Africa* (Athens, OH: Ohio University Press, 1995)

Bowman, N. M., 'Democracy without religion', *Life and work* 28:4 (October 1947), 111

Elphinck, R., and R. Davenport (eds.), *Christianity in South Africa* (Oxford: James Currey, 1997)

Esedebe, P. O., *Pan Africanism: the idea and movement* (Enugu: Fourth Dimension Publishers, 1980)

Gifford, P., *African Christianity: its public role* (Bloomington: Indiana University Press, 1998)

Hansen, H. B., and M. Twaddle (eds.), *Christian missionaries and the state in the third world* (Oxford: James Currey, 2002)

Hastings, A., *The church in Africa, 1450–1950* (Oxford: Clarendon Press, 1994)

Kalu, O. U., *Divided people of God: church union movement in Nigeria: 1876–1996* (New York: NOK Publishers, 1978)

   Power, poverty and prayer: the challenges of poverty and pluralism in African Christianity, 1960–1996 (Frankfurt: Peter Lang, 2000)

   'Doing mission through the post office: the Naked Faith people of Igboland, 1920–1960', *Neue Zeitschrift für Missionswissenschaft* 54:4 (2000), 263–80

Linden, I., *Catholics, peasants and Chewa resistance in Nyasaland, 1889–1939* (Berkeley: University of California Press, 1974)

Martin, Marie-Louise, *Kimbangu* (Oxford: Blackwell, 1975)

Papini, Robert, 'Carl Faye's transcript of Isaiah Shembe's testimony of his early life and calling', *Journal of religion in Africa* 1:1 (1967), 1–32

Peel, J., *Aladura* (London: Oxford University Press, 1968)

Roberts, A. D. (ed.), *The colonial moment in Africa* (Cambridge: Cambridge University Press, 1990)

Spear, T., and N. Kimambo (eds.), *East African expression of Christianity* (Oxford: James Currey, 1999)

Sundkler, B., and C. Steed (eds.), *A history of the church in Africa* (Cambridge: Cambridge University Press, 2000)

Tasie, G. O. M., *Thoughts and voices of an African church: Christ Army church, Nigeria* (Jos: Connack Nigeria Ltd, 1997)

Temu, A. J., *British Protestant missions* (London: Longmans, 1972)

Turner, H. W., 'Pagan features in west African Independent churches', *Practical anthropology* 12:4 (1965), 145–51

'A typology for African religious movements', *Journal of religion in Africa* 1:1 (1967), 1–32
Webster, J. B., *African churches among the Yoruba, 1888–1922* (Oxford: Clarendon Press, 1964)

Chapter 12

Aleyne, Mervyn, *Roots of Jamaican culture* (London: Pluto Press, 1998)
Austin-Broos, Diane, *Jamaica genesis: religion and the politics of moral orders* (Chicago: University of Chicago Press, 1997)
Bisnauth, Dale, *History of religions in the Caribbean* (Kingston, Jamaica: Kingston Publishers, 1996)
Curtin, Paul, *Two Jamaicas: the role of ideas in a tropical colony, 1830–1865* (Cambridge, MA: Harvard University Press, 1955)
   The rise and fall of the plantation complex (Cambridge: Cambridge University Press, 1990)
Dayfoot, Arthur Charles, *The shaping of the West Indian church 1492–1962* (Kingston, Jamaica: University of the West Indies Press, 1999)
Gerloff, Roswith, *A plea for British Black Theologies: the black church movement in Britain in its transatlantic cultural and theological interaction*, Intercultural History of Christianity 77, 2 vols. (Frankfurt am Main: Peter Lang, 1992)
   '"Africa as laboratory of the world": the African Christian diaspora in Europe as challenge to mission and ecumenical relations', in *Mission is crossing frontiers* (Pietermaritzburg: Cluster, 2003), pp. 343–81.
Glazier, Stephen D., *Perspectives on Pentecostalism: case studies from the Caribbean and Latin America* (New York and London: University Press of America, 1980)
Gordon, Shirley C., *God Almighty, make me free: Christianity in pre-emancipation Jamaica* (Burton Sankeralli: Trinidad and Tobago CCC, 1994)
Gossai, Hemchand, and Nathaniel Samuel Murrell, *Religion, culture and tradition in the Caribbean* (London and Basingstoke: Macmillan, 2000)
Lampe, Armands (ed.), *Christianity in the Caribbean – essays on church history* (Barbados: University of the West Indies Press, 2001)
Lawson, Winston Arthur, *Religion and race: African and European roots in conflict – a Jamaican testament*. Research in Religion and Family: Black Perspectives 4 (New York: Peter Lang, 1996)
Lowenthal, David, *West Indian societies* (London: Oxford University Press, 1972)
Osborne, Francis J., and G. Johnston, *Coastlands and islands* (Kingston, Jamaica: UTCWI, 1972)
Pulis, John W., *Religion, diaspora, and cultural identity: a reader in the Anglophone Caribbean* (Amsterdam: Gordon and Breach, 1999)
Russell, Horace O., *Foundations and anticipations: the Jamaica Baptist story 1783–1892* (Columbus, GA: Brentwood Christian Press, 1993)
Segal, Ronald, *The black diaspora* (London and Boston: Faber&Faber, 1995)
Simpson, George Eaton, *Black religions in the new world* (New York: Columbia University Press, 1978)
Stewart, Robert J., *Religion and society in post-emancipation Jamaica* (Knoxville: University of Tennessee Press, 1992)

Toulis, Nicole Rodriguez, *Believing identity: Pentecostalism and the mediation of Jamaican ethnicity and gender in England* (Oxford and New York: Berg, 1997)

Turner, Mary, *Slaves and missionaries: the disintegration of Jamaican slave society 1787–1834* (Urbana: University of Illinois Press, 1982)

Warner, R. Stephen, and Judith G. Wittner (eds.), *Gatherings in diaspora: religious communities and the new immigration* (Philadelphia: Temple University Press, 1998)

Williams, Lewin, *Caribbean theology*, Research in Religion and Family: Black Perspectives 2 (New York: Peter Lang, 1994)

Wilmore, Gayraud S., *Black religion and black radicalism*, 2nd edn (Maryknoll, NY: Orbis, 1983)

Yorke, Gosnell, 'The Bible in the black diaspora: links with African Christianity', in Gerald O. West and Musa W. Dube (eds.), *The Bible in Africa: transactions, trajectories and trends* (Leiden: Brill, 2000), pp. 127–49.

Chapter 13

Blumhofer, Edith L., *Aimee Semple McPherson: everybody's sister* (Grand Rapids: Eerdmans, 1993)

Burkett, Randall K., *Garveyism as a religious movement: the institutionalization of a black civil religion* (Metuchen, NJ: Scarecrow Press, 1978)

'The Baptist church in years of crisis: J. C. Austin and Pilgrim Baptist church, 1912–1950', in Hans A. Baer and Merrill Singer (eds.), *African-American religion in the twentieth century: varieties of protest and accommodation* (Knoxville: University of Tennessee Press, 1992)

Carpenter, Joel A., 'Fundamentalist institutions and the rise of evangelical Protestantism, 1929–1942', *Church history* 49 (1980), 62–75

Carpenter, Ronald H., *Father Charles E. Coughlin: surrogate spokesman for the disaffected* (Westport, CT: Greenwood Press, 1998)

Census of religious bodies, 1936, Washington, DC: Department of Commerce, 1939–1940

Conkin, Paul, *When all the gods trembled* (Lanham, MD: Rowman and Littlefield, 1998)

DeBerg, Betty A., *Ungodly women: gender and the first wave of American fundamentalism* (Minneapolis: Augsberg Fortress, 1990)

Egerton, John, *Speak now against the day: the generation before the Civil Rights movement in the south* (Chapel Hill: University of North Carolina Press, 1994)

Fauset, Arthur Huff (1944), *Black gods of the metropolis: Negro religious cults of the urban north* (Philadelphia: University of Pennsylvania Press, 2000)

Flynn, George Q., *American Catholics and the Roosevelt presidency* (Lexington: University of Kentucky Press, 1968)

Fox, Richard Wightman, 'Epitaph for Middletown: Robert S. Lynd and the analysis of consumer culture', in Richard Wightman Fox and T. J. Jackson Lears (eds.), *The culture of consumption* (New York: Pantheon Books, 1973)

Griffith, R. Marie, 'Female suffering and religious devotion in American Pentecostalism', in Margaret Lamberts Bendroth and Virginia Lieson Brereton (eds.), *Women and twentieth-century Protestantism* (Urbana: University of Illinois Press, 2002)

Halsey, William, *The survival of American innocence: Catholicism in an era of disillusionment 1920–1940* (Notre Dame: University of Notre Dame Press, 1980)

Handy, Robert T., 'The American religious depression, 1925–1935', *Church history* 24 (1960), 3–16

Hangen, Tona J., *Redeeming the dial: radio, religion, and popular culture in America* (Chapel Hill: University of North Carolina Press, 2002)

Heineman, Kenneth J., *A Catholic New Deal: religion and reform in Depression Pittsburgh* (University Park: Pennsylvania State University Press, 1999)

Kincheloe, Samuel C., *Research memorandum on religion in the Depression* (New York: Social Science Research Council, 1937)

Lynd, Robert S., and Helen Merrell Lynd, *Middletown in transition: a study in cultural conflicts* (New York: Harcourt, Brace, and Co., 1937)

Marty, Martin E., *The noise of conflict, 1919–1941* (Chicago: University of Chicago Press, 1991)

McDannell, Colleen, *Material Christianity: religion and popular culture in America* (New Haven: Yale University Press, 1995)

Picturing faith: photography and the Great Depression (New Haven: Yale University Press, 2004)

Miller, William D., *A harsh and dreadful love; Dorothy Day and the Catholic worker movement* (New York, Liveright, 1973)

O'Brien, David, *American Catholics and social reform: the New Deal years* (New York: Oxford University Press, 1968)

Orsi, Robert A., *The Madonna of 115th Street: faith and community in Italian Harlem* (New Haven: Yale University Press, 1988)

Thank you St. Jude: women's devotion to the patron saint of hopeless causes (New Haven: Yale University Press, 1996)

Stein, Judith, *The world of Marcus Garvey: race and class in modern society* (Baton Rouge: Louisiana State University Press, 1985)

Sterne, Evelyn Savidge, *Ballots and Bibles: ethnic politics and the Catholic Church in Providence* (Ithaca, NY: Cornell University Press, 2004)

Warren, Heather A., *Theologians of a new world order: Reinhold Niebuhr and the Christian realists, 1920–1948* (New York: Oxford University Press, 1997)

Watts, Jill, *God, Harlem U.S.A: the Father Divine story* (Berkeley: University of California Press, 1992)

Chapter 14

Breward, Ian, *A history of the churches in Australasia* (Oxford and New York: Oxford University Press, 2000)

Davidson, Allan, and Peter Lineham, *Transplanted Christianity: documents illustrating aspects of New Zealand church history*, 3rd edn (Palmerston North: Department of History, Massey University, 1995)

Engel, Frank, *Christians in Australia: times of change 1918–1978* (Melbourne: Joint Board of Christian Education, 1993)

Forman, Charles, *The Island churches of the South Pacific: emergence in the twentieth century* (Maryknoll, NY: Orbis, 1982)

Garrett, John, *The history of Christianity in Oceania. Vol. II Footsteps in the sea: Christianity in Oceania to World War II; vol. III Where nets were cast* (Suva: Institute of Pacific Studies with University of the South Pacific and World Council of Churches, 1992, 1997)

Harris, John, *One blood: 200 years of Aboriginal encounter with Christianity, a story of hope* (Sutherland, NSW: Albatross Books, 1990)

Henderson, J. M., *Ratana: the man, the church, the political movement* (Wellington: A. H. & A. W. Reed, 1972)

Howe, K. R., Robert C. Kiste and Brij V. Lal (eds.), *Tides of history: the Pacific Islands in the twentieth century* (St Leonards, NSW: Allen and Unwin, 1994)

Inglis, K. S., *Sacred places: war memorials in the Australian landscape* (Carlton, Vic.: Miegunyah Press at Melbourne University Press, 1999)

International Missionary Council, *Beyond the reef: records of the Conference of Churches and Missions in the Pacific, Malua theological college, Western Samoa, 22 April–4 May 1961* (London: International Missionary Council, 1961)

Kaye, Bruce (ed.), *Anglicanism in Australia: a history* (Carlton, Vic.: Melbourne University Press, 2002)

Macintyre, A. J., and J. J. Macintyre, *Country towns in Victoria: a social survey* (Carlton, Vic.: Melbourne University Press, 1944)

Massam, Katharine, *Sacred threads: Catholic spirituality in Australia 1922–1962* (Sydney: University of New South Wales Press, 1996)

O'Farrell, Patrick, *Catholic church and community: an Australian history*, 3rd edn (Sydney: University of New South Wales Press, 1992)

Phillips, W. W., 'Religion', in Wray Vamplew (ed.), *Australians: historical statistics* (Broadway, NSW: Fairfax, Syme & Weldon, 1987), pp. 421–7

Piggin, Stuart, *Evangelical Christianity in Australia: Spirit, word and world* (Melbourne: Oxford University Press, 1996)

Chapter 15

Actes et documents du Saint Siège relatifs à la seconde guerre mondiale (Vatican, 1972–5)

Austad, Torleiv, 'Eivind Berggrav and the Church of Norway's resistance against Nazism, 1940–1945', *Mid-stream: an ecumenical journal* 26:1 (1987), 51–61

'Der Widerstand der Kirche gegen den nationalsozialistischen Staat in Norwegen 1940–1945', *Kirchliche Zeitgeschichte* 1:1 (1988), 79–94

Beckman Joachim, and Johannes Schneider (eds.), *Kirchliches Jahrbuch für die Evangelische Kirche in Deutschland 1933–1944* (Gütersloh: C. Bertelsmann Verlag, 1948)

Bell, G. K. A., *The church and humanity 1939–1946* (London: Longman, 1946)

Bethge, Eberhard, *Dietrich Bonhoeffer: Theologe-Christ-Zeitgenosse* (Gütersloh, 1967); revd English edn by Victoria Barnett and Clifford Green (Minneapolis: Fortress Press, 2000)

Bonhoeffer, Dietrich, *Letters and papers from prison*, enlarged edn (London: SCM, 1972)

Boyens, Armin, *Kirchenkampf und Ökumene, 1939–45: Darstellung und Dokumentation unter besonderer Berücksichtigung der Quellen des ökumenischen Rates der Kirchen* (Munich: Chr. Kaiser Verlag, 1973)

Chadwick, Owen, 'The pope and the Jews in 1942', in W. J. Sheils (ed.), *Persecution and toleration*, Studies in Church History 21 (Oxford: Blackwell, 1984)

Britain and the Vatican during the Second World War (Cambridge: Cambridge University Press, 1986)

Conway, John S., *The Nazi persecution of the churches* (London: Weidenfeld & Nicolson, 1968)

Coppa, Frank J., *The modern papacy since 1789* (London: Longman, 1998)

Deutsch, Harold, *The conspiracy against Hitler in the twilight war: an account of the German anti-Nazi plot from September 1939 to May 1940 and the role of Pope Pius XII* (London: Andre Deutsch, 1968)

Duquesne, Jacques, *Les catholiques français sous l'occupation* (Paris: B. Grasset, 1996)

Gerlach, Wolfgang, *And the witnesses were silent: the Confessing Church and the persecution of the Jews*, trans. and ed. Victoria Barnett (Lincoln, NE and London: University of Nebraska Press, 2000)

Gildea, Robert, *Marianne in chains: in search of the German occupation 1940–45* (London: Macmillan, 2002)

Hallie, Philip, *Lest innocent blood be shed* (London: Michael Joseph, 1979)

Halls, W. D. (ed.), *Politics, society and Christianity in Vichy France* (London: Berg, 1995)

Hansard, the debates of the House of Lords, fifth series (London, 1939–45)

Helmreich, Ernst Christian, *The German churches under Hitler: background, struggle and epilogue* (Detroit: Wayne State University Press, 1979)

Jackson, Julian, *France: the dark years 1940–1944* (Oxford: Oxford University Press, 2001)

Lewy, Guenter, *The Catholic church and Nazi Germany* (London: Weidenfeld & Nicolson, 1964)

Ludlow, Peter, 'The international Protestant community in the Second World War', *Journal of ecclesiastical history* 29 (1978), 311–62

Marrus, Robert R., and Robert O. Paxton, *Vichy France and the Jews* (New York: Basic Books, 1981)

McLellan, David, *Simone Weil: utopian pessimist* (London: Macmillan, 1983)

von Oppen, Beate Ruhm, *Religion and resistance* (Princeton: Princeton University Press, 1971)

The persecution of the Catholic church in German-occupied Poland: reports presented by H. E. Hlond, primate of Poland, to Pope Pius II, Vatican broadcasts and other reliable evidence, preface by Cardinal Hinsley (London: Burns Oates, 1941)

van Roon, Ger, *Neuordnung im Widerstand: der Kreisauer Kreis innerhalb der deutschen Widerstandsbewegung* (Munich: Oldenbourg Verlag, 1967)

Roth, John K., and Carol Rittner (eds.), *Pope Pius XII and the Holocaust* (London: Leicester University Press, 2002)

Scholder, Klaus, *A requiem for Hitler and other new perspectives on the German church struggle*, trans. John Bowden (London: SCM, 1989)

Snoek, Johan M., *The grey book: a collection of protests against anti-semitism and the persecution of Jews issued by non-Roman Catholic churches and church leaders during Hitler's rule* (Assen: Van Gorcam & Comp, 1969)

Stoltzfus, Nathan, *Resistance of the heart: inter-marriage and the Rosenstrasse protest in Nazi Germany* (New York: W. W. Norton, 1996)

Visser 't Hooft, W., *Memoirs* (London: SCM, 1973)

Visser 't Hooft, W. (ed.), *The struggle of the Dutch church for the maintenance of the commandments of God in the life of the state* (New York, 1945)

Wilkinson, Alan, *Dissent or conform? War, peace and the English churches 1900–45* (London: SCM, 1986)

Zuccotti, Sandra, *Under his very windows: the Vatican and the Holocaust in Italy* (New Haven: Yale University Press, 2001)

Chapter 16

Aldrich, R. J., 'OSS, CIA and European unity', *Diplomacy and statecraft* 8 (1977), 186–227

Boorstin, D. J., *The genius of American politics* (Chicago: University of Chicago Press, 1953)

Coupland, P. M., 'British Christians and European integration', *The historian* 78 (Summer 2003), 33–8

Deutscher, I., *Stalin* (Harmondsworth: Penguin, 1972)

Ellwood, R. S., *The fifties spiritual marketplace: American religion in a decade of conflict* (New Jersey: Rutgers University Press, 1997)

Fairclough, A., 'Was Martin Luther King a Marxist?', *History workshop journal* 15 (Spring 1983), 117–25

Fogarty, M., *Christian democracy in western Europe, 1820–1953* (London: Routledge, 1957)

Foglesong, D. S., 'Roots of "liberation": American images of the future Russia in the early Cold War, 1948–1953', *International history review* 21 (March 1999), 57–79

Herberg, W., *Protestant, Catholic, Jew: an essay in American religious sociology* (Garden City: Doubleday, 1955)

Ignatieff, M., *Isaiah Berlin: a life* (London: Henry Holt, 1998)

Irving, R. E. M., *The Christian Democratic Parties of western Europe* (London: Allen & Unwin, 1979)

Kalyvas, S., *The rise of Christian democracy in Europe* (Ithaca: Cornell University Press, 1996)

Van Kersbergen, K., 'The distinctiveness of Christian democracy', in D. Hanley (ed.), *Christian democracy in Europe: a comparative perspective* (London: Pinter, 1994)

Kirby, D., 'The Church of England and the Cold War, 1945–56', PhD dissertation, University of Hull, 1991

    'The Church of England and the Cold War nuclear debate', *Twentieth century British history* 4 (1993), 250–83

    'Truman's holy alliance: the president, the pope and the origins of the Cold War', *Borderlines: studies in American culture* 4 (1997), 1–17

    'Divinely sanctioned', *Journal of contemporary history* 35 (2000), 385–412

    'Anglican–Orthodox relations and the religious rehabilitation of the Soviet regime during the Second World War', *Revue d'histoire ecclésiastique* 96 (2001), 101–23

Kirby, D. (ed.), *Religion and the Cold War* (Basingstoke: Palgrave-Macmillan, 2003)

Lernoux, P., *People of God: the struggle for world Catholicism* (New York: Penguin, 1989)

Lucas, S., *Freedom's war* (Manchester: Manchester University Press, 1999)

Marty, M. E., *Modern American religion: under God indivisible, 1941–1960*, 3 vols. (Chicago: University of Chicago Press, 1996)

May, E. R. (ed.), *American Cold War strategy: interpreting NSC 68* (Boston, MA: Palgrave-Macmillan, 1993)

Michel, P., *Politics and religion in eastern Europe* (Cambridge: Polity Press, 1991)

Miller, J. E., *The US and Italy, 1940–1950* (London: University of North Carolina Press, 1986)

Miller, W. L., *Piety along the Potomac* (Boston, MA: Houghton Mifflin, 1964)

Pollard, J., 'Italy', in Tom Buchanan and Martin Conway (eds.), *Political Catholicism in Europe 1918–1965* (Oxford: Clarendon Press, 1996)

Sherry, M. S. *In the shadow of war: the United States since the 1930s* (New Haven: Yale University Press, 1995)

Silk, M., *Spiritual politics: religion and America since World War II* (New York: Simon & Schuster, 1988)

Simpson, C., *Blowback: America's recruitment of Nazis and its effects on the Cold War* (New York: Weidenfeld, 1988)

Truman, H. S., *Mr. Citizen* (New York: Popular Library, 1961)

Visser 't Hooft, W., *Memoirs* (London: SCM, 1973)

    Has the ecumenical movement a future? (Belfast: Christian Journals Limited, 1974)

Williams, W. A., *The tragedy of American diplomacy* (New York: W. W. Norton, 1972)

Chapter 17

Alberigo, Giuseppe and Komonchak, Joseph A. (eds.), *History of Vatican II* (Maryknoll, NY: Orbis; Leuven: Peeters, 1995–)

Allen, John L., *Cardinal Ratzinger* (New York and London: Continuum, 2000)

Allitt, Patrick, *Catholic intellectuals and conservative politics in America 1950–1985* (Ithaca, NY and London: Cornell University Press, 1993)

Blake, Eugene Carson, 'Uppsala and afterwards', in Harold E. Fey (ed.), *The ecumenical advance: a history of the Ecumenical movement, volume 2, 1948–1968* (London: SPCK, 1970), pp. 411–45

Cox, Harvey, *The secular city* (New York: Macmillan, 1965)

    'The secular city twenty-five years later', *Christian century* 107 (1990), 1025–9

Cuneo, Michael W., *The smoke of Satan* (New York and Oxford: Oxford University Press, 1997)

Davis, Charles, *A question of conscience* (London: Hodder and Stoughton, 1967)

Edwards, David L. (ed.), *The Honest to God debate* (London: SCM, 1963)

Gillis, Chester, *Roman Catholicism in America* (New York: Columbia University Press, 1999)

Goodall, Norman, *Ecumenical progress: a decade of change in the Ecumenical movement 1961–71* (London: Oxford University Press, 1971)

Grootaers, J., *Actes et acteurs à Vatican II* (Leuven: Leuven University Press/Peeters, 1998)

Handy, Robert T., *A history of the church in the United States and Canada* (Oxford: Clarendon Press, 1976)

Hastings, Adrian, *A history of English Christianity, 1920–2000* (London: SCM, 2001)

Hebblethwaite, Peter, *John XXIII: pope of the council* (London: Geoffrey Chapman, 1984)

    Paul VI: the first modern pope (London: HarperCollins, 1993)

Kaiser, Robert Blair, *The encyclical that never was* (London: Sheed and Ward, 1987)

Kerkhofs, J. (ed.), *Catholic Pentecostals now, 1967–1977* (Canfield, OH: Alba Books, 1977)

Komonchak, Joseph A., 'The silencing of John Courtney Murray', in A. Melloni, D. Menozzi, G. Ruggieri and M. Toschi (eds.), *Cristianesimo nella storia: saggi in onore di Giuseppe Alberigo* (Bologna: Il Mulino, 1996), pp. 657–702

    '"The crisis in church–state relationships in the U.S.A.": a recently discovered text by John Courtney Murray', *The review of politics* 61 (1999), 675–714

Küng, Hans, *My struggle for freedom* (New York and London: Continuum, 2003)

Middleton, Neil, *The language of Christian revolution* (London: Sheed and Ward, 1968)

Perrin, Luc, *L'affaire Lefbvre* (Paris: Editions du Cerf, 1989)

Ranaghan, Kevin, and Dorothy Ranaghan, *Catholic Pentecostals* (New York: Paulist Press, 1969)

Rico, Herminio, *John Paul II and the legacy of 'Dignitatis humanae'* (Washington: Georgetown University Press, 2002)

Rynne, Xavier [F. X. Murphy], *Vatican Council II* (New York: Orbis, 1999)

Tanner, Norman P., *The councils of the church: a short history* (New York: Crossroad, 2001)

Walsh, Michael J., 'Spain on the move', *The month* (June 1972), 163ff.

'The conservative reaction', in Adrian Hastings (ed.), *Modern Catholicism* (London: SPCK; New York: Oxford University Press, 1991), pp. 283–8

'The thorny question of religious freedom', in Austen Ivereigh (ed.), *Journey unfinished* (London: Continuum, 2003), pp. 134–48

Weaver, Mary Jo and R. Scott Appleby (eds.), *Being right* (Bloomington: Indiana University Press, 1995)

Chapter 18

Bebbington, David, 'The secularization of British universities since the mid-nineteenth century', in George M. Marsden and Bradley J. Longfield (eds.), *The secularization of the academy* (New York: Oxford University Press, 1992), pp. 259–77

Bibby, Reginald W., *Fragmented gods* (Toronto: Stoddart, 1990)

Blaschke, Olaf, *Konfessionen im Konflikt: Deutschland zwischen 1800 und 1970: ein zweites konfessionelles Zeitalter* (Göttingen: Vandenhoeck und Ruprecht, 2001)

Briggs, Asa, 'Christ and the media', in Eileen Barker, Karel Dobbelaere and James Beckford (eds.), *Secularization, rationalism and sectarianism* (Oxford: Oxford University Press, 1993), pp. 267–86

Brown, Callum G., *The death of Christian Britain: understanding secularisation 1800–2000* (London: Routledge, 2001)

Bruce, Steve, *Religion in the modern world: from cathedrals to cults* (Oxford: Oxford University Press, 1995)

Chadwick, Kay, '*Accueillir l'étranger*: immigration, integration and the French Catholic church', in Kay Chadwick (ed.), *Catholicism, politics and society in twentieth-century France* (Liverpool: Liverpool University Press, 2000), pp. 175–96

Cholvy, Gérard, and Yves-Marie Hilaire, *Histoire religieuse de la France contemporaine, 1930–1988* (Toulouse: Privat, 1988)

Coleman, J. A., *The evolution of Dutch Catholicism, 1958–1974* (Berkeley: University of California Press, 1978)

Dittgen, Alfred, 'Évolution des rites religieux dans l'Europe contemporaine. Statistiques et contextes', *Annales de démographie historique* 2 (2003), 111–29

Dogan, Mattei, 'The decline of religious beliefs in western Europe', *International social science journal* 143 (1995), 405–18

Egerton, George, 'Trudeau, God and the Canadian constitution', in David Lyon and Marguerite van Die (eds.), *Rethinking church, state and modernity: Canada between Europe and America* (Toronto: Toronto University Press, 2000), pp. 90–112

Field, Clive, 'The haemorrhage of faith? Opinion polls as sources for religious practices, beliefs and attitudes in Scotland since the 1970s', *Journal of contemporary religion* 16 (2001), 157–75

Gaine, Michael, 'The state of the priesthood', in Adrian Hastings (ed.), *Modern Catholicism: Vatican II and after* (London: SPCK, 1991), pp. 246–54

Gilbert, Alan D., *The making of post-Christian Britain* (London: Longman, 1980)

Gill, Robin, *The myth of the empty church* (London: SPCK, 1993)

Hastings, Adrian, *A history of English Christianity, 1920–2000* (London: Collins, 2001)

Heelas, Paul, and Linda Woodhead, *The spiritual revolution* (Oxford: Blackwell, 2004)

Hilliard, David, 'The religious crisis of the 1960s: the experience of the Australian churches', *Journal of religious history* 21 (1997), 209–27

Kerkhofs, Jan (ed.), *Europe without priests?* (London: SCM, 1995)

Kosmin, Barry A., and Seymour P. Lachman, *One nation under God: religion in contemporary American society* (New York: Crown, 1993)

Lambert, Yves, *Dieu change en Bretagne* (Paris: Editions du Cerf, 1985)

'New Christianity, indifference and diffused spirituality', in Hugh McLeod and Werner Ustorf (eds.), *The decline of Christendom in western Europe, 1750–2000* (Cambridge: Cambridge University Press, 2003), 63–78

Machin, G. I. T., *Churches and social issues in twentieth-century Britain* (Oxford: Oxford University Press, 1998)

Murphy, Terence, and Roberto Perin (eds.), *A concise history of Christianity in Canada* (Don Mills ONT: Oxford University Press, 1996)

Pasture, Patrick, 'Christendom and the legacy of the sixties: between the secular city and the age of Aquarius', *Revue d'histoire ecclésiastique* 99 (2004), 82–116

Presser, Stanley, and Linda Stinson, 'Data collection and social desirability bias in self-reported religious attendance', *American sociological review* 63 (1998), 137–45

Robbers, Gerhard (ed.), *State and church in the European Union* (Baden-Baden: Nomos, 1996)

Roberts, Elizabeth, *Women and families: an oral history, 1940–1970* (Oxford: Blackwell, 1995)

van Rooden, Peter, 'Long-term religious developments in the Netherlands, c.1750–2000', in McLeod and Ustorf (eds.), *Christendom*, pp. 113–29

Roozen, David A., Jackson W. Carroll and Wade C. Roof, 'La génération née après-guerre et la religion instituée: un aperçu sur 50 ans de changement religieux aux Etats Unis', *Archives des sciences sociales de la religion* 83 (1993), 25–52

Sutcliffe, Steven, and Marion Bowman (eds.), *Beyond new age: exploring alternative spirituality* (Edinburgh: Edinburgh University Press, 2000)

Wuthnow, Robert, *Experimentation in American religion: the new mysticisms and their implications for the churches* (Berkeley: University of California Press, 1978)

After heaven: spirituality in America since the 1950s (Berkeley: University of California Press, 1998)

Chapter 19

Barnett, Simon, 'Religious freedom and the European Convention on Human Rights: the case of the Baltic states', *Religion, state & society* 29 (2001), 91–100

Beeson, Trevor, *Discretion and valour: religious conditions in Russia and eastern Europe* (London: Fount, 1982)

Borowik, Irena (ed.), *Church–state relations in central and eastern Europe* (Kraków: Nomos, 1999)

Bibliography

Bourdeaux, Michael, *Land of crosses: the struggle for religious freedom in Lithuania, 1939–1978* (Chulmleigh, Devon: Augustine Publishing Co., 1979)

Cantrell, Beth, and Ute Kemp, 'The role of the Protestant church in eastern Germany: some personal experiences and reflections', *Religion, state & society* 21 (1993), 277–88

Corley, Felix, 'Soviet reaction to the election of Pope John Paul II', *Religion, state & society* 22 (1994), 37–64

Davie, Grace, *Religion in Britain since 1945: believing without belonging* (Oxford: Blackwell, 1994)

Religion in modern Europe: a memory mutates (Oxford and New York: Oxford University Press, 2000)

Gordon, Arvan, 'The church and change in the GDR', *Religion in communist lands* 18 (1990), 138–54

Hornsby-Smith, Michael P., 'The Catholic church in central and eastern Europe: the view from western Europe', in I. Borowik and G. Babiński (eds.), *New religious phenomena in central and eastern Europe* (Kraków: Nomos, 1997), pp. 133–49

'The Hungarian Lutheran church and the "theology of diaconia"', *Religion in communist lands* 12 (1984), 130–48

Luxmoore, Jonathan, 'Eastern Europe, 1995: a review of religious life in Bulgaria, Romania, Hungary, Slovakia, the Czech Republic and Poland', *Religion, state & society* 24 (1996), 357–65

'Eastern Europe, 1997–2000: a review of church life', *Religion, state & society* 29 (2001), 305–30

Luxmoore, Jonathan, and Jolanta Babiuch, *The Vatican and the red flag* (London and New York: Geoffrey Chapman, 1999)

Merdjanova, Ina, *Religion, nationalism and civil society in eastern Europe: the post-communist palimpsest* (Lewiston, NY: Edwin Mellon Press, 2002)

Michel, Patrick, *Politics and religion in eastern Europe: Catholicism in Hungary, Poland and Czechoslovakia* (Cambridge: Polity Press, 1991)

'Religious renewal or political deficiency: religion and democracy in central Europe', *Religion, state & society* 20 (1992), 339–44

'Religion, communism, and democracy in central Europe: the Polish case', in William H. Swatos, Jr (ed.), *Politics and religion in central and eastern Europe: traditions and transitions* (Westport, CT: Praeger, 1994), pp. 119–31

Mojzes, Paul, *Religious liberty in eastern Europe and the USSR before and after the great transformation* (Boulder: East European Monographs, 1992)

Oestreicher, Paul, 'Christian pluralism in a monolithic state: the churches of East Germany 1945–1990, *Religion, state & society* 21 (1993), 263–75

Pungur, Joseph, 'Doing theology in Hungary: liberation or adaptation', *Religion, state & society* 21 (1993), 71–85

Ramet, Pedro (ed.), *Christianity under stress*, 3 vols. (Durham, NC: Duke University Press, 1988–92)

Ramet, Sabrina P., *Nihil obstat: religion, politics, and social change in east-central Europe and Russia* (Durham, NC: Duke University Press, 1998)

Sapiets, Marite, 'The Baltic churches and the national revival', *Religion in communist lands* 18 (1990), 155–68

Schönherr, Bishop, 'Church and state in the GDR', *Religion in communist lands* 19 (1991), 197–206

Tomka, Miklós, 'Religious change in east-central Europe', in Irena Borowik and Miklós Tomka (eds.), *Religion and social change in post-communist Europe* (Kraków: Nomos, 2001), pp. 11–27

Tomsky, Alexander, 'John Paul II in Poland: pilgrim of the Holy Spirit', *Religion in communist lands* 7 (1979), 160–5

Williamson, Roger, 'East Germany: the Federation of Protestant Churches', *Religion in communist lands* 9 (1981), 6–17

Chapter 20

Arns, Paulo Evaristo, *Brasil, nunca mais*, 10th edn (Petrópolis, Brazil: Vozes, 1985)

Cleary, Edward L., *Crisis and change: the church in Latin America today* (Maryknoll, NY: Orbis, 1985)

Cleary, Edward L., and Hannah Stewart-Gambino (eds.), *Conflict and competition: the Latin American church in a changing environment* (Boulder and London: Lynne Rienner, 1992)

Escobar, Samuel, *Changing tides: Latin America and world mission today* (Maryknoll, NY: Orbis, 2002)

Gutiérrez, Gustavo, *A theology of liberation: history, politics and salvation* (Maryknoll, NY: Orbis, 1973)

Latin American Bishops Conference, *The church in the present-day transformation of Latin America in the light of the council* (Bogotá: Latin American Bishops Conference, 1970)

Martin, David, *Tongues of fire: the explosion of Protestantism in Latin America* (Oxford: Blackwell, 1990)

Nida, Eugene A., 'The relationship of social structure to the problems of evangelism in Latin America', *Practical anthropology* 5 (1958), 101–23

Oficina Sociología Religiosa, *Datos estadísticos 1996: clero secular, congregaciones religiosas, sacramentación en Chile* (Santiago: Oficina Sociología Religiosa, 1997)

Peterson, Anna L., Manuel Vasquez and Philip J. Williams (eds.), *Christianity, social change, and globalization in the Americas* (New Brunswick: Rutgers University Press, 2002)

Ponce García, Jaime, and Oscar Uzín Fernández, *El clero de Bolivia* (Cuernavaca, Mexico: CIDOC (Centro Intercultural de Documentación), 1970)

Pro Mundi Vita Institute, *PMV special note* (Brussels: Pro Mundi Vita Institute) 15 (October 1970)

Secretaria Status, *Annuarium statisticum ecclesiae* (Vatican City: Typis Polyglottis Vaticanis, annual publication)

Smith, Brian H., 'Pentecostalism and Catholicism in contemporary Latin America', paper prepared with support of National Endowment for the Humanities, September 1996 *Religious politics in Latin America, Pentecostal vs. Catholic* (Notre Dame: University of Notre Dame Press, 1998)

Stoll, David, *Is Latin America turning Protestant? The politics of evangelical Growth* (Berkeley: University of California Press, 1990)

Williams, Philip, 'The limits of religious influence: the progressive church in Nicaragua', in Cleary and Stewart-Gambino (eds.), *Conflict and Competition*

www.providence.edu/las website on religion in Latin America

Chapter 21

Borer, Tristan Anne, *Challenging the state: churches as political actors in South Africa, 1980–1994* (Notre Dame: Notre Dame University Press, 1998)

Carson, C., et al. (eds.), *The eyes on the prize: civil rights reader* (New York: Penguin, 1991)

Cloete, G. D., and D. J. Smit, *A moment of truth: the confession of the Dutch Reformed mission church 1982* (Grand Rapids, Eerdmans, 1984)

Cochrane, James. *Servants of power: the role of the English-speaking churches 1903–1930* (Johannesburg: Ravan Press, 1987)

Cone, James H., *For my people: Black Theology and the black church* (Maryknoll, NY: Orbis, 1984)
Speaking the truth: ecumenism, liberation and Black Theology (Grand Rapids: Eerdmans, 1986)
A Black Theology of liberation, twentieth anniversary edn (Maryknoll, NY: Orbis, 1990)
Martin & Malcolm & America: a dream or a nightmare (Maryknoll, NY: Orbis, 1991)

Elphick, Richard, and Rodney Davenport (eds.), *Christianity in South Africa: a political, social and cultural history* (Cape Town: David Philip, 1997)

Franklin, John Hope, and Alfred A. Moss, Jr, *From slavery to freedom: a history of Negro Americans*, 6th edn (New York: McGraw-Hill, 1988)

Fredrickson, George, *Racism: a short history* (Princeton: Princeton University Press, 2002)

Garrow, David J., *Bearing the cross: Martin Luther King, Jr., and the Southern Christian Leadership Conference* (New York: William Morrow, 1986)

de Gruchy, John W., with Steve de Gruchy *The church struggle in South Africa* revd 3rd edn (London: SCM and Minneapolis: Fortress, 2004)

de Gruchy, John W., and Charles Villa-Vicencio (eds.), *Apartheid is a heresy* (Cape Town: David Philip, 1983)

Hofmeyer, J. W., and Gerald J. Pillay (eds.), *A history of Christianity in South Africa*, vol. 1 (Pretoria: Haum Tertiary, 1994)

Hopkins, Dwight N., *Black Theology USA and South Africa: politics, culture and liberation* (Maryknoll, NY: Orbis, 1989)
Down, up and over: slave religion and Black Theology (Minneapolis: Augsburg Fortress, 2000)

Kairos Theologians, *The Kairos document: challenge to the church*, revd 2nd edn (Johannesburg: Skotaville, 1986)

Motlhabi, Mokgethi, *The theory and practice of black resistance to apartheid: a socio-ethical analysis* (Johannesburg: Skotaville, 1985)

Motlhabi, Mokgethi (ed.), *Essays on Black Theology* (Johannesburg: Black Theology Project of UCM, 1972). Republished with some changes as Basil Moore (ed.), *The challenge of Black Theology in South Africa* (Atlanta: John Knox, 1973)

Sitkoff, Harvard, *The struggle for black equality, 1954–1992*. Rev. edn (New York: Hill and Wang, 1981, 1993)

Villa-Vicencio, Charles, *Trapped in apartheid* (Cape Town: David Philip, 1988)

Walshe, Peter, *Church versus state in South Africa* (Maryknoll, NY: Orbis, 1983)

Wilmore, Gayraud S., and James H. Cone, (eds.), *Black Theology: a documentary history, 1966–1979* (Maryknoll, NY: Orbis, 1979)

Wood, Forrest G., *The arrogance of faith: Christianity and race in America from the colonial era to the twentieth century* (New York: Alfred A. Knopf, 1990)

Chapter 22

Boulaga, F. Eboussi, *Christianity without fetishes* (Maryknoll, NY: Orbis, 1984)

Cross, S., 'Independent churches and independent states: Jehovah's Witnesses in east and central Africa', in E. Fashole-Luke, R. Gray, A. Hastings and G. Tasie (eds.), *Christianity in independent Africa* (London: Rex Collings, 1978), pp. 304–15

Ela, Jean-Marc, *African cry* (Maryknoll, NY: Orbis, 1986)

Fashole-Luke, E., R. Gray, A. Hastings and G. Tasie (eds.), *Christianity in independent Africa* (London: Rex Collings, 1978)

Freston, Paul, *Evangelicals and politics in Asia, Africa and Latin America* (Cambridge: Cambridge University Press, 2001)

Gifford, Paul, 'Bishops for reform', *Tablet*, 30 May 1992, pp. 672–4.

   'Some recent developments in African Christianity', *African affairs* 93:373 (1994), 513–34

   African Christianity: its public role (London: Hurst & Co., 1998)

Gifford, Paul (ed.), *The Christian churches and the democratisation of Africa* (Leiden: Brill, 1995)

Hansen, Holger B., and Michael Twaddle (eds.), *Religion and politics in east Africa: the period since independence* (London: James Currey, 1995)

Hastings, A., *A history of African Christianity, 1950–1975* (Cambridge: Cambridge University Press, 1979)

   The church in Africa 1450–1950 (Oxford: Clarendon Press, 1994)

Imo, Cyril, 'Evangelicals, Muslims and democracy: with particular reference to the declaration of Sharia in northern Nigeria', in Terence Ranger (ed.), *Evangelical Christianity and democracy in Africa* (Oxford: Oxford University Press, forthcoming)

Isichei, Elizabeth, *A history of Christianity in Africa: from antiquity to the present* (London: SPCK, 1995)

Jenkins, Philip, *The next Christendom: the coming of global Christianity* (New York: Oxford University Press, 2002)

Longman, Timothy, 'Church politics and the genocide in Rwanda', *Journal of religion in Africa* 31/2 (2001), 163–86

Lonsdale, John., 'Kikuyu Christianities: a history of intimate diversity', in David Maxwell (ed.) with Ingrid Lawrie, *Christianity and the African imagination: essays in honour of Adrian Hastings* (Leiden: Brill, 2002), pp. 157–97

Martin, D., *Pentecostalism: the world is their parish* (Oxford: Blackwell, 2001)

Maxwell. D., *Christians and chiefs in Zimbabwe: a social history of the Hwesa People c.1870s–1990s* (Edinburgh: International African Library, 1999)

   African gifts of the Spirit: Pentecostalism and the rise of a Zimbabwean transnational religious movement (Oxford: James Currey, forthcoming)

Mbiti, John, *African religions and philosophy* (New York: Praeger, 1969)

Ranger, T., 'Religious movements and politics in sub-Saharan Africa', *African studies review* 29:2 (1986), 1–69

   'Introduction', in Ranger (ed.), *Evangelical Christianity and democracy in Africa* (Oxford: Oxford University Press, forthcoming)

Robert, Dana, 'Shifting southward: global Christianity since 1945', *International bulletin of missionary research* 24:2 (2000), 50–8

Bibliography

Sanneh, L., 'A resurgent church in a troubled continent: review essay of Bengt Sundkler's *History of the church in Africa*', *International bulletin of missionary research* 25:3 (2001), 113–18

Sundkler, Bengt, and Christopher Steed, *A history of the church in Africa* (Cambridge: Cambridge University Press, 2000)

Ward, Kevin, 'Africa', in A. Hastings (ed.), *A world history of Christianity* (London: Cassell, 1999), pp. 192–233

Chapter 23

Arasaratnam, S., 'Christians of Ceylon and nationalist politics', in G. A. Oddie (ed.), *Religion in south Asia* (New Delhi: Manohar, 1991), 347–69

Baago, K., *A history of the National Christian Council of India, 1914–1964* (Nagpur: National Christian Council, 1965)

Boyd, Robin, *An introduction to Indian Christian theology* (Madras: Christian Literature Society, 1975)

Clarke, Sathianathan, *Dalits and Christianity: subaltern religion and Liberation Theology in India* (New Delhi: Oxford University Press, 1998)

David, M. D., *The YMCA and the making of modern India (a centenary history)* (New Delhi: National Council of YMCAs of India, 1992)

Frykenberg, Robert, 'India', in Adrian Hastings (ed.), *A world of history of Christianity* (London: Cassell, 1999)

Grafe, Hugald, *History of Christianity in India*, vol. IV, part 2: *Tamilnadu in the nineteenth and twentieth centuries* (Bangalore: Church History Association of India, 1990)

Hardgrave, Robert, *The Nadars of Tamilnad: the political culture of a community in change* (Berkeley: University of California Press, 1969)

Harper, Susan Billington, *In the shadow of the Mahatma: Bishop V. S. Azariah and the travails of Christianity in British India* (Grand Rapids: Eerdmans; Richmond, Surrey: Curzon Press, 2000)

Hocking, W. E., *Rethinking missions: a laymen's inquiry after one hundred years* (New York: Harper & Bros., 1932)

Houtart, François, and Geneviève Lemercinier. *Size and structures of the Catholic church in India: indigenization of an exogeneous religious institution in a society in transition* (Leuven: Université Catholique de Louvain, 1982)

Job, G. V., et al., *Rethinking Christianity in India.* (Madras: A. N. Sudarisanam, 1938)

Kim, Sebastian, *In search of identity: debates on religious conversion in India* (New Delhi: Oxford University Press, 2003)

Mallampalli, Chandra, *Christians and public life in colonial south India, 1863–1937* (London: RoutledgeCurzon, 2004)

Mathew, George, *Communal road to a secular Kerala* (New Delhi: Concept Publishing Co., 1989)

Mundadan, A. M., *History of Christianity in India, volume I: From the beginning up to the middle of the sixteenth century* (Bangalore: Theological Publications in India, 1984)

Nehru, Jawaharlal, *Discovery of India* (New Delhi: Oxford University Press, 1985)

Popely, H. A., *K. T. Paul, Christian leader* (Madras: Christian Literature Society, 1987)

Sundkler, Bengt, *Church of South India: the movement towards union, 1900–1947* (London: Lutterworth Press, 1954)

Thomas, George, *Christian Indians and Indian nationalism, 1885–1950: an interpretation in historical and theological perspectives* (Frankfurt: Peter Lang, 1979)

Webster, John C. B., *The Dalit Christians: a history* (New Delhi: ISPCK, 1996)

Chapter 24

Adeney, Frances S., *Christian women in Indonesia: a narrative study of gender and religion,* Women and religion (Syracuse, NY: Syracuse University Press, 2003)

Aragon, Lorraine V., *Fields of the Lord: animism, Christian minorities, and state development in Indonesia* (Honolulu: University of Hawai'i Press, 2000)

Barrett, David B., *World Christian encyclopedia*, 2nd edn (New York: Oxford University Press, 2001)

Chew, Maureen K. C., *The journey of the Catholic church in Malaysia, 1511–1996* (Kuala Lumpur: Catholic Research Centre, 2000)

Christie, Clive J., *A modern history of southeast Asia: decolonization, nationalism and separatism* (London: Tauris, 1996)

England, John C. (ed.), *Asian Christian theologies: a research guide to authors, movements, sources,* vol. II, *Southeast Asia* (Maryknoll, NY: Orbis Books ISPCK/Claretian Publishers, 2003)

Fox, Thomas C., *Pentecost in Asia: a new way of being church* (Maryknoll, NY: Orbis, 2002)

Hwa, Yung, 'Endued with power: the Pentecostal-Charismatic renewal and the Asian church in the twenty-first century', *Asian journal of Pentecostal studies* 6 (2003), 63–82

Keyes, Charles F., 'Being Protestant Christians in southeast Asian worlds', *Journal of southeast Asian studies* 27 (1996), 280–92

van Klinken, Gerry, *Minorities, modernity and the emerging nation: Christians in Indonesia, a biographical approach* (Leiden: KITLV Press, 2003)

Manikam, Rajah Bhushanam, *Christianity and the Asian revolution* (Madras: Christian Literature Society, 1955)

McKenzie, Douglas G., and I. Wayan Mastra, *The mango tree church: the story of the Protestant Christian church in Bali* (Brisbane: Boolarong Publications, 1988)

Rae, Simon, *Breath becomes the wind: old and new in Karo religion* (Dunedin, NZ: University of Otago Press, 1994)

Religious affiliation by provincial-level unit 1991 (accessed 23 January 2004). Available from http://www.indonesiaphoto.com/article247.html

Ricklefs, M. C., *A history of modern Indonesia since c.1200* (Basingstoke: Palgrave, 2001)

Roxborogh, John, 'Ministry to all the people? The Anglican church in Malaysia', in W. J. Shiels and Diana Wood (eds.), *The ministry: clerical and lay,* Studies in Church History (Oxford: Blackwell, 1989), pp. 423–31

'Contextualisation and re-contextualisation: regional patterns in the history of southeast Asian Christianity', *Asia journal of theology* 9:1 (1995), 30–46

'Südostasien', in Karl Müller and Werner Ustorf (eds.), *Einleitung in die Missionsgeschichte: Tradition, Situation und Dynamik des Christentums* (Stuttgart: Kohlhammer, 1995), pp. 143–58

Russell, A. Sue, *Conversion, identity, and power: the impact of Christianity on power relationships and social exchanges* (Lanham, MD: University Press of America, 1999)

Sakhong Lian, H., *Religion and politics among the Chin people in Burma (1896–1949)*, Studia missionalia Upsaliensia 80. (Uppsala: Uppsala University, 2000)

Steenbrink, Karel A., 'The rehabilitation of the indigenous: a survey of recent research on the history of Christianity in Indonesia', *Exchange. Journal of missiological and ecumenical research* 22 (1993), 250–63

Sunquist, Scott, *A dictionary of Asian Christianity* (Grand Rapids: Eerdmans, 2001)

Walker, Anthony R., *Merit and the millennium: routine and crisis in the ritual lives of the Lahu people*, Studies in sociology and social anthropology (New Delhi: Hindustan Pub. Corp., 2003)

Chapter 25

Baker, Don, 'From pottery to politics: the transformation of Korean Catholicism', in Lewis R. Lancaster and Richard K. Payne (eds.), *Religion and society in contemporary Korea*, Korea research monograph 24 (Berkeley: University of California Press, 1997), pp. 127–68

Barrett, David, et al. (eds.), *World Christian encyclopedia* (Oxford: Oxford University Press, 2001)

Bays, Daniel H., 'Chinese popular religion and Christianity before and after the 1949 revolution', *Fides et historia* 23 (1991), 67–77

'Indigenous Protestant churches in China, 1900–1937: a Pentecostal case study', in Steven Kaplan (ed.), *Indigenous responses to Western Christianity* (New York: New York University Press, 1995), pp. 124–43

'The growth of independent Christianity in China', in Bays (ed.), *Christianity in China: from the eighteenth century to the present* (Stanford: Stanford University Press, 1996), pp. 307–16

Ching, Julia, 'Twentieth-century Christianity in China', in Theodore de Bary and Richard Lufrano (eds.), *Sources of Chinese tradition*, 2nd edn, vol. II (New York: Columbia University Press, 2000), pp. 527–44

Clark, Allen D., *History of the Korean church* (New York: Friendship Press, 1961)

Erh, Deke, and Tess Johnston (eds.), *Hallowed halls: Protestant colleges in old China* (New York: United Board for Christian Higher Education in Asia, 1998)

Fairbank, John K. (ed.), *The missionary enterprise in China and America* (Cambridge, MA: Harvard University Press, 1974)

Gluck, Carol, *Japan's modern myths: ideology in the late Meiji period* (Princeton: Princeton University Press, 1985)

Grayson, James Huntley, 'Christianity and Korean religions: accommodation as an aspect of the emplantation of a world religion', in Keith Howard (ed.), *Korean shamanism: revivals, survivals, and change* (Seoul: The Royal Asiatic Society, Korea Branch, 1998), pp. 133–51

Korea – a religious history, revd edn (London and New York: RoutledgeCurzon, 2002)

Hunter, Alan, and Kim-kwong Chan (eds.), *Protestantism in contemporary China* (Cambridge: Cambridge University Press, 1993)

Jenner, W. J. F. (ed.), *Modern Chinese short stories* (Oxford: Oxford University Press, 1936)

Kang, Wi Jo, *Christ and Caesar in modern Korea: a history of Christianity and politics* (Albany: State University of New York Press, 1997)

Kurihara, Sadako, *Black eggs: poems of Kurihara Sadako*, trans. Richard H. Minear (Ann Arbor: Center for Japanese Studies, University of Michigan, 1994)

Latourette, Kenneth Scott, *A history of Christian missions in China* (New York: Russell and Russell, 1929)

Lutz, Jessie G., *Chinese politics and Christian missions: the anti-Christian movements of 1920–28* (Notre Dame: Cross Roads Books, 1988)

Mullins, Mark R., *Christianity made in Japan: a study of indigenous movements* (Honolulu: University of Hawai'i Press, 1998)

Mullins, Mark R., and Richard Fox Young (eds.), *Perspectives on Christianity in Korea and Japan: the gospel and culture in East Asia* (Lewiston, NY and Queenston, Ontario: Edwin Mellen Press, 1995)

Palmer, Spencer J., *Korea and Christianity* (Seoul: Royal Asiatic Society / Hollym, 1967)

Phillips, James, *From the rising of the sun: Christians and society in contemporary Japan* (Maryknoll, NY: Orbis, 1981)

Reid, David, *New wine: the cultural shaping of Japanese Christianity* (Berkeley: Asian Humanities Press, 1991)

Rubinstein, Murray A., *The Protestant community in Taiwan: mission, seminary, and church* (Armonk, NY and London: M. E. Sharpe, 1991)

'Statement on war responsibility of Nippon Sei Ko Kai: 49th Regular General Synod excerpt from May 23, 1996', *Anglican and Episcopal history* 65 (1996), 489–91

Tiedemann, R. G., 'China and its neighbors', in Adrian Hastings (ed.), *A world history of Christianity* (Grand Rapids and Cambridge, UK: Eerdmans, 1999), pp. 369–415

Wan, Sze-kar, 'The emerging hermeneutics of the Chinese church: the debate between Wu Leichuan and T. C. Chao and the Chinese Christian problematik', in Irene Eber et al. (eds.), *Bible in modern China: the literary and intellectual impact*, Monumenta Serica monograph series 43 (Sankt Augustin: Institut Monumenta Serica, 1999), pp. 351–82

Wang, Peter Chen-main, 'Christianity in Modern Taiwan – struggling over the path of contextualization', in Stephen Uhalley and Wu Xiaoxin (eds.), *China and Christianity: burdened past, hopeful future* (Armonk, NY and London: M. E. Sharpe, 2001), pp. 321–43

Wells, Kenneth M., *New God, new nation: Protestants and self-reconstruction nationalism in Korea, 1896–1937* (Honolulu: University of Hawai'i Press, 1990)

Wickeri, Philip L., *Seeking the common ground: Protestant Christianity, the Three-Self movement, and China's united front* (Maryknoll, NY: Orbis, 1988)

Chapter 26

Abbington, James (ed.), *Readings in African American church music and worship* (Chicago: GIA Publications, 2001)

Baker, Jonny, and Doug Gay, *Alternative worship: resources from and for the emerging church* (Grand Rapids: Baker, 2003)

Botte, Bernard, *From silence to participation* (Washington: Pastoral Press, 1988)

Burson, Malcolm C., *Worship points the way* (New York: Seabury Press, 1981)

Daniels, Harold M., *To God alone be glory* (Louisville: Geneva Press, 2003)

Dong-sun Kim, *The bread for today and the bread for tomorrow* (New York: Peter Lang, 2001)

Fenwick, John, and Bryan D. Spinks, *Worship in transition: the liturgical movement in the twentieth century* (Edinburgh: T&T Clark, 1995)

Liesch, Barry, *The new worship* (Grand Rapids: Baker, 2001)

Pecklers, Keith, SJ (ed.), *Liturgy in a postmodern world* (New York: Continuum, 2003)

Quere, Ralph W., *In the context of unity* (Minneapolis: Lutheran University Press, 2003)

Redman, Robb, *The great worship awakening: sharing a new song in the postmodern church* (San Francisco: Jossey-Bass, 2002)

Reid, Alcuin, OSB, *The organic development of the liturgy* (Farnborough: Saint Michael's Abbey Press, 2004)

Shepherd, Massey H., *The liturgical renewal of the church* (New York: Oxford University Press, 1960)

Spinks, Bryan D., and Iain R. Torrance (eds.), *To glorify God: essays on modern Reformed worship* (Edinburgh: T&T Clark, 1991)

Chapter 27

(i) Relations between Christians and Jews, 1914–2000

Bonhoeffer, Dietrich, *No rusty swords: letters, lectures and notes 1928–1936*, ed. and trans. Edwin Robertson (London: Collins, 1965)

Borcherdt, H. H., and Georg Merz (eds.), *Martin Luther: ausgewählte Werke*, 7 vols. (Munich: C. Kaiser, 1934–8)

Bovis, H. Eugene, *The Jerusalem question, 1917–1968* (Stanford: Hoover Institution Press, 1971)

Buber, Martin, *I and thou*, trans. Ronald Gregor Smith (Edinburgh: T&T Clark, 1994)

Cohn-Sherbok, Dan, *Messianic Judaism* (London and New York: Continuum, 2000)

Flusser, David, *Jesus*, trans. Ronald Walls (New York: Herder and Herder, 1969)

Foot-Moore, George, 'Christian writers on Judaism', *Harvard theological review* 14:5 (1921), 197–254

Geiger, Abraham, *Judaism and its history* (New York: M. Thalmessinger, 1866)

Herzl, Theodor, *The complete diaries of Theodor Herzl*, ed. Raphael Patai, trans. Harry Zohn, 5 vols. (New York and London: The Herzl Press, 1960)

Isaac, Jules, *The teaching of contempt: Christian roots of anti-semitism*, trans. Helen Weaver (New York: Holt, Reinhart and Winston, 1964)

Klausner, Joseph, *Jesus of Nazareth: his life, times, and teaching*, trans. Herbert Danby (New York: Macmillan, 1925; Hebrew original 1922)

Montefiore, Claude G., *Some elements in the religious teaching of Jesus* (London: Macmillan, 1910)

Niemoeller, Martin, *Here stand I!*, trans. Jane Lymburn (Chicago and New York: Willett, Clark & Co., 1937)

Parkes, James, *The conflict of the church and the synagogue: a study in the origins of antisemitism* (London: Soncino Press, 1934)

Rothschild, Fritz A. (ed.), *Jewish perspectives on Christianity* (New York: Crossroad, 1990)

Ruether, Rosemary Radford, 'Anti-semitism and Christian theology', in Eva Fleischner (ed.), *Auschwitz: beginning of a new era: reflections on the Holocaust* (Jerusalem: KTAV, 1977)

Faith and fratricide: the theological roots of anti-semitism (New York: Seabury Press, 1974)

Saperstein, Marc, *Moments of crisis in Jewish-Christian relations* (London: SCM, 1989)

Travers-Herford, Robert, *Judaism in the New Testament period* (London: The Lindsey Press, 1928)

The Pharisees (London: G. Allen & Unwin, 1924)

van Buren, Paul, *A theology of the Jewish-Christian reality*, 3 vols. (Lanham, MD and London: University Presses of America, 1995)

Weizmann, Chaim, *Trial and error; the autobiography of Chaim Weizmann* (London: Hamish Hamilton, 1949)

(ii) Relations between Christians and Muslims

Congregation for the Doctrine of the Faith, *'Dominus Jesus' on the unicity and salvific universality of Jesus Christ and the church* (Vatican City, 2000)

Gioia, F. (ed.), *Interreligious dialogue: the official teaching of the Catholic church (1963–1995)* (Boston: Pauline Books and Media, 1997)

Goddard, H., *A history of Christian–Muslim relations* (Edinburgh: Edinburgh University Press, 2000)

Huntington, S. P., 'The clash of civilizations?', *Foreign affairs* 72:3 (1993), 22–49

Kraemer, H., *The Christian message in a non-Christian world* (London: Edinburgh House Press, 1938)

Missionary Council of the Church Assembly, *The world call to the church, the call from the Moslem world* (London: Press and Publications Board of the Church Assembly, 1926)

Nielsen, J. S., *Muslims in western Europe*, 3rd edn (Edinburgh: Edinburgh University Press, 2004)

Pontifical Council for Interreligious Dialogue, 'Dialogue and Proclamation: reflections and orientations on interreligious dialogue and the proclamation of the gospel of Jesus Christ', *Bulletin* 26:2 (1991), 201–50

Qutb, Sayyid, 'That hideous schizophrenia', in P. Griffiths (ed.), *Christianity through non-Christian eyes* (Maryknoll, NY: Orbis, 1990), pp. 73–81

Rahner, K., 'Christianity and the non-Christian religions', *Theological investigations*, vol. v (London: Darton, Longman and Todd, 1966), pp. 115–34

Rocalve, P., *Place et rôle de l'Islam et de l'Islamologie dans la vie et l'oeuvre de Louis Massignon* (Damascus: Publications de l'I.F.E.A.D., 1993)

Samartha, S., 'Guidelines for dialogue', *Ecumenical review* 31 (1979), 155–62

Sullivan, F. A., *Salvation outside the church? Tracing the history of the Catholic response* (London: Geoffrey Chapman, 1992)

Tambaram-Madras series. International Missionary Council meeting at Tambaram, Madras, December 12th to 29th, 1938 (Oxford: Oxford University Press, 1939)

Vatican Secretariat for non-Christians, 'The attitude of the church towards the followers of other religions: reflections and orientations on dialogue and mission', *Bulletin* 19:2 (1984), 126–41

Waardenburg, J. (ed.), *Muslim–Christian perceptions of dialogue today, experiences and expectations* (Leuven: Peeters, 2000)

World Council of Churches, *Guidelines on dialogue with people of living faiths and ideologies* (Geneva: World Council of Churches Publications, 1979)

Zebiri, K., *Muslims and Christians face to face* (Oxford: Oneworld, 1997)

(iii) Relations between Christians and Buddhists and Hindus

Abishiktananda, *Hindu–Christian meeting point within the cave of the heart* (Delhi: ISPCK, 1976)

Brockington, J., *Hinduism and Christianity* (London: Macmillan, 1992)

Coward, H. (ed.)., *Hindu–Christian Dialogue: perspectives and encounters* (Maryknoll, NY: Orbis, 1989)

Cupitt, D., *Taking leave of God* (London: SCM, 1980)

Dalai Lama XIV, *The good heart* (London: Rider, 1996)

Griffiths, B., *The marriage of East and West* (London: Collins, 1982)

Gross, R. M., and T. C. Muck, *Buddhists talk about Jesus, Christians talk about the Buddha* (New York: Continuum, 1999)

Klostermaier, K., *Hindu and Christian in Vrindaban* (London: SCM, 1969)

Lai, W., and M. Bruck (eds.), *Christianity and Buddhism: a multi-cultural history of their dialogue* (Maryknoll, NY: Orbis, 2001)

Nirmal, A. P. (ed.), *A reader in Dalit theology* (Madras: Gurukul Lutheran Theological College and Research Institute, 1990)

Schmidt-Leukel, P., *Den Löwen brüllen hören* (Paderborn: Schöningh, 1992)

Sugirtharajah, R. S., and C. Hargreaves (eds.), *Readings in Indian Christian theology* (Delhi: ISPCK, 1993)

Thich Nhat Hanh, *Living Buddha, living Christ* (New York: Riverhead Books, 1995)

(iv) Theologies of religions

Amaladoss, M., *Making all things new: dialogue, pluralism and evangelisation in Asia* (Maryknoll, NY: Orbis, 1990)

Anderson, G. H., 'Theology of religions and missiology: a time of testing', in C. van Engen et al. (eds.), *The good news of the kingdom: mission theology for the third millennium* (Maryknoll, NY: Orbis, 1993)

Braybrooke, M., *Pilgrimage of hope: one hundred years of global interfaith dialogue* (London: SCM, 1992)

Courage for dialogue (Maryknoll, NY: Orbis, 1981)

D'Costa, G., *The meeting of religions and the Trinity* (Edinburgh: T&T Clark, 2000)

Dupuis, J., *Toward a Christian theology of religious pluralism* (Maryknoll, NY: Orbis, 1997)

Heim, S. M., *Salvations* (Maryknoll, NY: Orbis, 1995)

Hick, J., and B. Hebblethwaite (eds.), *Christianity and other religions* (London: Fount, 1980)

Knitter, P., *Introducing theologies of religion* (Maryknoll, NY: Orbis, 2002)

Panikkar, R., *The unknown Christ of Hinduism* (Maryknoll, NY: Orbis, 1981)

Race, A., *Christians and religious pluralism* (London: SCM, 1983)

Samartha, S., *One Christ, many religions: towards a revised christology* (Maryknoll, NY: Orbis, 1991)

Sharpe, E., *Comparative religion – a history* (London: Duckworth, 1986)

Chapter 28

Archbishop of Canterbury's Commission on Urban Priority Areas, *Faith in the city: a call for action by church and nation* (London: Church Information Office, 1985)

Arnal, Oscar L., *Priests in working-class blue: the history of the worker-priests (1943–1954)* (New York: Paulist Press, 1986)

Barth, Karl, 'The Christian community and the civil community', in *Against the stream: shorter post-war writings, 1946–52* (London: SCM, 1954)

Boff, Clodovis, and G. V. Pixley, *The Bible, the church and the poor* (Maryknoll, NY: Orbis, 1990)

Bonino, J. Miguez, *Revolutionary theology comes of age* (London: SPCK, 1975)

Brouwer, Steve, Paul Gifford and Susan Rose, *Exporting the American gospel* (New York: Routledge, 1996)

Busch, Eberhard, *Karl Barth: his life from letters and autobiographical texts* (London: SCM, 1976)

Congregation for the Doctrine of the Faith, *Instruction on Christian freedom and liberation* (Vatican City, 1986)

Dennis, Norman, and A. H. Halsey, *English ethical socialism: Thomas More to R. H. Tawney* (Oxford: Clarendon Press, 1988)

Fogarty, Michael, *Christian democracy in western Europe, 1820–1953* (London: Routledge and Kegan Paul, 1957)

Forrester, Duncan B., *On human worth: a Christian vindication of equality* (London: SCM, 2001)

Gorringe, Timothy J., *Karl Barth: against hegemony* (Oxford: Oxford University Press, 1999)

Griffiths, Brian, *Morality and the market place* (London: Hodder and Stoughton, 1982)

Gutiérrez, Gustavo, *A theology of liberation* (London: SCM, 1974)

   'Liberation praxis and Christian faith', in Rosino Gibellini (ed.), *Frontiers of theology in Latin America* (London: SCM, 1975)

Joseph, Keith, and Jonathan Sumption, *Equality* (London: John Murray, 1979)

Maritain, Jacques, *Scholasticism and politics*, 3rd edn (London: Bles, 1954)

Martin, David, *Tongues of fire: the explosion of Protestantism in Latin America* (Oxford: Blackwell, 1990)

Novak, Michael, *The spirit of democratic capitalism* (New York: Simon and Schuster, 1982)

   Catholic social thought and liberal institutions: freedom with justice, 2nd edn (New Brunswick: Transaction, 1989)

   Free persons and the common good (New York: Madison Books, 1989)

Petrie, John (trans.), *The worker priests: a collective documentation* (London: Routledge and Kegan Paul, 1954)

Pixley, Jorge, and Clodovis Boff, *The Bible, the church and the poor* (London: Burns and Oates, 1989)

Pope, Stephen J., 'Proper and improper partiality and the preferential option for the poor', *Theological studies* 54 (1993), 242–71

Tawney, Richard, *The acquisitive society* (London: Bell and Son, 1921)

   Religion and the rise of capitalism (London: John Murray, 1926)

Temple, William, *Christianity and social order* (Harmondsworth: Penguin, 1942)

US Catholic Bishops, *Economic justice for all: Catholic social teaching and the US economy* (Washington: National Conference of Catholic Bishops, 1986)

Chapter 29

(i) Marriage and the family

Archive of resolutions from Lambeth Conferences of Anglican Bishops. On-line at http://www.anglicancommunion.org/acns/archive/

Barton, Stephen C. (ed.), *The family in theological perspective* (Edinburgh: T&T Clark, 2000)

Book of Common Prayer, The, On-line at www.eskimo.com/~lhowell/bcp1662/

Browning, Don S., Bonnie J. Miller-McLemore, Pamela D. Couture, K. Brynolf Lyon and Robert M. Franklin, *From culture wars to common ground: religion and the American family debate* (Louisville: Westminster John Knox Press, 1997)

Browning, Don S., *Marriage and modernization: how globalization threatens marriage and what to do about it* (Grand Rapids and Cambridge, UK: Eerdmans, 2003)

Common Worship Marriage Service (2000). On-line at www.cofe.anglican.org/commonworship/marriage/

Dennis, Norman, and George Erdos, *Families without fatherhood* (London: Institute of Economic Affairs Health and Welfare Unit, 1993)

Dunn, James D. G., 'The household rules in the New Testament', in Barton (ed.), *The Family*, pp. 43–64

Gaudium et spes [Pastoral Constitution on the Church in the Modern World] (1965). On-line at http://www.vatican.va/archive/hist_councils/ii_vatican_council/documents

General Assembly Special Committee on Human Sexuality, Presbyterian Church (USA), *Keeping body and soul together: sexuality, spirituality and social justice* (Tampa, FL: Jan, 1991)

Halsey, A. H., 'Foreword', in Dennis and Erdos (eds.), *Families without fatherhood*, pp. ix–xiii

Hastings, Adrian, *Christian marriage in Africa* (London: SPCK, 1973)

Hogan, Margaret Monahan, *Finality and marriage*, Marquette studies in philosophy (Marquette: Marquette University Press, 1993)

Lord Chancellor's Advisory Group on Marriage and Relationship Support, *Moving forward together* (London: COI Communications, 2002)

One Plus One, Marriage and Partnership Research. On-line at http://www.oneplusone.org.uk

Paul VI, Pope, *Humanae vitae* (1968). On-line at http://www.vatican.va/holy_father/paul_vi/encyclicals/documents

Pius XI, Pope, *Casti connubii* [*Chaste marriage*] (1930). On-line at http://www.vatican.va/holy_father/pius_xi/encyclicals/documents/hf_p-xi_enc_31121930_casti-connubii_en.html

Post, Stephen G., *More lasting unions: Christianity, the family, and society* (Grand Rapids and Cambridge, UK: Eerdmans, 2000)

Robbins, Paul, 'Marriage nullity in the Catholic church: not every wedding produces a marriage', in Thatcher (ed.), *Celebrating Christian marriage*, pp. 1311–24

Southern Baptist Convention, *The Baptist faith and message* (2000). On-line at http://www.sbc.net/bfm/default.asp

Thatcher, Adrian, *Marriage after modernity* (New York: New York University Press; Sheffield: Sheffield Academic Press, 1999)

Living together and Christian ethics (Cambridge: Cambridge University Press, 2002)

Thatcher, Adrian (ed.), *Celebrating Christian marriage* (Edinburgh and New York: T&T Clark, 2001)

Whitehead, Barbara Dafoe, *The divorce culture* (New York: Vintage, 1998)

Witte, John, Jr, *From sacrament to contract: marriage, religion, and law in the Western tradition* (Louisville: Westminster John Knox Press, 1997)

Zion, William Basil, *Eros and transformation: sexuality and marriage – an Eastern Orthodox perspective* (Lanham, MD and London: University Presses of America, 1992)

(ii) Homosexuality

Anglican Church of Australia, *Faithfulness in fellowship: reflections on homosexuality and the church. Papers from the doctrine panel of the Anglican Church of Australia* (Melbourne: John Garratt Publishing, 2001)

Bailey, Derrick Sherwin, *Homosexuality and the Western Christian tradition* (London: Longmans, Green and Co., 1955)

Bates, Stephen, *A church at war: Anglicans and homosexuality* (London: I. B. Tauris, 2004)

Bradshaw, Timothy (ed.), *The way forward? Christian voices on homosexuality and the church* (London: Hodder and Stoughton, 1997, 2nd edn 2003)

Catechism of the Catholic church (Dublin: Veritas, 1994)

Catholic church, Congregation for the Doctrine of the Faith, *Letter to the bishops of the Catholic church on the pastoral care of homosexual persons* (London: Catholic Truth Society, 1986)

Church of England, General Synod Board for Social Responsibility, *Homosexual relationships: a contribution to discussion* (London: CIO Publishing, 1979)

Coleman, Peter, *Christian attitudes to homosexuality* (London: SPCK, 1980)

Edsall, Nicholas C., *Toward Stonewall: homosexuality and society in the modern Western world* (Charlottesville: University of Virginia Press, 2003)

Germond, Paul, and Steve de Gruchy (eds.), *Aliens in the household of God: homosexuality and Christian faith in South Africa* (Cape Town: David Philip, 1997)

Gill, Sean (ed.), *The Lesbian and Gay Christian Movement: campaigning for justice, truth and love* (London: Cassell, 1998)

Glasgow, Joanne, 'What's a nice lesbian like you doing in the church of Torquemada? Radclyffe Hall and other Catholic converts', in Karla Jay and Joanne Glasgow (eds.), *Lesbian texts and contexts: radical revisions* (New York: New York University Press, 1990), pp. 241–54

Heron, Alastair (ed.), *Towards a Quaker view of sex: an essay by a group of Friends* (London: Friends Home Service Committee, 1963)

Hilliard, David, 'UnEnglish and unmanly: Anglo-Catholicism and homosexuality', *Victorian studies* 25 (1982), 181–210

Jenkins, Philip, *Pedophiles and priests: anatomy of a contemporary crisis* (New York: Oxford University Press, 1996)

John Paul II, Pope, *Familiaris consortio* (1981). On-line at http://www.vatican.va/holy_father/john_paul_ii/apost_exhortations/documents/

  Letter to families (1994). On-line at http://www.vatican.va/holy_father/john_paul_ii/letters/documents/

Jordan, Mark D., *The silence of Sodom: homosexuality in modern Catholicism* (Chicago: University of Chicago Press, 2000)

Mader, Donald, 'Exclusion, toleration, acceptance, integration: the experience of Dutch Reformed churches with homosexuality and homosexuals in the church', *Journal of homosexuality* 25:4 (1993), 101–19

Moore, Gareth, *A question of truth: Christianity and homosexuality* (London: Continuum, 2003)

Moorhouse, Geoffrey, *Against all reason* (London: Weidenfeld and Nicolson, 1969)

Oraison, Marc (1952), *Vie chrétienne et problèmes de la sexualité*, new edn (Paris: P. Lethielleux–Fayard, 1972)

Pittenger, Norman, *Time for consent: a Christian's approach to homosexuality* (London: SCM, 1967, 3rd edn 1976)

Schneider, Laurel C., 'Homosexuality, queer theory, and Christian theology', *Religious studies review* 26 (2000), 3–12

Scroggs, Robin, *The New Testament and homosexuality: contextual background for contemporary debate* (Philadelphia: Fortress Press, 1983)

Siker, Jeffrey S. (ed.), *Homosexuality in the church: both sides of the debate* (Louisville: Westminster John Knox Press, 1994)

Vasey, Michael, *Strangers and friends: a new exploration of homosexuality and the Bible* (London: Hodder and Stoughton, 1995)

Ward, Kevin, 'Same-sex relations in Africa and the debate on homosexuality in east African Anglicanism', *Anglican theological review* 83 (2002), 81–111

Weeks, Jeffrey, *Coming out: homosexual politics in Britain from the nineteenth century to the present*, revd edn (London: Quartet, 1990)

(iii) Patriarchy and women's emancipation/(iv) The church as women's space

Alvarez, Sonia E., 'Women's participation in the Brazilian "People's church": a critical appraisal', *Feminist studies* 16 (1990), 381–408

Brown, Callum G., *The death of Christian Britain: understanding secularisation 1800–2000* (London and New York: Routledge, 2001)

Butler, Sara, 'The ordination of women: a new obstacle to the recognition of Anglican orders', *Anglican theological review* 78 (1996), 96–113

Camp, Richard L., 'From passive subordination to complementary partnership: the papal conception of a woman's place in church and society since 1878', *Catholic historical review* 76 (1990), 506–25

Chaves, Mark, 'Ordaining women: the diffusion of an organizational innovation', *American journal of sociology* 101 (1996), 840–73

Crawford, Janet, 'The community of women and men in the church: where are we now?', *Ecumenical review* 40 (1988), 37–47

'Women and ecclesiology. Two ecumenical streams?', *Ecumenical review* 53 (2001), 14–24

Fletcher, Brian H., 'Anglicanism and national identity in Australia since 1962', *Journal of religious history* 25 (2001), 324–45

Hamilton, Michael S., 'Women, public ministry, and American fundamentalism, 1920–1950', *Religion and American culture. A journal of interpretation* 3 (1993), 171–96

Huber, Mary Taylor, and Nancy C. Lutkehaus (eds.), *Gendered missions: women and men in missionary discourse and practice* (Ann Arbor: University of Michigan Press, 1999)

Isichei, Elizabeth, *A history of Christianity in Africa: from antiquity to the present* (Lawrenceville, NJ: Africa World Press Inc., 1995)

Korinek, Valerie J., 'No women need apply: the ordination of women in the United church, 1918–65', *Canadian historical review* 74 (1993), 473–509

Lindley, Susan Hill, *You have stept out of your place: a history of women and religion in America* (Louisville: Westminster John Knox Press, 1996)

MacCurtain, Margaret, 'Late in the field: Catholic Sisters in twentieth-century Ireland and the new religious history', *Journal of women's history* 7 (1995), 49–63

Malmgreen, Gail (ed.), *Religion in the lives of English women, 1760–1930* (Bloomington and Indianapolis: Indiana University Press, 1986)

Markkola, Pirjo (ed.), *Gender and vocation: women, religion and social change in the Nordic countries, 1830–1940* (Helsinki: Finnish Literature Society, 2000)

Muir, Elizabeth Gillan, and Marilyn Färdig Whiteley (eds.), *Changing roles of women within the Christian churches in Canada* (Toronto: University of Toronto Press, 1995)

Offen, Karen, *European feminisms 1700–1950: a political history* (Stanford: Stanford University Press, 2000)

Prelinger, Catherine M. (ed.), *Episcopal women: gender, spirituality, and commitment in an American mainline denomination* (New York and Oxford: Oxford University Press, 1992)

Robert, Dana L., 'From missions to mission to beyond missions: the historiography of American Protestant foreign mission since World War II', *International bulletin of missionary research* 18 (1994), 145–61

Ruether, Rosemary Radford, and Rosemary Skinner Keller, *Women and religion in America*. Vol. III: *1900–1968* (San Francisco: Harper & Row, 1986)

Salonen, Kari, Kimmo Kääriäinen and Kati Niemelä, *The church at the turn of the millennium: the Evangelical Lutheran Church of Finland from 1996 to 1999*. Publication no. 51. The Research Institute of the Evangelical Lutheran Church of Finland. http://www.evl.fi/kkh/ktk/english/p51.htm

Sharma, Arvind (ed.), *Women in world religions* (Albany: State University of New York Press, 1987)

Stuckey, Johanna, *Feminist spirituality: an introduction to feminist theology in Judaism, Christianity, Islam and feminist goddess worship* (Toronto: Centre for Feminist Research, York University, 1998)

Tentler, Leslie Woodcock, 'On the margins: the state of American Catholic history', *American quarterly* 45 (1993), 104–27

Vuola, Elina, *Limits of liberation; praxis as method in Latin American Liberation Theology and feminist theology* (Helsinki: The Finnish Academy of Science and Letters, 1997)

Yong Ting Jin, 'On being church. Asian women's voices and visions', *Ecumenical review* 53 (2001), 109–13

Chapter 30

Barbour, I. G., *Religion and science: historical and contemporary issues* (London: SCM, 1998)

Barnes, J., *Ahead of his age: Bishop Barnes of Birmingham* (London: Collins, 1979)

Behe, M., *Nature's black box: the biochemical challenge to evolution* (New York: Simon and Schuster, 1996)

Bowler, P. J., *The eclipse of Darwinism: anti-Darwinian evolution theories in the decades around 1900* (Baltimore: Johns Hopkins University Press, 1983)

The non-Darwinian revolution: reinterpreting a historical myth (Baltimore: Johns Hopkins University Press, 1988)

Reconciling science and religion: the debate in early twentieth-century Britain (Chicago: University of Chicago Press, 2001)

Clements, K. W., *Lovers of discord: twentieth century theological controversies in England* (London: SPCK, 1988)

Dillistone, F. W., *Charles Raven: naturalist, historian, theologian* (London: Hodder and Stoughton, 1975)

Durant, J. (ed.), *Darwinism and divinity: essays on evolution and religious belief* (Oxford: Blackwell, 1985)

Hastings, A., *A history of English Christianity, 1920–1985* (London: Collins, 1986)

Larson, E. J., *Summer for the gods: the Scopes trial and America's continuing debate over science and religion* (New York: Basic Books, 1998)

Matczak, S. A., *Karl Barth on God: the knowledge of the divine existence* (New York: St Paul's Publications, 1962)

Miller, Kenneth R., *Finding Darwin's God: a scientist's search for common ground between God and evolution* (New York: Perennial, 2000)

Moore, J. R., *The post-Darwinian controversies: a study of the Protestant struggle to come to terms with Darwin in Great Britain and America, 1870–1900* (New York: Cambridge University Press, 1979)

Numbers, R. L., *The creationists* (New York: Knopf, 1992)

Darwinism comes to America (Cambridge, MA: Harvard University Press, 1998)

Oppenheim, J., *The other world: spiritualism and psychic research in England, 1850–1914* (Cambridge: Cambridge University Press, 1985)

Peacocke, A. R., *Creation and the world of science* (Oxford: Oxford University Press, 1980)

Polkinghorne, J. C., *Belief in God in an age of science* (New Haven: Yale University Press, 1998)

Roberts, J. H., 'Psychoanalysis and American Christianity, 1900–1945', in D. C. Lindberg and R. L. Numbers (eds.), *When science and Christianity meet* (Chicago: University of Chicago Press, 2003), pp. 225–44

Stephenson, A. M. G., *The rise and decline of English modernism* (London: SPCK, 1984)

Chapter 31

(i) Literature and film

Babington, Bruce, and Peter Williams Evans, *Biblical epics: sacred narrative in the Hollywood cinema* (Manchester: Manchester University Press, 1993)

Barratt, David, Roger Pooley and Leland Ryken (ed.), *The discerning reader: Christian perspectives on literature and theory* (London: Inter-Varsity Press, 1995)

Butler, Christopher, *Early modernism: literature, music and painting in Europe, 1900–1916* (Oxford: Clarendon Press, 1994)

Cecil, Lord David, *The Oxford book of Christian verse* (Oxford: Oxford University Press, 1940)

Davie, Donald (ed.), *The new Oxford book of Christian verse* (Oxford: Oxford University Press, 1981)

Dawes, Gregory W. (ed.), *The historical Jesus quest* (Louisville: Westminster John Knox Press, 2000)

Detweiler, Robert, *Uncivil rites: American fiction, religion, and the public sphere* (Urbana and Chicago: University of Illinois Press, 1996)

Dillistone, F. W., *The novelist and the passion story* (London: Collins, 1960)

Doctrine Commission of the Church of England, *Believing in the church: the corporate nature of faith* (London: SPCK, 1981)

Eliot, T. S., 'Religion and literature' (1935), in *Selected essays*, 3rd edn (London: Faber & Faber, 1951), pp. 388–401

Fiddes, Paul, *The promised end: eschatology in theology and literature* (Oxford: Blackwell, 2000)

Jasper, David, *The study of literature and religion*, 2nd edn (London: Macmillan, 1992)

'The Bible in literature', in John Rogerson (ed.), *The Oxford illustrated history of the Bible* (Oxford: Oxford University Press, 2001), pp. 278–91

Jasper, David, and Colin Crowder (eds.), *European literature and theology in the twentieth century: ends of time* (London: Macmillan, 1990)

Kazantzakis, Nikos, *The last temptation*, trans. P. A. Bien (London: Faber and Faber, 1975)

Kinnard, Roy, and Tim Davis, *Divine images: a history of Jesus on the screen* (New York: Citadel Press, 1992)

Kuschel, Karl-Josef, *Jesus im Spiegel der Weltliteratur* (Düsseldorf: Patmos Verlag, 1999)

Langenhorst, Georg, *Jesus ging nach Hollywood: die Wiederentdeckung Jesu in Literatur und Film der Gegenwart* (Düsseldorf: Patmos Verlag, 1998)

Levi, Peter (ed.), *The Penguin book of English Christian verse* (Harmondsworth: Penguin, 1984)

Marsh, Clive, and Gaye Ortiz (eds.), *Explorations in theology and film* (Oxford: Blackwell, 1997)

O'Connor, Flannery, *Wise blood*, 2nd edn (London: Faber and Faber, 1968)

Pattison, George, *Art, modernity and faith: towards a theology of art* (London: Macmillan, 1991)

Péguy, Charles, *The portal of the mystery of hope*, trans. David Louis Schindler, Jr (Edinburgh: T&T Clark, 1996)

Salyer, Gregory, and Robert Detweiler, *Literature and theology at century's end* (Atlanta: Scholar's Press, 1995)

Sayers, Dorothy L., *The man born to be king: a play-cycle on the life of our Lord and Saviour Jesus Christ* (London: Victor Gollanz, 1943)

Scott, Jamie S., 'And the birds began to sing': religion and literature in post-colonial cultures (Amsterdam and Atlanta: Rodopi, 1996)

Sherry, Patrick, *Images of redemption: art, literature and salvation* (London and New York: T. & T. Clark, 2003)

Steiner, George (ed.), *The Penguin book of modern verse translation* (Harmondsworth: Penguin, 1966)

Whitelaw, Marjory, 'Interview with Christopher Okigbo, 1965', *Journal of Commonwealth literature* 9 (1970), 28–37

Wright, T. R., *Theology and literature* (Oxford: Blackwell, 1998)

(ii) Music and Christianity in the twentieth century

Begbie, J., *Theology, music and time* (Cambridge: Cambridge University Press, 2000)

Gelineau, J., *The liturgy today and tomorrow* (London: Darton, Longman and Todd 1978)

Humphreys, M., and R. Evans, *Dictionary of composers for the church in Great Britain and Ireland* (London: Mansell, 1997)

Leaver, R. A., 'British hymnody, 1900–1950', 'British hymnody since 1950', in R. F. Glover (ed.), *The Hymnal 1982 companion*, vol. I (New York: 1990), pp. 474–504, 555–99

Littlewood, A. R. (ed.), *Originality in Byzantine literature, art and music* (Oxford: Oxbow Books, 1995)

Overath, J. (ed.), *Sacred music and liturgy reform after Vatican II* (Proceedings of the Fifth International Church Music Congress, Chicago-Milwaukee, 1966 August 21–28) (Rome: Consociato Internationalis Musicæ Sacræ, 1969)

Routley, E. (1978), *Twentieth century church music* (Oxford: Oxford University Press, 2000)

Sadie, S. (ed.), *The new Grove dictionary of music and musicians*, 2nd edn, 29 vols. (London: Macmillan, 2001), including articles on Byzantine chant (vol. IV p. 734), gospel music (vol. X p. 168), Anglican Episcopalian church music (vol. I p. 658), Roman Catholic church music (vol. XXI p. 544), Baptist church music (vol. II p. 673), liturgy and liturgical books (vol. XV p. 1), Methodist church music (vol. XVI p. 521)

Spencer, J. M., *Protest and praise: sacred music of black religion* (Minneapolis: Fortress Press, 1990)

Wheaton, J., *Crisis in Christian music* (Oklahoma: Hearthstone, 2000)

Wilson-Dickson, A., *A brief history of Christian music from biblical times to the present* (Oxford: Lion, 1997)

In tune with heaven: the report of the Archbishops' Commission on Church Music (London: Church House Publishing, 1992)

(iii) Christianity and art

Apostolos-Cappadona, Diane (ed.), *Art, creativity, and the sacred: an anthology in religion and art* (New York: Continuum, 1998)

Barron, Stephanie with Sabine Eckmann, *Exiles and emigrés: the flight of European artists from Germany*, exhibition catalogue, Los Angeles County Museum, Los Angeles (23 February – 11 May 1997)

Dillenberger, John, *A theology of artistic sensibilities: the visual arts and the church* (London: SCM, 1986)

Duncan, Carol, *Civilising rituals* (London and New York: Routledge, 1995)

Eckart, Christian, Harry Philbrick and Osvaldo Romberg, *Faith: the impact of Judeo-Christian religion on art at the millennium*, exhibition catalogue, The Aldrich Museum of Contemporary Art, Ridgefield, CT (23 January – 29 May 2000)

De Gruchy, John W., *Christianity, art, and transformation: theological aesthetics in the struggle for justice* (Cambridge: Cambridge University Press, 2001)

Gercke, Hans, and Rainer Volp, *Die Glasbilder von Johannes Schreiter. The stained glass art of Johannes Schreiter* (Darmstadt: db Verlag Das Beispiel, 1988)

Mädler, Inken, *Kirche und bildende Kunst der Moderne. Ein an F. D. E. Schleiermacher orientierter Beitrag zur theologischen Urteilsbildung*, Beiträge zur historischen Theologie 100 (Tübingen: Mohr Siebeck, 1997)

Mennekes, Friedhelm, 'Between doubt and rapture – art and church today: the spiritual in the art of the twentieth century', *Religion and the arts* 2 (2000), 165–83

Newman, Barnett, *Selected writings and interviews* (New York: Alfred A. Knopf, 1990)

Nolde, Emil, *Das eigene Leben* (Berlin: Rembrandt-Verlag, 1931)

O'Meara, Thomas F., 'Modern art and the sacred: the prophetic ministry of Alain Couturier, O.P.', *Spirituality today* 38 (1986), 31–40

Ottaviani, Alaphridus (Adsessor), 'Instructio. Ad locorum ordinarios: "De arte sacra"' (Acta SS. Congregationum. Suprema Sacra Congregatio S. Officii, part 1), *Acta Apostolicae Sedis* 44 (1952), 542–5

Plate, S. Brent (ed.), *Religion, art and visual culture: a cross-cultural reader* (New York and Basingstoke: Palgrave, 2002)

Rahner, Karl, 'Zur Theologie des Bildes', in Rainer Beck, Rainer Volp and Gisela Schmirber (eds.), *Die Kunst und die Kirchen: der Streit um die Bilder heute* (Munich: Bruckmann, 1984), pp. 213–22

Vergo, Peter, and Felicity Lunn, *Emil Nolde* (London: Whitechapel Art Gallery, 1996)

West, Shearer, *The visual arts in Germany, 1890–1937: utopia and despair* (Manchester: Manchester University Press, 2000)

Worsdale, Godfrey, and Lisa G. Corrin, *Chris Ofili*, exhibition catalogue, Southampton City Art Gallery and Serpentine Gallery, London (1998)

(iv) Church architecture

Anson, P. F., *Fashions in church furnishings 1840–1940*, 2nd edn (London: Studio Vista, 1965)

Cope, Gilbert (ed.), *Making the building serve the liturgy* (London: A. R. Mowbray, 1962)

Debuyst, Frederic, *Modern architecture and Christian celebration* (London: Lutterworth Press, 1968)

Hammond, Peter, *Towards a church architecture* (London: The Architectural Press, 1962)

Hammond, Peter (ed.), *Liturgy and architecture* (London: Barrie and Rockcliff, 1960)

Heathcote, E. S., *Church builders* (Chichester: Academy Editions, 1997)

Hebert, A. G., *Liturgy and society: the function of the church in the modern world* (London: Faber and Faber, 1935)

Hurley, Richard, *Irish church architecture in the era of Vatican II* (Dublin: Dominican Publications, 2001)

Kidder-Smith, G. E., *The new churches of Europe* (London: The Architectural Press, 1964)

Little, Bryan, *Catholic churches since 1623* (London: Robert Hale, 1966)

Lockett, W. E. A. (ed.), *The modern architectural setting of the liturgy* (Liverpool: Liverpool University Press, 1964)

Maguire, Robert and Keith Murray, *Modern churches of the world* (London: Studio Vista, 1965)

Chapter 32

Bentley, James, *Martin Niemöller* (London: Hodder & Stoughton, 1984)

Chandler, Andrew (ed.), *The terrible alternative: Christian martyrdom in the twentieth century* (London: Cassell, 1998)

Cholvy, Gérard, and Yves-Marie Hilaire, *Histoire religieuse de la France contemporaine 1930–1988* (Toulouse: Privat, 1988)

Delumeau, Jean (ed.), *L'historien et la foi* (Paris: Fayard, 1996)

Folley, Malcolm, *A time to jump* (London: HarperCollins, 2000)

Gailus, Manfred, *Protestantismus und Nationalsozialismus: Studien zur nationalsozialistischen Durchdringung des protestantischen Sozialmilieus in Berlin* (Cologne: Böhlau, 2001)

Hastings, Adrian, *A history of English Christianity 1920–2000* (London: SCM, 2001)

Jeremy, David, *Capitalists and Christians: business leaders and the churches in Britain, 1900–1960* (Oxford: Oxford University Press, 1990)

'Twentieth-century Protestant Nonconformists in the world of business', in Alan P. F. Sell and Anthony R. Cross (eds.), *Protestant Nonconformity in the twentieth century* (Carlisle: Paternoster, 2003), pp. 264–312

Kent, John, *William Temple: church, state and society in Britain 1880–1950* (Cambridge: Cambridge University Press, 1992)

Martin, William, *The Billy Graham story: a prophet with honour* (London: Hutchinson, 1992)

Murray, Bill, *The old firm* (Edinburgh: John Donald, 1984)

Oates, Stephen B., *Let the trumpet sound: the life of Martin Luther King, Jr* (London: Search Press, 1982)

Pivato, Stefano, 'The bicycle as a political symbol: Italy 1885–1955', *International journal of the history of sport* 7 (1990), 173–87

Putney, Clifford, *Muscular Christianity: manhood and sports in Protestant America 1880–1920* (Cambridge, MA: Harvard University Press, 2002)

Shepherd, John, *George Lansbury: at the heart of Old Labour* (Oxford: Oxford University Press, 2002)

Snape, Michael, *God and the British soldier* (London: Routledge, 2005)

Steigmann-Gall, Richard, *The Holy Reich: Nazi conceptions of Christianity, 1919–1945* (Cambridge: Cambridge University Press, 2003)

Walsh, Michael, *John Paul II* (London: HarperCollins, 1994)

Wheatcroft, Geoffrey, *Le Tour: a history of the Tour de France* (London: Simon and Schuster, 2003)

Williams, Paul, *Mother Teresa* (Indianapolis: Alpha, 2002)

Williamson, Philip, *Stanley Baldwin: Conservative leadership and national values* (Cambridge: Cambridge University Press, 1999)

Wilson, Stephen (ed.), *Saints and their cults* (Cambridge: Cambridge University Press, 1983)

Woodward, Kenneth, *Making saints: inside the Vatican: who become saints, who do not, and why* (London: Chatto & Windus, 1991)

Chapter 33

Barrett, David B., George T. Kurian and Todd M. Johnson, *World Christian encyclopaedia*, 2 vols. (Oxford: Oxford University Press, 2001)

Bruce, Steve, *The rise and fall of the new Christian right: conservative Protestant politics in America 1978–1988* (Oxford: Oxford University Press, 1988)

Capps, Walter, *The new religious right: piety, patriotism and politics* (Columbia: Columbia University Press, 1994)

Chandler, Andrew, and Anthony Harvey, 'Introduction', in Andrew Chandler (ed.), *The terrible alternative: Christian martyrdom in the twentieth century* (London: Cassell, 1998)

Cox, Jeffrey, 'Master narratives of long-term religious change', in Hugh McLeod and Werner Ustorf (eds.), *The decline of Christendom in western Europe, 1750–2000* (Cambridge: Cambridge University Press, 2003), pp. 201–17

Davie, Grace, *Religion in modern Europe: a memory mutates* (Oxford: Oxford University Press, 2000)

Gifford, Paul, *African Christianity: its public role* (London: Hurst, 1998)

Gill, Robin, *Moral communities* (Exeter: Exeter University Press, 1992)

Hastings, Adrian, *A history of English Christianity 1920–2000* (London: SCM, 2001)

Inglis, Tom, 'Irish civil society: from church to media domination', in Tom Inglis, Zdzisław Mach and Rafal Mazanek (eds.), *Religion and politics: east–west contrasts from contemporary Europe* (Dublin: University College Press, 2000), pp. 49–67

Jenkins, Philip, *The next Christendom: the coming of global Christianity* (New York: Oxford University Press, 2002)

Lambert, Yves, *Dieu change en Bretagne* (Paris: Editions du Cerf, 1985)

Mach, Zdzisław, 'The Roman Catholic church and the dynamics of social identity in Polish society', in Inglis, Mach and Mazanek (eds.), *Religion and politics*, pp. 113–28

Perica, Vjekoslav, *Balkan idols: religion and nationalism in Yugoslav states* (Oxford: Oxford University Press, 2002)

Putnam, Robert D., *Bowling alone* (New York: Simon & Schuster, 2000)

Schmidt, Thomas, and Monika Wohlrab-Sahr, 'Still the most areligious part of the world: developments in the religious field in eastern Germany since 1990', *International journal of practical theology* 7 (2003), 86–100

Tang, Edmond, 'The second Enlightenment: the spiritual quest of Chinese intellectuals', in T. Murayama and W. Ustorf (eds.), *Identity and marginality: Christianity in north east Asia* (Frankfurt am Main: Peter Lang, 2000), pp. 55–70

Whyte, Bob, *Unfinished encounter: China and Christianity* (London: Fount, 1988)

Index

Index

Index